Teaching-Learning Theory and Teacher Education 1890 to 1950

by *Walter S. Monroe*

DISTINGUISHED PROFESSOR OF EDUCATION, EMERITUS
University of Illinois

GREENWOOD PRESS, PUBLISHERS
NEW YORK

PREFACE

Historical research in education reveals what has been; it does not provide an appraisal of the present or prove what should be. But the present is connected with the past. Educational theories and practices tend to persist. Even so-called new theories and practices have a history. Hence historical research, especially studies of the period since 1890, contributes to an understanding of the present which is a prerequisite step in dealing with problems of what should be.

The record of the development of teacher education in the United States reveals continuing problems and issues which are fundamental in the current situation. The discussions, controversies, investigations, and actions relative to these problems and issues help us understand the developing points of view and practices in teacher education and in appraising the present. Viewing the past from the vantage point of the present one becomes aware of the persistence of traditional beliefs and prejudices, instances of neglect and extreme emphasis in both theory and practice, and other aspects of the development which now appear to have been unfortunate. One also identifies instances of penetrating thinking and sagacious conclusions. Although the developing social and cultural setting calls for changes in teacher-education theory and practice, the mistakes and shortcomings of the past and the constructive views and actions of educational leaders may be suggestive in planning for the future.

Another connection of the present with the past is through the time spread of the education of the teacher-educator group. Although a person may modify his views as the result of continuing study and experience, the understandings and beliefs acquired during his student days, especially at the graduate level, tend to influence his thinking and actions. Thus the older members of the teacher-educator group approach current problems and issues with an orientation and background different from that of those who were graduate students during the thirties or later. These subgroups tend to think in terms of different concepts and points of view. Frequently there is a lack of mutual understanding. In addition to vocabulary differences, common terms are employed with different meanings. Study of the past, especially of the past half century, clarifies these differences and thus contributes to better communication within the teacher-educator group.

During the hundred years since the publication of Henry Barnard's *Normal Schools and Other Institutions, Agencies, and Means Designed for the Professional Education of Teachers* numerous historical studies of teacher education have been reported, especially since 1920. There have also been survey studies, committee reports, and significant writing by individuals. This accumulation of materials is a rich source of historical information but it tends to be fragmentary and some of it is not conveniently accessible to the interested student of teacher education. Several items are in the form of unpublished theses. A number were published in limited editions and are not to be found in some of the larger institutional libraries. Even in the case of publication in proceedings and yearbooks of educational organizations or in periodicals persistent search may be required.

The belief in the value of historical study and the recognition of the need for a comprehensive account of the development of teaching-learning theory and teacher education since 1890 motivated the present work. The author believes that the account of the thinking and practice of the period will contribute to a more adequate understanding of present thinking and practice in teacher education and of the problems and issues which teacher educators face today. He hopes that it will also afford some guidance in dealing with these problems and issues.

WALTER S. MONROE

CONTENTS

INTRODUCTION

The education of the successive generations of children is basic to the perpetuation and improvement of a social group. In a primitive society the means of this education was relatively simple, much of the responsibility being assumed by the family. As the group became larger and living became more complex, a special educational agency became necessary. Schools were established in the American colonies because the need for their services was recognized. As our civilization developed, the responsibility of the schools increased and the preparation of teachers for our schools became recognized as a matter of social importance.

The establishment of state normal schools, beginning in the second quarter of the nineteenth century, was an expression of the thesis that a teacher in an elementary school needed an education somewhat different from that provided by the higher schools of the time. The extension of our common schools to include grades nine to twelve resulted in the application of a corresponding thesis to teachers for secondary schools. Recognition of the thesis that teachers need some special preparation for their work created the complementary problems of what should be the nature of this special preparation and how should it be provided.

The story of the evolving solution of these problems is a complex one. It transcends an account of the development of practice in the education of teachers. Educational practice is a means for the realization of certain goals. In teacher education these goals are the qualifications considered necessary or desirable for teachers in our schools. The concept of these qualifications is derived from our understanding of the teacher's function, and so the story includes the evolving concept of the teaching-learning process which has been a major factor in the thinking about desired teacher qualifications.

1

The Developmental Period To Be Considered

This is not a study of beginnings; instead it deals with a period of relatively mature thinking and doing. Considerable evidence points to around 1890 as the time of the beginning of such a period of development. Although several American authors had written texts on teaching before 1885,[1] none of them presented a systematic theory of teaching. In a bibliography [2] published in 1886 there are only three English titles under the heading "Works on Systematic Pedagogy" and none of these was by an American author. In 1886 Payne [3] referred to the formulation of the "science of pedagogics" as the "need of the hour," thus implying that such a formulation had not yet been produced. Krusé appraised the teaching-learning theory of 1890 from the point of view of the definition of the area. From his examination of texts and other sources of that time he concluded that teaching-learning theory (principles of teaching), although frequently referred to, was undefined as a field of pedagogical thinking, being treated more or less incidentally in connection with "methods [techniques] of teaching" and/or with the "science of education" which he referred to as "a peculiar combination of faculty psychology and the theory of knowledge." [4]

Krusé referred to *Theory and Practice of Teaching* (1847) by David Page as "probably the most popular book on education ever written." E. C. Branson, who edited the edition published in 1899, stated that there had been no material change except for the addition of a chapter on "Fitness to Teach." Thus it may be inferred that after fifty years the thinking of typical American educationists relative to teaching theory had not advanced materially beyond Page's formulation of 1847. In the preface, Page stated that the volume consisted of lectures addressed to classes of the State Normal School at Albany, New York, of which he was principal. The purpose of the lectures was to inculcate "such practical views as would best promote the improvement of the teacher." They dealt with such topics as "The Spirit of the Teacher," "Personal Habits of the Teacher," "Right Views of Education," "Conducting Recitations,"

---

[1] Samuel A. Krusé, *A Critical Analysis of Principles of Teaching as a Basic Course in Teacher-training Curricula* (Contribution to Education, No. 63 [Nashville, Tennessee: George Peabody College for Teachers, 1929]). 168 pp. Appendix I bears the title, "Chronological list of the more important books on education published during the nineteenth century." Of sixty-nine titles bearing dates prior to 1885, all but about ten were by American authors.

[2] G. Stanley Hall and John H. Mansfield, *Hints Toward a Select and Descriptive Bibliography of Education* (Boston: D. C. Heath and Company, 1886).

[3] William H. Payne, *Contributions to the Science of Education* (New York: American Book Company, 1886), p. 3.

[4] Samuel A. Krusé, *op. cit.*, p. 15.

"The Teacher's Relation to the Parents of his Pupils," and "The Rewards of the Teacher." The treatments are in line with the implications of such titles, i.e. skillful formulations of sagacious advice to teachers derived from "the realities of the schoolroom." The term "theory" appears in the title but it is clear that the volume was not intended to be a "work on systematic pedagogy."

A Treatise on Pedagogy (1884) by Edwin C. Hewett and The Elements of Pedagogy (1886) by Emerson E. White were attempts to formulate a systematic pedagogy. In the preface to his volume Hewett stated his purpose as being "to present, in a brief and compact form, such principles as underlie and give form to all methods worthy of mention." White included among his purposes the "presentation of the fundamental principles of teaching." Thus these two volumes may be regarded as pioneer formulations of teaching-learning theory among American educationists and hence as representing beginnings of the development which is to be described in the following chapters.

The efforts to develop a systematic teaching-learning theory were motivated by the recognition of the need for more effective instruments to use in the education of teachers and by the belief that engendering a sound theory of teaching would add materially to the effectiveness of teaching. In 1869 the American Normal School Association appointed a committee to determine "What properly constitutes the 'Science of Education' as applicable to the Normal Schools and the teaching profession in general?" [5] There was an aggressive demand for writings by foreign authors. A translation of The Philosophy of Education (1848) by J. K. F. Rosenkranz was published in The Journal of Speculative Philosophy, 1872-74, and an edition of two thousand reprints was made available. The demand after this printing was exhausted was such that a revised translation was published in 1886. An American edition of The Philosophy of Education, or The Principles and Practice of Teaching by T. T. Tate, was published in 1884 at the insistence of Colonel Francis W. Parker. The printing of one thousand copies was soon exhausted and a second American edition was published in 1885. American educators were also reading Education as a Science (1879) by Alexander Bain.[6]

In spite of the availability of these works by foreign authors and numerous less systematic writings by American authors, presidents of normal schools and others directly concerned with the education of teachers felt the need for more adequate texts on teaching-learning theory. A. R. Taylor, president of the school at Emporia, Kansas, prob-

---

[5] Addresses and Proceedings (National Educational Association, 1869), p. 34. For the report of this committee, see Report of the Commissioner of Education, 1888-89, I, 294-95.

[6] There was an American printing in 1881.

ably reflected the general attitude in his address as president of the Department of Normal Schools in 1887.[7]

> In my intercourse with teachers, I am constantly reminded that they in general lack that acquaintance with recognized authorities on pedagogical subjects which is necessary to make them intelligent, consistent, and independent workers. . . . We have no great authorities to whom teachers appeal as do lawyers to Kent and Blackstone and Parsons. The curricula of our normal schools have not yet become so potent in the profession that they dictate what is orthodox pedagogy. It may be that the masters who are to give us the desired books are not yet among us. In any event, the fact remains and the confusion is lamentable.

The preface of White's *Elements of Pedagogy* (1886) begins with the statement: "This treatise has its origin in a belief that the time has come for such a study of school education as will ascertain the limitations of its maxims and the coordination and harmonizing of its apparently *conflicting methods.*"

Although most educators were not as explicit as Taylor and White, there is evidence of a persistent belief that a systematic formulation of a sound theory of teaching would contribute materially to the improvement of teaching. In his study of normal schools Krusé [8] characterized the period from 1868 to 1890 as one of "criticism and discontent." Writings of normal-school men and others concerned with teacher education around 1890 indicate that criticism was diminishing and that normal-school leaders were beginning to exhibit penetrating thinking about their work and were becoming more confident in regard to the function of normal schools.

The beginnings of professional education for teachers in colleges and universities were around 1850,[9] but the development was slow until the closing decade of the century. Again evidence points to 1890 as marking a time of significance. A specific event supporting this hypothesis is the legislative action in Michigan in 1891 giving the "Special Diploma," which had been issued by the University of Michigan for several years, the legal status of a license to teach in public schools. A national Herbart society was organized in 1895 as a means of promoting Herbartian teaching-learning theory which had been introduced into the United States a few years earlier. Other evidence is to be found in the record of meetings of the Department of Normal Schools and other departments of the National Education Association.

---

[7] A. R. Taylor, "Annual Address," *Addresses and Proceedings* (National Educational Association, 1887), pp. 469-71.

[8] Samuel A. Krusé, *op. cit.,* p. 53.

[9] G. W. A. Luckey, *The Professional Training of Secondary Teachers in the United States* (New York: The Macmillan Company, 1903), pp. 62f.

Considerable collateral evidence might be cited in support of the hypothesis that 1890 marks a time of significance, but space will be taken only to note two items. *The Principles of Psychology* by William James appeared in 1890. The Committee of Ten was appointed in 1892, the outcome of discussions and deliberations centering about 1890. Although the *Report of the Committee of Ten* (1894) dealt with the program of secondary schools, it indirectly influenced teacher education in colleges and universities.

The Purposes of This Study

The following chapters are grouped under three general heads: I. Development of teaching-learning theory; II. Evolution of teacher-education purposes; III. Development of practice in teacher education. These captions indicate the central problems considered. In describing the developments in these areas, attention will be given to the "mode of development" as well as the changes that occurred. Thus there will be mention of differences of opinion, controversies, and divergent practices. As a means of contributing to an understanding of the thinking and doing, certain background conditions will be noted.

Certain limitations should be noted. The development of teacher-education practice is restricted to state normal schools and teachers colleges and colleges and universities. Teacher education in secondary schools, city training schools, and private normal schools is noted only very incidentally. In-service teacher education is also dealt with incidentally. Finally, developments in particular institutions and in particular states are noted only for purposes of illustration.

Some Definitions

The total formal education of a teacher is represented by his schooling from nursery school, kindergarten, or first grade to the level at which he qualifies as a teacher or to which he extends his schooling on an in-service basis. However, in treatments of teacher education, attention is commonly focused upon the period of schooling beyond a certain level such as high-school graduation or junior status in college. During this period of his schooling the prospective teacher may continue his general education and devote time to academic specialization, but his program of study includes some work of a professional nature, i.e. courses explicitly planned as preparation for teaching. Hence, *professional education* is employed to designate that portion of the total education of a teacher which is explicitly designed as preparation for a type of teaching position.

The program of professional education includes *pedagogical* courses, i.e. courses offered in departments of education, and "teachers' courses" offered in subject-matter departments. Thus "professional education of teachers" is broader than "pedagogical training," sometimes referred to as "technical-professional education." Frequently the professional education of teachers is referred to as if it consisted of only pedagogical courses. This is a loose usage of the term, and will be avoided in this study.

The reader should bear in mind the definitions of terms indicated in the above paragraphs. *Teacher education* refers to the portion of the total formal education of prospective teachers beyond graduation from a secondary school (or the equivalent) or some other indicated level, such as the completion of the second year of college or even graduation from college. The program of this teacher education may include some courses for general-education purposes and typically it includes work in one or more teaching fields. The essential condition is that throughout the period of teacher education, the program includes one or more professional courses. *Professional education* designates the portion of the program of teacher education that is explicitly planned as preparation for a type of teaching position. The *pedagogical education* of a teacher consists of the courses called education (pedagogy). To avoid monotonous repetition, "training" is frequently used instead of "education" in the above terms.

Sources

This work is a combination of an account based on original sources and a summary of reported studies in the area of teacher education. Texts and other writings relating to teaching-learning theory constitute original sources for the thinking in this area. Statements by individuals, committee reports, and actions of associations are original sources for the thinking about the purposes of teacher education and attitudes relative to aspects of practice. Institutional records and statistical reports of the United States Office of Education are documentary sources for numerous items of practice. The research relating to teacher education includes some historical studies, but a considerable portion of it consists of studies of the survey type. Very little of the research may be regarded as experimental.

As a means of supplementing information from the above sources and especially as a means of checking the author's interpretations and hypotheses, a number of the older members of the teacher-education group were consulted. In some cases there was an exchange of letters and the author talked at some length with several persons. He also made direct inquiry into current practices at a number of institutions.

Part 1

Development of Teaching-Learning Theory

The purpose of teacher education is to engender the qualifications judged to be necessary for doing the work the teacher is called upon to undertake. The central phase of the teacher's work is instruction, i.e. stimulating, directing, and guiding the learning of pupils, and an understanding of the contemporary teaching-learning theory is an essential prerequisite for understanding the developing thinking about the purposes of teacher education, i.e. the desired teacher qualifications. Hence the central problem of Part One is to outline the evolving concepts of the complementary processes of teaching and learning.

A theory of teaching and learning is in effect largely an interpretation and application of certain aspects of psychology and philosophy. Consequently, attention will be directed first to certain developments in these areas as a background for understanding the evolution of teaching-learning theory. The thinking relative to teaching-learning theory has reflected much disagreement, sometimes to the level of acrimonious controversy, and some of the significant changes have been in the form of shifts of "majority" opinion on certain continuing controversial issues. In addition, the changing temper of the continuing controversy is a significant aspect of the development of thinking. Hence Chapter 2 is devoted to tracing the modification of "majority" opinion relative to (*a*) teaching as an art *versus* teaching as a science, (*b*) conditions for effective learning, (*c*) teacher control, mechanization, conformity *versus* pupil freedom, self-expression, independent thinking, and (*d*) individualized instruction *versus* class teaching. In Chapter 3 an attempt will be made to indicate changes in teaching-learning theory as a whole. As a means to this end four theories of teaching are recognized: (*a*) developing powers of the mind, (*b*) teaching subject matter, (*c*) directing learning activities, and (*d*) guiding pupil experiencing. In the final chapter of Part One, attention will be directed to certain "significant developments" of the period since 1890 and an attempt will be made to outline "current teaching-learning theory." Finally, under the heading, "An appraisal," certain comments will be made about the status of current teaching-learning theory and the "mode of progress" during the period.

The chapters of Part One are based on books and other writings which seem to represent the more authoritative thinking of the time and which seem to have been influential in the general teacher-educator thinking of the period. The account of teaching-learning theory is not intended to be an interpretation of school practice or of the thinking of educational reformers except as noted. Hence the treatment is somewhat selective in the sense that it is from the point of view of the bearing of the evolving teaching-learning theory upon the development of teacher education.

CHAPTER I

Background Developments
in Psychology and Philospohy

In 1890 the philosophical atmosphere of the United States was predominantly idealistic. Rosenkranz's *The Philosophy of Education* had been published as a translation in *The Journal of Speculative Philosophy*, 1872 to 1874, and made available in reprint form for philosophical students. The popularity of the work resulted in a second edition in 1886 with "a somewhat elaborate commentary" by William T. Harris, who like Rosenkranz was an exponent of the philosophy of Hegel. In an article in *A Cyclopedia of Education*, Vol. V (1913), E. F. Buchner referred to the volume as having "practically determined the course of serious reflection in this field" since its publication.

As a philosopher Rosenkranz was an idealist. To him "ultimate reality" was mental (spiritual) in nature and the purpose of education was the development of the child's mind (soul) or his "theoretical and practical reason." [1] The process of education involved attention to (absorption in) the material world and the "removal" of this state of mind, i.e. transcendence to the mental or spiritual (pp. 26-29), the latter phase being designated as "self estrangement." The tone of Rosenkranz's writing is dogmatic. The first sentence begins with the phrase, "The science of

[1] J. K. F. Rosenkranz, *The Philosophy of Education* (New York: D. Appleton and Company, 1886), p. 23. This is a translation of a volume originally published in 1848.

education. . . ." Although "education as an art" was recognized, and it was noted that in practice there must be adaptation to "existing circumstances," the "science of education," i.e. the principles, laws, etc., is unchanging (p. 12). The school and the teacher occupy an authoritarian position. They are to determine the course of study and the "formulae of teaching" as adaptations of the science of education to "existing circumstances." More than a third of the volume is devoted to the history of education which is thought of as containing "all the ideas and definitions of the nature of education" (p. 14, comment by Harris).

Although psychology had become generally recognized in theory as an "independent science" by 1890, there were many vestiges of the metaphysical in psychological writings and the designation "mental philosophy" was still occasionally employed. William James, whose *The Principles of Psychology* (1890) was a contribution of first rank, was also an outstanding philosopher and in the first sentence of the preface of this work he observed that it was more metaphysical than is suitable for beginning students. On the other hand, writings labeled "educational philosophy" explicitly dealt with psychological topics. For example, in Rosenkranz's *The Philosophy of Education* one chapter bears the title, "The act of learning." In *A Cyclopedia of Education*, Vol. III (1912), William T. Harris was referred to as "America's first great educational philosopher" but he was also the author of a volume bearing the title, *Psychologic Foundations of Education* (1898). John Dewey, generally thought of as a philosopher, published a volume under the title, *Psychology*, in 1886 (third revised edition, 1891) and contributed a number of articles on psychological topics.

In the first sentence of *The Principles of Psychology* (1890) James defined psychology as "the Science of Mental Life, both of its phenomena and of their conditions." In the first sentence of *Psychology* Angell referred to psychology as being "commonly defined as the science of consciousness." [2] These statements suggest a considerable degree of agreement among psychologists of the time, i.e. a common "school of psychology." This inference is supported by Woodworth's [3] summary classification of psychologists of 1900 as being in theory "mostly associationists, but not dogmatically so" and by his reference to the "established order of 1900."

Although the philosophical atmosphere was predominantly idealistic, there were seeds of discord. In the philosophic world, especially in England, realism had attained prominence. With reference to its influence

---

[2] James R. Angell, *Psychology* (4th ed.; New York: Henry Holt and Company, 1904, 1908), 468 pp.

[3] Robert S. Woodworth, *Contemporary Schools of Psychology* (New York: The Ronald Press Company, 1931), p. 12.

on educational thought the most significant effect was the engendering of a distrust of deductive reasoning as the method of arriving at the truth and the advocacy of induction as the method of science. Although the realists subscribed to the quest for certainty, they were inclined to question the conclusions of the idealists and to ask for scientific verification.

There were also beginnings of the pragmatic movement. The pragmatists took sharp issue with both idealists and realists relative to the nature of truth. The "truth" was not to be thought of in an absolute sense. It was what proved to be satisfying relative to a person's purposes and since one's purposes might change, "truth" was a relative matter. This was a revolutionary point of view and through the years following the turn of the century it resulted in a major disturbance of the philosophical atmosphere. Although the idealists were not in agreement with the realists and there were differences of opinion within both schools of thought, they tended to join hands in opposing the pragmatists.

The relatively noncontroversial status of psychology around the turn of the century also included seeds of discord. In his *Talks to Teachers* William James [4] referred "to something like a 'boom' in psychology." The nature of the "new psychology" is not described, but in the chapter on apperception James referred to his earlier comment and it may be inferred that he regarded the contemporary promulgation of apperception as a discordant note in the psychological atmosphere of the time. In the first paragraph of the preface to the 1904 edition of his *Psychology,* Angell referred to "investigating the *structure* of the mind" as the focus of the efforts of psychologists of the past and to the emerging "disposition to deal more fully with its functional and genetic phases." During the following years there was much controversy between the structuralists and the functionalists, although a contemporary writer [5] observed that the difference, "as the functionalists have so far stated the case, is unintelligible." In *Twenty-five Years of American Education,* Daniel B. Leary,[6] writing on the "Development of educational psychology," identified "two trends of thought" around the turn of the century. One, "personified in such people, say, as James, Dewey, and Thorndike," reflected the spirit of scientific inquiry and the inductive approach to educational problems; the other, represented by "De Garmo, Harris, Van Liew, Francis W. Parker, and perhaps Hall," was "more mystical, more moral in the popular sense of that term, more deductive than inductive, not particularly keen about concrete observation, prone to argue about tech-

---

[4] William James, *Talks to Teachers* (New York: Henry Holt and Company, 1899, 1900), p. 6.

[5] John B. Watson, *Behavior* (New York: Henry Holt and Company, 1914), p. 8.

[6] Daniel B. Leary, "Development of Educational Psychology," in *Twenty-five Years of American Education,* ed. I. L. Kandel (New York: The Macmillan Company, 1924).

nicalities, and inclined to worry about words" (p. 94). The teachings of
Thorndike, both through his writings and in the classroom, supplemented
by the rise of behaviorism and other influences, served to make the first
of these "two trends of thought" dominant during the following years.
As Leary's characterization suggests, this "trend of thought" was not much
concerned with philosophical matters. In particular, educational psychologists gave little attention to the mind-body problem. Learning was
studied objectively, i.e. in behavioristic terms.

By the close of the first quarter of the twentieth century the "psychological atmosphere" had become still more complicated and confused.
In addition to the structuralists (existentialists) and the functionalists
(dynamic psychologists), who thought of psychology as the science of
consciousness and whose method was primarily introspectional (subjective), and the behaviorists, who emphasized objective (scientific)
methods and viewed psychology as the science of behavior, there were
added the psychoanalysts, who were concerned with the unconscious
rather than the conscious life of the organism, the purposivists (hormic
psychologists), and finally the Gestaltists. Even this enumeration of
schools of psychology is an oversimplification of the picture. Within each
school there were divergencies of views and of emphases, and without
the schools there were individualists, such as E. L. Thorndike, and the
eclectics or middle-of-the-roaders. Such is the general picture around
1925. Even within some institutional departments of psychology there
were antagonisms and jealousies. In his editorial introduction to Ragsdale's *Modern Psychologies and Education* (1932), M. V. O'Shea referred to "six distinctive schools of psychology" being represented at
the University of Wisconsin, "each being expounded by a partisan and
each having adherents and votaries among students" (p. xv).

Thus as an aspect of the total setting within which teaching-learning
theory developed, psychology evolved from an "established order," in
which the structure of the mind and laws of association were matters
of focal concern, to the status of a number of opposing schools of
psychology. The result was that the psychological background, especially
following about 1910, was one of uncertainty and confusion to the educator who sought the "truth." Although not all authors were committed to
a particular school of psychology, the middle-of-the-road position, which
many attempted, tended to add to the confusion. In addition to the
conflicting psychologies, as represented by protagonists of the recognized
schools, and the eclectic views which frequently amounted to another
psychology, the educator was further confused by the specialization of
interests and hence of emphases in psychological writings and by the
varying technical terminology employed.

As psychology became more scientific (objective), less attention was given to philosophical matters and following the rise of behaviorism, even philosophical implications tended to be ignored. During the past fifteen to twenty years, educational philosophers have emphasized the necessity of psychology "putting its house in order" by developing or accepting from the philosophers a sound philosophical basis for the theories presented. The title of Bode's volume, *Conflicting Psychologies of Learning* (1929), is suggestive of the situation as viewed by philosophers. After reviewing "The dilemma of psychology" (Chapter XII), Bode pointed out that it "arises from the fact that it [educational psychology] cannot do business on the basis of traditional 'mind' or of traditional 'matter,' nor yet on the basis of the two put together" (p. 210). In *Modern Philosophies of Education* (1939) John S. Brubacher also emphasized the fundamental importance of philosophical questions in educational psychology. (See especially Chapter V, "Philosophical aspects of educational psychology.") [7]

Due to the tendency of psychology to divorce itself from philosophy, especially in the sense that educational psychologists gave little attention to philosophical questions, the developments of the period in the field of philosophy functioned less directly in the evolution of teaching-learning theory. However, it should be noted that during the nineties the pragmatism of William James was becoming arrayed against the idealism of Hegel as interpreted by Rosenkranz and Harris and against the realism of science and the scientific method. Later Dewey became an outstanding advocate of the pragmatic position which in recent years has been called "experimentalism." Although these three basic positions relative to the fundamental philosophic question of "What is the essential nature of human beings and of the universe in which they live" have been explained and interpreted with many variations, they may be characterized in general terms as follows: (*a*) The idealist thinks of education in terms of training the "mind" which, after the rejection of faculty psychology, was conceived of in terms of powers, mental functions, and critical intelligence. (*b*) The realist is interested in the external world and to him education is the process whereby the child comes to know this world. (*c*) The pragmatist is concerned with conduct (behavior in a broad sense) and the starting point in education is human purpose.

Such, in broad outline, is the psychological and philosophical background of the evolution of teaching-learning theory during the period

---

[7] Brubacher organized his discussion about the following: "(1) How shall the age-old problem of the relation of mind and body be stated to make the most exact and effective approach to the learning process? (2) Is mind to be conceived as aggressive in acquiring knowledge, or as a sort of container into which wisdom is poured? (3) What is the logic of learning, of capturing the unknown and reducing it to the status of the known?" (John S. Brubacher, *Modern Philosophies of Education* (New York: McGraw-Hill Book Company, Inc., 1939). 370 pp. (p. 103).

following 1890. As a means of providing a more adequate understanding of the more pertinent aspects of this background, the development of psychological and philosophical thought will be traced more fully relative to child development, psychology of learning, and individual differences.

The Child and Child Development

Up to about 1890 psychologists had been concerned almost wholly with the "science of mental life" of adults, and although they were aware that the child differed from the adult, they had postulated that the differences were mainly quantitative rather than qualitative. Thus there was little occasion for considering the nature of the child and his development. The index of James's *The Principles of Psychology* (1890) did not include a reference to the "child." However, by this time psychologists had generally rejected the belief that the child is a "man writ small" and the child-study movement, in which G. Stanley Hall was a prominent leader, was acquiring momentum. The theory that the child is a "little man" still dominated the popular thinking, and some educationists, especially the more conservative ones, generally regarded the "child mind" and the mind of the adult as being "the very same in kind, differing only in relative development and power." [8] Payne argued at some length in support of this belief. The trend of the time, however, is indicated by the number of treatises and other writings on child development published during the nineties.

By 1890 there was general acceptance of the "doctrine of development" in the sense that the "development" of the child's mind was characterized by qualitative changes, and the education of the child was beginning to be thought of largely in terms of such development. Within this general position there was much controversy during the following years. The definition of the issues varied, but with respect to the present purpose attention will be directed in the following questions: (*a*) What is the relative influence of nature and nurture in the child's development? (*b*) In the development process how does each of these factors function relative to the other? (*c*) What is the nature of the product (outcomes) of the development (educative) process? (*d*) Should the desired development be thought of as being toward a determined goal?

These questions and related ones provided opportunity for a variety of "theories" of child development and in writings of the years following 1890 there are numerous descriptive designations — unfoldment, recapitulation, "Nature is Right," preparation, adaptation, adjustment, self-realization, and so on. Instead of two or three clearly defined views,

---

[8] William H. Payne, *Contributions to the Science of Education* (New York: American Book Company, 1886), pp. 120f.

there were about as many theories as there were authoritative writers, some individualistic authors being arrayed against the field, others tending to be eclectic. The principal contributors up to 1900 appear to have been Rosenkranz and Harris, his American sponsor; Froebel, introduced through the kindergarten movement; the Herbartians, especially De Garmo and the McMurrys; G. Stanley Hall and others participating in the child-study movement; and William James.

Rosenkranz [9] asserted that what "we choose to call" faculties are "only different activities of the same power." The activities of "cognitive intelligence" he enumerated as "1) sense-perception, (2) representation [10] (or imagination), (3) thinking" (p. 74). The "perceptive faculty is most active in the infant, the representative faculty in the child, and the thinking faculty in the youth" (p. 74). Rosenkranz then dealt with these three "epochs" (stages) of the child's development. Later (pp. 141f.) he treated the "education of the will" which included "social culture" (becoming "civilized"), "moral culture," and "religious culture."

Rosenkranz thought of the child as being dynamic in the sense of possessing the "power" of attention (pp. 70f.) and the capacity for "self-estrangement" (pp. 26f.), but he defined "education" as "the influencing of man by man" to the end of leading "him to actualize himself through his own efforts" (p. 19). Thus the child developed along the lines noted above under the "influence" of the teacher and other educative agencies. Rosenkranz emphasized that influencing did not mean "training," which was a term to be used relative to "animals" not "man." However, the influencing was to be relatively coercive, punishment being justified when "all other efforts have failed" (p. 38). Rosenkranz did not deal explicitly with the goals of the child's development, but it is apparent that he thought of the development being influenced toward determined goals (p. 10). Tompkins [11] seems to have epitomized the view of Rosenkranz: "Teaching is the process by which one mind, from set purpose, produces the life-unfolding process in another." The phrase "from set purpose" makes explicit what Rosenkranz suggested at several places and the verb "produce" is more in keeping with the general tenor of the volume than our present interpretation of "influence." Thus according to Rosenkranz both nature and nurture functioned in the development (education) of the child which was to be directed toward determined goals. The outcomes of the development were not to be called "trained [disciplined] faculties" but rather "activities [powers] of the mind."

---

[9] J. K. F. Rosenkranz, op. cit., p. 73.

[10] In his editorial comment William T. Harris indicated (p. 74) that "conception" was the preferred term.

[11] Arnold Tompkins, The Philosophy of Teaching (Boston: Ginn and Company, 1891, 1894), p. 9.

Froebel's theory had been introduced in the United States, largely through the kindergarten movement beginning in 1856, and in 1887 a translation of *The Education of Man* was published under the editorship of William T. Harris who was a vigorous sponsor of the kindergarten.[12] The "doctrine of development" advocated by Froebel and his followers differed in certain respects from that set forth by Rosenkranz and tended to be thought of as an opposing view. In *The Education of Man* Froebel emphasized the dynamic qualities of the child and asserted that "the young human being . . . would seek . . . as a product of nature . . . that which is in itself best" (p. 8). "Education . . . should necessarily be *passive, following* (only guarding and protecting), *not prescriptive, categorical, interfering*" (p. 7). At other places there are certain qualifications of this position. For example, Froebel observed that "the original wholeness of the human being to be educated" may be "marred" and that when evidence to this effect is unmistakable, "directly categorical, mandatory education in its full severity is demanded" (p. 10). Also beyond the period of infancy "training prevails" (p. 94). This "training" (apparently in the sense of instruction) was to be conducted "in accordance with fixed and definite conditions lying *outside* the human being" (p. 95). As these qualifications indicate, Froebel conceived of the child's development being toward a goal which in terms of his philosophy (idealism tempered with religious mysticism) he defined as "knowledge and application, consciousness and realization in life, united in the service of a faithful, pure, holy life" (p. 4).

Froebel's statements relative to the nature of the outcomes of the development process are difficult to interpret in terms comparable to the ones employed by Rosenkranz. Among the terms which designate outcomes are "knowledge" (p. 95), "intellect," "will," (p. 96), "insight" (p. 128), and "consciousness" (p. 129). In the "conclusion" he referred to the "all-sided development and unfolding of his [the child's] nature" (p. 327). As this characterization suggests, Froebel conceived of the child's development as an "unfolding of his nature" and was only incidentally concerned with the "content" of the development beyond the qualities of "all-sided" and "Divine Unity" (p. 2). Froebel seems to have been little concerned with psychological aspects of the child's development beyond the thesis—Given the proper environment the child's nature would unfold as the result of his activity—but it is clear that he did not write in terms of faculty psychology.

The Herbartians advocated the recapitulation theory of child develop-

---

[12] See *Report of the Commissioner of Education, 1896-97* (U. S. Bureau of Education, 1898), I, 899-922. This chapter bears the title, "Early history of the kindergarten in St. Louis, Mo." and is taken from Harris' report as superintendent of schools for 1878-79.

ment [13] — the thesis that the child in his development recapitulates (traverses) the epochs of racial development (world culture). This claimed parallelism between the development of the child and that of the race was the basis of a curriculum theory referred to as "culture epochs." By the time the child entered school he was considered to have reached the stage in his development corresponding to the culture epoch represented by "folklore and fairy tales." During the following years he traversed succeeding epochs, attaining that of "social and political development, and scientific and philosophic mind" in the seventh and eighth grades.

The Herbartians also advocated the apperception theory of learning and its correlative concept of mind-content as the outcome of the development (educative) process. According to this psychology of learning, the ideas present in the child's mind at a given time (apperceptive mass) functioned as a "reception committee" relative to "new ideas" and the perception of objects.[14] As "new ideas" were welcomed they were assimilated, thus increasing the apperceptive mass. In the assimilation there was "comparison" and "generalization." The outcome of the development process was variously designated — "logical notions" [15] "character," "ideals" [16] — but it may be referred to as the "content" of the child's mind. This "content" consisted of "ideas" connected and organized into a harmonious whole.

Thus the total Herbartian theory of child development was a combination of the recapitulation thesis and the apperception concept of learning. From the point of view of the former, child nature was the determining factor in the sense that the environment (school curriculum) should be adjusted to the stages of the child's development. From the point of view of the latter, the environment, particularly school instruction, was the dominant influence. The child was regarded as relatively passive. Through childhood a succession of "powerful instinctive interests" appeared and each of these interests was to be seized and utilized "at the time of its greatest intensity" as a means of increasing the momentum of "all the child's efforts, both receptive and expressive." [17] The

[13] Charles C. Van Liew, "The Educational Theory of the Culture Epochs," *First Yearbook,* Herbart Society for the Scientific Study of Teaching (Chicago: University of Chicago Press, 1895), pp. 67-114; "In Reply to Some Comments on the Culture Epoch Theory," *Second Yearbook,* National Herbart Society (Bloomington, Illinois: Pantagraph Printing and Stationery Company, 1896), pp. 130-40.

[14] Charles A. McMurry, *The Elements of General Method* (New York: The Macmillan Company, 1903), pp. 257, 263.

[15] Charles A. McMurry and Frank M. McMurry, *The Method of the Recitation* (New York: The Macmillan Company, 1897, 1903), p. 51 *et passim.*

[16] William C. Bagley, *The Educative Process* (New York: The Macmillan Company, 1905), p. 220.

[17] Charles A. McMurry, *The Elements of General Method,* p. 116.

emphasis was upon the "powerful instinctive interests" as a condition of favorable receptivity. This view of the child is implied in the "steps" of Herbartian methodology. In the first "step" the child is "prepared," i.e. a condition of favorable receptivity is created for what is to be "presented." The "preparation" was facilitated by seizing and utilizing instinctive interests and the seizing and utilizing were facilitated by synchronizing the organization of selected subject matter (culture materials) with the child's development which was considered to be a recapitulation of racial development.[18]

The Herbartians were concerned mainly with the "how" of teaching and hence there was little reference to the aim of education in their writings. For example, in *The Method of the Recitation* the McMurrys stated: "It is taken for granted that the teacher has a definite object in view in each recitation" (p. 107). But there was no treatment of the question of what that object should be. In *Elements of General Method* a chapter was devoted to "The chief aim of education" which was designated as building "moral character." The criteria of "moral character" had been indicated by Herbart [19] but with respect to the present purpose the significant point is the assumption that the "teacher has a definite object in view," i.e. the child's development was to be directed toward determined goals.

The child-study movement under the leadership of G. Stanley Hall emphasized the child as a developing organism and directed attention to his distinctive characteristics at the several stages of his development. The direction of the effect of the movement is indicated by the fact that in 1913 Thorndike [20] characterized Hall as an advocate of the "Nature is Right" doctrine. The child-study group did not originate this doctrine. It is to be found in the writings of Froebel (see p. 16) and before him Rousseau had emphasized it. It had been supported by the Herbartians in their advocacy of the recapitulation and culture-epoch theories. Furthermore, Hall, in what presumably was a considered interpretation of child-study theory relative to educational procedure,[21] in effect qualified the "Nature is Right" doctrine in a significant respect.

He gave a limited description of the "ideal school" for children up to the age of eight or nine in which the "Nature is Right" doctrine is apparent. The period from eight or nine to the dawn of puberty

[18] *Ibid.*, pp. 114f

[19] See Charles De Garmo, *Herbart and the Herbartians* (New York: Charles Scribner's Sons, 1895), Part I, Chap. IV.

[20] Edward L. Thorndike, *Educational Psychology, Vol. I: The Original Nature of Man* (New York: Teachers College, Columbia University, 1913), p. 271.

[21] G. Stanley Hall, "The Ideal School as Based on Child Study," *Addresses and Proceedings* (National Educational Association, 1901), pp. 474-88.

should be mainly devoted to drill, habituation, and mechanism . . . discipline should be the watchword here. . . . It is the time to break in the human colt, which is by nature, in some sense, the wildest of all wild animals . . . arithmetic . . . should be mechanized, with plenty of mental exercises, and later with rules and processes for written work, with only little attempt at explanation. . . . Even with respect to morals and conduct the chief duty of the child at this age is to obey (pp. 477f.).

Although his "ideal school" was presented as being indicated by the nature of the child at this stage of his development, the content of the curriculum and to some extent the method of teaching were really Hall's ideas, and in effect he was proposing that during this period when the child's nature offered favorable conditions, the environment should be designed to mould (train, break in) the child in conformity with predetermined educational aims. Incidentally, it may be noted that Hall's views here tend to be in agreement with those of James relative to habit formation. During adolescence "the drill and mechanism of the previous period must be gradually relaxed, and an appeal must be made to freedom and interest." Hall criticized the American high school for its distrust of human nature.

Outside of Hall and others who were directly concerned with the child-study movement, American psychologists of the time seem to have been a relatively minor influence in the psychological atmosphere within which educators thought about teaching-learning theory until the publication of *Talks to Teachers* by William James in 1899. He described education as "the organization of acquired habits of conduct and tendencies to behavior." [22] This designation is not systematically analyzed and described. James referred to the function of the teacher as "mainly that of *building up useful systems of association* in the pupil's mind" (p. 83), but the significance of the qualification "mainly" is not made explicit. It appears that James thought of a very large proportion of conduct (behavior) as being controlled by habits (systems of association), but the appearance of "tendencies to behavior" in the description of education noted above indicates that he recognized other controls of conduct. This inference is supported by his use of such phrases as *"faculty of effort"* (p. 75), *"power of judging"* (p. 78), and *"power of voluntarily attending"* (p. 188). Relative to the process of development (education) James assigned the major role to the environment (teacher), the child's nature providing the opportunity for the optimum functioning of the school.

James was a major influence in psychological circles from 1890 until after the turn of the century. It is difficult to characterize his influence in the area of child development. He contributed to the reaction against

---

[22] William James, *op. cit.,* p. 29.

"formal discipline" and "transfer of training" which were still prominent in educator thinking in 1890, but he supported "training" as an educative process. He was critical of the contemporary child-study movement [23] and dealt with the child's development only incidentally. He conceived of the child more as plastic than dynamic. Instincts were transitory and "ripened" in a "certain determinate order" (pp. 60-61). He criticized "apperception" but tended to support Herbartian psychology in several respects.

At the beginning of the twentieth century the psychological and philosophical theory relative to the child and his development reflected a confused accumulation of views from Froebel, Herbart (or rather the Herbartians), James, Hall and other child-study devotees, and Rosenkranz and Harris plus a residue from faculty psychology and formal discipline. The presence of this "residue" is indicative of the confusion. Rosenkranz, writing in 1848, noted the rejection of faculty psychology by psychologists.[24] Herbartian theory was explicitly opposed to both faculty psychology and formal discipline. James had been emphatic in his opposition. Hence it would seem that by 1900 there would be no supporters of faculty psychology and formal discipline in psychological circles. However, this does not appear to have been the case. In *Education as Adjustment* O'Shea [25] cited a supporter of as late date as 1900 [26] and in *Democracy and Education* Dewey [27] criticized "Education as training of faculties" at some length, thus implying that the view was still current to an extent sufficient to justify such treatment.

There was little clarification of the situation during the first decade of the century. O'Shea advanced "adjustment" as the designation of the sound theory of child development.[28] Judd proposed that development be conceived of as "adaptation." [29] Both of these authors were endeavoring to promote an eclectic (average) view, but the proposed terminology was not widely used during the following years, and it does not appear that much clarification resulted from the efforts of these educational psychologists. William C. Bagley was more influential. In *The Educative Process* (1905) he presented an eclectic theory of development constructed about the apperception concept of learning. He stressed as the

[23] *Ibid.*, pp. 12-13.

[24] J. K. F. Rosenkranz, *op. cit.*, p. 73.

[25] M. V. O'Shea, *Education as Adjustment* (New York: Longmans, Green, and Company, 1903), p. 70.

[26] T. F. G. Dexter and A. H. Garlick, *Psychology in the Schoolroom* (New York: Longmans, Green, and Company, 1900). 413 pp.

[27] John Dewey, *Democracy and Education* (New York: The Macmillan Company, 1916), pp. 70-79.

[28] M. V. O'Shea, *op. cit.*, Chap. V to VIII.

[29] Charles H. Judd, *Genetic Psychology for Teachers* (New York: D. Appleton and Company, 1903), p. 135 *et passim*.

significant characteristic of the child his capacity to "profit" in his development "not only by his own experiences" but also "by the experiences of the race" (Chap. I). This capacity was conceived of largely in terms of the plasticity inherent in the child's nature (pp. 30-32), and the environment, particularly the school, was the "all-important" factor in the child's development (p. 36). However, the child by nature had the capacity for "passive attention," i.e. he "naturally" attended to certain stimuli of his environment (p. 97). Furthermore, he possessed the capacity for developing "secondary passive attention," i.e. the capacity for developing (acquiring) the functional equivalent of natural (instinctive) attention (p. 101). Hence Bagley did recognize the child as a dynamic factor in his development but only to a limited extent. In his conception of the outcomes of the development process he was explicitly eclectic. He recognized habits (both sensori-motor and ideo-motor) and "moral habits" (pp. 117-21); "concepts and apperceptive systems" (pp. 144f.); and "ideals" in terms of which he explained transfer of training (pp. 210f.). "Social efficiency" was the "ultimate aim of education" (p. 61) and hence the criterion of the child's development.

The trend of "majority" opinion around the end of the first decade seems to have been in the direction of agreement, at least in regard to the general aspects of the nature of the child and his development. The child's developing nature, particularly his instincts, provided the opportunity for the effective functioning of the environment which was thought of as the dominant influence in his education. A defined aim of education should be the principal criterion in selecting the school environment (curriculum), but the child's developing nature should be the dominant criterion in organizing the selected materials. The "majority" thinking in regard to the outcomes of the development (learning) process was along the lines of Bagley's proposal. It would, however, be a distortion of the facts not to note certain developing influences that disturbed the trend toward an "established order."

Although Thorndike did not deal systematically with child development in his three-volume *Educational Psychology,* the work was one of the major influences in the thinking of the following years. In Volume I, *The Original Nature of Man* (1913), a series of nine chapters was devoted to an inventory of "original tendencies," and it is clear that Thorndike credited the child with a considerable "natural" equipment and he indicated that his inventory represented a middle position among psychologists of the time (pp. 199f.). He criticized the recapitulation theory (pp. 245f.) and the theory that original tendencies appeared suddenly, remained for a brief period, and then disappeared "unless then and there fixed as habits," which afforded the basis of James's admonition "to strike the iron while hot" (pp. 264f.). He criticized at even greater length the

"Nature is Right" doctrine (pp. 271f.). Although he tempered his conclusion that "original nature is imperfect and untrustworthy" (p. 310) and observed that "we cannot deal with it wholesale" (p. 282), his argument doubtless contributed materially to the reaction against the unfoldment theory and other applications of the "Nature is Right" doctrine.

   Thorndike's positive contributions to the thinking about child development are less easy to identify. What the child becomes in the sense of "intellect, character, and skill" is "the result of the original nature of man, the laws of learning, and the forces of nature amongst which man lives and learns." [30] Since the "laws of learning" are included among the "original human tendencies," nature would appear to be the dominant influence in a child's development (education). In Volume III, *Mental Work and Fatigue and Individual Differences and Their Causes*, Thorndike [31] devoted a chapter to "The influence of the environment" as a cause of individual differences. After reviewing "the available facts" he stated that the "interpretation is left to the student" (p. 310) and then directed attention to "certain cautions." The principal point of these cautions is that the question of the relative contributions of nature and nurture to the child's development should not be dealt with on a "wholesale" basis. In the area of "the more primitive and fundamental traits in human nature such as energy, capability, persistence, leadership, sympathy and nobility," school environment can contribute little. In the area of intellectual and moral qualities the environment provided is a determining influence (p. 313). "To the real work of man for man,— the increase of achievement through the improvement of environment, — the influence of heredity offers no barrier" (p. 311).

   The outcomes of the learning process were conceived of as "situation-response connections," the total encompassed in an educated man's "intellect, character and skill" running "well up into the millions." [32] For convenience a "group of connections" may be referred to as a "mental function," but Thorndike did not attempt an enumeration or classification of the "mental functions" resulting from the educative process. However, a lengthy chapter is devoted to "The influence of improvement in one mental function upon the efficiency of other functions," a designation indicating his interpretation of the problem of transfer of training. He noted a marked change in psychological opinion since the publication of his earlier *Educational Psychology* in 1903 and an apparent tendency in 1913 of "some careless thinkers" to believe that "training is totally special-

   [30] Edward L. Thorndike, *Educational Psychology, Vol. II: The Psychology of Learning* (New York: Teachers College, Columbia University, 1913), p. 1.

   [31] Edward L. Thorndike, *Educational Psychology, Vol. III: Mental Work and Fatigue and Individual Differences and Their Causes* (New York: Teachers College, Columbia University, 1914), Chap. XIII.

   [32] Edward L. Thorndike, *Educational Psychology, Vol. II: The Psychology of Learning* (1913), p. 4.

ized" (pp. 364-65). As the second of these observations suggests, Thorndike in 1913 recognized the possibility of outcomes (groups of situation-
response connections) whose functioning would be "general," at least
to some degree (pp. 420f.).

Thorndike wrote as a psychologist and did not explicitly consider the
question of the end of the child's development. There are, however, a
few incidental implications that the child's learning was to be directed
toward determined goals.[33] He expressed approval of "the doctrine so
brilliantly and earnestly defended by Dewey, that school work must be
so arranged as to arouse the problem-attitude" and also of the "general
principle" that "school tasks must be significant at the time to those doing
them." [34] The explicit approval of these principles suggests development
stemming from child interests, needs, and purposes, but in the light of
earlier statements [35] and his criticism of the "Nature is Right" doctrine,
it is improbable that he intended this inference. It seems fair to say that
Thorndike assumed that a goal (aim) was to be set for the intellectual
and moral aspects of the child's development and that the environment,
especially the school environment, was to be selected and arranged with
that aim in view as the means of utilizing the child's original nature in
the developmental process. In this concept of development the emphasis
is upon the environmental stimuli rather than the child's dynamic
qualities.

John Dewey is generally recognized as a major influence in the thinking about child development, especially the aspects dealt with under the
head of education. The publication of *Democracy and Education* (1916)
was an influential event of the second decade. In this volume Dewey
stressed his concept of the child's development as the product of his
reactions to the environment within which he lived (p. 13). As a factor
in these reactions the child possessed the "power to grow" which was
described as a "positive force or ability" (pp. 50f.). Although Dewey emphasized that the child should not be thought of as a "dependent" and
"plastic" organism in the conventional sense, he tended to minimize
the child's dynamic qualities [36] and to regard the environment as the
determining influence in the child's development (pp. 86-88).

Dewey stressed development (education) as a growth process. As such
it is characterized by continuity in the sense that what the child learns

[33] *Ibid.*, p. 230.
[34] *Ibid.*, pp. 225-26.
[35] Edward L. Thorndike, *The Principles of Teaching* (New York: A. G. Seiler,
1906), pp. 3-6; "The Contribution of Psychology to Education," *Journal of Educational Psychology*, 1 (1910), 5-12.
[36] This statement is made with cognizance of Dewey's emphasis upon the child as a
dynamic factor in some of his earlier writings, for example *The School and Society*,
p. 55 *et passim*.

from one reaction to his environment is a factor, at least potentially, in subsequent experiencing. Thus education as a process is defined as "that reconstruction or reorganization of experience which adds to the meaning of experience, and which increases ability to direct the course of subsequent experience" (pp. 89-90). Dewey presented this concept of education (development) in a setting of criticism of other theories — "preparation," "unfolding," "training of the faculties" (formal discipline), "formation" (Herbartian theory), and "recapitulation and retrospection" (pp. 63-89) and thus created the impression that all other theories of development were wrong.

A principal point of criticism was the postulation of an "external goal" toward which the development was to be directed. Dewey asserted that "the educational process has no end beyond itself; it is its own end" (p. 59). Although he devoted some three pages to an explanation, a precise interpretation of this assertion and others of similar import requires careful reading of other sections and some interpolation. Dewey was emphasizing his protest against the traditional, and at the time of his writing still the popular, concept of development (education) as being directed toward preconceived goals. The basis of his protest was both philosophical and psychological. As a philosopher Dewey was a pragmatist and hence he did not accept the idealist thesis of absolutes and insisted that the criterion of value was inherent in the current situation, which, of course, was characterized by change. Thus a goal external, to the current situation and remote in time was contrary to his philosophy. Psychologically, Dewey insisted that a goal external to the current situation and remote in realization was lacking in motivating influence. Hence it was necessary to resort to extrinsic motivation and under such conditions the development (educative) process was inefficient.

On the other hand, Dewey did not mean that the development process was not to be directed. In a previous chapter he stated: "The natural or native impulses of the young do not agree with the life-customs of the group into which they are born. Consequently they have to be directed or guided" (p. 47). This direction or guidance was conceived of as residing in "the nature of the situation in which the young take part" (p. 47). Since the objective aspects of this situation (environment) are subject to control by the "group," especially in the case of school environment, the group (mainly the adults of the group) does in effect direct or guide the development of the young. Furthermore, the control of this environment (social as well as physical) was to be in accordance with a criterion [37] which at least implied a goal or end of the child's development (education) (p. 22). Unfortunately, Dewey's concept of this criterion is obscure. In one place he mentioned that the criterion implied a "particular social ideal" (p. 115); in another there is reference to a "truly shared or associated life" (p. 45). Then he further confused the matter by asserting in the chapter on "Aims in education" that his "whole conception forbids" seeking "an end [aim] outside of the educative process" (p. 117). Thus Dewey appears to deny what he implied at other places. What he meant was perhaps that the continuing experiencing should be directed to the end of optimum quality of future experiences. The quality of an experience, as Dewey observed later,[38] has two aspects — its "immediate aspect of agreeableness or disagreeableness" and "its influence upon later experiences." In *Democracy and Education* Dewey emphasized the second of these aspects but did not make clear the implied thesis that in the planning of current experiencing (selecting the environment), attention should be given to the probable influence upon future experiencing. In other words, the planner (teacher) should consider the question: Will this experience probably contribute to future experiences in the direction of agreeableness? Dewey postulated a changing, developing society rather than a static one and he appears to have believed that it would be inconsistent to specify what would promote agreeableness in the relatively remote future. It seems clear, especially in the light of later writings, that he recognized agreeable continued living in the sense of a "truly shared or associated life" as a goal. Such a goal is within the educative process in the sense that it is inherent in the reconstruction of experience.

Thorndike and Dewey were major influences in the thinking about the child and his development (education), but it is not easy to appraise the effect of either of them on the ideas of the time. Both seem to have been misinterpreted in the sense that certain aspects of their views were accepted without adequate recognition of other aspects which in effect constituted significant qualifications. Thorndike's concept of the outcomes as "situation-response connections" and his S-R bond terminology were widely accepted without recognizing that both the situation and the response might be "patterned," i.e. there might be outcomes which in the sense of their functioning were general in some degree rather than specific. The tendency on the part of some persons to classify Thorndike as a behaviorist represents another "misinterpretation." Judd's exaggerated criticism [39] of Thorndike, characterized as "one of the strongest opponents of the doctrine of formal discipline," may be cited as still

[38] John Dewey, *Experience and Education* (New York: The Macmillan Company, 1938), p. 16.

[39] Charles H. Judd, *Psychology of High-school Subjects* (Boston: Ginn and Company, 1915), Chap. XVII.

another misinterpretation. These and other misinterpretations [40] suggest that the effect of Thorndike's writings was not wholly in the direction of clarifying the psychological atmosphere.

Dewey's assertion that the developmental (educative) process "has no end beyond itself; it is its own end" [41] attracted attention and his somewhat obscure thesis that the development should be "directed" through the control of the environment in accordance with his concept of "democracy" [42] tended to be overlooked. This misinterpretation was perhaps suggested by Dewey's trenchant criticism of other theories of development, some of which as of the date of his writing tended to be "strawmen." Whatever the cause, Dewey on later occasions attempted to correct the "misinterpretation." In 1926 he characterized the completely child-centered school as "really stupid." [43] Again in *Experience and Education* (1938) he was repeatedly critical of those who conceived of the child's development as being unguided. Incidentally, it may be noted that although he emphasized the guidance function of the teacher (p. 64 *et passim*), he was only a little more communicative in regard to the criterion of the direction than in 1915. Probably the most explicit statement is the assertion that "the organized subject-matter of the adult and the specialist . . . represents the goal toward which education should continuously move" (p. 103). The interpretation is not made clear. Presumably Dewey did not intend that it be interpreted in the conventional sense, but the statement does emphasize one of the major points of the volume, namely, that the development (education) of the child was to be guided (directed).

The prestige of his institutional connection, his standing as a psychologist, and the "practical" quality of his writings combined to make Thorndike the dominant influence in the psychological atmosphere within which many members of the educator group thought about child development during the following years. For these persons there was relatively little confusion and disagreement until the attacks upon atomistic psychology and the intensified rivalry among schools of psychology. Thus for a time Thorndike's influence was in the direction of clarifying the psychological atmosphere for a considerable portion of the educator group. Dewey also had a following which became known as the Progressives. Although the Progressives acclaimed Dewey as their leader, the controversy within the ranks suggests that they thought in

---

[40] Arthur I. Gates, "Connectionism: Present Concepts and Interpretations," *Forty-first Yearbook*, Part II, National Society for the Study of Education, 1942, Chap. IV.

[41] John Dewey, *Democracy and Education*, p. 59.

[42] *Ibid.*, p. 45.

[43] John Dewey, "Individuality and Experience," *Journal of Barnes Foundation*, 2 (January, 1926), 1-6.

a confused atmosphere. Dewey has indicated, as shown above, that he was misinterpreted, or at least inadequately interpreted. It appears that some of the blame for this effect should be assigned to Dewey because of his failure to make explicit certain aspects of his position. Thus relative to clarifying the psychological and philosophical atmosphere of the time Dewey did not contribute much. In fact, it might be argued that the net effect up to about 1925 was in the direction of increased confusion.[44]

In presenting the Stanford Revision of the Binet-Simon Intelligence Scale, L. M. Terman proposed the IQ (intelligence quotient — ratio of mental age to chronological age) as a measure having predictive significance relative to the child's mental development.[45] This suggested use of the IQ was based "on the assumption that the intelligence quotient remains practically constant during the years of mental growth" (pp. 52-54). Terman interpreted the limited evidence of the time as supporting this assumption (hypothesis) "in a general way" (p. 55). In a companion volume [46] Terman wrote more positively in regard to the constancy of the IQ and its predictive value. A little later he stated,[47] "the IQ is sufficiently constant to make it a practical and serviceable basis for mental classification" and also "for predicting a child's later school progress" (p. 158).

Thus Terman made conspicuous two theses relative to child development: (a) nature practically determines the child's "mental development," deviations from the average nurture (environment) affecting the development very little; [48] and (b) the child's mental development (intelligence) practically determines his school progress or educative development (rate and quality of his school achievement). Although "most scientific students" of the nature-nurture problem at that time tended to assign a major role to heredity (nature) in the child's mental development (intelligence), relatively few subscribed to the extreme position proposed by Terman and his followers. [49] After reviewing "all experi-

[44] In support of this appraisal, see Michael Demiashkevich, *An Introduction to the Philosophy of Education* (New York: American Book Company, 1935), p. 136. Robert Ulich, *History of Educational Thought* (New York: American Book Company, 1945), pp. 334-36.

[45] Lewis M. Terman and Others, *The Stanford Revision and Extension of the Binet-Simon Scale for Measuring Intelligence* (Baltimore: Warwick and York, Inc., 1917), p. 56.

[46] Lewis M. Terman, *The Measurement of Intelligence* (Boston: Houghton Mifflin Company, 1916), p. 68.

[47] Lewis M. Terman, *The Intelligence of School Children* (Boston: Houghton Mifflin Company, 1919), pp. 149-50.

[48] *Ibid.*, pp. 10-15.

[49] As an example of the extreme position taken by some, see "The School as a Selective Agency" (an editorial), *Journal of Educational Research*, 3 (February, 1921), 138-39.

mental, statistical, and historical material thus far accumulated on the problems of mental heredity," Starch concluded that the evidence leads "one almost to a fatalistic philosophy." As the presence of the qualifying word "almost" suggests, Starch was reluctant to accept this view but his "note of optimism" was limited mainly to observing that "rarely does anyone do his best or attain his limit even in a single capacity" and hence that nature sets a limit rather than determines educational development.[50] Gates (*Psychology for Students of Education*, 1923) did not deal as specifically with the matter, but he tended to reflect the same position (p. 433 *et passim*).

On the other hand, some behaviorists, particularly J. B. Watson, tended toward an extreme antiheredity position in their emphasis on conditioning. Thorndike's S-R bond theory of learning, which was compatible with behaviorism in several respects, reflected the training concept of child development and minimized the dynamic qualities of the child. Dewey mentioned the matter only incidentally, but his general position may be interpreted as giving support to the environment as the controlling influence in the child's educational development. A paper presented at the 1922 meeting of the National Society of College Teachers of Education by Bagley [51] served to focus attention on the controversy which has continued through the years.

The nature-nurture issue, especially the question of the relative influence of the two factors upon the development of intelligence, was the basis of considerable research,[52] but the interpretation of the findings tended to be influenced by the bias of the investigator. The *Twenty-seventh Yearbook* (Parts I and II) (1928) was heavily weighted with the hereditarian position. The psychological atmosphere of the third decade, especially that of educational psychology, tended to be behavioristic, or at least Thorndikean, and hence the hereditarian view was not as dominant as might be supposed from an examination of the explicitly controversial literature. Many psychologists maintained a middle-of-the-road position, recognizing that both nature and nurture were factors in the child's development. Some pointed out that probably the relative influence of the two factors varied among children.[53]

During the years following 1928 the nature-nurture problem continued

<hr/>

[50] Daniel Starch, *Educational Psychology* (New York: The Macmillan Company, 1919), pp. 94-96.

[51] William C. Bagley, *Determinism in Education* (Baltimore: Warwick and York, Inc., 1925), Chap. I.

[52] For example, see *Nature and Nurture: Their Influence upon Achievement*, Twenty-seventh Yearbook, Part II, National Society for the Study of Education, 1928. 397 pp.

[53] Clarence E. Ragsdale, *Modern Psychologies and Education* (New York: The Macmillan Company, 1932), pp. 164-65.

to command the attention of numerous psychologists, and in 1940 the National Society for the Study of Education published another yearbook, entitled *Intelligence: Its Nature and Nurture*. The chairman of the committee, George D. Stoddard, was a leader among the environmentalists, and research favoring this point of view was given attention, at least equal to that favoring the opposing position. Environmentalist authors pointed to research that supported, if it did not prove, their position. The hereditarians did likewise in addition to directing attention to weaknesses and limitations in studies interpreted as supporting the environmentalist position. The appraisals of the yearbook by committee members reflected evaluations and interpretations in line with their respective positions.

This yearbook and some other writings of the time probably exaggerated the controversial status of the nature-nurture problem. Although there is still controversy among students of child development, the typical position is to recognize both nature and nurture as factors in the child's development and to be more concerned with understanding the functioning of environmental influences (home, school, community, etc.) to the end that the optimum interaction between nature and nurture may be provided rather than with establishing either a nature or a nurture doctrine. The psychological atmosphere is less deterministic than during the twenties, but there are few extreme environmentalists.

Viewed in retrospect it does not appear that the psychological and philosophical atmosphere of the area of child development has afforded a satisfying background for educators concerned with developing teaching-learning theory. There has been much criticism of opposing views and although numerous authors attempted to promote a middle-of-the-road position, the high visibility of controversial writings tends to create the impression that an educator seeking the "truth" was faced with an either-or situation. From the vantage point of the present it is easy to be critical of the past, but it does appear that some critics tended to set up strawmen as a means of attracting attention. On the other hand, authors of prestige and their followers have in many instances been guilty of exaggeration in presenting their beliefs, at least in the sense that they overemphasized certain items and failed to give prominence to qualifying statements.

Recently there has been less criticism of the type to be found in earlier writings and evidence of attempts to direct attention to the points of agreement rather than those of disagreement. One of the most significant of these attempts is represented by the Forty-first Yearbook, Part II, *The Psychology of Learning* (1942). Dewey [54] has commented on the

---

[54] John Dewey, *Experience and Education* (New York: The Macmillan Company, 1938) 116 pp.

unfortunate consequence of *"Either-Or* philosophies." A few years ago "nature *versus* nurture" was a fairly common designation; now "nature and nurture" is generally employed. "Transfer of training" is no longer an issue, at least in the former sense. Thus there appears to be emerging a clearer atmosphere relative to the nature of the child and his development.

Psychology of Learning

Although the differentiation should not be pressed too far, two levels of thinking may be noted in this background area — the psychologist's psychology of learning and the educator's psychology of learning. The psychologists have been concerned with *systems* of psychology within which "learning" is only a chapter. Thus in their thinking they have given attention to questions relating to the fundamental nature of learning and to other matters important in a system of psychology. The psychologists, except those who may be more appropriately designated as "educational psychologists," have been little interested until comparatively recently in schoolroom learning. Consequently, their treatment of the psychology of learning, in both spirit and terminology, has been of the pure-science type and relatively sterile with respect to obvious implications for teaching-learning theory. In contrast, educators, including some persons of standing as psychologists, have been more interested in learning as a process to be stimulated and directed by the teacher than in psychological systems, and they have tended to give little attention to some matters considered fundamental by psychologists. Consequently, their "psychologies of learning" have not always been psychologically respectable, but they tended to be more understandable to the educator and hence more influential with respect to teaching-learning theory as conceived by teacher educators. This differentiation was conspicuous for some years following 1890, but it gradually faded out and has little application to the period since about 1930.

The educators of 1890 thought of learning in terms of the mental activity of the pupil, i.e. learning occurred as the result of the pupil's mental activity. The mind (soul) was capable of several types of activity. Its capability for a type of activity, e.g. perceiving a material object or reasoning, was rather generally referred to as a "power" rather than a "faculty." Although the names employed to designate "powers" were much the same as those that had been used for "faculties," some writers made clear that they were not subscribing to the outmoded faculty psychology.[55] In other words, there was a distinct tendency to think of the mind in terms of its functioning. Learning referred to pupil activity as the

---

[55] For example, Emerson E. White, *The Elements of Pedagogy* (New York: American Book Company, 1886), p. 21 *et passim.*

means of acquiring "power, knowledge, and skill." This activity consisted of the "natural and harmonious activity" of the several powers of the mind.[56] Along with the departure from the outmoded faculty psychology there was a disposition to discard the formal-discipline concept of learning. However, the "natural and harmonious activity" of the several powers of the mind was thought of as having a disciplinary effect in the sense that the powers were "developed and trained" as the result of the mind's activity. White asserted that the "developing of power should be made the leading aim of teaching" (p. 123), but he made clear that repetition (drill) contributed little and might be harmful in the attainment of this aim. Philosophically, the psychology of learning of the educator group was idealistic. The mind (soul) was *real*, consisting of the sensibility, the intellect, and the will. The nervous system was the "organ" of the soul.

Most psychologists of 1890 were concerned with explaining and describing consciousness or mental states. There was little explicit attention to learning and what was said was under the head of "association" or "habit." In his *Talks to Teachers*,[57] developed from lectures first given in 1892, James included the following chapter titles: "The association of ideas," "The acquisition of ideas," and "The laws of habit." In view of the fact that these "talks" were explicitly addressed to teachers and that they were the product of an extended experience in presenting the material to teacher audiences, it is reasonable to assume that James had evolved a treatment of these topics that was more "practical" for teachers than that offered by typical psychological texts of the time. In the chapter on "The association of ideas," after directing attention to the "stream of consciousness," James stated the "two fundamental 'laws of association'" as an explanation of the succession of the "waves" which make up the "stream of consciousness." "The *Law of Contiguity* tells us that objects thought of in the coming wave [of consciousness] are such as in some previous experience were *next* to the objects represented in the wave that is passing away. . . . The *Law of Similarity* says that, when contiguity fails to describe what happens, the coming objects will prove to *resemble* the going objects, even though the two were never experienced together before" (p. 80).

In commenting on these laws, James observed that the educator's principal task was "to break up bad associations or wrong ones, to build others in, to guide the associative tendencies into the most fruitful channels" (p. 84), but that the application of the "laws" to this task was difficult. "Psychology can state the laws: concrete tact and talent alone can work them to useful results" (p. 84). Later in the discussion he

[56] *Ibid.*, p. 119.
[57] William James, *op. cit.*

offered a practical suggestion: ". . . in working associations into your pupils' minds, you must not rely on single cues, but multiply the cues as much as possible" (p. 89). The chapter on "The acquisition of ideas" is devoted largely to the importance of following the natural (instinctive) order of the "awakening of the faculties" (p. 149) in the process of education. The treatment of "The laws of habit" is somewhat more practical in that it is centered about certain "maxims" such as, "Never suffer an exception to occur till the new habit is securely rooted in your life" (pp. 68-69).

Angell, whose *Psychology* (1904, 1908) was widely used as a text in teacher-training institutions, dealt with "learning" even less explicitly. The term does not appear in either the chapter headings or the index, and it is rarely employed in the text. Although there are a few suggestive paragraph headings such as "the process of development of concepts," the volume tends to be sterile with respect to an explanation of the learning process. Judd, in *Genetic Psychology for Teachers* (1903), a volume written after "a number of years spent in teaching psychology to classes of teachers," dealt with "learning" more explicitly but the index includes only two entries under this head, "learning games" and "learning languages." There are other mentions of learning in the text but, on the whole, the treatment of learning is fragmentary and partial. In the index of Judd's *Psychology* (1907, 1917) there are three entries, "learning curve," "learning handwriting," and "learning, units of" but the volume does not provide a systematic treatment of learning.

The psychological atmosphere of the time included also physiological or "experimental" psychology, in which attention was focused on the nervous system and its functioning. It was assumed that mental states were accompanied by physiological processes, and since these physiological correlates could be studied objectively, there was opportunity to avoid the subjective (introspectional) methods of associationism. Although physiological psychology does not appear to have attained the status of a "school," it deserves recognition as a factor in the psychological atmosphere. Many associationistic authors devoted one or more chapters to physiological psychology. There was little explicit treatment of learning, but there was the obvious implication that it was the establishment of preferred (favorable) pathways or conduction units within the nervous system.

The general attitude of psychologists toward learning during the first decade of the twentieth century is indicated by Cameron's article on "learning" in *A Cyclopedia of Education* (1912). The text of this article occupies only one column and there are no cross references to other articles. Three types of learning are recognized — "formation and development of perceptual processes," "acquisition of bodily habits," and "acquisition of power of response through the medium of ideas." [58] The word "association" was not used in the article, but in both spirit and content the implied psychology is associationistic. The article is typical of the time in that there is no reference to "how children learn" beyond the observation that in school "most of these forms of learning are combined."

During this period (1890 to about 1910) when psychologists gave little explicit attention to learning, the Herbartian theory of learning, commonly referred to as "apperception," became the "psychology of learning" for many educators concerned with teaching-learning theory. For example, Bagley (*The Educative Process*, 1905) dealt with learning largely in terms of "apperception," [59] even though he acknowledged that the term "has fallen into something . . . akin to disrepute". (p. 81). In *Talks to Teachers* (1899, 1900) James devoted a chapter to "Apperception" in which he asserted that "psychology itself can easily dispense with the word, useful as it may be in pedagogics" (p. 157). The attitude of psychologists of the time is further shown by Dewey's observation that Herbartianism was "essentially a schoolmaster's psychology, not the psychology of a child." [60]

Thus from 1890 to about 1910 the psychological background relating to learning consisted of a mixture of the modified faculty psychology, Herbartian apperception, associationism (structural and functional), and physiological psychology. The first two of these ingredients were supplied by educator psychologists, the last two by psychologists who, with the possible exception of James, had little interest in a conception of learning that would provide a basis for developing a theory of teaching. Such a background must have been confusing to an educator who sought the "true" theory of learning. In the Herbartian theory of learning (apperception), the important outcomes were ideas (content); in the modified "faculty psychology," the important result was development (training) of the powers of the mind. Hence these two concepts of learning stood in opposition. In associationism the product of learning was associations which implied a mind theory similar to that of apperception. In physio-

----

[58] "Language, written and spoken," is explicitly included and inferentially skills (specific habits) in various school subjects.

[59] Bagley (1905) defined apperception as the "process of unifying and making 'meaningful' the data furnished by sensation" (p. 67). An often quoted illustration is that of the designation, "a pot of green feathers," given by a member of "a class of very young children" when the teacher exhibited "a pot of beautiful fresh green ferns" and asked what it was. The "body of ideas" (meanings) present in consciousness on a given occasion functioned as the "apperceiving mass," i.e. the child's active ideas were the means of apperceiving or assimilating new ideas. It is apparent that the apperception theory of learning is not wholly incompatible with the association theory.

[60] John Dewey, "Interest as Related to Will," *Herbart Yearbook for 1895*, Second supplement (Chicago: University of Chicago Press, 1895), p. 29.

logical psychology the result was "conduction units" which were thought of as physical rather than mental.

Following the turn of the century, E. L. Thorndike and gradually other psychologists began to give systematic attention to learning as a major topic. From the point of view of learning as a process the central question was how are tendencies to action (situation-response relationships) acquired. This general problem may be analyzed into the following sub-questions: [61] (a) How is the initial discovery of the adequate (satisfying) response accomplished? (b) How is the adequate response fixated (strengthened) and how are the inadequate responses eliminated (weakened)? (c) What is the explanation of the utilization (functioning) of fixated situation-response relationships? The last of these questions involves retention and "transfer of training." Before tracing the developments relative to these phases of the problem of learning ensuing from the efforts of Thorndike and other psychologists, attention will be given to a significant event on the educator level of thinking.

In *How We Think* John Dewey [62] dealt with learning from the point of view of the "training of thought." Learning as a process was problem solving or reflective thinking. The "aim of education" was referred to as "a disciplined mind" which was described as "original native endowment turned, through gradual exercise, into effective power." [63] Thus Dewey set forth a concept of learning which in effect was a "modernized" version of the disciplinary concept of learning supported by Rosenkranz, Harris, White, and others around 1890.

Dewey did not deduce this contribution to learning theory from contemporary psychology. Instead he resorted to logic as the means of analyzing a complete act of thought. Thus he arrived at

five logically distinct steps: (1) a felt difficulty; (2) its location and definition; (3) suggestion of possible solution; (4) development by reasoning of the bearings of the suggestion; (5) further observation and experiment leading to its acceptance or rejection; that is, the conclusion of belief or disbelief.[64]

Later (pp. 202f.) Dewey contrasted this concept of reflective thinking as a learning activity with the learning processes underlying the Herbartian Five Formal Steps. He noted a general similarity in that both involved induction and deduction, but he directed attention to a difference which he regarded as significant — "the Herbartian method makes no reference to a difficulty . . . as the origin and stimulus of the whole

---

[61] Arthur W. Melton, "Learning," in *Encyclopedia of Educational Research*, ed. Walter S. Monroe (New York: The Macmillan Company, 1941), pp. 667-86.

[62] John Dewey, *How We Think* (Boston: D. C. Heath and Company, 1910). 224 pp.

[63] *Ibid.*, p. 63.

[64] *Ibid.*, p. 72.

process." [65] In the above analysis Dewey viewed "a felt difficulty" and the succeeding defined problem functioning as the motive relative to the subsequent phases of the "act of thought." Although Dewey's emphasis on this point is perhaps more implicit than explicit, it seems clear that he viewed this "motivating condition" within the child as a basic factor in his concept of reflective thinking as a learning activity. In terms of the above analysis of the problem of learning, Dewey's emphasis was upon the question of the initial discovery of the "adequate response" to a problematic situation. By designating the outcome of the learning process (reflective thinking) as a "disciplined mind," he implicitly recognized transfer of training. It should be noted that Dewey did not deal explicitly with the other aspects of the problem of learning.

In the psychology-of-learning movement E. L. Thorndike was a leader. In *Elements of Psychology* (1905) there is some explicit treatment of "learning" (e.g. pp. 209f.) even though the term does not appear in either the table of contents or the index. But more significant is Thorndike's criticism of conventional laws of association (e.g. p. 243) and the introduction of the concept of the "law of effect" (p. 203). The growth of Thorndike's concern about learning as a psychological topic is indicated by the fact that a 452-page volume of his *Educational Psychology* (1913) was given the subtitle, *The Psychology of Learning*. In the introductory chapter of this volume he stated three laws of learning — Readiness, Exercise (Use and Disuse), and Effect — which described the process of learning, i.e. the process of forming situation-response connections (S-R bonds) which was his designation of the outcomes of the process. Both the situation and the response may be either external or internal — "an enormous majority [of the connections] begin and end with some state of affairs within the man's own brain — are bonds between one mental fact and another" (p. 55). Thus all learning is reduced to one type, namely, formation of S-R bonds. The "educated" person is "a wonderfully elaborate and intricate system of connections. There are millions of them" (p. 54). Such terms as character, interests, ideals, courage, and even ability to read and ability to add are interpreted as representing "compound tendencies, or groups of connections" (p. 56). Although situation-response psychology (connectionism) may be regarded as an outgrowth of associationism, especially as interpreted by the functionalists, it should be noted that Thorndike dealt with "laws of learning" rather than "laws of association." A complementary trend is indicated by the fact that to a much greater extent than previous writers he presented his theory as an interpretation of experimental findings.

Although Thorndike does not appear to have stressed the Law of

---

[65] *Ibid.*, p. 204.

Exercise,[66] it tended to occupy a dominant position in the thinking about learning, especially in the educator interpretation of the developing psychology of learning. James had emphasized the habit-formation concept of learning by viewing "thinking and feeling processes" as subject largely to the laws of habit.[67] The trend of the time is suggested by the title of a volume by S. H. Rowe in 1909 — *Habit-Formation and the Science of Teaching*. John B. Watson, in promoting behaviorism, emphasized frequency of repetition as a factor in learning.[68] Gates, a student and associate of Thorndike, began his exposition [69] of "The laws of learning" with a consideration of the Law of Use and the Law of Disuse. Later the Law of Effect was introduced as a supplementary explanation of the learning process.

During the years following the publication of Thorndike's *Educational Psychology* (1913) the psychology-of-learning movement reflected considerable confusion. Behaviorism emerged as a school of psychology. The psychological atmosphere was further confused by the advocacy of purposivism or hormic psychology by William McDougall [70] and others. The central thesis of hormic psychology is that man is a goal-seeking organism and hence that the point of departure in studying behavior is to identify and define man's instinctive tendencies. Learning occurs somewhat incidentally as man endeavors to attain his goals or realize his purposes. In other words, the hormic (purposive) psychologist is concerned with motivation rather than with the learning process.

Within this confused psychological atmosphere, some psychologists, in addition to Thorndike, attempted to formulate a psychology of learning which would communicate to educators sound views relative to the process and its outcomes. For example, in *How Children Learn* Frank N. Freeman [71] attempted "to present briefly those general facts and principles of mental growth which have most direct application to the problems of teaching." In this presentation Freeman recognized four "types of learning": [72] (1) "Acquiring skill" (sensori-motor learning) — connect-

[66] According to Sandiford, the Law of Effect was the first one to emerge in Thorndike's study of learning and it received major emphasis in his writings. Peter Sandiford, "Contributions to the Laws of Learning," *Teachers College Record*, 27 (1926), 523-31.

[67] William James, *op. cit.*, p. 79.

[68] John B. Watson, *Behavior* (New York: Henry Holt and Company, 1914), p. 61 and Chap. VII.

[69] Arthur I. Gates, *Psychology for Students of Education* (New York: The Macmillan Company, 1923), Chap. X.

[70] William McDougall, *An Introduction to Social Psychology* (London: Methuen and Company, 1908; Boston: J. W. Luce and Company, 1909).

[71] Frank N. Freeman, *How Children Learn* (Boston: Houghton Mifflin Company, 1917). Preface, p. viii.

[72] See also Frank N. Freeman, *Experimental Education* (Boston: Houghton Mifflin Company, 1916), p. 12.

ing "movements already under control with perceptual elements," e.g. learning to drive a car, "organization of new movements in response to their stimuli," e.g. handwriting, and more complex series of movements, e.g. typewriting or piano playing; (2) "Building up perceptions" — discrimination between sensations, combining sensations into perceptions of objects, and recognition of the meaning of complex symbols; (3) "Association and memorizing"; and (4) "Problem-solving or thinking." Freeman did not mention either Thorndike's "Laws of Learning" or behaviorism and his psychology of learning in as far as he presented it seems to have been his own "brand." However, his recognition of "types of learning" is in line with Cameron's treatment in 1912 (see p. 32).

As a second illustration of the attempt of psychologists to interpret learning to educators, we may note *The Psychology of Learning* (1921) by W. H. Pyle, who announced his intention as being to present an impartial summary of "every thing that is known about learning" (Preface). He defined learning as "the process of forming habits and acquiring knowledge" (p. 1), but later (p. 4) he also said: "It is evident that all learning is connecting stimulus with response, idea with idea," and although a separate chapter is devoted to "Ideational learning" (Chap. VI), he observed in the second sentence that "In the last analysis . . . there is little if any difference between habit and knowledge" (p. 91). Hence while Pyle did not employ the symbol "S-R bond" and did not deal explicitly with "laws of learning" [73] there is much evidence of compatibility with Thorndike's theory. But he did not mention Watson or behaviorism. On the whole, the volume was not very satisfying to an educator who was seeking guidance from psychology. It is significant to note that by his definition of learning Pyle took a stand in opposition to the recognition of "types of learning," thus indicating that by 1921 the tendency to analyze learning into types was disappearing among educational psychologists.

Thorndike's psychology of learning, referred to under various names — situation-response psychology, S-R bond psychology, connectionism, and the like — has been something of a "maverick" among schools of psychology. In *Contemporary Schools of Psychology* (1931) Woodworth dealt with Thorndike's early work in a chapter on "Behaviorism" but observed that the "main lines" of his theory were "in accordance with the association doctrine" (p. 54). Ragsdale, in *Modern Psychologies and Education* (1932), did not list Thorndike among the founders and leading representatives of the six modern psychologies he recognized, but in the chapter on "Learning" he observed that "stimulus-response psychology has grown out of functionalism." In the *Forty-first Yearbook*, Part II, of the National Society for the Study of Education, Sandiford presented

---

[73] This item does not appear in the index.

connectionism as having been evolved from an associationistic background (pp. 102-9) and as having been shaped in its early development by Thorndike's studies in animal psychology which dated back to 1896-97 (pp. 110-11).

Another significant characteristic of connectionism is its evolutionary modification through the years. Although Thorndike's 1913 formulation of the laws of Readiness, Exercise, and Effect (pp. 1-4) and the array of supporting experimental evidence doubtless tended to create an impression of finality, he modified and extended the theory of connectionism, especially the Law of Exercise, in the light of his continuing experimental studies.[74] In addition to this evolution of Thorndike's own thinking, there have been variations of interpretation and modifications by a host of other authors. Thus we came to have varieties of situation-response psychology, among which there are differences of the order of those exhibited between two opposed schools of psychology.

In considering situation-response psychology (connectionism) as an aspect of the psychological atmosphere, within which teaching theory developed following the publication of Thorndike's *Educational Psychology* in 1913, it should be noted that his theory of learning was subjected to criticism from various sources. One point of attack was his explanation of "transfer of training" by means of a theory of "identical elements." [75] Judd,[76] Orata, [77] and others vigorously criticized the theory of identical elements and inferentially Thorndike's situation-response psychology. Hullfish [78] dealt more comprehensively with Thorndike's psychological theories. He concluded that Thorndike, although tending to be behavioristic, was essentially eclectic and that his theory was not "internally consistent."

Following the publication of Ogden's translation of Koffka's *Growth of the Mind* in 1924, Gestaltism became an influence in the psychological atmosphere. Gestalt psychology may be viewed as a revolt against the analytical approach implicit in associationism, behaviorism, and Thorndike's situation-response psychology. The Gestaltists directed attention to the total situation and the total response and insisted that the "whole was greater than the sum of the parts." They characterized the "dis-

[74] For example, see Edward L. Thorndike, *The Fundamentals of Learning* (New York: Bureau of Publications, Teachers College, Columbia University, 1932). 638 pp.

[75] Edward L. Thorndike, *Educational Psychology, Vol. II: The Psychology of Learning* (New York: Teachers College, Columbia University, 1913), pp. 358f.

[76] Charles H. Judd, *op. cit.*, Chap. XVII.

[77] Pedro T. Orata, *The Theory of Identical Elements* (Columbus, Ohio: The Ohio State University Press, 1928). 204 pp.

[78] H. Gordon Hullfish, *Aspects of Thorndike's Psychology in Their Relation to Educational Theory and Practice* (Columbus, Ohio: The Ohio State University Press, 1926). 113 pp.

covery" phase of learning as one of "insight" rather than "trial and error." They also maintained that learning should be conceived of as a process of maturation and that exercise (repetition), although a factor in the learning process, was not an independent cause of learning. It has been observed [79] that as a means of attracting attention the Gestaltists tended to set up "men of straw" as a basis for their attack upon the psychologies of the time. Regardless of the merits of this "observation," it seems clear that the introduction of Gestaltism during the third decade served to add to the confusion.

The status of psychology of learning toward the close of the third decade is indicated by the title of a volume by Bode published in 1929 — *Conflicting Psychologies of Learning*. Within the educator group Thorndike was regarded as the dominant authority. Gates, writing in the *Forty-first Yearbook,* Part II, observed that Thorndike's foremost purpose had been "to develop an arrangement of propositions or concepts which would be of highly practical service for the guidance of the professional activities of teachers." [80] The record shows that this purpose of "practical service" was realized to a high degree. In 1931 H. H. Remmers reported a summary of the responses to a questionnaire addressed to members of the National Society of College Teachers of Education. The replies to the question, "How is the theory of learning presented to your beginning students in education," indicated behaviorism (defined as S-R bond psychology) to be the most popular theory.[81]

Remmers also reported that 85 per cent of the usable replies were to the effect that "a combination of the various points of view was presented." These "various points of view" were indicated as structural, functional, behavioristic, Gestalt, psychoanalytical, and laboratory-factual. The first two of these "theories of learning" go back to the turn of the century or earlier and seem to have played a supplementary role in the systematic thinking about learning. Behaviorism, which may be dated from the publication of Watson's volume in 1914, had developed to the point of a basis for an elaborate set of laws of learning [82] in which the Law of Exercise was emphasized and the Law of Effect was not recognized. Gestalt psychology stood in opposition to behaviorism and to associationism (functionalism). Psychoanalysts were interested in a restricted aspect of learning, i.e the environmental (life-history) conditions leading to the acquisition of antisocial behavior.

The "psychology of learning" of around 1930 seems to have been

[79] For example, see Robert S. Woodworth, *op. cit.*, pp. 122-23.

[80] Arthur I. Gates, *op. cit.*, p. 142.

[81] H. H. Remmers, "Typical Points of View on Learning Presented to Beginning Students of Education," *Journal of Applied Psychology,* 15 (1931), 155-67.

[82] Percival M. Symonds, "Laws of Learning," *Journal of Educational Psychology,* 18 (1927), 405-13.

something of a synthesis of these several views. In 1928 Dashiell, writing from the point of view of a behaviorist but attempting a "survey of the psychological field," set forth an account of learning [83] which probably is not far from the average view. Learning was designated as habit-building, but habit was given a flexible meaning. The Law of Effect was emphasized (p. 344), which was contrary to Watson's theory. Dashiell appears to have approved interpretations of "insight," "thinking" as a learning activity, and some other views not subscribed to by orthodox behaviorists.

It is somewhat hazardous to appraise the evolution of the psychology of learning since around 1930, but some statements seem justified. In 1932 Thorndike published a group of studies [84] bearing on certain aspects of the psychology of learning. With reference to the present purpose it is significant that on the basis of the reported studies Thorndike materially modified his 1913 formulation of the laws of learning. He gave the Law of Exercise a different orientation which in effect was a repudiation of the Law as it seems to have been interpreted.[85] The Law of Effect in a somewhat modified form was viewed as the basic law.[86] Thorndike also commented on the significance of the restrictive provision, "other things being equal." The "set" of a person, temporary or permanent, may be a very potent factor in his learning.[87] The implication of this "law" is that the operation of other factors in the learning process is to be viewed as relative to the total situation, especially the "set" of a person.

In describing the status of the "psychology-of-learning movement" during the years prior to 1930, attention was directed to the disagreement and rather general confusion. Soon after 1930 there emerged a rather definite tendency toward rapprochement. In a brief summary on "Theoretical aspects of learning" in 1936, W. A. Brownell [88] devoted a section to "Controversial articles" and one to "Common ground among the conflicting schools." Under the first of these heads, Gestaltists appear as the aggressor psychologists, their principal target being behaviorism and Thorndike's psychology of learning. Eight references are listed. Under the second head attention is directed to three articles as suggest-

---

[83] John F. Dashiell, *Fundamentals of Objective Psychology* (Boston: Houghton Mifflin Company, 1928), Chap. XII.

[84] Edward L. Thorndike, *The Fundamentals of Human Learning* (New York: Bureau of Publications, Teachers College, Columbia University, 1932). 638 pp.

[85] *Ibid.*, pp. 62-63, 170.

[86] *Ibid.*, pp. 176f., 181, 276, *et passim*.

[87] *Ibid.*, p. 393.

[88] William A. Brownell, "Theoretical Aspects of Learning and Transfer of Training," *Review of Educational Research*, 6 (1936), 281-90.

ing "the desirability of holding to the gains already made at the same time that room is being made for the newer findings of Gestalt on learning" (p. 284). An article by Dashiell [89] is referred to as presenting "this position with special clarity and force."

Three years later Brownell [90] contributed another summary on the topic. In an introductory paragraph he observed that greater prominence was given to "critical discussions as contrasted with purely experimental investigations" (p. 255). However, he did not employ "controversial articles" as a section heading. This seems to reflect the spirit of the "critical discussions." Apparently acrimonious controversy was on the wane. Brownell specifically noted the current interest of psychologists in the question "whether or not all learning can be explained in terms of a single theory." Some psychologists, although recognizing apparent "types of learning," had *attempted* to account for all learning under one theory. In the concluding section Brownell noted several trends, among which the following is significant with reference to the present purpose: "the more common effort to seek relationships among apparently unlike positions and theories" (p. 266). Brownell interpreted this and the other trends noted to indicate that "psychology is about to make valuable contributions to the practical enterprise of education" (p. 267). In commenting on this observation he noted that up to date "little help" has been forthcoming from the "psychology of learning."

The trend noted by Brownell is also evident in two other summary writings. In the article on "Learning" in the *Encyclopedia of Educational Research* (1941), Arthur W. Melton cited certain authorities in support of his presentation of "the scientific psychology of learning" without "adherence to any one of the popular systems of psychology" (p. 681). In accordance with this position, which he viewed as the "current trend among students of learning," he pointed out that names of the process — "*association* (meaning the process of formation of an association), *conditioning, memorization, reasoning, insight*" — and names of the product — "*association, S-R bond* or *connection, habit, conditioned response, memory, insight*" — have "essentially similar definitions when one considers the basic operations in the demonstration and measurement of the phenomena to which they refer" (pp. 667-68).

The Committee on the Psychology of Learning of the National Society for the Study of Education stated one of its purposes as being to show that the different theories of learning are to a considerable degree complementary, each making a useful contribution to a comprehensive

[89] J. F. Dashiell, "A Survey and Synthesis of Learning Theories," *Psychological Bulletin,* 32 (1935), 261-75.

[90] William A. Brownell, "Theoretical Aspects of Learning and Transfer of Training," *Review of Educational Research,* 9 (1939), 255-73.

description of the learning process.[91] In Chapter VII, "Reconciliation of learning theories," T. R. McConnell, chairman, pointed out that the differences in learning theories — conditioning, connectionism, and field theory — were due to a large extent to differences in the type of learning situation implied, and that all of the forms of learning occur in both children and adults (p. 255). Then McConnell directed attention to nine fundamental similarities in the several points of view (pp. 256-79). In view of the fact that conditioning and connectionism have been criticized as "atomistic psychologies," it is significant that the first "fundamental similarity" declared that in learning "both situation and response are complex and patterned phenomena" (p. 256). In the following discussion McConnell argued that the Gestaltists' emphasis upon the whole being greater than the sum of its parts is largely an exploitation of a position that is accepted in the other two theories of learning. As a qualification it should be noted that Sandiford, in his presentation of connectionism, explicitly stated that it was "atomistic rather than holistic or organismic" (p. 98). However, Gates sharply disagreed with Sandiford and cited evidence in support of his contention that Thorndike and Woodworth tended to be in agreement with the Gestaltists (p. 258).

The emerging spirit of rapprochement suggests the question — What appears to be the "common" psychology of learning? Although determination of the details of this "common" psychology of learning must await further experimental research and unbiased interpretation and synthesis by competent psychologists, certain general statements seem to be justified. Since Melton dealt with learning without "adherence to any one of the popular systems of psychology," his article in the *Encyclopedia of Educational Research* [92] will be taken as the point of departure.

Learning according to Melton is "the process of adjustment of the organism to a problem situation in which the obstacles to the satisfaction of a motivating condition cannot be overcome by the direct utilization of innate or previously acquired modes of behavior" (p. 668). The "motivating condition" is a condition (physiological and/or psychological) within the organism. As such it may be thought of, particularly in its psychological aspects, as the resultant of the interaction of the organism and its environment at the time. In Melton's definition this motivating condition within the organism is an essential factor in the learning process. It *energizes* the organism relative to overcoming the

[91] T. R. McConnell, "The Purpose and Scope of the Yearbook," *The Psychology of Learning*, Forty-first Yearbook, Part II (National Society for the Study of Education, 1942), p. 3.

[92] After the following paragraphs were written, Melton revised his article for the 1950 edition of the *Encyclopedia of Educational Research*. Since this revision is in essential agreement with the 1941 article on the points dealt with here, the following account may be considered applicable to the later date.

obstacles of the problem situation, it *directs* the "variable and persistent activity of the organism" to this end, and it affords the criterion of satisfaction or relief and hence fulfills a *selective* or *emphasizing* function. A second factor is a "problem situation" in which there are "obstacles" to the satisfaction of the motivating condition. Thus the "problem situation" is dependent upon the motivating condition within the organism. In other words, the "problem situation" is the resultant of the interaction of the organism, including the developing motivating condition, and his environment. An essential aspect of the "problem situation" is an "obstacle" to the satisfaction of the accompanying motivating condition "which cannot be overcome by direct utilization of innate or previously acquired modes of behavior." In this setting Melton described the learning process relative to initial discovery of the adequate response, fixation of the adequate response and elimination of inadequate responses, and factors determining the rate of learning.

How the initial discovery of the adequate response (adequate with respect to the motivating condition) is accomplished has been a problem of major concern to students of learning. The older explanation in terms of "trial and error" was challenged by the Gestalt school which used "insight" to designate the process. After considering the experimental evidence, Melton pointed out that the commonly accepted position is that insight, reasoning (covert trial-and-error), and overt trial-and-error represent a continuum. He then added: "The range, specific nature, and plasticity of the trial behavior of the organism are determined by the motivating condition of the organism, when considered as a persistent stimulus, and by the *associative spread* from previous learning" (p. 673). Although employing somewhat different phraseology, McConnell [93] indicated substantial agreement.

It should be noted that the "trial behavior" is relative to the problem situation, which in the classroom is subject to modification by the guidance efforts of the teacher. Thus the pupil's problem situation may be made relatively easy by the teacher's suggestions, explanations, illustrations, etc. By such guidance efforts the teacher limits the scope of the trial behavior in the discovery process. Thus Melton's statement quoted above should be interpreted as applying to the more typical problem situations.

From the point of view of teaching-learning theory the psychological explanation of *how* the initial discovery of the adequate response is accomplished is less important than the recognition that the motivating condition and the associative spread from previous learning are deter-

[93] T. R. McConnell, "Reconciliation of Learning Theories," *The Psychology of Learning*, Forty-first Yearbook, Part II (National Society for the Study of Education, 1942), pp. 272-74.

mining factors. The motivating condition not only energizes the organism but also directs the trial behavior. Thus without a motivating condition relative to the problem situation there will be no trial behavior and hence no discovery. Furthermore, the discovery of the adequate response is contingent upon the associative spread from previous learning. Incidentally it may be noted that this thesis is implied in Dewey's principle of continuity in the reconstruction of experience (see pp. 23-24).

With reference to the "fixation of the adequate response and elimination of inadequate responses," Melton stated that there is almost universal acceptance of the "empirical law of effect" which makes the motivating condition the determining factor in the sense that it "defines the adequate response and in some way strengthens it." As the phrase "in some way" suggests, psychological research has not answered the question of how the strengthening of the adequate response is accomplished. However, it appears to be generally agreed that the motivating condition is influential in this phase of the learning process. In another place (p. 672), Melton indicated that the "active and individual discovery of the adequate response is a necessary part of the fixation." This observation appears to mean that limiting the discovery process through guidance may make a negative contribution to the fixation.

The term "fixation" as employed here refers to the relative strengthening of the adequate response on the occasion of the organism's successful (satisfying) reaction to the problem situation. There has been fixation, or learning has taken place in the sense that if and when the organism is again confronted with the situation, the adequate response occurs sooner, and fewer inadequate responses enter into the reaction. However, learning, as it is commonly thought of, usually requires several repetitions. Psychological research has not yet adequately explained this phase of learning, but it seems clear that frequency of repetition (amount of practice) is only one of several factors.

By listing "associative spread from previous learning" as a factor in the discovery process Melton recognized "transfer of training" and he specifically noted that "unless there were transfer of training, there would be no pyramiding of the learning activities of the organism, and mental development would be sorely limited" (p. 679). Thus "transfer of training" in this modern sense is basic to the concept of learning as presented by Melton. Furthermore, "retention" is basic to transfer of training.

Melton's account of learning dealt with the process following the development of the motivating condition and the related problem situation. The article includes only incidental references to how the motivating condition and the related problem situation develop in the organism. Although motivation has been the topic of much psychological and pedagogical discussion and considerable research, it appears that psychological knowledge is limited, especially relative to the development of motivating conditions and attendant problem situations which function as bases for desired learning.[94] Melton noted that the motivating condition might be psychological ("a want, interest, or attitude which fulfills the demands of instructions imposed by one's self or other persons") and implied that such motivating conditions were contributed to by previous learning. In the article on "Motivation" in the *Encyclopedia of Educational Research,* Young suggested as a convenience the use of "motives" to refer to factors within the organism and "incentives" to refer to environmental factors.[95] In this sense the "motives" of the child in school are largely products of his previous experience. Ryans [96] noted the following in a partial list of "motives" — wants and needs, traits, attitudes, interests, habits and skills, purposes, and affective and emotional conditions.

At a given time the motivating condition of the organism is the resultant of active "motives" plus its reactions to "incentives" (environmental factors). Young emphasized that the organism's reaction to "incentives" is relative to the "whole configuration" of the environmental situation and the active "motives" within the organism (p. 741). Although Melton did not deal with the matter, supporting implications are apparent in his article. Ryans included a section on "relativity of motivation" which is a suggestive designation of the principle emphasized by Young.

This outline of the "common" psychology of learning is an oversimplification in the sense that attention has not been directed to items of uncertainty and even of disagreement. However, many problems of serious concern to psychologists are of limited significance to educators. In commenting on the research relating to transfer of training, Brownell pointed out that "many of the problems which intrigue psychologists and which in a sense may be truly fundamental are essentially nonexistent for the educationalist." [97] Griffith (1935) suggested a generalization of this position when he expressed himself as being doubtful "whether it is essential that the teacher should know what learning really is." [98] An "outline" psychology of learning is essential for the formulation of a sound theory of teaching and it is significant that psychologists are

[94] David G. Ryans, "Motivation in Learning," *The Psychology of Learning,* Forty-first Yearbook, Part II (National Society for the Study of Education, 1942), p. 303.

[95] Paul Thomas Young, "Motivation," in *Encyclopedia of Educational Research,* ed. Walter S. Monroe (New York: The Macmillan Company, 1941), pp. 735-42.

[96] David G. Ryans, *op. cit.,* p. 309.

[97] William A. Brownell, "Theoretical Aspects of Learning and Transfer of Training," *Review of Educational Research,* 9 (1939), 272.

[98] Coleman R. Griffith, *An Introduction to Educational Psychology* (New York: Farrar and Rinehart, Inc., 1935), p. 385.

beginning to say to educationists: We are in substantial agreement, except perhaps in matters of phraseology, to a sufficient extent to present a common psychology of learning and although there are still questions that intrigue us, they probably have little bearing upon the stimulation and direction of learning in the classroom.

Individual Differences and the Educability of Children

Recognition of individual differences in the sense that children differ in respect to their capacity to learn can be traced back to ancient times,[99] but the scientific study of the topic was just beginning in 1890.[100] Psychologists gave relatively little attention to individual differences until some years after the turn of the century. The index of *The Principles of Psychology* (1890) by William James does not include any reference to "individual differences." This is also true of *Psychology* (1904, 1908) by James R. Angell and of *Psychology* (1907, 1917) by Charles H. Judd. Preston W. Search studied at Clark University from 1896 to 1898 and from his zealous interest in individualizing instruction it would be expected that in *An Ideal School* (1901) he would support his proposal by references to psychological writings in which statements had been made relative to the existence and nature of individual differences. Yet in a chapter devoted to "individual variations" his argument relative to "psychic variations" is mainly inference from variations in physical characteristics. In a footnote Search mentioned that C. W. Hetherington, an instructor at Clark University, "has for several years been working on a Psychology of Individual Differences, which, when completed, will open up an enormous field of possibilities" (p. 165). In *The Elements of Psychology* (1905, 1907) E. L. Thorndike mentioned briefly the existence of individual differences and stated that little is known about them (p. 291).

The typical thinking of the time seems to be similar to that expressed by Rosenkranz which Harris epitomized in his editorial comment as follows:

Abstractly speaking, each human being has the possibility in him of every talent that has appeared or will appear in the human race. But, practically, there is immense difference in the facility with which individuals can realize this possibility. Hence we have the scale: (1) incapacity (pure dunce); (2) mediocrity (mechanical intelligence, who can do the average task as others do); (3) the talent and genius who have great self-activity.[101]

---

[99] For example, Plato's *Republic*.

[100] Frank N. Freeman, *Mental Tests* (Boston: Houghton Mifflin Company, 1926), p. 1.

[101] J. K. F. Rosenkranz, *op. cit.*, p. 109.

The significance of the first sentence of this excerpt is not made apparent by either Rosenkranz or Harris, but the following statement makes it clear that for "practical" purposes, presumably the intellectual education of children, "human beings" were to be thought of as characterized by individual differences. The classification of human beings under three types suggests a discrete scale of capacity to learn rather than a continuum. Even after tabulations of test scores demonstrated that the distribution of an unselected group with reference to a particular trait tended to be normal rather than multimodal, the continued use of such terms as "feeble-minded," "moron," "gifted," and "introvert," indicates the persistence of the tendency to classify children into a few types. Thus the thinking about individual differences tended to be in terms of categories, within which little or no variation was recognized.[102]

In the third volume of *Educational Psychology* (1914), Thorndike devoted ten chapters to "individual differences and their causes." The numerous references to quantitative studies in this treatment are indicative of the growing interest in individual differences during the preceding years. The development of psychological and educational tests, which was under way by 1914, made possible more extended study in this field, and today there is a vast accumulation of data bearing on the nature and extent of individual differences and on related problems. Distributions of intelligence and achievement test scores for age and typical grade groups served to emphasize the extent of individual differences in the traits measured by such tests, and "individual differences" became a major topic in the field of educational psychology. Since the publication of Thorndike's monumental work, psychologists have recognized that the distribution of unselected individuals relative to a trait was continuous rather than discrete and that the distribution tended to be normal in shape. Although the practice of classifying children under a limited number of types has persisted, it has been recognized that such classification was a convenience and not a truthful representation of the facts.

The statement by Harris suggests that capacity to learn is a unitary trait. This appears to have been Binet's concept of intelligence.[103] As intelligence tests came into use, the translation of the scores into mental-age measures and the use of the IQ implied the hypothesis that intelligence was a unitary trait or at least could be treated as such. According to this theory, the observed unevenness of an individual in school achievements or in other areas was explained as being due to variation in moti-

[102] Edward L. Thorndike, *Educational Psychology, Vol. III: Mental Work and Fatigue and Individual Differences and Their Causes* (New York: Teachers College, Columbia University, 1914), pp. 152-53.

[103] Edith J. Varon, "Alfred Binet's Concept of Intelligence," *Psychological Review*, 43 (1936), 32-58.

vation and training in the respective areas of performance. In other words, the development of a child's intelligence tended to present an even front, even though his school achievement might appear uneven.

The concept of intelligence as a general trait characterized by evenness of learning potentialities in an individual was contrary to a rather widespread popular belief that there might be rather extreme unevenness in the abilities possessed by an individual. In a volume [104] published in 1912 the first two chapter titles were "Born short" and "Born long." In the first of these chapters several instances are mentioned of persons judged to be of average or possibly superior intelligence on the basis of their total attainments, who had been unable, they reported, to learn certain specific matters generally regarded as relatively simple. In the second chapter cases of phenomenal performance along a particular line are cited and the author asserted that practically all persons he knew were "long" in some respect. In the following chapter he subscribed to the thesis of compensation, persons "born long" in certain respects typically possessed compensating "shortages," and *vice versa*. In the discussion it was emphasized that this applied to the "great bulk of humanity." Although Smith should not be regarded as a representative psychologist of the time, his position appears to have had numerous adherents.[105] In particular, "geniuses" were not infrequently regarded as "queer," i.e. they were very "short" in other respects.

The limited psychological research of the time tended to disprove these popular beliefs. In 1914 Thorndike, after referring to a number of published studies, stated, "It is very, very hard to find any case of a negative correlation between desirable mental functions." [106] He added that this seems to be especially true in the case of "original capacities." In other words, the observed unevenness in the performance of individuals was probably due more to training than to original nature.

Although a few investigators gave attention to the problem of the nature of intelligence, most psychologists were not seriously concerned until around 1925. "A symposium" published in the 1921 volume of the *Journal of Educational Psychology* provides a sample record of the thinking of American psychologists, especially of those commonly referred to as educational psychologists. As one reads the statements of the thirteen persons who responded to the invitation of the editors of the journal, it seems that relatively few of them had given serious consideration to the nature of "intelligence." One said frankly that he was "not very much

---

[104] William Hawley Smith, *All the Children of All the People* (New York: The Macmillan Company, 1912). 346 pp.

[105] Edward L. Thorndike, *op. cit.*, p. 360.

[106] *Ibid.*, p. 362.

interested in the question." [107] Those who explicitly dealt with the matter admitted that probably intelligence was not a unitary trait, but they varied in their concepts of the analytical structure and generally implied that for practical purposes "intelligence" might be thought of as a unitary trait, at least in the sense of an average or general level.

During the third decade a number of studies of the unevenness of abilities were reported. A review [108] published in 1926 revealed general agreement that children exhibited unevenness in their development, but the author noted "considerable disagreement" among the findings in regard to the relative degree of unevenness among dull, normal, and bright children. His own findings indicated that "dull boys and bright boys show an equal amount of unevenness in all the abilities" which he considered (p. 109). In a study by Woodrow [109] the findings were interpreted as revealing a relationship between IQ and degree of unevenness, normal children (IQ's 96–104) exhibiting less than those above and below these limits. However, this position has not been generally supported.

The publication of Spearman's *The Abilities of Man* in 1927 stimulated research directed toward the identification of the analytical structure of intelligence. Both the two-factor theory which Spearman advocated and the multiple-factor theory advanced by Thurstone are in opposition to the unitary concept of intelligence. Today few, if any, psychologists would defend intelligence as a unitary trait, but there is far from agreement in regard to the analytical structure. However, the rejection of the unitary hypothesis in theory, if not entirely in practice, is significant. Although questions relating to special abilities have commanded the attention of numerous investigators, the findings tend to be disappointing. In fact, it has been stated that "the existence of special abilities has not been adequately established." [110] But it is rather generally agreed that the assumption of the existence of special abilities is justified as a working hypothesis.

The existence of special disabilities is generally recognized, but as cases of grossly unsatisfactory achievement in particular areas have been studied, it has become clear that in many instances the cause was not a special shortage in intelligence such as suggested by the term "born

[107] S. L. Pressey, "Intelligence and Its Measurement: A Symposium—VII," *Journal of Educational Psychology*, 12 (1921), 144-47.

[108] Andrew W. Brown, *The Unevenness of the Abilities of Dull and of Bright Children* (Contributions to Education, No. 220 [New York: Bureau of Publications, Teachers College, Columbia University, 1926]), p. 14.

[109] Herbert Woodrow, "Mental Unevenness and Brightness," *Journal of Educational Psychology*, 19 (1928), 289-302.

[110] Howard Easley, "Child Development—XII. Abilities—Special and General," in *Encyclopedia of Educational Research*, ed. W. S. Monroe (New York: The Macmillan Company, 1941), p. 167.

short." Cases of special disability tend to vary widely with reference to details of causation. Travis [111] gave six rubrics: "(a) perceptual disabilities, (b) deficiencies in visual and auditory memory span, (c) alexia, or word-blindness, (d) aphasia, (e) agraphia, (f) amusia." In some cases other conditions function as contributory causes.

In the first sentence of the statement by Harris (see p. 46), he appears to say that in theory all human beings are educable to the same degree, but it is clear from the remainder of the statement that "practically" an individual's position on the "scale," i.e. his classification, defines his degree of educability. Rosenkranz did not comment upon "incapacity" beyond the explanatory phrase, "the want of all gifts," which suggests the same interpretation as "pure dunce" used by Harris. It is apparent that both writers considered that, "practically," children belonging to the class of "incapacity" were not educable. The description of "mediocrity" as "mechanical intelligence" suggests a limit to the educability of children belonging to this category.

This deterministic position tended to persist. According to the hereditarian view, which was dominant, a child's nature determined his intelligence and his position in the scale of intelligence (his IQ) was an expression of his educability. Children on the lower levels might profit from schooling adjusted to their respective capacities, but in each instance their nature (intelligence) determined their educational potentials.[112] Following 1920 the hereditarian position was vigorously attacked (see p. 28). Recently a modified stand has prevailed. In the article on "Nature and Nurture" by Gladys C. Schwesinger, in the *Encyclopedia of Educational Research* (1941), she stated that except in cases of extreme deprivation or advantage, nature is the major factor in determining individual differences but that "a purely deterministic position need not be taken" (p. 745) and that the possibilities of environmental influences are sufficient "to stimulate educators to every effort to provide cultural help so that maximal potentials can be realized in as many cases as possible" (p. 746).

Regardless of the position taken in regard to environmental modification of intelligence, there is the question of what might be possible in the case of a given child in school whose achievement is unsatisfactory or who exhibits some special disability. Studies of such pupils have revealed that frequently the unsatisfactory achievement could not be explained on the basis of the child's intelligence and that when the responsible factors were removed or alleviated, the pupils improved in

[111] Lee Edward Travis, "Intellectual Factors," *Thirty-fourth Yearbook* (National Society for the Study of Education, 1935), pp. 43-44.

[112] L. M. Terman, *The Intelligence of School Children* (Boston: Houghton Mifflin Company, 1919), pp. 268-69.

achievement. As the result of studies along the line of diagnosis and remedial instruction, there has developed a spirit of optimism in regard to the achievement possibilities of pupils who are not mentally defective. Likewise studies of cases of special disability have revealed possibilities of eliminating or at least alleviating the underlying causes.[113] Although it is generally held that a child's intelligence level, commonly expressed in terms of his IQ, indicates a ceiling relative to educability, the point is generally made that the possibilities under this ceiling are seldom fully realized. Hence for most children who are not mentally inferior there is little justification for not maintaining an attitude of optimism relative to their educability.

[113] For example, see Grace M. Fernald, *Remedial Techniques in Basic School Subjects* (New York: McGraw-Hill Book Company, Inc., 1943). 349 pp.

CHAPTER 2

Shifts in "Majority" Opinion
on Certain Continuing Issues

An illuminating aspect of the evolution of teaching-learning theory is furnished by the controversial discussions of the period, especially those relating to continuing issues. The caption of this chapter directs attention to the shifts in "majority" opinion in the thinking on certain issues, but the "mode of educational progress" reflected by the controversies is also significant. Furthermore, a "lesson" may be drawn from the modification of the temper of controversial discussion.

Numerous references in the literature of the period suggest that the educator group has been divided into two defined "parties," rather frequently referred to as "conservatives" and "progressives." Such an inference tends to be an exaggeration. For several years there was little attempt toward the formulation of an "educational platform" by either "party" and the division on particular issues varied. There have been some educational leaders and probably many of the "rank and file" who tended to subscribe to a middle-of-the-road (eclectic) position. However, as an introduction to the consideration of the shifts in "majority" opinion, a summary of characterizations of the two "parties" will be noted.

General Characteristics of the "Conservatives" and the "Progressives"

In *Contributions to the Science of Education,* published in 1886, William H. Payne, professor of the science and the art of teaching, University of Michigan, made numerous mentions of the "so-called reform party" and of the "adherents of the *status quo*" (p. 104 *et passim*). Payne described these "parties" in terms of attitudes and "mental constitution" rather than educational beliefs. In commenting upon the "mental constitution" of the "adherents of the *status quo*" he credited them with a disproportion of the "reflective habit" which "almost inevitably entails some slowness of motion and an indisposition to move out of beaten tracks" (p. 105). Thus, as the designation suggests, the "adherents of the *status quo*" opposed "reforms," but Payne emphasized that they did not consider contemporary educational theory perfect. He credited them with a conviction that "the future is doubtless to exhibit a continuous series of changes for the better." A fundamental "plank" of their position, as Payne interpreted it, was the belief that "the main lines of educational theory have been pretty firmly and correctly established" and that "changes for the better" would be of the nature of extensions and coordinations of "these lines of thinking" (p. 103). Thus they opposed "reforms," which involved a "break with the past," as dangerous. "Continuity of growth" was a condition for progress.

Colonel Francis W. Parker, an aggressive "reformer" of the time, was less charitable in his characterization of the "conservative" party. Under the designation, "stationary followers of the Old Education," he ascribed to the conservatives of his time "limited ideals" and an attitude of "perfect pedantic satisfaction (utter complacency)" relative to them.[1] Although Parker's statement may have been applicable on occasion to some individuals, Payne's description appears to be a more valid characterization of conservatives as a "party." Payne, who was a conservative, did not reflect an attitude of "utter complacency" in his volume of 1886. In fact, he stressed the formulation of a more complete and perfect "science of pedagogics" as the "need of the hour" (p. 3). Thus the "adherents of the *status quo*" may be thought of as *slow* to approve proposed innovations and disposed to believe that progress would be achieved most effectively by considered interpretation and coordination of what seemed to them the fundamental beliefs inherited from the past rather than as a "party" maintaining that the millennium in education had been attained and that the *status quo* should be maintained.

In contrast, the "so-called reform party" was critical of the *status quo*. Payne (1886) referred to reformers as claiming that "the whole exist-

---

[1] Thomas T. Tate, *The Philosophy of Education* (Syracuse, New York: C. W. Bardeen, Publisher, 1884, 1885), Preface to the American Edition.

ing order of things in education, at least on the practical side, is almost hopelessly bad" (p. 102). Thus the "reformers," as this appellation implies, advocated change. In referring to their "mental constitution" Payne observed that they tended to be more "emotional" and less "reflective" than the members of the opposing party. "An excess of feeling leads to great energy of movement, but it is usually accompanied by a marked defect in the power of clear insight" (p. 105). Although this characterization of the "reform party," later designated as the Progressives, tends to be extreme,[2] it directs attention to this group's attitude toward established views and practices, their aggressiveness in promoting change, and their tendency to make dogmatic assertions and to advocate innovations in school practices which, at least in retrospect, reflect a lack of comprehensive and critical thinking.

Parker, as an aggressive advocate of the "New Education," defined the position of its disciples: "They believe that there is an immense margin between the known and the unknown in education."[3] The setting in which this sentence appears suggests an interpretation along the lines of Payne's statement quoted above. Certainly the disciples of the New Education were critical of contemporary theory and practice, especially the latter. Furthermore, they advocated innovations (reforms), which at least in some instances, appeared as revolutionary. It should also be noted that Parker asserted: "No one can tell what the so-called New Education really is. . . ." The "belief" noted above, viewed in conjunction with this assertion, implies that the disciples of the New Education were committed to change, i.e. something different, before they had defined the nature of the change. They were convinced that contemporary theory and practice, especially the latter, were unsound ("almost hopelessly bad"), but they had not formulated constructive proposals in which they, as a group, had strong confidence.

As the record since around 1890 is examined, it appears that the conservative party has continued to reflect much of the general point of view and "mental constitution" which Payne credited it with in 1886. The "conservatives" have opposed innovations (reforms), at least in the sense of urging caution. To some extent they have appeared as "adherents of the status quo," but, in general, they have not defended the "present" as perfect. Insofar as the conservatives can be said to have had a "platform," it has been materially modified by the psychological and philosophical developments of the period and the "victories" of the reformers. Some conservatives have been relatively aggressive in promoting modifications of theory and practice.

---

[2] Payne's characterization of the "reform party" is not extreme in the sense that other persons have expressed similar appraisals. For a recent criticism of the Progressive Education movement which is at least equally "extreme," see Wilbur A. Yauch, "Progressive Education Comes of Age," *School and Society*, 61 (1945), 97-100.

[3] Thomas T. Tate, *op. cit.*, Preface to American Edition.

In 1884 Francis W. Parker asserted: "The followers of the New Education count in their ranks every great thinker and writer upon education from Socrates to Horace Mann, 'who point to higher worlds and lead the way.'" [4] This assertion seems to be equivalent to saying that disciples of the New Education included all who proposed plausible innovations (reforms) in theory or practice. This interpretation, however, is not in accord with the record. During the nineties the "progressives" joined with the "conservatives" in opposing two proposed innovations — individualized instruction by Search [5] and the recognition of pupil achievement as the criterion of teaching success by Rice.[6] Thus it appears that to propose any sort of innovation was not sufficient to obtain admission to the circle of disciples of the New Education.

Although the "progressives" supported the culture-epoch theory, Herbartian methodology, and other less well defined innovations,[7] they cannot be said to have had a "platform" until toward the close of the second decade. The "progressives" attained organizational status in 1919 but "it took the whole group weeks of labor . . . to evolve the set of seven principles" which constituted the "platform" of the Progressive Education Association.[8] The first three of these principles bear rather directly upon teaching-learning theory.

I. Freedom to Develop Naturally

The conduct of the pupil should be governed by himself according to the social needs of his community, rather than by arbitrary laws. Full opportunity for initiative and self-expression should be provided, together with an environment rich in interesting material that is available for the free use of every pupil.

II. Interest, the Motive of All Work

Interest should be satisfied and developed through: (1) direct and indirect contact with the world and its activities, and use of the experience thus gained. (2) application of knowledge gained, and correlation between different subjects. (3) the consciousness of achievement.

III. The Teacher a Guide, not a Taskmaster

It is essential that teachers should believe in the aims and general principles of progressive education and that they should have latitude for the development of initiative and originality.

Progressive teachers will encourage the use of all the senses, training the

---

[4] Thomas T. Tate, *op. cit.*, Preface to American Edition.

[5] See pp. 101f.

[6] See p. 61.

[7] Charles A. McMurry, *Conflicting Principles in Teaching* (Boston: Houghton Mifflin Company, 1914), p. 262.

[8] Stanwood Cobb, "The Romance of Beginnings," *Progressive Education*, 6 (1929), 67.

pupils in both observation and judgment, and, instead of hearing recitations only, will spend most of the time teaching how to use various sources of information thus acquired, and how to express forcefully and logically the conclusions reached.

Ideal teaching conditions demand that classes be small, especially in the elementary-school years.[9]

The statement of principles was revised in 1929, but the changes in the principles just quoted seem to be primarily matters of emphasis. In a publication of the Progressive Education Association — *Progressive Education Advances* — issued in 1938 it was stated that "no comprehensive statement of the philosophy of progressive education" had been officially issued and that probably no such statement could be formulated to which all members would agree. In fact, it was observed that the philosophy is inherently dynamic, i.e. "responsive to ever changing social and educational needs and . . . flexible enough to allow for the original contributions of many minds" (p. 10). This "official" observation reflects what had been a significant plank of the progressive (reform) platform, viz. the party stood for change, even in their platform, and did not consider it necessary, possibly not desirable, that there be agreement within the group except on the thesis of freedom for members to contribute to change. However, some writers have attempted to identify and formulate the central beliefs. In an address at the 1941 meeting of the New Education Fellowship, Kilpatrick presented a statement of the "common doctrines of the group." [10] The only direct reference to teaching-learning theory is in the fifth principle, which is among those "held widely in common among all who advocate 'the new education'": "Learning goes on best in the degree that the individual himself sees and feels the significance, to his own felt needs, of what he does." In another article published during the same month, this author gave the following as the first of the "planks" of Progressivism:

The center and nub of what is here advocated is that we start with the child as a growing and developing person, and help him live and grow best; live now as a child, live richly, live well; and thus living, to increase his effective participation in surrounding social life so as to grow steadily into an ever more adequate member of the social whole.[11]

In such a "two party" setting there was naturally much controversy

[9] Progressive Education Association, *Progressive Education Advances,* Report on a Program to Educate American Youth for Present-day Living (New York: D. Appleton-Century Company, Inc., 1938). 70 pp. (See p. 5.)

[10] William H. Kilpatrick, "The Philosophy of the New Education," *School and Society,* 54 (1941), 481-84.

[11] William H. Kilpatrick, "The Case for Progressivism in Education," *N.E.A. Journal,* 30 (1941), 231-32.

within the area of teaching-learning theory. In general, the conflicts have been between "older" views rooted in conventional psychological and philosophical beliefs and expressed in the popular terminology of the time and "newer" views stemming from "new" psychological and philosophical beliefs and involving a terminology which often was inadequately defined and consequently frequently misinterpreted. As a means of illustrating the conflicts and of indicating the changing temper of controversial discussion, the shift of "majority" of opinion will be traced relative to four continuing issues.

Teaching as an Art *Versus* Method of Teaching

In the first sentence of *The Method of the Recitation* (1897, 1903) the McMurrys referred to the "long-standing dispute" concerning "whether or not the processes of instruction must conform to any fixed and uniform regulatives." Although the focal point of the issue has varied, this "dispute" has continued through the years since the turn of the century and today is included in the disagreement between Essentialism and Progressivism. The course of the dispute has been marked by periods of relatively formal debate during which the participating educators tended to divide into two opposing parties and by intervening periods characterized by reorientation of thinking dominated by the spirit of eclecticism.

The "majority" position around 1890 was that teaching is an art. Within this general characterization there were some who asserted that success in teaching depended upon "the divine skill of the born teacher's instincts." [12] "A teacher is born, not made" was a common slogan. In *Talks to Teachers* [13] William James maintained essentially this position: "Psychology is a science, and teaching is an art; and sciences never generate arts directly out of themselves. An intermediary inventive mind must make the application, by using its originality." [14]

There were others who subscribed to a more moderate art-of-teaching position. In *The Elements of Pedagogy* (1886) White expressed his position as follows: "It is assumed in this study of teaching that it is an *art*, and as such has its underlying principles which determine its methods." [15] He then stated seven "fundamental principles . . . deduced from psychical facts, and tested by the best school experience known to the writer" (Preface, iii). Payne (1886) expressed essentially the same position when

---

[12] Josiah Royce, "Is There a Science of Education?" *Educational Review*, 1 (1891), 22, 132.

[13] The published account of lectures first delivered in 1892.

[14] William James, *Talks to Teachers* (New York: Henry Holt and Company, 1899, 1900), pp. 7-8.

[15] Emerson E. White, *The Elements of Pedagogy* (New York: American Book Company, 1886), p. 100.

he described "educational science" as "the doctrines, principles, or laws that are involved in the art of education." [16]

In opposition to the art-of-teaching position, certain "progressives" of the time asserted that the processes of instruction should be regulated by specifications of methodological procedure. In *The Method of the Recitation* (1897, 1903) Charles A. McMurry and Frank M. McMurry set forth eight laws of teaching (pp. 288f.) and argued that these laws "furnish a fair basis for the assertion that there is a scientific method of teaching" (p. 296). This "scientific method of teaching" was described in terms of "Five Formal Steps": (1) preparation, (2) presentation, (3) comparison, (4) generalization, and (5) application. This prescription of the "processes of instruction" was declared to be "universal" (pp. 288f.). Thus teaching was not to be practiced as an art, each one making his own method in accordance with his "divine skill" or even in the light of "underlying principles," but in all cases the instructional process should be "regulated" by conforming to these Five Formal Steps.

The issue involved divergent psychological and philosophical beliefs. In defending his position Royce summarized the argument of a contemporary German philosopher, Wilhelm Dilthey, who maintained that a "science of education" was based on the assumptions of uniformity (universality) of "human nature" and of a determination of the end of education ("the highest moral perfection" of the child) and that these assumptions were not sound. Human nature is variable, i.e. in present terminology, children exhibit individual differences, and there is no agreement (and inferentially never will be) in regard to a "moral system" defining the end of education. Royce accepted this argument and did little more than elaborate and emphasize it. On the other hand, the authors of *The Method of the Recitation* declared that "logical notions [general truths] are the goal of all instruction" (p. 51) and devoted most of the volume to the argument that the "movement of the mind" in learning (acquiring knowledge) was uniform in sequence and hence that the Five Formal Steps defined a universal plan of instruction.

During the last decade of the century the method-of-teaching position gained supporters. A factor in this change was the organized aggressiveness of the Herbartians. In 1895 the National Herbart Society for the Scientific Study of Teaching was organized for the avowed purpose of "aggressive discussion and spread of educational doctrines." [17] The organization provided for "local clubs" with a minimum membership of four. Although the Five Formal Steps do not appear as a topic in the

[16] William H. Payne, *Contributions to the Science of Education* (New York: American Book Company, 1886), p. 13.

[17] National Herbart Society, "Plan and Purpose of the National Herbart Society," *Herbart Yearbook for 1895,* First supplement (Bloomington, Illinois: Pantagraph Printing and Stationery Company, 1895), p. 204.

Yearbooks of the Society, the advocacy of other Herbartian doctrines tended to support the method-of-teaching position advanced by the McMurrys, who were prominent in the activities of the organization. By the turn of the century Herbartian methodology was "quite generally" taught in normal schools.[18]

Following the turn of the century, there was less explicit discussion of this issue. However, a change is to be noted. The McMurrys and others advocated the Five Formal Steps as the "universal" method of teaching, i.e. all instruction was to conform to the pattern defined by these "steps." In *The Art of Teaching* (1901) White stressed "that the method of teaching knowledge is determined primarily by the nature of the knowledge taught" (p. 35). Later he observed that although "there are lessons, especially in higher grades, in which Herbart's five formal steps may be used with advantage," there are many lessons in which these "steps" are not appropriate (p. 112). Although White did not explicitly renounce his qualified art-of-teaching position, these statements appear to indicate an emerging position in which the regulation of the processes of instruction is apparent. For example, in 1905 Bagley [19] advocated the following "types of lessons" (general methods):

> (1) The Development Lesson
>> (a) The Inductive Development Lesson
>> (b) The Deductive Development Lesson
>
> (2) The Study Lesson
> (3) The Recitation Lesson
> (4) The Drill Lesson
> (5) The Review Lesson
> (6) The Examination.

A list of this general character was a feature of most method texts published during the next few years. The several "general methods" approved by the author were usually presented with the implication that they were recipes or formulas for effective teaching, selection to be made on the basis of the nature of the subject and the purpose of the lesson. For example, Strayer in 1911 observed that "the actual work of the teacher varies greatly as she strives now for one end and again for another," [20] and then devoted a chapter to each of several types of lessons.

The point of view reflected by the writings of Bagley, Strayer, and

---

[18] Lois Coffey Mossman, *Changing Conceptions Relative to the Planning of Lessons* (Contributions to Education, No. 147 [New York: Teachers College, Columbia University, 1924]), p. 37.

[19] William C. Bagley, *The Educative Process* (New York: The Macmillan Company, 1905), p. 284.

[20] George D. Strayer, *A Brief Course in the Teaching Process* (New York: The Macmillan Company, 1911), p. 38.

others was eclectic, but it may be characterized as a modified method-of-teaching position. The "method-whole" was a composite of lesson types, each of which was prescribed as to form, at least in general outline. The teacher exercised his art in the selection of the lesson type or types and within the prescriptions of the selected type or types. The art-of-teaching thesis was subordinated to the method-of-teaching position. However, around 1915 "majority" opinion shifted in the direction of emphasis upon teaching as an art. In 1913 Suzzallo [21] referred to a "newer view" in which the "method-whole" typically included various "types [methods] of teaching," each succeeding the other "as the nature of the problem, the child's psychological need, and the teacher's immediate purpose dictate." In 1915 Earhart gave her text the title, *Types of Teaching,* and devoted separate chapters to the Herbartian Five Formal Steps and to other general methods. However, one of the author's central theses was that in attaining the various aims (ends), "different types of teaching are employed" and "several may occur in the same lesson period" (p. 36). In the Introduction Suzzallo referred to this book as "a new volume on the art of teaching." Later he said: "*There is no one best method for school teachers.* . . . the teacher must be versatile in the use of methods . . . the best that theory can do is to suggest the spirit and the law of the teaching adjustment and to describe those types of teaching which in real practice are found only in infinite variation" (pp. xv-xvi).

This statement by Suzzallo suggests the trend of the thinking from about 1915. S. C. Parker published two volumes — *Methods of Teaching in High Schools* (1915) and *General Methods of Teaching in Elementary Schools* (1919) — but contrary to the suggestive character of these titles and his support of the "science of education" in the field of method,[22] these volumes do not present "methods" in the sense of definite plans of instruction or teaching formulas. In fact, both volumes reflect the "new" art-of-teaching point of view, the second more explicitly (p. 2) than the first. The recession from the method-of-teaching position is also reflected in Mossman's study of lesson planning in teacher education and in school practice.[23] Around the turn of the century lesson planning on the basis of the Five Formal Steps was fashionable in normal schools, but soon there was a growing tendency toward more variable and flexible lesson plans (pp. 37, 51). By 1923 there was "wide diversity in opinion as to the form of the plan" (p. 47).

[21] Henry Suzzallo, "Recitation, Method of," in *A Cyclopedia of Education,* ed. Paul Monroe (New York: The Macmillan Company, 1913), V, 125.
[22] S. Chester Parker, "The Present Status of Education as a Science: Educational Methods," *School Review Monographs,* No. II (Chicago: University of Chicago Press, 1912), pp. 135-50.
[23] Lois Coffey Mossman, *op. cit.*

This, however, is not the whole story of what had been going on in the evolution of this aspect of teaching-learning theory, especially during the second decade. Rice's presentation of his study of spelling [24] based upon test results at the meeting of the Department of Superintendence in 1897 focused attention on a related issue. Leonard P. Ayres described the occasion as follows:

The presentation of these data threw that assemblage into consternation, dismay, and indignant protest. But the resulting storm of vigorously voiced opposition was directed, not against the methods and results of the investigation, but against the investigator who had pretended to measure the results of teaching spelling by testing the ability of the children to spell.

In terms of scathing denunciation the educators there present, and the pedagogical experts, who reported the deliberations of the meeting in the educational press, characterized as silly, dangerous, and from every viewpoint reprehensible the attempt to test the efficiency of the teacher by finding out what the pupils could do. With striking unanimity they voiced the conviction that any attempt to evaluate the teaching of spelling in terms of the ability of the pupils to spell was essentially impossible and based on a profound misconception of the function of education.[25]

Although Rice's study explicitly dealt with the question of the time to be devoted to the teaching of spelling, the reaction to the report was in terms of the implications relative to teaching-learning theory. Rice's procedure implied the thesis that the "efficiency of the teaching" and inferentially the effectiveness of the method employed was to be judged on the basis of "what the pupils could do." It is difficult to understand why this thesis was regarded as a radical innovation. In 1891 White had written approvingly of examinations conducted by a superintendent as a means of ascertaining the "character of the teacher's work" and "whether the methods employed have been such as to afford right training." [26] In 1914 Coffman [27] reported that there was a "prevailing tendency . . . to rate teachers according to an examination given the pupils." Hence it is likely that the tendency noted by Coffman in 1914 existed, at least to some degree, in 1897. Another confusing factor is that Rice's procedure

---

[24] This study concerned the relation between the minutes per day devoted to the teaching of spelling and the spelling ability of the pupils. For the original report, see J. M. Rice, "The Futility of the Spelling Grind," *The Forum*, 23 (1897), 163-72, 409-19. These articles also appear as Chapters V and VI in J. M. Rice, *Scientific Management in Education* (New York: Hinds, Noble, and Eldredge, 1912). Rice's account of the reception of his report is given on pages 17-18 of this reference.

[25] Leonard P. Ayres, "Measuring Educational Processes Through Educational Results," *School Review*, 20 (1912), 300.

[26] Emerson E. White, *Promotions and Examinations in Graded Schools*, U. S. Bureau of Education, Circular of Information No. 7, 1891, p. 58.

[27] Lotus D. Coffman, "The Rating of Teachers in Service," *School Review Monographs*, No. V (Chicago: University of Chicago Press, 1914), p. 15.

was scientific and there were many supporters of the science-of-education thesis.

However, the explanation now appears to have been somewhat as follows. The last decade of the nineteenth century was a period of strong advocacy of "pet" theories and methods of teaching and, in spite of the talk about a science of education, there was little of the scientific attitude among educationists. For example, the Herbartian method (Five Formal Steps) was declared to be scientific on the grounds that it followed from certain "laws of teaching." It was not a proposed method to be appraised in the light of results. Likewise the art-of-teaching proponents were unwilling that their position be evaluated in this manner. Consequently, "progressives" of the time joined with "conservatives" in resisting what they considered to be a radical innovation in the evaluation of teaching.

During the years immediately following 1897 the "debate"on this issue was between Rice, who continued with studies on arithmetic and language, and the field. In *Scientific Management in Education* (1912) Rice stated that the first support that came to his attention was an article by Paul H. Hanus in 1902 (p. 18). Oliver P. Cornman [28] referred to Rice's study as "very suggestive," and it appears to have been both suggestive and stimulating to E. L. Thorndike who became an outstanding leader in the measurement movement which attained prominence during the early years of the second decade of the century. Following the reference to the reception of Rice's study quoted above, Leonard P. Ayres observed that at the 1912 meeting of the Department of Superintendence forty-eight addresses and discussions were devoted to tests and measurements of educational efficiency based on the proposition "that the effectiveness of the school, the methods, and the teachers must be measured in terms of the results secured." Ayres interpreted the occasion as evidence that "a transformation has taken place [since Rice's report in 1897] in what we think as well as in what we do in education." Implicit in this interpretation is the thesis that the "goals of instruction" are known and that progress toward them can be measured by means of objective tests.

It appears, however, that opposition to this "progressive" movement still persisted. The program of the first session of the National Council of Education at the 1915 meeting of the Department of Superintendence was announced as being planned "to give full hearing to those who are skeptical about the desirability of standardization, tests, measurements, and other exact forms of evaluating school work." Ten years later Charles H. Judd referred to this meeting in the following words:

---

[28] Oliver P. Cornman, *Spelling in the Elementary School: An Experimental and Statistical Investigation* (Boston: Ginn and Company, 1902). 98 pp.

There are many here who will recall the meeting of the National Council in 1915 when the forces of conservatism gathered for a last stand and a battle was fought to determine whether measurement of mental and moral traits was to be recognized as permissible.

There can be no doubt as we look back on that council meeting that one of the revolutions in American education was accomplished by that discussion. Since that day tests and measures have gone quietly on their way, as conquerors should. Tests and measures are to be found in every progressive school in the land. The victory of 1915 slowly prepared during the preceding twenty years was decisive.[29]

During the years that the "measurement of mental and moral traits" was becoming "recognized as permissible," there was some experimental evaluation of methods and techniques of teaching. In an article, "The Present Status of Education as a Science: Educational Methods," in 1912 S. Chester Parker [30] asserted with respect to the field of methodology that education had attained the status of an "experimental science," at least in connection with certain problems. The development of instruments for measuring pupil traits and achievements and of techniques of controlled experimentation was slowed down during the period of World War I, but beginning about 1920 there was a phenomenal growth in the production of experimental studies relating to teaching theory. The title of William A. McCall's volume, *How to Experiment in Education* (1923), is suggestive of the trend of the times. The announced purpose of the author was "to assemble or originate a fairly complete methodology of research" (Preface). The general tone of the volume is indicated by the sentence: "Everywhere there are evidences of an increasing tendency to evaluate educational procedures experimentally" and by the assertion that "experimental education" is the "most important current movement in education" (p. 2). The thesis that comparable methods or techniques of teaching could be evaluated experimentally implied that the better (or best) procedure should be employed by all teachers, at least in similar situations.

Thus out of the "victory" of 1915 there developed the modern research (scientific) movement which, although extending its activities to educational procedures generally, reflected, at least by implication, the method-of-teaching point of view. Comparable methods and techniques could be evaluated scientifically and as the better ones were identified, the "processes of instruction" would be regulated through conformity with them. This implication does not appear to have received

---

[29] Charles H. Judd, "The Curriculum: A Paramount Issue," *Addresses and Proceedings* (National Education Association, 1925), pp. 806-7.

[30] S. Chester Parker, "The Present Status of Education as a Science: Educational Methods," *School Review Monographs*, No. II, 1912, pp. 135-50.

much attention from contemporary writers on teaching-learning theory, possibly because during the years following 1915 the comprehensive experimental identification of the better (best) methods and techniques was merely something to contemplate. Furthermore, stemming from the preachings of Francis W. Parker, John Dewey, J. L. Meriam, and others, there had developed the Progressive education party [31] which attained organizational status as the Progressive Education Association in 1919. This "new" party was aggressive in promoting its views which included a position relative to the curriculum as well as one on the regulation of the "processes of instruction." The latter was generally discussed under the head of the "project method." Despite its designation the "project method" was "a point of view," a general principle or a philosophy of teaching rather than a prescription of instructional procedure. It has been referred to as "opportunistic" teaching in contrast to "systematic" teaching. The issue suggested by this contrast may be defined as teaching regulated only by a point of view, a general principle, *versus* teaching according to planned-in-advance procedures and techniques.

This statement of the issue will be recognized as similar to the one forming the basis of the "long-standing dispute" referred to by the McMurrys before the turn of the century. There was, however, a difference. The project-method advocates insisted upon the recognition and application of "a point of view" deduced from their philosophy and psychology of education. Although they insisted upon teacher freedom, it was to be exercised within the framework of this point of view. Thus in contrast to the art-of-teaching party of around 1890, they held that success in teaching was dependent upon an appropriately indoctrinated intelligence rather than upon "the divine skill of the born teacher's instinct."

The position of the opposition "party" of 1920 also differed from that of the method-of-teaching advocates of the earlier period. The "party" of 1920 maintained that the "processes of instruction" should be regulated to the extent of being planned in advance in terms of the best synthesis of principles and procedures. In particular, they advocated planned-in-advance assignments and they recognized that the influence of the teacher would tend to be coercive. They did not, however, advocate the regulation of the "processes of instruction" to the extent of conformity to a teaching formula or recipe.

The opposition to the project method crystallized during the third decade of the century. However, researchers interested in the field of methodology tended to look upon the project method as another method of teaching to be evaluated experimentally, and, in general, the wide-

---

[31] For an account of more remote origins, see Reuben R. Palm, "The Origins of Progressive Education," *Elementary School Journal*, 40 (1940), 442-49.

spread spirit of eclecticism tempered the reactions of even the more conservative writers. In a symposium [32] of 1921 Bagley, representing the opposition, began his address as follows:

> The project method represents a synthesis of movements and tendencies in educational theory that have been gathering momentum for several years — some of them indeed for several decades. . . . it already ranks as a constructive achievement of the first magnitude. It is quite within the realm of possibility that it may work a complete transformation in school life.

During the 1920's the thinking relative to regulation of the "processes of instruction" exhibited considerable confusion and uncertainty. Most authors treated methodology in terms of principles and an exposition of the learning process, individual differences, and other related topics, but in some quarters there was emerging a conviction that principles were inadequate as guides to effective teaching [33] and that to be efficient the teacher needed to have an extensive repertoire of specific techniques or "devices" from which to draw in meeting particular situations. In the preface to *Modern Methods in High School Teaching* (1926) Harl R. Douglass made clear that the principal purpose of the volume was to present an exposition of the "more common details of teaching technique." Although some reference was made to general method, most of the chapter titles designate "procedures which go to make up the professional skill of the master teacher," and it is clear that the author was not recommending any definite pattern or plan for the teaching process. Instead it appears to have been the author's central thesis that effectiveness in teaching is to be attained by selecting and adapting techniques to the purposes of secondary education and to the capacities and needs of the pupils being dealt with. The last chapter of the volume is devoted to "The technique of controlled classroom experimentation" which is presented as a means for determining "the relative efficacy of different forms of instruction — visual instruction, the project method, socialized recitation, supervised study, the problem method, the Dalton plan" (p. 507).

Although the project-method position was not accepted as *the* point of view in teaching outside of Progessive circles, the aggressive advocacy of it by Kilpatrick and others did influence the thinking of several authors during the later years of the decade, especially to the extent of shifting the emphasis in the teacher's function from that of a taskmaster and "hearer of lessons" to that of a director of learning. For

---

[32] William H. Kilpatrick and Others, "Dangers and Difficulties of the Project Method and How to Overcome Them — A Symposium," *Teachers College Record*, 22 (1921), 283-321.

[33] W. W. Charters, "The Inadequacy of Principles of Teaching," *Educational Administration and Supervision*, 4 (1918), 215-21.

example, in *Directing Learning in the High School* (1927) Monroe dealt with the procedures of teaching in a series of chapters concerned with directing the learning activities which result in various types of outcomes. Furthermore, this author, although he believed that most of the instruction at the secondary level would "inevitably be based" on teacher assignments, recognized the merits of the project method and recommended its use on suitable occasions (pp. 446-47). The volume, however, reflects a conviction that the "processes of instruction" should be regulated to the extent of thoughtful lesson planning in accordance with the principles of learning and teaching.

In *The Nature and Direction of Learning* (1929) William H. Burton referred to the opposing positions. At one extreme, he pointed out, there were those who maintained that pupil purposes, motives, and interests afforded the basis of all really effective learning activities and who "viewed with alarm" prescribed methods or other forms of "teacher domination" of the learning process. At the other extreme, there were method-of-teaching advocates who conceived of teaching as a relatively arbitrary application of a "formula and rule" (pp. 56-58). These extreme positions, however, involved relatively few persons and many authors of the period, like Burton, gave the matter only the passing mention of observing that neither extreme position was tenable.

The position of Burton, which tended to be typical of much of the thinking of the time, may suggest that the controversial discussion stimulated by the Progressives was disappearing from the scene. This, however, was not the case. In the continuing controversy the issue was defined in terms of relative functions of philosophy and research in determining educational theory and practice. The "philosopher group," which consisted mainly of Progressive educationists, maintained that the "research group" was extending the scientific method to educational areas in which the philosophic method (philosophizing) was required.[34] In opposition, the "research group" insisted that scientific study, especially in the area of educational psychology, was the basic source of teaching-learning theory.

A session of the 1928 meeting of the National Society of College Teachers of Education was devoted to the question: "Where does one go for fundamental assumptions in education?" Arguments were presented for four sources — philosophy by B. H. Bode, psychology by F. N. Freeman, history of education by E. H. Reisner, and educational sociology by C. C. Peters.[35] It appears that these participants looked upon the occasion as

[34] For example, Boyd H. Bode, *Modern Educational Theories* (New York: The Macmillan Company, 1927), pp. 345f.

[35] The four papers were published in *Educational Administration and Supervision*, 14 (1928), 361-92.

a "debate" and their respective papers tend to be "arguments" rather than tempered expositions of the issue. The redefined issue received more specific attention the following year by the American Educational Research Association in a symposium under the general title "Philosophy and Research." [36]

The research position was "defended" by F. N. Freeman under the title "The Contribution of Science to Education." Although he explicitly recognized shortcomings of current educational research and, in general, attempted to avoid an extreme position, it is apparent that he assigned a broad and fundamental role to scientific method. For example: "I think it safe to say that we are never justified in trying to settle a question by mere thought [meaning philosophizing] when it is possible to solve it by means of scientific investigation." [37] William H. Kilpatrick assigned a complementary but relatively broad and essential role to "philosophizing." For example: ". . . education can never become a science. . . . but always . . . will there be problems, nay regions of problems, with which the processes of 'exact' science are insufficient to cope. With such what is here called philosophizing is forever essential." [38]

Although it may be argued from a careful reading of the two articles that Freeman and Kilpatrick were near enough together to justify one who was not "defending" a position to accept most of what both men said, it appears that the controversy continued. Two years later (1931) Kilpatrick again addressed the American Educational Research Association. In the published paper [39] he quoted from the letter of invitation in which W. W. Charters, president of the Association, referred to the continued difference of opinion. Kilpatrick pointed out that the crux of the matter "seems to lie in the meanings that we are to give to the terms philosophy, science, and research." He then noted "three fundamental problems of life and education" and commented on the role of philosophy and science with respect to them. His conclusion was that philosophy and science, as he conceived them, "are not antagonistic but complementary processes."

The period since around 1930 is so recent that it is somewhat hazardous to attempt to identify the trends in the evolution of the thinking relative to the regulation of the "processes of instruction," but it appears to be characterized in part by a modification of the meaning associated with the phrase "method of teaching." To the Herbartians around the

[36] The four papers were published in *School and Society,* 30 (1929), 39-52, 103-12.

[37] Frank N. Freeman, "The Contribution of Science to Education," *School and Society,* 30 (1929), 107-12. (See p. 109.)

[38] William H. Kilpatrick, "The Relations of Philosophy and Science in the Study of Education," *School and Society,* 30 (1929), 39-48. (See p. 48.)

[39] William H. Kilpatrick, "The Relation of Philosophy to Scientific Research," *Journal of Educational Research,* 24 (1931), 97-114.

turn of the century this phrase meant a formula or recipe specifying the procedure of the teaching process. This meaning tended to cling to the term even though "method" was not infrequently used when this interpretation was obviously inconsistent. For example, when the project concept of teaching was introduced it was generally referred to as the "project method." The word "method" had become embedded in our pedagogical vocabulary and proposals of substitutes have not gained general recognition.

In *The Practice of Teaching in the Secondary School* (1926) Henry C. Morrison rejected the term "method" because of the associated meaning of "method-to-be-followed stereotype" and used "teaching cycle" to designate the organization of the phases of the teaching process which he advocated (pp. 220f.). Although Morrison expressed adherence to the "science of education" position, it is clear that to him a "method of teaching" did not mean a specification of instructional procedures to be followed in routine fashion but rather a general organization of the "teaching cycle" within which the teacher would exercise his initiative, resourcefulness, and skill. Other authors have employed other terminology in emphasizing a similar general concept of "method of teaching." For example, Umstattd [40] used the rather cumbersome phrase "Integration and elaboration of the unit procedures" as the title for the chapter in which he described his concept of the "plan of teaching."

The efforts to replace the term "method of teaching" have not been very effective to date, but it seems clear that when the term is used, the meaning is along the line just indicated. In the first sentences of the preface to *Fundamentals of Secondary-school Teaching*, Billett [41] stated that his purpose has been to construct "a general method of teaching at the secondary-school level." With reference to this "general method" he emphasized two fundamental theses: (*a*) The essential aspect of the learning activity, especially at the secondary-school level, is problem solving (pp. 118-19, 174, 471). (*b*) The basis of the teaching unit, typically extending over three to four weeks (p. 603), is an assignment unit which is described as "a tentative but systematic plan for teacher-and-pupil activities likely to produce the [desired] increment of educative growth" (p. 173, see also pp. 504, 506).

The general method is described in terms of four phases (steps): (1) introductory phase; (2) laboratory phase; (3) pooling-of-experiences phase; (4) estimating-educative-growth phase (pp. 599f.). Although Billett referred in several places (e.g. pp. 461, 477) to "the general

[40] J. G. Umstattd, *Secondary School Teaching* (Boston: Ginn and Company, 1937). 459 pp.

[41] Roy O. Billett, *Fundamentals of Secondary-school Teaching* (Boston: Houghton Mifflin Company, 1940). 671 pp.

method developed in this volume," it is apparent that the word "method" is not used in the sense of a teaching formula. Instead the general method proposed is to be regarded as only an outline of the teaching-learning cycle associated with a unit assignment. He referred to teaching as "a conscious problem-solving activity" (p. 138), and in the exposition of the four phases he makes clear that teacher procedures must be adjusted to the development of the teaching-learning situation.

Aspects of the art-of-teaching point of view are apparent in such a concept of method. Some relatively recent authors have made this point of view more explicit. For example, William C. Ruediger whose bibliography in *Teaching Procedures* (1932) included 156 titles — 17 published before 1900 — asserted that "teaching is an art" and that although principles "may be helpful in perfecting an art," observance of them does not necessarily make teaching efficient. "For this an additional factor, an inborn knack for teaching, is also required" (pp. 9-10). This is only a slight modification of the position defended by Royce in 1891, but Ruediger, at the time of his writing, was more an eclectic than a ultra-conservative.

An interpretation of the current situation is hazardous, but an attempt is made as a conclusion to the story of the continuation of the "long-standing dispute" to which the McMurrys referred before the turn of the century. Although it seems clear that few, if any, of the more authoritative writers now use "general method" or even "method" in the sense of a "pattern method" or "teaching formula" and instead think of these terms, when used, as referring to a rather general outline of the teaching-learning cycle, it appears that there is still a difference of opinion in regard to the extent to which the "processes of instruction" should be regulated.

Under the chapter heading, "Foundations of progressive educational practices" Macomber (1941) listed as one of fifteen principles: "The teacher is a guide rather than a director of the educational process." [42] The issue implied by this principle is not made very clear by Macomber, but the designation of the teacher as a "guide" is intended to mean that the teacher's instructional actions are to be governed by his "judgment." This judgment, however, should be informed and considered and exercised within the framework of the Progressive point of view. Thus the "processes of instruction" are to be regulated by pronouncements of teaching-learning theory only in a very general sense. The teacher is to be "free" to exercise judgment.

The interpretation of the contrasting designation of the teacher as a "director" is more obscure. Apparently Macomber was thinking of a

[42] Freeman G. Macomber, *Guiding Child Development in the Elementary School* (New York: American Book Company, 1941), p. 314.

"director of the educational process" as implying a considerable degree of regulation by authoritative prescriptions of methodology, for he contrasts the exercise of judgment by the teacher with "rule-of-the-thumb" ways of knowing what to do. The current opposition position, as indicated above, is distinctly more liberal than the phrase "rule-of-thumb" suggests, but present-day conservatives and even the eclectics do advocate regulation of the "processes of instruction" to the extent of conformity to a proposed analysis of the "teaching-learning cycle" in terms of sequential "steps" or "phases." The teacher is to exercise judgment, but his decisions are to be regulated by recognition of the proposed outline of the instructional process rather than by merely "a point of view" or a "philosophy of teaching."

The contrast just presented is limited to the opposing positions relative to the regulation of the "processes of instruction." Each of these positions constitutes only one "plank" in the total teaching-learning theories of the respective parties and the difference between their stands on the regulation of the "processes of instruction" becomes more meaningful when it is viewed in the light of related aspects of their respective beliefs.

The "method-of-teaching" advocates recognize that learning is an active process but minimize the dynamic potentialities of the child; their philosophy is not systemized but tends in the direction of realism; their confidence in objective tests implies an atomistic psychology; teaching is conceived of more in terms of training and even discipline than as merely guidance; and there is the persistent hope that eventually research will reveal the specifications of efficient instruction in terms of experimentally evaluated plans and techniques of teaching.

In contrast, the Progressives emphasize the dynamic character of the child and tend to stress the growth aspect of learning; their philosophy is also not well systemized but is more pragmatic than otherwise, especially in the recognition of pupil purposes; they criticize atomistic psychology and are skeptical of the fundamental soundness of educational tests; guidance is dominant in the concept of the teaching process; and their research hope is that eventually we will know enough about child nature and his reactions to the various aspects of the schoolroom situation and other environmental factors that teaching may be intelligently artistic.

Conditions for Effective Learning

The psychological (motivating) condition within the child and the correlative educational conditions (selection and organization of subject matter and instructional procedures and techniques) that make for the optimum effectiveness of learning activity have been a matter of major concern throughout the period. In an essay published as the Second Supplement to the *Herbart Yearbook for 1895* John Dewey referred to the "educational lawsuit of interest *versus* effort." As this phrase suggests, there were at this time two "schools of thought" in educational circles about the general nature of the motivating condition under which the activity of a learner would be most educative. Both groups recognized focalization of attention as an essential aspect of the requirement for effectiveness in learning; they disagreed on the optimum attending affective aspect of consciousness and the relative merits of two approaches in stimulating pupil activity and obtaining focalization of attention. The older (conservative) school, conceiving of the educative process as disciplinary in nature, held that "effort" leading to voluntary activity, i.e. activity resulting from the functioning of the will, represented the condition for effectiveness in learning. The other (progressive) school insisted that "interest" (a state of consciousness involving nonvoluntary focalization of attention) represented the condition under which learning would be most effective.

In defending their respective positions, and especially in criticizing the opposing position, both "schools of thought" emphasized the effect of motivating procedures and techniques upon the child's moral (personality) development, but they differed in their conception of the concomitant outcomes. The doctrine-of-effort advocates tended to make "training of the will" the dominant criterion in appraising motivation techniques. White's treatment [43] of "school incentives" (motivation) was introduced by sections on "The will" and "The training of the will" under the general head of "Moral training." Dewey's essay, referred to above, was under the title, "Interest as Related to Will." The doctrine-of-effort advocates regarded the child as relatively passive (see pp. 15f.) and the doing of school tasks was to be stimulated by means of "school incentives" applied by the teacher. The pupil's motive pertained to a goal (immunity from some duty, approbation, school mark, escape from punishment, etc.) extrinsic to the task at hand. In thus stimulating pupil activity, the teacher should endeavor to employ those incentives that contributed most effectively to the training of the will to the end that the pupil would come to do school tasks from a "sense of duty."

This position was emphasized by White. He asserted: "It is not enough that the teacher secures diligence in study, good order, and proper behavior in school. The vital question is, *To what motives does he appeal in gaining these ends?*" [44] From the point of view of their postulated effects upon the child's will, White condemned the use of "artificial in-

---

[43] E. E. White, *Elements of Pedagogy* (New York: American Book Company, 1886), pp. 313f.

[44] *Ibid.*, p. 320.

centives" — prizes, privileges, and immunities — and enumerated "natural incentives" in ascending order of merit under the title, "Royal Seven":

1. A desire for standing or rank, including the desire to excel.
2. A desire for approbation — of equals and superiors.
3. A desire for activity and power.
4. A desire for knowledge.
5. The hope for future good.
6. A sense of honor.
7. A sense of duty. [p. 321.]

This enumeration implies that from the point of view of the total effect (moral training as well as acquisition of skills and knowledge) the motivating condition designated as "a sense of duty" was the optimum condition for learning. From this ideal motivating condition the less desirable but still "recommended" motivating conditions ranged through this enumeration to "a desire for standing or rank, including the desire to excel" as the least desirable of these "natural incentives."

During the following years several authors seem to have accepted the position expressed by White without major qualification. In *Classroom Management* (1907) Bagley devoted a series of four chapters to "The problem of attention." Although the title of the volume suggests a treatment of the managerial aspects of the teacher's work, the author made it clear that he was appraising the "methods" with respect to their contributions to the "ultimate end of education." [45] Bagley criticized White's categories of "natural" and "artificial" and proposed instead "positive incentives" — "those that depend for their efficacy upon the hope of a reward," and "negative incentives" — "those that depend upon fear of punishment" (p. 161). The basis of this classification, as Bagley pointed out, is the postulated effect of the incentive upon the child. If an object induces the "hope of a reward," the incentive is positive; if an object induces the "fear of punishment," the incentive is negative. [46]

Bagley's position was that "in general, incentives should appeal to the pupil from the positive rather than the negative point of view," but he hastened to observe that "this general rule is certainly subject to some qualifications" (p. 162). In extreme cases it was justifiable to employ "corporal punishment" and occasionally even "scolding" (p. 165). Prizes were listed as the lowest of the positive incentives and Bagley asserted that "penalties for poor work" were a preferable means of motivation. He also disapproved of "immunities" (granting of holidays and exemption from examination) (p. 171). Care should be exercised in em-

---

[45] William C. Bagley, *Classroom Management* (New York: The Macmillan Company, 1907), p. 138.

[46] This distinction is suggestive of Thorndike's Law of Effect. See p. 35.

ploying privileges (monitorial positions, favored seats, honor roll, and the like) (p. 172). Grades (marks), promotion, and nonpromotion are "good" incentives if certain cautions are kept in mind (pp. 174f.). "Praise, commendation and adulation" are, "perhaps, the most effective of all incentives" provided they are employed judiciously (pp. 180f.). "Pupils' pride in the good name of the school" is "one of the most powerful incentives," but its utilization is limited and certain dangers should be avoided (pp. 182f.). "Ideals" (sense of duty, sense of self-respect, and the like) are highest in order of merit but little is known about their development (pp. 184f.). These qualifications and cautions are indicative of differences of opinion among authors of texts on teaching-learning theory around the turn of the century. For example, Dutton [47] listed marks, prizes, special privileges and favors and commendation and reproof under the head of "artificial and objectionable incentives" and concluded that "they are to be looked upon with suspicion and used only guardedly and sparingly."

The doctrine-of-interest advocates subscribed to the thesis that "interest in the subject-matter of instruction is the *sole* condition under which it can be properly acquired." The Herbartians went further and asserted "interest to be the highest aim of instruction, and ideas to be the means by which that object can be reached." [48] Thus among Herbartians engendering interests (an attitude of mind toward school tasks and subject matter) was an aim corresponding to "training the will" emphasized by the effort advocates. Furthermore, they regarded interests as contributing to the will.[49]

The interpretation of the "doctrine of interest" in terms of motivation procedures and techniques was not very explicit and systematic in the teaching-learning theory of the Herbartians. In the first place they encountered difficulty in "communicating" their concept of interest. One writer pointed out that the "essential nature" of interest was not included in the common meaning: [50] "first, that we are attracted toward something; second, that we find pleasure in attending to it; and third, that attending to it is easy." "The chief element in interest," he asserted, "is spontaneous activity, a tendency of the soul of greater or less strength to

[47] Samuel T. Dutton, *School Management* (New York: Charles Scribner's Sons, 1903), pp. 100f.

[48] Frank M. McMurry, "Interest: Some Objections to It," *Educational Review*, 11 (1896), 147.

[49] Charles A. McMurry, *The Elements of General Method* (New York: The Macmillan Company, 1903), pp. 303f.

[50] Several writers of around the turn of the century and even later quoted, or at least implied agreement with, a definition given in Dexter and Garlick's *Psychology in the Schoolroom:* "Interest is the name given to the pleasurable or painful feelings which are evoked by an object or idea, and which give that object or idea the power of arousing and holding the attention" (p. 31).

go forward in the pursuit of an object." [51] The "pleasure" resulted not
from the easiness of the task but rather from "overcoming resistance."
In *The Elements of General Method,* C. A. McMurry devoted a chapter
of 78 pages (nearly one-fourth of the volume) to "Interest." He did not
present a formal definition, but it is apparent that like Wilson he did
not accept the popular meaning. "The kind of interest which we think
is so valuable for instruction is direct and intrinsic. It reaches down
into those spontaneous and instinctive forces in child-life out of which
all strong activity must spring" (p. 92).

McMurry's general position relative to motivation is indicated by his
summary enumeration of the

preliminaries and predispositions which condition the rise and continuance of
the feeling of interest in school exercises. First is a wholesome, healthy, bodily
status; second, knowledge selected for its adaptability to awaken spontaneous
interest; third, the skilful use of familiar previous experiences, of the strong
apperceiving masses of knowledge in the mind — this implies a sympathetic
and expert method on the teacher's part; fourth, the will, which gives the first
direction and impulse in the mental attack, and issues sharp commands from
time to time in the call to pressing duty.[52]

The inclusion of "will" is surprising, but McMurry insisted that "the
friends of the doctrine of interest" were in agreement (p. 157). Thus it
appears that under the "doctrine of interest," at least as presented in
Herbartian teaching-learning theory, the doing of school tasks was to be
motivated by (*a*) formulating and selecting school tasks so that they
would be most likely to appeal to pupils by reaching down into appropriate "spontaneous and instinctive forces in child-life," (*b*) "preparing"
pupils' minds by stimulating consciousness of appropriate "old ideas,"
and (*c*) training the will "by a proper cultivation of the other powers,
feeling and knowing." [53]

Although the positive positions of the two "parties" involved fundamental differences, the controversial writings were devoted largely to
criticisms of school practices assumed to represent applications of the
opposing theories. It appears that in the typical application of the "doctrine of effort," pupil attention to school tasks was obtained by means
of incentives which authorities subscribing to this doctrine condemned.
White implied that "artificial incentives" —prizes, privileges, and immunities — were extensively employed in school, but he asserted they did
not "stand the decisive test of character" (p. 321). In *The Educative
Process* (1905) Bagley characterized school practice under this view

---

[51] W. E. Wilson, "The Doctrine of Interest," *Educational Review,* 11 (1896), 256.

[52] Charles A. McMurry, *op. cit.,* pp. 138-39.

[53] *Ibid.,* p. 298.

as follows: "The child 'learned his lessons' under compulsion. His common motive was to avoid pain" (p. 109). Wilson and Wilson [54] referred to the "effort doctrine" as having been interpreted by some extremists to mean that "subject-matter was made more valuable for training by its lack of inherent interest or vital appeal to the child." Such characterizations of school practice by "conservatives" indicate that the doctrine-of-interest advocates found much to criticize, but, in general, their criticisms were of practices not approved by the conservatives.

Application of the "doctrine of interest" likewise frequently resulted in practices that were not in accord with authoritative presentations of the theory. For example, children like to play games; hence games with a modicum of school content were introduced. Sometimes a game or other pleasurable activity was offered largely as a bribe for doing a school task. Among the lesson plans given by Strayer is one which he described as "an illustration of the principles involved in good drill work." He represented the teacher as saying: "If you learn it [half of the table of fours], we will play our game for ten minutes." [55] Another erroneous application of the doctrine of interest implied the thesis that pupils dislike "hard" tasks; hence school work is made interesting by making it "easy." C. A. McMurry [56] inveighed against such practices. " 'Making things interesting to children,' " he said, "suggests a wholly erroneous point of view as to what is meant by true interest" (p. 93).

It [true interest] is awakened by the inherent quality of the subject and not by a thin whitewash of agreeable devices. . . . It is inevitable that a teacher . . . spicing and sugar-coating, in fun and jokes, and entertaining by-play . . . will spoil the children with sweetmeats and herself fall a prey to unworthy motives and trivial devices [p. 96].

Both "parties" obtained "aid and comfort" from psychological writings of the time. In *Talks to Teachers* (1899, 1900) James stated as a maxim: "Keep the faculty of effort alive in you by a little gratuitous exercise every day. That is . . . do every day or two something for no other reason than its difficulty" (p. 75). Later he asserted: "The exercise of voluntary attention in the schoolroom must therefore be counted one of the most important points of training that take place there; and the first-rate teacher . . . will provide abundant opportunities for its occurrence" (p. 189). At other places James appears to support the doctrine of interest. "The teacher, therefore, need never concern himself about *in-*

[54] H. B. Wilson and G. M. Wilson, *The Motivation of School Work* (Boston: Houghton Mifflin Company, 1916), p. 38.

[55] George D. Strayer, *A Brief Course in the Teaching Process* (New York: The Macmillan Company, 1911), p. 180.

[56] Charles A. McMurry, *op. cit.*, pp. 92f, 97f.

venting occasions where effort must be called into play. Let him still awaken whatever sources of interest in the subject he can by stirring up connections between it and the pupil's nature, whether in the line of theoretic curiosity, of personal interest, or of pugnacious impulse" (p. 110). He even indicated agreement "in principle" with the "Herbartian doctrine of interest" (p. 111).

The functional psychologists emphasized instinct as an important means in the adaptation process and hence afforded support to the doctrine of interest. The child-study group led by G. Stanley Hall gave attention to the identification of interests, both native and acquired, as manifested by children at various stages of their development. A basic psychological principle was expressed by William James: "Any object not interesting in itself may become interesting through becoming associated with an object in which an interest already exists." [57] From the point of view of this principle the procedure in "making things interesting" was first to ascertain what things children are interested in and then to associate school tasks with them. An "object" which appealed to a native or acquired interest was immediately interesting and hence constituted a point of departure in applying the "association principle" expressed by William James.[58]

Although the "educational lawsuit of interest *versus* effort" did not result in a verdict for either "party," the doctrine of interest tended to become the "majority" position in the sense that there was a growing emphasis upon procedures and techniques that evoked immediate (intrinsic) interest. In *The Principles of Teaching* (1906) Thorndike observed that interest was a necessary condition for learning and that the "problem" was "from what the interest shall be derived" (p. 54). In explaining this "problem" Thorndike distinguished between "immediate or intrinsic" interest and "derived" interest. In the first case the child is attracted by the "intrinsic qualities of the work"; in the second his interest derived from consequences or connections extrinsic to the work. Under the caption "practical precepts" he said: "Having decided what an individual or a class ought to learn, arouse as much interest in it as is needed. . . . Other things being equal, work with and not against instinctive interests" (p. 55).

Within this general position systematic attention was given to the identification of "instinctive interests" and especially to the description of procedures and devices by means of which school work would evoke

---

[57] William James, *op. cit.*, p. 94. See also *Principles of Psychology,* Vol. I, 1890, pp. 416f.

[58] William James, *Talks to Teachers*, pp. 95-96. See also William C. Bagley, *The Educative Process* (New York: The Macmillan Company, 1905), pp. 110f.; George D. Strayer, *A Brief Course in the Teaching Process* (New York: The Macmillan Company, 1911), pp. 15f.

such interests.[59] Games are immediately interesting to children and games were devised for use in teaching a variety of subject matter items.[60]

In his discussion of the "educational lawsuit of interest *versus* effort" in 1895 Dewey [61] pointed out that both the "doctrine of effort" and the "doctrine of interest" as he interpreted them involved a common erroneous assumption, namely, "the externality of the object or idea to be mastered, the end to be reached, the act to be performed, to the self." Later (p. 22) he gave his definition of interest: ". . . it is impulse functioning with reference to an idea of self-expression." And in the summary of the section, ". . . normal interest and effort are identical with the process of self-expression" (p. 25). In the concluding paragraph of the essay (p. 33) Dewey implied that the optimum conditions for learning are to be attained by finding "the child's urgent impulses and habits" and by setting "them at work in a fruitful and orderly way, by supplying proper environment." Thus Dewey dismissed the "lawsuit" and attempted to direct attention to a different position relating to the optimum conditions for learning.

Since Dewey became a major influence in later thinking about the optimum conditions for learning, his position of 1895 is worthy of further exposition. With reference to describing this optimum condition Dewey proposed the employment of "self-expression" instead of either "effort" or "interest." The intended effect of this change in terminology was to direct attention to "the conditions that lie back of and compel interest" and/or effort. Dewey employed "urgent impulses and habits" and "needs" as descriptive of these conditions. In other words, Dewey proposed that instead of arguing over the relative merits of "effort" and "interest" as descriptions of the motivating condition within the pupil, we think of it as being characterized by the child's purposing stemming from his urgent impulses and habits, needs, difficulties, problems, and the like. Back of this proposed change in terminology there appears to have been the contention that, although "effort" or "interest" might be useful on occasion as a characterization of the process of self-expression, neither was appropriate as a description of the motivating condition within the pupil.

[59] For typical treatments, see Stuart H. Rowe, *Habit-Formation and the Science of Teaching* (New York: Longmans, Green, and Company, 1909), pp. 74-78, 136f.; H. B. Wilson and G. M. Wilson, *The Motivation of School Work* (New York: Houghton Mifflin Company, 1916), pp. 47-53.

[60] Arithmetic was a favorite area for games. See David E. Smith and Others, "Number Games and Number Rhymes," *Teachers College Record*, 13 (1912), 385-495. For an illustration in another area, see W. W. Charters and Harry G. Paul, *Games and Devices for Improving Pupils' English* (U.S. Bureau of Education, Bulletin 1923, No. 43). 88 pp.

[61] John Dewey, "Interest as Related to Will," *Herbart Yearbook for 1895*, Second supplement (Chicago: University of Chicago Press, 1895), p. 9.

Dewey also proposed an approach for obtaining this motivating condition, namely, "find the child's urgent impulses and habits" and "set them at work in a fruitful and orderly way, by supplying proper environment." The use of incentives is not mentioned. The teacher is merely to *find* the "child's urgent impulses and habits" and to "set them at work." Dewey's writing of 1895 attracted attention,[62] but it is difficult to appraise the influence of his position and the related ideas he advanced in other writings during the following years. Although the approach is apparent in Rousseau's *Émile,* it was a radical innovation with respect to the thinking of the advocates of both "effort" and "interest." Furthermore, Dewey did not elaborate this phase of his proposal in 1895. It is apparent in *The School and Society* (1900), but again visibility of the proposal is not high.

In 1903 Charles A. McMurry quoted from Dewey's *The School and Society* and in one place referred to a "project" which children "themselves have conceived" and observed "if this kind of energy could be let loose in school studies, it would save the teacher a good deal of anxiety." [63] Thus it appears that at this time McMurry was aware of Dewey's ideas, but his motivation theory was still essentially that of the "doctrine of interest." In the University Elementary School at the University of Missouri (opened in 1905) the basic thesis of Meriam was: "the great purpose of the elementary school is to help boys and girls do better in all those wholesome activities in which they normally engage."[64] This principle is in line with Dewey's verdict in 1895, but his influence on Meriam appears to have been limited.

Meanwhile an eclectic tendency developed. In 1905 Bagley offered an interpretation of the Herbartian doctrine of apperception as a basis for "clearing up the problem of interest." [65] Although he leaned toward the doctrine of effort, he subscribed to a modified doctrine of interest as an ideal.[66] Charters, who had a background of student experience under Dewey at the University of Chicago, had been principal of the elementary school and supervisor of practice teaching at the State Normal School, Winona, Minnesota, and had been associated with Meriam at the University of Missouri, stated in the conclusion of the chapter on "Motives": "Energy is focalized when there is some value to control, some need to

[62] For example, see *Educational Review*, Vol. 12, 1896 and *Public School Journal*, Vol. 15, 1895-96.

[63] Charles A. McMurry, *The Elements of General Method* (New York: The Macmillan Company, 1903), p. 97.

[64] Junius L. Meriam, *Child Life and the Curriculum* (Yonkers-on-Hudson: World Book Company, 1920), p. 147.

[65] William C. Bagley, *The Educative Process* (New York: The Macmillan Company, 1905), p. 106.

[66] *Ibid.*, p. 113; p. 110.

be satisfied, some interest to be fulfilled, or some problem to be solved." [67] This statement reflects the rejection of the "effort" point of view,[68] a selective recognition of the "interest" theory, and an attempt to apply Dewey's theory within a modified subject-matter-to-be-learned point of view. According to this view, which Charters claimed was held by the "great majority of educators" (p. 117), the curriculum was to be restricted to "important" (useful) subject-matter items "so arranged that each will be taught at the time when the child has potentially within him, the motive for studying that particular thing" (p. 117). Thus the approach to effective learning was not from "the child's urgent impulses and habits" as Dewey suggested in 1895, but through the selection and organization of subject matter to the end that what is to be learned at a given time will be consonant with the child's potential "impulses and habits."

Within the general eclectic position authors varied in emphases. Strayer (1911) quoted Dewey and asserted: [69] "The standard of efficiency [in teaching] is found in ability to present to the child a need, a purpose, or a problem which solicits his attention." However, he immediately noted that this standard was an ideal and in practice the realization might be imperfect. Later he tended to support the doctrine of interest.[70] In 1914 Charles A. McMurry expressed his position relative to the opposing doctrines by saying: [71] "The solution . . . is not found in the acceptance of one and the rejection of the other. We must learn . . . to combine them as closely as possible in all important studies." The nature of this "combination" is not explained beyond general statements, but it is apparent that at this time C. A. McMurry accepted "hard problems" as appropriate bases of learning activities and spoke of a combination of "a strong interest and a rugged will" as a motive.[72] In *The Motivation of School Work* (1916) the Wilsons defined motivation as "that attack upon school work which seeks to make its tasks significant and purposeful to each child, by relating them to his childish experiences, questions, problems, and desires" (p. 15). This point of view is the central theme of the volume. "The ideal way of taking up the study of any new subject is to meet a problem or need which may be solved or satisfied by its mastery" (p. 23). However, in the volume there are numerous suggestions reflecting the doctrine-of-interest point of view.

[67] W. W. Charters, *Methods of Teaching* (Chicago: Row, Peterson and Company, 1909), p. 114.

[68] This rejection is more explicit elsewhere, e.g. p. 117.

[69] George D. Strayer, *A Brief Course in the Teaching Process* (New York: The Macmillan Company, 1911), p. 25.

[70] *Ibid.*, pp. 36-37.

[71] Charles A. McMurry, *Conflicting Principles in Teaching* (Boston: Houghton Mifflin Company, 1914), p. 127.

[72] *Ibid.*, p. 128.

Parker's treatment of motivation in both *Methods of Teaching in High Schools* (1915, 1920) and *General Methods of Teaching in Elementary Schools* (1919, 1922) was in terms of the utilization of "interests" derived from instincts. Although it appears that Parker tended to deviate from the position expressed by Charters and the Wilsons, there is evidence of the spirit of eclecticism. For example, in the second volume he approved "sugar-coating" devices if they result in "properly directed attention" (p. 207). Colvin (*An Introduction to High School Teaching*, 1917) treated motivation only incidentally, but his position tended to be eclectic. An extreme position was expressed by H. W. Nutt (*Principles of Teaching High School Pupils*, 1922): ". . . it does not matter what it is that impels the effort to learn . . ." (p. 109).

Although most of the writings noted above reflect something of Dewey's point of view, it is apparent that the authors were not thinking of "the child's urgent impulses and habits" being utilized as the determining origin of learning activity. Instead the teacher was to select and organize the subject matter to the end that the assignments would appeal to the child as "significant" things to do. The "progressive" position of the time is perhaps more explicit in Klapper's *Principles of Educational Practice* (1912). After reviewing Dewey's essay of 1895 and giving an illustration of a "project" involving learning division of fractions, he devoted a chapter to "How to arouse interest and effort." The principles for arousing interest related to the adaptation of the subject matter and method to the "capabilities and mental development" of the pupils, variety in drill and review, novelty and concreteness, teacher enthusiasm, and the "practical, the real value of the contents of the subject taught" (pp. 211f.).

In 1918 Kilpatrick stated that he had developed the conception of "wholehearted purposeful activity proceeding in a social environment" in response to his feeling of "the need of unifying more completely a number of important related aspects of the educative process." He then "named" this idea a "project," even though he recognized that the term was being used to designate other meanings.[73] In his attempt to clarify the concept underlying his use of the term, Kilpatrick drew heavily from Thorndike's treatment of the psychology of learning and referred to Dewey only in connection with the "problem type" of project which he feared might be overemphasized. In a later writing,[74] however, Kilpatrick assigned major credit to Dewey's analysis of reflective thinking [75] in the development of the "project method" (p. 241). He also referred to

---

[73] William H. Kilpatrick, "The Project Method," *Teachers College Record,* 19 (1918), 319-35.

[74] William H. Kilpatrick, *Foundations of Method* (New York: The Macmillan Company, 1925). 383 pp.

[75] John Dewey, *How We Think* (Boston: D. C. Heath and Company, 1910), Chap. VI.

Dewey's essay of 1895 on "Interest as Related to Will." Hence in retrospect Kilpatrick recognized Dewey's influence.

Viewing Kilpatrick's writing of 1918 in its historical setting, it is apparent that he should not be credited with much originality in evolving his concept of "wholehearted purposeful activity" as descriptive of the optimum condition for learning. A contemporary writer suggested that it was "just what has been meant by the doctrine of interest and the problem solving method for the last generation" [76] and certainly the essentials of the idea were expressed by Dewey in 1895 (see p. 77). But Kilpatrick should be credited with a "practical" formulation and with aggressive advocacy.

The project method, as developed by Kilpatrick included the thesis that learning activity is most effective when a "dominating purpose, as an inner urge, (1) fixes the aim of the action, (2) guides its processes, and (3) furnishes its drive, its inner motivation." With reference to the origin of such purposes Kilpatrick stated in 1921 that "either the child or the teacher may originate the suggestion." [77] However, he emphasized as the essential condition for optimum learning that "while the activity is in process the child or children so feel the purpose that it operates as an inner urge to define the end, guide the pursuit, and supply the drive." Thus instead of employing incentives and other procedures to stimulate (motivate) the doing of school tasks (assignments), the teacher's effort in this phase of instruction would be directed toward discovering appropriate pupil purposes and, when such exploratory attempts were not successful, stimulating appropriate purposing.

The project method was a synthesis of "movements and tendencies in educational theory" that had been "gathering momentum for several years — several of them indeed for several decades," [78] and the opposition was, in part, one of suspended judgment relative to the efficacy of incidental learning and of skepticism in regard to the practicality of the project method as a universal pattern of instruction. In the 1921 "Symposium" Bagley [79] explicitly questioned the efficacy of incidental (instrumental) learning and indicated that there was "some indirect evidence" supporting the thesis that information acquired as a means was "*not* so long retained nor so easily recalled as . . . information that is mastered

[76] William C. Ruediger, "Projects and the Project Method," *School and Society*, 14 (1921), 240-43.

[77] William H. Kilpatrick, "Dangers and Difficulties of the Project Method and How to Overcome Them—A Symposium. I. Introductory Statement: Definition of Terms," *Teachers College Record*, 22 (1921), 283-88.

[78] William C. Bagley, "Dangers and Difficulties of the Project Method and How to Overcome Them—A Symposium. II. Projects and Purposes in Teaching and in Learning," *Teachers College Record*, 22 (1921), 288-97.

[79] *Ibid.*, pp. 290f.

with the intent to make its mastery permanent." He also emphasized the point that much of our racial heritage — "skill, knowledge, standard, and ideal" — was not instrumental at least in "the narrow meaning of the term" and hence that there was a "place for logical organization and systematic treatment in practically all of the content subjects." The desirability of "purposeful" pupil activity was generally accepted,[80] but the "conservatives" were unwilling to accept the purposing potentialities of the child, even as developed under teacher guidance, as the determining criteria of learning activity. Thus the conservatives, although approving of capitalizing pupil purposes when they appeared appropriate, maintained that much of the instruction, perhaps most of it in the typical school beyond the elementary level, should be based on teacher-planned learning exercises and that efficient learning activity could be stimulated by skillful application of wise motivation procedures and by skillful performance in other teaching functions.

As implied in the preceding paragraph, the arguments of the "conservatives" transcended consideration of the optimum conditions for learning. In fact, much of the contention between the project-method advocates (the Progressives) and the "conservatives" has been in the realm of educational purposes. Here there are fundamental psychological and philosophical differences. In the project-method theory the emphasis is upon the child's dynamic and purposing potentialities and his education as a growth process commonly described as "experiencing." The goal of the educative process is the child's growth (development), i.e. self-realization of his potentialities. The stimuli and regulatives of this growth develop from within the process.[81] In the opposing view the child's dynamic and purposing potentialities are minimized and, although his education is to be accomplished through his own activity, this activity must typically be stimulated and his development is to be directed toward ends determined from without, i.e. by the school.

Argument along the lines just indicated tended to obscure or even to distract attention from the issue raised by Bagley in his questioning the efficacy of incidental (instrumental) learning. When learning is instrumental, the focus of the child's purpose is on a goal (result) to which the learning is related as a means. The learning is incidental to the realization of the purpose. Of course, the focus of the purpose may shift to the needed learning as a primary goal, but this shift of the purpose goal is not explicit in the project-method position. In fact, it appears that a substantial case could be made for the thesis that in the project method the goal of the purpose was not to be learning. In other words, instru-

[80] *Ibid.*, p. 289.

[81] John L. Childs, *Education and the Philosophy of Experimentalism* (New York: D. Appleton-Century Company, 1931), pp. 87f., *et passim*.

mental learning was inherent in the project-method position.[82] Although there was general acceptance of "purpose" as a characterization of the motivating condition for optimum learning, there was in effect an issue in regard to the goal of the purposing.

Although the two positions stand out in rather sharp contrast when attention is focused upon their fundamental psychological and philosophical beliefs, both schools of writers, when dealing with motivational aspects of teaching-learning theory, tended to be somewhat eclectic. In the 1921 "Symposium" Kilpatrick emphasized that "the idea that we propose to turn children loose to make their own decisions, to decide their own course" was a serious misconception. The accumulated racial experience was to be recognized as "the basis of guidance" and the teacher was to be in "complete charge," on proper occasion demanding and receiving "obedience instant and willing." [83] Furthermore, his fourth type of project, in which the purpose is to acquire some item or degree of knowledge or skill, provides for the pupil to purpose "his own education at a specific point." This, in effect, means that there is compatibility with project-method theory, as advanced by Kilpatrick, if a school task becomes significant to the pupil at the time he is doing it. Macomber,[84] writing from the Progressive point of view, said: "Definite and required assignments may be necessary at times, and there may be situations where something more than suggestion is necessary to get the work of the day completed." This qualification, which Macomber indicated was generally accepted by Progressives, is essentially that, in practice, it may be necessary to depart from the project-method theory of motivation, but it is significant that he observed that when this is done the learning activity is likely to be less effective.

Among the "conservatives" there were many who went far in accepting the project-method position relative to motivation, especially when it was qualified as by both Kilpatrick and Macomber. Kilpatrick [85] stated that Bagley's position was "not far removed" from that which he maintained and evidence could be cited to support a similar conclusion with respect to other "conservatives." Even Morrison [86] recognized an "inner drive" as a necessary condition for learning and found a place for "supple-

---

[82] Kilpatrick did propose recognition of learning projects as one type, but this proposal did not meet with general approval.

[83] William H. Kilpatrick, "Dangers and Difficulties of the Project Method and How to Overcome Them—A Symposium. VI. A Review and Summary," *Teachers College Record*, 22 (1921), 310-21.

[84] Freeman G. Macomber, *Guiding Child Development in the Elementary School* (New York: American Book Company, 1941), p. 309.

[85] William H. Kilpatrick, *op. cit.*, p. 317.

[86] Henry C. Morrison, *The Practice of Teaching in the Secondary School* (Rev. ed.; Chicago: University of Chicago Press, 1926, 1931), p. 107.

mentary projects." [87] Billett,[88] writing from the point of view of unit assignments and the problem method of teaching, recognized the project as "a special case of problem-solving" and approved of projects as "optional related activities." Thus, although there are still fundamental differences and some controversial discussion, the spirit of rapprochement is probably the more significant characteristic of the current scene.

The reader has perhaps noted that in this account of the evolution of teaching-learning theory pertaining to motivation there has been practically no reference to the contemporary developments in the psychology of learning. Since the concern of the authors mentioned was with the motivating condition for optimum learning, it would be reasonable to assume that their thinking would have stemmed from the contemporary psychology of learning. However, it appears that there are few identifiable contributions from psychologists other than Thorndike, who should be regarded as an *educational* psychologist. It appears that the thinking of the educationists concerned with the matter stemmed largely from the writings of Herbart, Froebel, Dewey, and other educationists and from their own observation and contemplation of the teaching-learning situation. Today the project method, or rather the more inclusive designation "Progressive education," is generally associated with Gestalt psychology, but since this school of psychology was relatively unknown in the United States until after Ogden's translation of Koffka's *Growth of the Mind* in 1924, it cannot be assigned a causal relationship to the development of the project method.

There is, however, one line of psychological development that may be noted. In his *Psychology of Learning* (1913) (*Educational Psychology,* Vol. II) Thorndike dealt with the factors and conditions of improvement under four heads: (1) "external conditions" ("length of practice period, time of day, amount of food, and the like"); (2) "physiological conditions" ("dosing with alcohol or caffein or attack by certain diseases"); (3) "psychological conditions"; and (4) "educational conditions" (pp. 193f.). The treatment of "psychological conditions" was from the point of view of the "law of effect," i.e. a condition which leads to "a satisfying state of affairs" contributes to learning and a condition which leads to "an annoying state of affairs" has a negative influence upon learning. Hence, the problem of identifying the conditions for effectiveness in learning, assuming a state of readiness, is that of determining the conditions or combinations of conditions that result in the optimum "satisfying state of affairs."

This view places the emphasis upon the consequential effects of the

[87] *Ibid.,* p. 90.
[88] Roy O. Billett, *Fundamentals of Secondary-school Teaching* (Boston: Houghton Mifflin Company, 1940), pp. 499f.

learning activity rather than the motivational approach. The emphasis is on creating a motivating (psychological) condition within the pupil such that the effect of the ensuing activity is an optimum "satisfying state of affairs." The approach in building up such a motivating condition is inconsequential except as a means. Furthermore, it is made clear that the continuing motivating condition is influenced by the environmental setting and even aspects of the learning activity.

Under "psychological conditions" Thorndike recognized eight factors as most "noteworthy": "ease of identification of the bonds to be formed or broken, ease of identification of the states of affairs which should satisfy or annoy, and ease of application of satisfaction or annoyance to them," and the " 'interest series' — interest in the work, interest in improvement, an active, inquiring attitude, attention, and acceptance of the work as significant to the worker's wants" (p. 215). The consideration of the first three leads to the following as conditions contributing to learning: (a) definite and understandable (to the learner) goals, as, for example, in typewriting and (b) obviousness of success (correct answer or response) and of failure (wrong answer or response). In commenting on the "interest series" Thorndike referred to Dewey as having advocated the doctrine that "school work must be so arranged as to arouse the problem-attitude" (p. 225) and indicated that this principle was generally accepted in the sense that a problem-attitude (active, inquiring attitude) contributed to a desirable motivating condition. Thorndike also indicated general acceptance of "the general principle of modern educational theory that school tasks must be significant at the time to those doing them," significant being defined as comprehending the "nature and purport" of the work involved (p. 226). It should be noted that the reference to Dewey does not appear to constitute an approval of the view expressed in 1895 (see p. 77). In effect, Thorndike described the desired motivating condition within the pupil as one characterized by the "problem attitude" and an understanding of the "nature and purport" of the work (assignment). This characterization appears to indicate a concept of the motivating condition different from that suggested by the designation, "urgent impulses and habits." Thus Thorndike introduced a fourth concept of the optimum motivating condition.

By his analytical consideration of "psychological conditions" Thorndike implied that the motivating condition in the learner was the resultant of several factors and that in attempting to build up the optimum motivating condition a combination of procedures may and, in general, should be employed. This interpretation is supported by the exposition of "educational conditions" as factors contributing to the motivating condition in the learner. There is also the supplementary point that the teacher's "approval, criticism and amendment of the pupil's responses" contribute to the motivating condition (pp. 230f.). More generally those school incentives — praise, punishments, rewards, school marks, and the like — which resulted in "satisfying states of affairs" would contribute to effectiveness in learning.

In his writing in 1913 Thorndike was able to cite relatively few experimental findings in support of the "psychology of motivation" outlined above. In *The Fundamentals of Learning* (1932) Thorndike referred to the "psychology of motivation" only rather incidentally, apparently because he had no experimental evidence to present (p. 397). In 1940 he asserted that the "scientific knowledge of human motivation," which he characterized as relatively small, was as yet not organized.[89] Thus, although psychologists are agreed that the motivating condition in the child is basic in his learning (see pp. 42f.), it is not possible to describe the optimum motivating condition beyond general terms, and perhaps more significant it is not possible to describe systematically the conditions and procedures by which this motivating condition is to be built up and maintained.

Much of the more strictly educational research on motivation has dealt with social incentives, i.e. "with environmental factors which act as spurs and checks upon behavior." Underlying this research is the thesis, more or less explicitly accepted, that regardless of the motivational approach in teaching it is desirable, if not crucially important, that school marks, promotion, evaluation of pupil work, praise and reproof, goals (objectives), and other aspects of the school environment be regulated to the end that optimum conditions for learning will prevail. Although there is substantial experimental basis for some general statements — e.g. informing pupils of their progress contributes to their learning — it is not possible to write a composite prescription for motivational procedures leading to optimum learning conditions. In fact, it now seems likely that the influence of any factor is relative to the total motivating situation. If this inference is sound it follows, for example, that praise may be more effective in one situation and reproof more effective in another.

The effect of the psychology-of-motivation development traced in the preceding pages upon educationist thinking has been in the direction of modification and refinement of the concept of the optimum conditions for learning. "Purpose" has become widely used as a designation for the optimum motivating condition but few authors have attempted to specify the meaning associated with the term. However, Burton's exposition [90]

[89] Edward L. Thorndike, *Human Nature and the Social Order* (New York: The Macmillan Company, 1940), p. 97. See also David G. Ryans, "Motivation in Learning," *Forty-first Yearbook*, Part II (National Society for the Study of Education, 1942), pp. 289-331.

[90] William H. Burton, *The Guidance of Learning Activities* (New York: D. Appleton-Century Company, 1944), pp. 101f.

seems to be in line with current usage. He distinguished between "purpose" and "impulse, desire, and wish." Furthermore, he presented purpose, not as initiating experience (activity), but as emerging out of experience. The developed purpose involves a desired goal and a plan of action for its attainment.[91] The "desired goal" and the "plan of action" are relative terms in the sense that there are stages (degrees) of definition and of commitment on the part of the individual. A purpose does not emerge full-fledged but as a developing motive.

The process of purpose development is not fully understood, but it seems to be in line with current thinking to conceive of a purpose as a learning outcome and as such the laws of learning are applicable, especially the empirical law of effect. Thus as activity (experiencing) proceeds under the stimulus of environmental conditions, the developing purpose is modified and strengthened by the effects stemming from the total situation. This concept of the development of purpose implies that the task of obtaining the optimum motivating condition should not be thought of as being completed during the approach phase of instruction. Instead this task continues and the teacher contributes to the motivating condition in various ways.

Thus it appears that whether "purpose" or some other phraseology is employed as the designation, there is emerging an agreement in regard to the general nature of the desired motivating condition within the pupil. Most of the disagreement in this area appears to relate to the means (procedures) for obtaining this motivating condition, but again the evidence indicates an emerging understanding and agreement.

Teacher Control, Mechanization, Conformity *Versus* Pupil Freedom, Self-Expression, Independent Thinking

This caption designates a broad area of disagreement which ramifies into educational purposes and the curriculum. There necessarily will be some reference to these matters, but the emphasis will be upon the opposing positions relative to classroom management and aspects of the teacher's function in the instructional process. The definition of the issue has varied and as will be shown the disagreements, especially during recent years, have involved more than two "parties." However, in general terms the conflict has been between (1) those who conceived of the teaching-learning situation as being characterized by (a) teacher control (domination) in classroom management, assignments, conduct of recitations, evaluation of student performances, and the like, (b) a planned-in-advance program, systematic prescription relative to pupil activity even

---

[91] Hollis L. Caswell and Doak S. Campbell, *Curriculum Development* (New York: American Book Company, 1935), pp. 194f. David G. Ryans, "Motivation in Learning," *Forty-first Yearbook*, Part II (National Society for the Study of Education, 1942), pp. 289-331.

to the level of mechanization, and (c) conformity in learning, i.e. memorizing the text or statements of the teacher; and (2) those who would (a) place the emphasis upon pupil freedom, self-realization, and initiative, (b) minimize teacher assignments, direction, and evaluation, and (c) endeavor to stimulate pupils to think for themselves rather than merely to conform.

Although classroom management is now generally treated as a minor subtopic in teaching-learning theory, it was an area of controversial discussion during the first two or three decades of the period being considered here. By 1890, due to the evolving social situation and to influences within the educator group emanating largely from Pestalozzi, Froebel, and Herbart, there had been some amelioration of the disciplinary concept of school management with its harsh punishments,[92] but mechanized routine and "pin-drop" order were generally considered desirable, if not essential characteristics of good teaching. "Order is Heaven's first law" was a generally accepted maxim, and "good order" in the classroom was a dominant criterion of teaching success. "Inability to maintain good order" or "poor discipline" was a frequent cause of teacher failure, especially at the elementary level.[93] In well-managed classes the pupils responded to the signal for "attention" by assuming an erect posture in their seats, folding their arms, and looking forward; passing to the blackboard and to and from the classroom was a "military maneuver" performed in response to a series of signals; in many schoolrooms the reciting group "toed the mark"; and in other ways the teacher was the ruler, the pupils his subjects. The spirit of the times is indicated by the use of "The teacher as governor" as a major section (chapter) title in White's *School Management* published in 1893.

The teacher was also a "governor" in the instructional process. Under the recitation method the teacher assigned pages of the text to be studied (memorized) or other exercises to be done. During the class period the pupils *recited*, i.e. responded to teacher requests, their answers being pronounced "right" or "wrong" by the teacher. The mechanized routine of classroom management was extended into the instruction. "Methods of calling on pupils" was a pedagogical topic of importance. The "consecutive method" was perhaps the fashion of the time but unison (simultaneous) recitation was a fairly common practice. Some teachers recognizing the defects of these procedures employed the "promiscuous

---

[92] Herbert A. Falk, *Corporal Punishment* (Contributions to Education, No. 835 [New York: Bureau of Publications, Teachers College, Columbia University, 1941]), pp. 106-7.

[93] William C. Ruediger and George D. Strayer, "The Qualities of Merit in Teachers," *Journal of Educational Psychology*, 1 (1910), 272-78.

method" but, since it was considered desirable, if not essential, that the pupils have equal opportunity to recite, some mechanical device was introduced to insure that no pupils were neglected. Frequently pupil responses were required to conform to a prescribed formula. Pupil questions and other expressions of initiative were not encouraged. The aim of the pupils tended to be to become able to give responses that the teacher would accept as "right" which usually meant "in conformity with the text."

Back of the theory of school management of the time were the concept of the child as "a bad little man" and a faith in strict discipline as a means of "moral training." The majority position of the time was probably expressed by William T. Harris, then United States Commissioner of Education, in *The Third Yearbook of the National Herbart Society* (1897) under the title "The Relation of School Discipline to Moral Education." He stated "four cardinal rules" relating to school discipline suggested by the assertion: "The child must be regular and punctual, silent and industrious" (p. 59). He considered these rules not only necessary for efficient instruction but also important in the "building of character" (p. 65). He emphasized the necessity of obedience, even mechanical obedience at first, but he also referred to "an arbitrary and tyrannical teacher" as a "fearfully demoralizing influence in a community" (p. 69). In this connection he criticized the practice of corporal punishment. Harris would have school discipline strict but not too strict: ". . . strictness which is indispensable must be tempered by such an administration as causes the pupils to love to obey the law for the law's sake" (p. 72).

The implied theory of classroom management is apparent. The pupils were to be governed by the teacher, but he was not to be "arbitrary and tyrannical" in fulfilling this function. He was to maintain a "happy medium" between "lax discipline" and "too strict discipline." The teacher was to obtain regularity and punctuality in attendance and in other matters; the pupils were to be required to be "silent," i.e. refrain from whispering and doing other things that would interfere with the industry of their classmates; and the routines of the classroom were to be mechanized but not overemphasized. In obtaining obedience to authority in respect to these matters and "systematic industry" teachers should endeavor to engender the "sense of responsibility" and the "law of duty."

The record of the nineties and even earlier furnishes evidence of opposition to "teacher control, mechanization, and conformity." This opposition, frequently referred to as the "New Education," was not organized and its effectiveness was conditioned in other ways. Francis W. Parker, a prominent progressive of the time, wrote approvingly of Tate's *Philosophy of Education* in the Preface to the American Edition (1884).

Tate, characterized by Parker as "a firm, undaunted believer in the New Education," asserted that "instruction should give pleasure to children" and that "a teacher should govern his pupils by the principle of love rather than by that of fear" (p. 132). In the following discussion he observed that "we should endeavor to avoid, as far as possible, the imposition of tasks" (p. 140). In another place, "we should foster voluntary efforts" (p. 112). Under the head of "School discipline" the first rule is — "The teacher should endeavor to establish a principle of limited self-government in his school" (p. 395). On the other hand, Tate made clear that the teacher was to "govern" the school, even having recourse to punishment as a "last hope" (p. 143-44) and he gave limited approval to concert (simultaneous) reciting. He would have pupils "marched in and out of their classes in regular military order" and they should be drilled to respond t₌ certain commands in prescribed ways (p. 400). Thus if Tate was "a firm, undaunted believer in the New Education" it appears that the "New Education" of that time included more than a trace of the "Old Education."

Francis W. Parker was an aggressive "progressive" from his superintendency of the Quincy (Mass.) schools to his death in 1902, and he has been recognized as "the father of the progressive educational movement." [94] Although Parker was a vigorous and severe critic of the prevailing teaching theory and practice of his time, his "New Education" tended to be a changing, developing thing rather than a systematically formulated theory. A fundamental aspect of his position was implied in an address on "The Quincy Method" in 1900. "There never was a Quincy method or a Quincy system, unless we agree to call the Quincy method a spirit of study and the Quincy system one of everlasting change." [95] He was not a writer [96] but a teacher, an inspirer of students and associates. Although Parker was a leader of the opposition, his contribution to a "party platform" was only in general terms.

In *Talks on Pedagogics* (1894) Parker was concerned with presenting the "theory of concentration," but he included a chapter on "school government and moral training" in which he reflected a "progressive" position. "A school is a community; community life is indispensable to mental and moral growth" (p. 337). Although he criticized the "unnatural dis-

---

[94] John Dewey, "How Much Freedom in New Schools?" *New Republic*, 63 (July 9, 1930), 204. For supporting evidence, see Edward Dangler, "Francis W. Parker, 'Father of the Activity Program,'" *School and Society*, 56 (1942), 370-74.

[95] Report of the Commissioner of Education for the year 1902, Vol. I, p. 240.

[96] ". . . he himself refused to impose a creed upon his followers, or even to suggest a watchword under which disciples in the future might assemble. . . . He has left but few books, and these he himself outlived." Wilbur S. Jackman, "Colonel Francis Wayland Parker," *Addresses and Proceedings* (National Educational Association, 1902), p. 401.

cipline in schools" (p. 364), he did not develop the point of view indicated by his statement. Neither did he develop his ideas relative to the aspects of the teacher's function with which he was here concerned, but his emphasis on "the social factor in education" (p. 421) and the general tone of the volume make it clear that he stood for a considerable degree of pupil freedom and especially for self-expression.

The Herbartian movement included a number of "progressive" ideas among which a general method of teaching purporting to provide for or even to insure inductive thinking by pupils was perhaps most conspicuous. Thus Herbartian methodology (Five Formal Steps) stood in opposition to the textbook-recitation method, but although the character of the recitation activity was changed, the teacher dominated the pupil "thinking." The teacher "prepared" the pupils, "presented" the "individual notions," and directed the subsequent steps. Hence, the contribution of Herbartian methodology to the opposition was limited. The "doctrine of interest" which was supported by Herbartians was opposed to the coercive procedures of teacher control, but the extreme practices indulged in by some teachers weakened its influence.

The child-study movement focused attention on the child, but it appears that it made little direct contribution to the opposition. In 1901 G. Stanley Hall presented "The Ideal School as Based on Child Study." [97] In view of the fact that child study had been prominent for several years, it is significant that he referred to this writing as "a first attempt to formulate a practical program of this great movement." Most of Hall's description of his "ideal school" is concerned with the education of children at two stages of their development — from seven or eight years of age to thirteen or fourteen and the period of adolescence. The "ideal school" for the first of these periods would be characterized by "drill, habituation, and mechanism . . . discipline should be the watchword here." Obedience was to be stressed. ". . . the ideal teacher at this age will be the captain of the child's soul . . . will be a stern disciplinarian, genial withal, but rigorous and relentless in his exactions." At the adolescent level "the drill and mechanism of the previous period must be gradually relaxed, and an appeal must be made to freedom and interest."

In *The School and Society* (1900) John Dewey told of his experience in seeking pupil desks and chairs for the University Elementary School that he started in January, 1896. After a number of unsuccessful inquiries for equipment compatible with the type of school he desired to establish, one dealer remarked: "I am afraid we have not what you want. You want something at which the children may work; these [conventional school desks of the time] are all for listening" (p. 48). This observation is suggestive of the teaching-learning theory of the nineties and of the degree

---

[97] *Addresses and Proceedings* (National Education Association, 1901), pp. 474-88.

to which Dewey's school departed from it.[98] Little is said in the volume about "discipline and order," but it was noted that the school "has perhaps suffered most from misunderstanding and misrepresentation" with respect to this aspect of its work. There is also reference to "more than the usual amount of freedom" (p. 128). In another place the recitation is described as "the social clearing-house, where experiences and ideas are exchanged and subjected to criticism, where misconceptions are corrected, and new lines of thought and inquiry are set up" (p. 65). This description of the recitation reflects a concept of the teacher's function which stands in sharp contrast to that of the teacher in the lesson-hearing type of recitation.

Thus during the nineties the revolt against "teacher control, mechanization, and conformity" was not an organized movement. Francis W. Parker was a vigorous critic of conventional teaching practice and theory and an aggressive reformer, but he did not formulate a systematic teaching theory. The teaching theory of the Herbartians (Five Formal Steps) modified teacher control rather than encouraged pupil freedom and initiative. The child-study movement, although implying opposition to the "Old Education," did not become a positive factor of much weight. Dewey's work did not bear fruit until later. Furthermore, the theory of concentration, culture-epoch theory, and other curriculum matters were commanding considerable attention. Hence the "New Education" of the nineties was many things. There was opposition to "teacher control, mechanization, and conformity," especially as exemplified in the more conventional schools of the time, but the psychological and philosophical beliefs now associated with "pupil freedom, self-expression, and independent thinking" had not emerged in systematized form. However, the "progressives" of the time tended to conceive of learning as a process in which field trips, construction enterprises of various sorts, pupil discussion, and the like, were important educative activities. The child was a dynamic developing organism rather than a passive, plastic one to be moulded and disciplined.

Following the turn of the century the opposition developed slowly. The Francis W. Parker School of Chicago was opened in 1901 under the leadership of Flora J. Cooke and a staff, most of whom had served under Parker at the Cook County Normal School, as a means of developing and

---

[98] Although it is clear that Dewey's teaching theory as developed in his experimental school was in sharp contrast to the prevailing practice and theory of the time and that he has been a major influence in the evolution of the "New Education" since the turn of the century, the reader should realize that much, or even essentially all, of his theory is to be found in American writings reaching back beyond the middle of the nineteenth century. However, Dewey probably should be credited with developing his teaching theory from his psychological and philosophical beliefs. See Thomas Woody, "Historical Sketch of Activism," *Thirty-third Yearbook,* Part II (National Society for the Study of Education, 1934), pp. 9-43.

exemplifying Parker's educational theories. However, it was not until 1912 that a systematic attempt was made to "advertise" the work of the school.[99] The University Elementary School at the University of Missouri was opened in 1905 under the leadership of J. L. Meriam, but as in the case of the Francis W. Parker School, the teaching-learning theory exemplified was not "advertised" for several years.[100] In 1904 Dewey left the University of Chicago to become professor of philosophy at Columbia University, but writings relating to teaching-learning theory continued to appear: *How We Think*, 1910; *Interest and Effort in Education*,[101] 1912; *Democracy and Education*, 1916. Thus until after the middle of the second decade Dewey was the only author of prominence actively and consistently opposing this phase of conservative teaching-learning theory.[102]

During this period there was some modification of the conservative position. In the first chapter of *School Management* (1903) Dutton asserted: "The whole theory of school government has changed" (p. 6). But, although he may have thought of his position as being "progressive," it seems more appropriate to characterize it as a modified "conservative" one. In his thinking "law and order are still enthroned in the school" (p. 6). The school virtues (punctuality, silence, obedience, industry, etc.) are the "fruit of life" (p. 89), making assignments is a teacher function (p. 151), and the Five Formal Steps are "simply an application and amplification" of the principle of teaching he advocated (p. 161). On the other hand, "Spontaneous self-directed conduct is more important than passive obedience" (p. 5) and "self-control is the very beginning of right discipline" (p. 92).

In 1907 *(Classroom Management)* Bagley referred to "two opposing theories of school management" — the "conservatives" favoring "some measure of reversion to the old-time school fashion of rigid discipline and machine-like organization" and the "progressives" disapproving of "anything that resembles a military organization of the schools" (p. 30). It should be noted, however, that Bagley hastened to add that these characterizations are somewhat exaggerated. His own position was liberal for the time. He would have routine activities mechanized. These include "the passing of lines," "fire drills," "assuming a position of attention," "passing to the blackboard," and the like. He would, however, guard against the "machine spirit" being carried over to the work of instruction. An essential condition for "effective discipline" was respect for "the authority of

---

[99] Francis W. Parker School Yearbook, *The Social Motive in School Work* (Chicago: Francis W. Parker School, 1912), Vol. I, 139 pp.

[100] Junius L. Meriam, *op. cit.*

[101] This monograph is in part a revision of *Interest as Related to Will*, 1895.

[102] Francis W. Parker died in 1902.

the teacher," but in exercising this authority the teacher should be tactful, persistent, just, and good-natured. Penalties were to be employed but with restraint and corporal punishment was to be a last resort. He commended praise and commendation as positive incentives. Bagley mentioned "pupil self-government" with some skepticism but admitted that it had attained "a measure of success" in some schools and reproduced as suggestive the "charter of the Arsenal School City, Hartford, Connecticut" (p. 291).

In 1914 Bagley, writing under the title *School Discipline*, exhibited some change from the position set forth in 1907. ". . . the conception of school discipline must continue to reflect some measure of arbitrary dominance and repression" (p. 7), but he devoted more space to "positive and noncoercive" methods than to "restrictive and repressive" procedures. He defined the "well-disciplined school as one in which the 'fashion' or 'mode' of good order, courteous behavior, and aggressive industry has been firmly established" (p. 3). A chapter was devoted to "stimulating group responsibility" (pp. 90f.), and he emphasized that "the old idea of the teacher as a master" must be modified (p. 91). Writing in the same year under the title *The Discipline of the School*, Morehouse described the "ideal teacher" as "a benevolent despot in his school" and, in general, reflected a position similar to that of Bagley's.

In *Methods of Teaching in High Schools* (1915, 1920) S. C. Parker included a chapter on "Economy in classroom management" in which he argued for the application of the "principles of business management" in the classroom on the basis of economy of time and effort. Although he appears to have thought of the teacher as being in "command" and to have favored a considerable degree of mechanized routine, Parker defended his position on the grounds of economy. This was a distinct departure from the argument of the "conservatives" of the earlier period who insisted that the management of the classroom afforded an opportunity for desirable "moral training." Bagley implied the "economy argument" in *Classroom Management* (1907), but Parker elaborated it and rested his case on it.

Pupil self-government to which Bagley referred in 1907 received considerable attention following the development of the George Junior Republic during the nineties. "School cities" were organized in several school systems. The reactions of school administrators and of authors of texts on classroom management are indicative of the general attitude toward "pupil freedom." Bagley, as has been noted, did not condemn self-government as being contrary to sound principles but doubted its general applicability (p. 290). Dutton was less explicit but implied a similar attitude (p. 93). At the 1908 meeting of the Department of Superintendence two papers were presented on the topic, "Principles and

Methods of Pupil Government," [103] one speaker advocating the "school city" and the other opposing it. The latter asserted that "the great majority of educators seem to regard the paternal form of government that obtains in schools generally to be the legitimate form for school purposes and the method by which the best character training can be most successfully accomplished" (p. 290).

In instruction both theory and practice, outside of the limited number of experimental child-centered schools, supported teacher control but there was a disposition, at least in theory, to get away from the traditional textbook-recitation method. Development lessons were generally advocated by authors of texts on teaching-learning theory. The assignments were to be more than a mere indication of pages of the text to be studied; the "study lesson" was generally included as one type; and topical recitations were generally approved. Some authors explicitly disapproved mechanization in instruction (e.g. Bagley, 1907, p. 36). But pupil initiative and self-expression received very limited support and independent thinking little more. Charters, who had been a student under Dewey at Chicago and who had observed Meriam's work at Missouri, took a middle-of-the-road position in 1912.[104] He used the verb "assist" in defining the teacher's function (pp. 9, 119), argued that pupils should study subject matter only when they feel an intrinsic need for it [105] (p. 174), favored the problem method of teaching (pp. 174f., 261), and referred to the "progressive" practices and theories of Dewey, Meriam, and others with implied approval, at least in certain respects (pp. 230f.). On the other hand, he approved a modification of the Herbartian Five Formal Steps (pp. 323f.), recognized oral questioning for testing pupil acquisition of subject matter as an appropriate instructional activity but would have memory questions limited (pp. 299f.), and included chapters on "The assignment of lessons" and "The lesson plan." The lesson plan is defined as "a guess at what the teacher will have to do in the recitation" (p. 415). Thus the activities of the classrom were to be teacher controlled, but this control was to be adjustable to the emerging needs and interests of the pupils.

During the following years other authors reflected somewhat the same general position. The instruction was to be "controlled" by the teacher but pupil needs and interests were to be recognized and thinking by the pupils was to be stimulated. The teacher was to make assignments but they should be *good* assignments including suggestions and directions

---

[103] *Addresses and Proceedings* (National Education Association, 1908), pp. 285-93.

[104] W. W. Charters, *Methods of Teaching* (Rev. ed.; Chicago: Row, Peterson and Company, 1912). 444 pp.

[105] It should be noted that Charters expected the teacher to be resourceful and skillful in arousing pupil needs.

for study. Supervised study was generally given a chapter treatment. The recitation was retained as an appropriate instructional activity, but it was urged that memory questions be minimized. There was some advocacy of the socialized recitation. The problem method received considerable emphasis and as the project method came into the picture it received a degree of approval. In the revised edition (1922) of *General Methods of Teaching in Elementary Schools,* originally published in 1919, S. C. Parker added a chapter of five pages on "Project teaching." He approved such teaching but not as an exclusive type. He maintained that there was "a large place in the school for the learning of organized systems of facts from textbooks, and for drill in acquiring routine skills" (p. 327).

During the time that the conservative position was becoming liberalized, the Progressive party increased in membership, attained a degree of organization, and became increasingly aggressive in criticizing even the liberalized beliefs and practices of conservatives and in promoting tenets of the "New Education." During the third and fourth decades "project method," "Progressive education," "child-centered school," "activity program," and other phrases emerged as slogans designating this opposition party. Numerous references to the controversy that has "raged" since around 1920 suggest that the educator group has been divided into two parties, each committed to a fairly definite platform. This, however, has not been the case and a significant feature of the controversy has been the individualism, dissension, and criticism within the ranks of both parties. The conservative party included at one extreme persons subscribing to a philosophy of idealism and thinking in terms of a psychology in which learning was in part disciplining (training) the mind and at the other persons whose eclectic position included partial acceptance of Progressive beliefs. In the Progressive party there has been much individualism and consequently diversity of beliefs and criticism within the ranks.

Thus the controversy of the twenties and thirties was not merely between the conservatives and the Progressives, but also within each party. The conservatives "argued" about the relative merits of procedures and techniques of teacher control — objective tests *versus* essay examinations, form of lesson plans, form and technique of assignments, Morrison unit method *versus* some other method of teaching, means of adapting instruction to individual differences, sequence of recitation and laboratory work in science classes, and the like. The research movement was in full swing. Enthusiastic researchers attempted to answer these and other questions of means of teacher control, but within the ranks of the conservatives there were many who doubted the efficacy of controlled experimentation as a means of solving the problems raised, and even among the friends of research there were some who were critical of the techniques of reported studies and of the interpretation of the findings.

The record of the Progressive movement exhibits a picture of even acrimonious discord within the ranks. In the foreword to *The Child-Centered School* (1928) Harold Rugg referred to the urgent need for "sympathetic criticism" and in the volume a series of four chapters was devoted to "criticism." In 1930 *The New Republic* published a symposium on "The New Education Ten Years After." [106] The final article of the series was by John Dewey under the title, "How Much Freedom in New Schools?" In this writing Dewey criticized the left-wing Progressive schools for carrying "the thing they call freedom nearly to the point of anarchy," and it is clear that in his opinion a degree of adult control and direction is necessary in the proper education of children. "To fail to assure them guidance and direction is not merely to permit them to operate in a blind and spasmodic fashion, but it promotes the formation of *habits* of immature, undeveloped and egoistic activity" (p. 205). The differences and dissension within the "family" have been described by Pedro T. Orata in an article with the suggestive subtitle, " 'Fifty-seven Varieties' of Progressive Education." [107] Three "main varieties" are recognized: (*a*) "the extreme right" advocating progressive methods to put over traditional subject-matter, (*b*) the reconstruction-of-the-social-order variety which may be analyzed into two subvarieties, and (*c*) the "extreme left wing" ("let-freedom-ring" variety) advocating creative self-expression, the pupils to do what they want to do, and the like.

Part II of *The Thirty-third Yearbook* of the National Society for the Study of Education (1934) was devoted to "The Activity Movement." Definitions of the activity school (curriculum) were obtained from forty-two "experts," twenty-five curriculums, and fifteen books. The tabular analysis of the data revealed much diversity of concepts and of emphases (pp. 47-55). William H. Kilpatrick, who was assigned the task of finding and stating the "prevailing tendency," found differences of opinion relative to the desirable degree of teacher control and systematic instruction for engendering "customary content of fact and skill and knowledge" (p. 63). In a chapter presenting "Comments and criticisms by some educational leaders in our universities," Boyd H. Bode, John Dewey, Frank N. Freeman, and Goodwin Watson all emphasized the variation of position. The " 'Activity Movement' in education is both comprehensive in scope and obscure in meaning" (Bode, p. 78). "The term [activity] is elastic enough to cover dissimilar affairs in education" (Dewey, p. 81). "The activity program means many different things to different people"

---

[106] Vol. 63, pp. 61, 93, 123, 145, 172, and 204.

[107] Pedro T. Orata, "Conflicting Viewpoints in Contemporary American Education," *Educational Administration and Supervision*, 22 (1936), 361-74.

(Freeman, p. 89). "Each writer has set forth his idea of what a school ... ought to be" (Watson, p. 99). In Chapter VIII, "Controversial issues," William S. Gray and Adelaide M. Ayer attempted "to identify significant issues" both between the conservatives and the opponents of traditional practices and within the ranks of the "proponents of the activity movement." Several of "the significant issues" related to the meaning of "basic terms," the "objectives sought," and the "curriculum," but "nature of the learner," "method of learning," and "the teacher's place [function] in the program" also appeared as major captions. Although it was perhaps not the intention of these writers to direct attention to the controversial issues within the "movement," the chapter suggests that the internal dissension and controversy tended to dominate the scene.

Other records of the period since 1920 support this interpretation. As has been noted the conservative party had become liberalized, at least in the sense that numerous leaders tended to be eclectic. When such persons expressed themselves relative to the project method, the activity movement, the Progressives, and the like, they tended to be restrained in their criticisms and frequently indicated their open-mindedness by proposing that the Progressive theories be subjected to experimental evaluation. In the 1921 "Symposium" W. C. Bagley referred to the project method as "a constructive achievement of the first magnitude" and limited his criticism to pointing out the need for experimental validation of three assumptions.[108] Bagley's position seems to have been that of an eclectic. In an address of February, 1933, he explicitly stated: "These [activity programs], I believe, should dominate the earlier stages of education . . . [and] throughout the elementary and secondary schools there should be abundant opportunities for the learner to follows the learning 'leads' that his interests suggest." [109] However, in the following comment he made it clear that this recognition of activity programs was limited and that they should not dominate the work of the school beyond the earlier stages. Essentially the same position was advocated by William C. Ruediger.[110] Frederick S. Breed [111] argued at some length in support of his thesis that the difference between the "liberal group in education" and the "progressive minus radicals" was "mainly one of words." In an

[108] William C. Bagley, "Dangers and Difficulties of the Project Method and How to Overcome Them—A Symposium. II. Projects and Purposes in Teaching and in Learning," *Teachers College Record*, 22 (1921), 288-97.

[109] William C. Bagley, "Modern Educational Theories and Practical Considerations," *School and Society*, 37 (1933), 409-14.

[110] William C. Ruediger, *Teaching Procedures* (Boston: Houghton Mifflin Company, 1932), Chap. 18.

[111] Frederick S. Breed, "The Liberal Group in Education," *Educational Administration and Supervision*, 22 (1936), 321-30.

address [112] in 1931 Charles H. Judd after defining the issue, devoted his
time to a "statement of the reasons" for his beliefs. The spirit of his dis-
course is indicated by his proposal of a "new progressivism" and by his
statement that he was "quite willing to make a liberal concession to the
old progressives" in regard to the curriculum but he stood for a curriculum "well ordered and arranged in advance."

The criticisms of "conservative" teaching-learning theory by Progressives
have been more severe and in the case of the more radical Progressives
there has been something of a tendency to exaggerate the dissension by
directing attention to reactionary conservatives and thus ignoring the
liberal majority or by selecting "data" to make their case. An illustration
of criticism in which the position of certain "conservatives" was mis-
represented in some respects is furnished by Norman Woelfel's *Molders
of the American Mind* (1933), a doctoral dissertation written under the
direction of W. H. Kilpatrick. In an extended critical review of the
volume, Michael J. Demiashkevich [113] characterized the writing as involving "gross misstatements . . . crude thinking, and . . . grossly un-
scholarly vagaries" (p. 643).

An appraisal of the period since 1940 relative to the conflict is not
easy to formulate. Controversial writings continue to appear which imply
a dichotomous classification of the educator group — the Progressives
versus the "conservatives"—but it is apparent that any such differentiation
is an over-simplification. There is still dissension within the Progressive
group. In *Progressive Education at the Crossroads* (1938) Bode directed
attention to the basic issue within "progressivism" and attempted to point
the way to the "democratic principle on which progressive education is
properly based." Although this principle — "the democratic philosophy
of life" — is not made very explicit, Bode's criticism of child-centeredism,
growthism, activityism, and the like is very apparent. His position with
regard to Progressive education is suggested by the sentence: "It is the
lack of an adequate social ideal that has burdened the progressive movement with a heavy load of trivialities and errors" (p. 113).

One writer [114] noted "three strains of thought in Progressivism:" (*a*)
the "naturalistic" group which would center the educational program in
the "child's impulses, drives, and interests" and which is opposed to
teacher control, (*b*) the "pragmatic" group which stresses "knowledge as
a tool of social adjustment and as ground for reflective living," and hence

---

[112] Charles H. Judd, "The Training of Teachers for a Progressive Educational Program," *Elementary School Journal*, 31 (1930-31), 576-84.

[113] Michael J. Demiashkevich, "'Traditionalists' Before a 'Progressive' Tribunal,"
Educational Administration and Supervision, 19 (1933), 641-51.

[114] Alfred L. Hall-Quest, "Three Educational Theories: Traditionalism, Progressivism, Essentialism," *School and Society*, 56 (1942), 452-59.

stresses instrumental (incidental) learning, and (c) the "social" group which stresses the "interaction between individual and group" as a major phase of the educative process. The lines of demarcation are not very clear, but it is obvious that this writer found differences among the Progressives which he considered significant.

In another analysis of the situation two groups are recognized — pragmatic Progressives and organic Progressives.[115] After observing that "all progressives advocate the democratic procedure in the group life of the class" the writer mentions the central beliefs of the two groups. It seems to this writer that both groups, or at least many members of both groups, are somewhat vague, if not uncertain, about their beliefs.

The "non-progressives" are likewise not unified. The Essentialist Committee for the Advancement of American Education was formed in 1938. Although this committee has not emerged as a promoter of a third party, the platform set forth by Bagley,[116] a member of the committee, presents a conservative position in that it emphasizes teacher direction and a considerable degree of control as "the right of the immature learner" and a planned-in-advance program of studies. On the other hand, the platform is not reactionary. There is explicit recognition of the weaknesses of our schools, but the solution is not a return to traditional practices. In the article noted above Hall-Quest distinguished between Essentialism and Traditionalism. The proponents of Traditionalism are described as believing that "education is synonymous with rigid, intellectual training through the logical use of symbols" (p. 455). This characterization implies teacher control and conformity to a somewhat greater degree than is supported by the Essentialists.

Thus the continuing controversy is not merely between "conservatives" and "progressives" but also within these groups and neither of these labels stands for a definite "platform." Occasionally, a writer suggests that the "battle" is largely one of words, the actual differences of position being little more than differences in emphasis.[117] Certainly no authority on teaching theory now argues for the "brand" of teacher control, mechanization, and conformity that was dominant during the nineties. Risk's treatment [118] seems to be rather typical of the conserva-

---

[115] A. Gordon Melvin, "Confusion Among Progressive Educators—and Others," *Educational Administration and Supervision,* 30 (1944), 129-38.

[116] William C. Bagley, "An Essentialist's Platform for the Advancement of American Education," *Educational Administration and Supervision,* 24 (1938), 241-56.

[117] For example, see George H. Deer, "Must Every Teacher Have an Ism?" *Educational Administration and Supervision,* 28 (1942), 369-74.

[118] Thomas M. Risk, *Principles and Practices of Teaching in Secondary Schools* (New York: American Book Company, 1941), Chap. XXIX. See especially pages 696-97.

tive position. He contended for routine in classroom management as a means of economy of time and effort, but he also favored as much freedom as possible in learning activities. Progressives point out that they do not advocate unrestricted pupil freedom and do believe in a degree of teacher control and, possibly, of conformity. It may be an exaggeration to characterize the current scene as one in which the spirit of rapprochement is emerging, but with respect to the issue considered here, it does not appear that, if the reactionary conservatives and the radical Progressives are excluded, the actual differences are sufficient to justify characterizing the educator group as divided into two opposing parties. The beliefs of this "majority" have not crystallized into a defined "platform," but their position on this issue is in the direction of a modified progressivism.

Individualized Instruction *Versus* Class Teaching

In *The Evolution of the Common School* (1930) Reisner employed the chapter title, "In the grip of the school machine," as descriptive of conditions prevailing during the "generation following the Civil War." Two features of this "school machine" were the graded system and the accompanying class (group) teaching. However, by 1890 the graded system and class teaching were being challenged. Some argued for greater flexibility in the graded system by means of semi-annual or even quarterly promotion, multiple-track plans providing for varying rates of progress, and other organizational schemes. Others proposed that the recognized "evils" of class teaching be minimized by means of improved instructional procedures and techniques. A few insisted that class teaching be abolished and the instruction individualized. During the last decade of the century the controversy attained considerable prominence.

At the meeting of the Department of Superintendence in 1895 Preston W. Search, then City Superintendent of Schools of Los Angeles read a paper on "Individualism in Mass Education." [119] After pointing out "the weaknesses of the graded school system" and the accompanying group instruction he argued for the superiority of the "school of individualism." The nature of this "school of individualism" is only indicated in this paper, but presumably Search had in mind the laboratory method of teaching, commonly referred to as the "Pueblo Plan," which he had developed in the Pueblo (Colo.) Industrial Public Schools during his superintendency there, 1888-94.[120] The presentation of the paper stimu-

---

[119] Preston W. Search, "Individualism in Mass Education," *Addresses and Proceedings* (National Educational Association, 1895), pp. 398-406.

[120] *An Ideal School* (Search, 1901) describes other individual instruction plans.

lated considerable discussion [121] from the opposition which was the majority position.[122] The following excerpts from the comments of William T. Harris, United States Commissioner of Education, indicate the general attitude.

> In some cases the graded school system is so managed that it is made to do harm to all pupils except those of average ability. . . . But the class system is really one of the greatest inventions ever made in pedagogy. A class recitation is a great means of instruction; far more potent than any device of individual instruction. Some have supposed that the ideal of instruction is the private tutor with his single pupil; but the pupil in the class has the opportunity of hearing his fellow-pupils tell what they have learned by their study. . . . The private tutor when at his best cannot arouse the interest of the individual pupil so well as the average class recitation can do it.[123]

The spirit of the discussion and the general spirit of the time are suggested by the remarks of A. E. Winship, editor of the *Journal of Education,* who stated that he was not "an out-and-out believer in individualism."

> Superintendents, like others, worship the new thing that is their own. Their attack on what is not their own newness is often amusing, never more so than in this instance, when three men who stood pre-eminently for the most advanced thought in school administration turn upon Mr. Search with peculiar delight when he brings something newer than their newest.
> Superintendent Search has brought us an idea that has been designated as individualism, and all of these speakers have at once arrayed themselves for a redefense of the class system; a thing they have done, probably, regularly for thirty years. There is certainly nothing new in this defense.[124]

It is easy to understand why school people generally could not visualize a system of "individual instruction and individual progress" as practical in the typical city school. To most school administrators the retention of class instruction was demanded by practical considerations — the number of pupils per teacher, the plan of school buildings and their equipment, and the lack of teachers skilled in individual instruction. And, as Winship suggested, professional jealousy was probably a factor. How-

---

[121] The reported discussion occupies five and one half pages of small type.

[122] Although the discussion was strongly against Search, it appears that there were some educators of the time who agreed with him, at least to a considerable extent. For example, see Charles W. Eliot, "Undesirable and Desirable Uniformity in Schools," *Addresses and Proceedings* (National Educational Association, 1892), pp. 82-95. In this address Eliot urged "individualization of instruction," though perhaps not the one hundred per cent form that Search advocated.

[123] *Addresses and Proceedings* (National Educational Association, 1895), p. 407.

[124] *Ibid.,* p. 409.

ever, there appears to have been a more fundamental consideration. Although the point is not very explicit, the majority (conservative) party appears to have held that it was desirable to have the instruction so organized that pupils would have group (common) experiences. In supporting this position, mention was made of the stimulating (motivating) effect of a group and desirable educative effects of membership in the class group. There seems to have been also the implication that although the individual pupil should have the opportunity to advance commensurately with his capacity and motivation, it was desirable that this opportunity be provided in a setting of undifferentiated instruction beyond what might be provided within and supplementary to class teaching. Search explicitly opposed this implied position and maintained that the instruction should be organized so that there would be "perfect adaptation to the working ability of each individual."

Although following 1895 there appears to have been little explicit discussion of the issue defined by Search's advocacy of the "school of individualism," it seems to have been in the picture. The "majority" position on this issue was a consequence of, or at least compatible with, the American tradition of equal opportunity and freedom for the exercise of individual initiative and the concept of the educative process as being disciplinary. In his reply to the opposing arguments Search emphasized that in the "ideal school of individualism" each individual would be provided with an educational opportunity adapted to his "necessities." Thus opportunity was to be equal in the sense of being equally adapted to the individual needs of the several pupils rather than in the sense of being the same for all pupils of the class. Search did not deal directly with the nature of the learning process but in the discussion E. E. White observed that "the Herbartian pedagogy, as explained by its American advocates, leads logically to individual instruction and to the abandonment of class instruction." [125] This logical consequence does not appear to have been in the minds of other participants and Search did not cite Herbartian doctrines in support of his position.

As indicated by the statement of A. E. Winship quoted above, there was little support of the "school of individualism" in 1895 and the shift of opinion was slow during the following years. However, the majority party was not unmindful of the need for correcting the "evils" of mass teaching. E. E. White expressed what was probably the typical position in *The Art of Teaching* published in 1901. In a chapter on "Class instruction" he criticized the "doctrine of individualism" and defended "class teaching." In the argument he minimized the significance of individual differences and emphasized the assumption of the "modern school" "that

[125] *Ibid.*, p. 410. See also "Discussion" by E. E. White, pp. 346-47, and by N. M. Butler, pp. 347-49.

children are endowed with common powers, and that they face common interests and needs, those of the common civilization into which they are born" (p. 133). On this basis he argued that although economy was an important consideration, the "prime reason" for class teaching was "its efficiency as a means of preparation for both individual and social life" (p. 134). He, however, admitted "errors" in class teaching and expressed his position by saying, "What is needed is not the abandonment of the class system but higher skill in teaching pupils in classes, — a skill that is sufficiently keen eyed to note individual characteristics while training common powers" (p. 135).

In *An Ideal School* (1901) Search elaborated his criticisms of class teaching and the argument for individualized instruction. In both connections he cited results of studies, a rather surprising number considering that educational research was not the fashion. Search also described the Pueblo plan and numerous other departures from conventional class teaching and cited considerable circumstantial evidence in support of the effectiveness of the innovations. The volume was published in the International Education Series, edited by William T. Harris, who was an advocate of class instruction. The Editor's Preface was primarily an explanation or even an apology for including it in the Series. Harris did not believe in the "educational reform" advocated by Search, but he appears to have justified the publication of the volume in his Series on the grounds that the "reading of books on educational reform" is "stimulating to the teacher" and will not be harmful if supplemented by "a reading of the history of education" as an antidote. The volume also included an "Introduction" by G. Stanley Hall in which he observed that "while there are a few minor matters in which I differ from the author, it is, on the whole, a book I wish I could have written myself; and I can think of no single educational volume in the whole wide range of literature in this field that I believe so well calculated to do so much good at the present time."

The persistence of the "conservative" position is indicated by the fact that in *A Cyclopedia of Education* (1912) only a definition paragraph was devoted to "individual teaching" and "individual differences" was given only one column. Neither of these terms appears in the index of Bagley's *The Educative Process* (1905). In *Classroom Management* (1907) this author commended the "Batavia system" as a "compromise between the individual and class methods" (p. 215). This "system," developed by Superintendent John Kennedy in the public schools of Batavia, New York, beginning in 1898, involved two teachers for a given classroom, one providing class instruction and the other individual instruction for the "weaker members of the class" which included sixty to seventy pupils. In the first edition of *Methods of Teaching* (1909) Charters did not treat individual differences, but he included a brief treatment in the revised edition (1912). It is significant to note that he appears to have believed that in a "well-graded class" the differences are not sufficiently important to justify individualizing instruction beyond what may be accomplished incidentally (pp. 121f.).

Although White referred to the "doctrine of individualism," explicit advocacy of the "school of individualism" seems to have been limited, and Search retired from the "battle" following the publication of his volume *An Ideal School*.[126] Thus the "movement" tended to subside. Doubtless the opposition [127] to the broader "Nature is Right doctrine" was a factor. However, evidence of individual differences in grade and class groups was being brought to the attention of teachers and others interested in educational methodology. Thorndike emphasized individual differences.[128] Distributions of test scores of successive grade groups furnished striking evidence of individual differences. Perhaps the most influential were distributions of measures of intelligence. The trend of the times is reflected by Parker's *Methods of Teaching in High Schools* (1915, 1920), in which a chapter is devoted to "Adapting class instruction to differences in capacity." The Pueblo plan, "the Batavia scheme," and some other departures from conventional class instruction are described.

Around 1915 a second protagonist of individualized instruction emerged. Beginning in 1913 an "individual system" was developed in the training school department of the San Francisco Teachers College under the leadership of Frederic L. Burk who was Search's direct successor in the individualizing of instruction.[129] Under his direction the faculty of the training school department developed a series of "textbooks that would be fundamentally self-instructive." A detailed record of pupil progress was kept and the results of the study were published under the title, "Monograph C," in 1915. Burk's ideas were further developed and elaborated at Winnetka, Illinois, by Carleton W. Washburne who had served as a member of Burk's faculty.

Numerous educational writings during the third decade of the century furnish evidence of widespread recognition of the existence of

---

[126] For supporting evidence, see L. Belle Voegelein, "An Annotated Bibliography on Adapting Schools to Individual Differences," *Twenty-fourth Yearbook*, Part II (National Society for the Study of Education, 1925), pp. 287-363.

[127] See p. 22.

[128] Edward L. Thorndike, *Educational Psychology, Vol. III: Mental Work and Fatigue and Individual Differences and Their Causes* (New York: Teachers College, Columbia University, 1914), pp. 142-388. These pages present a revision of a volume originally published in 1903 and revised in 1910. Edward L. Thorndike, *The Principles of Teaching* (New York: A. G. Seiler, 1906). 293 pp.

[129] H. G. Good, "Individualism in Teaching: Two Pioneers," *School and Society*, 46: 551-55, 1937.

marked individual differences in typical grade groups and of the desirability, or even necessity, of effecting a better adaptation of the school to pupils differing in capacity to learn and in other respects. By 1925 there had been a variety of experimental attempts to deal with the problem.

"Ability grouping," which had become popular by this time, was in many cases essentially a scheme to provide for varying the rate of progress for groups of pupils. In such plans the adaptation of instructional procedure was typically left to the teacher and usually very little was done beyond varying the pace of the assignments. Another means of adaptation within the class organization was some form of "coaching" or additional instruction for the "laggards." The "Batavia system" noted above was one such scheme. Forms of supervised study such as "study coach" and the "conference plan" served the same purpose. Some schools developed "hospital classes" and, of course, many teachers on their own initiative kept pupils after school or in other ways provided "coaching" for the "laggards." The record provides relatively little information concerning the instructional techniques employed. It seems reasonable to assume that teachers, especially the more resourceful ones, developed considerable skill in adapting the instruction to their "laggards," but it is likely that in many cases, perhaps in most cases, the adaptation was essentially more of the same sort of instruction as obtained during the class period. Surveys of "supervised study" practice indicate little systematic effort in the direction of developing techniques for adapting instruction to individual differences. Even under such schemes of individualized instruction as the Pueblo plan or the Dalton plan the nature and extent of use of the adaptive techniques are uncertain. At least in the case of the Pueblo plan, the adaptation to individual differences was largely through varying the rate of progress.

Another attack upon the problem of individual differences is represented by "differentiated assignments." Although there have been variations in the details of this technique and it has been supplemented by curriculum changes and other innovations, the basic feature is adjustment of the difficulty and number of learning exercises to the respective abilities and capacities of the members of an instructional group. The employment of a pre-test in spelling results is a rudimentary form of a differentiated assignment. The words missed on the pre-test by the respective pupils constitute assignments adapted to their individual needs. An informal type of differentiated assignment is accomplished by suggesting optional supplementary readings or other exercises or by inviting volunteers for special reports. Ingenious and highly systemized schemes of differentiated assignments were developed in arithmetic under the general title of "practice tests." For example, The Courtis

Standard Practice Tests, "designed to cover every known difficulty in the development of ability in the four operations with whole numbers," provided a diagnosis of needs and remedial instruction for each pupil. As interest in adapting instruction to individual differences increased, schemes of differentiated assignments were developed in other subject-matter areas. One such scheme that was widely publicized is commonly referred to as Miller's contract plan. Within each integral portion of the course (topic, unit, or "challenge") a classified series of assignments was developed. The exercises of the first group were required of all members of the class, i.e. they were looked upon as embodying the "minimum essentials" within the area being dealt with; the remaining groups of exercises were "optional" assignments, i.e. opportunities for supplementary learning.

In Miller's contract plan the mark a pupil received depended upon the number of "blocks of material" he "mastered." If he "mastered" only the first "block" of the "challenge" his mark was "fair"; "mastery" of the second "block" was recognized by a mark of "good"; and "excellent" was given for the "mastery" of all three "blocks." [130] A somewhat similar scheme was reported by Dalman [131] for elementary algebra. In the University High School (University of Chicago) [132] differentiated assignments were employed as a means of providing opportunity for "capacity work" by each pupil, but instead of making the mark depend upon the amount of work completed, a "descriptive report" was made to the administrative office and then to the parents, the emphasis being upon the degree to which the pupil was doing work commensurate with his capacity. In addition, meritorious work was commended and remedial instruction was provided for pupils whose work was judged unsatisfactory.

The "disagreement of the inquiring" since about 1920 has been characterized to a considerable degree by the spirit of scientific inquiry. In 1925, thirty years after Search's presentation stimulated controversial discussion, the issue of individualizing instruction again received attention at a national meeting. This time the treatment was in the form of a committee report published as *The Twenty-fourth Yearbook*, Part II, of the National Society for the Study of Education. The volume bears the title "Adapting the Schools to Individual Differences," but the editor of the Yearbook stated the issue as: "Is it desirable and practicable to

---

[130] H. L. Miller and Dorothy Johnson, "Directing Study for Mastery," *School Review,* 30 (1922), 777-86.

[131] Murray A. Dalman, "Hurdles, a Series of Calibrated Objective Tests in First Year Algebra," *Journal of Educational Research*, 1 (1920), 47-62.

[132] W. C. Reavis, "Differentiated Requirements in the University of Chicago High School," *Twenty-fourth Yearbook*, Part II (National Society for the Study of Education, 1925), pp. 49-52.

carry the differentiation [of instruction] . . . to the complete individualization of instruction?" This statement of the issue and the title implies
general recognition and appreciation of individual differences among
the members of a grade group and of the pedagogical inefficiency of
traditional class teaching. Over a period of thirty years the conservative
position had shifted from a defense of class teaching based upon its educative and socializing value and the impracticality of individual teaching [133] to arguments for "homogeneous grouping" or some form of coaching laggards plus special assignments for the brighter pupils. Meanwhile
the "reformers" had refined and elaborated techniques for individualized
instruction and in some cases, e.g. the Winnetka system, group work was
retained in some areas of school activity. However, there was still disagreement but on a different level from that reflected by the discussion
of Search's paper in 1895.

Two major sections of the report of the 1925 Committee — Carleton
W. Washburne, chairman — bear the following titles: "Typical attempts
to adjust schools to individual differences" and "Statistical results of
experiments with individualization." Under the former a subsection is
devoted to "adjusting to individual differences while retaining the organization and the method of the class system." The "statistical results" presented were judged inadequate to answer some of the questions considered but it was asserted:

There are enough data, however, to make these conclusions reasonably safe:

Ability-grouping does not adequately provide for individual differences;
individual instruction saves the time of many children; it tends to raise the level
of efficiency in the tool subjects.[134]

The presentation of the committee report attracted an audience of
some three to four thousand persons — one of the largest ever attending
a meeting of the National Society for the Study of Education.[135] The
official report of the meeting [136] mentioned that there was discussion, but
from the names of the speakers listed it may be inferred that the opposition to individualized instruction was not very vocal. This inference is

---

[133] Referring to "individual instruction" John R. Kirk in 1907 said, "If this were
practicable it would be unwise, because it could offer nothing to compensate for the
interplay of student upon student which in a well-managed class of any rank or grade
is almost as valuable as the instruction given by the teacher." *Addresses and Proceedings* (National Education Association, 1907), p. 224.

[134] *Twenty-fourth Yearbook*, Part II (National Society for the Study of Education,
1925), p. 215.

[135] W. Carson Ryan, Jr., "The Department of Superintendence at Cincinnati,"
School and Society, 21 (1925), 273-79.

[136] *Twenty-fifth Yearbook*, Part II (National Society for the Study of Education,
1926), p. 242.

supported by Ryan's brief account. In the committee report there is a chapter, "An effort at appraisal" by Kilpatrick in which he criticized both "contestants" on the ground that they "have assumed that education properly consists in acquiring fixed-in-advance subject matter presumably to be used at some later time, typically in adult life." [137] However, his final conclusion was, "We must have both individualized work and group work."

This general conclusion seems to have been in line with typical opinion of the time, but there was disagreement in regard to the relative proportion of the two types of instruction and particularly in regard to the means to be employed. There was also disagreement in regard to a basic issue. The first "plank" of the "platform" of the Progressive Education Association, organized in 1919, was under the caption, "Freedom to Develop Naturally" and during the following years the attention of the Association was focused upon "developing the methods and techniques that would promote the growth of children through guidance of their natural activities." [138] The development of this point of view was traced in the volume by Harold Rugg and Ann Shumaker, *The Child-Centered School* (1928). In the foreword Rugg referred to "two opposing camps" — "those who center education on adjustment to Society" and "the protagonists of self-expression and maximum child growth." Although Rugg aligned himself and his coauthor with the latter "camp," the central purpose of the volume was to criticize the child-centered school sympathetically. The criticism directed attention to certain "mistakes" and shortcomings of the protagonists of the child-centered school, but the volume in effect, was an argument for the child, individually and collectively, as the "true center" of educational thinking.

In the foreword Rugg recognized the believers in the "philosophy of adaptation" as the majority party and referred to the advocates of "development of personality, individuality" as a "militant minority." The "platform" of this majority party was not that of the advocates of class teaching of 1895. The typical majority position may be indicated by "adaptation to individual differences (individualized instruction) within the framework of class teaching." Correspondingly the position of the "militant minority" may be suggested by "individualized instruction supplemented by class teaching."

The modification of opinion since 1930 is not easy to appraise. In the article on "Individual Differences" in the *Encyclopedia of Educational Research* (1941) the advocates of adaptation to individual differences as

---

[137] *Twenty-fourth Yearbook*, Part II (National Society for the Study of Education, 1925), p. 277.

[138] Progressive Education Association, *Progressive Education Advances* (D. Appleton-Century Company, 1938), p. 7.

fundamental in the education of children are referred to as forming a vigorous and growing group. There seems to be the implication that this group represented the ascendant point of view at the time of this writing. The Educational Policies Commission, viewing educational purposes from the point of the American concept of democracy, appears to support the "doctrine of individualism," at least to a considerable degree,[139] but the significance of the pronouncement of this group is not clear. Burton [140] criticized the volume referred to as naïvely lacking in "analysis, discrimination, and organization." In this criticism Burton was not specific relative to the "doctrine of individualism," but at other places he appears to support adaptation to individual differences within the framework of class teaching.[141] Billett, to whose study of provisions for individual differences Burton referred as being suggestive, proposed [142] "optional related activities" as opportunities for individualized instruction, but as this designation suggests the instructional program of the school would be organized on a class basis.

In a brief appraisal of the "individual-instruction movement" Dean [143] concluded that it was on the decline. Dean cited Carleton W. Washburne, an individual-instruction enthusiast, as subscribing to this conclusion and it seems to be in line with other evidence. It should be noted, however, that this conclusion, as Dean indicated, does not mean an emerging indifference relative to providing effectively for individual differences. In this connection it is perhaps significant that under either class teaching or individualized instruction "a systematic and persistent plan of adaptation to individual differences" seems to yield good results.[144]

[139] Educational Policies Commission, *The Purposes of Education in American Democracy* (National Education Association, 1938), pp. 21, 146, *et passim.*

[140] William H. Burton, *The Guidance of Learning Activities* (New York: D. Appleton-Century Company, 1944), p. 269, footnote.

[141] For example, *ibid.*, p. 532.

[142] Roy O. Billett, *op. cit.*, p. 507.

[143] Ray B. Dean, "What Has Become of the Individual-instruction Movement?" *School and Society,* 58 (1943), 164-67.

[144] Gertrude Hildreth, "Individual Differences," in *Encyclopedia of Educational Research,* ed. W. S. Monroe (New York: The Macmillan Company, 1941), p. 598.

CHAPTER 3

Changes in

Teaching-Learning Theory

In view of the controversies that have prevailed it is apparent that there has not been at any time a teaching-learning theory that was universally accepted. However, the record suggests certain theories which, at least in general outline, were widely accepted for a time and it seems justifiable relative to the present purpose to recognize the following: (*a*) Developing the powers of the mind, (*b*) Teaching subject matter or transmitting racial experience, (*c*) Directing learning activities, and (*d*) Guiding pupil experiencing.

The first was the dominant theory around 1890. The second, a characterization of Herbartian methodology and its subsequent modifications, was dominant from around the turn of the century until it was replaced by the third, which became prominent following the publication of *Methods of Teaching in High Schools* by S. C. Parker in 1915. The change from "developing the powers of the mind" to "teaching subject matter" was relatively abrupt and complete. The change from the latter to "directing learning activities" was more gradual and less complete. The rise to prominence of "guiding pupil experiencing" came at the time when the "directing-learning-activities" theory was still developing and for some years they were regarded as competing points of view. There have been modifications in both theories and recently there has been a tendency to think of them as complementary. This change has been gradual and the final stage is probably not yet fully apparent.

The following descriptions of these four theories are based upon what appear to be the more authoritative writings, mainly texts on methodology, and hence the accounts should be regarded as representing the thinking of the authors of the selected writings rather than the theory implicit in school practice or the ideas expressed in the more casual writings of the period. Furthermore, it should be recognized that up until about 1915 most authors were writing with the elementary-school situation in mind. The directing-learning-activities theory was presented mainly in writings pertaining to high-school teaching, while the guiding-pupil-experiencing theory was advanced mainly by authors who were thinking primarily in terms of the elementary-school situation.

As employed here the term, teaching-learning theory, refers to how the complementary processes of learning and teaching are conceived. The total process is complex, and no attempt is made to present the following descriptions under a formal organization. However, a teaching-learning theory includes a position relative to the following items: (a) teaching as an art or a science, (b) nature of the child, (c) learning process and conditions for effective learning, (d) general nature of learning outcomes, (e) purpose of teaching in terms of the focus of emphasis relative to the several types of outcomes, and (f) teacher's responsibilities and functions relative to the teaching-learning situation. General developments relative to the first three of these items have been dealt with in sections of the preceding chapters and the reader will note some duplication.

Developing Powers of the Mind

Although it was frequently asserted that a "teacher is born, not made" and Josiah Royce [1] maintained that success in teaching depended to a large degree upon "the divine skill of the born teacher's instinct," White probably expressed the typical position of the time, at least among "frontier" thinkers: ". . . it (teaching) is an *art*, and as such has its underlying principles which determine its methods." [2] The statement that

---

[1] Josiah Royce, "Is There a Science of Education?" *Educational Review*, 1 (1891), 22.

[2] Emerson E. White, *The Elements of Pedagogy* (New York: American Book Company, 1886), p. 100. Krusé cited a statement by Horace Mann in 1843: "Teaching is an art. Like the other arts, it rests upon definite and fixed principles," ("Normal Schools," *Common School Journal*, 5 (1843), 327) and observed that many authors had "paraphrased Mann's assertion." Samuel A. Krusé, *A Critical Analysis of Principles of Teaching as a Basic Course in Teacher-training Curricula* (Contributions to Education, No. 63 [Nashville, Tennessee: George Peabody College for Teachers, 1929]), p. 124.

"teaching is an art" is repeated in several connections and its seems clear that White thought of the teaching act being determined in its "method," especially the details, by the teacher rather than by pedagogical prescription. This, however, is only one aspect of White's position. The teacher's determination of his "method" was not to be by means of "the divine skill of the born teacher's instinct" but on the basis of the art's "underlying principles."

Although White made only an incidental reference to the teacher's personality as a factor in teaching, it is apparent from other writings of the time that "personality" was generally emphasized as an important qualification. Putnam (1895) asserted it was "first in importance" and supported his statement by quotations from several sources.[3] In explaining the meaning of the term Putnam said he was using it to include "everything which can be expressed by the words individuality and character" (p. 255). Some authors were more analytic in describing the "personality" of the teacher. In discussing the "elements of governing power," White [4] (1893) emphasized "heart power; i.e., love for pupils," "will power," "common sense," and "moral character." In the "edited" publication of Page's *Theory and Practice of Teaching* (1899) E. C. Branson inserted a chapter on "Fitness to teach" in which he used "insight," "sense," "sympathy," "conscience," and "courage" as the basis of his discussion of "native fitness" (pp. 27f.). From these descriptions and other writings of the time it is apparent that there was agreement upon "good moral character" as an essential teacher qualification, but the argument for it seems to have been based upon the thesis that the teacher's "character and life" should constitute a "fit model for the young to copy." [5] This argument and the treatments of teacher personality generally suggest that personal qualities were looked upon more as factors in "governing" the class and in character (moral) training than as functioning in the instruction of pupils. There is evidence of some faith in certain qualities, e.g. sympathy, contributing directly to the effectiveness of instruction, but most of the contribution in this direction was thought of as being made through the governing of the class and through engendering the functioning of the higher incentives.

Rosenkranz, White, and other authorities of around 1890 recognized that psychologists had discarded the traditional faculty psychology.[6] They, however, adhered to the belief that the mind was developed by appropriate activity. The psychologists of the time had not formulated

---

[3] Daniel Putnam, *A Manual of Pedagogics* (New York: Silver, Burdett and Company, 1895). 330 pp.

[4] Emerson E. White, *School Management* (New York: American Book Company, 1893), pp. 30f.

[5] *Ibid.*, p. 47.

[6] See pp. 20, 30.

a substitute psychology of learning, and educationists dealing with teaching theory subscribed to a modified faculty psychology. In the place of "faculties" they postulated "powers" of the mind. This change in terminology was intended to suggest an "integrated" mind rather than a composite of "separate faculties." [7] Occasionally "power" seems to be used as referring to a type of functioning of the mind.[8] Although it is customary to characterize the educationists of around 1890 as thinking in terms of faculty psychology, it seems clear that they were endeavoring to be psychologically respectable, and in view of the barrenness of contemporary psychology relative to learning, they should not be unduly censured.

The child was considered a developing organism whose nature, especially his "powers of mind," evolved (changed) as he advanced in age. This view of the child had become generally accepted, at least as a general thesis. White [9] referred to it as "an obvious fact — too obvious to require proof." But within this general view there was a difference of opinion in regard to the nature of the child and his development. The child was thought of in terms of certain phases or lines of development. Physical development was recognized and Rosenkranz dealt with physical education briefly.[10] There are only very incidental references to the physical aspect of the child in White's volume. The psychical aspect of the child, i.e. his mind or soul, was commonly analyzed into certain "powers." The designations varied. White employed (a) presentative (sense perception), (b) memory, (c) imagination (and phantasy), (d) conception, (e) judgment, (f) reason, and (g) will. However, he noted that although these "powers" were "distinct," they were not "independent" (pp. 21, 84f.), i.e "the power of the soul to put forth any given activity depends more or less on its power to put forth other distinct but related activities" (p. 22). This position was taken also by Rosenkranz (p. 55).

There was considerable interest in the description of the child's development in terms of the appearance of the several powers and their relative activity at a given stage of his development. White presented as the "true theory" the belief that the "variation in the intellectual capability of pupils" from year to year was due to "a variation in the *relative* activity and energy of the several mental powers" (pp. 101, 103). Thus all "powers" were to be found in the child when he entered school, but

[7] Emerson E. White, *The Elements of Pedagogy* (New York: American Book Company, 1886), p. 21.

[8] *Ibid.*, p. 99.

[9] *Ibid.*, p. 101.

[10] J. K. F. Rosenkranz, *The Philosophy of Education* (New York: D. Appleton and Company, 1886), pp. 59-68.

certain ones, especially "sense-perception," were more active (p. 90). The opposing position was that the "age differences" were due to the *"absence* or *non-activity"* of certain powers, e.g. reasoning, during the earlier years, and the "successive awakening of these powers to activity as pupils grow older" (p. 101). The attention given to the identification of the stages of child development indicates considerable support of this position. However, the disagreement relative to the nature of the child's development is less significant than the fact that the child was generally recognized as a developing organism.

Although it was recognized that children of a given age differed with reference to "capability," practically no attention was given to individual differences in the teaching theory of the time. The topic does not appear in the volume by White. Rosenkranz [11] recognized three classes as a "practical matter": "(1) incapacity, as the want of all gifts; (2) mediocrity; (3) talent and genius." However, nothing is said about the education of "incapacity," presumably because a child lacking "all gifts" was, as a "practical matter," not educable. The class of "talent and genius" is dismissed with some brief observations. "Mediocrity" is thought of as including the "great mass of intelligences" and the discussion of teaching-learning theory apparently assumed "mechanical intelligence" which characterized mediocrity. White's references to *the* child suggest that he thought of all children at a given stage of development as being essentially alike. This inference is supported by the fact that in commenting on the principle, "Teaching, both in matter and method, must be adapted to the capability of the taught" (p. 100), he deals only with adaptation to the stage of development.

In discussing the "limits of education," Rosenkranz stated that the "individuality of the youth" sets a "definitive (insurmountable) limit" relative to his education, but a person's "actual education" only approximated this limit and the decision relative to "what the real essence of anyone's individuality consists can never be made with certainty till he has left behind him his years of development" (p. 47). These qualifications appear to mean that "in practice" the teacher was to think of children, except the "pure dunces," as being potentially equally educative. White did not deal explicitly with the question, but his writing tends to suggest conformity with the position expressed by Rosenkranz.

Although the child was generally thought of as a growing, developing organism, his dynamic qualities received only limited recognition as assets relative to his education. The prevailing tendency was to regard the child primarily as plastic material to be moulded and trained by the school. In his chapter on "Habit" William James stated as his "first proposition": "the phenomena of habit in living beings are due to the plasticity of the

[11] *Ibid.,* p. 107.

organic materials of which their bodies are composed." [12] Later (p. 122)
he emphasized that habits should be formed "as early as possible," i.e.
while the child was more plastic. Although he did not explicitly introduce the question of the dynamic qualities of the child, he tended to
imply at least in one place (p. 105) that the formation of habits is the
result of external influences. In a paper on "The Ideal School as Based
on Child Study" G. Stanley Hall [13] recognized dynamic qualities, but he
emphasized training (drill and sternness in discipline) up to the beginning
of adolescence. Thus Hall's teaching theory at the elementary-school
level seems to have been influenced very little, if at all, by his recognition
of the child's dynamic qualities.

White referred to the mind as "self-active" (p. 111) and later added:
"The human soul is not a machine that can be put into action by turning
a crank. Its activity is the result of a self-exerted energy" (p. 120). These
statements suggest that White was thinking of the child as dynamic relative to learning activity. However, it should be noted that he repeatedly
referred to the teacher "*occasioning*" pupil activity and following the sentences quoted above he warned against the inference that "the child is
capable of teaching himself, only needing an opportunity for his self-
activity to manifest itself" (p. 121). Rosenkranz referred to the "passi-
vity" of "mechanical natures" which characterize the "majority of man-
kind" (p. 108). On the other hand Tate [14] observed that "children like
to discover things, and to do things, for themselves" and other authors
of the time tended to recognize dynamic qualities of the child. However,
there was only limited application of this recognition in connection
with expositions of instructional procedures. Tate appears to have been
somewhat more "progressive." He commended the "suggestive method
of instruction" and the fostering of "voluntary efforts" (p. 112). Francis
W. Parker also credited the child with dynamic qualities. Proper external
conditions ("objects and their movements in space") will lead to "educative self-effort." [15] In his editorial comment on Rosenkranz's *Philosophy
of Education* (1886) Harris indicated a "conservative" position by defining "education" (in the sense of teaching) as "the influence of the
individual [the teacher] upon the individual [the pupil], exerted with
the object of developing his powers in a conscious and methodical manner" (p. 23). Thus in 1890 the child in the elementary school was gen-

[12] William James, *The Principles of Psychology* (New York: Henry Holt and Company, 1890), Vol. I, p. 105.

[13] *Addresses and Proceedings* (National Educational Association, 1901), pp. 474-88.

[14] Thomas T. Tate, *The Philosophy of Education* (Syracuse, New York: C. W.
Bardeen, Publisher, 1884, 1885), p. 111.

[15] Francis W. Parker, *Talks on Pedagogics* (New York: E. L. Kellogg and Company, 1894), p. 138.

erally thought of as a developing (growing) organism, but the emphasis was upon his plastic qualities rather than his dynamic nature.

As was noted in Chapter 1 the psychologists of 1890 tended to deal with "learning" only incidentally and frequently only by implication. Somewhat the same condition obtained in the pedagogical writings of the time. However, certain beliefs relating to learning are apparent. Writers of the time generally stressed the thesis that the child learned as the result of his own activity. White stated as one of a group of seven "principles of teaching": "The several powers of the mind are developed and trained by occasioning their natural and harmonious activity." [16] In another place he emphasized this "principle" by saying: "The mind . . . is not a vessel that can be filled from without, or a sponge that can be filled by mechanical absorption" (pp. 111-12). Rosenkranz was not as explicit, but his position seems to have been essentially the same. It appears that learning was generally regarded as being accomplished through the doing of exercises (tasks) set or otherwise determined by the teacher. This "doing" included a variety of pupil activities — observing (sense perception), repeating (drill), listening, reading, memorizing, thinking (reasoning), and the like. There was considerable emphasis upon "doing" under the immediate guidance (direction) of the teacher. White (1886) distinguished between "recitations" (oral testing) and "lessons" (instruction and drill exercises) and asserted that "lessons" had become a prominent teaching activity (pp. 164-65). Development lessons were recognized (p. 139), but White gives the impression that the concept of such lessons and other types had not yet been very adequately developed. Tompkins [17] described learning as a process of inductive development. This fact and the rapid rise of Herbartian methodology during the nineties suggest that by 1890 inductive thinking was becoming recognized as an important learning activity. However, it should be noted that although this recognition is apparent, the thinking conceived of was "thinking *under guidance*." [18]

Payne [19] referred to, "We learn to do by doing" as "the creed of the 'New Education,' so far as it has been been formulated." The meaning associated with this "creed" is not very clear. Payne criticized it by pointing out that on the basis of historical thought and contemporary practice "knowing" was antecedent to "doing." White characterized the

---

[16] Emerson E. White, *The Elements of Pedagogy* (New York: American Book Company, 1886), p. 119.

[17] Arnold Tompkins, *The Philosophy of Teaching* (Boston: Ginn and Company, 1891, 1894), p. 5.

[18] Emerson E. White, *op. cit.*, p. 121.

[19] William H. Payne, *Contributions to the Science of Education* (New York: American Book Company, 1886), p. 129.

"creed" as "only a half truth" (p. 127) and asserted that acceptance of it as the concept of learning would exclude "the idea of teaching" (p. 121). The point of these criticisms is not very clear. White had emphasized activity as the means of learning and Payne appears to have been in agreement.[20] Apparently they interpreted "doing" in a physical sense and were insisting that physical activity was not educative. White went farther and stressed the inadequacy of "mere practice." Thus it appears that the concept of learning activity was a restrictive one.

The outcomes of learning activity were rather commonly designated as skill, knowledge, and power.[21] The first of these categories appears to designate controls of conduct of the specific-habit type, and knowledge seems to have been used with much the same meaning as today. The definition of the third category was a matter of some discussion if not controversy. In his discussion White stated that he was using "power" in "the active sense of capability for self-activity, or for activity when called forth, and also in the more passive sense of capacity to receive or resist, but usually in the active sense of capability" (pp. 98-99). This explanation is elaborated by pointing out that "intellectual power," the aspect considered in this connection, included:

(1) the power to acquire original knowledge [i.e. by observation and thought]; (2) the power to acquire recorded or expressed knowledge; (3) the power to express knowledge in language, oral and written; and (4) the power to apply or use knowledge, the last two including skill [p. 99].

Tate presented the "object of education" as being "to develop all the faculties of our nature — physical, intellectual, and moral; and that, too, in harmony with one another" (p. 63). In the following discussion "individual faculties" are designated by such terms as "perception," "attention," "observation," "memory," "conception," "imagination," "abstraction," "judgment," and "reason" (p. 78). The difference between White's concept of the "ends of teaching" and that set forth by Tate, which appears to have been more representative of the "rank and file" thinking of the time, is more than the use of "power" in the place of "faculty." Although White's list of "powers" (p. 83) is similar to the conventional lists of "faculties" of his time, it appears that the list was introduced only as a means of describing his concept of child development (pp. 84f.).

In spite of the confusion or at least lack of clear understanding in regard to nature of the powers or faculties of the mind, there appears to have been a general conviction that the outcomes of learning activity included more than skill and knowledge and that the additional phase or aspect of educative growth was highly important. White stressed the

[20] *Ibid.*, p. 69-73.

[21] For example, see Emerson E. White, *op. cit.*

value of the "mental power" gained from the process of acquiring knowledge.[22] This "mental power" seems to have been regarded as a collateral (incidental) outcome. Payne maintained much the same position.[23]

There was general agreement that the educative effect of the pupil's activity depended upon the degree of attention involved. Focalization of the attention upon the matter at hand was a necessary condition for effective learning. There was, however, disagreement in regard to the means whereby this focalization of attention should be attained. The "doctrine of effort" adherents argued for focalization of attention by means of the exercise of the will and evaluated school incentives (motivation procedures) largely on the basis of assumed effect on the will. The "doctrine of interest" advocates argued for "making" school work interesting by devising learning exercises that appealed to children or by other effective means. However, they were not indifferent in regard to "will training." In fact, they were inclined to defend their proposed motivation on the grounds of its contribution to this end. White (1886) seems to have been eclectic, perhaps leaning in the direction of the "doctrine of effort." He recognized attention as a product of the exercise of the "will" (pp. 37-38) and his systematic treatment of "school incentives" is under the chapter title, "Moral training," which was interpreted as "will training." His statement, "the most fruitful learning is self-impelled and self-directed" (p. 136), seems to have been intended to say that learning activity was most educative when it involved the exercise of the will. However, in another place he apparently recognized that the necessary focalization of attention might result from interest. ". . . the attention is most easily given when the mind is attracted to or interested in the object observed" (p. 43). White's position seems to have been the majority view in 1890.

The teacher was generally thought of as being charged with the responsibilities of *managing* the class and *teaching* the pupils. The first of these responsibilities was considered a means of certain aspects of moral training and hence highly important. In practice the effectiveness of the teacher in managing the class in conformity with the norms of the time was the dominant criterion of his success as a teacher. White [24] described teaching as including "both instruction and training." Instruction was defined as "the act of presenting objects and subjects of knowledge to the pupil's mind in such manner as to occasion those mental activities that result in knowledge." Training was "the occasioning and directing of the pupil's activities [doing or practice] in such manner as to result in power and skill."

---

[22] *Ibid.*, pp. 122-24.

[23] William H. Payne, *op. cit.*, p. 56 *et passim.*

[24] Emerson E. White, *op. cit.*, p. 134.

It seems clear that in connection with both instruction and training the teacher was charged with responsibility for occasioning (motivating) pupil activity. White specified that the teacher was to direct pupil activity in practice (drill). "Presenting objects and subjects of knowledge" seems to have been thought of as involving more than mere motivation. In elaborating his concept of instruction, White (pp. 141-42) referred to the teacher "directing" the pupil's "observation and thought," "leading" him to "recall concepts or ideas of objects," and by "skillful direction" leading him "to discover or discern" desired knowledge. Such direction occurred in oral teaching.

White maintained that "book study" should be introduced to a limited extent in "primary classes" and that the amount of such learning activity should be increased from year to year in the following grades to the end that "book study" would predominate at the secondary level. It does not appear that the teacher was assigned much directional responsibility relative to "book study." Thus although directing pupil activity was recognized as a teacher responsibility in the teaching-learning theory of 1890, it appears to have been thought of as a relatively minor one which was to be fulfilled mainly during the presentation of "objects and subjects of knowledge." This interpretation is supported by Hinsdale's [25] statement in 1900 that the art of study "receives little conscious attention on the part of either teacher or pupil."

White (1886) recognized "the testing of the results of instruction and learning" as one of the three processes of teaching (p. 147), but he immediately noted that the propriety of doing so had been questioned. Apparently the opposition to testing as a teaching function was a part of the reaction against the recitation (oral testing) as the dominant classroom activity and the extensive administration of examinations and the use of the results in determining pupil promotion and even in evaluating teachers. White recognized the examination "evils" (pp. 199f.), but he maintained that, in addition to its motivating influence, testing "throws needed light on the work of the teacher, disclosing imperfect results, and thus indicating what future instruction and training may be needed" (p. 147). In thus stressing testing as a teaching function and in recognizing what we now refer to as "diagnosis and remedial teaching," White tended to be ahead of his contemporaries.

Although White implies [26] that the teacher should plan lessons, he does not deal with the matter as a teacher activity. Mossman stated that although several authors advised teachers to plan lessons, she found no suggestions relative to "planning lessons" in writings up to 1890.[27] Ap-

---

[25] B. A. Hinsdale, *The Art of Study* (New York: American Book Co., 1900), p. 7.

[26] Emerson E. White, *op. cit.*, p. 168.

[27] Lois Coffey Mossman, *Changing Conceptions Relative to the Planning of Lessons* (Contributions to Education, No. 147 [New York: Teachers College, Columbia University, 1924]), p. 9.

parently it was generally agreed that planning lessons was a teacher responsibility and so far as teaching-learning theory was concerned the matter rested at that stage. Tompkins explicitly advocated lesson planning and treated the topic at some length.[28] The appearance of the volume by Tompkins in 1891 and the systematic treatment of the topic in many later texts indicate an emerging trend which was scarcely discernible during the years up to 1890.

Although the question of the "how" of teaching had been a topic of some prominence during the years prior to 1890 and several method names are to be found in the literature of the time, the emphasis upon teaching as an *art* was incompatible with a treatment of "methods of teaching" or lesson types such as was typical during the years following the turn of the century. Under the heading, "Methods in lessons," White (1886) stated that "it is not practicable to give detailed instructions for the teaching of any branch of knowledge" and he warned against copying "model lessons" as "patterns." ". . . the human soul can not be unfolded, informed, and enriched by operatives following prescribed forms" (p. 168). This position was in conformity with White's thesis that teaching is an art (p. 100). However, White insisted that the "methods" of this art should be in conformity with its "underlying principles."

Among the "underlying principles" White presented [29] he emphasized the adaptation of the matter and method of teaching to "the capability of the taught" as a "fundamental axiom of teaching." This "principle" did not refer to adaptation of "matter and method" to individual differences but to adaptation to the stage of the child's development. Later (p. 168) he asserted that "the particular method to be employed in giving a lesson will depend on the nature of the knowledge to be taught, and the mental condition of the pupils." In concluding the section on "Methods in lessons" he observed: "Skillful teaching requires . . . a quick insight into determining conditions, and a ready adaptation of means to ends" (p. 172). It seems clear that he did not attach much importance to the "method" of a lesson provided there was conformity with principles.

In his treatment of the recitation (pp. 173f.) White discussed the relative merits of the "question method" and the "topic method." He also discussed in the same way "methods of calling pupils" — consecutive, promiscuous, and simultaneous. In the first instance he recommended "the union of the methods in a practical manner." He disapproved of the simultaneous (concert) method of calling on pupils except in certain situations, but favored a combination of the other two methods. In a concluding statement (p. 190) White observed: "It is not what the teacher says or does that tells. . . ." Thus again White placed on the

---

[28] Arnold Tompkins, *The Philosophy of Teaching* (Boston: Ginn and Company, 1891, 1894), pp. 11-35.

[29] Emerson E. White, *op. cit.*, p. 100.

teacher the responsibility of determining the *form* of his method and gave only the guiding admonition that the use of the "concert" method be restricted to appropriate situations.

Although the teaching-learning theory outlined in the preceding pages was soon overshadowed by the Herbartian movement, the leaders around 1890, especially White, should be recognized as formulating a sagacious teaching-learning theory in terms of the psychological and philosophical beliefs of the time.

Teaching Subject Matter — Transmitting Racial Experience

The teaching-learning theory designated by this caption was aggressively promoted during the nineties by Charles De Garmo, C. A. McMurry, F. M. McMurry, and other persons subscribing to Herbartian doctrines. The first systematic presentation was a volume by Charles De Garmo in 1889, *The Essentials of Method*. The subtitle, *A Discussion of the Essential Form of the Right Methods in Teaching*, is suggestive of a basic thesis of Herbartian methodology which became thought of in terms of a pattern method referred to as the Five Formal Steps. In 1886 White closed his consideration of "method in lessons" with an emphasis upon his thesis that "teaching is an art" (p. 172). In *The Method of the Recitation* (1897, 1903)[30] the McMurrys asserted that the Five Formal Steps defined the scientific method of teaching, i.e. they were presented as outlining *the* method of teaching in all school subjects.[31] This thesis was widely accepted particularly in normal-school circles.

The title, *The Method of the Recitation*, tends to be misleading. White[32] analyzed "teaching exercises" (instructional activities) into "lessons" and "recitations" and urged that this classification be "universally recognized in school literature." The term "recitation" was to be employed as the designation of "a test exercise, or an exercise in which the test is the chief element" (p. 165). The use of this term was to be restricted to its original meaning. In contrast, "lesson" was to be used as the designation of "an instruction or drill exercise, or an exercise com-

[30] In *Changing Conceptions Relative to the Planning of Lessons* Mossman listed a volume by C. A. McMurry in 1890 with the title, *How to Conduct the Recitation and the Principles Underlying Methods of Teaching*. This volume is also listed by Krusé, a copy being in the library of George Peabody College for Teachers. But it is not mentioned by De Garmo in the bibliography of Herbart and the Herbartians (1895) and no reference is made to it in the 1903 edition of *The Method of the Recitation*. However, it is likely that the 1890 publication was in effect a "first edition" of the later volume which became widely used as a text, especially in normal schools.

[31] Charles A. McMurry and Frank M. McMurry, *The Method of the Recitation* (New York: The Macmillan Company, 1897, 1903), p. 288.

[32] Emerson E. White, *The Elements of Pedagogy* (New York: American Book Company, 1886), p. 164.

bining both instruction and drill" (p. 164). Thus "lesson" was to refer to "exercises" (teacher-pupil activities) designed to advance pupil learning. Referring to school practice, White stated that in "many schools" the "recitation" had been largely displaced by "lessons." There is the implication that White did not approve of this extreme practice, but he thought that the two kinds of teaching exercises should be used as "*complementary means* of school training" (p. 165).

From White's treatment and other writings of the time it appears that "the passing of the recitation" was definitely under way in 1890, even in practice at the elementary-school level. In the *Art of Teaching* (1901) White commented on this "passing of the recitation" as the most marked "change in teaching in the last twenty-five years" and indicated his disapproval by observing that "teaching has become the giving of lessons, too largely talking" by the teacher and that "pupils are coming to the high school with little power and less habit of study, and their dependence upon the teacher 'to make all things clear' is increasing" (p. 57). Thus if we accept White's estimate of practice, "the passing of the recitation" had been largely accomplished at the elementary-school level by the turn of the century and hence the title of the volume by the McMurrys — *The Method of the Recitation* (1897, 1903) — is definitely a misnomer. In the volume "lesson" is frequently used in the sense that White proposed and a more correct title would have been *The Method of the Lesson*.

The change from "teaching as an art with underlying principles" to "teaching in conformity with a pattern method" — Five Formal Steps, and the change from "recitation teaching" to "lesson teaching" are significant aspects of the development in teaching-learning theory, but with respect to the present purpose attention is directed to the change in the concept of the dominant function of teaching, i.e. from "developing powers of the mind" to "teaching subject matter." In 1892 and 1894 F. M. McMurry [33] emphasized engendering (developing) "a lively, permanent interest" as the "highest immediate purpose of instruction." "Mere knowledge is entirely subordinate to it." However, the trend was in the direction of emphasis upon teaching subject matter. In *The Method of the Recitation* (1897, 1903) a chapter was devoted to the topic, "Why general notions or concepts are the goal of instruction." After reviewing the literature, Mossman stated: [34] "All discussions found on planning of lessons

[33] Frank M. McMurry, "Value of Herbartian Pedagogy for Normal Schools," *Addresses and Proceedings* (National Educational Association, 1892), pp. 421-33; "Recent Educational Theory," *Addresses and Proceedings* (National Educational Association, 1894), pp. 843-50.

[34] Lois Coffey Mossman, *Changing Conceptions Relative to the Planning of Lessons* (Contributions to Education, No. 147 [New York: Teachers College, Columbia University, 1924]), p. 37.

assume that the center of gravity is in the teacher or subject matter, not in the child." This statement, viewed in the light of writings of the period to which it applied, suggests teaching subject matter as the guiding purpose and the method of teaching (type of lesson) as a means to this end.

Consideration of the selection and organization of subject matter became a large "chapter" in the literature of this teaching-learning theory. In *The Elements of General Method* (1903) C. A. McMurry devoted a chapter of 65 pages to "Relative value of studies" and one of 53 pages to "Correlation." Bagley did not include an explicit treatment of subject matter in *The Educative Process* (1905), but the series of chapters devoted to methodology appear under the general caption, "The Transmission of Experience and the Technique of Teaching." Since subject matter may be regarded as recorded racial experience, it appears that Bagley in effect was viewing "technique of teaching" as a means of teaching subject matter. Charters (*Methods of Teaching*, revised 1912) devoted a series of chapters to subject matter and related topics. Again there is evidence of somewhat the same point of view.

Within the teaching-subject-matter view there was emphasis on the organization as a means of facilitating learning, i.e. the pupil's acquisition of the subject matter. The *First Yearbook* (1895) of the Herbart Society for the Scientific Study of Teaching consisted of four articles: "Most Pressing Problems Concerning the Elementary Course of Study" by Charles De Garmo; "Concentration" by Frank M. McMurry; "The Educational Theory of the Culture Epochs" by C. C. Van Liew; and "Correlation of Studies with the Interests of the Child for the First and Second School Years" by Lida B. McMurry. Most of De Garmo's article was devoted to the "psychological correlation" of selected subject matter under which four problems were listed:

1. When shall a study be first introduced?
2. Upon what principle shall it unfold, or what shall determine the sequence of its parts?
3. What shall be the organization within an important department, such, for instance, as science?
4. How shall its relations to kindred subjects be established so as to involve the minimum of time and labor, and to secure the maximum of interest, knowledge, and development of character? [35]

These problems are ones of organization of subject matter. The second relates to the sequential organization within a study (school subject), the third to the organization within a department or somewhat general area, and the first and fourth to the general aspects of the course of study.

---

[35] Charles De Garmo, "Most Pressing Problems Concerning the Elementary Course of Study," *First Yearbook*, Herbart Society for the Scientific Study of Teaching (Chicago: University of Chicago Press, 1895), pp. 7-27.

According to De Garmo, "the apperceptive capacities and interests of the child" should be the principal basis of the solution of these problems. This thesis was generally accepted among the Herbartian group, but a variety of solutions was proposed. According to the "theory of culture epochs," the "intellectual, emotional, and volitional development" of the child paralleled in significant respects that of the race, and hence the general sequential organization of subject matter should be that of its racial development and its chronological positions in the course of study should be in conformity with the corresponding stages of the child's development.[36] Van Liew quoted Rein's scheme in which the "materials of instruction" for the first and second school years were designated as "folklore and fairy tales" and "Robinson Crusoe," and those for the eighth year as "Luther-Nationalization" (p. 93). Parker proposed a plan of concentration in which geography (broadly defined) was to be the central subject of study.[37] In his article Frank M. McMurry[38] proposed "literature and history" as the "center for concentration." A somewhat different proposal appeared in the report of the Committee of Fifteen[39] under the designation, "Correlation of studies."

The appearance of these proposals and the attention given to them and others of a similar nature in educational writings of the time are evidence of the emphasis upon the organization of subject matter as a means of facilitating learning which the Herbartians conceived of in terms of apperception. After the decline of the Herbartian movement, the principle was continued under the designation "psychological organization." In 1912 Charters mentioned the "culture-epoch theory" with the comment that "it will not work."[40] He presented the concepts of "correlation and concentration" with approval, especially the former (pp. 226f.), but his principal treatment was in terms of psychological organization (pp. 208f.).

Although child study was an area of much activity until some years after 1900, the nature of the child and his development received relatively little attention in writings on teaching-learning theory. However, the child was recognized as a developing organism. This recognition was explicit in the culture-epoch theory. Charles A. McMurry emphasized

---

[36] Charles C. Van Liew, "The Educational Theory of the Culture Epochs," *First Yearbook*, Herbart Society for the Scientific Study of Teaching (Chicago: University of Chicago Press, 1895), pp. 67-114.

[37] Francis W. Parker, *Talks on Pedagogics* (New York: E. L. Kellogg and Company, 1894), pp. 27f.

[38] Frank M. McMurry, "Concentration," *First Yearbook*, Herbart Society for the Scientific Study of Teaching (Chicago: University of Chicago Press, 1895), pp. 28-66.

[39] *Addresses and Proceedings* (National Educational Association, 1895), pp. 287-350.

[40] W. W. Charters, *Methods of Teaching* (Chicago: Row, Peterson and Company, 1912), p. 137.

that the child's development exhibited "a successive rise of powerful instinctive interests." [41] In *The Educative Process* (1905) Bagley dealt briefly with the stages of development and asserted that "the child at different levels of his growth has different needs and capacities that must be catered to in different ways" (pp. 200-201). Charters did not list either "child" or "child development" in the index of *Methods of Teaching* (revised 1912). Since Charters dealt briefly with "individual differences," and "genetic differences," these omissions from the index indicate that the "center of gravity" of his thinking was not in the child.

Bagley [42] referred to infancy as a "period of plasticity" and it appears that few writers credited the child with dynamic qualities. This interpretation is supported by the emphasis upon interest and motivation. Charles A. McMurry wrote of "instinctive interests" as being "seized" and "utilized" by the teacher.[43] In another place he defined interest as, "the natural bent or inclination of the mind to find satisfaction in a subject when it is properly presented" (p. 85). This definition and other less explicit statements indicate that he thought of "instinctive interests" not as active (dynamic) urges to action but rather as potentialities which could be stimulated by *proper presentation* of subject matter. He referred to John Dewey in *The School and Society* (1900) as going "a step farther." No specific reference is given but he might have had in mind the following: [44] "He [the child] is not a purely latent being. . . . The child is already intensely active, and the question of education is the question of taking hold of his activities, of giving them direction." In this statement Dewey seems to be thinking of the child in school as dynamic (already intensely active), but in another place he referred to certain interests as "the natural resources, the uninvested capital, upon the exercise of which depends the active growth of the child" (p. 61). The phraseology of this description of certain interests suggests a position close to that expressed by McMurry.

If Dewey went "a step farther," W. C. Bagley probably should be described as being "a step behind." In *The Educative Process* (1905), he asserted: "Children are seldom 'lazy,' but they are normally and constitutionally 'indolent' . . . they are averse to continued effort along a given line" (pp. 103-4). In the following discussion there is some qualification of this assertion. The child is recognized as having "primitive interests"

---

[41] Charles A. McMurry, *The Elements of General Method* (New York: The Macmillan Company, 1903), p. 116.

[42] William C. Bagley, *The Educative Process* (New York: The Macmillan Company, 1905), p. 30.

[43] Charles A. McMurry, *op. cit.*, p. 116.

[44] John Dewey, *The School and Society* (Chicago: University of Chicago Press, 1900), p. 53.

which the teacher should "seize" and "turn" to the ends of education. However, it is clear that Bagley thought of the child primarily in terms of potentialities rather than dynamic qualities.

Charters treated "Motive" in terms of interest, need, and problem.[45] Children were recognized as having "certain native and immediate interests and values which determine the direction that their activity is to take," but the emphasis was upon "potential interests and values which could be made active" (p. 183). Charters appears to have credited the child with more in the way of dynamic qualities than Bagley, and in doing so, he was in line with the trend of the time. Even Bagley seems to have receded somewhat from his earlier position.[46]

Herbart, "one of the greatest psychologists of modern times," was a leader in the reaction against the traditional faculty psychology. His psychology of learning, commonly referred to as "apperception," was basic in the "scientific method of teaching" proposed by the McMurrys. In *The Method of the Recitation* (1897, 1903) "three great topics" were recognized: "individual notions" (percepts or ideas), "general notions" (concepts, principles, etc.), and "application of general notions." [47] This "outline of method" suggests three phases of learning: apperception, induction, and deduction or acquiring skill in application. Apperception was defined as "the assimilation of ideas by means of ideas already possessed." [48] Thus the "ideas already possessed" (apperceiving mass) were assigned an active part in the learning process. The "meaning" given to the data furnished by sensation on a particular occasion depended upon the ideas making up the active apperceiving mass at that time. The active apperceiving mass also functioned as a reception committee for new ideas as they were presented.

The process of assimilation was continued in induction, but the characterizing aspect of this phase of learning was the development of general notions. The Herbartians stressed inductive development as a phase of learning. In the first sentence of the chapter on induction the McMurrys observed that often learning did not extend beyond the acquisition of individual notions [49] and then emphasized that it was "unsafe to stop

[45] W. W. Charters, *op. cit.*, Chap. IX, X, and XI.

[46] William C. Bagley, *Educational Values* (New York: The Macmillan Company, 1911), p. 8.

[47] Charles A. McMurry and Frank M. McMurry, *The Method of the Recitation* (New York: The Macmillan Company, 1897, 1903), p. 72.

[48] Charles De Garmo, *Herbart and the Herbartians* (New York: Charles Scribner's Sons, 1895), p. 32. See also Charles A. McMurry, *The Elements of General Method* (New York: The Macmillan Company, 1903), p. 257.

[49] Charles A. McMurry and Frank M. McMurry, *The Method of the Recitation* (New York: The Macmillan Company, 1897, 1903), p. 185.

short of the abstract truths, the rules, laws, or definitions" (p. 188). The process of induction was analyzed into two stages, "comparison and abstraction" and "definition," which furnished the bases of the third and fourth of the Five Formal Steps. The designation "definition" is significant. In this stage of induction the result of the "comparison and abstraction" was to be formulated (worded) "clearly and accurately," [50] but it was emphasized that the goal was "clear insight" rather than "verbal mastery."

The McMurrys asserted: "The end of instruction has not been reached until skill in the actual application has been developed," [51] and "the acquisition of skill in the ready use of principles" was referred to as "the child's most difficult problem." [52] Since occasions for application vary, the assimilation process was continued as "skill in the actual application" was developed, and there was likely to be also further abstraction and definition. It should be noted, however, that in *The Elements of General Method* (1903) Charles A. McMurry mentioned deduction (application) only briefly (p. 253), and, in general, the emphasis in Herbartian writings was upon the first two phases of learning, i.e. assimilation and induction.

Although the McMurrys cited "the law of self-activity" as one of the laws of teaching underlying the Five Formal Steps [53] and at several places referred to the pupil as an active agent in his learning, the emphasis in Herbartian methodology was upon the arrangement of the content and instruction (teacher activity) as the determining factors. The effectiveness of the apperception depended upon the appropriateness of the "apperceiving mass" relative to the presented "individual notions" and this appropriateness was under the teacher's control through the arrangement of the content of instruction and the step of preparation. The teacher was also an active agent relative to the other phases of learning.[54]

In *The Method of the Recitation* (1897, 1903) the McMurrys asserted: "The law of interest expresses one great condition of effective instruction" (p. 294). In *The Elements of General Method* (1903) Charles A. McMurry devoted a chapter to "interest" and in several places indicated that the pupil being interested in the matter at hand is an asset in his learning.[55] There are several mentions of "interesting problems" and some other suggestions that the teacher should endeavor to stimulate in-

[50] *Ibid.*, p. 198.
[51] *Ibid.*, p. 208.
[52] *Ibid.*, p. 207.
[53] *Ibid.*, p. 292.
[54] Ernest N. Henderson, "Apperception," in *A Cyclopedia of Education*, ed. Paul Monroe (New York: The Macmillan Company, 1911), Vol. I, pp. 141-44.
[55] For example, see pp. 116 and 144.

terest as a means of contributing to the efficacy of learning. However, as indicated above, the emphasis in Herbartian theory was upon the selection and arrangement of subject matter and the instructional procedure as the dominant factors in pupil learning.

The Five Formal Steps — preparation, presentation, comparison, generalization, and application — prescribed the order and general nature of the instructional procedure. With the general method thus outlined it was natural that the Herbartians should emphasize lesson planning. In the final chapter of *The Method of the Recitation* the suggested form consists of two parallel columns — subject matter and method of presentation. The first two items under the latter would be more properly classified as pertaining to the step of preparation. Some of the later items seem to relate to the steps following presentation. In view of the emphasis in earlier chapters of the volume upon the learning being carried beyond the acquisition of "individual notions," it is strange that so much of the planned instructional procedure was under "method of presentation." Perhaps this aspect of the form of a lesson plan is indicative of a tendency to think of instruction as being characterized by the "presentation" step. The frequency of the appearance of the words "present" and "presentation" in writings on methodology seems to support this hypothesis.

Except for the emphasis upon the "presentation" of subject matter (individual notions), the instructional responsibilities (functions) of the teacher were not dealt with systematically in Herbartian methodology as expounded by the McMurrys. It is apparent that the teacher was thought of as responsible for "preparing" the pupils. The "first duty of the teacher" was described [56] as being "to direct attention to the past related experiences," i.e. to stimulate recall of past experiences which would constitute an appropriate apperceiving mass. The step of "preparation" also included "statement of aim." The "aim" was referred to as being "given to the children at the beginning of the recitation" (p. 110). The teacher's responsibilities in steps beyond "presentation" are less apparent. In the discussion of the third step (comparison and abstraction) there is reference to the teacher suggesting "the generalizations intended" (p. 192). Later it was asserted: "It is the duty of teachers to give children training in this work [comparison and abstraction] and to lead them to reach important generalizations correctly in all school studies" (pp. 197-98). The teacher's function relative to the "definition" of the generalization is not clear. It is stated that the wording of the generalization "should come from the child himself" (p. 205). Presumably the teacher was thought of as having a responsibility relative to this pupil action, but the nature of this responsibility was not dealt with explicitly. In concluding this description of the Herbartian concept of teacher functions, it

[56] Charles A. McMurry and Frank M. McMurry, *op. cit.*, p. 91.   See also p. 100.

may be noted that adaptation to individual differences, diagnosis and remedial instruction, and measurement or testing do not appear.

Herbartian doctrines were energetically advocated by members of the National Herbart Society [57] organized in 1895 and Herbartian methodology (Five Formal Steps) became widely accepted. There was, however, criticism [58] and the decline of pure Herbartianism was soon apparent.[59] *The Educative Process* (1905) by William C. Bagley is indicative of the trend of modification. There is no explicit discussion of whether teaching is to be thought of as a "science" or an "art," but statements in *Classroom Management* (1907) indicate that Bagley thought of teaching as an art, even though it appears that he would have it a "regulated" art. He accepted "apperception" and even amplified it as a theory of learning. He also recognized habit formation as a type of learning.[60] The "culture-epoch theory" is not listed in the index of *The Educative Process* and "concentration" and "correlation" are treated with reservations.[61] But the most obvious departure from Herbartian doctrines was the recognition of several lesson types in addition to that defined by the Five Formal Steps.

It probably would not be a valid characterization to say of *The Educative Process* that the "center of gravity is in the teacher or subject matter, not in the child," but there are numerous indications of the teaching-subject-matter view.[62] The teacher's function was to "give" "condensed experiences" to the pupil or to "lead" the pupil to develop judgments (subject matter). Bagley stressed the "leading" function [63] and thus departed from the Herbartian emphasis upon "presentation." Bagley recognized the "recitation" and the "examination" as lesson types. In the treatment of the former there is the suggestion of diagnosis as a teacher responsibility.

The Herbartians emphasized "logical notions" (concepts) as "the goal of all instruction" [64] and did not explicitly recognize drill as an in-

[57] This organization was an outgrowth of the Herbart Club formed in 1892. For an account of activities of members of this Club see Charles De Garmo, *Herbart and the Herbartians* (New York: Charles Scribner's Sons, 1895), pp. 205-14.

[58] For a brief account, see Lois Coffey Mossman, *Changing Conceptions Relative to the Planning of Lessons* (Contributions to Education, No. 147 [New York: Teachers College, Columbia University, 1924]), Chap. IV.

[59] Mossman reported that the peak year in the amount of space in the *Proceedings* of the National Education Association and in the *Educational Review* devoted to discussion of Herbartian doctrines was 1896. *Op. cit.*, p. 21.

[60] William C. Bagley, *The Educative Process* (New York: The Macmillan Company, 1905), pp. 122f., 328f.

[61] *Ibid.*, pp. 179f.

[62] For example, see *ibid.*, p. 256.

[63] *Ibid.*, pp. 260f.

[64] Charles A. McMurry and Frank M. McMurry, *op. cit.*, p. 51.

structional process. Bagley included the "drill lesson" in his list [65] and similar recognition is to be found in several subsequent treatments of teaching-learning theory. This addition of the "drill lesson" may be considered a modification of Herbartian methodology. The engendering of habits had been strongly supported by James [66] and it is likely that his advocacy contributed to the modification. Rowe [67] commented on the neglect of this "subdivision of methodology." Later he asserted: "The methods by which an idea is learned and a habit gained are distinctly different" (p. 37). Drill was essential in engendering many habits. The importance of drill was emphasized by Charters in the first edition of *Methods of Teaching* (1909). Probably referring to Herbartian methodology, he asserted that in recent years there had been "a pernicious tendency afloat in pedagogical literature and practice to the effect that what is needed is that pupils *understand* what they study rather than that they should memorize it," and that "there is the most urgent necessity for memorizing and drill, for review and re-review" (pp. 230-31).

The development of the teaching-subject-matter theory seems to have been essentially completed by 1910. *A Brief Course in the Teaching Process* (1911) by G. D. Strayer, "Revised and enlarged" edition of *Methods of Teaching* (1912) by Charters, and *Types of Teaching* (1915) by Lida B. Earhart reflect this theory of teaching with little change.

Directing Learning Activities

The transition from the teaching-subject-matter view to the directing-learning-activities concept of teaching involved several changes. The "center of gravity" shifted from subject matter to the learning process; the apperception theory of learning was replaced by the activity theory of learning; and there was a shift in emphasis from teacher activity (method of teaching) to pupil activity (responses to stimuli). The development of the "new" teaching-learning theory was gradual. However, the publication of *Methods of Teaching in High Schools* by S. C. Parker in 1915 may be taken as the "event" marking the change. In this volume methods of teaching are dealt with in terms of directing "types of learning in high-school subjects" — (a) acquiring motor control, (b) associating symbols and meanings, (c) practice or drill (automatizing motor and mental associations), (d) reflective thinking (problem-solving and acquiring abstract and general meanings), (e) forming habits

[65] William C. Bagley, *op. cit.*, pp. 328f.

[66] William James, *Talks to Teachers* (New York: Henry Holt and Company, 1899, 1900), Chap. VIII and IX.

[67] Stuart H. Rowe, *Habit-formation and the Science of Teaching* (New York: Longmans, Green, and Company, 1909). 308 pp.

of harmless enjoyment, and (f) training in expression. A date of around 1915 is also suggested by other evidence. Judd pointed to 1915 as the date of the final "battle" for the recognition of educational tests as appropriate (see p. 63). Also around this date there was a tendency among educational psychologists to recognize "types of learning" (see p. 37).

Although 1915 seems justified as the date for the emergence of the point of view designated by the phrase "directing learning activities," it should be noted that one of the most explicit treatments from the point of view of "teaching in terms of lesson types," *Types of Teaching* by Lida B. Earhart, was published in that year. On the other hand, suggestions of the directing-learning point of view are to be found in earlier writings. In the preface of *Methods of Teaching in High Schools*, Parker referred to Thorndike's *Principles of Teaching* (1906) as having influenced his thinking. He does not give specific references, but Thorndike's position is apparent in the following:

> Education should be considered not as a moulding of perfectly plastic substances, nor as a filling of empty minds, nor as a creation of powers, but rather as the provision of opportunity for healthy bodily and mental life, of stimuli to call forth desirable activities in thought, feeling and movement, and of means for their wise direction, for the elimination of their failures and futilities, and for the selection of their useful forms.[68]

This general point of view, which Thorndike referred to as the "doctrine of self-activity," received little recognition until after the appearance of Parker's writing. In *How to Study and Teaching How to Study* (1909) F. M. McMurry deplored the emphasis upon teacher activity (p. 294) and insisted that the "center of gravity" should be placed in the learner (p. 296). However, the general definition of study was given as "the work that is necessary in the assimilation of ideas" (p. 26), and in other respects the volume reflects the teaching-subject-matter view. Charters referred to Thorndike's volume in several connections but there is no mention of the "doctrine of self-activity."

The "types of learning" recognized by Parker may be regarded as counterparts of the "types of lessons" which had been a feature of the teaching-learning theory since the appearance of Bagley's *The Educative Process* (1905). But in centering his discussion about "types of learning" rather than "types of lessons" Parker shifted the focus of attention from the teacher to the learner. There is no mention of whether teaching is to be regarded as an art or a science, but it is apparent that he thought of teaching as an art subject to guiding principles.

In the directing-learning-activities concept of teaching assignments

---

[68] Edward L. Thorndike, *The Principles of Teaching* (New York: A. G. Seiler, 1906), p. 39.

(requests) by the teacher function as "stimuli to call forth desirable activities in thought, feeling, and movement." Parker did not deal systematically with the formulation of assignments, but the matter became an explicit topic in later texts.[69] The emphasis was on the construction of learning exercises compatible with the objectives recognized by the school, i.e. requests that would "call forth desirable activities," and on skillful techniques in making assignments as means of obtaining optimum conditions for learning. Parker devoted a chapter to "Interests, the basis of economy in learning," in which he stressed the utilization of pupils' active interests as the means of obtaining economy (efficiency) in learning. This utilization was to be accomplished by the teacher's skillful arranging of educative situations (learning exercises). Although not explicitly mentioned, it appears that Parker subscribed to the general educational principle stated by Thorndike in 1913 (see p. 85). Much the same point of view is reflected in the writings of other exponents of the directing-learning-activities point of view.

There has been some variation in the types of learning recognized,[70] but the differentiation has been mainly on the basis of the types of desired outcomes. Thus "motor skill" was the basis of one type, "knowledge" that of another, and so on. Parker dealt with each of the "types of learning" from the point of view of how the teacher should direct it. It would transcend the present purpose even to summarize his pronouncements and suggestions. Instead attention will be directed to the following general developments: (a) assignments, especially as means of directing learning activity; (b) instructional procedures and aids for "assisting" pupils in classroom learning activities; (c) supervised (directed) study; (d) diagnosis and remedial instruction.[71]

Assignments. The assignment refers to that phase of the teaching act in which the teacher requests the pupil to do certain exercises — read (study) certain pages in the text or supplementary references, solve certain problems, determine the answers to certain questions, write a theme, prepare a report on a specified topic, do certain laboratory exercises, and the like.

---

[69] For example, see Walter S. Monroe, *Directing Learning in the High School* (Garden City, New York: Doubleday, Page and Company, 1927), pp. 45-48, *et passim.*

[70] Walter S. Monroe and Ruth Streitz, *Directing Learning in the Elementary School* (Garden City, New York: Doubleday, Doran and Company, 1932), Chap. V to X; William H. Burton, *The Nature and Direction of Learning* (New York: D. Appleton and Company, 1929), Units III and IV; Robert W. Frederick, Clarence E. Ragsdale, and Rachel Salisbury, *Directing Learning* (New York: D. Appleton-Century Company, 1938), Part III; Thomas M. Risk, *Principles and Practices of Teaching in Secondary Schools* (New York: American Book Company, 1941), Unit II.

[71] Adaptation of instruction to individual differences might appropriately be added, but since the shifting of opinion relative to this matter has been dealt with elsewhere (see pp. 101f.), it is not included.

Such exercises afford bases for learning activities. The teacher's requests may be supplemented by directive procedures such as suggestions or instructions for doing the exercises, explanations designed to assist the pupils in understanding what they are to do, and even actual assistance relative to anticipated difficulties. During the period since 1915 there have been developments relative to both learning exercises and the associated directive procedures.

In *Methods of Teaching* (revised and enlarged, 1912) Charters advised directive procedures but referred to the formal textbook assignment (take from page — to page —) as the "ideal form toward which the teacher's effort should be directed" (p. 397). Charters mentioned "definite statement of problem" (assignment questions) and "assistance in solutions" as directive procedures (pp. 393, 408). Colvin [72] closed a brief treatment of the assignment with an elaboration of the assertion: "The chief function of the assignment is to teach the pupil how to study." Thus it appears that around 1915 little attention was given to the nature of assignment, but in the limited treatments there was emerging a recognition of its potentialities as a means of directing learning activity.

Following 1920 increased attention was given to the assignment, especially the learning-exercise phase. An essential feature of the Dalton plan [73] was the "job assignment." The "contract plan" involved a system of differentiated assignments.[74] In both cases the assignment was presented in written form. By 1931 the "written assignment" (instruction sheet, job sheet, workbook) had become a widespread practice.[75] In some cases the teacher prepared his own written assignments, but a large number of published workbooks were available. Umstattd described his own collection as containing "more than two hundred different workbooks covering secondary-school fields." Teacher-made "workbooks" varied from a compilation of topics with "assigned" or "suggested" readings to a series of carefully developed "units of work." Some of the published "workbooks" were prepared to be used with a particular text; in certain instances this type of workbook was incorporated in the text. Other workbooks were prepared without reference to any text but were designed to cover a field of study.

The workbook provides an opportunity for convenient application of

[72] Stephen S. Colvin, *An Introduction to High School Teaching* (New York: The Macmillan Company, 1917), p. 240.

[73] Helen Parkhurst, *Education on Dalton Plan* (New York: E. P. Dutton and Company, 1922). 278 pp.

[74] H. L. Miller, "The Contract Plan of Assignment and Some Implications Concerning Procedure," *Educational Administration and Supervision*, 12 (1926), 238-50.

[75] J. G. Umstattd, *Secondary School Teaching* (Boston: Ginn and Company, 1937), p. 176.

several assignment techniques generally regarded as desirable: clear statement of objective, questions or problems as points of departure in study, suggestions and directions with reference to the study process, self-instructive devices, provisions for optional work, and the like. Umstattd presented an analysis of 201 workbooks designed for use at the secondary-school level which showed "instruction to students" and "self-instructive devices" as the most common features. "Introductory remarks" were found in about one-third of the workbooks examined. "Objectives" and "provision for choice of work" appeared in slightly less than 10 per cent.

Some authors directed attention to the nature of the "requests" of assignments. Textbook assignments, i.e. requests to study certain pages, were generally criticized.[76] In *Directing Learning in the High School* (1927), Monroe pointed out that an "outline assignment" was "nothing more than a systematic enumeration of topics about which something is to be learned" and was not a good assignment (p. 417). In this volume, learning exercises are emphasized as "stimuli" of learning activities and the point was made that the learning exercises should be of such a nature that the outcomes of the activities will be the abilities specified as immediate objectives (p. 46). Thus the teacher viewing the defined immediate objectives was to infer the types of learning activities that seem to be effective relative to these objectives and then devise learning exercises to serve as "stimuli" for the desired learning activities.

Yoakam classified assignments as "old-type" and "new-type" and indicated that these categories reflected a change in "philosophy of education" and "a better understanding of the nature of learning."[77] Unfortunately Yoakam did not make this change clear, but his volume and other writings of the period afford a basis for some inferences. *Methods of Teaching* (revised and enlarged, 1912) by Charters may be taken as representative of the position Yoakam designated as "old-type assignment." Charters referred to "methods of teaching" as dealing "with the ways in which the child gets control of subject matter" (p. 142). This statement, which expresses a fundamental phase of his teaching-learning theory, may be interpreted as follows: The function of the assignment and other phases of the teaching act is to stimulate and assist the child in acquiring selected racial subject matter which Charters defined as "a way of acting" (p. 33). In other words, the assignment was regarded as an instrument employed in the "teaching of subject-matter." [78]

---

[76] For example, see William H. Burton, *The Nature and Direction of Learning* (New York: D. Appleton and Company, 1929), pp. 446 *et passim*.

[77] Gerald A. Yoakam, *The Improvement of the Assignment* (New York: The Macmillan Company, 1932), pp. 36f.

[78] This phrase is the title of Chapter VIII of the volume by Charters.

In the contrasting view, associated with "new type assignments," the assignment was thought of as a basis (stimulus) of educative activity, i.e. learning activity considered an effective source of outcomes compatible with the defined immediate objectives of the area of instruction. Racial subject matter, as recorded in books and other forms, was regarded as material to be utilized as resources in the learning activity. This view was suggested in part by Monroe in the volume referred to above. It is rather clearly implied in several more recent writings. For example, Risk [79] referred to subject matter as, "what is used rather than what is learned or memorized." Billett seems to maintain much the same view.[80]

A related aspect of this development is generally referred to under the designation "unit assignment." The thesis that related outcomes from learning activities distributed over a period of time and even among two or more school subjects should be synthesized (integrated) into larger wholes can be traced back to Herbartian methodology. For example, in *The Method of the Recitation* (1897) the McMurrys stated: "To work out such a lesson unity . . . may require several recitation periods" (p. 257). However, the "unit idea" did not become prominent in connection with the assignment until after the publication of *The Practice of Teaching in the Secondary School* by H. C. Morrison in 1926. The term "unit" has been used with a variety of meanings,[81] but as used in connection with assignment, it means that learning exercises are organized in relatively large unified groups rather than as relatively isolated daily installments. Thus a "unit assignment" may provide a basis of learning activity in a course for a period of several weeks.

Treatments of new-type assignments typically include explicit provisions for directing learning activity. A clear statement of a definite objective is generally emphasized. Various other techniques are recommended — pre-test, class discussion of how to attack the requests, questioning relative to meaning of assignment, comments or other forms of assistance relative to anticipated difficulties, reviewing related matters, and the like. In "unit assignments" there is usually provision for a "laboratory" phase during which the teacher has opportunity to extend directive activities.

Instructional procedures and aids for "assisting" pupils. Parker in-

---

[79] Thomas M. Risk, *Principles and Practices of Teaching in Secondary Schools* (New York: American Book Company, 1941), p. 267.

[80] Roy O. Billett, *Fundamentals of Secondary-school Teaching* (Boston: Houghton Mifflin Company, 1940), p. 173.

[81] Hollis L. Caswell and Doak S. Campbell, *Curriculum Development* (New York: American Book Company, 1935), pp. 400f.

cluded a chapter [82] on "The art of questioning." Most of the space is devoted to questioning for recitation (oral testing) and drill purposes, but in the concluding paragraph he asserted: "The recitation should be regarded as primarily a place for group thought, and many of the details of the technique of questioning should be determined by this attitude." During the following years increasing attention was given to questioning as a means of stimulating and directing thinking during the class period. In a study of the use of thought questions, Monroe and Carter [83] reported a list of twenty types. Referring to this list Douglass [84] stated: "The teacher who aspires to be a successful director of educative mental activity in the recitation period should include in his repertoire of question-types a large part of the twenty types." The phraseology of this statement indicates that Douglass recognized the directive function of questioning. The growth of the recognition of this function is suggested by a subtitle employed by Risk: "Directing classroom activities through questioning."

The appraisal of pupil responses to thought questions and other classroom learning performances has received little explicit treatment, but several of the limited references to it indicate recognition of the teacher's appraisal techniques and attitude as having significant directive effects. In *Directing Learning in the High School* (1927) Monroe observed that "the teacher's evaluation and criticism of answers [of thought questions] are probably the most important phase of his instruction in training students to follow effective procedures" (p. 263). In reporting his observational study of "good and poor teachers" of the social studies, Barr [85] stated that the least frequently recommended type of appraisal of pupil responses was a categorical statement by the teacher and the most frequently recommended was "teacher-appraisal plus free class discussion." The next most frequent recommendation was "class appraisal." Risk [86] referred to "the teacher's handling of pupil responses" as important.

Since about 1920 there has been a growing emphasis upon a variety

[82] S. Chester Parker, *Methods of Teaching in High School* (Boston: Ginn and Company, 1915, 1920). Chap. XX.

[83] Walter S. Monroe and Ralph E. Carter, *The Use of Different Types of Thought Questions in Secondary Schools and Their Relative Difficulty for Students* (University of Illinois, Bureau of Educational Research Bulletin No. 14, 1923). 26 pp.

[84] Harl R. Douglass, *Modern Methods in High School Teaching* (Boston: Houghton Mifflin Company, 1926), p. 37.

[85] A. S. Barr, *Characteristic Differences in the Teaching Performance of Good and Poor Teachers of the Social Studies* (Bloomington, Illinois: Public School Publishing Company, 1929), p. 108.

[86] Thomas M. Risk, *op. cit.*, pp. 530-31.

of instructional aids as means of "assisting" pupils in learning. Douglass [87] devoted two chapters to the topic. During recent years "visual education" has become an area of considerable research.[88] Although authors typically call attention to certain "limitations and dangers;" [89] there is general approval of a variety of material devices as means of "assisting" pupils.

Supervised (directed) study. As employed here, "study" refers to learning activity engaged in outside the regular class (recitation) period. For some years prior to 1915 certain educators had directed attention to the teacher's responsibility relative to such learning activity. At first the emphasis in dealing with this problem was upon "teaching pupils how to study." In *The Art of Study* (1900) B. A. Hinsdale advocated the "study-recitation" (pp. 55f.) and the "study-lesson" (pp. 68f.). *How to Study and Teaching How to Study* (1909) by F. M. McMurry and *Teaching Children to Study* (1909) by Lida B. Earhart were more serious attempts in this area of teaching-learning theory. McMurry's treatment of techniques for teaching pupils how to study is limited. He recommended class exercises in which pupils are asked to formulate the "principal thought" of paragraphs (p. 106) or to propose "marginal headings" (p. 108). The marking of the text to "indicate relative values" was suggested. The preparation of summaries was commended. This exercise might be done as a group activity during the class period (p. 130), or the pupils might be asked to prepare separate summaries of a designated text and the class period be used for comparison and discussion. Although some additional "practical suggestions" were given, this description of McMurry's treatment is indicative of the status of the thinking about techniques for teaching pupils how to study at the time of his writing. School practice, of course, lagged far behind his suggestions.

During the second decade of the century, "pupil study" became a major center of interest. Parents reported difficulties in "helping pupils get their lessons." [90] Conditions under which "home study" was done were investigated,[91] and it became generally recognized that the typical study of pupils was rather grossly inefficient. Under these conditions one would expect that following the pioneer attempts of McMurry and Earhart, there would be commendable progress in developing techniques

---

[87] Harl R. Douglass, *op. cit.*, Chap. VI and VII.

[88] Edgar Dale and Charles F. Hoban, Jr., "Visual Education," in *Encyclopedia of Educational Research*, ed. Walter S. Monroe (New York: The Macmillan Company, 1941), pp. 1323-34.

[89] Thomas M. Risk, *op. cit.*, pp. 572f.

[90] Ernst R. Breslich, "Teaching High-school Pupils How to Study," *School Review*, 20 (1912), 505-15; "Supervised Study as a Means of Providing Supplementary Individual Instruction," *Thirteenth Yearbook*, Part I, National Society for the Study of Education, 1914, pp. 32-72.

[91] W. H. Heck, "A Study of Home Study," *School Review*, 23 (1915), 577-606.

for "teaching pupils how to study." What happened is suggested by the term "supervised study" which was introduced about 1910. Rather typically the energies of teachers and school administrators were directed toward "supervising" the study of pupils, i.e. "helping them get their lessons," rather than toward engendering study habits.

Hall-Quest's *Supervised Study* (1916) provides a record of the trend of practice up to 1915. A large room, commonly designated the study hall, was provided in many high schools (p. 96). Here pupils studied during their vacant periods under the "supervision" of the person in charge. Some schools had developed a "conference plan" under which pupils voluntarily or by request consulted with their teachers; other schools employed a "study coach" or an "unassigned teacher." In a number of schools a study period was provided for each subject during the school day and the pupils studied under the "supervision" of the respective teachers (pp. 127f.). This provision was accomplished in several ways: (*a*) Under the "divided-period plan" the "question and answer" recitation was minimized and during a portion of the period the teacher worked "*with* the pupils . . . in the preparation of the new lesson" (p. 129). (*b*) Under the "double-period plan" a second period was provided during which the pupils studied under the direction of the teacher. Hall-Quest also described a variety of special study periods — one hour a week, "daily-extra period," "home rooms," and "occasional study periods."

Hall-Quest's discussion of the various "schemes of supervised study" included references to "teaching pupils how to study." The apparent purpose was "to help the pupil to overcome difficulties in preparing lessons" (p. 127). In the treatment of techniques Hall-Quest stressed the assignment. "Supervised study is simply an elaborate assignment or a cooperative assignment" (p. 143). This "elaborate assignment" included specifications of the "limits of the new lesson," "direction of study," and "explanations." After the assignment was completed, the teacher was to "supervise the pupils at work" (p. 149). As a means of doing this effectively, the pupils should be classified into three groups — superior, average, and inferior. The teacher's "supervising" activities were devoted to the second and third groups, especially the latter. The teacher answered questions, inspected work, made suggestions, called attention to wrong methods being employed, and "when absolutely necessary" provided needed information. The engendering of study habits appears to have received little explicit attention. What was accomplished to this end was done incidentally, or perhaps accidentally.

The general picture of the status of "supervised study" provided by Hall-Quest's text is corroborated by a summary [92] account in 1919. The need for "supervised study" had become generally recognized; numerous

---

[92] Karl J. Holzinger, "Periodical Literature on Supervised Study During the Last Five Years," *Elementary School Journal*, 20 (1919), 146-54.

"plans" had been developed, especially in high schools; but "the technique of directing the study habits of children does not appear to have progressed very far" (p. 153). After a critical review of the literature, Brownell [93] stated in 1925: ". . . relatively too much attention in educational writing and thinking has been paid to the technique of supervised study [organization of the school to provide for supervised study], and too little attention to pupil-direction in study. . . . Our plea, then, is for a change in emphasis in thinking and in practice. We need to be less anxious about the type of technique [organization] which the administrator chooses for his school, and more concerned with the quality of pupil-direction which the teacher gives in the period of study" (p. 45).

This statement provides a considered appraisal of the "supervised-study movement" at the time of Brownell's writing. It appears that the objectives of "supervised study" had not been adequately defined.[94] Critical students of the matter regarded "helping pupils to do assignments" as an incidental function,[95] but there was not a clear understanding in regard to what controls of conduct should be engendered in teaching pupils how to study.

In 1928 Flemming and Woodring [96] reported an analysis of the problems listed by 230 teachers engaged in junior- and senior-high-school instruction. Sixty-five of these teachers reported "that their most difficult problem in directing the study of high school pupils" arose "from their own lack of knowledge of the psychology of learning" (p. 321). No other source of difficulty was reported by as large a number of these teachers. This finding suggests that writers dealing with "supervised study" did not have an adequate understanding of the psychology of learning. Since this was a time of confusion in this area (see p. 36), this "lack of knowledge" was, in effect, a reflection of the status of the psychology of learning.

Meanwhile, there were attempts to teach pupils how to study. A popular procedure was to place a list of "rules for study" in the hands of pupils. Whipple's *How to Study Effectively* was widely used following its publication in 1916. By 1923, 49,000 copies had been printed. Other authors [97] also compiled lists of general rules, some for the study of

[93] William A. Brownell, *A Study of Supervised Study* (University of Illinois, Bureau of Educational Research Bulletin No. 26, 1925). 48 pp.

[94] Cecile White Flemming, "Directing Study," in *Encyclopedia of Educational Research*, ed. Walter S. Monroe (New York: The Macmillan Company, 1941), p. 402.

[95] For example, see Harl R. Douglass, *op. cit.*, p. 135.

[96] Cecile W. Flemming and Maxie N. Woodring, "Problems in Directing Study of High School Pupils," *Teachers College Record*, 29 (1928), 318-33.

[97] For example, A. W. Kornhauser, *How to Study* (Chicago: University of Chicago Press, 1924), p. 43.

particular subjects.[98] Numerous schools formulated lists. However, this technique did not prove effective. Knowledge of a rule did not insure its application in study.[99]

In an article in 1921 Carter [100] urged the systematic teaching of "study habits" by direct or indirect procedures. Although he did not advocate a "how to study course," he mentioned it as a possible means of providing for such teaching and such a course was developed in numerous high schools and colleges. In some cases, the work was incorporated in one of the English courses. In others it was offered as a noncredit course, the time given to it being limited, e.g. one period per week. Several texts for such work were published during the twenties.[101] Several reports indicate that the course was worthwhile.[102] However, some of the experimental evaluations were conflicting,[103] and the trend has been toward engendering study skills and habits by the teachers of the respective subjects and in connection with particular assignments.

During the twenties there was considerable interest in identifying good study habits. One approach was to ascertain how good students study, but comparative studies of groups of good and poor students failed to reveal clear-cut differentiations in study habits. Another approach was experimental evaluation of particular study procedures.[104] Various research workers were inquiring into the study deficiencies of particular

---

[98] For example, R. D. Armstrong, "Some Aspects of Supervised Study in History," *History Teacher's Magazine*, 8 (1917), 42-59.

[99] Joseph S. Butterweck, *The Problem of Teaching High School Pupils How to Study* (Contributions to Education, No. 237 [New York: Bureau of Publications, Teachers College, Columbia University, 1926]). 116 pp. Ruth Strang, "Another Attempt to Teach How to Study," *School and Society*, 28 (1928), 461-66.

[100] Ralph E. Carter, "Teaching a Study-Habit," *School Review*, 29 (1921), 695-706, 761-75.

[101] For example, R. L. Lyman, *The Mind at Work in Studying, Thinking, and Reading* (Chicago: Scott, Foresman and Company, 1924). 349 pp.

[102] For example, William F. Book, "Results Obtained in a Special 'How to Study' Course Given to College Students," *School and Society*, 26 (1927), 529-34; C. C. Crawford, "Some Results of Teaching College Students How to Study," *School and Society*, 23 (1926), 471-72.

[103] For example, Mazie E. Wagner and Eunice Strabel, "Teaching High-school Pupils How to Study," *School Review*, 43 (1935), 577-89; Henry C. Mills, "How to Study Courses and Academic Achievement," *Educational Administration and Supervision*, 21 (1935), 145-51.

[104] William A. Barton, Jr., *Outlining as a Study Procedure* (Contributions to Education, No. 411 [New York: Bureau of Publications, Teachers College, Columbia University, 1930]). 115 pp.; Charles E. Germane, "The Value of the Controlled Mental Summary as a Method of Studying," *School and Society*, 12 (1920), 591-93; Carter V. Good, "The Appeal Made to High School Graduates by College Catalogues," *School and Society*, 23 (1926), 149-52; Edwin H. Reeder, *A Method of Directing Children's Study of Geography* (Contributions to Education, No. 193 [New York: Bureau of Publications, Teachers College, Columbia University, 1925]), pp. v, 98.

pupils.[105] Diagnostic techniques were being developed. An interest was manifested in work-type reading. The trend of the times is indicated by Monroe's *Directing Learning in the High School* (1927) in which a chapter is devoted to "Directing the acquiring of knowledge through reading" in addition to one on "Directing and supplementing learning activity outside of the recitation period."

In 1928 Woodring and Flemming [106] stated that "the emphasis has shifted from the administration of study direction to the quality of the activities engaged in by pupils" and in two later articles in the series[107] they dealt first with "diagnosis as a basis for the direction of study" and then with "training high school pupils in study procedures with emphasis upon reading." The basis of the treatment of diagnosis was a list of "specific study activities" derived from analyzing several hundred assignments given to high-school pupils. Techniques for "teaching pupils how to study" were presented under nine heads: (1) Rapid reading for meaning in general, (2) Skimming, (3) Directed or controlled comprehension, (4) Outlining and summarizing material read, (5) Comparing two or more presentations, (6) Note-taking (on materials read), (7) Understanding and following directions, (8) Problem-solving, and (9) Use of books and materials. Diagnosis was emphasized as an essential prerequisite step for engendering "work skills and habits." The discussion of techniques for "teaching pupils how to study" was documented with references to reports of investigations and other writings and thus constitutes a synthesis of the more advanced thinking and practice of the time. It is apparent that by 1928 considerable progress had been made in devising techniques, but the authors pointed to the need for further investigation in evaluating the suggested techniques and in developing others for study situations.

In 1935 Woodring and Flemming [108] expressed several observations in regard to trends.

. . . the assignment has increased in importance until it is at present the center around which revolves the entire study program [p. 28]. The classroom is

[105] For example, Walter S. Monroe and Dora Keen Mohlman, *Training in the Technique of Study* (University of Illinois, Bureau of Educational Research Bulletin No. 20, 1924). 66 pp.

[106] Maxie N. Woodring and Cecile W. Flemming, "A Survey of Investigations on Study," *Teachers College Record*, 29 (1928), 527-49.

[107] Maxie N. Woodring and Cecile W. Flemming, "Diagnosis as a Basis for the Direction of Study," *Teachers College Record*, 30 (1929), 46-64, 134-47; Cecile W. Flemming and Maxie N. Woodring, "Training High School Pupils in Study Procedures, with Emphasis upon Reading," *Teachers College Record*, 30 (1929), 589-610.

[108] Maxie N. Woodring and Cecile W. Flemming, "Recent Trends in Study," *Teachers College Record*, 37 (1935), 27-49.

rapidly becoming a workshop where teachers and pupils work through problems together. . . . The teacher always alert to needs, quickly diagnoses difficulties, senses obstacles, and provides the necessary guidance and help. . . . Home study becomes "unfinished business" or voluntary leisure pursuits, and the study hall (if there be one) is a place for concentrated, independent work [pp. 30-31].

In increasing numbers and in varied types of schools teachers are comprehending the significance of reading skill as a factor in school success and are realizing the responsibility of the high school teacher for diagnostic and remedial effort to improve reading activities [p. 40].

In the *Thirty-sixth Yearbook* of the National Society for the Study of Education (1937) Snedaker and Horn [109] emphasized the "basic importance of reading ability in study." In discussing the "problems of study growing out of the enrichment of the curriculum," they stated that "the importance of skills involved in selecting, appraising, and organizing data has become increasingly apparent" (p. 149). They also emphasized that "training in methods of study" should be adapted to the "specific needs of each field of subject matter" (p. 150), and they would "place the responsibility for the efficient study of a subject squarely upon the teacher of that subject" (p. 151). Every assignment should be carefully analyzed "as to the study skills required for its completion" and specific training be provided in these skills. The chapter closes with a "limited sampling of exercises that have proved helpful in developing specific reading abilities" (p. 163). Another indication of the trend in the clarification of objectives is the explicit recognition of "investigatory skills." [110]

An analysis of thirty-eight How-To-Study Manuals designed for secondary-school pupils and published in the United States between 1926 and 1939 provides a basis for statements relative to the status of identifying developing study techniques.[111] In the thirty-eight manuals a total of 517 "study habits and skills" were mentioned; 313 were mentioned in four or more of the manuals and 35 in twenty or more of the manuals. In the report of this analysis it is pointed out that the authors of several of the manuals stated that the "rules" for study are the product of their experience with how-to-study classes. The report also suggested that few of the "rules" have any basis in research findings. It was also noted that a rule recommended by one author is condemned by another. The fact that so many how-to-study manuals were published within a period of

---

[109] Mabel Snedaker and Ernest Horn, "Reading in the Various Fields of the Curriculum," *Thirty-sixth Yearbook,* Part I, National Society for the Study of Education, 1937, pp. 133-82.

[110] Cecile White Flemming, "Directing Study," in *Encyclopedia of Educational Research,* ed. Walter S. Monroe (New York: The Macmillan Company, 1941), p. 403.

[111] Samuel R. Laycock and David H. Russell, "An Analysis of Thirty-eight How-To-Study Manuals," *School Review,* 49 (1941), 370-79.

fourteen years indicates widespread interest in study techniques. On the other hand, the variation in the frequencies of the study procedures dealt with and the lack of agreement with regard to rules for study are indicative of immaturity.

Diagnosis and remedial instruction. There is no reference to "diagnosis" in the index of Parker's *Methods of Teaching in High Schools* (1915, 1920), but by 1920 attention was being directed to the diagnostic function of educational tests.[112] In *Modern Methods in High School Teaching* (1926) Douglass dealt briefly with diagnosis in the chapter on "Individual differences" (pp. 476-82). In 1929 Burton [113] devoted a section of 19 pages to the topic: "How may diagnostic procedures be used in improving teaching?" The report of the Committee on Educational Diagnosis of the National Society for the Study of Education in 1935 extended over 523 pages.[114] The article on "Diagnosis and Remedial Teaching" was one of the major contributions to the *Encyclopedia of Educational Research* (1941).

Recent authors vary in their treatment of this phase of teaching theory. There is no systematic mention of either "diagnosis" or "remedial instruction" in *Secondary School Teaching* (1937) by Umstattd and the index of the volume by Risk includes only a reference to "diagnostic testing." Billett's treatment is on about the same level. In *The Guidance of Learning Activities* (1944) Burton devoted a chapter to "Diagnosis of learning difficulties." However, it should not be inferred that authors who treated the matter only incidentally were not duly cognizant of the development designated by the phrase "diagnosis and remedial instruction." What happened seems to be that the diagnosis and remedial instruction had permeated the thinking relative to teaching conceived of as directing learning activity. Evidence of this interpretation is apparent in Morrison's *The Practice of Teaching in the Secondary School* (revised edition, 1931). His "mastery formula" — "Pre-test, teach, test the result, adapt procedure, teach and test again to the point of actual learning" (p. 81) — is essentially an assertion that teaching should be conceived of as diagnosis and remedial instruction. Later (pp. 640-41) he observed that if the teaching, as thus conceived, is efficient there will be few pupils (remedial cases) requiring formal diagnostic and remedial procedures. This trend is also reflected by the change of the title of

---

[112] For example, see Walter S. Monroe, *Measuring the Results of Teaching* (Boston: Houghton Mifflin Company, 1918). In the preface it is stated that "much space is given to the interpretation of scores or measures and the corrective instruction which should be given to correct unsatisfactory scores."

[113] William H. Burton, *The Nature and Direction of Learning* (New York: D. Appleton and Company, 1929), pp. 538-56.

[114] "Educational Diagnosis," *Thirty-fourth Yearbook* (National Society for the Study of Education, 1935). 563 pp.

Brueckner's article in the revision of the *Encyclopedia of Educational Research* to "Diagnosis in Teaching." [115]

Guiding Pupil Experiencing

The beginnings of the teaching-learning theory, here designated as guiding pupil experiencing, may be traced far back in educational history.[116] With respect to the present purpose it is sufficient to note that aspects of the theory may be identified in the "New Education" which Francis W. Parker and a few other educators were writing about around 1890 and that it was a basic thesis in Dewey's University Elementary School (University of Chicago, 1896), Francis W. Parker School of Chicago (1901), Meriam's University Elementary School (University of Missouri, 1905), and other child-centered schools. Much of the development of this teaching-learning theory was included in the account of shift of "majority" opinion in regard to "teacher control, mechanization, conformity *versus* pupil freedom, self-expression, independent thinking" (see pp. 87-101), and hence the present treatment will be limited.

By 1920 guiding pupil experiencing was being promoted as a teaching-learning theory under the title of "project method" and "A Symposium"[117] of March, 1921, may be recognized as the "event" marking the beginning of widespread recognition of the theory. Bagley began his contribution[118] to the "Symposium" with the observation that the "project method," as then conceived, represented "a synthesis of movements and tendencies in educational theory that have been gathering momentum for several years — some of them indeed for several decades." This characterization suggests that Bagley viewed the project method as an eclectic concept of teaching. However, later in the introductory paragraph he asserted: "In a very real sense we are standing today at the parting of the ways."

The phrase, "parting of the ways," implies that the project method was contrasted with an opposing teaching-learning theory. Although

---

[115] Leo J. Brueckner, "Diagnosis in Teaching," in *Encyclopedia of Educational Research*, ed. Walter S. Monroe (Rev. ed.; New York: The Macmillan Company, 1950), pp. 314-21.

[116] Thomas Woody, "Historical Sketch of Activism," *Thirty-third Yearbook*, Part II (National Society for the Study of Education, 1934), pp. 9-43.

[117] William H. Kilpatrick and Others, "Dangers and Difficulties of the Project Method and How to Overcome Them—A Symposium," *Teachers College Record*, 22 (1921), 283-321.

[118] William C. Bagley, "Dangers and Difficulties of the Project Method and How to Overcome Them—A Symposium. II. Projects and Purposes in Teaching and in Learning," *Teachers College Record*, 22 (1921), 288-97.

It may be noted that in *Foundations of Method* (1925) (pp. 233f.) Kilpatrick indicated Dewey's *How We Think* had been a major influence in the development of his teaching theory.

directing learning activities had not become fully established as a teaching-learning theory, at least in practice, it appears that Bagley had it in
mind. The differences between directing-learning-activities theory and
guiding-pupil-experiencing theory ramify into educational purposes and
the curriculum, but for the present purpose it will suffice to note the
difference in the approach in initiating pupil activity and developing an
effective motivating condition. In the directing-learning-activities theory
the activity is initiated by assigning learning exercises designed as a
basis of the outcomes implied in the recognized objectives of the school.
The desired motivating condition is to be developed by a skillful assignment and supplementary motivational procedures. In the guiding-pupil-
experiencing theory the teacher utilizes a purpose which the child, or
a group of children, brings to the school or stimulates the development
of a purpose (motivating condition) by means of conversational techniques. Then the things to be done (learning activities) are planned
cooperatively within the framework of the developed purpose. From one
point of view the difference between these teaching-learning theories is
one of the relative priority of the planning of the learning exercise (or
learning activity) and the development of the motivating condition
(purpose). From another it is one of relative emphasis on pupil initiative and freedom and teacher control and direction. Perhaps the most
significant difference is in the degree of explicit teacher control. In the
directing-learning-activities theory the teacher control is direct. The
teacher plans the learning exercise, assigns it, and directs the pupils'
responses. In the guiding-pupil-experiencing theory the teacher control
is through "setting the stage" and by means of comments, suggestions,
and questions. Furthermore pupils participate in the planning.

The contrast between these two concepts of teaching is extended by
noting certain associated differences. In his contribution to the "Symposium" James F. Hosic pointed out that different methods of teaching
resulted in different educational outcomes.[119] Kilpatrick alluded to a
possible curricular difference (p. 287) and William C. Bagley commented
on it.[120] Under the project method what the pupil learns is instrumental
relative to his purposes as they develop under the stimulation of his
environment, which, of course, includes the teacher. Thus the curriculum
was not to be planned in advance except in very general terms but was
thought of as emerging as the pupil realized his purposes.[121] In the

[119] James F. Hosic, "Dangers and Difficulties of the Project Method and How to
Overcome Them—A Symposium. IV. The Project Method," *Teachers College Record*,
22 (1921), 305-6.

[120] William C. Bagley, "Dangers and Difficulties of the Project Method and How
to Overcome Them—A Symposium. II. Projects and Purposes in Teaching and in
Learning," *Teachers College Record*, 22 (1921), 288-97.

[121] This position is implied in the symposium discussion and was more explicit in
later writings of Kilpatrick and others. See pp. 152, 169.

directing-learning-activities concept the curriculum was to be planned in advance, and the teacher's efforts were to be directed toward engendering the outcomes specified by the defined immediate objectives. This associated difference is suggested by the contrasting terms, "opportunistic" and "systematic" which have occasionally been used as designations.[122]

Closely connected with the difference just noted, Kilpatrick and others subscribing to the guiding-pupil-experiencing view went far in crediting the child with dynamic qualities. The child would form purposes, if given the opportunity, at least if given guiding encouragement. "There is no normal boy but has already many socially desirable interests and is capable of many more." [123] Meriam repeatedly referred to the activities in which children normally engage [124] thus implying that if given opportunity they would form purposes. Authors subscribing to the directing-learning-activities view did not deny the dynamic qualities of children, but they maintained a more conservative position. Parker [125] referred to interests as "dynamic active tendencies in human beings," but his treatment was in terms of *utilizing* interests and did not emphasize the child as a dynamic organism. Douglass stated that his volume was written from the point of view of "assisting child nature to grow and unfold" [126] and he devoted a chapter to "Project teaching," but his treatment of this topic is conservative, at least in the sense that project teaching was not to be the method of all high-school instruction.[127] Monroe's position was about the same.[128]

In "A Review and Summary" of the Symposium report, Kilpatrick mentioned the recognition of concomitant learnings as a significant thesis of the project method.[129] This thesis was given more prominent emphasis during the years after the introduction of Gestalt psychology (see p. 38). Kilpatrick asserted that the "older way," in effect, denied or ignored

---

[122] For example, see Arthur I. Gates and Others, "A Modern Systematic Versus an Opportunistic Method of Teaching," *Teachers College Record*, 27 (1926), 679-700.

[123] William H. Kilpatrick, "The Project Method," *Teachers College Record*, 19 (1918) 328.

[124] Junius L. Meriam, *Child Life and the Curriculum* (Yonkers-on-Hudson, New York: World Book Company, 1920), p. 147 *et passim*.

[125] S. Chester Parker, *Methods of Teaching in High Schools* (Rev. ed.; Boston: Ginn and Company, 1915, 1920), p. 338.

[126] Harl R. Douglass, *Modern Methods in High School Teaching* (Boston: Houghton Mifflin Company, 1926), p. xvii.

[127] *Ibid.*, p. 338.

[128] Walter S. Monroe, *Directing Learning in the High School* (Garden City, New York: Doubleday, Page and Company, 1927), pp. 86, 447.

[129] William H. Kilpatrick and Others, "Dangers and Difficulties of the Project Method and How to Overcome Them—A Symposium," *Teachers College Record*, 22 (1921), 313f.

the possibility of concomitant learnings, such as attitudes, interests, study habits, prejudices, and the like. Kilpatrick did not identify the proponents of the "older way," but presumably he was referring to those who represented the teaching-subject matter view. Assuming this to be the case, Kilpatrick's observation is at least an exaggeration.

The thesis of concomtiant outcomes is, in effect, a modernized version of "transfer of training." Statements of authors writing in terms of "developing powers of the mind" may be interpreted as expressing the thesis of concomitant outcomes. In 1886 White stated as a "maxim of elementary teaching": "Whatever knowledge is taught a child should be so taught that the act of acquiring it shall be of greater value than the knowledge itself." [130] In his argument for the use of "natural" incentives rather than "artificial" ones, White also, in effect, recognized concomitant outcomes.[131] Herbart was a major influence in the rejection of faculty psychology in terms of which transfer of training and formal discipline were conceived. In the United States the introduction of Herbartian theory came at the time of the reaction against transfer of training and formal discipline [132] stemming from James's assertion in 1890.[133] It became unfashionable to appear as a believer in transfer of training, but the possibility of concomitant learning was not denied or even totally ignored.

Many-sided interest, emphasized by Herbartians, is, in effect, a concomitant learning. Although he did not employ the phrase, Bagley rather explicitly subscribed to the thesis of concomitant outcomes.[134] Thorndike indicated the possibility of such by-products of the teaching act.[135] In his summary treatment of "transfer of training," Freeman asserted: "It is generally agreed that there is some transfer of training." Later he indicated that the degree of transfer depended largely upon the organization of the subject and the way it is taught.[136] Thus it cannot be said that the possibility of concomitant outcomes had been wholly ignored. Furthermore, it does not appear that any of the prominent authors

---

[130] Emerson E. White, *The Elements of Pedagogy* (New York: American Book Company, 1886), p. 124.

[131] *Ibid.*, p. 321.

[132] B. A. Hinsdale, "The Dogma of Formal Discipline," *Addresses and Proceedings* (National Educational Association, 1894), pp. 625-37.

[133] William James, *The Principles of Psychology* (New York: Henry Holt and Company, 1890), Vol. I, p. 667.

[134] William C. Bagley, *The Educative Process* (New York: The Macmillan Company, 1905), p. 218. William C. Bagley, *Educational Values* (New York: The Macmillan Company, 1911), pp. 202f.

[135] Edward L. Thorndike, *The Principles of Teaching* (New York: A. G. Seiler, 1906), p. 8.

[136] Frank N. Freeman, *How Children Learn* (Boston: Houghton Mifflin Company, 1917), pp. 265, 284.

denied the possibility of such outcomes unless the absence of specific mention is interpreted as a denial.

In 1926 Douglass explicitly recognized concomitant outcomes [137] and similar mention is to be found in many subsequent writings of persons subscribing to the directing-learning-activity view. Thus if Kilpatrick's assertion in 1921 is interpreted as indicating a real difference in recognition of concomitant outcomes, the difference later became largely a matter of degree of emphasis.

Another associated difference relates to the teacher-pupil relationship. In his "Introductory statement" Kilpatrick referred to "the child as a 'free moral agent'" being "an original and necessary factor in the project method" (p. 287). On the other hand, in "A review and summary" he emphasized that the project method did not mean that the pupils were to be "turned loose" or permitted to do what they might want to do (pp. 314-17). It is apparent that he encountered difficulty in explaining his concept of teacher-pupil relationship. The crux of the matter was that the teacher, on occasion, was to be a number of different persons — "leader, chairman, chief interlocutor, coach, umpire, taskmaster, authority, judge, adviser, sympathetic listener, chief performer, examiner, guide, or friend." [138] Under the directing-learning-activities concept the emphasis was on the teacher as a *director*, a designation that Hosic and Chase did not include. The omission was perhaps unintentional, but in recent years the difference in the concept of the teacher-pupil relationship has been discussed in terms of the verbs *direct* and *guide*, project-method advocates insisting that their concept differed from that held by those who conceived of teaching as *directing* learning activities. The difference seems to be mainly a matter of the degree of *control* exercised by the teacher.

As indicated above, the "project method" included certain curricular ramifications, and following 1921 attention was focused upon the curricular aspects. The phraseology of the title — *An Experiment with a Project Curriculum* — used by Collings in 1923 is suggestive of the trend. Later "child-centered school" and "activity movement" became widely used designations. The teaching-learning theory of the project method and its curricular associate became identified with Progressive Education. Thus the record of the further development of the teaching theory of the project method is to be found mainly in writings of wider scope. The project-method concept of teaching has become an integral aspect of a theory of education.

The proponents of the guiding-pupil-experiencing view have exhibited

---

[137] Harl R. Douglass, *op. cit.*, pp. 24-26.

[138] James F. Hosic and Sara E. Chase, *Brief Guide to the Project Method* (Yonkers-on-Hudson, New York: World Book Company, 1924), p. 28.

considerable disagreement among themselves. For some years there was argument over the definition of the term "project." In 1918 Kilpatrick, who became a prominent proponent of the guiding-pupil-experiencing view, stated that he was using the term "project" as the designation for a "purposeful act with the emphasis on the word purpose." [139] In the "Introductory statement" of the "Symposium" Kilpatrick defined a project as a unit of activity (experience) "which is in fact actuated by a dominating purpose," i.e. a purpose that "(1) fixes the aim of the action, (2) guides its process, and (3) furnishes its drive, its inner motivation." In 1925 Kilpatrick [140] explicitly pointed out that if the purpose should "die away," an activity begun as a project would become a "mere task." A contrasting definition was proposed by Stevenson: [141] "A project is a problematic act carried to completion in its natural setting." Other persons proposed still other definitions. Reviewing the controversy in 1929, Burton [142] pointed out that there were two contrasting definitions — (a) "a problem-solving exercise of a practical nature" and (b) "any whole-hearted purposeful activity."

Such differences of opinion "within the ranks" are not pertinent to the present purpose beyond serving as a warning that the guiding-pupil-experiencing concept of teaching has been variously interpreted. As noted in the preceding paragraph, Kilpatrick stressed purposefulness of the activity as the identifying criterion. In other words he emphasized the motivating condition within the pupil, described as a "dominating purpose," as an essential requirement of this view of teaching. Although few authors subscribing to the directing-learning-activities view explicitly commented on the function of motivation in learning, motivation was the topic of an important "chapter" in their teaching-learning theory and intrinsic motivation was considered more effective than extrinsic motivation.[143] Following his review of the controversy over the definition of the project in 1929 Burton asserted: [144] "Whole-hearted purposeful activity is an excellent description of all good learning situations." Recently students of the psychology of learning have emphasized the function of the motivating condition within the pupil as a determining factor in the

---

[139] William H. Kilpatrick, "The Project Method," *Teachers College Record*, 19 (1918), 320.

[140] William H. Kilpatrick, *Foundations of Method* (New York: The Macmillan Company, 1925), p. 348.

[141] John A. Stevenson, *The Project Method of Teaching* (New York: The Macmillan Company, 1921), p. 89.

[142] William H. Burton, *The Nature and Direction of Learning* (New York: D. Appleton and Company, 1929), pp. 264-68.

[143] Walter S. Monroe and Max D. Engelhart, *Stimulating Learning Activity* (University of Illinois, Bureau of Educational Research Bulletin No. 51, 1930), pp. 8-10, 58.

[144] William H. Burton, *op. cit.*, p. 268.

learning process (see pp. 42f.). Thus Kilpatrick, as an advocate of the guiding-pupil-experiencing view of teaching, was emphasizing a principle now widely accepted.

In arguing for the "purposeful act [as] the typical unit of instruction," Kilpatrick [145] in 1918 drew support from the laws of learning as set forth by Thorndike [146] in 1913. In his "theory of learning" Kilpatrick emphasized the laws of readiness, effect, and set or attitude, and minimized the law of exercise which tended to be stressed in contemporary teaching-learning theory. Thus in the beginning Kilpatrick's teaching-learning theory, which he named the "project method," was differentiated from the contemporary theory by this difference of emphasis upon Thorndike's laws of learning which were basic in the directing-learning-activities view of teaching.

Outside of the argument on the definition of a project, the writings of Kilpatrick and others around 1920 reflect a considerable degree of agreement in regard to the "project method" as a teaching-learning theory. In his concluding remarks at the time of the Symposium, Kilpatrick stated that "our personal points of view are remarkably close" (p. 310). However, as the movement developed, a variety of terms were introduced and the "project method" became an area of differences of opinion, or of differences of phraseology, and, hence, of confusion. The *Thirty-third Yearbook,* Part II, of the National Society for the Study of Education, 1934, dealt with the matter under the title of *The Activity Movement.* A "definition" of the "activity curriculum" was obtained from forty-two "experts." Kilpatrick, who reported the analysis and summary of the definitions, seemed to find evidence of substantial agreement except in regard to the degree of teacher control in determining the "content and succession of the activities" and the extent to which supplementary instruction should be provided for engendering "some customary content of fact and skill and knowledge" (p. 63). However, in the following chapters it is apparent that there was much disagreement among activists [147] and that this disagreement was more than verbal.

It is difficult to appraise the situation since the Yearbook of 1934. In his volume of 1941 Macomber at some places implied substantial agreement among well-informed persons.[148] The same year Kilpatrick, under the title, "The Philosophy of the New Education," stated what seemed to

[145] William H. Kilpatrick, "The Project Method," *Teachers College Record,* 19 (1918), 319-35.

[146] Edward L. Thorndike, *Educational Psychology, Vol. II: The Psychology of Learning* (New York: Teachers College, Columbia University, 1913), pp. 1-16.

[147] For example, see Chapter VIII, "Controversial issues."

[148] Freeman G. Macomber, *Guiding Child Development in the Elementary School* (New York: American Book Company, 1941), p. 309.

him the "common doctrines" of the New Education Fellowship,[149] a designation similar to American Education Fellowship the successor of the Progressive Education Association. As the epitomized statement of the "common doctrines" is examined, it is apparent that in Kilpatrick's judgment there was substantial agreement except on the question of the extent to which the curriculum should be planned in advance. Kilpatrick reaffirmed his advocacy of the "emerging curriculum." However, on another occasion he recognized that his position was extreme (see p. 169) and hence the exception to substantial agreement loses much of its significance as evidence of a deviation from "common doctrines."

From another point of view this exception is significant. If it represents a distinctly minority view, and there is evidence to support the hypothesis,[150] the trend of the development of the guiding-pupil-experiencing view has been in the direction of minimizing the differences between this concept of teaching and that of directing learning activities. As one of the "common doctrines," Kilpatrick stated the following: [151] "Learning goes on best in the degree that the individual himself sees and feels the significance, to his own felt needs, of what he does." This "common doctrine" is little more than a paraphrase of Thorndike's statement [152] of a "general principle of modern educational theory" in 1913 (see p. 85). The burden of Meriam's argument is a protest against the trend of practice in employing the "project (activities) method" as a means of teaching a planned-in-advance curriculum. In thus protesting he in effect admits that project-method practice was in the direction of agreement with the directing-learning-activities view, or perhaps more meaningfully, that in practice the two teaching-learning theories were intermingled to the extent that guiding pupil experiencing did not characterize the teaching act.

At the theory level intermingling of the sort that Meriam criticized is not approved; instead there is a tendency to recognize directing learning activities and guiding pupil experiencing as complementary procedures. The latter is considered appropriate for young children and "beginners on almost any level, and in the area of general education"; the directing-learning-activity procedure is more appropriate "as students attain more maturity, become able to learn through abstractions, and enter upon areas of specialization." [153] The appropriateness of either teaching-learn-

---

[149] William H. Kilpatrick, "The Philosophy of the New Education," *School and Society*, 54 (1941), 481-84.

[150] For example, see Junius L. Meriam, " 'Activities' in the School Curriculum," *Teachers College Record*, 44 (1943), 510-18.

[151] William H. Kilpatrick, *op. cit.*, p. 482.

[152] Edward L. Thorndike, *Educational Psychology, Vol. II. The Psychology of Learning* (New York: Teachers College, Columbia University, 1913), p. 220.

[153] William H. Burton, *The Guidance of Learning Activities* (New York: D. Appleton-Century Company, 1944), Preface, p. vii.

ing is relative to the educational status of the learners and to the purpose.

In practice, the distinction between directing learning activities and guiding pupil experiencing is not always clear and there is sometimes confusion in descriptions of teaching-learning situations. There has been careless usage of project, project method, activity, and other terms. In some instances what is called guiding pupil experiencing or "activity teaching" is essentially directing learning activity. However, such confusion and erroneous designation do not invalidate the recognition of guiding pupil experiencing as a teaching-learning theory.

CHAPTER 4

A Summary Statement

In 1886 Payne referred to the three stages in the development of group understanding proposed by Herbert Spencer [1] — "the unanimity of the ignorant, the disagreement of the inquiring, and the unanimity of the wise." Payne appraised the contemporary status as being of the second stage,[2] and the record of the time reveals much divergence of opinion, in some cases at the level of acrimonious controversy. The interest in developing a science of education exhibited during the following years reflects the hope that the third stage, "the unanimity of the wise," would soon be attained. The record, however, shows continued controversy in the area of teaching-learning theory. In 1914 Charles A. McMurry [3] expressed an appraisal similar to that by Payne in 1886 and in conclusion asserted than "in nearly every case, there is no cause for lasting controversy or contradiction" (p. 278) and that "A science of education should balance up and combine these opposing tendencies, removing all unnecessary causes of friction" (p. 281). Thus McMurry like Payne implied the hope, if not the expectation, that "unanimity of the wise" was not far in the future.

---

[1] Herbert Spencer, *Education: Intellectual, Moral, and Physical* (New York: D. Appleton and Company, 1860), p. 101.

[2] William H. Payne, *Contributions to the Science of Education* (New York: American Book Company, 1886), p. 104.

[3] Charles A. McMurry, *Conflicting Principles of Teaching* (Boston: Houghton Mifflin Company, 1914). 290 pp.

154

Disagreements and controversies continued, but since about 1930 there has been less of the controversial spirit and several writers have commented on the weakness of the either-or type of thinking.[4] A spirit of rapprochement has emerged in the psychology of learning (see pp. 40f.) and in other areas. Thus it appears that the current status of teaching-learning theory may appropriately be characterized as that of the third stage, or at least as approaching the third stage. This progress from the "disagreement of the inquiring" to the "unanimity of the wise" is a very significant development.

The "mode of educational progress" in this development is worthy of note. In the preface of his volume (1886) Payne employed the nautical term "tacking" as description of the current mode and elaborated as follows:

In his recoil from what seems to be a serious error in schoolroom practice, the reformer catches hold of some neglected truth, concentrates his whole soul on his new discovery, denounces the whole existing order of things as irretrievably bad, and by his declamation incites the unthinking and the malcontent to a revolution in methods. Finally the grain of wheat is winnowed from the bushel of chaff, and the pendulum of opinion swings back towards the abandoned truth.[5]

This characterization emphasizes one aspect of the mode of educational progress, but a complete understanding requires that the conservative party be also recognized. As noted in the accounts of "shifts in majority opinion" (Chapter 2), the conservatives tended to present an uncompromising opposition. Such opposition was conspicuous in the cases of Search's proposal of a means of adapting instruction to individual differences (see p. 102) and Rice's implied thesis that pupil achievement should be recognized as the criterion of the effectiveness of instruction (see p. 61). In these instances the opposition crumbled after a time and the proposed changes became generally accepted.

A comprehensive view of the mode of educational progress includes a composite of these aspects. Around 1890 there was a tendency to classify educationists into two parties, the reformers (progressives) and the "adherents of the *status quo*" (see pp. 53f.). From one point of view the mode of educational progress was acrimonious argument, "lawsuit," "battle," and the like. Although there is still argument, the mode of educational progress is now on a different level. As noted above there is a disposition to condemn the either-or type of thinking. This condemnation seems to be a way of saying we should be more open-minded and

---

[4] For example, John Dewey, *Experience and Education* (New York: The Macmillan Company, 1938), p. 1 *et passim.*

[5] William H. Payne, *op. cit.*, p. vii.

should react to criticisms and to proposals at the level of critical intelligence, seeking to ascertain what is supported by the available evidence rather than to defend a position. There is evidence of a trend in this direction since around 1930, and it seems appropriate to characterize the current mode of progress relative to teaching-learning theory as that of critical, but open-minded inquiry. The change from "tacking" combined with uncompromising opposition to this mode of progress qualifies as a significant development in the thinking about teaching-learning theory.

Within the development of teaching-learning theory four general views are identifiable — (a) developing powers of the mind, (b) teaching subject matter, (c) directing learning activities, and (d) guiding pupil experiencing. The first of these concepts represents the teaching-learning theory of around 1890. The second developed during the nineties and was dominant until about 1920. As the designation implies, the purpose of instruction was to teach subject matter. Within this theory there developed concern about the practical value of the subject-matter items the pupil was to learn, and curriculum construction on the basis of adult needs, and to some extent child needs, became an area of much activity. Pupil learning was facilitated by the psychological organization of the selected subject matter, but the emphasis was on the teacher conforming to a pattern method.

Following 1915, the directing-learning-activities theory gradually replaced the teaching-subject matter concept, but the latter view persisted in the thinking of many persons, especially in academic circles. About 1920 the guiding-pupil-experiencing concept of instruction emerged as the opposition teaching-learning theory. Since 1940 there has been a tendency to consider the two theories as complementary, each being appropriate under certain conditions.

Comparisons of 1890 and 1950

Although few recent authors explicitly characterize teaching as an art, the tendency to deal with "method" in terms of an outline of the teacher's functions relative to pupil learning and to emphasize understandings, points of view, and principles in teacher education indicates that teaching is regarded as an art rather than an activity prescribed by specified procedures and rules. Thus current thinking relative to this point appears to be somewhat similar to that of 1890. In view of the popularity of Herbartian methodology (general method) around the turn of the century, the later emphasis upon "lesson types," and the more recent enthusiasm for experimental identification of "best" methods and devices, it is significant that now there is a tendency to return to a concept that was stressed in 1890. Of course, the present concept of artist

teaching differs from that of 1890, but this fact does not constitute a re-
futation of the claim of the indicated similarity.

The teacher personality as a factor in the teaching-learning situation
is a related point of similarity. Although it is not often dealt with beyond
incidental mention in texts on "methods of teaching," numerous recent
writers, especially students of the preservice selection of teachers have
pointed to teacher personality as a potent factor of teaching success.
In this recognition there is a similarity to the teaching theory of 1890.
Although at that time the optimum teacher personality was only vaguely
defined, there was general agreement that the personal aspects of "fitness
to teach" were important.

A third point of similarity is to be found in the concept of the child.
In 1890 it was emphasized that the child was a developing organism, not
"a little man." White stressed as a principle (see p. 115) that instruction,
in both its content and method, should be adapted to the stage of the
child's development. The culture-epoch theory was one proposed adaptation. There has been continued recognition of the child as a developing
organism and research in the area of child development, especially since
about 1920, has added to our understanding.

Psychological developments relating to learning make this area one
in which changes are conspicuous, but certain similarities may be noted.
The child learns as the result of his own activity and the 1890 emphasis
is comparable to that of the present time. Although the current concept
of the outcomes of learning activity differs in certain respects from that
of 1890, it may be noted that at the earlier date three rubrics were recognized — skill, knowledge, and power. The corresponding rubrics today
are specific habits, knowledge, and general patterns of conduct (emo-
tionalized controls). In both instances the third category is thought of
as consisting largely of collateral (incidental) learnings. Thus in general
outline there is a similarity in the concept of learning outcomes.

The principle that, in appraising teaching methods (devices), consideration should be given to the total effect upon the child's educative
development appears in the teaching theory of 1890 as well as that of
the present time. White [6] asserted as a "maxim of elementary teaching"
that knowledge "should be so taught that the act of acquiring it shall be
of greater value than the knowledge itself." This is in agreement
with his contention that "the developing of power should be made the
leading aim of teaching" (p. 123). Although White was thinking in
terms of the psychology of 1890, it seems clear from these and other
statements that he was in effect proposing that in appraising a "method"
of teaching considerations should be given to the by-products as well as

---

[6] Emerson E. White, *The Elements of Pedagogy* (New York: American Book Company, 1886), p. 124.

the direct (knowledge and skill) outcomes. In the "educational lawsuit of interest *versus* effort" both parties pointed to incidental effects in supporting their respective positions. The principle is implied rather than explicit in most recent writings, but it is likely that few, if any, authoritative authors would deny it. Thus there is a similarity in the sense of a common principle and also in the status of its recognition.

These similarities and some others that might be noted make it clear that the teaching theory of 1890 was not wholly "bad." Considering the psychological and philosophical setting of the time, the frontier thinkers deserve commendation for their insight into the teaching-learning situation. The test of time indicates the soundness of their views on several points. But some of the changes in teaching-learning theory appear to be significant gains.

Although there is some variation of opinion, the child is now generally credited with dynamic qualities. This position relative to an aspect of child nature is in contrast to the tendency in 1890 to regard the child as passive and to point to his plasticity as the significant quality. At that time the teacher was charged with the responsibility of motivating the child, i.e. of arousing him to action. In present teaching theory the teacher is thought of as capitalizing pupil purposes, managing the release of pupil energy, and the like.

A second significant change is the recognition of individual differences and the emphasis upon adapting instruction to them. Although psychologists had recognized individual differences prior to 1890, practically all members of the educator group disregarded variations within classes and dealt with teaching-learning theory as if class groups were homogeneous. Hence the present recognition of individual differences and the associated emphasis upon the adaptation of instruction to them constitute a *new* development.

Developments in the psychology of learning since 1890 have led to some changes in teaching-learning theory. The current concept of the motivating condition within the pupil as a determining factor in the educative effectiveness of his activity is a significant development. In 1890 the motivating condition within the pupil, which was generally thought of as characterized by either effort or interest, was considered a factor in learning primarily as a condition contributing to "will training." So far as acquiring skill and knowledge (and perhaps power), focalization of attention was the essential consideration, the nature of the motive (incentive) being of little moment aside from the effect upon the pupil's will. In other words two functions were ascribed to the motivating condition — stimulating a state of focalized attention and training the will. Effective fulfillment of the first was essential and aside from the effect in the area of the will (moral) training the motivating condition was not consideration provided it was effective relative to the first function.

In current teaching-learning theory the concept of will training has been eliminated, but there is recognition of collateral learnings, which may be thought of as the current counterpart; and the motivating conditon is considered a potent factor relative to these learnings. Thus the change relative to the by-product effect of the motivating condition tends to be one of redefinition of collateral learnings, rather than a reversal of position. A much more significant development is that the motivating condition within the pupil is now considered to contribute to the direction of the learning activity and the selection and retention of satisfying responses. Although there is some difference of opinion relative to the optimum "goal" of the motivating condition, there is general agreement that through its directive, selective, and retentive functions the motivating condition in the pupil is a potent factor in his specific-habit and knowledge learning. This emphasis is commonly expressed by saying that the pupil's activity should be purposeful.

Associated with the above development, there has been a modification of the concept of learning activity. In 1890 learning activity was thought of almost wholly in terms of doing conventional school exercises. Knowing was considered a prerequisite to doing and "learning by doing" was not generally recognized except in the sense of application as a culminating step. It was maintained that there was a "natural order in which the powers of the mind should be exercised"[7] and "learning by doing" was in opposition to this dictum. The current recognition of experiencing as educative activity and of the "project method" is evidence of a broader concept of learning activity. The doing of school exercises is still generally recognized as educative, and the emphasis upon learning exercises of the problem type suggests some recognition of "learning by doing" even in the case of assigned "tasks." Although some authors have questioned the efficacy of instrumental learning, especially when "learning by doing" is emphasized as learning activity, the possibility of instrumental learning is generally recognized. On the whole, there has been a significant change in the concept of the kind of activity that is recognized as educative. A basic thesis in this connection is that the "whole child" reacts to his total environment. This makes the pupil's activity complex and an appraisal relative to its educative effect should include consideration of all aspects. In 1890 the appraisal was based largely upon the degree of focalization of attention exhibited.

Current Agreements and Disagreements

The frequent references in recent educational writings, especially around 1940, to disagreements between the Progressives and the Essentialists (and/or conservatives) suggest the recognition of two opposing teach-

---

[7] *Ibid.*, p. 104.

ing theories. It is, however, the considered judgment of the present writer than the disagreements are actually fewer and less significant than an uninformed person would infer; some of the apparent disagreements are essentially verbal, some stem from comparisons with "straw men," and others are differences in relative emphasis. Insofar as the directing-learning-activities and guiding-pupil-experiencing views are identifiable as distinctive theories of teaching, the present trend appears to be to regard them not as opposing positions but rather as complementary aspects of a common theory; the former representing an interpretation with respect to more mature learners, especially in areas of specialization, and the latter an interpretation relative to less mature learners, especially in the area of general education.

A verbal difference occurs when two terms purporting to represent different concepts are employed with essentially the same meaning. Such a situation involves a lack of adequate definition of one or more often both of the terms. Confusion about the meaning of crucial terms employed in expositions of teaching theory has been noted by several authors. Billett directed attention to evidence showing that by 1930 in "both the thought and practice of teachers in better-than-average secondary schools" the terms "project" and "problem" were given essentially the same meaning.[8] In another place he commented on the confusion relative to the meaning of the term "unit," noting that Morrison appeared to be inconsistent in his usage.[9] Meriam was severely critical [10] of the usage of both "units" and "activities." More general assertions supporting the thesis of verbal differences are to be found in a number of recent writings.[11]

Caswell [12] reported, from an examination of the literature, that the "subject curriculum" attributed by the "Progressives" to the "conservatives" was a fiction, a "straw man" and that the "opportunistic [experience] curriculum" attributed by the "conservatives" to the "Progressives" was not what the latter advocated. This appraisal was stated with reference to the curriculum, but the situation in the area of teaching-learning theory appears to be much the same. It has been characteristic of both "parties" to use ill-considered statements and extreme practices as bases for the position credited to the opposition. Designations such as child-

---

[8] Roy O. Billett, *Fundamentals of Secondary-school Teaching* (Boston: Houghton Mifflin Company, 1940), pp. 496-97.

[9] *Ibid.*, p. 464.

[10] Junius L. Meriam, "Activities in the School Curriculum," *Teachers College Record*, 44 (1943), 510-18.

[11] For example, see George H. Deer, "Must Every Teacher Have an Ism?" *Educational Administration and Supervision*, 28 (1942), 369-74.

[12] Hollis L. Caswell, *Education in the Elementary School* (New York: American Book Company, 1942), p. 9.

centered school *versus* adult-centered school, project method *versus* text-book-recitation, and teacher domination *versus* pupil freedom imply an either-or type of thinking which is contrary to the attitude reflected in an increasing number of recent writings.

The trend toward viewing the directing-learning-activities and the guiding-pupil-experiencing concepts of teaching, as modified in recent years, as complementary theories of teaching has been specifically noted by Burton.[13] Project-method advocates, activity enthusiasts, and other proponents of guiding pupil experiencing have, for the most part, written with the elementary school in mind, while authors writing in terms of the directing-learning-activities view have generally envisaged education at the secondary level. It is likely that much of the apparent disagreement has stemmed from this difference in setting. Furthermore, most advocates of each position recognize that there are occasions when the other view of teaching is applicable. Within this general situation more specific statements are made relative to several aspects of current teaching-learning theory.

a. Teaching as an art versus *teaching as a science.* Recent educational writings include few explicit references to "teaching as an art *versus* methods of teaching" and hence the position relative to this issue, which commanded attention around the turn of the century, must be deduced largely from general statements relative to teacher education and from related aspects of current teaching-learning theory. The attention given to methodology, educational psychology, and practice teaching in the technical-professional phase of teacher education is evidence of a general belief that effectiveness in teaching depends, at least in large part, on adequate training in these areas. But the large volume of studies directed toward the identification of personality traits contributing to success in teaching and the inclusion of personal fitness in schemes of preservice selection of teachers are evidence of continued recognition of teacher qualifications associated with the teaching-as-an-art point of view. Odenweller, on the basis of an extensive investigation, concluded that "who" does the teaching is more important than "how" it is done.[14] Although few, if any, other investigators have been so positive in their conclusions, there appears to be general agreement that the teacher as a person is an important factor in the teaching-learning situation. Thus the current

[13] William H. Burton, *The Guidance of Learning Activities* (New York: D. Appleton-Century, 1944), Preface. As Appendix C Burton gives a classified bibliography under the title, "The historical development of principles of teaching in the United States." The final section of this bibliography has the subtitle, "An emerging, coherent and integrated theory of learning and principles of teaching."

[14] Arthur L. Odenweller, *Predicting the Quality of Teaching* (Contributions to Education, No. 676 [New York: Bureau of Publications, Teachers College, Columbia University, 1936]), p. 122.

position may be indicated by saying that teachers are *both* born *and* made, or that teaching is *both* an art *and* a science.

It should be noted, however, that teaching as a science is not conceived of as meaning conformity to a pattern method except in a general sense. In fact, most authors emphasize understandings, points of view, and principles, and if a method of teaching is advocated it is conceived of not as a formula or recipe but rather as a general outline of procedure within which the teacher is to exercise his resourcefulness and ingenuity in conformity with the advocated understandings, points of view, and principles. Thus teaching is not considered an art in the sense that success depends upon "the divine skill of the born teacher's instinct." It is rather a cultivated art, the process of cultivation (professional education of teachers) involving systematic study of teaching-learning theory and experience (practice teaching). If a simple designation of the teaching process is desired, "problem solving" would seem to be in conformity with current thinking.

b. Child nature. There is general agreement in current teaching-learning theory that the child is a dynamic rather than a passive organism. He brings to the schoolroom interests, purposes, urges to actions. It is his nature to be active. But there is some divergence of opinion in regard to the nature and extent of the child's dynamic qualities. In Progressive teaching-learning theory, "the child is an active, curious individual, anxious to learn." [15] In contrast, Morrison [16] asserted "we hate to learn." Both of these characterizations of the child as a pupil in school are exaggerations of the respective positions. Macomber observed that "there may be situations where something more than suggestion is necessary to get the work of the day completed" and that "definite and required assignments may be necessary at times" (p. 309). These observations and other statements make it clear that Macomber did not think of the child as being at all times "anxious to learn," at least "anxious to learn" along lines compatible with the purposes of the school. The context of Morrison's assertion tends to modify its meaning. He explicitly recognizes that "curiosity" is an innate trait of children, and it appears that he introduced the assertion quoted above as a means of emphasizing his contention that "native curiosity" is typically inadequate as a motive even in the "most favorable experiential surroundings." Thus the difference of position relative to the dynamic quality of the child tends to be one of degree of confidence in child "curiosity" as a source of motivation for learning. Macomber, who may be regarded as a typical

---

[15] Freeman G. Macomber, *Guiding Child Development in the Elementary School* (New York: American Book Company, 1941), p. 311.

[16] Henry C. Morrison, *The Practice of Teaching in the Secondary School* (Rev. ed.; Chicago: University of Chicago Press, 1926, 1931), p. 108.

("average") Progressive, professes a high degree of confidence but recognizes that at times the motivation may not be adequate. Morrison, who probably should be regarded as somewhat to the right of the typical "conservative" position, recognizes "native curiosity" as a source of motivation but maintains that it should not be regarded as adequate. Even this contrast should perhaps be toned down because Macomber wrote relative to teaching at the elementary-school level, while Morrison was dealing with teaching-learning theory more especially at the secondary level.

It seems to be in line with "average" thinking to say that typically the child is regarded as dynamic in the sense that he comes to the school with some purposes, interests, curiosities, and the like and that under a skillful teacher he is responsive to the school environment. Children differ in this respect, but this statement is considered applicable to the great majority, especially at the elementary-school level.

The child is a developing organism and the growth process involves qualitative changes. Thus the child is not a "little man," but changes both qualitatively and quantitatively as he develops from an infant to adult status.[17] At a given time the child's developmental status is the resultant of the interaction of his nature and the nurture (environment) within which he lives. The relative influence of nature and nurture varies among the several aspects of the child's development. In the case of his intelligence (capacity to learn), nature tends to be the determining factor. Consequently, the ratio of a child's mental age to his chronological age tends to be constant and hence, the IQ is useful as an indicator of future school achievement. However, the possibilities of error in measuring intelligence and variation in the influence of nurture are such that a purely deterministic position is not justified. Furthermore, in many cases, probably typically, a child's achievement is not commensurate with his educational potentials. Thus the teacher should approach his task as an instructor with faith in the educability of his pupils. This principle is seldom given prominence in treatments of teaching-learning theory, but it is generally implicit, especially in sections dealing with educational diagnosis and remedial instruction.

The fact that the child's development involves qualitative changes as well as quantitative augmentation affords the basis of a pedagogical principle to the effect that the content and method of instruction should be adapted to the stage of the child's development. This principle was emphasized by White in 1886, and it has been generally recognized through the years since that time. In current teaching-learning theory there is

---

[17] For a summary of research on this general statement see "Child Development," in *Encyclopedia of Educational Research,* ed. Walter S. Monroe (Rev. ed.; New York: The Macmillan Company, 1950), pp. 137-97.

some variation in interpretation. Advocates of the guiding-pupil-experiencing concept of teaching tend to think of the adaptation of content as stemming largely from the emergence of the child's purposes. Some stress learning as a growth process and thus introduce the pupil's previous experiencing as a second determining factor. In contrast, some directing-learning-activities proponents make the child's intelligence (mental age) the dominant determining factor. From this point of view the adaptation of content (grade placement of subjects and topics), when determined, would be relatively fixed. The current position relative to the adaptation of method is less explicit. The thesis of the complementary relationship of the two teaching-learning theories (see p. 52) is in effect an affirmation of the principle.

c. Individual differences. The members of grade groups exhibit differences in a variety of traits which are factors in the learning process. The fact of such individual differences is not disputed, and it is generally recognized that, in spite of what may be accomplished by classifying pupils for instructional purposes, class groups typically exhibit differences which should be explicitly provided for in the plan of teaching. Some writers emphasize individualized instruction, making group work supplementary. Others advocate group instruction with supplementary provisions for individual differences. [18] Within these opposing positions there is a common recognition of the socializing value of group work and of the need for instructional adaptations to individual differences. The difference of opinion is largely a matter of emphasis.

d. General nature of learning activity. A child learns as the result of his own activity, i.e. his learnings (skills, knowledges, attitudes, and so on) are outcomes of what he does. This view of the learning process is universally accepted, at least in the sense that no recent writers have explicitly dissented from it. Furthermore, expositions of teacher functions and of procedures relating to the learning process tend to be in terms of phraseology suggesting the functioning of this principle. Instead of writing about the teacher "presenting" a topic or unit of subject matter, "telling" pupils, "preparing" pupils, and the like, authors tend to emphasize the function of the teacher as a guide or director relative to pupil activity.

Within this general view there are variations in emphasis upon "types" of learning activity. Some stress what they designate as "experiencing," i.e. the child's reactions to his environment, including the school. The teacher's control of experiencing is largely through the manipulation of the environment. The teacher may suggest or even ask questions, but there is no assignment of exercises to be done. The pupil's activity is his attempts to realize his purpose under the guidance of the teacher. Others

[18] Thomas M. Risk, *Principles and Practices of Teaching in Secondary Schools* (New York: American Book Company, 1941), p. 652.

think of learning activity as problem solving. The problem may develop out of the pupil's reaction to his environment, but more typically it is suggested, or even assigned, by the teacher. Still others recognize the doing of other types of assignments as appropriate learning activities. Such differences stem to a considerable extent from having in mind different aspects or areas of the child's education. It is likely that with reference to a given aspect of a child's education there would be relative agreement in regard to the nature of the learning activity involved.

e. Learning outcomes. The outcomes of learning activity are now generally conceived of as controls of conduct, i.e. as dispositions, tendencies, and abilities to *do,* not mere acquisitions of subject matter. Progressives emphasize this concept.[19] Morrison (1926, 1931) implied agreement by his emphasis upon "mastery" (pp. 36f.). Billett's (1940) use of the phrase "capacity for behavior" (p. 139 *et passim*) indicates a more explicit endorsement. Some authors, however, by their emphasis upon the use of objective tests and in other ways suggest the subject-matter concept of the goal of instruction. Although a case can be made for this interpretation, it is perhaps unfair to conclude that such authors are actively opposed to the thesis that the desired outcomes of instruction should be conceived of in terms of "mastery," "capacity for behavior," "dispositions, tendencies, and abilities to do," and the like. There may be some divergence of opinion, especially in matters of emphasis, but the appearance of disagreement probably stems largely from the persistence of terminology and testing procedures from the past.

Most authors employ a scheme of classification as a means of directing attention to differences in the nature of the outcomes. Although there is variation in the terminology employed, there is fairly close agreement in regard to the nature of the controls of conduct under the following categories: (*a*) specific habits or "specific abilities" — motor skills (abilities, fixed associations or memorized responses to specific questions such as the multiplication facts, and other "ready-made" controls of conduct, (*b*) knowledge — facts, principles, understandings, concepts of complex relationships, and the like, which function in responding to problematic situations, and (*c*) general patterns of conduct — attitudes, interests, ideals, points of view, dispositions, general habits, skills in thinking, and the like.[20]

Although there are differences of opinion in regard to the explanation [21] of the "transfer of training," the fact of "transfer" is generally recognized in the sense that outcomes resulting from responding to one situation may function in situations that differ from the one in which the learning oc-

---

[19] For example, see Freeman G. Macomber, *op. cit.,* p. 314.

[20] For an illustrative account, see Thomas M. Risk, *op. cit.,* pp. 90f., 117, 175f.

[21] *Ibid.,* pp. 96-99.

curred.[22] It is also generally recognized that the "transfer" quality of a child's learning is itself a learning outcome and that if the "transfer" quality is desired, it should be included in the concept of the "desired outcomes." Since the designation "general patterns of conduct" implies generalization of functioning, which is "transfer," recognition of the "transfer" quality in the concept of the "desired outcomes" is accomplished, at least to a considerable extent, by the inclusion of controls of conduct of this category and by emphasis upon generalizing their functioning.

f. Motivation. The motivating condition that develops in the pupil is a determining factor in the educative effectiveness of his activity. In addition to energizing the pupil, the motivating condition directs the activity, provides criteria for the selection of adequate responses, and contributes to strengthening such responses as controls of future behavior.[23] Thus the means of obtaining the optimum motivating condition is a consideration of vital importance. It is not sufficient that there be aggressive, persistent pupil activity, or in other words, that the pupil be appropriately energized. It is also necessary that the motivating condition be such that it *directs* the pupil's activity along lines of effective learning relative to the purpose of education, that it *provides* criteria for the selection of adequate responses, and that it contributes to *strengthening* the selected responses as controls of future behavior.

The argument over the verbal description of the optimum motivating condition has largely subsided. There are, however, significant differences of position relative to the nature of pupil activity and accompanying motivating condition that make for maximum educative effectiveness. The issue is complex. First there is the question of the desirability, if not possibility, of specifying in advance the desired outcomes, especially as objectives allocated with respect to instructional area and grade level. A second question pertains to the efficacy of incidental (instrumental) learning. A third point of disagreement relates to the approach in obtaining the desired motivating condition.

Conservatives (Essentialists) regard pupil activity as the means by which desired outcomes (determined-in-advance objectives) are to be achieved. "Maximum educative effectiveness" is to be attained by (*a*) determining the "desired outcomes," specifying in appropriate detail the increments of educative growth in terms of controls of conduct, (*b*) initiating pupil activity envisaged as directly productive of the "desired outcomes," particularly those of skill and knowledge types, by means of skillful assignment of learning exercises wisely planned relative to the

---

[22] Roy O. Billett, *op. cit.*, p. 158.

[23] Arthur W. Melton, "Learning," in *Encyclopedia of Educational Research*, ed. Walter S. Monroe (Rev. ed.; New York: The Macmillan Company, 1950), pp. 673-74.

pupil's readiness to learn and his interests, needs, and the like, and (c) stimulating an adequate motivating condition by means of appropriate procedures and techniques.[24] This position implies that "desired outcomes" are to be determined in advance and in detail, that it is appropriate to allocate them relative to instructional areas and grade levels, and that when thus determined and allocated they constitute the basic criterion of educative effectiveness of pupil activity.

The conservatives recognize the motivating condition as a factor in learning, and they accept the thesis that the pupil's activity should be purposeful, but their concept of the optimum motivating condition is one characterized by the *purpose of learning* in the skill or knowledge area defined by the specified objectives.[25] Since the motivating condition fulfills a directive function, the pupil activity would be *directed* toward the attainment of the specified objectives (goals). Conservatives consider incidental (instrumental) learning resulting from pupil activity of the experience type as not efficient from the point of view of the time involved and likely to be incomplete, if not "hit-and-miss," relative to stated-in-advance objectives.[26] It should be noted, however, that the conservatives do not deny the possibility of instrumental learning. Furthermore, they definitely recognize the possibility of concomitant learnings of the general-pattern type.

The conservatives recognize that a verbal statement by the teacher of the determined-in-advance objectives may not result in the pupil purposing the doing of assigned exercises as a means of attaining the goals thus indicated. They also recognize that, although the pupil may be energized by means of extrinsic incentives, the optimum motivating condition may not obtain. On the positive side, the conservatives recognize that the development of the optimum motivating condition in the pupil poses an important teacher problem. In dealing with this problem, they would have the teacher plan learning exercises wisely, being guided by pupil interests, needs, and the like as well as by the determined-in-advance objectives and they would have the assignments skillfully made. The result, they hope, will be an adequate motivating condition, and they maintain that responding to learning exercises, especially if the activity is satisfying, may lead to the pupil purposing learning in the area.[27] They also emphasize contributions to the motivating condition from teacher appraisal and direction during the learning activity.

---

[24] For example, see Roy O. Billett, *op. cit.*, pp. 150-51; Frank A. Butler, *The Improvement of Teaching in Secondary Schools* (Chicago: University of Chicago Press, 1939), p. 141.

[25] Roy O. Billett, *op. cit.*, p. 174.

[26] Boyd H. Bode, *Modern Educational Theories* (New York: The Macmillan Company, 1927), p. 151.

[27] Thomas M. Risk, *op. cit.*, pp. 500-501.

The contrasting view relative to the development of the motivating condition in the pupil is so interrelated with the question of the goals of the pupil activity that it is presented in connection with that topic.

g. *Goals of pupil activity.* In Progressive teaching theory learning is referred to as "experiencing" which has been described as "an active process of interaction between the human organism and its natural and social environment." [28] The end of this "process of interaction" is the realization of purposes and interests, the satisfaction of needs, the overcoming of difficulties, and the like. In the process, knowledge is acquired, habits are formed, and ideals and attitudes emerge as instrumental learnings. The Experimentalist, who may be regarded as a "radical" Progressive, maintains that education should not "serve fixed, external ends," that "growth is its own end," and that "maximum meaningful living in the present is the best preparation for the future." [29] Such assertions suggest a lack of concern about what the pupil learns, i.e. what the outcomes of pupil activity will be. In other words, the Experimentalist seems to say that purposeful activity (maximum meaningful living) on the part of the pupil should be the objective of the teacher without regard for the goals of his purposes or the outcomes of the activity.

Careful reading of Experimentalistic writings reveal restrictive qualifications. For example, Kilpatrick [30] stated: "The work of the school . . . is . . . to build before adulthood useful social ideals, habits of democratic study and action, and actual social intelligence." Back of this statement is Kilpatrick's concept of a democratic society, but, since we are living in a changing civilization and presumably this condition will continue, this desired democratic society cannot be defined except in terms of general criteria.[31] Consequently, "useful *social* ideals, habits of *democratic* study and action, and actual *social* intelligence" also are not to be defined except in general terms and then only tentatively. However, Kilpatrick's specification of "the work of the school" does imply that the teacher should be concerned about what the pupil learns, but, and this seems to be the crux of his position, he would have this concern stem from a point of view (the philosophy of Experimentalism) rather than from stated-in-advance objectives in terms of controls of conduct to be acquired. Kilpatrick does recognize that the outcomes of pupil activity

[28] John L. Childs, *Education and the Philosophy of Experimentalism* (New York: The Century Company, 1931), p. 8.

[29] *Ibid.*, p. 89.

[30] William H. Kilpatrick, "The Teacher's Place in the Social Life of Today," *School and Society*, 46 (1937), 129-34.

[31] William H. Kilpatrick, "Philosophy of Education from the Experimentalist Outlook," *Forty-first Yearbook*, Part I (National Society for the Study of Education, 1942), p. 54. See also pp. 65-66.

should include "a considerable body of common knowledge and common skills," but he insists [32] that specifying the items in advance, especially stating when they should be learned, is not the helpful way to begin. In other words the process of the pupil's education will be more effective if the teacher is concerned primarily with the quality of pupil activity. If this activity is purposeful, vigorous, wholesome, creative, and so on, the desired outcomes will "emerge," provided the activity is wisely guided. Kilpatrick indicated that his position tends to be extreme among Experimentalists and that many wish to "prescribe in some manner or degree what shall be learned." It is probably fair to say that in the typical Experimentalistic theory the teacher is to be guided by a prescription of desired outcomes, the prescription being in relatively general terms and subject to modification in the light of our evolving society. The more conservative Progressives tend to agree with those who would have the teacher formulate relatively specific aims,[33] but these "aims" seem to be a combination of what is *desired* from the point of view of the purposes of the school (conduct objectives) and what is *anticipated* from the envisaged experience unit.

It is apparent that Progressives make the motivating condition a criterion in appraising the educative effectiveness of pupil activity, but, with the possible exception of the more radical ones, they also give consideration to "desired outcomes." It is difficult to ascertain the relative weight of these two criteria, but the typical position seems to be that during the beginning stages of the teaching-learning activity the motivating condition is the prime consideration, i.e. what the pupil is starting to do should be something he *wants* to do. In guiding the developing activity (experience) the teacher may appropriately appraise it as a means of the attainment of the "desired outcomes," but, since these are not to be thought of as "fixed, external ends," this appraisal is largely a matter of identifying increments of educative growth that may be regarded as desirable. However, such an appraisal should be interpreted by the teacher as suggestive relative to her guidance efforts and not as indicative of need for coercive action that might materially lessen the purposefulness of the pupil activity. In other words, an appraisal relative to educative growth in the direction of "desired outcomes" is to be regarded as somewhat secondary to the appraisal from the point of view of the motivating condition. Progressives favor appraisal in terms of resulting outcomes at the conclusion of pupil activity (experience), provided that all phases of educative growth are considered and that the valuing of the several increments is based upon appropriate criteria.

---

[32] *Ibid.*, p. 77.

[33] For example, see Freeman G. Macomber, *op. cit.*, pp. 93-100.

h. Incidental (instrumental) learning. The Progressive position implies faith in incidental (instrumental) learning. Some years ago Bode [34] characterized the project method as "the method of *instrumental* or *incidental* learning." Recent writers seem to avoid an explicit commitment, but the emphasis upon the activity being purposeful without qualification relative to the goal of the purpose, the persistent use of "experiencing" as a designation of pupil activity, and other emphases and phraseologies suggest faith in incidental learning. In addition, it is argued that the outcomes of instrumental learning have a quality that enhances their functioning as controls in future behavior. Since the Progressives decline to commit themselves to stated-in-advance objectives beyond a general outline designation, they are not much concerned about the possibility of incidental (instrumental) learning being a "hit-and-miss" affair, and if it should appear after a career of rich, purposeful experiencing that there are deficiencies in the pupil's education, they can be corrected by systematic instruction.

The conservatives generally recognize that instrumental learning may be effective so far as what is learned, but they tend to emphasize the probable "hit-and-miss" quality and to give priority to systematic instruction, at least beyond the beginning stages of learning in an area. Thus the difference is largely one of relative priority and emphasis.

i. Organization of learning activity. Most authorities emphasize that the "desired outcomes" should have the organizational quality indicated by the designation "unitary" or "integrated." From the point of view of this emphasis, the interrelation of the activities of a pupil is a factor in the educative effectiveness of a segment of learning activity. Integrative organization of controls of conduct is to be regarded as a learning outcome, and, if it is desired that the outcome elements be unified or integrated, then the activity of the pupil must be such that this quality will result. Thus unit assignments or experience units are generally advocated as means contributing to outcomes having the organizational quality implied by the widely-used term "educative growth."

Although there is general agreement that at least a large portion of pupil activity should be in terms of units, typically large units, instead of relatively isolated daily "lessons" (assignments), there are differences of opinion in regard to the nature of the unit and especially the instructional procedures relating to the unit.[35] Those who are committed to experience units make pupil purposing as developed under teacher guidance the basic criterion of the "content" of the unit. Opposed to this position there are those who take the desired outcomes, including organization and in-

---

[34] Boyd H. Bode, *op. cit.*, p. 149.

[35] J. G. Umstattd, *Secondary School Teaching* (Boston: Ginn and Company, 1937), Chap. VII; M. L. Goetting, *Teaching in the Secondary School* (New York: Prentice-Hall, Inc., 1942), Chap. XV.

tegration considerations, as the point of departure in planning unit assignments.[36] However, with respect to the present purpose this difference of opinion and the variations relative to instructional procedure should not obscure the general agreement that pupil learnings should be appropriately matured and integrated, and that the plan of instruction should explicitly provide for this result.

Although emphasized mainly in Progressive writings, it is generally recognized, at least in the sense that there is little or no explicit dissent, that the "whole child" is affected by the instruction he receives. In addition to what he learns within subject-matter fields, there are contributions to his interests, purposes, attitudes, ideals, study habits, and even to his physical health. Thus instructional procedures and techniques should be planned and judged not solely on the basis of the resulting school achievements of the pupils, but their effects upon the pupil's total development should also be recognized. The differences of opinion relative to this principle are largely variations in emphasis. To the Progressives it is a basic thesis.[37] In contrast, conservative authors mention the matter only incidentally or not at all, and the use of objective tests as means of measuring results has been pointed to as evidence of failing to recognize the whole child.

j. Teacher functions. In current teaching-learning theory the teacher is assigned a wide range of responsibilities. With respect to the present purpose the more important instructional functions are: (*a*) managerial (mainly in classroom), (*b*) planning, (*c*) initiating and motivating pupil activity, (*d*) guiding (directing) pupil activity, (*e*) diagnosis and remedial instruction, and (*f*) evaluation (measurement). These teacher functions are generally recognized, but there are some differences in relative emphasis and, more important, certain differences in the concept of what the teacher should do in performing certain ones.

As an explicit topic in recent texts the treatment of classroom management is generally restricted to a single chapter and some authors advocate student self-government procedures. Thus it might be argued that the managerial responsibility of the teacher is regarded as a minor one. On the other hand, it appears to be generally agreed that classroom management is important. The apparent minimization of the teacher's managerial responsibility is due to emphasis on other functions and the criteria by which the management is appraised. The principal difference of opinion relates to the question of the extent to which the management should be "democratic." Some authors would have the teacher conceive of his managerial function primarily in terms of leadership.[38] Others, although rejecting the dictatorial and harsh procedures of the past,

---

[36] Thomas M. Risk, *op. cit.*, pp. 287f.

[37] Freeman G. Macomber, *op. cit.*, p. 313.

[38] For example, see *ibid.*, p. 239.

favor a considerable degree of authoritarian control by the teacher, or at least their advocacy of "democratic" methods is very limited.[39]

Writings of experience-curriculum enthusiasts (project-method advocates) sometimes appear to imply that the teacher's planning responsibility is restricted largely to the period of cooperative planning and that here the principal concern is that the ensuing pupil activity be vigorous. However, typical Progressives stress planning-in-advance as a teacher function.[40] Thus it may be said that planning is generally regarded as an important teacher responsibility, but there is some difference of opinion in regard to the nature of the planning to be done, particularly in regard to specifying the outcomes desired (objectives) and formulating plans for pupil activity.

It is generally agreed that in fulfilling his responsibilities as an instructor the teacher should be guided by appropriate purposes (objectives). Many authors stress conception of purposes in terms of controls of conduct (specific habits or skills, knowledges, and general patterns) to be engendered. Some would have the definition of these controls of conduct carried to a high level of specificity.[41] The more radical Progressives (Experimentalists) maintain that objectives should not be specified in advance except in general terms (see p. 169). At the other extreme there are some conservatives (idealists) who tend to think of objectives in terms of racial subject matter (expressions in terms of words and other symbols of ways of acting that have evolved from our racial experience). If these extreme groups are disregarded, the differences of opinion relative to teacher planning in the area of objectives appear to be of a minor order. Progressives tend to stress recognition of outcomes under the designations "attitudes and appreciations" and "essential abilities" (tool skills and work habits).[42] Although conservatives do not disregard these categories of outcomes, they tend to emphasize specific-habit and knowledge (understanding) outcomes.[43]

It is generally agreed that the teacher should also develop plans for fulfilling his responsibilities as an instructor, particularly plans relative to initiating pupil activity and developing the attendant motivating condition,[44] but again there is a difference of opinion with reference to the type of planning to be done. Authors generally favor planning in terms

[39] Thomas M. Risk, *Principles and Practices of Teaching in Secondary Schools* (New York: American Book Company, 1941), Chap. XXIX.

[40] For example, see Freeman G. Macomber, *op. cit.*, p. 95.

[41] M. L. Goetting, *Teaching in the Secondary School* (New York: Prentice-Hall, Inc., 1942), p. 131.

[42] Freeman G. Macomber, *op. cit.*, pp. 99-101.

[43] Thomas M. Risk, *op. cit.*, pp. 404-5.

[44] For example, see M. L. Goetting, *op. cit.*, pp. 220f.

of large units rather than daily lessons. In their study of contemporary practice Caswell and Campbell recognized two general types — subject-matter units and experience units.[45] These designations suggest two contrasting approaches in planning. In the case of a "subject-matter unit" the focus of the planner's attention is a body of subject matter which in effect constitutes an expression of objectives, and learning exercises are developed which are judged to function as bases for pupil activity which will result in the desired outcomes.[46] In planning an experience unit, the approach is from pupil purposes, needs, and interests, as initial criteria of the learning activity.[47] The difference between these planning approaches, especially in practice, is in part a matter of relative priority of desired outcomes (objectives) and pupil purposes, needs, and interests.

Since the approach in planning an experience unit is from pupil purposes, interests, and needs, they are to be considered the dominant criterion. However, experience-unit advocates, except possibly the extremists, would have the teacher appraise his plan with reference to its compatibility with desired outcomes (recognized objectives) and make such modifications as may be indicated, provided the unit is not "forced" out of its "natural paths of development." [48]

The occasions for teacher functioning beyond the initial stages of the teaching-learning situation cannot be anticipated except in general terms and hence the planning for supplementary motivation, direction (guidance) of learning activity or experiencing, and diagnosis and remedial instruction is not to be extended beyond the levels of a general outline with details tentative. Although most authors appear to believe that the teacher should plan relative to these functions, the plan should be regarded as suggestive and flexible rather than a schedule of teacher activity to be followed.

The teacher's function relative to initiating and motivating pupil activity is an area of teaching-learning theory which is characterized by considerable controversy. The issue is related to the one noted in connection with the optimum conditions for learning. In fact, it might be said to be the same issue viewed from the point of view of instructional procedure. In conservative teaching theory the initiation and motivation of pupil activity is to be accomplished by the skillful assignment of learning exercises wisely planned relative to desired outcomes (objectives) as well as pupil interests, needs, and purposes and by the skillful employ-

[45] Hollis L. Caswell and Doak S. Campbell, *Curriculum Development* (New York: American Book Company, 1935), p. 406.

[46] Thomas M. Risk, *op. cit.*, pp. 388-90, 436; M. L. Goetting, *Teaching in the Secondary School* (New York: Prentice-Hall, Inc., 1942), p. 334.

[47] Freeman G. Macomber, *op. cit.*, p. 93; J. G. Umstattd, *Secondary School Teaching* (Boston: Ginn and Company, 1937), p. 247.

[48] Freeman G. Macomber, *op. cit.*, p. 97.

ment of appropriate motivation procedures. In Progressive teaching theory the initiation and motivation of pupils is to be accomplished by means of "cooperative planning" in which the teacher participates mainly by raising questions, making suggestions, manipulating the class and school environment ("setting the stage"), and the like. The teacher should have a "plan" for pupil activity, but there is to be no assignment except as a last resort.

It is to be noted that conservatives recognize that under a well-ordered program of studies and competent instruction commendable pupil purposes may emerge [49] and they would have the teacher encourage and capitalize such purposing.[50] It should be noted also that Macomber explicitly advocates teacher-planned "learning exercises" as supplementary to the experience-unit type.[51] The significant differences between Macomber's position and that of the typical conservative are: (a) The teacher's plan lists "potentialities" of the unit, i.e. possible learning activities or exercises rather than the learning exercises to be assigned. (b) The assignment is to be accomplished by means of "cooperative planning," i.e. pupils are to participate in deciding upon the activities they will engage in, rather than by means of explicit teacher procedures. These differences, however, are somewhat modified when it is noted that Macomber recognized that "definite and required assignments may be necessary at times" (p. 309) and that Risk (a liberal conservative) recognized that the cooperative assignment "can be used to advantage in many classes" (p. 399). Thus although there are two approaches for initiating and motivating pupil activity, the difference between the conservative position and that of the Progressives is in part a matter of relative emphasis. Both groups typically recognize both approaches. The conservatives, however, think of the "assignment" approach as basic and look upon the "cooperative-planning" approach as an optional procedure to be employed as may appear feasible and desirable. The Progressives make "cooperative planning" the basic approach and think of the "assignment approach" as supplementary when needed.

In Progressive teaching theory motivation, after initiating pupil activity, is to be accomplished by commendation and other noncoercive means. It appears to be assumed that if the activity initiated is purposeful, and this condition is basic in their theory, there will be little need for supplementary motivation. Thus motivation in the usual sense is not recognized as a "chapter" in Progressive theory. Conservative authors typically present a systematic treatment of the topic. Although much of

[49] Henry C. Morrison, *op. cit.*, p. 108.
[50] J. G. Umstattd, *op. cit.*, p. 116.
[51] Freeman G. Macomber, *op. cit.*, pp. 93-99.

what they say applies to initiating pupil activity, they recognize that there is likely to be need for supplementary motivation, even of the coercive type in some cases. However, conservatives tend to agree with the Progressives on what is desirable.

Guiding (directing) pupil activity is generally regarded as an important teacher function. The difference of opinion in regard to procedures is suggested by the verbs "guide" and "direct." The Progressives employ "guide" and emphasize that there should be a minimum of coercion (dictation) by the teacher. The conservatives, who rather typically use "direct," do not advocate coercive measures, but they see considerable need for teacher direction. Thus the difference tends to be a minor one.

Diagnosis and remedial instruction are stressed more by conservatives than by Progressives. The latter do not oppose recognition of these teacher functions, but since they are not committed to stated-in-advance goals (objectives), except in rather general terms, the occasion for systematic diagnosis and remedial instruction is somewhat limited.

The evaluation (measurement) of pupils relative to the outcomes from learning activity is generally regarded as an essential teacher responsibility. Progressives have introduced the term "evaluate" as a means of emphasizing that "measurement" in the conventional sense does not constitute an adequate appraisal of educative growth. They insist that the appraisal should encompass all aspects of educative growth — work habits, interests, attitudes, skills in thinking, and the like — as well as subject-matter achievement. The conservatives do not protest evaluation as something undesirable. In fact, they probably agree that evaluation is desirable, but they tend to be satisfied with what is accomplished by means of conventional examinations and tests.

k. Pattern methods of teaching. In fulfilling his instructional responsibilities in the classroom relative to a teaching-learning unit the teacher follows a course of procedure (method of teaching). Within this method he employs *devices* (specific techniques) as means of initiating, motivating, and guiding (directing) pupil activity, diagnosing pupils relative to their learning and providing remedial instruction, and evaluating outcomes.[52] Examination of educational writings reveals a large number of method names — recitation method, lecture (telling) method, socialized recitation, Dalton plan, unit method, and the like. In several instances, the name obviously refers to a device — e.g. sentence method (in teaching reading), contract method, and case method — and hence designates a method of teaching only in the sense that the method is one

---

[52] Thomas M. Risk, *op. cit.*, pp. 500-501. Although "method" and "device" are on occasion used by other authors with different meanings, it has seemed wise to adopt the definitions given by Risk.

in which the device is employed. Other names refer to a "course of procedure" — e.g. Morrison unit-mastery plan. An attempt [53] to identify the different general methods resulted in the following enumeration: (1) lecture method, (2) recitation method, (3) object teaching, (4) development methods, (5) laboratory method, (6) project method, (7) problem method, (8) socialized recitation, and (9) Morrison unit-mastery plan. It is to be noted, however, that in some cases the line of demarcation was recognized as not being very clear. Hence, this enumeration may not be the answer to the question: What are the different "methods of teaching?"

Several other authors have given some consideration to this question. Morrison differentiating on the basis of the nature of the learning process involved and the resulting outcomes recognized five "types [methods] of teaching": (1) science type, (2) appreciation type, (3) practical-arts type, (4) language-arts type, and (5) pure-practice type.[54] Risk, viewing the teaching-learning activity relative to the degree of teacher control and the correlative pupil initiative, recognized "two general methods of teaching" — (1) "authoritative" and (2) "developmental." [55] As an organization for summarizing research in this area, Stiles employed three categories: (1) teacher-centric patterns (recitation, lecture method); (2) pupil-centric patterns (laboratory method, project method, dramatic method); (3) cooperative group patterns (socialized recitation, group discussion, teacher-pupil planning). [56]

Some writers seem to be thinking in terms of a single pattern method. Billett, regarding all learning activity as being essentially "problem-solving," [57] recognized only a single "general method." [58] This "general method" is in effect only an outline of the "teaching-learning cycle" in terms of its "steps or phases" — "(1) introduction, (2) individual-work or laboratory period, (3) period of class discussion, and (4) testing period." Umstattd described his method of teaching (unit idea) in similar terms.[59] Risk described the "unit-plan operative technique" in terms of three steps: [60] (1) "introducing or initiating the unit," (2) "developing the unit," and (3) "culminating the unit." Macomber recognized four

[53] Walter S. Monroe and Arlyn Marks, "General Methods of Teaching," *Educational Administration and Supervision*, 24 (1938), 497-512.

[54] Henry C. Morrison, *op. cit.*, pp. 91-99.

[55] Thomas M. Risk, *op. cit.*, pp. 11-12.

[56] Lindley J. Stiles, "Methods of Teaching," in *Encyclopedia of Educational Research*, ed. Walter S. Monroe (Rev. ed.; New York: The Macmillan Company, 1950), pp. 745-53.

[57] Roy O. Billett, *op. cit.*, pp. 118, 470-71.

[58] *Ibid.*, pp. 595f.

[59] J. G. Umstattd, *op. cit.*, pp. 197-98.

[60] Thomas M. Risk, *op. cit.*, pp. 433-46.

"phases" of guiding pupil experiencing: (1) "introduction and orientation stage," (2) not specifically named but referred to as "the period of
broad pupil experiencing," (3) "culmination of the unit," and (4)
"evaluation." [61]

The above citations and others that might be made seem to indicate an
emerging tendency to recognize a single "pattern method of teaching"
described in terms suggesting the teacher instructional responsibilities
noted above. In other words there appears to be a tendency to think of a
"method of teaching" in terms of an ordered enumeration of the teacher's instructional responsibilities rather than of "methods of teaching,"
each defined in terms of an organization of teaching "devices." This tendency fits in with the emerging emphasis on understandings of and principles relating to the teaching-learning process.

l. Teaching devices. As defined here, there is a multitude of teaching
devices, and much has been written describing and advocating certain
devices and criticizing others. In addition, there is a considerable accumulation of experimental research directed toward determining the
relative merits of devices having a common function and of comparable
organizations of devices. Since we are dealing with current teaching
theory, our concern here is with the implications of arguments and research findings relative to principles bearing on the selection and use of
devices. Although the evidence is fragmentary and in some cases only
implied, it seems that a case can be made for the emerging recognition
of certain principles.

The educative effectiveness of a given device is relative to the teaching-learning situation. This principle has been explicitly noted in interpreting the findings of research on motivation devices.[62] It is implicit in
the thesis that the instruction should provide for individual differences.

In appraising a device relative to a particular teaching-learning situation collateral (incidental), outcomes should be recognized as well as
those under the categories of specific habits and knowledge. Although
few authors have explicitly directed attention to this principle, it is
suggested in numerous educational writings and probably few if any
persons who have inquired into the matter would oppose it. Psychologists tend to agree [63] that responses to situations are "complex and patterned." Dewey has noted: "collateral learning in the way of formation
of enduring attitudes, of likes and dislikes, may be and often is much

---

[61] Freeman G. Macomber, *op. cit.*, pp. 109-11.

[62] Benjamin Brenner, *Effect of Immediate and Delayed Praise and Blame upon
Learning and Recall* (Contributions to Education, No. 620 [New York: Bureau of
Publications, Teachers College, Columbia University, 1934]), pp. 48-49.

[63] T. R. McConnell, "Reconciliation of Learning Theories," *Forty-first Yearbook,*
Part II (National Society for the Study of Education, 1942), pp. 256f.

more important than the spelling lesson or lesson in geography that is learned." [64] The possibility of collateral or concomitant outcomes (by-products) and their importance as controls of conduct are generally recognized.[65]

There is a dearth of statements bearing on the factors of the teaching-learning situation that contribute to concomitant outcomes. This condition, however, is doubtless due to the lack of knowledge about this aspect of learning [66] and should not be interpreted as evidence of opposition to the above principle. On the positive side, it may be noted that there are some investigations which indicate that in particular situations the teaching devices employed did contribute to certain concomitant outcomes.[67] The "social climate" of the classroom appears to be a contributing factor.[68] The system of final examination and marks, especially when scholastic competition is stimulated, has been pointed to as a factor contributing to outcomes considered undesirable.

These principles relating to teaching "devices" and the tendency to think of "method" as a "course of procedure" outlined in terms of a sequential enumeration of the teacher's instructional responsibilities have implications which are significant relative to teaching-learning theory. The teacher is to develop his method (organization of devices) being guided by his understanding of child nature, the learning process, the responsibilities of a teacher, and the teaching-learning situation he faces and by principles relating to teaching devices. A method of teaching in the sense of an organization of particular devices, such as the Dalton plan or the socialized recitation, is to be regarded as illustrative or suggestive and not as a prescribed "course of procedure."

An Appraisal

A critical reading of the preceding account will doubtless result in a number of questions. One of the more fundamental of such questions may be expressed as follows: Does this account of recent thinking represent an approximation, at least in general outline, to a sound teaching-learning theory or should one expect a continuation of development in-

---

[64] John Dewey, *Experience and Education* (New York: The Macmillan Company, 1938), p. 49.

[65] Thomas M. Risk, *op. cit.*, p. 353.

[66] Ross Stagner, "Attitudes," *Encyclopedia of Educational Research*, ed. Walter S. Monroe (Rev. ed.; New York: The Macmillan Company, 1950), pp. 79, 83.

[67] For example, see Arthur I. Gates and Guy L. Bond, "Some Outcomes of Instruction in the Speyer Experimental School," *Teachers College Record*, 38 (1936), 206-17.

[68] Kurt Lewin, Ronald Lippitt, and R. K. White, "Patterns of Aggressive Behavior in Experimentally Created Social Climates," *Journal of Social Psychology*, 10 (1939), 271-99.

volving changes, more or less revolutionary, in our thinking about learning and teaching?

An appraisal of current status is hazardous. In 1886 Payne appraised what he considered the authoritative views of the time as approaching a "science of pedagogics." There was need for the "addition of omitted principles" and for a systematic formulation, but it is clear that in his opinion there would be no revolutionary changes in teaching-learning theory.[69] White seems to have held a similar opinion.[70] The McMurrys presented Herbartian methodology as *the* scientific method of teaching[71] and thus implied that, in their opinion, a sound theory of teaching had been attained. It is now apparent that these men were in error. In view of this fact what assurance is there that an appraisal at the present time would be dependable.

Although it is impossible to be certain in regard to the future, there is, in the opinion of the present writer, substantial support for the hypothesis that the current theory of teaching is sound in general outline and that future developments will be of the order of refinements and systematization of formulation. A strong line of support is supplied by the development of the psychology of learning. At the time White wrote, faculty psychology, which had been basic in the dominant thinking about teaching, was outmoded, but the psychologists had not yet developed an adequate substitute. Consequently, White wrote in terms of a modified faculty psychology. Since the publication of Thorndike's *Educational Psychology* in 1913, psychology of learning has been a major area of study. For some time the development was characterized by divergent theories, but during recent years the trend has been in the direction of agreement, at least in regard to the general outline of the psychology of learning (see pp. 40f.). In view of the large amount of research underlying the present thinking about learning, it seems unlikely that revolutionary discoveries will be made.

The psychology of learning as now presented by psychologists [72] is generally accepted by educationists writing authoritatively on teaching-learning theory. In fact, it appears that some educationists have been in advance of contemporary psychological thinking about certain aspects of learning. For example, at the time when Kilpatrick began to stress pupil purposing as a dominant factor in learning, psychologists were

---

[69] William H. Payne, *op. cit.*, pp. 3, 130f.

[70] Emerson E. White, *op. cit.*, Preface.

[71] Charles A. McMurry and Frank M. McMurry, *The Method of the Recitation* (New York: The Macmillan Company, 1897), pp. 288-96.

[72] For a summary account see Arthur W. Melton, "Learning," in *Encyclopedia of Educational Research*, ed. Walter S. Monroe (Rev. ed.; New York: The Macmillan Company, 1950), pp. 668-90.

thinking of repetition (Law of exercise) as the dominant factor after the initial connection was formed [73] and the motivating condition was defined in terms of attention.[74] Thus current psychology of learning, especially in some of its more significant aspects, has been basic in teaching-theory thinking for some time.

A third line of support for confidence in current teaching-learning theory is afforded by the relatively noncontroversial status of the field of child development.[75] Although there are still unanswered questions, it appears that there is general agreement in regard to most of the understandings and principles that are most significant relative to teaching-learning theory. For example, with the possible exception of a few extremists there is now agreement that both nature and nurture contribute to the child's development, the relative influence varying with reference to the several lines of growth.

As a final line of evidence, we may note the tendency during recent years to get away from the either-or point of view in our thinking. The emerging tendency to think of the directing-learning-activities and guiding-pupil-experiencing views of teaching as complementary rather than opposing theories of teaching was noted in the introductory pages of the preceding section. In his summary of research relating to learning Melton characterized "insight" and trial-and-error learning as extremes of a continuum.[76]

Thus the present writer is inclined to characterize the current status of teaching-learning theory as that of the "unanimity of the wise" or at least as the beginning of that stage. In practice, however, there is still "disagreement of the inquiring."

NOTE. This chapter was written before the publication of *Learning and Instruction, Forty-ninth Yearbook*, Part I, of the National Society for the Study of Education, 1950, and no citations from this source have been introduced. It should be noted, however, that this volume is in general agreement with the present account. Although certain issues are recognized (e.g. pp. 339-41) it is clear that the authors of the volume believe that we have attained a sound teaching-learning theory, at least in general outline. The contrast of directing learning activities and guiding pupil experiencing is minimized. Like Burton (see p. 152) they view these characterizations of instruction as complementary aspects of a general teaching-learning theory.

[73] William H. Pyle, *The Psychology of Learning* (Baltimore, Maryland: Warwick and York, Inc., 1921), p. 36.

[74] *Ibid.*, p. 53.

[75] For a brief summary of research, see "Child Development," in *Encyclopedia of Educational Research*, ed. Walter S. Monroe (Rev. ed.; New York: The Macmillan Company, 1950), pp. 137-97.

[76] Arthur W. Melton, *op. cit.*, pp. 667-86.

Evolution of Teacher-Education Purposes

The purpose of teacher education is to engender in prospective teachers the qualifications considered necessary for effective service in our schools. During the years since 1890 there have been significant changes in the concept of the needs of this service resulting from the developing understanding of the teaching-learning process, the evolving objectives of our schools, and the expanding function of teachers. The development of teaching-learning theory has been dealt with in Part One and this account should be kept in mind in reading the chapters of Part Two. It is especially important to remember that the teaching-subject-matter theory, which emphasized pattern methods, was dominant during the time when professional training became accepted as desirable for secondary teachers and when normal schools were developing into teachers colleges.

The present study does not include a systematic account of the evolution of the purposes and the curriculum of our schools, but from time to time reference will be made to changes in our schools as a means of explaining changes in the thinking about the purposes of teacher education or as a factor in appraising this thinking. There is also no systematic consideration of the expanding function of teachers, but changes in this area are reflected in the developing program of our schools and to some extent in the evolution of teaching-learning theory.

Writings dealing with purposes of teacher education reflect recognition of four areas of teacher qualifications: (a) personal fitness, (b) liberal (general) education, (c) teaching knowledge, and (d) pedagogical knowledges and skills. The meanings associated with these designations will be apparent in the following sections, but brief comments on the last two may be helpful here.

Around 1890 "teaching knowledge" was employed to designate the knowledge in the fields of school subjects which a teacher "needs simply because he is a teacher." The thinking of this time was about the qualifications of teachers for elementary schools, and teaching knowledge referred to learnings in the areas of the subjects to be taught in addition to what the prospective teacher had learned as a pupil studying them and to his general education resulting from study of the conventional subjects beyond the elementary level. This knowledge was also in addition to the outcomes of his pedagogical training. Although the teaching-knowledge area has not been explicitly recognized in some discussions of purposes, and when mentioned, a different terminology has frequently been employed, the phraseology of 1890 will be used in the present treatment. It should be noted that the designation refers to a qualification area, not to a particular concept of the qualification. Subject-matter courses designed to engender teaching knowledge will be referred to as being professionalized, or as especially designed for teachers.

The designation, "pedagogical knowledges and skills," refers to qualifications resulting from the study of courses, including student teaching, of the kind now commonly labeled "education." Special-method courses are included, even when such a course is given by a subject-matter department. The area is not coextensive with professional education, unless the latter is narrowly conceived.

The record since around 1890 reveals several persistent issues in the area of teacher qualifications. Three of the most significant ones have related to (a) the nature of the teaching-knowledge qualification, (b) the nature and amount of the pedagogical training, and (c) the relation of pedagogical training to the other phases of teacher education. In addition to the shifts in "majority" opinion relative to these items, the development since around 1890 has involved changes in the approach in thinking about teacher qualifications.

The chapters of Part Two deal with the thinking of teacher educators, especially the leaders, about the purposes of teacher education, i.e. the desired teacher qualifications. The sources are mainly committee reports, pronouncements of selected individuals, and certain pertinent studies. Purposes announced by institutions or reflected in teacher-education practice are noted only incidentally. The emphasis is on what teacher-educators *thought* the qualifications should be.

CHAPTER 5

Teacher-Education Purposes
Around 1890

The purposes of the education of teachers for elementary schools and the correlative question of the normal-school course of study had been matters of major concern for several years prior to 1890. An address by S. S. Parr as President of the Department of Normal Schools of the National Educational Association in 1888 may be taken as a "text" for an exposition of the considered opinion of the time in regard to desired teacher qualifications at the elementary-school level.[1]

Parr's Approach to the Definition of Teacher Qualifications

His approach was from the point of view of the thesis: "What the teacher must be is determined by the nature and needs of the training [teaching] process." The nature of the work the teacher is to do was the point of departure in attempting to identify and describe the qualifications of the "roundly-equipped teacher." Parr did not elaborate the phrase, "nature and needs of the training process," apparently because he believed there was general agreement that the function of the teacher was to stimulate and direct pupil activity to the end of developing the several faculties (powers) of the mind.[2] This concept of teacher function

---

[1] S. S. Parr, "The Normal-school Problem," *Addresses and Proceedings* (National Educational Association, 1888), pp. 467-76.

[2] Although Parr did not mention it, there was also general agreement in regard to a coordinate aim of education, i.e. the moral (character) development of the child.

reflects the dominant concept of the purpose of the schools at that time. For an elaboration of this concept, see Chapter 3.

Outline of Teacher Qualifications

Proceeding from this thesis, Parr outlined the qualifications of the "roundly-equipped teacher":

a. Personal fitness.

b. A good academic knowledge of subjects.

c. The teaching-knowledge which is derived from viewing the various subjects in the order fixed for them by their nature and by that of the mind which acquires them.

d. Knowledge of the process of development under the stimulation of the teaching-act and the function of the several faculties, acts, and products, and of the successive phases of mental growth.

e. An understanding of method as the scientific application of the means of stimulation to the ends of development.

f. Acquaintance with the historical development of pedagogical principles.

g. A comprehension of the science of mind as an energy, and of that of mental stimulation.

h. Such an acquaintance with the art of teaching as a reasonable experience will give.[3]

The first three of these items coincide with the first three qualification areas noted above and the remaining five statements furnish an analytical elaboration of Parr's concept of the desired pedagogical qualifications. The formal list was followed by comments which afford further insight into his thinking.

Personal Fitness

"Personal fitness" was not discussed and it may be inferred that this omission was due to a general agreement in regard to the importance and the concept of this qualification area. In fact, there was a tendency to stress its importance even though it was defined only in general terms. "Good moral character" was a commonly used designation for one aspect of personal fitness. Satisfactory evidence of this quality was a legal requirement for a teacher's license in some states (See *Report of U.S. Commissioner of Education, 1893-94*, p. 1063). The teacher's personality was also emphasized. Some trait names (e.g. sympathy, tactfulness, and self-reliance) were mentioned, but for the most part the phraseology was not very definitive.

The Report of the Committee on Elementary Education of the National Council on Education in 1890 concluded with an enumeration of teacher qualifications which reflects the emphasis upon personal fitness: "A clear

---

[3] S. S. Parr, *op. cit.*, pp. 467-68.

knowledge of the subjects to be taught; personal habits that illustrate good character; tact in management and discipline that will secure the willing cooperation of the pupils; ability to awaken attention and to concentrate it upon the particular subject before the class; readiness in discovering the mental conditions of each pupil, and facility in supplying the needed guidance; skill in training the mind in correct habits of learning; and the magnetism of kindness and justice that shall develop noble traits of character."[4]

In school practice personal qualities and effects attributed largely to them were made paramount criteria in judging teaching success. In 1895 the Sub-committee (of the Committee of Fifteen) on the Training of Teachers of the Department of Superintendence,[5] after submitting a list of pertinent questions to "all persons throughout the country whose opinions might be considered of value" reported what may be considered the consensus, especially among city superintendents. The following questions were designated as some of those "one must answer before he pronounces any [elementary-school] teacher a success or failure."

"Do her pupils grow more honest, industrious, polite? Do they admire their teacher? Does she secure obedience and industry only while demanding it, or has she influence that reaches beyond her presence? Do her pupils think well and talk well? As to the teacher herself: Has she sympathy and tact, self-reliance and originality, breadth and intensity? Is she systematic, direct, and business-like? Is she courteous, neat in person and in work? Has she discernment of character and a just standard of requirement and attainment?"[6]

It is significant that, with the possible exception of the reference to pupils' thinking and talking well, this list includes no question relating to pupil achievement in school subjects or to the teacher's competence in these subjects. It is not unlikely that had the committee been pressed on the point it would have added some other questions relative to pupil achievement. There was, however, no reference to this matter in the reported discussion. Thus it appears that in 1895 "personal fitness" was the dominant criterion of teaching success as conceived by school superintendents and probably by most normal-school men.[7]

---

[4] Committee on Elementary Education, National Council of Education, "Essentials in Elementary Education," *Proceedings* (National Council of Education, 1890), p. 68 (*Addresses and Proceedings* [National Educational Association, 1890], p. 352).

[5] This sub-committee consisted of five city superintendents.

[6] "Report of the Sub-committee on the Training of Teachers." *Addresses and Proceedings* (National Educational Association, 1895), p. 248.

[7] This interpretation is supported by the hostile reception accorded J. M. Rice's report of his spelling study at the meeting of the Department of Superintendence in 1897. The discussion indicated that "mental training" and perhaps some "moral training" were considered more important as outcomes, and hence as objectives, than ability to spell. Test scores were not permissible evidence of the effectiveness of teaching spelling.

Liberal (general) Education

Parr did not elaborate the second qualification, "a good academic knowledge of subjects," but he doubtless had in mind what another writer of the time designated as "that [knowledge] which he [a teacher] has learned, not because he is to follow this or that occupation, but because he is a man." [8] This qualification, which may be regarded as the counterpart of what is now commonly referred to as "general education," was generally emphasized in discussions of teacher qualifications. It was generally agreed that the teacher's academic study should transcend the subjects he actually taught. In its 1895 report the Sub-Committee on the Training of Teachers said: "It is a widely prevalent doctrine, to which the customs of our best schools conform, that teachers of elementary schools should have a secondary or high school education, and that teachers of high schools should have a collegiate education." [9] A committee report [10] of 1899 gave the designation "Tappan's Law" to the generalization: "A teacher should be trained in an institution of a higher grade than the one in which he teaches." [11]

The definition of the general-education qualification was quantitative. There was no specification of the subjects to be studied in the "institution of higher grade." Hence, it may be inferred that the ones to be studied were those commonly taught in the secondary schools and colleges of the time. The qualifying term "academic" employed by Parr indicates that no professionalization of the subjects was intended. However, it should be borne in mind that in 1890 the normal-school group recognized "a good academic knowledge of subjects" as an important qualification of the "roundly-equipped teacher." In this area there was no disagreement, at least at the theory level.

Teaching Knowledge

Parr argued at some length in support of "teaching knowledge of subjects" as a phase of the professional education of elementary teachers. His concept of this qualification is indicated in the following statement:

[8] J. P. Gordy, *Rise and Growth of the Normal-school Idea in the United States* (Circular of Information No. 8 [U. S. Bureau of Education, 1891]), p. 129.

[9] "Report of the Sub-committee on the Training of Teachers," *Addresses and Proceedings* (National Educational Association, 1895), p. 238.

[10] "Report of the Committee on Normal Schools," *Addresses and Proceedings* (National Educational Association, 1899), p. 838.

[11] The thesis expressed by this statement is mentioned approvingly in several writings, but this is the only characterization of it as "Tappan's Law" which was found. The source may have been an address, "Public Education," by Henry Tappan, president of the University of Michigan, delivered in 1857. This address does not include a formal statement of the "law," but the thesis is argued as a basis for support of the University.

An analysis of the process of teaching shows that there is a special knowledge in each subject that belongs to instruction. This is quite distinct from academic knowledge. It differs from it in purpose, in its relation to the facts in things, and in the mode by which it is obtained. The ideas of an academic subject are arranged in an order which is determined by their own relations. The order of the same ideas, when they are arranged for teaching, is determined by their relation to the learning mind. The purpose of academic knowledge is acquaintance with series of beings in the order of their necessary dependence. The purpose of teaching-knowledge is acquaintance with the processes of the learning mind in the order of mastery.[12]

There was opposition to this view and this qualification area had been the focus of controversial discussion for years. The history of this discussion has been described in detail by Randolph under the title, *The Professional Treatment of Subject-matter*.[13] The issue involved the scope of the normal-school program. Those who maintained that adequate subject-matter preparation for teaching elementary subjects was to be obtained through the study of "higher branches" made the point that a normal school which included the "higher branches" in its curriculum duplicated facilities already provided by secondary schools and colleges and insisted that such duplication was undesirable.

Many normal-school men supported this position, notably President Thomas G. Gray of the institution at St. Cloud, Minnesota, who argued that the work of the normal school should be restricted to professional (pedagogical) courses. In the *Report of the United States Commissioner of Education* for 1885-86 it was stated that normal schools "fall naturally into two classes: one including the schools that combine academic and professional training, and the other those that confine themselves to professional work" (p. 310). The Committee on Normal Education of the National Council of Education in 1889 asserted: "The normal schools ought to, and perhaps the normal schools of the future will, leave to the common schools [elementary and secondary] all academic work." [14]

Following the report of the Committee on Normal Education in 1889, the *Proceedings* of the National Council of Education include a communication from William T. Harris, United States Commissioner of Education, in which he commented on a difference between academic instruction in the normal school and in "the high school or the grammar school." "In the latter the pupil learns each branch as a step to the mastery of the next higher branch, while in the normal school he learns each branch of study as reflecting all other branches." In the light of the reported dis-

[12] S. S. Parr, *op. cit.*, p. 469.

[13] Edgar D. Randolph, *The Professional Treatment of Subject-matter* (Baltimore: Warwick & York, Inc., 1924). 204 pp.

[14] "Report of the Committee on Normal Education," *Addresses and Proceedings* (National Educational Association, 1889), p. 395.

cussion (pp. 400-403), it appears that the majority of the participants supported the committee in its contention that normal schools should be concerned only with the pedagogical qualification area. On the other hand, in 1890 Gordy, who argued that the "teacher's professional preparation" should include "the acquisition of that knowledge of the subject he is to teach which he needs simply because he is a teacher," stated: ". . . unless I am very much mistaken, the tide of opinion among normal-school men is setting very steadily in the direction of the position I am advocating." [15]

Within this controversy it appears that the concept of teaching knowledge was inadequately defined,[16] and means (courses and methods) for engendering this teacher qualification had not been developed to the level of a systematic procedure generally approved by the advocates of teaching knowledge. It also appears that in only a few normal schools were there concerted, continued attempts to engender teaching knowledge beyond review courses and special methods. The degree of success attained doubtless depended upon institutional leadership and the ingenuity and resourcefulness of individual instructors. The Indiana State Normal School (Terre Haute), under the leadership of President William Parsons, is mentioned by Randolph [17] as an institution where the teaching-knowledge thesis was emphasized over a period of years.

The teaching-knowledge issue involved not only the scope of professional training, but also the relation of pedagogical study to academic study. If "all academic work" were left to the common schools, then the pedagogical training was something *added* to the previous academic study. On the other hand, instruction for engendering teaching knowledge was an opportunity for *combining* (integrating) pedagogical training *with* the study of subject matter. This aspect of the issue was given little explicit attention in the discussions around 1890, but the proponents of the teaching-knowledge qualification were, in effect, also arguing for an integration of pedagogical training and subject-matter study.

Pedagogical Knowledges and Skills

A variety of analyses has been employed in expositions of the pedagogical qualification area, but no standard categories have emerged. For the present purpose the following will be employed: (a) educational ideas, (b) psychological knowledge, (c) principles (theory) of methodology, (d) procedures and devices, and (e) teaching skills. It may be noted that the first three of these rubrics refer to what is frequently

---

[15] J. P. Gordy, *op. cit.*, p. 130.

[16] Edgar D. Randolph, *op. cit.*, pp. 65f.

[17] *Ibid.*, pp. 78-79.

called the "theoretical" aspects of pedagogical training and the last two to the "practical" phases.

In his discussion of "educational ideas" Parr did not elaborate his concept beyond the implication of history of education being the means of engendering them. However, the explicit recognition of the category indicates an extension of the thinking about the purposes of the theoretical phase of teacher education beyond psychology and principles of methodology.

The category of "psychological knowledge" was stressed in the thinking of 1890. Parr gave it prominence by referring to it in two items of his enumeration (d and g; see p. 184), and psychology or educational psychology was generally included in any listing of pedagogical subjects. There was, however, a lack of specification of what psychological knowledge should be engendered. The caption, "educational psychology, not general psychology," employed by Parr indicates that contemporary practice in normal schools was not compatible with his concept of this aspect of the "roundly-equipped teacher." His descriptive statements emphasize child development and the learning process as topics, but he dealt with them only in general terms.

Although Parr listed "an understanding of method as the scientific application of the means of stimulation to the ends of development," he noted later that the "science of general method . . . is yet to be created," and it appears that this category received little attention in the thinking of the time about the pedagogical purposes of teacher education. However, Parr's explicit recognition of it indicates an emerging differentiation between principles (general method) and procedures (specific rules) and devices.

"Procedures and techniques" designate a generally recognized category, but Parr emphasized that "special method," the means of engendering the desired qualification, should be thought of as "the culmination of the science of education." This category of technical-professional qualifications should not be thought of as referring to an assemblage of empirical devices but rather to applications deduced from educational psychology, "principles of general method," and history and philosophy of education.

Parr emphasized "teaching skills" which were to be engendered by means of practice teaching differentiated with respect to individual needs to give "freedom of action in class-teaching." His reference to the "limitations of our present environment" and other comments makes it clear that he attached more importance to this category than was reflected in contemporary practice. His total discussion of pedagogical qualifications indicates a well-balanced recognition of the theoretical and practical aspects.

The Thinking of Other Normal-School Leaders

No discussion of Parr's address was reported but other writings of the time suggest that, although probably few, if any, normal-school leaders would have criticized seriously his general outline of teacher-education purposes, the thinking of the time was highly opinionated, particularly relative to details of desired pedagogical qualifications. In the "Report of the Chicago Committee" on "methods of instruction and courses of study in normal schools," the chairman in summarizing the responses to the questions: "Would a conference of normal-school teachers and professors of pedagogy to formulate such a course of study be of service to the cause of education? Is such a thing feasible?" remarked [18] that the replies were not always "complimentary to those in the vocation." Some respondents asserted that "we are too opinionated to confer together over a course of study for normal schools." Later the chairman noted that his study had resulted in the belief that there had been "a decided advance in the conception of what the sphere of pedagogical training really is" (p. 584).

This interpretation of the situation, however, should be viewed in the light of conditions existing during the preceding years. Krusé [19] characterized the period from 1868 to 1890 as one of "criticism and discontent." Normal-school leaders exhibited faith in pedagogical training, but both opinion and practice reflected disagreement and uncertainty about the details of the purposes of this phase of teacher education. Many writers did not go beyond an enumeration of the pedagogical subjects considered desirable — history of education, educational psychology, "methods," observation and practice, and the like. Such designations of the pedagogical qualifications are indicative of the confusion in regard to this aspect of the purpose of teacher education. On the other hand, Parr's address and other writings of the time reflect penetrating thinking by several individuals.

Curricular requirements in normal schools indicate the quantitative definition of professional (pedagogical) training to have been about one-fourth of the schooling period.[20] Since the normal schools of 1890 tended to be institutions of secondary grade, this means that the quantitative

[18] "Report of the 'Chicago Committee' on Methods of Instruction and Courses of Study in Normal Schools," *Addresses and Proceedings* (National Educational Association, 1889), p. 582.

[19] Samuel A. Krusé, *A Critical Analysis of Principles of Teaching as a Basic Course in Teacher-training Curricula* (Contributions to Education, No. 63 [Nashville, Tennessee: George Peabody College for Teachers, 1929]), p. 53.

[20] A. L. Thomasson, *A Half Century of Teacher Training in State Normal Schools and Teachers Colleges of the United States, 1890-1940* (Unpublished Ph.D. dissertation, University of Illinois, 1942), pp. 62, 65.

emphasis upon professional training at the secondary level tended to be slightly greater than that reflected in present practice at the college level. This attention to pedagogical study plus the time devoted to "review courses" materially reduced the amount of "academic study." Thus, although normal-school administrators in discussions generally stressed general education and teaching knowledge, normal-school practice reflected an emphasis upon pedagogical training that tended to minimize these qualification areas.

Other Views of Teacher Qualifications

Outside of the normal-school group the thinking about desired teacher qualifications was focused upon personal fitness and "academic knowledge of subjects." The evaluation of pedagogical qualifications varied. Among school administrators there were many who, although they considered pedagogical training desirable, assigned it a position subordinate to scholarship (academic competence in subjects taught).[21] Others considered pedagogical training less important or even undesirable, since the time devoted to it lessened the amount of academic training. In college circles there was little support of pedagogical training for high-school teachers. President Eliot of Harvard referred to his faculty, "in common with most teachers in England and the United States," as feeling "but slight interest or confidence in what is ordinarily called pedagogy." [22] He did not explain his use of the term "pedagogy," but one may infer that he had in mind the sort of pedagogical courses that were taught in normal schools.

Three General Points of View

Three concepts of the professional education of teachers are reflected in this sketch of the thinking around 1890. In normal-school circles, where the concern was mainly about elementary teachers, a large group, possibly a majority, thought of professional education for teachers as encompassing the engendering of "teaching knowledge" as well as "pedagogical knowledge and skills." This group accepted a "good academic knowledge of subjects" as a desirable, probably essential, phase of the total education of teachers and considered it an appropriate function of normal schools to provide facilities for academic schooling. Although the point was seldom explicitly mentioned, this group tended to think of the professional education as being *combined with* academic training.

A second group took the position that the professional education should

---

[21] See *Report of the U.S. Commissioner of Education*, 1889-90, chapter on "Educational discussions."

[22] *Report of the U.S. Commissioner of Education*, 1890-91, p. 1076.

be limited to engendering "pedagogical knowledge and skills." Some members of this group maintained that the function of normal schools should be limited to providing this professional education, leaving to the "common schools [elementary and secondary] all academic work." Thus professional education was to be *added to* academic training.

A third group, which included a large proportion of school administrators as well as members of college and university faculties, considered teacher education as essentially equivalent to a good academic (liberal) education. Some pedagogical knowledge and skills might be added, provided the time for academic study was not lessened, but pedagogical knowledge and skills were not regarded as essential; some members of this group considered them superfluous if not detrimental.

With this summary account of the thinking around 1890 about desired teacher qualifications as a background we turn to the developments during the following years. The treatment is organized in terms of three chronological periods: (*a*) from 1890 to 1907, the date of the report of the Committee of Seventeen which recommended a program of professional training for secondary teachers; (*b*) from 1907 to 1933, the publication date of the report of the National Survey of the Education of Teachers; and (*c*) the period since 1933. Although the dates, 1907 and 1933, should not be regarded as epochal, they do serve to mark out distinguishable periods in the evolution of the definition of the purposes of teacher education.

CHAPTER 6

Modifications of Desired
Qualifications, 1890 to 1907

The major developments of this period were (*a*) the subsidence of argument for the teaching-knowledge qualification, as expressed by Parr and others around 1890, and the correlative acceptance of a "good academic knowledge of subjects" (scholarship) as adequate for teaching purposes, (*b*) the extension of the thesis of pedagogical training being a desirable phase of teacher education to the preparation of teachers for secondary schools, and (*c*) a trend in the direction of a standard program of pedagogical (education) courses which reflects a tendency toward agreement about the desired pedagogical qualifications. Although an explicit statement was seldom made, the theoretical thinking tended to be in terms of the thesis enunciated by Parr in 1888: "What the teacher must be is determined by the nature and needs of the training process." Teacher-education practice of the later years of the period reflects much compromise thinking, apparently motivated largely by the desire of normal-school people and other educationists to be accepted as academically respectable.

General Setting of Period

By 1890 there were 204 state, city, and private normal schools and teachers' courses were offered in 114 colleges and universities. In only a few of these higher institutions were the teachers' courses of college

193

grade, and professional training for secondary teachers was at the level of "small beginnings" (see Chapter 12). During the years following 1890 a major problem of the state normal school was to obtain increased support. Around the turn of the century the normal schools became concerned about their articulation with colleges and universities and with obtaining recognition as institutions for the preparation of secondary teachers (see Chapter 10). The pressure of these and other practical problems tended to distract attention from the definition of teacher qualifications.

By 1890 the public high school had become the most frequent type of secondary school and by 1910 the number of public high schools had increased by approximately 300 per cent. This development increased the demand for secondary teachers. During this period the colleges and universities shaped the development of the secondary curriculum through the reports of the Committee of Ten (1894) and the Committee on College Entrance Requirements (1899) and through the development of accreditation. The academic subjects of the secondary curriculum became largely elementary phases of the corresponding college subjects.

Finally, it should be noted that Herbartian methodology was introduced during the nineties and following the turn of the century, the teaching-subject-matter theory became dominant. Knowledge of subject matter was to be engendered by means of pattern methods.

A 1905 Outline of Teacher Qualifications

In an address as president of the Department of Normal Schools of the National Education Association in 1905, Charles C. Van Liew enumerated the "elements which should enter into the make-up of a teacher":

(1) That general knowledge and culture which constitute the common stock in trade of the average citizen; but such knowledge and culture must be liberally, not meagerly, acquired. (2) Native teaching personality. (3) Professional culture, i.e., the ideas which belong peculiarly to the teachers profession. (4) Skill in teaching, as demonstrated by actual practice, including skill in the ability to select, grasp, group, and arrange the materials of instruction with respect to the goals to be reached.[1]

The Concept of the Teaching-Knowledge Qualification

The conspicuous difference between this statement and the corresponding one by Parr in 1888 (see p. 184) is the absence of any explicit reference to "teaching knowledge," and it may be inferred that Van Liew thought of the "general knowledge and culture which constitute

---

[1] Charles C. Van Liew, "A Statement of the Issues Before the Department," *Addresses and Proceedings* (National Educational Association, 1905), p. 520.

the common stock in trade of the average citizen" as including adequate knowledge for teaching purposes, provided that such knowledge and culture "be liberally, not meagerly, acquired." However, the significance of this qualification of his general statement is not commented on and apparently Van Liew considered graduation from a "high-grade secondary school" as sufficient evidence of the attainment of this qualification in the case of elementary teachers. Since Van Liew introduced his enumeration by the assertion that it was "practically agreed" upon, there is the implication that by 1905 the teaching-knowledge qualification had "practically" disappeared as an explicit item in the general outline of teacher-education purposes and when included it was considered to be satisfied by appropriate academic study. In practice, the "review courses," generally offered in the normal schools of the time, may be regarded as rudimentary attempts in the direction of "professionalized study," but normal-school people tended to apologize for their presence on the grounds of necessity and as these institutions attempted to attain academic respectability and to offer approved preparation for secondary teachers, they developed academic departments along more or less conventional lines.

In view of the emphasis around 1890 on the teaching-knowledge aspect of professional training and the opposition to the duplication of educational facilities one would expect that when academic departments were developed in normal schools, the work would have been weighted in the direction of engendering teaching knowledge. Such was not the case. In fact, there appears to have been a lessening of relative emphasis upon pedagogical training within the normal-school function.

A statement by Learned and Bagley referring to the development in Missouri following 1900 presents an interpretation of the attitude of the normal schools of that state:

In effect the school has unconsciously said to the student: "This academic foundation is your education . . . as a teacher-preparing agency we are obliged to hang in your belt certain tools that will get you a license and may be useful if you teach, but they are not big enough to be in the way if you do not, and an educated person ought to have them anyhow." [2]

Learned and Bagley implied that this description was applicable to normal schools in general. This implied generalization is supported by the broader study of Randolph.[3]

Some normal-school people seem not to have been in sympathy with

---

[2] William S. Learned, William C. Bagley, and Others, *The Professional Preparation of Teachers for American Public Schools* (New York: The Carnegie Foundation for the Advancement of Teaching, Bulletin No. 14, 1920), p. 77.

[3] Edgar D. Randolph, *The Professional Treatment of Subject-matter* (Baltimore: Warwick & York, Inc., 1924), p. 34.

the trend of the times. In 1907 one normal-school president, referring to
"where there is a strong accentuation of the academic idea and a rich
development of it at the expense of the professional idea," suggested
that the institution "ought not to call itself a normal school, but an academy or college with a pedagogical annex." [4] However, the development
of conventional academic work and the isolation of professional study in
normal schools tended to be the fashion from about the turn of the
century.[5]

As "departments of education" were established in colleges and universities the same general concept of professional training for teachers
prevailed, i.e pedagogical training supplementary to academic study. The
graduate of a college or university was "professionally" trained for teaching if he had included in or added to his liberal-arts course a minimum
number of hours of education (pedagogy). The nature and distribution
of his academic study were governed by the requirements of the institution. Due to the popularity of the elective system,[6] these requirements
were very limited, but the thinking of persons concerned with teacher
education in colleges and universities emphasized "a detailed and specialized study of the subjects to be taught" as a teacher qualification.[7]

Thus in spite of the apparent trend around 1890 and occasional vigorous arguments for explicit recognition of teaching knowledge during the
following years,[8] this teacher qualification came to be thought of as
being satisfied by an adequate general education [9] plus specialized academic study in the case of teachers for secondary schools. A dominant
influence in this trend was the desire of normal-school leaders and of
educationists in colleges and universities to have their work recognized

[4] John W. Cook, "Capacity and Limitations of the Normal School in the Professional
Preparation of High-school Teachers," *Addresses and Proceedings* (National Education
Association, 1907), p. 633.

[5] Randolph gives 1903 as the date marking the transition. See *op. cit.*, pp. 28, 33,
90; also *Addresses and Proceedings* (National Educational Association, 1903), pp.
539-93.

[6] R. Freeman Butts, *The College Charts Its Course* (New York: McGraw-Hill Book
Company, Inc., 1939). 464 pp.

[7] See "Joint Recommendations of the Committee of Seventeen on the Professional
Preparation of High-school Teachers," *Addresses and Proceedings* (National Education Association, 1907), p. 536.

[8] For example, James M. Green, "The Academic Function of the Normal School,"
Addresses and Proceedings (National Educational Association, 1894), pp. 853-57.

[9] This position was explicitly expressed by the Sub-Committee (of the Committee of
Fifteen) on the Training of Teachers of the Department of Superintendence in 1895.
The question of professionalized study of the subjects to be taught was dismissed with
the assertion that the requirement of "sufficient preparation for admission" to normal
schools would settle the matter. However, "some review of the branches which are
to be taught" was to be included under "methodology." See "Report of the Sub-
Committee on the Training of Teachers," *Addresses and Proceedings* (National Educational Association, 1895), p. 240.

as academically respectable. A secondary influence was the failure to develop professionalized subject-matter courses which met with general approval, even among educationists.

The elimination, or at least the minimization, of the teaching-knowledge qualification restricted the professional education of teachers to pedagogical training which was to be *added to* subject-matter study. In retrospect this development appears to represent compromise thinking and to have been a definite loss for the professional education of teachers. However, the teacher educators of the time should not be criticized too severely; there were extenuating circumstances which will be noted in Part Three.

Pedagogical Qualifications

The development of the thinking in the area of pedagogical qualifications is not easy to describe. As indicated above (see p. 190) the thinking of 1890 in regard to pedagogical purposes was confused and reflected disagreement and uncertainty, especially in the interpretations represented by the programs of courses offered in normal schools. This confusion, disagreement, and uncertainty continued in spite of a persistent request for an authoritative specification of the pedagogical program. The situation during the nineties is indicated by the record of a committee created in 1895 by the Department of Normal Schools of the National Education Association to report "upon such educational matters as directly concern the department." The following year this committee recommended that a committee be appointed to undertake a program of inquiry. The preliminary report [10] (1897) included a section on "variations that exist in normal schools of the United States because of geographical location" in which it was asserted: "There is no typical course of study for teachers to get a certain preparation for the business. There are no single ideas that are common to all schools that are called by the name 'normal'" (p. 713). The committee was instructed to continue "investigation on the lines proposed and also to submit a course of study with minimum professional instruction for state normal schools of the United States" (p. 709). The "preliminary report of the committee on the formulation of a course of study" presented the following year was devoted to summary descriptions of practices in different sections of the country.

The 1899 report [11] began with a section on the "function of the normal school." The committee's general concept of purpose was ". . . the

---

[10] "Report of the Normal School Committee," *Addresses and Proceedings* (National Educational Association, 1897), pp. 710-21.

[11] "Report of the Committee on Normal Schools," *Addresses and Proceedings* (National Educational Association, 1899), pp. 836-903.

teaching of subjects that they in turn may be taught . . . the development of character that it in turn may be transfigured into character . . . a preparation for life that it in turn may prepare others to enter fully, readily, and righteously into their environment" (p. 838). In the following elaboration the committee stressed giving "an interpretation of the child and child life" as a function of the normal school. The recommended "provisional minimum course" included under the head of "professional work" one year each of "psychology," "pedagogy," "observation," and "practice teaching." The purposes to be served by the year of "pedagogy" were not indicated beyond the implication that this professional work was to consist of philosophy of education, science and art of teaching, history of education, and social economics.

The fact that the committee did not develop its thinking about the purposes of teacher education beyond this general, and hence somewhat platitudinous, level was probably due, at least in part, to differences of opinion. However, it is significant that the committee, which at first gave no explicit attention to defining the purposes of teacher education, included this section in its final report. The functional point of view is clearly reflected. The purpose of the normal school was to prepare teachers for service in the schools which were then considered to be in a state of change. With reference to "professional work" it is apparent that the committee viewed engendering "an interpretation of the child and child life" and teaching skill through observation and practice teaching as the dominant functions of the normal school. In the outline of "centers of interest" the committee included "man in society." This recognition and the paragraph on "the function of the normal school in its relation to the social mind or society" reveal that the committee's concept of teacher education included learnings in the area designated by the phrase "man in society." The failure of the committee to formulate purposes in more definitive terms was probably intentional, because the status of pedagogics was referred to as "*nascent*."

When this committee report is compared with statements by individuals, such as that by Parr in 1888, it appears that whereas an individual was able to formulate a systematic and somewhat definite statement of pedagogical purposes and outline a program of courses, a committee, even after persistent study, was not able to agree upon a formulation beyond one couched in general terms. It appears that normal-school practice was moving somewhat in the direction of a "standard" program of pedagogical course offerings. Krusé [12] stated:

By 1910 the standard professional course [program or curriculum] in normal

---

[12] Samuel A. Krusé, *A Critical Analysis of Principles of Teaching as a Basic Course in Teacher-training Curricula* (Contributions to Education, No. 63 [Nashville, Tennessee: George Peabody College for Teachers, 1929]), p. 62.

schools and teachers colleges consisted of the following courses: (1) educational psychology; (2) history of education; (3) classroom management; (4) principles of teaching; (5) practice teaching; and (6) a group of special methods.

Although Krusé did not define the term "standard professional course," it is probable that "standard" was intended to mean "average." At least writers of around 1910 and later investigators revealed marked variations in the pedagogical course offerings in normal schools. However, Krusé's statement and other evidence indicate a trend toward agreement in the thinking about the purposes of the pedagogical phase of teacher education, especially during the first decade of the twentieth century. Although there were differences of opinion in regard to details and variations in emphasis, the general situation may be described.

"Psychological knowledge" was stressed and due to the child-study movement and the development of adolescent psychology, there was an increased content under the designation, educational psychology. "Principles (theory) of teaching" (general method) had become established as an outcome of the Herbartian movement and related developments. The category of "educational ideas" may also be regarded as established. In colleges and universities history of education was frequently supplemented by comparative education or principles (philosophy) of education. The status of "procedures and techniques" was about the same as in 1890, but "teaching skills" was commanding greater recognition.

The first three of these categories were frequently contrasted with the last two under the designations, "theoretical" and "practical." In practice, theoretical aspects of teacher education were emphasized. But the effectiveness of theoretical training was being questioned. In 1902 Homer H. Seerley, president of Iowa State Normal School, said: "The normal schools have made and still make too much of theory, dogma, and philosophy and too little of the real, the practical, and the essential." [13] In *Conflicting Principles in Teaching*, Charles A. McMurry [14] devoted a chapter to "The gulf between theory and practice." The treatment is somewhat historical and many of his statements may be taken as descriptive of the period being considered here. "The actual teachers are much in need of rational theory to guide their practice" (p. 243), but later, "Our teachers have had an overdose of theory not well related to practice" (p. 247).

The *Third Yearbook*, Part I, of the National Society for the Scientific Study of Education (1904) was devoted to "the relation of theory to

[13] H. H. Seerley, "Defects in the Normal Schools that are Responsible for the Opposition and Criticism Urged Against Them in Many Parts of the United States," *Addresses and Proceedings* (National Educational Association, 1902), p. 542.

[14] Charles A. McMurry, *Conflicting Principles in Teaching* (Boston: Houghton Mifflin Company, 1914). 290 pp.

practice in the education of teachers." The trend of the discussion in this volume as well as in McMurry's chapter is not that theory purposes should be minimized but rather that more effective means (courses) should be developed. It should be noted also that these writings and others of the period include arguments for a greater degree of attention to "practical" purposes.

Development of Professional Qualifications for Secondary Teachers

Accompanying the agitation for a standard program of pedagogical courses, there was an increased acceptance of pedagogical training as a desirable phase of teacher education. This development is most apparent in connection with the thinking about the qualifications of teachers for secondary schools and their education. Until about 1900 very little attention was given to "the necessary qualifications of teachers for secondary schools." [15] The Committee of Ten on Secondary School Studies [16] was concerned primarily with the curriculum, but it was sufficiently realistic to give some attention to the training of teachers required to implement certain of the recommendations (pp. 17-18). One of the eleven questions considered by the conferences in the several subject-matter fields is as follows: "Can any description be given of the best method of teaching this subject throughout the school course?" The statements in the several conference reports pertaining to this question and to the more general matter of teacher qualifications relate for the most part to details of the teacher's academic preparation or to special methods. It appears that, in general, the several conference groups believed that the most important need in the training of teachers was more adequate academic preparation. Professional (pedagogical) training is implied in certain places, but it appears that the conference groups did not believe that it need extend beyond special methods. There is no explicit reference to pedagogical courses such as history of education, philosophy of education, or general methods. The following statement under geography appears to be typical of the general point of view. "The Conference hold it to be of first importance that every teacher should become so familiar with the subject as to be able freely to depart from any proposed method according as the special conditions of the school shall indicate" (p. 217). This statement clearly places methods of teaching subordinate to adequate academic training.

The Sub-Committee (of the Committee of Fifteen) on the Training

---

[15] James E. Russell, "The Training of Teachers for Secondary Schools," *Addresses and Proceedings* (National Educational Association, 1899), p. 285.

[16] *Report of the Committee of Ten on Secondary School Studies* (New York: American Book Company, 1894). 249 pp.

of Teachers [17] (1895) gave limited attention to the training of secondary teachers (pp. 249f.). Specific mention is made of the scholarship qualification which "is by common consent fixed at a collegiate education" (p. 250). The program of technical-professional training suggested is similar to that for elementary teachers except for the addition of "philosophy of education," and the expansion of "school economy" to include the study of the school systems of England, France, and Germany as well as the "leading" ones of the United States. However, the tone of the treatment indicates the committee's realization that recognition of technical-professional training for secondary teachers was limited.

From these and other writings up to the turn of the century it appears that the thinking about teacher qualifications at the secondary level was as follows. There was general recognition of the need for more adequately trained teachers, but it seems to have been assumed that graduation from college, which was generally regarded as an essential qualification, insured adequate general education and competent special knowledge of the subjects to be taught. The desirability of technical-professional training was being advocated from above, i.e. by educationists in colleges and universities and in the more ambitious normal schools, and secondary school principals and city superintendents were beginning to accept the general proposition.[18] "Skill in teaching" was regarded as an important qualification, but as Russell observed a teacher's ability to teach was rather generally interpreted in terms of his "ability to maintain order in the class-room, to get work out of his pupils, to satisfy casual supervisors and examiners, to keep fine records, and to mystify parents." [19]

In discussing the training of secondary teachers Russell [20] argued for qualifications under four heads: (a) general knowledge, (b) professional knowledge, (c) special knowledge, and (d) skill in teaching. With reference to the first of these categories he expressed approval of "general education" as represented by four years of college study. Professional study should result in the teacher being

able to view his own subject and the entire course of instruction in its relations to the child, and to society of which the child is a part. . . . The true educator must know the nature of mind; he must understand the process of learning, the formation of ideals, the development of will, and the growth of character. The secondary teacher needs particularly to know the psychology of the adolescent period. . . . But more than man as an individual the teacher needs

---

[17] "Report of Sub-Committee on the Training of Teachers," *Addresses and Proceedings* (National Educational Association, 1895), pp. 238-59.

[18] G. W. A. Luckey, *The Professional Training of Secondary Teachers in the United States* (New York: The Macmillan Company, 1903), p. 175.

[19] James E. Russell, *op. cit.*, p. 290.

[20] *Ibid.*, pp. 285-96.

to know the nature of man as a social being. No knowledge, I believe, is of more worth to the secondary teacher than the knowledge of what standards of culture have prevailed in the past or now exist among various peoples, their ideas of life and their methods of training the young to assume the duties of life. . . . I should also include such information as can be gained from a study of school economy, school hygiene, and the organization, supervision, and management of schools and school systems at home and abroad.

Although Russell emphasized "special knowledge," his brief exposition suggests that his thinking was in terms of adequate subject-matter specialization in the field of teaching. At least he did not argue for teaching knowledge in contrast with academic knowledge. "Skill in teaching" was not very clearly defined, but the attainment of this qualification was to be by means of observing "good teaching," studying "its methods under guidance," and giving "instruction under normal conditions long enough to demonstrate" ability to teach.

During the first decade of the twentieth century there was a growing interest in the training of secondary teachers and the related question of their qualifications. The first "standards" adopted by the North Central Association of Colleges and Secondary Schools in 1902 expressed the belief "that the efficiency of the average college or university graduate is materially enhanced by professional study, observation, and training in practice teaching under so-called supervision" and advised that accredited secondary schools "be urged to give due preference to teachers possessing such preparations." [21] Although this "standard" was not retained and a mandatory requirement of professional training was not adopted [22] until 1914, it is significant that the first "standards" of this association included a declaration in favor of professional training for secondary teachers.

The *Fourth Yearbook*, Part I, of the National Society for the Scientific Study of Education (1905), bore the title, "The education and training of teachers," one chapter of which was a symposium on "What constitutes the ideal secondary teacher." This symposium was contributed to by five persons [23] with extended acquaintance with high schools, especially in the North Central area. The emphasis was upon personality with specific mention of "sympathy" for adolescents, "imagination," "sense of humor," and "moral character." Scholarship was included by all except Halleck who stated that he was leaving this "requirement" to others,

[21] John E. Grinnell, "The Rise of the North Central Association," *North Central Association Quarterly*, 10 (January, 1936), 368.

[22] *Ibid.*, p. 497. April, 1936.

[23] Reuben Post Halleck, Principal, Boys' High School, Louisville, Ky., J. Stanley Brown, Superintendent, Township High School, Joliet, Ill., Stratton D. Brooks, Supervisor of Schools, Boston, Mass., A. F. Nightingale, County Superintendent of Cook County, Chicago, Ill., J. F. Brown, Inspector of High Schools, State University of Iowa, Iowa City, Iowa.

because it had been his custom to base recommendations largely upon personality. The scholarship envisaged by the other four writers was more than "knowing one's subject." There is definite suggestion of what is today commonly designated as "general education." The ideal teacher was interested in his field, he exemplified the "spirit of research," and he knew his subject in terms of the level of his students. Pedagogical preparation was also included by all except Halleck, but within this area the psychology of the adolescent was the dominant phase. Brooks definitely disparaged the usual study of methods of teaching but indicated a higher estimate of philosophy of education and of history of education. J. F. Brown was the only one that mentioned observation and practice teaching. J. S. Brown mentioned participation in the life of the community and this characteristic was suggested by some of the others.

In somewhat more general terms the composite picture of the "ideal secondary teacher" was a person with a good personality, a broad general education, a mastery of the subject he teaches, an interest in and an understanding of adolescents, and an acquaintance with philosophy of education and history of education. In addition, he should be interested in teaching at the secondary level and in serving his community.

The Recommendations of the Committee of Seventeen

In 1905 the Department of Secondary Education of the National Education Association authorized the appointment of a committee "to consider the subject of securing proper professional preparation for high-school teachers." The report of this Committee of Seventeen, "The professional preparation of high-school teachers," was made in 1907, a "banner year" in the discussion of teacher education.[24] With reference to "academic preparation" the report [25] specified "a detailed and specialized study of the subjects to be taught"; "one or more subjects from a group including history, economics, and sociology, which will give the teacher a proper outlook upon the social aspects of education"; and "a course in general psychology and at least one from a group of subjects including history of philosophy, logics, and ethics, which will give the teacher a proper outlook upon education as the development of the individual."

---

[24] The program of the Department of Superintendence included two papers: "Minimum qualifications of the elementary teacher" by Ashley van Storm and "Minimum qualifications for the training and certification of secondary school teachers" by Henry Suzzallo. At a joint session of the departments of higher education, secondary education, and normal schools three papers were presented on the preparation of high-school teachers.

[25] "Joint Recommendations of the Committee of Seventeen on the Professional Preparation of High-school Teachers," *Addresses and Proceedings* (National Education Association, 1907), pp. 536-38.

The "joint recommendations" bearing on technical-professional training were as follows:

    II. That definite study be given to each of the following subjects, either in separate courses or in such combinations as convenience or necessity demands:
        A. History of Education.
            1. History of general education.
            2. History of secondary education.
        B. Educational psychology with emphasis on adolescence.
        C. The principles of education, including the study of educational aims, values, and processes. Courses in general method are included under this heading.
        D. Special methods in the secondary school subjects that the students expect to teach.
        E. Organization and management of schools and school systems.
        F. School hygiene.
    III. That opportunity for observation and practice teaching with secondary pupils be given (p. 537).

The Committee recommended that the "subjects mentioned under II be distributed thru the last two years of the college course" and that the time given to them be not less than 15 semester hours. Thus the Committee viewed professional study exclusive of "observation and practice teaching" as appropriate for inclusion in the work toward the baccalaureate degree. In other words, the "subjects mentioned under II" were regarded as academically respectable, but apparently "observation and practice teaching" were to be "extras" not worthy of academic credit.

These recommendations of the Committee of Seventeen and other evidence indicate that by 1907 the "normal-school idea" had become rather generally accepted among colleges and universities and the enumeration of "subjects" suggests a trend toward a "standard professional course," corresponding to the one noted by Kruse among normal schools. The supplementary discussions by members of the Committee of Seventeen reflect a considerable degree of agreement. It is clear that, in general, "history of education" and "educational psychology with emphasis on adolescence" were considered the more important phases of the professional education of secondary teachers. Some members questioned the effectiveness of "observation and practice teaching" [26] and expressed a preference for teaching experience in the elementary schools or "cadet teaching." This difference of opinion, however, pertains to means rather than to purposes.

---

[26] *Ibid.*, p. 545 (Barrett); p. 563 (De Garmo); and p. 627 (Buchner).

Concept of Teacher Qualifications in Colleges and Universities

The Committee of Seventeen consisted of four school administrators, ten professors of education, two normal-school presidents, and the secretary of the Massachusetts State Board of Education. Consequently, the Report should not be interpreted as reflecting the general opinion in colleges and universities in regard to the desirable nature of the education of secondary teachers. By 1907 most of the larger institutions and some of the smaller ones had established a "department of education" and in a few cases a college (school) of education. However, the establishment of such provisions for the professional phase of teacher education does not necessarily reflect general approval of including technical-professional study, such as recommended by the Committee of Seventeen, within the work for the baccalaureate degree. At a joint session of the departments of Higher Education, Secondary Education, and Normal Schools of the National Education Association in 1907, A. F. Lange, dean of the faculty of the College of Letters, University of California (Berkeley), spoke on "The Preparation of High-school Teachers from the Standpoint of the University." [27] Although he appears to have approved of pedagogical training, including observation and practice teaching, he asserted that he regarded "segregation and training in pedagogical technique before the bachelor's degree has been obtained as justifiable only on the ground of temporary expediency." Since Lange had been a member of the Education Department and shortly after became head of the department, his approval of "pedagogical" training was perhaps not generally shared by his academic colleagues.[28] His stand for "training in pedagogical technique" at the postbaccalaureate level probably was supported by a number of persons.

Lange's concept of the academic phase of the prospective teacher's preparation is also worthy of note. He emphasized "the modern liberal culture that a bachelor's degree represents" plus "a certain scientific mastery of at least one subject, not necessarily the one the candidate expects to teach." Thus Lange included major study as a part of the prospective teacher's liberal (general) education rather than as a major specialization in a teaching field. Furthermore, the omission of any reference to study at the college level of the subjects to be taught in high school implies that if one has a liberal (general) education with "a cer-

---

[27] Alexis F. Lange, "The Preparation of High-school Teachers. II. From the Standpoint of the University," *Addresses and Proceedings* (National Education Association, 1907), pp. 718-23.

[28] For support of this hypothesis see Timothy F. O'Leary, *An Inquiry into the General Purposes, Functions, and Organization of Selected University Schools of Education* (Ph.D. thesis; Washington, D.C.: The Catholic University of America Press, 1941), p. 262.

tain scientific mastery of at least one subject" he is thereby academically qualified in any high-school subject, except perhaps the so-called special subjects. This view is in significant contrast to the position of the Committee of Seventeen. It is, however, a view which had many adherents.

Personal Fitness and the General-Education Qualification

Accompanying the subsidence of arguments for the teaching-knowledge qualification and the developments relative to pedagogical knowledge and skills, there were minor changes in the thinking about personal fitness and the general-education qualification. There was a decrease in explicit attention to personal fitness, but it continued to be recognized as important. A few new trait designations were introduced, but they do not appear to indicate significant modifications of the concept of this area of teacher qualification.

As indicated by Van Liew's enumeration in 1905 (see p. 194), the general-education qualification persisted in the thinking about the purposes of teacher education, but there was little attention to its definition. In 1895 the Sub-Committee on the Training of Teachers described it as the "scholarship, culture, and power gained by four years of study." [29] As long as the philosophy of idealism dominated the thinking and education was conceived of as a process of disciplining the mind, there was no occasion to be concerned about a qualitative definition of general education for teachers. However, toward the close of the period there was some tendency to differentiate general education of teachers from that considered desirable for the "average citizen." In 1905 Van Liew [30] supplemented his specification of "that general knowledge and culture which constitute the common stock in trade of the average citizen" (see p. 194) by saying that "such knowledge and culture must be liberally, not meagerly, acquired." In 1907 the Committee of Seventeen recommended that the academic preparation of high-school teachers include "one or more subjects from a group including history, economics, and sociology, which will give the teacher a proper outlook upon the social aspects of education" (p. 536). However, this tendency was not prominent and there was little reflection of it in teacher-education practice. There was also, as noted above, a tendency in some academic circles to insist that specialized study in at least one field was a necessary phase of a liberal education.

---

[29] "Report of Sub-Committee on the Training of Teachers," *Addresses and Proceedings* (National Educational Association, 1895), p. 238.

[30] Charles C. Van Liew, "A Statement of the Issues Before the Department," *Addresses and Proceedings* (National Educational Association, 1905), pp. 519-24.

Concluding Statement

When the thinking of this period is viewed from the vantage point of current teacher-education theory and practice, certain gains may be noted, but there were also significant losses. On the credit side of the ledger the most significant items are: (*a*) a developing recognition of professional (pedagogical) training as a desirable phase of the education of teachers for secondary schools and (*b*) a trend in the direction of a "standard" pedagogical program. On the debit side the significant developments were: (*a*) the rejection of the teaching-knowledge qualification, as argued for by Parr and others around 1890, and the support of the position that this qualification was satisfied by appropriate academic study, including "a detailed and specialized study of the subjects to be taught" in the case of teachers for secondary schools and (*b*) the consequent isolation of pedagogical training from the other phases of the teacher's education. It may also be noted that the thinking of the period reflects the teaching-subject-matter view of instruction.

CHAPTER 7

Modifications of Desired
Qualifications, 1907 to 1933

In 1890 practically all of the thinking about the purposes of teacher education related to the preparation of teachers for elementary schools, which was regarded as the function of normal schools. From about 1900 there was an increasing group of normal-school leaders who maintained that the function of normal schools should be extended to include the education of teachers for secondary schools. Paralleling this development, there was a growing concern in colleges and universities about the preparation of secondary teachers. This interest in the education of teachers for secondary schools resulted in the appointment of the Committee of Seventeen and its report in 1907.

During the years from 1907 to 1933, especially after about 1920, the education of teachers for secondary schools was a major concern in normal schools and teachers colleges as well as in colleges and universities. Although normal schools and teachers colleges continued to recognize their responsibility for the education of teachers for elementary schools, the thinking of their faculties about this function tended to be overshadowed by their concern about the preparation of teachers for secondary schools. Hence in this chapter the emphasis will be on the qualifications of teachers for secondary schools.

General Status of the Thinking in 1907

The general status of the thinking about the purposes of teacher education at the beginning of this period has been indicated in the preceding chapter, but a brief summary statement will be helpful as a means of directing attention to certain aspects which are significant relative to the development during the years following 1907. Although professional (pedagogical) training had become widely recognized as a desirable part of the education of both elementary and secondary teachers, it tended to be thought of as being *added to* academic training. Even in normal schools the education department tended to be isolated from the subject-matter departments within which the instruction tended to be academic except in special methods (teachers') courses. For the most part these courses were unrelated to the general-methods instruction in the department of education.

Although the record of around 1907 reflects differences of opinion in regard to details and relative emphasis, the thinking about the purposes of teacher education tended to be in the direction of agreement, especially among normal schools. This statement is supported by Van Liew's pronouncement in 1905 that there was practical agreement in regard to the "elements which should enter into the make-up of a teacher" (see p. 194). In 1910 Joseph H. Hill,[1] addressing the Department of Normal Schools of the National Education Association as president, asserted that the general outline of professional study was "so obvious that it needs in this presence no discussion." Presumably both Van Liew and Hill were referring primarily to the normal-school group, but the report of the Committee of Seventeen in 1907 and other evidence indicate a tendency toward agreement within the more general group of educationists.

The record of around 1907 does not provide adequate evidence of the extent to which members of subject-matter departments agreed with educationists. Probably the most common attitude among academic departments in colleges and universities was one of indifference toward teacher education, except as it might be accomplished by providing the means for a liberal education and a departmental teacher's course. There were some academic instructors who did not approve of pedagogical courses; on the other hand there were some instances of friendly support, at least for some courses.[2] Outside of the pedagogical-qualification area there was general agreement. Educationists emphasized the "schol-

---

[1] Joseph H. Hill, "The Distinctively Professional Content of Normal School and College Courses," *Addresses and Proceedings* (National Education Association, 1910), pp. 564-68.

[2] This statement is based largely on the writer's experience as a graduate student at the University of Missouri, 1909-11. However, he recognizes that this institution was probably not typical of universities of that time.

arship" qualification of teachers, which tended to be thought of as encompassing both general education and subject specialization. This emphasis is apparent in the writings of normal-school presidents, especially in connection with the preparation of high-school teachers.[3] It is also apparent in writings of "professors" of education in colleges and universities.[4] The "scholarship" qualification was not very clearly defined, but it was thought of in terms of "academic training." Within this general concept, some writers included qualitative specifications along the line of the recommendation of the Committee of Seventeen (see p. 203). There were still many who thought mainly in quantitative terms, i.e. years of "academic training" under some form of the elective system.

General Setting of the Period

The research movement in education began to influence educational thinking following 1907. Psychologists began to give systematic attention to learning as a major topic and following 1915 two additional teaching-learning theories were promoted. Education developed as a field of scholarly study and by the end of the period it had become a major area of graduate study.

During the period there were significant developments in our schools. There was serious concern about the curriculum and gradually changes were made in the programs of both elementary and secondary schools. Unfortunately, teacher educators, especially those contributing to general-education and subject-matter preparation, failed to maintain adequate contacts with the schools and hence tended not to have an adequate understanding of the work teachers were being called upon to do.

Lack of Explicit Concern about Purposes of Teacher Education

During the years following 1907 there was relatively little systematic discussion of purposes. The Betts, Frazier, and Gamble *Selected Bibliography on the Education of Teachers*[5] included a total of 1,297 references, mainly of the period 1907 to 1933, but only five were classified under "objectives and aims in the education of teachers." The outstand-

---

[3] For example, see Joseph H. Hill, "The Preparation of High-school Teachers. I. From the Standpoint of the Normal School," *Addresses and Proceedings* (National Education Association, 1907), pp. 712-18.

[4] For example, see "Papers on the Professional Preparation of High-school Teachers" in the "Report of the Committee of Seventeen," *Addresses and Proceedings* (National Education Association, 1907). Elwood P. Cubberley, p. 556; Paul H. Hanus, pp. 564f.; E. O. Holland, p. 580; C. H. Judd, p. 582; George W. A. Luckey, p. 589; M. V. O'Shea, p. 598.

[5] Gilbert L. Betts, Benjamin W. Frazier, Guy C. Gamble, *Selected Bibliography on the Education of Teachers*, National Survey of the Education of Teachers, Vol. I (U.S. Office of Education, Bulletin 1933, No. 10). 118 pp.

ing treatment of teacher education prior to the National Survey of the Education of Teachers (1933) was *The Professional Preparation of Teachers for American Public Schools* by William S. Learned, William C. Bagley, and others. This volume, published in 1920, bears the subtitle, *A Study Based Upon an Examination of Tax-supported Normal Schools in the State of Missouri.* As the general title suggests it is more than a report of a survey of a group of teacher-training institutions in one state and, in view of the personnel involved, the criticisms of practices and especially the recommendations may be taken as indicative of the advanced thinking of the time. The extended attention given to administrative matters, institutional relations, and staff qualifications reflects major centers of interest of persons concerned with normal schools as institutions for the education of teachers. It is not surprising, therefore, that the authors did not present a systematic exposition of purposes. Their general position, however, is apparent.

There is practically no reference in the volume [6] to the general-education qualification. Perhaps this omission was due to the fact that the study was focused upon the professional preparation of teachers, but it suggests that the definition of general education for teachers was being given little attention in the thinking of the time. The authors gave considerable attention to the teaching-knowledge qualification in the several subject-matter fields. Although there are only rather incidental observations in regard to what was considered to constitute a satisfactory teaching knowledge in the several fields, the persistent reference to the desirability of professionalized treatment of subject matter makes it clear that this qualification area was prominent in the thinking of the authors. Extended attention was given also to provisions for engendering pedagogical qualifications. Current practices were severely criticized relative to the lack of planned programs of professional study (pp. 167f.). On the constructive side, the authors urged curriculums differentiated relative to type of position and the organization of the curriculums about "observation, participation, and practice teaching" as the "central and critical elements" (p. 192). The second of these recommendations, however, was not intended to emphasize "skill in teaching" to the neglect of attention to the "broader professional intelligence and insight of the teacher" (p. 393).

Further evidence of the limited extent of the concern about the definition of purposes of teacher education is provided by the Addresses and Proceedings of the National Education Association, the Yearbooks of the American Association of Teachers Colleges, and the Monographs and Yearbooks of the National Society of College Teachers of Education. For

---

[6] William S. Learned, William C. Bagley, and Others, *The Professional Preparation of Teachers for American Public Schools* (New York: The Carnegie Foundation for the Advancement of Teaching, Bulletin No. 14, 1920). 475 pp.

example, the index of the first of these publications for 1925 listed twenty-two committee reports, but not one of them concerned teacher-education purposes. The table of contents of the volume included three items relating to teacher education. One was a plea for recognizing "Training for health education in the school" in the education of teachers; the second was a report on "The teaching or service load in state teachers colleges"; and the third dealt with "The development of the teachers' college" and it was noted incidentally that "an ideal course of study has not yet been found." The 1925 Yearbook of the American Association of Teachers Colleges included an address under the title, "The present status of the teachers college curriculum and what to do about it." The present status was characterized as "chaos work," and a plea was made for co-ordinated research as a means toward a "scientifically constructed course of study." The curriculum was dealt with in some of the other addresses but almost wholly in terms of current practices. The 1925 Yearbook of the National Society of College Teachers of Education did not include any articles dealing explicitly with the purposes of teacher education. In the Yearbook for the following year the Committee on teacher-training curriculums presented a brief "report of progress" to the effect that it had not yet anything to report.

The status of the thinking about purposes at the close of the period is indicated by the National Survey of the Education of Teachers. There is no explicit reference to the purposes or objectives of teacher education in the table of contents of the *Summary and Interpretation* (Vol. VI) and it appears that the Survey was not planned to include any systematic consideration of purposes. In Volume III, *Teacher Education Curricula*, a chapter is devoted to "Objectives and functions of teacher education" in normal schools and teachers colleges. The treatment is concerned with the recognition of general aspects or phases of the total education of teachers, i.e. with general institutional aims. "Education of teachers" is shown to rank first among the "aims" of both normal schools and teachers colleges. "Knowledge of subject matter" is second. Lower ranking aims include "scholarly and scientific attitudes," "training for life needs," and "training for wise use of leisure" (p. 35). Further attention is given to purposes under the subheading "Functions of teacher education" (pp. 38f.), but again the treatment is in general terms and thus contributes little to the definition of purposes. Under "Proposals" a plea is made for the formulation of objectives that specify "in some detail what is implied in terms of the outcomes expected" (p. 42). The corresponding treatment relating to colleges and universities contributes even less to definition of purposes.

A Change in the Approach in Thinking about Desired
Teacher Qualifications

The record of the period, however, indicates some general developments in the thinking about the purposes of teacher education. A significant development was a shift in the approach from the "nature and needs of the training process" as the basis of planning and evaluating teacher education to the scientific study of teachers as they are as a means of identifying and evaluating teacher qualifications. Meriam's pioneer investigation [7] (1905) is indicative of the emerging trend. In evaluating aspects of teacher education he calculated coefficients of correlation as a means of ascertaining the degree of relationship between measures of teacher qualifications and criterion measures of "teaching efficiency." In 1915 Boyce [8] referred to "a movement toward analysis of the qualities of teachers as they are." The trend of the times as indicated by the 1912 volume of Addresses and Proceedings of the National Education Association. In contrast to the volumes of preceding years, which consist almost wholly of discussions by individuals and of reports from deliberative groups, a considerable number of the 1912 "addresses" include references to findings from systematic investigations. For example, in a paper on "The professional training of high-school teachers" William C. Bagley [9] introduced findings from four studies. The spirit of this paper is indicated by the treatment of the "personal-fitness" qualification. Instead of directing attention to the conventional arguments Bagley was concerned with the questions: (a) What are the "qualities" involved in personal fitness for teaching? (b) What is the relative importance of these qualities? These questions were answered in terms of the findings of a systematic investigation.

During the following years there were numerous studies directed toward the identification and evaluation of teacher traits [10] and the evaluation of phases of teacher education. The account of the purposes and planning of the National Survey [11] furnishes evidence of the status of the "movement toward analysis of teachers as they are" in 1930. The list of

---

[7] Junius L. Meriam, *Normal School Education and Efficiency in Teaching* (Contributions to Education, No. 1 [New York: Teachers College, Columbia University, 1905]). 152 pp.

[8] Arthur C. Boyce, *Methods for Measuring Teachers' Efficiency*, Fourteenth Yearbook, Part II (National Society for the Study of Education, 1915), p. 29.

[9] William C. Bagley, "The Professional Training of High-school Teachers," *Addresses and Proceedings* (National Education Association, 1912), pp. 686-91.

[10] Certain illustrative studies will be noted under "personal fitness."

[11] E. S. Evenden, *Summary and Interpretation*, National Survey of the Education of Teachers, Vol. VI (U.S. Office of Education, Bulletin 1933, No. 10), pp. 1-13.

controversial issues "presented to the board of consultants at its second policy-determining meeting" (p. 17) was expressed in the phraseology of research problems. The employment of such phraseology appears to have been a reflection of the attitude with which problems and issues of teacher education were being approached. At one of the planning conferences the majority of those present seemed to favor confining the Survey to an intensive analytical study of "a small group — about 1,000 sixth grade teachers . . . so chosen that they would represent as many as possible of the controversial issues" (p. 20). The majority position at this meeting was, in effect, that the findings from an "intensive analytical study" of an appropriately selected population of teachers in the schools would provide the solutions of the problems of teacher education.

This change in the approach to the definition of purposes of teacher education furnishes a partial explanation of the limited number of explicit writings on the topic. It was not fashionable to issue pronouncements of the qualifications of the "ideal teacher." Instead of attempting to deduce the desired teacher qualifications from the "nature and needs of the training process," which would be opinion, one should be "scientific" and determine the qualifications by ascertaining the characteristics and qualities of the "good" teachers in the schools. Until this was adequately accomplished, institutions and staff members within institutions should be free to "experiment."

Differentiation of Teacher Education Relative to Type of Position

A second general development was a trend in the direction of thinking of prospective teachers as preparing for the specific types of positions in which they expected to be employed. This view is apparent in several writings [12] and is reflected in the differentiation of teacher education with respect to teaching fields. During the period from 1890 to 1907 there was little curriculum differentiation relative to type of position. In his study of the catalogs of a sample of forty-five state normal schools and teachers colleges, Deyoe [13] reported that in 1902-3 the dominant types of curriculums were "general professional" and "general elementary." With the exceptions of "high school" and "kindergarten," other types were offered in less than 10 per cent of the institutions studied. Such practice indicates that a "roundly-equipped" elementary teacher was a generalist, i.e. adequately prepared to teach at any grade level. Soon after 1907 special curriculums for the primary, intermediate, and grammar grades became

[12] For example, see *Journal of Educational Research,* 10 (October, 1924), 175-256.

[13] George P. Deyoe, *Certain Trends in Curriculum Practices and Policies in State Normal Schools and Teachers Colleges* (Contributions to Education, No. 606 [New York: Bureau of Publications, Teachers College, Columbia University, 1934]), pp. 29f.

the general practice.[14] Later there were curriculums for special-subject fields.[15]

Deyoe reported that by 1932-33 the "general professional" curriculum had disappeared and the frequency of the "general elementary" had decreased from 76 per cent to 47 per cent (p. 30). He cites several other studies which support his findings (pp. 32-34).

The Committee of Seventeen, reporting in 1907, recommended "a detailed and specialized study of the subjects to be taught" (see p. 203). The major-minor compromise of the elective system provided for a degree of subject-matter specialization and later curriculums for various subject positions were introduced. Hall-Quest's analysis of the catalogs of 59 teachers colleges for the year 1923-24 revealed 390 "professional secondary curricula" distributed among 58 types of positions.[16] In the 1926 Yearbook of the National Society of College Teachers of Education, M. E. Haggerty reported on the development of "specialized curricula in teacher-training" at the University of Minnesota and announced that the next "college bulletin" would list "thirty-five different curricular programs" leading to the baccalaureate degree.[17] The National Survey, Vol. III, reported findings bearing on practice around 1930. An analysis of the catalog announcements of 66 teachers colleges and normal schools revealed a total of 170 "different titles of curricula" (p. 55). Among the four-year curriculums there were 29 titles with a frequency greater than 5 per cent. The canvass of opinion revealed a distinctly favorable attitude toward a "definitely prescribed sequence of courses for every type of teaching position."

Although practice in colleges and universities was in the direction of curriculums differentiated relative to type of teaching position, there were those who did not subscribe to this view. Reference has already been made to an address by A. F. Lange (see p. 205) in 1907 in which he asserted that the intensive study need not be of a subject the candidate expects to teach. This point of view seems to have had many supporters in academic circles. In the National Survey [18] the vote of several groups was obtained with respect to the proposition: "The program of teacher

[14] Guy E. Maxwell, "Differentiation of Courses in Normal Schools," *Addresses and Proceedings* (National Education Association, 1913), pp. 536-41.

[15] M. J. Nelson, "An Analysis of the Two-year Curricula Offered in Thirty Teacher-training Institutions," *Educational Administration and Supervision,* 16 (1930), 59-62.

[16] Alfred L. Hall-Quest, *Professional Secondary Education in Teachers Colleges* (New York: Teachers College, Columbia University, 1925), p. 42.

[17] M. E. Haggerty, "Specialized Curricula in Teacher-training," *Fifteenth Yearbook* (National Society of College Teachers of Education, 1926), pp. 3-25.

[18] Earle U. Rugg and Others, *Teacher Education Curricula,* National Survey of the Education of Teachers, Vol. III (U.S. Office of Education, Bulletin 1933, No. 10). 547 pp.

education should be general rather than specialized; teachers should be trained with but slight attention to specific positions or levels — in other words, we should educate teachers, not specialists, such as primary teachers, physical education teachers, or mathematics teachers." The vote of academic instructors in colleges and universities was 51 per cent "yes." Only 20 per cent of education instructors voted "yes" (pp. 246-47).

Relation of Pedagogical Training to Subject-Matter Study

In 1907 the department of education was generally isolated from the other departments contributing to the education of teachers. This tended to be true in normal schools as well as in colleges and universities. The pedagogical training of a prospective teacher was something *added to* his academic education. Even when education courses were distributed over two or more years of the college course, there was intermingling rather than integration of pedagogical training and subject-matter study. This situation changed slowly. By the time of the National Survey, college and university faculties strongly approved professional treatment of some subject-matter courses and the majority of the respondents from twenty-four selected colleges and universities favored the "professionalization of nearly one third of the curriculum." [19] However, a study of practice resulted in the conclusion that "professional treatment of so-called subject-matter courses for teachers is almost negligible in liberal arts colleges and universities and that full responsibility for developing the professionalization of the field has occurred in separate special-methods courses" (p. 277).

The Thinking Relative to the Four Qualification Areas

The following accounts of the changes within the four qualification areas should be interpreted in the light of these general developments. For the most part the thinking of the period, especially following 1920, was within the framework of the thesis that the desired qualification of teachers could be determined by studying teachers as they are. Associated with this thesis was the view, especially among educationists, that the education of teachers should be conceived of as explicit preparation for their respective jobs.

Personal fitness. In an address before the National Council of Education in 1913, Henry Suzzallo [20] described the teacher from the point of view of the "ideal of expert service," but his enumeration of qualifications in-

---

[19] *Ibid.*, p. 276.

[20] Henry Suzzallo, "The Reorganization of the Teaching Profession," *Addresses and Proceedings* (National Education Association, 1913), pp. 362-75.

cluded no mention of personal fitness. At the meeting of the Department of Normal Schools in 1914, David Felmley [21] indicated desired teacher qualifications, but again there was no specific mention of personal fitness. This qualification area appears to have been given little systematic attention in the thinking about the purposes of teacher education during the following years of the period.

It should not be inferred, however, that personal fitness was regarded as unimportant as a teacher qualification. Numerous investigators sought the causes of teacher failure by compiling reasons for dismissal or nonre-ëmployment as recorded or as given in response to a questionnaire inquiry. Such studies from the pioneer ones by Moses [22] and by Littler [23] revealed a great variety of "causes" among which "poor discipline" and undesirable personality qualities tended to be prominent. A large number of teacher rating scales were devised following E. C. Elliott's presentation of his "Provisional Plan for the Measure of Merit of Teachers" in 1910. In each case the immediate purpose was to determine a list of the items on which a teacher was to be rated as a means of arriving at a measure of his general merit. Several of the authors gave systematic attention to the identification of significant items and some subjected the constructed instrument to critical evaluation.

A study of 57 teacher rating scales,[24] published in 1931, revealed a total of 199 different items (traits) with the frequencies ranging from 43 to 1. Some of the variability is due to employing different phraseologies for designating essentially the same trait, but examination of the partial list of items given in the report makes clear that there was considerable disagreement in regard to the items that should be included in a teacher rating scale. It is also apparent that many of the items refer to aspects of the teaching-learning situation rather than teacher traits. However, the higher frequency items probably are indicative of teacher traits generally considered to be significant: discipline (43),[25] cooperation (36), adequate scholarship (29), voice (27), sympathy (27), care of individual differences (27), skill in assignment (27), class response (26), health (26), loyalty (25), command of English (25), daily preparation (25), care of physical condition: heat, ventilation, and light (25).

[21] David Felmley, "The Reorganization of the Normal School Curriculum," *Addresses and Proceedings* (National Education Association, 1914), pp. 498-504.

[22] Cleda Virginia Moses, "Why High-school Teachers Fail," *School and Home Education*, 33 (1914), 166-69.

[23] Sherman Littler, "Causes of Failure Among Elementary School Teachers," *School and Home Education*, 33 (1914), 253-56.

[24] Charles W. Knudsen and Stella Stephens, "An Analysis of Fifty-seven Devices for Rating Teaching," *Peabody Journal of Education*, 9 (1931), 15-24.

[25] The numbers in parentheses are frequencies.

The Commonwealth Teacher-Training Study (1929) included a comprehensive and systematic attempt to identify and evaluate teacher traits. The first step was to interview a number of persons, including pupils and parents as well as school people, as a means of ascertaining traits considered significant by the interviewees. The analysis and classification of the interview records resulted in a list of trait names and a longer list of statements descriptive of trait actions. Dictionaries were consulted in formulating "standard definitions" for each of the trait names, and then the trait actions were classified under the defined trait names.[26] It appeared that in several instances two or more trait names referred to very similar teacher characteristics and by telescoping the original list of eighty-three items was reduced to one of twenty-five. This final list was submitted for evaluation to a group of twenty-five "experienced school administrators" selected to serve as a jury. The total procedure, of course, yielded only a consensus in regard to desired teacher traits but it was elaborately and systematically obtained and the reliability of the consensus was checked at various points.

The relative importance of the twenty-five teacher traits tended to vary with the educational level (p. 18). For example, "breadth of interest (interest in community, interest in profession, interest in pupils)" had first rank in grades 10 to 12, second in rural schools, tenth in grades 7 to 9, eleventh in grades 3 to 6, and fifteenth in kindergarten and grades 1 and 2. Considering all educational levels "good judgment (discretion, foresight, insight, intelligence)" was the most important trait (ranks 1 to 4) and "self-control (calmness, dignity, poise, reserve, sobriety)" was second (ranks 2 to 6). "Magnetism (approachability, cheerfulness, optimism, pleasantness, sense of humor, sociability, pleasing voice, wittiness)" had a high rank (3 to 5) except in senior high schools (rank 11) and rural schools (rank 9). The rank of "adaptability" ranged from 6 to 10 except for rural schools where it was first.

Since Meriam's investigation [27] in 1905, a large number of correlation studies have been reported. The teacher characteristics investigated include chronological age, height, height-weight ratio, years of experience, test scores in various areas (e.g. intelligence, reading, and teaching field), scholarship marks (general and in particular areas), personality ratings, and scores on professional tests. The motive in most cases has been the desire to contribute to the development of a means of selection at some preservice level, but the findings have implications relative to the objectives of teacher education, i.e. the desired teacher qualifications.

---

[26] W. W. Charters and Douglas Waples, *The Commonwealth Teacher-Training Study* (Chicago: University of Chicago Press, 1929), pp. 223-44.

[27] Junius L. Meriam, *Normal School Education and Efficiency in Teaching* (Contributions to Education, No. 1 [New York: Teachers College, Columbia University, 1905]). 152 pp.

Knight [28] (1922) studied 156 teachers (118 elementary and 38 secondary) employed in three cities in Massachusetts. The interpretation of the statistical results, as Knight observed, is not very apparent but he suggested as the "most reasonable explanation" that the "general factor of interest in one's work" was the "dominant factor" in determining the degree of teaching success attained. A study of 560 elementary teachers (kindergarten through the sixth grade), graduates of the two-year course of the Cleveland School of Education (1922-28) and employed in the Cleveland City Schools, was made by Odenweller.[29] The criterion of teaching efficiency was a "composite" measure determined from rankings by principals, assistants, and supervisors. Correlations were calculated for twenty-six trait measures. Excluding the measure of personality as rated by principals and supervisors where the operation of a "halo effect" is apparent, the coefficients range from .533 ("personality by three teachers of the building") and .307 ("fitness-personality" by faculty and student-teaching supervisors) to —.004 ("intelligence — median scores") (p. 38). The findings, including coefficients of partial correlation, are interpreted by Odenweller as indicating personality, defined as "a power or an ability to influence other persons," (p. 52) to be "the outstanding trait, the one most closely associated with effectiveness in teaching" (p. 51).

A third approach to the identification of desired teacher qualifications is to observe teachers at work for the purpose of noting the qualities, procedures, and techniques associated with success. This investigational procedure may be illustrated by a study reported by A. S. Barr[30] in 1929. A preliminary phase of the investigation was the identification of a group of forty-seven "good" teachers of the social studies in junior and senior high schools and an equal group of "poor" teachers of the social studies in similar schools. Then teaching performances of each of these teachers were systematically observed. The characteristic differences between the teaching performances of the "good" teachers and those of the "poor" teachers were determined by an analytical comparison of the two groups of observational records. For example, under "teaching posture" the item, "stands in front of desk," had a frequency of six for the group of "poor" teachers and a frequency of twenty-three for the "good" teachers.

---

[28] Frederic B. Knight, *Qualities Related to Success in Teaching* (Contributions to Education, No. 120 [New York: Teachers College, Columbia University, 1922]). 67 pp.

[29] Arthur L. Odenweller, *Predicting the Quality of Teaching* (Contributions to Education, No. 676 [New York: Bureau of Publications, Teachers College, Columbia University, 1936]). 158 pp.

[30] A. S. Barr, *Characteristic Differences in the Teaching Performance of Good and Poor Teachers of the Social Studies* (Bloomington, Illinois: Public School Publishing Company, 1929). 127 pp.

A revealing general outcome of this investigation was the variable character of the teaching performances within both the group of "good" teachers and that of the "poor" teachers. Although certain performance items, e.g. "very attentive" to pupil responses, laughing with the class, and utilizing pupil experiences, and certain personal qualities, e.g. self-control and enthusiasm, were noted more frequently among the "good" teachers than among the "poor" ones, neither group exhibited a clearly defined pattern of either teaching performance items or teacher qualities. Furthermore, performance items and personal qualities tending to be characteristic of "good" teachers were very generally exhibited by some "poor" teachers and *vice versa*. This general finding was doubtless due in part to variability in teaching effectiveness within each of the groups and possibly to an overlapping between the groups, but in the light of other studies bearing on the matter it seems more probable that neither "poor" teaching nor "good" teaching is to be associated with a particular pattern of performance items and that particular personal qualities are not "critical" in the determination of the degree of teaching success attained. However, Barr concluded that "the chief sources of weaknesses among poor teachers are defective characteristics of personality" (p. 117). This conclusion should be interpreted in connection with the finding that with reference to "personal appearance, personal charm, and attractiveness," the "poor" teachers as a group were judged to be superior to the "good" teachers (p. 72). The defects of personality appear to have been mainly in areas of enthusiasm, self-control, appreciativeness, and sympathy.

The accumulation of studies of the types illustrated in the preceding pages added to the understanding of the personal-fitness qualification. For example, the definitions of teacher traits, both formal and in terms of trait actions, contributed by *The Commonwealth Teacher-Training Study* may be used to make discussion of this area of teacher qualifications more meaningful. Correlation studies revealed the relative unimportance of individual differences in various traits. On the other hand, it cannot be said that the research resulted in revolutionary changes in the thinking within this area of teacher qualification. At the beginning of the period personality traits, although not given as much prominence as previously, were considered important; at the time of the National Survey the thinking was at about the same level. There had been, however, some shift in the focus of emphasis. For example, the consensus of "experts" reported in *The Commonwealth Teacher-Training Study* [31] revealed high evaluations of "good judgment," "enthusiasm," and "self-control" and for secondary teachers of "forcefulness" and "leadership." Although the common trait designations of the earlier period — good moral character, sympathy, tactfulness, and self-reliance — were not well-

---

[31] W. W. Charters and Douglas Waples, *op. cit.*

defined, it appears that the concept of the ideal teacher person revealed by *The Commonwealth Teacher-Training Study* emphasized somewhat different personality qualifications.

In appraising the thinking of the period relative to the personal-fitness qualification, one should inquire into the extent to which programs of teacher education included provisions for engendering traits considered desirable. Although the evidence is fragmentary, it appears that teacher-training institutions of the period gave very little, if any, systematic attention to engendering desired personality traits. *The Commonwealth Teacher-Training Study* asserted that they "must be systematically provided for in building any professional curriculum" (p. 15). However, the chapters devoted to curriculum construction were restricted to suggestions for the use of the "master-list of teachers' activities." "Complete approval" of "provision for development of social and individual traits of teachers" is reported in the National Survey,[32] but apparently there was no systematic inquiry into the provisions in teacher-training institutions for this purpose, possibly because such an inquiry seemed to be fruitless.

The publication of *The Teacher's Health* by L. M. Terman in 1913 directed attention to an aspect of personal fitness that had received scant attention in the thinking about teacher qualifications. Many normal schools and teachers colleges came to require a physical examination or a health certificate from a physician as a condition of admission. In 1926 Rogers [33] reported that in only 67 of 190 institutions from which information was obtained "no examination of any students and no physician's certificate" were required. Most of the institutions also were endeavoring to do something "for the health of the students." However, it appears that only a few institutions were explicitly recognizing the improvement of health as a purpose of teacher education.[34]

General education. In 1908 the Committee on Statement of Policy Regarding the Preparation and Qualification of Teachers of Elementary and High Schools recommended that the "standard normal course" for the preparation of teachers for elementary schools be two years beyond high-school graduation or the equivalent.[35] This recommended extension of the total schooling of elementary teachers suggests an increase of the general-education preparation beyond that represented by high-school graduation. However, the curriculums for prospective elementary teachers presented in the "provisional suggestions formulated and issued by

---

[32] Earle U. Rugg and Others, *Teacher Education Curricula*, National Survey of the Education of Teachers, Vol. III (U.S. Office of Education, Bulletin 1933, No. 10), p. 41.

[33] J. F. Rogers, *The Health of the Teacher* (U.S. Office of Education, School Health Studies, No. 12, 1926), p. 37.

[34] *Ibid.*, pp. 42-43.

[35] *Addresses and Proceedings*, National Education Association, (1908), p. 735.

the Carnegie Foundation for the Advancement of Teaching" in 1917 were devoted to teaching knowledge and professional study. Comparative data presented by Class [36] indicate only slight changes from 1905 to 1930 in general-education requirements in the two-year course. Thus relative to two-year post-high-school curriculums for elementary teachers there does not appear to have been much quantitative change in the definition of general education. It may be noted, however, that by 1930 some normal schools and teachers colleges were offering three- and four-year curriculums for elementary teachers, and a portion of the additional time provided by such curriculums was devoted to general education.[37]

The Committee of Seventeen [38] recommended that the academic preparation of high-school teachers include:

(a) One or more subjects from a group including history, economics, and sociology, which will give the teacher a proper outlook upon the social aspects of education;

(b) A course in general psychology and at least one from a group of subjects including history of philosophy, logics, and ethics, which will give the teacher a proper outlook upon education as the development of the individual.

These recommendations and the outline statements by both Suzzallo [39] and Felmley [40] suggest an emerging tendency to define the general-education qualification as including more than "that general knowledge and culture which constitutes the common stock in trade of the average citizen" (specified by Van Liew in 1905). However, this tendency does not appear to have become prominent in the thinking about the purposes of teacher education, especially in the case of teachers for secondary schools.

Deyoe's analysis of curricular prescriptions in teachers colleges and normal schools revealed that from 1912-13 to 1932-33 there was an increase in both the range of departments and subjects included in the general education provisions and, with minor exceptions, in the proportion of institutions specifying such requirements.[41] He also found evidence of some adaptation of required courses to the function of teacher education.

---

[36] Edward C. Class, *Prescription and Election in Elementary-school Teacher-Training Curricula in State Teachers Colleges* (Contributions to Education, No. 480 [New York: Bureau of Publications, Teachers College, Columbia University, 1931]), p. 57.

[37] *Ibid.*, pp. 54f.

[38] *Addresses and Proceedings* (National Education Association, 1907), p. 536.

[39] Henry Suzzallo, *op. cit.*

[40] David Felmley, *op. cit.*

[41] George P. Deyoe, *Certain Trends in Curriculum Practices and Policies in State Normal Schools and Teachers Colleges* (Contributions to Education, No. 606 [New York: Bureau of Publications, Teachers College, Columbia University, 1934]), p. 67.

The National Survey, Volume III, reported an analysis of the general-education (nonspecialized) requirements included in certain curriculums offered in 66 teachers colleges and normal schools. The findings (p. 98) reflect considerable emphasis upon general education but they were interpreted (p. 104) as implying "a narrow concept of liberal or general education." "Fine arts, health and physical education, and home and family relationships" were considered relatively neglected and history appeared to be "emphasized at the expense of the other social studies." A questionnaire inquiry revealed that 49 out of 145 institutions responding "claimed to have orientation courses" and opinion strongly favored such courses. However, the concept of survey-orientation courses was judged to be lacking in compatibility with the general-education needs of teachers.

The report on the general education of prospective teachers in colleges and universities (pp. 200-221) is not in a form that permits precise comparison. When the "general education pattern of high-school and college work" taken by "1,000 graduates of 20 teachers colleges" (p. 101) is compared with the patterns of work taken by "1,000 prospective teachers from 24 universities and colleges" (p. 209), it appears that teachers-college graduates tended to take significantly more work in fine arts and vocational subjects while prospective teachers in colleges and universities took more in foreign languages.

The general evaluation given in the *Summary and Interpretation* (Volume VI) may be taken as an indication of the status of the definition of this qualification area.

Data collected by the National Survey of the Education of Teachers showed that teachers in the United States were generally deficient in the contacts made in high school and college with the larger fields of organized knowledge; in their contacts with the special fields, such as art and music which are certain to play an increasingly important part in their work as teachers as well as in their lives as individuals; in their reading interests and habits; and in their participation while in college in the extra-curricular activities which as teachers they will be expected to stimulate, organize, and perhaps direct. In most respects these lacks are not the result of the failure of institutions of higher education to provide facilities, but are, instead, due to the failure of institutions to guide the prospective teachers among their students into these desirable experiences.[42]

The final sentence of this appraisal is significant with reference to the definition of general-education purposes in the education of teachers. The "failure of institutions" is in effect a reflection of a relative indifference in regard to this qualification area. During the period from 1907 to 1933 academic respectability was a major concern of normal schools and teachers colleges and they tended to follow curricular practices of col-

---

[42] E. S. Evenden, *op. cit.*, p. 92.

leges and universities. Under the elective system, which prevailed in these institutions, general education was defined only in terms of limited requirements, specific and group; specialization was fashionable and students frequently used their privilege of election to extend study in their respective majors beyond the minimum requirement.

A study of a sampling of the 1929 seniors in ten selected institutions [43] probably indicates the general situation. Approximately two-fifths of the courses taken by 507 seniors were to satisfy requirements — specific, group, major or minor, etc. The reasons given for the selection of the remaining courses taken indicate little attention to general-education considerations. "Culture" was given as the reason for selecting 8 per cent of the total of the courses taken, but "occupation" and "subject matter" accounted for one-third of the elections. It is likely that a considerable portion of the courses taken for the latter reasons added to the work in major fields, thus extending specialization beyond institutional requirements. The extreme to which specialization was carried by some students is revealed by the analysis of records of 1,771 prospective teachers graduating from twenty-four colleges and universities.[44] The maximum credits in major ranged from 34 (physics) to 117 (music) semester hours and even the median credits ranged from 24 (physics) to 60 (agriculture) semester hours. Such specialization is indirect evidence of the limited attention to the general-education qualification of teachers.

Teaching knowledge. By 1907 the teaching-knowledge qualification tended to be thought of in terms of conventional academic study within a teaching field (see pp. 195f.) plus a special-methods (teachers') course, and the agitation for "professional treatment of subject matter" had practically disappeared from contemporary writings. In some quarters there appears to have been a disposition to minimize the desirability of a "detailed and specialized study of the subjects to be taught" (see p. 205). This low ebb of concern about the teaching-knowledge qualification was doubtless contributed to by the rise of the "elective system" which implied at least qualified acceptance of the thesis that all academically respectable subjects were equal in value for a liberal education. By 1910 practically all colleges and universities had adopted some compromise form of the "elective system." [45] This situation promoted competition among departments for students. This competition together with the emphasis upon "research" in connection with the developing graduate work contributed to the multiplication of course offerings, typically in

[43] Helen Foss Weeks, *Factors Influencing the Choice of Courses by Students in Certain Liberal Arts Colleges* (Contributions to Education, No. 465 [New York: Bureau of Publications, Teachers College, Columbia University, 1931]). 62 pp.

[44] Earle U. Rugg and Others, *op. cit.*, p. 534.

[45] R. Freeman Butts, *The College Charts Its Course* (New York: McGraw-Hill Book Company, Inc., 1939), pp. 239ff.

the form of narrow courses designed to prepare for further specialization.[46] In the absence of an effective guidance program the effect often was that a prospective teacher either elected "popular" courses and hence obtained a smattering of knowledge in a variety of fields or under the advice of a faculty member elected advanced courses in that "professor's" department.

Many normal schools of the time were attempting to be academically respectable so that they would be recognized as appropriate institutions for the education of high-school teachers. As a means to this end they tended to develop academic departments with course offerings similar to those provided in colleges and universities. They also adopted the "elective system." Under these conditions the concern about the teaching-knowledge qualification was at about the same level as among colleges and universities.

Within this situation there developed dissatisfaction with the subject-matter competence of teachers. Several factors contributed to this adverse appraisal. The findings of experimental studies led to the rejection of the theories of formal discipline and transfer of training. Curricular changes began to appear in our schools. The junior-high-school movement began about 1910. The Commission on the Reorganization of Secondary Education, appointed in 1912 and 1913, proposed its "seven cardinal principles" in 1918. Bobbitt's *The Curriculum* appeared in the same year.

One line of evidence indicating concern about the teaching-knowledge qualification of teachers is furnished by studies of teaching assignments and the college credits of teachers relative to these assignments. In the *Eighteenth Yearbook,* Part I, of the National Society for the Study of Education (1919) L. V. Koos and Clifford Woody reported a study of teachers in the accredited high schools of the state of Washington.[47] On the basis of questionnaire returns from about one-third of the teachers in these schools it was shown that a considerable proportion of teachers, especially in the smaller high schools, had "very meager preparation in higher institutions" in some of the secondary-school subjects which they were teaching. During the following years a number of similar studies were reported. Davis found on the basis of data for some fourteen thousand teachers that 57.2 per cent were teaching only subjects that they had prepared to teach.[48] Since only secondary schools accredited by the

[46] *Ibid.*, p. 266.

[47] Leonard V. Koos and Clifford Woody, "The Training of Teachers in the Accredited High Schools of the State of Washington," *Eighteenth Yearbook,* Part I (National Society for the Study of Education, 1919), pp. 213-57.

[48] C. O. Davis, "The Training and Experience of the Teachers in the High Schools Accredited by the North Central Association," *School Review,* 30 (1922), 335-54. See p. 346.

North Central Association of Colleges and Secondary Schools were included, this finding probably is not representative of the teaching assignments of college graduates during their first years of teaching. In a study of high-school science teachers Hutson [49] concluded that "large numbers of the science teachers are insufficiently prepared for the sciences they are teaching."

These findings are typical of the results from a large number of studies.[50] It should be noted, however, that the teaching assignments in the schools are not controlled by the training institutions and hence such studies should not be interpreted as meaning that these institutions gave no attention to engendering teaching knowledge in the prospective teacher's announced fields.

In 1914 a normal-school president [51] reported that, when he assumed the position in 1910, he addressed a questionnaire to "one hundred representative city superintendents of schools throughout the country" and that approximately 70 per cent of those responding listed "lack of scholarship" as the most notable shortcoming of normal-school graduates. The author interpreted this finding as meaning that the normal school should require high-school graduation for admission. He also approved extending the curriculum of the normal school one year which should be devoted to "academic instruction in the subjects the teacher will have to teach." The significance of "academic" in this phrase is not indicated, but it may be presumed that this normal-school president had in mind conventional academic instruction rather than instruction designed to engender professionalized teaching knowledge.

Thompson's position illustrates one developing point of view, namely, that more adequate subject-matter competence of normal-school graduates could be engendered by increasing the time devoted to "academic instruction." As normal schools developed into teachers colleges, high-school graduation, or the equivalent, became a standard entrance requirement, and there was a tendency to reduce the pedagogical requirement in the teacher-education curriculums (see pp. 231f.).

The utilization of the time devoted to "academic instruction" varied. By 1907 a number of colleges and universities had adopted the "major and minor system" and this compromise form of the elective system tended to become the common practice. In the case of prospective secondary teach-

[49] P. W. Hutson, "High-school Science Teachers: A Study of Their Training in Relation to the Subjects They Are Teaching," *Educational Administration and Supervision*, 9 (1923), 423-38.

[50] A brief summary of sixty-odd investigations is reported by Harl R. Douglass, "Subject-matter Preparation of High School Teachers," *Educational Administration and Supervision*, 21 (1935), 457-64.

[51] Alfred C. Thompson, "Notable Shortcomings of State Normal Schools," *Addresses and Proceedings* (National Education Association, 1914), pp. 554-59.

ers the major and minor requirements may be considered as representing quantitative provisions for the teaching-knowledge qualification.
Practice in regard to subject-matter majors varied. In a study of a
limited number of colleges and universities Ruediger [52] reported a range
from 18 to 60 semester hours in the requirement for a major.

A catalog study of sixty-six teachers colleges and normal schools, reported in the National Survey,[53] revealed a more extreme range of major
requirements in four-year curriculums than Ruediger found in 1926.
The most striking variations in practice were in the "special subject"
fields — art, 10 to 78 semester hours; commercial education, 16 to 89 semester hours; music, 15 to 72 semester hours; physical education for men,
19 to 82 semester hours. But the findings for academic fields also showed
significant variations — e.g. English, 15 to 47 semester hours; mathematics, 13 to 36 semester hours; biological science, 18 to 49 semester hours;
history, 22 to 43 semester hours. A similar study of fifty-seven colleges
and universities revealed practices of the same order (p. 530). The
median practice among teachers colleges and normal schools ranged from
16 semester hours for library science and 20 semester hours in German
to 34 semester hours for home economics and music and 35 semester
hours for science and social science. Among the colleges and universities
the medians ranged from 24 semester hours for history, biology, botany,
physics, zoology, art, and industrial arts to 45 semester hours for music
and 49 semester hours for agriculture.

These findings reflect a lack of agreement in regard to the quantitative prescription of teaching knowledge in a given field. It is apparent,
however, that the thinking was in the direction of academic specialization amounting to one-fifth or more of the work taken toward the baccalaureate degree. Opinion favored a major amounting to one-third or
more, and students tended to supplement the requirements by electives
(p. 70). In reporting the study of teachers colleges and normal schools,
it was observed that "with few exceptions" these institutions "have not
been much concerned with limitations on the extent of the major" (p.
71). The direction of the efforts within these "few exceptions" is perhaps
suggested later (p. 81) by the reference to the experimental use of
"qualifying examinations" as a means of determining the "competency
of students."

In teachers colleges and colleges (schools) of education within universities there was some tendency to regulate specialization (major and
minor study) from the point of view of the needs of teaching positions
(Vol. III, pp. 63, 80, 166; Ruediger, p. 51), but for the most part little

---

[52] W. C. Ruediger, "The Academic Major in Schools of Education Compared with
the Major in Liberal Arts Colleges," *Fifteenth Yearbook* (National Society of College
Teachers of Education, 1926), p. 51.

[53] Earle U. Rugg and Others, *op. cit.*, pp. 517-18.

attention was given to the qualitative aspects of the specialization. In liberal arts colleges qualitative specifications of teaching majors were largely from the point of view of the requirements for later scholarly study in the field (Vol. III, pp. 241f.). Thus during the period from 1907 to 1933 the "major and minor system" was capitalized to only a limited extent in these institutions as a means of providing for an appropriate teaching knowledge.[54] Subject-matter departments offered few courses explicitly designed relative to the needs of secondary teachers and the record of courses taken by prospective teachers reflects little concern about these needs in advising students relative to programs of study.

Within the situation described in the preceding pages there emerged some agitation for provisions for engendering a more adequate teaching knowledge. In 1918 W. C. Bagley,[55] who was then engaged in a study of the tax-supported normal schools of Missouri, made a plea for "professionalized subject-matter courses." The development of such courses, a few of which Bagley stated he had observed, was conceived of as involving a "fundamental reorganization of all our work with the professional end constantly in view." The courses should be designed as means of engendering teaching knowledge relative to the subjects of instruction in elementary and secondary schools. These courses were, however, to be of "real university grade."

The effect of Bagley's plea in 1918 and the elaboration of his position in the report [56] of the "study based upon an examination of tax-supported normal schools in the state of Missouri" is difficult to evaluate. From his examination of the announcements of one hundred normal schools and teachers colleges for 1921, Randolph [57] found some evidence of the development of "professional treatment of subject-matter." However, in 1927 E. U. Rugg on the basis of "a personal study of the courses in 26 representative teachers colleges and normal schools" and personal consultations with instructors in these institutions stated that "aside from methods courses, there is as yet little trend toward making required materials in fields aside from education and psychology professional in character." [58] Data obtained in the National Survey were interpreted as revealing little professionalization of subject-matter courses in normal

[54] Supporting evidence is provided by several studies. For example, see E. A. Fitzpatrick and P. W. Hutson, *The Scholarship of Teachers in Secondary Schools* (New York: The Macmillan Company, 1927). 208 pp.

[55] W. C. Bagley, "A Distinction Between Academic and Professional Subjects," *Addresses and Proceedings* (National Education Association, 1918), pp. 229-34.

[56] William S. Learned, William C. Bagley, and Others, *The Professional Preparation of Teachers for American Public Schools* (New York: Carnegie Foundation for the Advancement of Teaching, Bulletin No. 14, 1920), pp. 228-47 *et passim*.

[57] Edgar D. Randolph, *The Professional Treatment of Subject-matter* (Baltimore: Warwick and York, Inc., 1924). 204 pp. (p. 105).

[58] Earle U. Rugg, "The Trend Toward Standardization in Teachers Colleges," *Yearbook* (American Association of Teachers Colleges, 1927), pp. 84-99.

schools and teachers colleges.[59] However, among "academic subject instructors" in these institutions opinion was slightly in favor of "professionalization of practically all subject-matter courses." Other faculty groups were more favorable.[60]

Among colleges and universities there was less growth in the concern about the teaching-knowledge qualification. At the time of the National Survey the opinion of "academic subject instructors" was "not favorable" to the professionalization of all subject-matter courses. Even "teachers of education" in these institutions were slightly unfavorable.[61] However, it should be noted that some professionalization was strongly favored,[62] the central tendency being nearly one-third of the four-year curriculum. This favorable opinion was not aggressive and in practice there was little professionalization beyond what was accomplished in special-methods courses.[63]

The discrepancy between opinion and practice is probably due largely to uncertainty and disagreements in regard to professionalized subject-matter courses. Hurd [64] reported attempts to determine criteria for judging professionalized subject matter in science. Although certain criteria received majority approval, there was also serious minority criticism. Such criticism causes one to wonder about the extent to which the majority approval represented considered opinion. It is clear that at the time of Hurd's inquiries there were serious disagreements in the area of science education.

In the chapter of the National Survey on "Specialization and Differentiation for Teaching" it was pointed out that there were those who did not regard specialization as necessary for secondary teaching in a given field. It was the contention of such persons that a liberal education which included a "heavy concentration" in a college-subject department "essential for the appreciation of the depth of all knowledge" was sufficient preparation for a "selected person with good habits of study" to teach in related fields in which he had had introductory courses.[65] There is no indication of the size of the group holding this view. However, it probably pervaded the thinking of a considerable proportion of subject-matter instructors.

The increased concern about the adequacy of the preparation of teach-

[59] Earle U. Rugg and Others, *Teacher Education Curricula*, National Survey of the Education of Teachers, Vol. III (U.S. Office of Education, Bulletin 1933, No. 10), pp. 93, 134.

[60] *Ibid.*, p. 510.

[61] *Ibid.*, p. 510.

[62] *Ibid.*, p. 276.

[63] *Ibid.*, pp. 273, 277.

[64] A. W. Hurd, "Professionalization of Subject-matter Courses in the Education of Science Teachers," *Educational Administration and Supervision*, 19 (1933), 173-80.

[65] E. U. Rugg and Others, *op. cit.*, p. 223.

ers relative to the subjects they taught is a significant development of the period. This concern was common to all seriously interested in the education of teachers for elementary and secondary schools, especially the latter. There was, however, disagreement in regard to the nature of the desired teaching-knowledge qualification. The record of the period reflects three positions: (a) professional treatment of subject matter, (b) specialized academic study in the areas of the subjects to be taught, and (c) general education with a "heavy concentration" in a college-subject department "essential for the appreciation of the depth of all knowledge." The first of these positions had few aggressive supporters, the second was probably the view of the majority.

Pedagogical qualifications. The report of the Committee of Seventeen in 1907 (see p. 203) has been taken as marking the general acceptance of professional training as a desirable phase of the preparation of teachers for secondary schools. It should not be inferred, however, that the pedagogical training as outlined by the Committee of Seventeen was unanimously considered an essential phase of teacher education in academic circles. There were still "unbelievers" among those participating in the education of teachers, but for some years they were not aggressive in voicing their objections. Certification and accreditation requirements did not make it necessary for prospective teachers to devote a very large amount of time to education courses. Furthermore, departments of education in colleges and universities had attained a considerable degree of academic respectability, and history of education, comparative education, philosophy of education, educational psychology, and some other theory courses were not regarded as inappropriate electives. Even if they did not contribute much to professional competence, they probably added to a prospective teacher's liberal (general) education.

This more or less amicable situation did not long continue. The phenomenal growth of pedagogical (education) subject matter, the aggressiveness of educationists in promoting their sphere of teacher education, and the general faith in the efficacy of pedagogical training resulted in the specification by certificating and accrediting agencies of pedagogical requirements which made it necessary for even liberal arts colleges to establish a "major" requirement in education for prospective teachers. An analysis of the prescriptions in fifty-seven selected colleges and universities, reported in the National Survey,[66] revealed the same range of prescriptions in education (18 to 59 semester hours) as in academic majors. This position of pedagogical study in the collegiate program of prospective teachers was new and it tended to be regarded in academic circles as an encroachment. Some members of the subject-matter departments regarded education courses as futile; others argued that "even if

---

[66] *Ibid.*, p. 194.

valuable, they crowd out necessary general education or specialization at the undergraduate level" and that pedagogical training should be at the graduate level (p. 254). Practices in normal schools and teachers colleges tended to be similar to those in colleges and universities.[67]

In the *Summary and Interpretation* of the National Survey (Vol. VI) by E. S. Evenden, Chapter III is introduced by comments on the question: "Are there any distinctive elements in the education of a teacher which are not found in the education of any well-educated person?" (p. 72). The reference to this question as being "raised more frequently than any other" indicates that the place of professional training in the education of teachers, especially for secondary schools, was a major issue in 1930. It is significant, however, that Evenden pointed out that the question should not be given an "either-or" interpretation, i.e. the issue was not between a "well-educated person" (one having a liberal education including academic specialization) and a person having pedagogical training but an inadequate knowledge of the subjects he is to teach. Instead the issue was the question of the relative balance between academic study and professional education.

This statement of the issue seems to reflect the status of the thinking at the time of the National Survey. Evenden stated that most students of the problem (presumably mostly educationists) favored emphasis upon subject-matter study but not to the exclusion of appropriate attention to the pedagogical aspects of teacher education. In another volume of the report the authors concluded, on the basis of the data obtained, that "the majority attitudes of college and university instructors were favorable to courses in education, to student teaching, to observation, and to special methods." [68]

The evidence bearing on the thinking of the period from 1907 to 1933 relative to the balance between academic study and professional education is fragmentary. It appears that there was a slight tendency among normal schools and teachers colleges to decrease the pedagogical requirements. Thomasson's analysis [69] of four-year general curriculums showed that the average of education requirements decreased from 27.61 semester hours in 1910-11 to 26.07 semester hours in 1930-31. In the suggested curriculums "formulated and issued by the Carnegie Foundation for the Advancement of Teaching" in 1917, 23⅓ semester hours of professional work were proposed in addition to special-methods courses. In 1926 Evenden proposed "required courses in education" totaling only 14

---

[67] *Ibid.*, pp. 77-78.

[68] *Ibid.*, p. 257.

[69] A. L. Thomasson, *A Half Century of Teacher Training in State Normal Schools and Teachers Colleges of the United States, 1890-1940* (Unpublished Ph.D. dissertation, University of Illinois, 1942), p. 348.

semester hours in a four-year curriculum for elementary teachers.[70] Although this total tends to misrepresent Evenden's thinking, due to placing special methods in the subject-matter departments, it is apparent that he would have minimized requirements in education beyond contemporary practice in teachers colleges. No discussion of this proposal is reported in the *Yearbook,* but it is likely that some teachers-college administrators were in sympathy with the general proposition of decreasing the amount of required pedagogical work. In addressing the American Association of Teachers Colleges in 1922 Thomas W. Butcher[71] asserted: "The school that requires above twenty-five hours of professional courses for its degree is living close to the danger line between content and method." In the National Survey the "average" opinion of teachers-college instructors (all groups) was reported to be 20 semester hours (Vol. III, p. 259).

The recommendation of the Committee of Seventeen in 1907 was in terms of pedagogical subjects for definite study "either in separate courses or in such combinations as convenience or necessity demands," (see p. 204). An indication of the quantity of pedagogical study is provided by the chairman's statement that when the prospective teacher's preparation did not extend beyond the baccalaureate degree "at least one-eighth of his undergraduate work should be devoted to such professional branches." It is likely that majority opinion of the time favored somewhat less than this amount, and it appears that in 1907 the thinking in colleges and universities relative to the amount of pedagogical work was in terms of 12 to 15 semester hours. The National Survey reported the "average" opinion of both academic instructors and education instructors to be 23 semester hours of pedagogical work (Vol. III, p. 259). Thus with reference to the quantitative definition of the purposes of the teacher education the trend of the period in colleges and universities was to increase the amount of time devoted to pedagogical work.

Comparison between normal schools and teachers colleges on the one hand and colleges and universities on the other must be made with caution because of differences in the classification of courses, but it seems clear that while opinion in normal schools and teachers colleges was changing in the direction of reducing the amount of time devoted to pedagogical work, opinion in colleges and universities was changing in the direction of increasing the amount of such study. If probable differences in the classification of courses are recognized, it appears that the two groups approached agreement by 1930.

---

[70] E. S. Evenden, "What Courses in Education Are Desirable in a Four-year Curriculum in a State Teachers College? What Should Be Their Scope?" *Yearbook* (American Association of Teachers Colleges, 1926), pp. 57-71.

[71] Thomas W. Butcher, "Immediate Problems of the Teachers Colleges of the United States," *Yearbook* (American Association of Teachers Colleges, 1922), p. 27, 28.

Hill's statement in 1910 (see p. 209) and other evidence of this time indicate a degree of complacency in regard to further definition of purposes within the area of technical-professional training and the record of the period reveals little penetrating consideration of the matter. However, there was some change in the thinking. In the recommendations of the National Survey Evenden outlined the purposes in the "distinctly professional" area in terms of seven phases:

(a) Professional orientation — the relationship of education to society and the possibilities open in educational service.

(b) Educational "service" courses — the essential concepts and techniques used frequently in other courses and in educational literature.

(c) An understanding of the children to be taught.

(d) A knowledge of the essential methods of teaching for the grade or subject to be taught.

(e) A knowledge of the organization and management of class instruction in various types of schools.

(f) Acquisition of a "safety minimum" of teaching skill through observation, participation, and practice teaching.

(g) A summarized and integrated "working philosophy" of education and an understanding of the individual's relationship to education and society.[72]

When this recommendation of the "distinctly professional elements in the education of teachers" is compared with that of the Committee of Seventeen in 1907 (see p. 204) and certain earlier pronouncements, some indications of "progress" may be noted. There is a change from designations in terms of organizations of professional subject matter (e.g. history of education and educational psychology) to specifications of areas of professional learnings. This change in terminology reflects a closer identification of the objectives of teacher education with the "nature of the work the teacher is to do." At the earlier time the "thinking" was (a) the teacher should have "a comprehension of the science of mind as an energy, and of that of mental growth and mental stimulation," (b) educational psychology was the subject of instruction to provide this "comprehension," and (c) thus "educational psychology" was employed as a qualification designation. The 1933 statement implies that "an understanding of the children to be taught" is to be kept in mind as a designation of purpose, educational psychology being looked upon as a means to this end. Another change is the explicit recognition of "professional orientation" and of a "working philosophy" as important teacher qualifications. Although some traces of these teacher qualifications may be noted in writings of the period up to 1907, they may be regarded as "new." The teacher was to be more than a classroom technician.

---

[72] E. S. Evenden, *Summary and Interpretation,* National Survey of the Education of Teachers, Vol. VI (U.S. Office of Education, Bulletin 1933, No. 10), pp. 173-74.

A significant development in the definition of the purpose of the professional phase of teacher education was a change in relative emphasis upon the subareas of pedagogical study. The analysis of the development of the period from 1890 to 1907 (see pp. 199f.) was in terms of five subareas: (a) educational ideas, (b) psychological knowledge, (c) principles (theory) of methodology, (d) procedures and techniques, and (e) teaching skills. Although it is somewhat difficult to apply this analysis to the thinking of the later years of the period from 1907 to 1933, it will be employed as a means of indicating the trend of the definition of the purposes of pedagogical phase of teacher education.

During the years immediately following 1907 "educational ideas" were given considerable emphasis as a subarea of professional training, especially in colleges and universities. In 1915 Bolton [73] stated that history of education "still continues to be one of the leading subjects in the curriculum." His study also revealed principles of education to be a relatively popular course. Philosophy of education was given in fewer institutions and attracted relatively few students. Walk's study [74] of fifty pairs of normal school catalogs showed that forty-five of the institutions required history of education in 1904 and forty-four in 1914. At both times it was next to "psychology" in frequency of requirement. Philosophy of education had decreased in frequency from 13 to 9.

A questionnaire study reported by Stoutemeyer [75] in 1918 suggests that history of education had declined as a requirement in normal schools. In 1915 Bolton noted a growing belief in departments of education that "history of education yields less valuable results for the undergraduate than most of the other branches." [76] Thomasson's study [77] revealed a decline in the average semester-hour requirements in history of education, principles of education, and philosophy of education from 5.23 in 1910-11 to 4.27 in 1930-31. A study of opinion of the relative value of seven education courses at the time of the National Survey placed history of education last and philosophy of education fifth. This was true for both theory teachers and nontheory teachers. [78] A request for an evaluation of "courses in general educational theory (as now taught)" re-

[73] Frederick E. Bolton, "Curricula in University Departments of Education," *School and Society*, 2 (1915), 829-41.

[74] George E. Walk, "A Decade of Tendencies in Curricula of State Normal Schools," *Education*, 37 (1916), 209-29.

[75] J. H. Stoutemeyer, "The Teaching of the History of Education in Normal Schools," *School and Society*, 7 (1918), 571-80.

[76] F. E. Bolton, *op. cit.*

[77] A. L. Thomasson, *op. cit.*

[78] Obed J. Williamson, *Provisions for General Theory Courses in the Professional Education of Teachers* (Contributions to Education, No. 684 [New York: Bureau of Publications, Teachers College, Columbia University, 1936]), p. 112.

vealed [79] that 59 per cent of nontheory teachers and 82 per cent of theory teachers regarded these courses as "of great value" or "indispensable in a teacher-training program." Certain other findings [80] suggest that the opinion relative to general education theory then being taught was somewhat less favorable than these findings indicate.

The record of the period (1907-33) reflects continued emphasis upon "psychological knowledge." Thomasson's study of the four-year general curriculums in normal schools and teachers colleges revealed practically no change in the psychology requirements from 1910-11 to 1930-31, but there was a large increase in the elective courses offered.[81] This development suggests an increased emphasis upon the psychological area of teacher education. The emphasis in colleges and universities was possibly greater. In addition to the continued and perhaps somewhat increased emphasis upon psychological knowledge, there was some tendency to broaden the area, under the designation of educational science, in the direction of biology, physiology, and sociology.

Principles (theory) of methodology, which in 1907 appeared to be developing as a rather definite subarea of professional training, did not become a distinctive course area and hence it is difficult to appraise the modification of emphasis on it. It appears, however, that in the typical thinking, principles (theory) of methodology came to be minimized as an area of professional training. In 1918 Charters [82] asserted that principles of teaching were inadequate as guides to efficient classroom teaching and argued for engendering "specifics." In reporting the study of Missouri normal schools, the authors observed that "in spite of their nebulous character, the courses in general method and the principles of teaching seem to meet a real need," but it was found that teachers rating professional subjects in the order of their importance gave a slightly higher value to special-methods courses than those in general method.[83] In 1926 Evenden [84] reported that about one-third of the teachers colleges gave "courses in general methods" but in most cases the content tended to be a composite of special methods. Kruse's analy-

---

[79] Ibid., pp. 106-7.

[80] Ibid., p. 104.

[81] A. L. Thomasson, op. cit., pp. 236, 241.

[82] W. W. Charters, "The Inadequacy of Principles of Teaching," Educational Administration and Supervision, 4 (1918), 215-21; "The Administration of Methods of Teaching," Educational Administration and Supervision, 4 (1918), 237-44.

[83] William S. Learned, William C. Bagley, and Others, The Professional Preparation of Teachers for American Public Schools (New York: The Carnegie Foundation for the Advancement of Teaching, Bulletin No. 14, 1920), pp. 189, 442.

[84] E. S. Evenden, "What Courses in Education Are Desirable in a Four-year Curriculum in a State Teachers College? What Should Be Their Scope?" Yearbook (American Association of Teachers Colleges, 1926), pp. 57-71.

sis [85] of catalogs of 116 teachers colleges for 1927-28 revealed that a course in "principles of teaching" was required by 51 per cent of these institutions in their two-year curriculums. In 1930 Merrill [86] reported a controlled experiment in which the findings favored general methods.

The decline in the emphasis upon "educational ideas" (history of education, philosophy of education, and the like) in the thinking about the purposes of teacher education was accompanied by an increased emphasis upon "procedures and techniques" (educational measurements, statistics and other research techniques, and procedures of supervision and administration as well as instructional techniques) and upon "teaching skills." The trend is reflected in the education courses proposed as required in a four-year curriculum for the preparation of elementary teachers.[87] Thirteen quarter-hours were to be devoted to elementary statistics and measurement, classroom procedures, and practice teaching and only three quarter-hours to history and philosophy of education. This comparison probably exaggerates the minimization of "educational ideas," because there was considerable infiltration of educational theory and educational history into a number of courses such as "introduction to education" which was a recommended requirement. However, it is clear that Evenden was placing major emphasis upon "procedures and techniques" and "teaching skills" and was assigning a minor and perhaps incidental position to "educational ideas."

Williamson reported the vote on certain propositions which probably reflects the general appraisal of "procedures and techniques" as a subarea in the professional training of teachers. One of the most revealing of these propositions was: "The need for courses in general educational theory in teacher-training institutions should gradually disappear as a growing science of education shall continually improve our techniques and objective tests and measures." [88] Although this proposition was favored by considerably less than 50 per cent of the respondents, it is significant that it was favored by 16 per cent of the theory teachers. On the proposition of increasing the "place given to specific techniques and measurements," 49 per cent of the theory teachers gave a favorable vote.

The changes in relative emphasis among the subareas of professional training suggest practicality as the dominant criterion in the thinking

[85] Samuel A. Krusé, A Critical Analysis of Principles of Teaching as a Basic Course in Teacher-training Curricula (Contributions to Education, No. 63 [Nashville, Tennessee: George Peabody College for Teachers, 1929]), pp. 70-88.

[86] R. C. Merrill, "The Efficacy of Special vs. General Methods Courses in a Teacher-training Program," Educational Administration and Supervision, 16 (1930), 338-44.

[87] E. S. Evenden, op. cit., p. 68.

[88] O. J. Williamson, op. cit., pp. 103f.

about the purposes of the pedagogical education of teachers. There is considerable evidence to support this hypothesis. In January, 1919, the department of education of the University of Kansas formerly approved the following statements.

(1) Courses as they are now offered in most departments of education have rarely been tested as to their practical values to teachers; (2) The present movement for determining minimum essentials in elementary school subjects is just as valid when applied to the training of teachers; (3) The evaluation of courses in education by recently trained and successful teachers and school administrators is one of the most reliable sources of information for determining minimum essentials.[89]

Although this action by an institutional group of educationists should not be taken as necessarily typical of the thinking of the time, it seems to have reflected an emerging trend.

Kelly also reported a study in which a questionnaire was addressed to a "selected list of 500 superintendents, principals, and high school teachers in Kansas" soliciting their appraisals of the "practical value" of professional courses and of representative topics within certain courses. The following conclusion is indicative of the developing attitude. "There is an insistent demand [by teachers and school administrators] that the professional courses be planned with a view to meeting specifically the problems of the profession." Following this study other investigators attempted similar evaluations. In 1922 C. O. Davis reported a summary of the opinions of high-school teachers.[90] Two similar studies at the University of Minnesota are mentioned in the National Survey (Vol. III, p. 261). The findings of these and other studies indicated a relatively high evaluation of educational psychology, "special methods," and practice teaching and a relatively low evaluation of history of education.

Another line of evidence is afforded by the appearance of job-analysis studies of teaching. In *The Commonwealth Teacher-Training Study* (1929) an inquiry was made to locate "studies containing analysis of teaching." A total of 219 studies "completed, in preparation, or contemplated" was located.[91] Twenty studies were listed bearing dates ranging

---

[89] F. J. Kelly, "A Study of the Values Assigned to Courses in Education and Related Fields by 249 High School Teachers and School Administrators in Kansas," *Studies in Education*, Educational Monographs, No. IX (Society of College Teachers of Education, 1920), p. 3.

[90] C. O. Davis, "The Training, Experience, Salaries, and Educational Judgments of 24,313 of the High-school Teachers in North Central Accredited Schools," *Proceedings*, Part I (North Central Association of Colleges and Secondary Schools, 1922-23), p. 33.

[91] W. W. Charters and Douglas Waples, *The Commonwealth Teacher-Training Study* (Chicago: University of Chicago Press, 1929), p. 80.

from 1920 to 1926.[92] The study itself included an elaborate and systematic analysis resulting in a list of 1,001 activities evaluated with reference to types of teaching positions.[93] A chapter of the report is devoted to illustrating the use of the list in constructing new courses in special methods, school management, and educational psychology.

Although it cannot be described in quantitative terms, it seems evident that during the period from 1907 to 1933 there was a significant shift in the thinking from faith in the efficacy of theory courses (general method or principles of teaching, history of education, and the like) to emphasis upon courses considered to be more immediately practical. Within this trend, however, there was little organized and comprehensive consideration of teacher needs. From about 1920 on, there were some institutional attempts to develop more practical courses and curriculums, but in the National Survey it was observed in the case of normal schools and teachers colleges that curriculums expanded "largely from specialized interests within departments" (Vol. III, p. 51). The situation was found to be similar in colleges and universities (p. 177). Thus as the thinking shifted in the direction of emphasis upon "practical" objectives, the actual definition of purposes in the development of courses tended to be by individuals whose thinking was influenced by their specialized interests. The effect was a state of considerable confusion.

Concluding Statement

During the period from 1907 to 1933 the approach in defining desired teacher qualifications was through studying teachers as they are, and few of the developments in the thinking about the purposes of teacher education can be regarded as major changes. There were many studies directed toward identifying and defining desired teacher qualifications, but there were very few deliberative reports of significance. In fact, the record of the period includes very little systematic consideration of the purposes of teacher education from the point of view of the needs of the profession (see pp. 210f.).

The report of the Committee of Seventeen in 1907 was interpreted as indicating widespread acceptance of pedagogical training as desirable in the education of teachers for secondary schools. Although it was recognized that some persons, especially in academic circles, did not approve of the recommendations of the committee, the difference of opinion does not appear to have resulted in much controversial discussion until later. In the National Survey the "question which is more frequently

---

[92] *Ibid.*, pp. 78-80.
[93] *Ibid.*, pp. 493-646.

raised than any other" was expressed as follows: "Are there any distinctive elements in the education of a teacher which are not found in the education of any well-educated person?" (see p. 231). As stated, the question is misleading. It seems clear that by 1933 the disagreement, except for a few extremists, related to the balance between subject-matter study and pedagogical training, and findings reported in the National Survey indicate that the average opinion of academic instructors in colleges and universities in regard to the amount of education study was the same (23 semester hours) as that of education instructors. Comparable data for the beginning of the period are not available, but it is likely that the proportion of academic instructors who believed that pedagogical training was desirable had increased, perhaps materially. However, the change cannot be regarded as especially momentous.

During the early years of the period there was little concern about the teaching-knowledge qualification beyond what was implied by the term "scholarship." In academic circles there were many who maintained that a liberal education, including a "heavy concentration" in one high-school teaching field to obtain an "appreciation of the depth of all knowledge," was adequate preparation for "a selected person with good habits of study" to teach in any field "related to his major" in which he has had an introductory course. This position denies even academic specialization in anticipated teaching fields as a necessary qualification. In other words, the teacher was thought of as a generalist rather than a specialist. At the time of the National Survey 51 per cent of academic instructors in colleges and universities expressed adherence to this position. There were significant numbers of adherents in other groups — education instructors, 20 per cent; teachers-college instructors (all types), 32 per cent (Vol. III, p. 247).

In between this position and that represented by the proponents of professionalized treatment of subject matter, there were those who believed that an adequate teaching knowledge in a prospective teacher's major and minor fields could be obtained by appropriate prescriptions and other regulations of elections. Some institutions announced curriculums for various types of teaching positions. In some cases these curriculums and the major and minor requirements in other institutions reflect belief in the desirability of professionalized treatment of subject matter. This was more often true of normal schools and teachers colleges than of colleges and universities.

The presence of these three rather clearly defined positions created a situation in which one would expect to find considerable controversial discussion. However, outside of the writings of Bagley and other proponents of professionalized treatment of subject matter, the literature of the period includes very little that may be regarded as controversial.

In the *Summary and Intrepretation,* National Survey of the Education of Teachers, a number of problems and issues are listed (pp. 17-20). The only one definitely concerned with the teaching-knowledge qualification is a question in regard to the amount of college work. Hence it appears that the concern about this qualification area was below the level of a controversial issue.

In the National Survey it was reported that practically all (97 per cent) of college and university faculties favored some professionalized study of subject matter and that the average opinion favored the "professionalization of nearly one-third of the curriculum" (Vol. III, p. 276). These findings, however, should be interpreted in the light of the report that the "professional treatment of so-called subject-matter courses for teachers is almost negligible in liberal arts colleges and universities" (Vol. III, p. 277). In explaining this discrepancy between belief and practice it was pointed out that the "proposal is not widely known." This implies that the aggressive proponents of professional treatment of subject matter were not numerous. However, in view of the low ebb of interest in this phase of teacher education in 1907, it seems clear that significant gains had been made by 1933.

In 1907 educationists were in general agreement in regard to desired pedagogical qualifications and seemed to have had faith in the courses they were offering as means for engendering these qualifications. However, uncertainty, if not skepticism, developed and immediate practicality became a major criterion in their thinking. The emphasis in the pedagogical-qualification area shifted from educational ideas to specifics; the desired teacher qualifications tended to be those of the technician. This change and the phenomenal multiplication of education courses during the 1920's suggest confusion in the thinking of educationists. A few individuals and some institutional groups made progress in clarifying their thinking, but within the total group of educationists there was much confusion.

CHAPTER 8

Modifications of Desired
Qualifications, 1933 to 1950

At the 1933 meeting of the American Association of Teachers Colleges a session was devoted to the National Survey of the Education of Teachers.[1] E. S. Evenden, associate director of the Survey, presented a "few selected facts" from the findings and certain "proposals." "Preliminary reports" on certain topics had been published in *School Life,* but Evenden's presentation seems to have been the first opportunity for the American Association of Teachers Colleges, which had been instrumental in promoting the Survey, to react to a systematic account. The discussion was opened by W. P. Morgan, a member of the Board of Consultants and one of the leaders in promoting the Survey. He expressed himself as being considerably disappointed in the Survey, because it had not yielded "scientific" answers to problems of teacher education. The other participants in the discussion had little acquaintance with the Survey and on the whole were noncommittal in their remarks. R. W. Fairchild did note the lack of a consideration of the "relationship of teacher education to the schools." However, neither Morgan's extended discussion nor the following reactions suggest any serious concern about defining the purposes of teacher education. Morgan explicitly subscribed to the proposition that the qualifications to be desired were those of the "good" teachers in our schools.

---

[1] *Twelfth Yearbook* (American Association of Teachers Colleges, 1933), pp. 99-145.

In 1934 the Yearbook Committee of the National Society of College Teachers of Education was asked to "present to the Society a criticism of the National Survey of the Education of Teachers." In the *Twenty-third Yearbook* (1935) the Committee criticized the Survey for not giving more attention to the "trends in elementary and secondary education" as a basis of evaluating "current programs of teacher preparation" and as a source of constructive proposals (pp. 7-8). This is a significant criticism. It suggests a general principle relative to the definition of the purposes of teacher education — namely, the starting point should be a consideration of the purposes of our schools, elementary and secondary. This principle, which had been emphasized by Charles H. Judd[2] in 1933, stands in contrast to the approach through studying teachers as they are, which characterized the thinking of the preceding period and dominated the deliberations of those who planned the National Survey. It should be noted also that this principle is essentially the same as the thesis underlying the thinking of Parr in 1888 (see p. 183).

Further evidence of the emerging thesis implied by the criticism of the National Survey by the Yearbook Committee of the National Society of College Teachers of Education is furnished by the activity of the American Council on Education which culminated in the organization of the Commission on Teacher Education in 1938. Preliminary deliberations beginning early in 1936 resulted in a subcommittee report[3] under the title, *Major Issues in Teacher Education*. In the subcommittee report the exposition of "some typical problems" begins with the heading, "The objectives of teacher education need a thorough revision and restatement" (p. 10). In the argument justifying this asserted need the subcommittee noted the lack of an adequate formulation of teacher-education purposes and emphasized recognition of the purposes of our schools as basis in developing the objectives of teacher education. Thus it appears that between the planning of the National Survey and its publication[4] there had been a change in the general point of view relative to the basis for constructive thinking about teacher education.

The American Association of Teachers Colleges became a center of activity in defining the purposes of teacher education from the point of view of the contemporary concept of the aim of education. The program of the 1937 meeting of the Association included two addresses reflecting

---

[2] Charles H. Judd, "Next Steps in the Improvement of Teacher Training," *Twelfth Yearbook* (American Association of Teachers Colleges, 1933), pp. 25-31.

[3] Subcommittee on Teacher Education Problems, *Major Issues in Teacher Education*, (American Council on Education Studies, Series I, Vol. II, No. 4, 1938). 44 pp. This report was made early in 1937 but was not published until the following year.

[4] Although the National Survey of the Education of Teachers was published as Bulletin 1933, No. 10, of the U.S. Office of Education, the actual printing seems to have been completed during 1935.

concern about the definition of the purposes of teacher education. W. W. Charters [5] pointed out that a "thorough understanding of children" had been "a paper objective in the training of teachers from the beginning." This observation and the following discussion imply that this objective had not been sufficiently defined in the thinking of those who had planned programs of teacher education. George F. Zook [6] speaking on "what ought to be done" listed first the development of "a concise but comprehensive statement of objectives for the education of teachers." The implication of this statement, which Zook made clear, is that the purposes of teacher education had not been adequately defined.

In view of the limited explicit attention to objectives of teacher education in the literature of the period from 1907 to 1933 and in the National Survey, especially in the planning of the project, this emphasis upon the need for defining the purposes of teacher education indicates a significant general development. Further evidence of the change in the attention to the formulation of objectives of teacher education is furnished by a study by a subcommittee of the Committee on Standards and Surveys of the American Association of Teachers Colleges reported in 1940. Questionnaire returns were obtained from 150 institutions. The section under "curriculum objectives" begins with the statement: "Two-thirds of the faculties have formulated or accepted a set of curriculum 'objectives' — in most cases since 1935, and with the students participating in 8 per cent of the institutions." [7] Although it is not specifically indicated, this reported finding is probably to be interpreted as meaning that prior to 1935 relatively few of the institutions had developed or adopted a formulation of curriculum objectives.

The emerging recognition of the need for a "thorough revision and restatement" of the objectives of teacher education and the change in the approach to considering the purposes of our schools, elementary and secondary, as the basis of planning teacher education were the resultant of influences that had been gaining momentum for several years before 1933. A major influence was the revolutionary change in the secondary school, its purposes, and curriculum.

During the second decade of the century, opposition developed to the pattern of secondary education set by the Committee of Ten (1894) and by the Committee of College Entrance Requirements (1899) and enforced by the entrance requirements of colleges and universities. Fol-

---

[5] W. W. Charters, "Education Neglects Its Fundamental Bases," *Sixteenth Yearbook* (American Association of Teachers Colleges, 1937), pp. 10-15.

[6] George F. Zook, "Teacher Education as I See It," *Sixteenth Yearbook* (American Association of Teachers Colleges, 1937), pp. 34-40.

[7] E. S. Evenden, "Some Interpretive Comments on the Report on Curriculum Practices in Normal Schools and Teachers Colleges in the United States," *Nineteenth Yearbook* (American Association of Teachers Colleges, 1940), pp. 140-43.

lowing 1920, this opposition became more extensive and more insistent. Curriculum innovations were introduced in numerous secondary schools, but within the framework of the entrance requirements of the higher institutions of the respective states. However, the changes occurring in secondary schools do not appear to have impressed teacher educators as having significant implications relative to the purposes of teacher education.

In 1932 the Commission on the Relation of School and College of the Progressive Education Association obtained the cooperation of "more than 300 colleges and universities" for the Eight-year Study. This cooperation involved releasing recommended graduates of participating secondary schools from the "usual subject and unit requirements for college admission for a period of five years, beginning with the class entering college in 1936.[8] This action by a large group of colleges and universities appears to symbolize an emerging recognition among higher institutions that secondary schools were becoming different and that consequently the traditional qualifications would not provide teachers adequately prepared for service in these schools.

Paralleling changes in the program of secondary schools there emerged a new concept of the teacher's function. For years teachers had been spoken of as teaching subjects — reading, arithmetic, algebra, Latin, history, etc. (see pp. 122f.). Following the publication of S. Chester Parker's *Methods of Teaching in High Schools* in 1915 the teacher became thought of as a director of learning activities (see pp. 131f.). About the same time the development of the project method focused attention on the teaching-learning theory designated as "guiding pupil experiencing" (see pp. 145f.). Although school practice, especially at the secondary level, lagged behind these developments in teaching-learning theory, by 1933 the teacher was becoming more than one who merely taught school subjects. This development, which has continued, also focused attention on the need for redefining the objectives of teacher education.

An Illustration of Change in Thinking

Since little explicit attention had been given to defining the purposes of teacher education during the years preceding 1933, it is difficult to identify changes in the concept of purposes. However, certain changes are reflected in a comparison of writings of E. S. Evenden in 1926 with a statement made in 1938. In 1926 he addressed the National Council of Education [9] on the topic: "Criteria for the Construction of Teachers Col-

[8] Wilford M. Aikin, *The Story of the Eight-year Study* (New York: Harper and Brothers, 1942), p. 12.

[9] E. S. Evenden, "Criteria for the Construction of Teachers College Curricula," *Teachers College Record*, 27 (1925-26), 882-93.

lege Curricula." The following was listed as one of the five "specific problems of most pressing importance today in the preparation of teachers in this country": "What should be the approved professional, cultural, and social equipment of teachers for the various positions in the public schools?" In the brief discussion of this question Evenden stated that "we need an actual listing of the things done by each kind of teacher and of the skills and knowledge needed in the performance of his tasks." He then dismissed the matter by saying "such studies are now under way." Later he indicated his concept of the general-education qualification by saying that the adequately trained teacher should be "well grounded in practically all of the better known fields of human knowledge — language, literature, social science, natural and physical science, mathematics, music, fine and industrial arts, and health."

The same year Evenden addressed the American Association of Teachers Colleges on the topic: [10] "What Courses in Education are Desirable in a Four-year Curriculum in a State Teachers College? What Should Be Their Scope?" Although he observed that these questions should be answered by means of experimental study, he approached them in this paper by reporting an analysis of the catalogs of 102 teachers colleges relative to the "required" courses in education. Six "required" courses were proposed for teachers in the intermediate grades: (1) Introduction to teaching (or education), (2) Elementary educational statistics and measurements, (3) Educational psychology, (4) Classroom procedures, (5) Practice teaching, and (6) History and principles of education.[11] Under each of these courses Evenden listed "principal purposes." Taken together the statements emphasize the following teacher qualifications: (1) "an intelligent interest in children, their development, interests, and methods of work;" (2) knowledge of "principles of measurement — mental and educational" and "principles of conducting simple educational experiments;" (3) acquaintance with "elements of classroom management;" and (4) "a reasonable degree of proficiency in the art of teaching."

In 1938 E. S. Evenden [12] after emphasizing the importance of defining purposes, outlined the "large objectives in teacher education" as follows:

---

[10] E. S. Evenden, "What Courses in Education Are Desirable in a Four-year Curriculum in a State Teachers College? What Should Be Their Scope?" *Yearbook* (American Association of Teachers Colleges, 1926), pp. 57-71.

[11] A seventh course—Observation and specialized practice teaching—was proposed for those who interrupted their preparation at the end of two years and then completed the four-year curriculum after some years of teaching.

[12] E. S. Evenden, "What is the Essential Nature of an Evolving Curriculum of a Teachers College," *Seventeenth Yearbook* (American Association of Teachers Colleges, 1938), pp. 5-16.

1. Knowledge of the individuals to be taught.

2. A broad cultural background in the principal fields of organized knowledge. [In the elaboration under this head Evenden emphasized "a sympathetic over-view of the society and the social conditions under which children are living" and "an understanding of the principles of the American and other forms of government and the significance of a democracy."]

3. A broad scholarly mastery of the field or fields to be taught and a supporting knowledge of the most closely related fields.

4. An understanding of the relationships between education and society and a realization of the important contributions that the teacher can make toward the "social, political and economic stability and betterment" of our American form of government.

5. [Supplemenary to 1] An understanding and mastery of the professional knowledge and skills needed for successful initial teaching experience. [In the elaboration Evenden employed such phrases as "laws of learning," "principles of teaching," "educational measurements," "most approved methods of teaching," "teaching skill," "essential technics of guidance," and "mechanical aids."]

6. A well-rounded and well-integrated personality such as will assure a position of leadership in the school and community.

7. A guiding philosophy both of education and of life.

Comparison of this pronouncement with Evenden's writings of 1926 indicates significant changes in his thinking about the purposes of teacher education. In 1926 the reference to personal-fitness qualifications was limited to saying that the "personal and social equipment of the teacher" shquld be strengthened and developed. In 1938 "a well-rounded and well-integrated personality" was listed as one of the "large objectives of teacher education." Furthermore, this personality was defined as one which would "assure a position of leadership in the school and community."

The change in the general-education qualification area is indicated by Evenden's emphasis in 1938 on "a sympathetic over-view of the society and the social conditions under which children are living" and "an understanding of the principles of the American and other forms of government and the significance of a democracy." The teacher should also be cognizant of the contribution he is in position to make toward "the social, political and economic stability and betterment" of our American form of government. In the light of later developments (see p. 246), one is tempted to interpret these items as implying that the teacher should be equipped to promote the development of a democratic social order, but Evenden's comments do not appear to justify this interpretation. Although the general-education qualification was stressed in 1926, the emphasis in Evenden's statement was on being "well grounded in practically all of the better known fields of human knowledge." The change from this concept of general education for teachers to that indicated by his 1938 specification is a significant development.

Within the teaching-knowledge qualification area the 1938 reference to "a supporting knowledge of the most closely related fields" and the employment of the phrase "broad scholarly mastery" indicate an emphasis upon breadth of learning. Since Evenden did not deal specifically with the teaching-knowledge qualifications in his 1926 writings, the change in his thinking relative to this area is not very apparent. In 1926 there were some rather incidental references to the professionalization of subject-matter courses and it appears that the focus of emphasis in his thinking about the teaching-knowledge qualification shifted from this aspect to "broad scholarly mastery" of the teaching field and acquaintance with related fields.

The more significant changes in Evenden's thinking relative to the pedagogical qualification area are indicated by items 4 and 7 in the above list. They refer to what may be designated as a modernized version of "educational ideas." These phases of the technical-professional qualification area were not explicitly mentioned in his 1926 writings and hence they apparently represent an expansion of his concept of professional training. In 1926 the emphasis was on professional training for technician efficiency. This phase of the professional qualification was not minimized in 1938, except perhaps relatively, but there was emphasis upon what may be referred to as professional education for "constructive efficiency."

The General Development

The changes relative to the definition of the purposes of teacher education reflected by Evenden's writings in 1926 and in 1938 appear to be representative in several respects. In summarizing a study of curriculum requirements in fifty-five state teachers colleges in 1928 and 1938, Sprague [13] noted several changes relative to apparent purpose: in the general-education area — "a richer cultural background," "a clearer understanding of present day life," and "away from formal academic courses"; in the teaching-knowledge area — "more adequate scholarship" and "broader majors for specialization purposes"; and in the pedagogical qualification area — "away from courses which emphasize teaching skills and routine in management" toward "courses or types of subject matter which emphasize 'points of view'" or "interpretative background." The changes thus indicated correspond closely to those inferred from Evenden's writings. No similar comparison of requirements in colleges and universities has been reported, but fragmentary evidence indicates the development of thinking relative to purposes of teacher education corresponds to that among teachers colleges.

---

[13] H. A. Sprague, *A Decade of Progress in the Preparation of Secondary School Teachers* (Contributions to Education, No. 794 [New York: Bureau of Publications, Teachers College, Columbia University, 1940]). 170 pp.

In 1940 E. S. Evenden [14] as chairman of a subcommittee of the Committee on Standards and Surveys of the American Association of Teachers Colleges reported on the "curriculum practices" of normal schools and teachers colleges. The section of the questionnaire bearing on objectives was apparently organized in terms of Evenden's outline of the "large objectives in teacher education" presented in 1938. The summary of the questionnaire responses showed general recognition of these large objectives, but the reported variations in means provided for realizing them suggest varying interpretations and/or inadequate application in reconstructing the curriculum. It is significant that all institutions reporting stated that they were attempting by specific means to contribute to the development of "well-rounded and well-integrated personalities." Ninety-nine per cent reported assembly programs as one of the means employed. With respect to the realization of recognized objectives it is perhaps significant that under "a guiding philosophy of both education and life" Evenden noted certain elements reported as "needing *more* attention."

A "platform of principles, suggesting a national concept of teacher education" was published in 1940.[15] This formulation was prepared by a joint committee of the National Education Association and the American Association of Teachers Colleges and a large number of educational leaders contributed to it. The "platform" begins with the statement: "Teacher education in a democracy must have a definite objective." It is indicated that this objective should include the following goals: (1) an understanding of the purposes and functions of education in our democracy, (2) an understanding of the major problems of social life, (3) an understanding of the vital problems in connection with the growth and development of children, (4) an understanding of the organization and control of learning programs in the school, (5) development of leaders in the major learning areas and learning levels, and (6) knowledge and understanding of the application of methods and uses of materials suited to the different learning levels.

In 1941 the American Association of Teachers Colleges revised its Standard VII to specify that the professional objectives of an institution [16]

. . . should include at least the following: (1) an understanding of the development and characteristics of the individuals to be taught; (2) a broad cultural background enriched by varied experiences; (3) a broad scholarly

---

[14] E. S. Evenden, *Nineteenth Yearbook* (American Association of Teachers Colleges, 1940), pp. 140-43.

[15] *Addresses and Proceedings* (National Education Association, 1940), pp. 910-11. Also published in leaflet form, May, 1940. The formulation was tentatively adopted by the National Education Association in 1939.

[16] *Twentieth Yearbook* (American Association of Teachers Colleges, 1941), p. 147.

mastery of the field or fields to be taught and an ability and willingness to use the methods of critical inquiry in such fields; (4) an understanding of the relationship between education and society, particularly a democratic society, and a desire to promote and to implement democratic ideals; (5) a "safety minimum" mastery of the professional knowledge and skills needed by teachers and a desire to continue professional growth; (6) a well-rounded and well-integrated personality and the ability to assist others to develop such personalities; and (7) a guiding philosophy of education and of life.

It will be noted that this list of objectives follows closely the outline formulated by Evenden in 1938 (see p. 246), which may be considered as representing a preliminary stage in the development. The modifications in phraseology in items 3, 4, 5, and 6 appear to introduce supplementary qualifications. In addition to possessing certain personal qualities, understandings, knowledges, and skills, the teacher should be willing "to use the methods of critical inquiry" in his field or fields of teaching, should have a desire "to continue professional growth," should be able "to assist others to develop" well-rounded and well-integrated personalities, and should have the "desire to promote and implement democratic ideals." The last of these supplementary qualifications is especially significant; it designates a teacher-education purpose which had been emerging during the two or three preceding years as a result of the developing world conflict.

The significance of the action of the American Association of Teachers Colleges in 1941 becomes more apparent when the above formulation is compared with the preceding statement of Standard VII adopted in 1932. In this statement [17] there is no reference to objectives. The point of emphasis was that there must be "definite requirements with reference to sequence of courses." The Proceedings of the Association during the following years reflect dissatisfaction with the standards adopted in 1932 and in 1936 the Committee on Standards and Surveys proposed that it be authorized to develop "qualitative" standards.[18] The revision of the Standard VII adopted in 1941 is a product of the efforts of this Committee to develop a qualitative standard relative to the curriculum.

A questionnaire study of the status of teachers colleges relative to the objectives of Standard VII was reported in 1943.[19] The details of the report are too numerous to mention here and only a few general statements will be made. The findings were interpreted as justifying "professional satisfaction" in regard to some elements of the inquiry. Professional objectives, presumably along the lines of Standard VII, had

[17] *Eleventh Yearbook* (American Association of Teachers Colleges, 1932), p. 21.

[18] *Fifteenth Yearbook* (American Association of Teachers Colleges, 1936), p. 166.

[19] E. S. Evenden, "A Study of Educational Objectives in Normal Schools and Teachers Colleges in the United States in 1942-43," *Twenty-second Yearbook*, 1943, pp. 104-18.

been adopted by 84 per cent of the institutions. The increase from two-thirds in 1940 (see p. 243) to this proportion indicates the growing concern about the objectives of teacher education. The objective, "an understanding of the development and characteristics of the individuals to be taught," was generally considered to be satisfactorily provided for by the courses in child psychology and "human growth and development." General education was considered well cared for, especially in the social sciences, science, and mathematics. General satisfaction was expressed relative to courses dealing with principles and theory of education and educational psychology as means of engendering a philosophy of education and of life.

A report by the Commission on Teacher Education, published in 1944, provides a statement of the considered thinking of a group of leaders in teacher education.[20] This Commission, a group of sixteen persons appointed in 1938, represented "a wide variety of educational interests." The first draft of the report, prepared by Karl W. Bigelow, was discussed by the Commission and then revised in the light of the criticisms and suggestions made. This procedure was continued until the statement expressed the "common convictions of the Commission." Thus the published report is the product of persistent group thinking about the purposes of teacher education and in view of the "wide variety of educational interests represented," the fact that it is announced as an "official Commission statement" of the "common convictions" of the membership makes the report one of major significance.

The treatment of "qualities needed in teachers" is in general terms and it is emphasized that good teachers will not be identical. Within this setting the "balance and integration of qualities" exhibited by a teacher are recognized as a significant aspect of that teacher's qualifications. Following this general principle, the more "general" qualities are discussed under "respect for personality," "community-mindedness," "rational behavior," and "skill in cooperation." The more "professional" qualities are dealt with under "increasing knowledge [general and specialized]," "skill in mediating knowledge," "friendliness with children," "understanding children," "social understanding and behavior," "good citizenship in the school as society," and "skill in evaluation." "Faith in the worth of teaching" is noted as a "broad" quality.[21]

This outline of "qualities needed in teachers" appears in the final pages of the volume, and presumably the preceding argument represents the thinking of the Commission in arriving at its "common convictions" relative to teacher-education purposes. The immediately preceding sections

[20] Commission on Teacher Education, *Teachers for Our Times* (Washington, D. C.: American Council on Education, 1944). 178 pp.

[21] *Ibid.*, pp. 154-75.

are under the titles: Our Country, Our People and Our Children, Our Schools. It is clear that the Commission approached the defining of the "qualities needed in teachers" on the basis of what our schools are doing and should attempt to do. The validity of the Commission's thinking is indicated by Peik's comment that the outline of teacher qualifications is in agreement with the conclusions [22] arrived at from the "best clues from carefully interpreted research of the last fifteen years."

The pronouncements noted in the preceding pages make clear that the period following the National Survey (1933) was one of major significance relative to the evolution of the definition of purposes. In contrast to the relative indifference of the preceding period toward the purposes of teacher education, there emerged a commitment to the formulation of appropriate, definite objectives of teacher education. The approach in this formulation was from the purposes of education in our democracy and the conceived functions of teachers in our schools rather than a dependence upon scientific studies of teachers as they are. The thinking tended to be in terms of qualitative rather than quantitative considerations and in terms of desired learnings (competencies) rather than subject-matter areas of study. In its pronouncement the Commission on Teacher Education deliberately avoided quantitative specifications.[23]

An Emerging Integration

One student [24] of the matter has noted a trend toward an integration of the teacher's education beyond the first two years of collegiate study under the general designation of "professional," thus eliminating the differentiation of further general-education and teaching-knowledge purposes from pedagogical purposes. Although the Commission on Teacher Education did not make an explicit statement in its report, the assignment of the general qualities of "respect for personality," "community-mindedness," "rational behavior," and "skill in cooperation" to general education [25] and the inclusion of "increasing knowledge" under "professional" qualities definitely imply the extension of professional training into the areas of general education and subject-matter concentration. In a report prepared for the Commission on Teacher Education there is the explicit statement that the "professional education" should begin in

[22] W. E. Peik, "The Preservice Preparation of Teachers," *Review of Educational Research*, 13 (1943), 228-40.

[23] Qualitative specifications are emphasized in a number of recent writings. For example, see Hugh S. Bonar, "What Shall We Emphasize in the Selection and Training of Teachers?" *Educational Administration and Supervision*, 27 (1941), 683-91.

[24] H. M. Lafferty, "The Professional Education of Teachers," *Educational Administration and Supervision*, 27 (1941), 195-207.

[25] Commission on Teacher Education, *Teachers for Our Times* (Washington, D. C.: American Council on Education, 1944), p. 162.

the freshman and sophomore year.[26] Hence pedagogical training *combined with* general education and subject-matter specialization seems to be an emerging trend in the thinking of educationists. In academic circles, however, much of the thinking is still in terms of pedagogical training *added to* the other phases of the teacher's education.

Within the framework of these general developments, certain more detailed changes may be noted. They are summarized under the four rubrics employed in dealing with the preceding periods.

Personal Fitness

Evenden's enumeration of the "large objectives in teacher education" in 1938 included "a well-rounded and a well-integrated personality" and it is clear that he had in mind an objective of teacher education and not merely a desirable teacher qualification. The absence of explicit reference to personal fitness in the 1940 "platform of principles" and in other writings of the period suggests limited recognition of personality development as an objective of teacher education. However, insofar as there has been recognition the emphasis has tended to be on "a well-rounded and well-integrated personality" rather than certain identified and evaluated traits.

In 1932 Haggerty[27] proposed that the important consideration was the quality of the teacher-pupil relationship established rather than the absolute status of personality traits of the teacher. The record reveals some recognition of this thesis. Brookower[28] employed a scale for rating teacher-pupil relationships and reported evidence indicating that the quality of relationship was a factor in teaching effectiveness. Bush[29] studied the nature of effective teacher-pupil relationships. On the basis of his findings, he proposed an hypothesis relative to the conditions involved in an optimum relationship. With reference to the teacher's personal fitness· this hypothesis points to fairness and sympathy in dealing with pupils, an informed acquaintance with pupils, and a disposition to counsel with pupils. However, Bush noted that no factor appeared "crucial in all cases" and that "each student-teacher relationship has its own pattern of characteristics."

Haggerty's thesis is compatible with the implications of such a desig-

[26] W. Earl Armstrong, Ernest V. Hollis, and Helen E. Davis, *The College and Teacher Education* (Washington, D. C.: American Council on Education, 1944), p. 306.

[27] M. E. Haggerty, "The Crux of the Teaching Prognosis Problem," *School and Society*, 35 (1932), 545-49.

[28] Wilbur B. Brookower, "Person-Person Interaction between Teachers and Pupils and Teaching Effectiveness," *Journal of Educational Research*, 34 (1940), 272-87.

[29] Robert N. Bush, "A Study of Student-Teacher Relationship," *Journal of Educational Research*, 35 (1942), 645-56.

nation as "a well-rounded and well-integrated personality," but since the emphasis is upon the effect of teacher-pupil interaction rather than upon the specification of teacher traits, its contribution to the definition of the purposes of teacher education is limited. The thinking about "a well-integrated personality" has been in the direction of focusing attention upon the mental health of teachers as an area of teacher-education purposes. Within this area the emphasis has been on the elimination, or at least the amelioration of neurotic tendencies. On the positive side there has been emphasis upon engendering qualities of leadership. Although recent thinking relative to the personality qualification indicates considerable change from that during the years prior to 1933, the recognition of this qualification as an objective of teacher education is still limited and hence the change must be regarded as a relatively minor one.

The thinking of recent years has reflected considerable emphasis upon physical aspects of personal fitness. But again there has been limited recognition as an objective of teacher education. Evenden made no reference to physical fitness in his list of the "large objectives in teacher education."

General Education

The general-education qualification has tended to become less clearly differentiated from the pedagogical qualification. This suggests a tendency toward agreement that the general education of teachers should be professionalized, i.e. it should not be thought of as simply the general education desired for the average citizen. The definition of the general education desired for teachers emphasizes a broad cultural background encompassing the principal fields of organized knowledge and especially an intelligent understanding and appreciation of the social, economic, and political aspects of American life. It is perhaps significant that the definition is in terms of learnings rather than the study of any particular courses. There is also little specification of any quantitative measures of the desired general education of teachers.

Teaching Knowledge

The teaching-knowledge qualification is designated by means of general, qualitative terms. The emphasis is upon "a broad scholarly mastery," the teacher being a "leader" and a student in his field, and understanding "one's own fields in relation to the whole society and its trends and needs." Such designations suggest that the teaching-knowledge qualification is conceived of as including the ability to make adaptations to curricular developments in our schools and to exercise leadership in such changes. Although there have been few explicit references to professionalization of subject-matter courses, this emphasis indicates a type of such study.

The caption, "increasing knowledge," employed by the Commission on Teacher Education, may be regarded as the counterpart of "teaching knowledge." In its exposition of this qualification the Commission recognized the appropriateness of subject-matter specialization but emphasized that a teacher needs also "a background of broad information" and a "considerable acquaintance" with fields of learning closely allied to his specialty. The teacher's "increasing knowledge" from these sources should exhibit the qualities of "breadth, interrelationships, and applications to the solution of personal and social problems." The Commission also emphasized as an aspect of this qualification "that inner drive that results in continuous learning." The use of the designation, "increasing knowledge," suggests that this inner drive is a fundamental quality of this qualification and it may be inferred that "continuous learning" is definitely more important than the quantity of knowledge (study). This implication, together with the Commission's recognition of individual differences among teachers, suggests that the quantitative aspects of this qualification may well vary among teachers educated for teaching in a given subject-matter area, e.g. English.

The Commission's emphasis upon qualitative aspects of the teaching-knowledge qualification, particularly breadth and integration, stands in contrast to the quantitative specifications found in teacher-education curriculums, certificating requirements, and standards of accrediting agencies. In the light of other evidence [30] it appears that the Commission's position represents an emerging trend. As long as the teacher's functions was conceived of primarily in terms of teaching certain school subjects, quantitative specifications were consistent. When the concept of the teacher's function became different, consistency required a change in the thinking about teacher qualifications.[31]

Pedagogical Training

In the area of pedagogical qualifications "knowledge of the individuals to be taught" is interpreted in the direction of emphasis upon personality development as well as intellectual development. This qualification area also includes "an understanding and mastery of the professional knowledge and skills needed for successful initial teaching experience." This "professional knowledge" is not defined beyond rather general designa-

[30] For example, see Alonzo G. Grace, "Teacher Certification—A Problem in Teacher Education," *Educational Record,* January, 1942, Supplement No. 15, pp. 22-33.

[31] For an elaboration, see Allen D. Patterson, "Teacher Certification—Credits or Competencies," *Educational Research Bulletin,* 23 (1944), 233-39.

tions, but it is apparent that principles and laws are to receive considerable emphasis. There is a strong emphasis upon an understanding of the purposes of education in a democracy. The designation, "guiding philosophy of education and of life," indicates a general qualification strongly emphasized by some educationists, especially in teacher education at the graduate level.[32] It should be noted, however, that this "philosophical" qualification, like others in the professional area, has not yet been defined beyond rather general statements.

Concluding Statement

Although taken singly the several changes are perhaps not very impressive, in the composite they mark a very significant development in the thinking about the purposes of teacher education. The "ideal teacher" of the 1920's for a given type of position was a person possessing the traits, knowledges, and skills which scientific investigation would eventually reveal as necessary for performing the various duties involved in that type of position. Some fragmentary scientific studies had been reported, more comprehensive ones were in process, and as the National Survey was planned, many persons hoped that it would contribute much to a scientific definition of the purposes of teacher education. Meanwhile, the balance of opinion was in the direction of (a) providing a broad general education for teachers, (b) engendering teaching knowledge (subject-matter specialization) in two or more subjects, and (c) minimizing professional training by observing the criterion of practicality.

In contrast during the 1940's there was a strong emphasis upon the formulation of definite objectives from the point of view of the purposes of education in our democracy. The "ideal teacher" was a constructive and adaptable member of the school staff, competent to participate in determining school policies and programs and interested in doing so, as well as an efficient instructor in the classroom. The teacher's general education should be broad but, more important, weighted in the direction of social understandings. With reference to teaching knowledge his competence should be at the level of "scholarly mastery" and he should be a student and leader in his field. In the professional qualification area the "ideal teacher" was to be technically competent, but in a broad rather than a narrow sense, and, in addition, he was to have "educational ideas." Finally, the "ideal teacher" possessed personal qualities that would contribute to desirable teacher-pupil relationships in classroom situations.

---

[32] For example, see A. J. Klein and Others, *Adventures in the Reconstruction of Education* (Columbus: Ohio State University, College of Education, 1941), pp. 27, 162, *et passim*.

There is fragmentary evidence suggesting an emerging belief that the teacher should not only have adequate social understandings but should also have the desire to promote and implement democratic ideals. The "ideal teacher" should be committed to inculcating the American way of life.

In the second paragraph of this chapter, attention was called to the criticism of the National Survey by the Yearbook Committee of the National Society of College Teachers of Education that insufficient attention had been given to the "trends in elementary and secondary education" as a basis for evaluating current programs of teacher preparation and as a source of constructive proposals. During the period since that time increasing attention has been given to the evolving programs of our schools and it has become increasingly clear that "teaching" certain conventional subjects is becoming less and less descriptive of the service a teacher is called upon to render. In the first place, conventional subjects are disappearing from the curriculums of our schools. Instead of "teaching" certain subjects the teacher is asked to stimulate and guide learning in certain areas. Second, the teacher is expected to contribute to the improvement of the program of the school by participating in curriculum revision and in other ways. He is expected to work with the community agencies and organizations.[33] Thus from the point of view of purposes teacher education is undergoing a revolutionary change.

---

[33] W. Earl Armstrong, Ernest V. Hollis, and Helen E. Davis, *The College and Teacher Education* (Washington, D. C.: American Council on Education, 1944), p. 302.

Part **3**

Development of Practice in Teacher Education

Teacher-education practice, as used here, is a general designation for institutional actions relative to such matters as conditions of admission, scope, and general character of the educational program, curricular requirements, and institutional organization for the teacher-education function as well as the actions of individual staff members in developing courses of instruction and other phases of their work. In the following chapters attention is directed to the phases of teacher-education practice which appear most significant relative to the preparation of teachers for effective service in our schools.

The development of teacher-education practice since 1890 has been the result of many influences. Many teacher educators, especially staff members immediately concerned with the technical-professional work, have been aggressive in promoting institutional action which they thought would facilitate the engendering of the qualifications they considered desirable for teachers in our schools, but they worked within the contemporary educational and social setting. In understanding the development of teacher-education practice, it is necessary to inquire into the influence of this setting. Some aspects of it will be described in connection with particular developments, but its importance justifies a limited treatment as an introduction.

The development of teacher-education practice since 1890 will be dealt with in a series of chapters — "Normal Schools," "From Normal Schools to Teachers Colleges," "Teacher Education in Colleges and Universities," "Teacher Education Since the National Survey," and "The Technical-Professional Program." The treatment in these chapters will be from the point of view that effectiveness in preparing teachers for our elementary and secondary schools requires: (1) meaningful definition of the qualifications to be engendered; (2) appropriate organizational and administrative provisions in an institution purporting to prepare teachers for our schools; and (3) an educational program, including technical-professional courses, planned and administered on the basis of the purposes of our schools, the nature of the teaching-learning process, and the services asked of teachers. The final chapter is devoted to "Appraisal and Interpretation."

CHAPTER 9

The Educational and
Social Setting

The educational and social setting in which teacher-education practice developed following 1890 includes a number of interrelated factors. In addition to being complex this setting has not been uniform among the several states and sections of the country. Thus a brief description will tend to be an oversimplification. The following account is limited to certain factors which seem to be especially significant relative to the present purpose and there is only incidental mention of the variations among the several states.

Our Schools

In 1890, 14,181,415 children were enrolled in public schools of the United States. By 1930 the number had increased to 23,588,479. Following this date elementary-school enrollments decreased until after 1946.[1] Enrollment in public high schools increased from 357,813 in 1890 to 4,799,867 in 1930 and to 7,113,282 in 1940.[2]

These increases in the number of children being served by our schools

[1] Wayne W. Soper, "Elementary Education—II. Pupil Population," in *Encyclopedia of Educational Research*, ed. Walter S. Monroe (Rev. ed.; New York: The Macmillan Company, 1950), p. 363.

[2] Clifford P. Archer, "Secondary Education—II. Student Population," in *Encyclopedia of Educational Research*, ed. Walter S. Monroe (Rev. ed.; New York: The Macmillan Company, 1950), p. 1156.

are impressive, but changes in the educational program and in the work of the teachers are probably more significant relative to the development of teacher-education practice. In 1890 the teacher's task was to maintain order in the classroom and to teach the school subjects as defined by the adopted texts. There was little concern for the pupils that failed to "pass." Only twenty-six states had compulsory-attendance laws. In many cases these laws were inadequate and the enforcement was lax. By 1930 the curriculum had been "enriched" and changed in other respects. The teacher's task as an instructor was thought of as being to teach children rather than school subjects. Compulsory attendance was relatively effective and adaptation of school work to individual differences was being emphasized. Systematic diagnosis and remedial teaching were appearing in school practice and teachers were being asked to assume responsibilities in connection with extracurricular activities. In some schools they were being encouraged and stimulated to study a variety of school problems.

Developments along these lines have continued and in our better schools the teacher's work is a complex task. In addition to the responsibilities mentioned in the preceding paragraph, the teacher is asked to participate in the formulation of school policies and in the development of the educational program. The teacher is also being assigned responsibilities in the developing of pupil personnel programs. Thus during the years since 1890 the work of the teacher has evolved from the simple task of keeping order in the classroom and teaching formal school subjects to one involving various services, and as an instructor the teacher's function is to guide and/or direct learning in subject-matter areas rather than to teach school subjects.

The Demand for Teachers

In 1890 the number of teachers employed in the public schools of the United States was 363,922, of which 9,120 were in high schools. The corresponding data for 1900 are 423,062 and 20,372. Thus during the closing decade of the nineteenth century the total number of teachers employed in public schools increased by nearly 6,000 each year, the increase being proportionately much greater at the secondary level.

There is no accurate information in regard to the number of teachers retiring or otherwise leaving the teaching profession in the public schools each year. On the basis of a careful inquiry in the public schools of Milwaukee, Wisconsin, in 1887 and 1888 it was estimated that the rate of change was between 10 and 12 per cent.[3] In 1889 it was estimated that

[3] William E. Anderson, "Qualification and Supply of Teachers for City Public Schools," *Addresses and Proceedings* (National Educational Association, 1891), pp. 422-30.

of the total of 31,726 teachers employed in the schools of the State of New York some six or seven thousand were inexperienced persons.[4] In 1894 it was stated that the "average teaching life" of women in America was not greater than three and one half years and it was observed that it was presumably but little longer in city schools.[5] If it is assumed that the "average teaching life" of men was somewhat longer, it seems reasonable to estimate that in 1890 the total replacements in the public schools amounted to about 25 per cent of the total teaching personnel. Thus the total annual demand for new teachers (replacements and additions) may be estimated to have been between 90,000 and 100,000 during the period from 1890 to 1900.

On the basis of data for the period from 1916 to 1928, the Research Division of the National Education Association gave 110,000 to 120,000 as a "conservative estimate" of the annual demand for "new" teachers in the United States and asserted that this demand tended to be constant from year to year.[6] In Volume II of the National Survey the number of "additional new teachers," replacements and new positions for 1930-31, was estimated as 82,580 (p. 99). This estimate is substantially below the minimum of the "conservative estimate" for the period from 1916 to 1928 and hence suggests a trend in the direction of a materially reduced demand for teachers. The decrease in the demand may have been somewhat less than the comparison indicates.[7] Data for the period since 1930 indicate considerable fluctuation in the annual demand. During the thirties the demand decreased and then increased following the beginning of World War II. Present predictions indicate a high demand during the fifties.[8]

With respect to the present purpose the absolute demand is less significant than the relation of the demand to the supply of teachers being educated in normal schools and teachers colleges and in colleges and universities. The enrollment data show the number of persons "preparing for teaching" in these institutions in 1890 was far below the estimated demand. In other words the market (number of "new" teachers needed) was greatly in excess of the production (number of "graduates," i.e. persons other than ones already employed as teachers and qualifying for a

[4] John A. MacDonald, "Professional Training of Teachers by Educational Publications," *Addresses and Proceedings* (National Educational Association, 1894), pp. 106-14.

[5] Aaron Gove, "Sources of Supply of Teachers in City Schools," *Addresses and Proceedings* (National Educational Association, 1894), p. 374. See also p. 92.

[6] National Education Association, Research Division, "Teacher Demand and Supply," *Research Bulletin*, 9 (November, 1931), 313.

[7] For a criticism of the study by the Research Division of the N.E.A., see Alonzo F. Myers, "Teacher Demand and the Supply," *School and Society*, 35 (1932), 210-15.

[8] Earl W. Anderson and Reuben H. Eliassen, "Supply and Demand in Teaching," *Review of Educational Research*, 19 (1949), 179-84.

certificate or diploma by attendance at one of these institutions). One can only speculate in regard to the ratio of the market to this production, but it may be noted that the *Report of the Commissioner of Education*, 1889-90, gave the total of "normal graduates" from both public and private institutions as 5,237 (pp. 1030 and 1932). Presumably a "normal gradua-ate" was one who qualified for a certificate or diploma and doubtless a number of such persons were employed as teachers during the school term of 1889-90. Hence the number of "new" teachers produced by the normal schools was probably less than the number of "normal graduates."

The demand for "new" teachers continued to exceed the supply of professionally trained persons until after 1920 when "production" be-gan to exceed "consumption." On the basis of data collected in the Na-tional Survey, it was estimated that the "production" of 1930-31 was thirty thousand in excess of the "consumption." Thus during the third decade of the century the teacher-training institutions were operating in a situa-tion in which the demand for "new" teachers was less than the supply of professionally trained persons, and there was an added stimulation for improving their product. This situation appears to have furnished the central motivation of the National Survey.[9] A teacher shortage developed during World War II, but this was an unusual condition and it seems clear that since about 1925 the teacher-education "plant" of the country has been capable of a "production" in excess of the normal "consumption" under prevailing standards of certification and other conditions of em-ployment.

Requirements for Employment in Public Schools

The minimum qualifications for a given type of public school position are those specified by law for the lowest grade of certificate applicable to that position. In 1890 the licensing requirements varied among the several states and even within a state, but they may be illustrated by those of Virginia for 1892, which Elsbree [10] referred to as "typical of those which prevailed in most of the states prior to 1900." The school law of Virginia in 1892 specified that "the county superintendent shall ex-amine persons applying for license to teach in the free public schools, and, if satisfied as to their capacity, acquirements, morals, and general fitness, he shall grant them certificates of limited duration subject to revocation, all under the supervision of the State superintendent." The county superintendent was also to hold examinations "for those desiring to teach in his county for the school year at such time and place as may

[9] E. S. Evenden, *Summary and Interpretation*, National Survey of the Education of Teachers, Vol. VI (U.S. Office of Education, Bulletin 1933, No. 10), p. 224.

[10] Willard S. Elsbree, *The American Teacher* (New York: American Book Com-pany, 1939), p. 348.

be required by a district board." These examinations were to be given "in orthography, reading, writing, arithmetic, grammar, geography, physiology and hygiene, and for a first- or second-grade certificate, in the theory and practice of teaching. Applicants to teach schools in which the higher branches have been introduced must be examined upon those branches also." [11]

A study by E. P. Cubberley,[12] reported in 1906, revealed "low standards" of certification and a "great lack of uniformity" among states. In "more than half of the states" a prospective teacher could obtain a third-grade certificate (local) by "passing" examinations in the common-school subjects (reading, grammar, geography, orthography, arithmetic, penmanship, United States history, and physiology and hygiene) and "perhaps a little theory and practice of teaching" (p. 29). For a first-grade certificate an examination in one or more additional subjects was required — civics, algebra, physics, geometry, state history, physical geography, English composition, and literature being most frequently mentioned. The requirement of "theory and practice of teaching" was more common than in the case of a third-grade certificate. For a "state certificate" the requirements were somewhat higher, the median number of subjects being 19 for the highest grade.

From the point of view of teacher education it is significant to note that the Virginia school law of 1892 did not mention any schooling requirement as a prerequisite for a license to teach. Apparently any person desiring to teach was admitted to the examination. Even by the time of Cubberley's study only a very few states specified a schooling requirement for admission to the examinations,[13] and it appears from the tabulation given that in the typical state the scope of examinations for the highest grade of state certificate did not encompass schooling beyond the tenth grade, provided the student select his subjects wisely.

The first state to require high-school graduation as a condition for all licenses to teach was Indiana in 1907.[14] By 1921 fourteen states had taken similar action and four others required high-school graduation plus some professional training. By 1926 fifteen states did not stipulate a schooling requirement, but of the other thirty-three all but six required more than high-school graduation. In 1937 there were only eight states in which the "minimum scholarship prerequisites for certificating inexperienced teachers" did not stipulate a definite schooling requirement and in thirty-two

[11] U. S. Bureau of Education, "Digest of Public Schools," *Report of Commissioner of Education*, 1893-94, Vol. II, p. 1127.

[12] "The Certification of Teachers," *Fifth Yearbook*, Part II (National Society for the Study of Education, 1906), p. 73.

[13] *Ibid.*, p. 56.

[14] Harlan Updegraff, "Teachers Certificates Issued under General State Laws and Regulations," (U.S. Bureau of Education, Bulletin 1911, No. 18), p. 186.

states a year or more of college or normal-school study was required.[15]

The Virginia school law of 1892 specified that the county superintendent was to include an examination in "the theory and practice of teaching" among those given for a first- or second-grade certificate. Such a requirement was not common at this time. According to Cook,[16] an examination in professional subjects was required by only seventeen states in 1898. A tabulation by Updegraff in 1911 showed six states not requiring an examination in "professional subjects" for a first-grade certificate or the equivalent.[17] Of the states requiring a professional examination for a first-grade certificate or the equivalent 20 specified one subject, 12, two subjects, and 2, three subjects. (Information not given for 8 states.) According to Cook,[18] two states did not require an examination in professional subjects for the lowest grade of certificate in 1919. Until after 1903 no state required professional training as a prerequisite for a certificate of the lowest grade. In 1911 there were two states having such a requirement and by 1919 the number had increased to only seventeen states.[19]

The general development of authority to issue certificates has been from local (town and township) officials, to county superintendents, to the state department of education, but these stages of development have overlapped, both among the several states and within particular states. Multiple certification within a state tended to result in varying requirements. Furthermore, a given authority issued two or more grades of certificates. The change from this chaotic situation was slow. Bachman's comprehensive studies [20] describe the requirements of about 1930. The general situation was one of "ill-defined and low certification requirements."

The slow development of a schooling requirement as a prerequisite for obtaining a license to teach and the limited pedagogical requirements up to about 1910 indicate that prospective teachers were under little pres-

---

[15] Benjamin W. Frazier, "Development of State Programs of Certification of Teachers" (U.S. Office of Education, Bulletin 1938, No. 12), p. 73.

[16] Katherine M. Cook, *State Laws and Regulations Governing Teachers' Certificates* (U.S. Bureau of Education, Bulletin 1921, No. 22). 244 pp.

[17] Harlan Updegraff, *op. cit.*, pp. 188-89. Cook, apparently referring to Updegraff's findings, stated that in forty-two states "professional subjects" were included in "examination for certificates (all grades or lowest grade)" in 1911, but the present author's examination of Updegraff's tabulation resulted in a count of only thirty-two states plus Massachusetts for which no entries appear.

[18] Katherine M. Cook, *op. cit.*, p. 13.

[19] *Ibid.*

[20] Frank P. Bachman, *Training and Certification of High School Teachers* (Field Studies No. 2 [George Peabody College for Teachers, 1930]). 175 pp. See especially Chapter II. Frank P. Bachman, *Education and Certification of Elementary Teachers* (Field Study No. 5 [George Peabody College for Teachers, 1933]). 223 pp. See especially Chapter II.

sure to seek professional study in normal schools or in colleges and universities. Such study was not essential. But one may inquire concerning the extent to which it was an asset to teachers. In 1890 normal-school diplomas were recognized in some states as licenses to teach [21] and by 1897 normal-school graduates were exempted from examinations in more than half of the states. [22]

By 1910 the school laws of thirty-nine states provided for certificates based on graduation from standard colleges and this scholastic attainment was recognized in some of the other states as a basis of certification. Of this group, ten states had no requirement relative to professional study and ten other states issued two certificates, one not requiring professional study on the college level. The remaining nineteen states required that "certain amounts of professional study be pursued either during the college course or in postgraduate study" as a condition for a certificate based on graduation from a standard college. The amount of professional study varied, but in only 4 of the 26 states making specifications was it less than 11 semester hours. A larger number of states (41) had laws providing for certification upon completion of certain normal-school curriculums.[23]

By 1937 one or more kinds of certificates were issued in all states on the basis of college credentials and in only twenty states was a certificate issued upon examination. For high-school certificates issued to inexperienced persons on the basis of college credentials all states specified a minimum requirement in professional courses (including student teaching) ranging from 8 to 25 semester hours. The median requirement was 18 semester hours. In at least ten states "the state normal school or college boards, or individual college or normal school boards or executive officers" had been delegated authority to issue certificates directly, or the degrees or diplomas constituted licenses to teach.[24]

In addition to being a means of obtaining exemption from examinations for a certificate, professional training was something of an asset in obtaining better teaching positions. The subcommittee on the supply of teachers of the Committee of Twelve on Rural Schools reporting in 1897 noted that although normal schools were "originally established for the benefit of the common school," the graduates of these institutions tended to obtain employment in "graded schools." By way of explanation the subcommittee observed that current rural-school salaries were not suffi-

[21] This was true in California as early as 1863. See Willard S. Elsbree, *op. cit.*, p. 341.

[22] Katherine M. Cook, *op. cit.*, p. 12.

[23] Harlan Updegraff, *Teachers' Certificates Issued Under General State Laws and Regulations* (U.S. Bureau of Education, Bulletin 1911, No. 18), pp. 172-73, 182.

[24] Benjamin W. Frazier, *Development of State Programs of Certification of Teachers* (U.S. Office of Education, Bulletin 1938, No. 12), pp. 13-14, 40, 63.

cient to "remunerate one for the expense of a normal-school course." [25] Coffman's study revealed a difference in median salary of $201.00 between men with four years of training beyond the elementary school (mostly high-school graduates) and men with six years of training (mostly normal-school graduates). For women the corresponding difference was $86.00.[26] These salary differences suggest that teachers with professional training tended to be stronger candidates for the better teaching positions. On the other hand, it appears that in some schools professional training was a relatively minor factor in obtaining appointment and promotion. In an article relating to "teachers" in *A Cyclopedia of Education* (1913) it was stated that "the promotion, as well as the appointment, of teachers is largely conditioned by elements of favoritism, partisanship, or mere chance rather than by those of personal merit or professional efficiency."[27]

A recent summary [28] reveals variations in schooling and professional requirements among the several states. In Nebraska a certificate to teach in elementary schools is issued to graduates of the high-school normal training course. In ten other states the minimum schooling requirement for an elementary-school certificate is from 24 to 32 semester hours of college study. In contrast there are seventeen states that require a bachelor's degree for the lowest regular elementary certificate. The range of the professional requirement is from no requirement (six states) to 36 semester hours. For the lowest regular certificate for teaching in high schools the variations are somewhat similar. Texas requires only 30 semester hours of college study, and three states, 60 semester hours. At the other extreme four states require a fifth year of schooling. The range for the professional requirement is from zero semester hours (one state) to 24 semester hours. State certificates are not issued in Massachusetts.

The preceding statements refer to the lowest regular teaching certificates issued by the state authority on the basis of credentials. In Missouri county superintendents are authorized to issue third-grade certificates on the basis of examinations. Some form of certificate is issued in five other states on the basis of examinations.

With reference to future developments it is significant that in thirty-nine states certification requirements are prescribed by the state board of

[25] *Addresses and Proceedings* (National Educational Association, 1897), pp. 462-64.

[26] Lotus D. Coffman, *The Social Composition of the Teaching Population* (Contributions to Education, No. 41 [New York: Teachers College, Columbia University, 1911]), pp. 46-47.

[27] Edward C. Elliot, *Teachers, Promotion of*, in *A Cyclopedia of Education*, ed. Paul Monroe (New York: The Macmillan Company, 1913), V, 505.

[28] T. M. Stinnett and Others, "Interstate Reciprocity in Teacher Education-certification," *Journal of Teacher Education*, 1 (1950), 56-80.

education or some other state agency and in five other states the prescription is jointly by the state authority and the legislature. Such conditions facilitate modifications of requirements.

The Economic and Social Status of Teachers

In viewing the demand as a factor in the development of teacher education, it is necessary to consider also the economic status of teaching. The *Report of the United States Commissioner of Education for 1890-91* gave the "average monthly salary" [29] of male teachers in public schools (elementary and secondary) as $44.89 and that of female teachers as $36.65. The total "average annual earnings" of a teacher at this time have been estimated to be $246.00.[30] The increase from this low level was slow until after 1915 when the average salary for teachers of both sexes was $543.00.[31] Even the increase indicated by this figure is greater than the increase in the "purchasing power of the salary." With the average for the period 1890 to 1899 as a base, the "average real earnings" of teachers have been estimated to have been $246.00 in 1890 and $425.00 in 1915.[32]

Beginning in 1919 average salary increases were relatively large until 1930, but due to the decline in the purchasing power of the dollar, the "real" increases were much less. For example, the average salary in 1919 was $736.00 with a purchasing power, based upon 1913 salaries as 100, of $370.00; the corresponding figures for 1923 are $1,020.00 and $593.00.[33]

It is apparent that from the point of view of the salary received teaching has not, in general, been an attractive profession. Numerous comparisons of teacher salaries with those of other occupational groups have revealed the low status of teachers in this respect. Table 1 gives "average salaries or wages" for certain occupational groups at five-year intervals from 1890 to 1926. A compilation by the Research Division of the National Education Association [34] for the five-year period 1929-1933 showed teachers (including principals and supervisors) to occupy the lowest position among eleven occupational groups except in 1933 when their position was tenth by a margin of $2.00 per year over "state and county employees" exclusive of those in public education.

[29] The calculations were made from state reports from thirty-eight states and the District of Columbia, the missing ones being distributed as follows: South Atlantic, three; South Central, three; and Western, four. It was noted that some state reports were based on incomplete data.

[30] Willard S. Elsbree, *op. cit.,* p. 434.

[31] National Education Association, Research Division, "Teachers Salaries and Salary Trends in 1923," *Research Bulletin,* 1 (July, 1923), 27.

[32] See Willard S. Elsbree, *op. cit.,* p. 434.

[33] National Education Association, Research Division, *loc. cit.*

[34] National Education Association, Research Division, "The Teacher's Economic Position," *Research Bulletin,* 13 (September, 1935), 243.

TABLE 1. Average salaries or wages for certain groups.

Year	All persons gainfully employed	Employees in manufacturing industries	Clerical and low-salaried workers in manufacturing and transportation	Ministers	Government employees, Washington, D.C.	Teachers
1890		$ 439	$ 880	$ 794		$ 252
1895		416	980	787	$1,104	286
1900		435	1,029	731	1,033	325
1905		494	1,112	759	1,072	386
1910	$ 809	558	1,189	802	1,108	485
1915	861	568	1,291	984	1,152	543
1920	1,859	1,358	2,159	1,468	1,648	871
1925	1,971	1,293	2,141	1,712	1,786	1,252
1926	2,010	1,309	2,141	1,744	1,809	1,275

Source: N.E.A. *Research Bulletin*, 5 (1927), 176.

Averages do not reveal the effect of a "normal-school education" or other professional training upon the salary received, but it is probably safe to say that up to about 1920 the anticipated effect was not a strong motivating influence for attending normal schools and teachers colleges and colleges and universities. The "average teaching life" and other evidence indicate that in 1890 and to a slowly decreasing extent during the following years, teaching was regarded as a "stepping stone" to more remunerative employment. A study reported in the National Survey showed 6.5 per cent of the predecessors of new elementary teachers in 1930-31 as having "entered another profession or occupation." There were also 6.4 per cent of the predecessors who entered college, some of them doubtless intending to prepare for some other profession. The percentages at the junior- and senior-high-school levels entering another profession or occupation were somewhat higher, 7.2 and 9.1 respectively.[35] However, we do not know the extent to which the salary motive was operative.

It is reasonable that other motives were influential in at least some cases. Several other conditions combined with low salaries to limit the attractiveness of teaching as a profession. In many instances working conditions, social standing in the community, and employment practices added to the unattractiveness. Although dismissals for "political" reasons do not appear to have been as frequent as some have considered them to be,[36] the fact that some teachers were dismissed for such reasons points to one of the hazards of the teaching profession. The preference given to local residents in many communities, bargaining and "pull" through

[35] Edward S. Evenden and Others, *Teacher Personnel in the United States*, National Survey of the Education of Teachers, Vol. II (U.S. Office of Education, Bulletin 1933, No. 10), p. 92.

[36] R. L. C. Butsch, "Teacher Personnel—IX. Tenure," in *Encyclopedia of Educational Research*, ed. Walter S. Monroe (New York: The Macmillan Company, 1941), p. 1270.

relatives or friends as means of obtaining a position, "blue laws" relative to teacher out-of-school behavior, and other employment practices
doubtless tended to limit the attractiveness of the profession.

The Academic Environment

Normal schools were established as independent institutions, i.e. there
was no articulation with either the secondary schools or the colleges
of the time. But following 1890 the relationship of normal schools to
colleges and universities became a matter of concern. Some graduates
of normal schools, who had extended their schooling beyond the twelfth
year, sought admission to colleges and universities with advanced standing but these higher institutions tended to maintain that the work was
not of college grade. The normal schools supported their graduates, insisting that advanced standing should be granted, but gradually they
submitted to the requirements and standards of the higher institutions
and thus the academic environment of the time became an influence in
the development of the normal schools.

Teacher education in colleges and universities developed within the
academic environment. If credits in pedagogical courses were to be
counted toward a liberal-arts degree it was necessary that such courses
be approved as conforming to academic standards. As colleges of education were organized, proposals from this unit were submitted to the
general legislative body of the institution. Furthermore, except in special
fields, some four-fifths of a prospective teacher's collegiate education was
provided by the subject-matter departments.

The colleges and universities were established institutions at the
beginning of the period considered here. They had developed requirements and standards which seemed desirable relative to the purposes of
a liberal education. As graduate work was developed, there were added
requirements and standards relative to the preparation of scholars. The
atmosphere of these institutions was academic. The courses of instruction
were expected to represent an adequate scholarly content. Little attention was given to vocational or other practical values.

The Educational-Research Movement

In Chapter 7 the research approach was noted as influencing the thinking about desired teacher qualifications from 1907 to 1933. Research in
education influenced teacher-education practice in numerous other ways.
Although few problems and issues of practice have been settled by educational research, reported findings have been widely used in planning
and in supporting proposed changes. A major influence has been through
the contributions to the developing pedagogical content which has been

a factor in the expansion of the technical-professional program. The development of educational research created a new field of endeavor for educationists and, although many research workers maintained a strong interest in the preparation of teachers for our schools, education staffs tended to divide into two groups — those primarily concerned with the preservice education of teachers and those whose time was devoted largely or wholly to research and the instruction of graduate students interested in administration or in positions in colleges and universities. The present writer was told of one institution where this division of interest resulted in opposition within the department of education to proposed developments in teacher education.

Concluding Statement

A complete account of the educational and social setting within which teacher education developed following 1890 would include mention of other factors such as the agencies accrediting secondary schools, teachers' associations and other organized groups concerned with the improvement of our schools, the social status accorded teachers, and educational leaders who were aggressive in promoting their views. However, the preceding sketch should be sufficient to make clear that the development of teacher-education practice was influenced by a number of factors.

Some of the factors of the setting handicapped the efforts of teacher-educators in developing programs compatible with their concept of desired teacher qualifications. For example, the demand for teachers and the low requirements for employment were adverse influences, especially during the first half of the period here considered. Some factors of the setting have supported the efforts to develop more effective teacher education. For example, accrediting agencies have supported professional training for teachers.

The nature and effect of the setting have varied among the states. In some the state university exercised considerable leadership, especially with respect to the professional education of secondary teachers. In a few the state university is regarded as having been a handicap. The leadership of some normal schools and teachers colleges succeeded in developing strong institutions. A study of teacher education in California resulted in the conclusion that the development in that state was the result of social forces.[37]

[37] Evelyn Atkinson Clement, *The Evolution of Teacher Training in California as a Phase of Social Change* (Unpublished Ph.D. dissertation, University of California, 1936).

CHAPTER 10

Normal Schools

Normal Schools of 1890

The *Report of the United States Commissioner of Education for 1889-90* gave statistics for 135 public normal schools and 43 private normal schools (Vol. 2, pp. 1056-61). The ostensible purpose of these normal schools was the preparation of teachers, mainly for elementary schools, but in many instances, especially in the more sparsely settled areas, they functioned as regional institutions for schooling beyond the eighth grade. Although the normal schools of 1890 were generally referred to as being of secondary grade, preparation for college was seldom explicitly recognized as a function. Thus the normal school tended to be a dead-end institution, i.e. its program was not a section of the educational ladder.

The characterization of the normal schools of 1890 as being of secondary grade was a reflection of their admission requirements. A promise or a declaration of intention to teach for a specified number of years was required by law in some states as a condition of admission. Frequently there were also specifications of a minimum age and evidence of a "good moral character," which was a requirement for a license to teach in a number of states. Usually alternative scholastic conditions were announced. High-school graduation was announced as a sufficient condition by many institutions and probably acceptable in all. A license to teach, especially one beyond the lowest grade, was another sufficient scholastic condition in a number of normal schools. Admission on the basis of examination was a general practice. Practically no attention was given to the schooling status of the applicant, except in city training schools where high-school graduation was generally required. The scope of the examinations seldom extended beyond the "common branches," i.e. the subjects taught in the elementary schools of the time [1] and in practice examination standards appear to have been low. In 1888 Wickersham [2] stated: ". . . schools can be found that welcome to a place in their classes all who come, with little regard to age, scholarship, or fitness."

Admission practices at the Illinois State Normal University are probably suggestive of those of the better normal schools of the time. Holders of a first-grade certificate were admitted without examination and applicants with a second-grade certificate were admitted on "a kind of probation." Other applicants were admitted on examination. These examinations were not perfunctory. During a period of several years 32 per cent of those examined were rejected. After 1874 a "preparatory class was maintained in the Model School" for those who failed to pass the examination or who did not do satisfactory work after being admitted.[3]

The students were heterogeneous relative to schooling and teaching experience. In Indiana about 22 per cent of the entrants were graduates of a high school or academy and about 10 per cent more had attended a secondary school for one or two years. There were a few college graduates. From 60 to 65 per cent of the entrants had completed only a rural school or the elementary school of a city system. In some cases this schooling had been supplemented by private study. At a given time about half of those attending had had "more or less experience" in teaching.[4]

Illinois State Normal University was an outstanding normal school and its student body was doubtless above the average, but certain facts are indicative of general conditions, at least in the Middle West. About three-fourths of its students came from farm homes and most of the remainder were from homes on the lower economic level. The average age of the entrants in 1890 was 20 years and 1 month. The average age of the graduating classes from 1858 to 1888 was 26 years and 3 months. Students in the normal schools of the East were somewhat younger.[5] The difference

---

[1] "Report of the 'Chicago Committee' on Methods of Instruction and Courses of Study in Normal Schools," *Addresses and Proceedings* (National Educational Association, 1889), pp. 570-87.

[2] J. P. Wickersham, *Adequacy of Normal Schools* (United States Bureau of Education, Circular of Information, 1888, No. 6), p. 71.

[3] Charles A. Harper, *Development of the Teachers College in the United States* (Bloomington, Illinois: McKnight and McKnight, Publishers, 1935), pp. 101-17.

[4] William W. Parsons, "The Normal School Curriculum," *Addresses and Proceedings* (National Educational Association, 1890), pp. 718-24.

[5] Charles A. Harper, *op. cit.*, pp. 101-17.

between the above averages reflects the fact that many students attended
for a few months and then dropped out to teach for a term or to engage
in other remunerative activity as a means of obtaining funds for continuing their preparation for teaching. In another source it was reported
that 72 per cent of the students of Illinois State Normal University did
not progress beyond the work of the first year.[6]

The normal schools of 1890 had small incomes. The Illinois State Normal University was one of the "richer" schools, but its "annual revenue"
was only $40,000.00 in 1890. At this time its enrollment in the Normal
Department was 677 and in the Model School, 503.[7] The *Report of the
Commissioner of Education* for 1889-90 [8] gives a total of $1,312,419.00
received for "support" of normal schools from state, county, and city [9]
sources. The number of institutions included is not specified, but the
preceding table gives data for 135 "normal schools supported in whole
or in part by public funds." Using this figure, the average appropriation
per institution was $9,729.00 or approximately $930.00 per staff member.
In addition, there was income from other sources of $1,273.00 per insti-
tution, or about $120.00 per staff member.

Averages obscure the situation with reference to the less favored institutions. The amounts received from "state, county, or city" in 1890 are
given by states and so it is not possible to determine the appropriations
to particular institutions. The amounts for some states are such that
very inadequate support is apparent. For example, the income of the
normal schools of Ohio totaled $4,500.00 from public sources and $1,000.00
from other sources. In another table (p. 1058) four normal schools with
a total of 226 "normal" students are given for this state. Hence the income
per school was very limited.

There were significant variations in the general nature of the courses
of study (curriculums) designed for the preparation of elementary
teachers, but certain central tendencies are apparent. The regular courses
of study for prospective teachers ranged from two to four years in
length. These courses consisted of "reviews" of elementary-school subjects, "higher branches" similar to the academic offerings of the high
schools and academies of the time, and pedagogical subjects. Some of the
larger normal schools undertook to prepare teachers for high-school
positions and hence offered academic subjects similar to ones taught in
colleges. The program of pedagogical offerings varied but the modal sub-

[6] Charles De Garmo, "The German System of Normal Schools," *Addresses and
Proceedings* (National Educational Association, 1887), p. 489.

[7] Charles A. Harper, *op. cit.*, pp. 90-92.

[8] *Report of the Commissioner of Education, 1889-90* (Washington, D.C.: Government Printing Office, 1893), II, 1031.

[9] Many city normal schools not included.

jects were psychology, history of education, school economy and management, one or more special methods, principles of teaching,[10] and practice teaching and/or observation.[11]

The course of study of the Illinois State Normal University was three years in length, but a number of "optional studies" were offered and many students extended their period of study to four years. In 1889 these "optional studies" included Latin, Greek, German, French, astronomy, advanced algebra, trigonometry, surveying, analytical geometry, calculus, advanced science, political science, and advanced pedagogy. In the three-year course of study the following subjects were designated: first year — history and method of education, reading, spelling, grammar, arithmetic, geography, history; second year — metaphysics, rhetoric, criticism, algebra, trigonometry, geography, history, chemistry, botany; third year — history and method of education, constitutions of United States and Illinois, school laws of Illinois, English literature, natural philosophy, astronomy, bookkeeping, drawing, physiology. In addition, "teaching," writing, and zoology were listed without a time specification, and physical training was emphasized. This enumeration is based on the course of study for 1874, but it is stated that there was little change up to 1900 except that the time given to geography and spelling was reduced and that given to reading, grammar, and arithmetic was increased.[12]

The course of study of the Illionis State Normal University was more stable than that of most normal schools of the time. Typically there was considerable change over a period of a few years and there were differences between schools. The variations in the general nature of the courses of study for the education of teachers reflect three points of view relative to means. In many normal schools the emphasis was on a thorough understanding of the subjects taught in elementary schools. The curriculum for this purpose consisted of "reviews" of these subjects plus higher branches. The instruction tended to be academic, i.e. similar to that in the elementary and secondary schools of the time. Pedagogical training, limited largely to courses in methods, classroom management, and "psychology," was included but was considered to be secondary in importance. Although this pedagogical training was mingled with academic study in student programs, a teacher's education tended to consist of academic study *plus* pedagogical training.

Criticisms of normal schools during the seventies and eighties as being

[10] The title varied, a common one being "science and art of teaching" or simply "art of teaching."

[11] Benjamin W. Frazier and Others, *Special Survey Studies*, National Survey of the Education of Teachers, Vol. V (U.S. Office of Education, Bulletin 1933, No. 10), pp. 26-27.

[12] Charles A. Harper, *op. cit.*, pp. 124-25.

mainly academic institutions [13] indicate that this type of program was widely prevalent. However, it was opposed by a number of normal-school leaders who maintained that "reviews" of the academic type and instruction in higher branches similar to that provided in the high schools and academies of the time did not result in the sort of knowledge a teacher needed. They argued that the subject matter should be professionalized, i.e. selected and organized with the needs of the teacher in mind and that the instruction should also be directed to this end.[14] The extent to which this point of view was exemplified in practice is uncertain. No widely accepted technique for professionalizing subject matter and instruction had been developed and what was accomplished depended largely upon the insight and ingenuity of individual instructors. However, it appears that by 1890 professional treatment of subject matter was being attempted in a number of normal schools, especially in the better ones.[15] Where there was effective professional treatment, there was also an integration of subject-matter study and pedagogical study.

In contrast with these two positions, both of which emphasized the teacher's understanding of the subjects to be taught, there were some normal-school leaders who advocated that the normal school should be a "strictly professional" institution, leaving to the common schools, elementary and secondary, the instruction in the subjects to be taught and in the higher branches. The advocates of the "strictly professional" school observed that professional schools were maintained to prepare lawyers, physicians, and divines, and argued that teaching was a service of comparable importance and that corresponding schools for the education of teachers should be established. This argument had been advanced by Thomas Gallaudet [16] in 1825 and it reappeared many times [17] in support of the contention that the normal school should be a "strictly professional" institution.

The crucial weakness of the "strictly professional" normal school was in the implicit assumption that a person's common-school experience would result in an adequate knowledge of the subjects to be taught. Although this assumption now seems naïve, it does not seem to have attracted much attention until the seventies. Randolph [18] credits an

---

[13] Edgar D. Randolph, *The Professional Treatment of Subject-matter* (Baltimore: Warwick & York, Inc., 1924), p. 32.

[14] Some of the arguments for this position were reviewed in Part Two. See pp. 187f.

[15] Edgar D. Randolph, *op. cit.*, p. 72. See also Part Two, p. 188.

[16] See J. P. Gordy, *Rise and Growth of the Normal-school Idea in the United States* (Bureau of Education, Circular of Information No. 8, 1891), p. 14.

[17] Randolph reports forty instances in the literature up to 1900 (*op. cit.*, p. 14).

[18] Edgar D. Randolph, *op. cit.*

address by E. C. Hewett [19] in 1877 as marking "the first effective breach
in the armor of Gallaudet's analogy." Hewitt maintained that by
giving instruction in the common-school subjects a normal school was
providing training as essential as that represented by the pedagogical
courses. During the following years other normal-school leaders supported Hewett's position.[20]

Although the argument persisted, no normal school became "strictly
professional." Probably the nearest approach was the institution at St.
Cloud, Minnesota, under the administration of Thomas J. Gray. Persons
holding or "capable of securing a second-grade county certificate" were
admitted to the lowest class as a matter of expediency, and during the
first two years an effort was made "to fill out the academic conception of
subjects." A two-year program of teacher education followed, the first
being devoted to history of education, psychology, methodology, and
school economy. During the final year attention was given to the common branches as the "objective ground for all methodology." This work
appears to have been a combination of review courses and special
method. To it was added "several months of actual daily teaching in the
model school." Gray believed that the academic work provided in the
first two years should be "thrown back upon" the high schools, academies, and colleges, and the normal school he envisaged would offer only
the work indicated for the last two years.[21]

Many of the normal schools of the period preceding 1890 reflected the
educational ideas of their respective presidents or principals. Under a
continuing administration of a strong head some normal schools became
institutions of considerable prestige. In such cases the ideas developed
at one institution spread to others through its graduates and former
staff members. Harper shows how the normal school at Bridgewater,
Massachusetts, influenced the Illinois State Normal University,[22] and this
institution in turn influenced others.[23] "Object teaching," developed at
the Oswego State Normal and Training School, spread to a number of
institutions.[24] Thus some of the normal schools of 1890 exhibited certain
similarities.

---

[19] E. C. Hewett, "The Range and Limits of Normal-school Work," *Addresses and
Proceedings* (National Educational Association, 1877), pp. 146-54.

[20] See Edgar D. Randolph, *op. cit.*, pp. 70f.

[21] Thomas J. Gray, "The Normal-school Idea as Embodied in the Normal School
at St. Cloud," in J. P. Gordy, *Rise and Growth of the Normal-school Idea in the
United States* (Bureau of Education, Circular of Information No. 8), 1891, pp. 90-97.

[22] Charles A. Harper, *op. cit.*, pp. 78-89.

[23] *Ibid.*, pp. 162f.

[24] Ned H. Dearborn, *The Oswego Movement in American Education* (Contributions
to Education, No. 183 [New York: Bureau of Publications, Teachers College, Columbia University, 1925]), pp. 98f.

Differences in certification requirements and other influences contributed to variations. The Report of Normal-School Committee in 1897 included a summary [25] of an inquiry by Homer J. Seerley in regard to the "variations that exist in normal schools of the United States because of geographical location." These schools were characterized as "provincial" and as exhibiting "large variation in the courses of study." The normal schools of the Middle Atlantic states, especially New York and Pennsylvania, provided for those "seeking a secondary education alone." The New York Normal College (Albany) was noted as an exception. It professed "to do no academic work." In contrast there were normal schools that claimed "to be colleges in fact." The normal schools of New England were referred to as having a "special professional character" and as being "peculiar in their organization and management." Those of the North Central states were "gradually growing to be more and more of a factor in general education" and were commonly recognized by universities as "fitting [preparatory] schools."

Major Problems Recognized by Normal-School Leaders Following 1890

In 1890 and for some years following, normal-school leaders were interested in defining desired teacher qualifications (see Chapters 5 and 6) and in otherwise improving the education of teachers. However, circumstances caused them to give attention to two more immediately practical problems. In view of the meager support of state normal schools from public sources in 1890, a problem of major practical importance was to obtain larger incomes. Developments to this end will be noted under the headings: Attracting and holding students, and normal schools as institutions for nonprofessional purposes.

The place of the normal school in the American educational system was a controversial matter. Many normal-school leaders, perhaps a majority, maintained that their work beyond the twelfth year of schooling, should be accepted as transfer credit by the colleges and universities. However, they recognized that the decision was in the hands of the higher institutions, and reluctantly they faced the problem of modifying their practices to the end that the work of their graduates would be recognized by colleges and universities. The practical problems of increasing enrollments and attaining recognition as being academically respectable materially influenced the development of the normal schools during the years following 1890. Shortly after 1900 the normal schools began the struggle to become teachers colleges. This phase of their development is dealt with in the following chapter.

---

[25] "Report of Normal-School Committee," *Addresses and Proceedings* (National Educational Association, 1897), pp. 711-13.

Admission Requirements Following 1890

In 1890 the State Normal School at Albany, New York, adopted high-school graduation as a condition of admission and Massachusetts took similar action relative to its normal schools in 1894.[26] These actions appear to mark the beginning of requiring high-school graduation or the equivalent for admission to state normal schools. On the basis of a study of the catalogs of fifty normal schools for 1895, Gwinn [27] reported thirty-seven of the institutions having the requirement of graduation from the eighth grade. Only four institutions required the completion of four years of high-school work. McNeil described the situation in 1910 as follows: "A few of the schools had the requirement of high school graduation for entrance and the tendency was pointing in this direction. . . . The majority of normal schools maintained preparatory departments which allowed entrance of candidates with almost any degree of academic standards." [28]

The tendency to require high-school graduation for admission reported by McNeil has been revealed in other studies. For example, within the group of forty-five normal schools and teachers colleges studied by Thomasson [29] the number of institutions specifying this requirement increased from 1 in 1900-01 to 6 in 1910-11. Following 1910 the number of normal schools and teachers colleges requiring high-school graduation for admission continued to increase. Within the group of institutions studied by Thomasson, nine required high-school graduation by 1920-21.

The data of the preceding paragraphs indicate a reluctance on the part of normal schools to adopt completion of a four-year high-school course as a requirement for admission, i.e. to elevate their program of teacher education to the collegiate level. From around the turn of the century reported opinion among normal-school administrators favored the action. The Report of the Committee on Normal Schools, presented in 1899, asserted: "For entrance into the normal school the applicant should have a high-school education." [30] A recommendation to this effect was repeated

---

[26] Jessie M. Pangburn, *The Evolution of the American Teachers College* (Contributions to Education, No. 500 [New York: Bureau of Publications, Teachers College, Columbia University, 1932]), p. 35.

[27] J. M. Gwinn, "Tendencies in Entrance Requirements," *Education*, 28 (1905), 233-37.

[28] Mellicent McNeil, *A Comparative Study of Entrance to Teacher-training Institutions* (Contributions to Education, No. 443 [New York: Bureau of Publications, Teachers College, Columbia University, 1930]), p. 58.

[29] A. L. Thomasson, *A Half Century of Teacher Training in State Normal Schools and Teachers Colleges of the United States, 1890-1940*, (Unpublished Ph.D. dissertation, University of Illinois, 1942). 460 pp. (p. 87).

[30] *Addresses and Proceedings* (National Educational Association, 1899), p. 840.

in 1907 [31] and in 1908.[32] The minutes of the Department of Normal
Schools specify that the "preliminary report" of 1907 was "adopted," but
there is no record of action on the final report presented the following
year. It is, however, significant that one member of the committee in discussing the recommendation qualified his endorsement by saying it was
"unwise at present to turn away young men and women from the farms
who have not attained this academic rank" (p. 737).

This statement indicates a motive for delaying the adoption of "a
high-school education" as a requirement for admission. Experience, particularly beyond the eastern states, had revealed that many young men
and women from rural areas, where four-year high schools frequently
were not available, were able to do satisfactory work in the course of
study which normal schools offered for the education of teachers. Furthermore, many of those admitted without a high-school education had,
after graduation from the normal school, demonstrated their competence
as teachers. In view of the demand for teachers it did not seem appropriate to deny admission to those not high-school graduates. There was
also another reason.

Attracting and Holding Students

Certain evidence supports the hypothesis that attracting and holding
students was a major concern of normal schools of the time. In 1890
there were 135 "state normal schools" with a total enrollment of 26,917
"students preparing for teaching"; in 1899-1900, 127 state normal schools
reporting, the corresponding enrollment was 41,655.[33] If allowance is
made for the decrease in the number of schools reporting,[34] the increase
in enrollment may be estimated to be somewhat greater than 50 per
cent. In 1889-90 the "state normal schools" enrolled also 16,080 students
"not in professional department." By 1899-1900 the number of such students in these schools was 47,091.[35] The increase in "normal students" was
doubtless due in part to an increased "demand" for professionally trained
teachers, but the much larger relative increase in students "not in professional department" is evidence of aggressiveness in seeking students.
In addition to adding to the size of the institution, and thus increasing its

---

[31] *Addresses and Proceedings* (National Education Association, 1907), p. 739.

[32] *Addresses and Proceedings* (National Education Association, 1908), p. 735.

[33] Benjamin W. Frazier and Others, *Special Survey Studies*, National Survey of the
Education of Teachers, Vol. V (U.S. Office of Education, Bulletin 1933, No. 10),
pp. 66-67.

[34] This decrease seems to be due to classifying as "private normal schools" in 1899-
1900 some institutions listed as "state normal schools" in 1889-90.

[35] Benjamin W. Frazier, *op. cit.*, pp. 66-67.

prestige, such students were a fruitful source of income.[36] Continued aggressiveness in attracting students is indicated by increases in enroll-ments during the years following the turn of the century. The enrollment of "students preparing for teaching" in state normal schools and teachers colleges was 47,783 in 1904-5, 71,447 in 1909-10, 86,248 in 1914-15, 119,024 in 1919-20, and 243,047 in 1925-26.

The practices indulged in as means of attracting and holding students were more or less institutional secrets and hence the published record provides relatively little information. In the study of the state normal schools of Missouri this state is referred to as "fairly typical" with re-spect to the problem of preparing teachers for the public schools,[37] and it is likely that the practices reported were "fairly typical" among many, if not most, of the normal schools of the country. In 1890 there were three state normal schools located at Cape Girardeau, Kirksville, and Warrens-burg. In 1906 others were established at Maryville and Springfield. There was a separate board of control for each institution and there was compe-tition among the normal schools of the state as well as between them as a group and the state university and other institutions within the state.

The University of Missouri as an accrediting agent maintained a high-school inspector. In the report it is indicated that this official, who is referred to as one of the institution's "most effective aids in developing its tributary high schools," [38] tended to be viewed with suspicion by the normal schools of the state and as a means of combating his assumed influence upon high-school graduates they created a "'field agent,' either to serve expressly as a drummer for students and positions for graduates or to unite that function with certain more dignified extension duties." In addition, the presidents and other staff members capitalized their op-portunities as lecturers and commencement speakers to advertise their respective institutions. Such means of attracting students were of course in addition to the "catalogues" and other official literature distributed by the normal schools of the state. It is noted that with one exception this literature had been "restrained and considerate in tone," but the fact that there was one exception is not without significance. Since there were five normal schools in the state, if one was more aggressive along one line then the others were forced to meet the competition by other means.

[36] In several cases the legislative act establishing a state normal school provided that students who signed a pledge to teach were granted "free tuition" or reduced rates. (See *Report of U.S. Commissioner of Education, 1898-99,* Vol. II, pp. 2263-2470.) Even when not required by law, it appears that rather generally students "not in pro-fessional department" were charged higher fees and tuition.

[37] William S. Learned, William C. Bagley, and Others, *The Professional Preparation of Teachers for American Public Schools* (New York: Carnegie Foundation for the Advancement of Teaching, Bulletin No. 14, 1920), p. 20.

[38] *Ibid.,* p. 52.

From the report of the study, based mainly on data for the years from about the turn of the century to 1914-15, it is apparent that the normal schools of Missouri "offered" numerous inducements which would speed up a student's advancement toward a license to teach and/or the completion of a curriculum. These inducements began with liberalization of or exceptions to admission requirements and extended to permission to carry excessive programs and credit for "experience." No one of the institutions could afford to maintain "standards" higher than the others were willing to observe. It is reported that one normal school announced in its catalog (date not given) that it would "meet 'whatever favors either of the other schools will grant and no more.'"[39] In 1904 two of the three schools of that date desired to make graduation from an approved secondary school the requirement for admission, but one institution insisted upon the "proving up" policy and the others conformed. According to this policy, a student was admitted and classified upon his own representation and not until he became a candidate for a certificate or diploma were his scholastic credentials asked for and evaluated.[40]

Typically the president evaluated a student's secondary work and his requests for advanced standing, and in view of the obvious competition, it is easy to imagine that the president's action was not infrequently tempered by the desire to attract and hold students. A number of instances supporting this hypothesis are cited in the Missouri report. Such exercise of presidential prerogative seems to have been somewhat common. The *Annual Announcement of the Northern Arizona (Flagstaff) Normal School* for 1909-10 gave the admission requirement as follows: "Candidates for admission to the Normal course proper must present suitable credentials, or satisfy the President by examination or otherwise that they are prepared to enter upon the course of study with profit to themselves and credit to the institution" (p. 34). After examining the catalogs of fifty normal schools for the period from 1895 to 1905 Gwinn [41] commented on the vagueness of the statements of admission requirements. "One feels on reading these statements that the vagueness is intentional so that if a candidate is not able to enter by one route, he may get in by another, which is often by grace of the president." Other regulations, when announced, were similarly couched in general terms and the head of the institution exercised his administrative prerogative subject to few restrictions.

---

[39] *Ibid.*, p. 50.

[40] *Ibid.*, p. 311.

[41] J. M. Gwinn, *op. cit.*

The Support of Normal Schools

In describing the normal schools of 1890, it was noted that the support from public sources was limited. A report in 1899 on the support of state normal schools is introduced by the statement: "For a number of years the legislatures of the various states have been quite liberal in their appropriations." [42] As one examines the information given for the several states, this generalization does not appear to be entirely in accord with the facts. In some states the appropriations were probably "liberal," at least relatively; but the amounts appropriated in several states seem to be very meager.[43] In the study of the normal schools of Missouri it was noted that in 1893 the state appropriation to the institution at Warrensburg "lacked $5000 of the amount needed to pay the teachers alone" (p. 38). As one reads institutional histories, he frequently finds references to inadequate funds and to endeavors, not always successful, to obtain appropriations for desired developments. The inadequate support of normal schools resulted in a high student-teacher ratio. A report of 1894 placed this ratio as being 40 to 50 students to a teacher in comparison to about 10 students to a teacher in a "good college or university." [44]

Although it seems clear that during the nineties many state normal schools received inadequate appropriations and that even among the more liberally supported institutions funds were not available for desired improvements in the education of teachers, the trend was in the direction of increased appropriations. The average operating income per institution from public funds was $17,105.00 in 1899-1900, $34,948.00 in 1909-10, $49,597.00 in 1919-20, and $133,371.00 in 1929-30. The relative increases shown by the amounts are impressive, but it should be noted that during this period the total enrollments in these institutions also increased. When these enrollment increases are taken into account it is likely that many normal schools were seriously handicapped by a lack of funds, at least until after 1920.

General Curriculum Developments

In 1890 normal schools tended to announce several curriculums, the principal basis of differentiation being the schooling level and the period

---

[42] "Report of the Committee on Normal Schools," *Addresses and Proceedings* (National Educational Association, 1899), p. 874.

[43] This interpretation is supported by a normal-school president who asserted in 1902: "The normal schools are commonly conducted, maintained, and supported on a cheap plan." Homer H. Seeley, "Defects in the Normal Schools that are Responsible for the Opposition and Criticism Urged Against Them in Many Parts of the United States," *Addresses and Proceedings* (National Educational Association, 1902), p. 543.

[44] "Report of Committee on the Relation of Normal Schools to Universities," *Addresses and Proceedings* (National Educational Association, 1894), p. 824.

of time covered. Thomasson's analysis of the catalogs of forty-five normal schools revealed a total of thirty-two different curriculum titles and under most of these designations there were two or more curriculums varying in length. Among this group of institutions there were twenty-two one-year, thirty two-year, thirty three-year, and thirty-six four-year curriculums.[45] The range per school was one to eight. In only a few instances was a curriculum designed to prepare for a particular type of teaching position. The actual curriculum differentiation relative to period of study appears to have been somewhat greater than Thomasson's findings indicate. Deyoe, whose study covered the period from 1902-3 to 1932-33, reported[46] that frequently the official publications of the institutions indicated that "a certificate or diploma would be made available at the completion of practically any year of a given curriculum." Since Deyoe stated that this practice was more frequent during the earlier years of the period he studied, it may be inferred that it was a relatively common practice in 1890.

The curriculums as announced were largely, and in some cases wholly prescribed, but administrative policies and practices tended to be liberal in 1890 and it is likely that numerous exceptions were made in registering students and even in granting diplomas. Although the placement of the several courses within a curriculum implies gradation and sequence, the available evidence (mainly of a little later date) suggests that in the registration process little attention was given to either the indicated grade level of a course or the sequential relationships among courses.

Following 1890, especially after the turn of the century, normal schools and teachers colleges announced larger and larger programs of course offerings. Although it appears that this development was encouraged by the institutional administration, the nature of the courses added was determined largely by the interests and initiative of individual staff members. There was little change in the number of announced curriculums until following 1910, but meanwhile the elective system was being adopted. This development is indicated by Thomasson's findings relative to the average total of requirements in the four-year general curriculum — 1890-91, 123.68 semester hours; 1900-01, 118.00 semester hours; 1910-11, 104.74 semester hours; 1920-21, 66.15 semester hours.[47]

For the period 1910 to 1920 Thomasson found the average number of curriculums increased from 2.7 to 4.9 (p. 119). Thus the marked extension of the elective system was accompanied by a corresponding increase

---

[45] A. L. Thomasson, op. cit., pp. 45-46.

[46] George P. Deyoe, Certain Trends in Curriculum Practices and Policies in State Normal Schools and Teachers Colleges (Contributions to Education, No. 606 [New York: Bureau of Publications, Teachers College, Columbia University, 1934]), p. 52.

[47] A. L. Thomasson, op. cit., p. 348.

in the number of announced curriculums. The increase in number of curriculums involved a change in type. It was noted above that in 1890 the differentiation of the curriculums was primarily on the basis of schooling level and the period of time. Following this date, there were more and more curriculums designed to prepare for particular types of teaching positions. Deyoe's tabulation [48] of catalog data from forty-five normal schools and teachers colleges for the years 1902-3, 1912-13, 1922-23, and 1932-33 shows the general trend of this development. In 1902-3 the principal curriculums were "general professional" offered by 33 per cent of the institutions; "high school," 27 per cent; kindergarten, 31 per cent; and "general elementary," 76 per cent. None of the other categories had a frequency amounting to as much as 10 per cent and there was no curriculum for "junior high school" or "secondary administration and supervision." By 1932-33 the "general elementary" had dropped to 47 per cent. "Junior high school" and "secondary administration and supervision" had frequencies of 44 per cent and 4 per cent respectively. The other categories exhibited increased frequencies except in the case of "kindergarten" which dropped to 4 per cent. This latter change is offset by an increase in "kindergarten-primary" from 4 per cent to 56 per cent. Deyoe also presented data showing increases in the number of institutions offering curriculums for "teachers of special subjects" and for "high school teachers of academic subjects" and for "combinations" of such subjects.[49] Thus the general picture is one of a marked trend toward differentiation of curriculums with respect to type of teaching service. Deyoe's tabulation shows that the development was most rapid during the period from 1912-13 to 1922-23 and he stated that "there is some reason for believing that there may be a slight tendency in the direction of decreased differentiation" at the time of his study.

The extension of the elective system and the multiplication of curriculums contributed to a situation in which students were subject to few restrictions in attaining successive certificates and diplomas by accumulating credits from the elaborate arrays of course offerings. Referring to the situation in 1916-17 the report of the study of the normal schools of Missouri [50] characterized the collegiate curriculums announced by four of the five institutions as "rather large program patterns from which individual curricula may be constructed." In another place [51] the general organization of the curriculums is referred to as "ladder-like," i.e. the two-year curriculum consisted of 30 semester hours, including a small

---

[48] George P. Deyoe, *op. cit.*, p. 30.

[49] *Ibid.*, pp. 34 and 36.

[50] William S. Learned, William C. Bagley, and Others, *op. cit.*, p. 167.

[51] *Ibid.*, p. 163.

amount of prescribed work, beyond the one-year curriculum and so on. Thus a student who had obtained the one-year certificate could qualify for the two-year diploma by accumulating 30 semester hours of additional credit by attending spring terms and summer sessions provided the limited prescribed courses were included or approval of "substitutes" was obtained. A student holding the two-year diploma could qualify for the three-year diploma under similar conditions. Then a fourth year of study, subject to limited prescriptions, would satisfy the requirements for the baccalaureate degree. Such a situation, which appears to have been rather typical, reflects a policy of catering to the desires and convenience of students rather than making the "needs of the service" the dominant consideration. Although it is likely that no institution explicitly announced this policy, at least without some qualification, there is much evidence indicating its functioning in the administration of normal schools and teachers colleges up to 1915 and even later.

Ten individual curriculums are described in the report on the normal schools of Missouri.[52] The general picture is one in which the student was permitted to take courses in accordance with his desires and convenience. The National Survey reported an analysis of the records of a sampling of students completing seventeen different four-year major curriculums in twenty teachers colleges.[53] Although this group of institutions is not the same as that for which the analysis of technical-professional requirements was made, a comparison indicates considerable laxness in administering registration. Since the curriculums provided for "free electives" (range of median amounts, 24 to 48 semester hours) it is to be expected that some professional courses would be taken as "free electives" and it appears that the amount of such electives was large in numerous instances. The maximum amounts of professional courses taken in the seventeen four-year curriculums ranged from 25 to 57 semester hours. The corresponding range of maximum requirements was from 24 to 29 semester hours. When these facts are considered in connection with the findings bearing on the general education of graduates (p. 104), the picture of administrative laxness is reinforced. Apparently students who desired to do so were encouraged to elect technical-professional courses. In case they were "interested" in other courses, they were permitted to elect them.

Another item of curricular policy relates to the gradation and sequential organization of courses. In registering students little attention was given

---

[52] *Ibid.*, pp. 411-16.

[53] Earle U. Rugg and Others, *Teacher Education Curricula*, National Survey of the Education of Teachers, Vol. III (U.S. Office of Education, Bulletin 1933, No. 10), p. 525.

to either of these matters. In 1890 and for many years afterwards a student was permitted to enroll in almost any of the technical-professional courses offered,[54] i.e. prerequisites, either specific courses or academic status, were observed for very few courses. Much the same practice prevailed in other departments except when the nature of the courses imposed a sequence. Preparatory students were permitted to enroll in college courses and *vice versa*. Hence class groups were frequently rather extremely heterogeneous with reference to both previous study and academic status. The change from this situation was slow.

Normal Schools as Institutions for Nonprofessional Purposes

State normal schools were established as institutions for the education of teachers. In some cases the legislative action establishing a normal school specified a "pledge to teach" as a condition of admission.[55] However, local and regional pressures and the desire for larger and larger enrollments resulted in the admission of students "not in professional department." On page 277 reference was made to a report of 1897 in which it was stated that the normal schools of the North Central states were "gradually growing to be more and more of a factor in general education." A similar development was noted in most of the normal schools of the Middle Atlantic states.

The change in function indicated by these general statements may be illustrated by the story of the normal schools of Missouri. The five institutions of this state were established as follows: Kirksville and Warrensburg, 1870; Cape Girardeau, 1873; Springfield and Maryville, 1906. Up to about the turn of the century the Missouri normal schools adhered fairly closely to the function of preparing students for teaching, but by 1909 the institutions at Cape Girardeau and Kirksville were frankly soliciting students who were not preparing to teach. The Kirksville normal school employed the caption "Peoples College" in a publication of 1909. In contrast the Warrensburg normal school adhered to the teacher-education function as did the institutions at Maryville and Springfield.[56]

Within normal schools professing to adhere to the professional function there were students who did not expect to teach and many others who were interested in teaching only as a "stepping stone" to further education or to other vocational activity. It is reported that at the time of the Missouri study 60 per cent of the students in the five schools "declared

[54] Clarence Linton, *A Study of Some Problems Arising in the Admission of Students as Candidates for Professional Degrees in Education* (Contributions to Education, No. 285 [New York: Bureau of Publications, Teachers College, Columbia University, 1927]), p. 30.

[55] The pledge required in Missouri is quoted by William S. Learned, William C. Bagley, and Others, *op. cit.*, p. 73.

[56] William S. Learned, William C. Bagley, and Others, *op. cit.*, pp. 70-73.

that they did not intend to teach permanently." The proportion among
men was 78 per cent.[57]

The conditions prevailing in Missouri seem to have been rather typical.
In his study of the catalogs and other publications of forty-five state normal schools Deyoe [58] reported about one-third of the institutions announced and provided for nonprofessional functions during the period
from 1902-3 to 1932-33. Deyoe mentions a few institutions which explicitly stated that they did not wish students who were not interested
in preparing for teaching.

Increasing Academic Emphasis

Associated with the promotion of nonprofessional functions by some
normal schools there was a widespread trend toward subject-matter
courses of the academic type. In the account of the evolution of the
thinking about the purposes of teacher education it was noted that
around 1890 the consensus seemed to be in the direction of professional
treatment of subject-matter courses (see p. 188). This date, however,
marked the height of favorable opinion, and from about the turn of the
century the trend was toward subject-matter courses of the academic
type.

Several influences doubtless contributed to this development. The normal schools wished to be recognized as academically respectable, at
least to the extent that their work would be accepted by colleges and universities as transfer credit. By the turn of the century the normal schools
were seeking recognition as appropriate institutions for the preparation
of secondary teachers. From around 1910 many normal schools became
concerned with being recognized as collegiate institutions conferring the
baccalaureate degree. Meanwhile, the normal-school product was being
criticized as weak in "scholarship," and this appraisal was widely regarded as a major obstacle in achieving these desires.

In improving the academic quality of the subject-matter program departments were organized similar to those of liberal arts colleges and
academically trained persons were appointed to staff positions. The
effect of these developments was to create a liberal-arts group within
the institution. Although this group was more friendly to professional
training for teachers than the liberal-arts group in colleges and universities and some staff members were concerned about the subject-matter
needs of teachers in our schools, the emphasis was on courses that would
be regarded as academically respectable. In commenting on the situation
around the turn of the century, Randolph characterized the normal

---

[57] *Ibid.*, p. 74.
[58] George P. Deyoe, *op. cit.*, pp. 5-17.

school as being "typically two schools, with rival purposes; two institutions set side by side — the bond between them mainly their common students looking toward a common vocation."[59] In the Missouri study this detachment of the so-called "professional" work is cited as "a striking weakness in efforts to provide professional preparation for teachers, not only in the Missouri normal schools, but in the colleges and universities and in nearly all normal schools that are organized on the collegiate model." [60]

Coordination of Normal Schools with Colleges and Universities

In 1892 Charles De Garmo, president of the Normal School Department, addressed the meeting on the topic, "Co-ordination of the normal school and the university in the training of teachers." [61] In the first sentence he declared: "No co-ordination of the normal school and the university now exists." In discussing this situation he was critical of both classes of institutions. With reference to normal schools he said: "The natural tendency for the normal school, finding itself discredited at the higher seats of learning, is to crawl into the shell of its own individuality, proclaiming itself a peculiar institution, quite sufficient unto itself." De Garmo urged that the normal schools "strive constantly to raise the standards of qualification for admission" and more important try "to infuse new life into the faculty by the employment of highly educated instructors." This statement implies that, in general, normal-school faculties were not adequately educated according to academic standards. Although comprehensive data are not available, this implied appraisal seems to have been valid. This condition and the indifference of normal-school presidents toward academic standards tended to prevail until after 1910. However, the normal schools of the time became insistent that their work should be accepted for transfer credit.

Presumably as a result of De Garmo's address and the ensuing discussion the Department voted "that the Chairman appoint a committee of three to nominate at tomorrow's session a committee to report on what can be done to secure the co-ordination of normal schools and universities in the training of teachers." In 1894 the committee thus created presented a report based upon catalog information from twenty-five "representative normal schools" and information from twenty-three universities.[62] With reference to the attitude of the universities toward the

---

[59] Edgar D. Randolph, *op. cit.*, p. 34.

[60] William S. Learned, William C. Bagley, and Others, *op. cit.*, p. 168.

[61] Charles De Garmo, "Co-ordination of the Normal School and the University in the Training of Teachers," *Addresses and Proceedings* (National Educational Association, 1892), pp. 411-14.

[62] "Report of Committee on the Relation of Normal Schools to Universities," *Addresses and Proceedings* (National Education Association, 1894), pp. 821-32.

normal schools the committee reported that it "found a somewhat unex-
pected liberality." Two state universities and six nonstate universities
refused to "admit normal school graduates without Latin to any course
whatever." Two state universities (Iowa and Wisconsin) "admitted non-
classical normal school graduates to advanced standing in some cases."
The general situation is reflected by the statement: "To the credit of
American universities, it must be said that they have gone farther to
meet the normal schools than the normal schools have to meet them. The
universities manifest little inclination to debar normal school graduates
from pursuing studies they are able to master."

The report did not include any explicit recommendations and its acceptance probably was not intended to indicate approval by the normal-
school group of this conclusion. Referring to the appointment of the committee the president of the department in 1912 said: "It required some
courage in these days, when public sentiment was favorable to university
education and, in the main, ignorant of or antagonistic to normal schools,
to undertake a co-ordination of the products of these two types of institutions." [63] In the light of this comment and other evidence it appears
that in 1892 only a few members of the normal-school group were seriously concerned with the coordination of the normal schools and the universities. Charles De Garmo, then president of Swarthmore College,
was appointed chairman of the committee and he doubtless influenced
its deliberations. The other members of the committee were R. G. Boone,
Ph.D. (Michigan State Normal School); Charles McMurry,[64] Ph.D.
(Illinois State Normal University); N. M. Butler, Ph.D. (New Jersey
State Board of Education); G. Stanley Hall, Ph.D. (Clark University);
James M. Green, Ph.D. (New Jersey State Normal School); and Superintendent D. L. Kiehle (Minneapolis, Minnesota). The committee does not
appear to have been representative of the normal-school group and this
condition together with the absence of evidence of a follow-up activity
strengthens the inference that the normal schools as a group were little
concerned with elevating their work to the level of collegiate respectability. Consequently, the creation of the committee and the acceptance
of its report in 1894 must be regarded as a premature attempt by a limited group to stimulate normal schools to raise their standards to the end
that their work would be recognized by colleges and universities.

General recognition of post-high-school study in normal schools as
worthy of acceptance as college credit was not attained until several
years later. Pangburn has characterized the development in California
as typical among the "state universities of the West" where the accrediting of normal schools by "institutions of higher learning seems to have

[63] W. J. Hawkins, "The Attitude of the Normal Schools Toward Education," *Addresses and Proceedings* (National Education Association, 1912), p. 811.

[64] Appointed but not included among the signatories of the report.

begun." Up to 1911 normal-school work was recognized by the University of California only at the level of entrance requirements. Beginning in that year, "recommended state normal school graduates" who were also graduates of accredited high schools were allowed "forty-eight units toward the required sixty-four units for the junior certificate." [65]

Concluding Statement

The preceding account has dealt mainly with the development of normal schools as normal schools. Their evolution into teachers colleges is the topic of the following chapter.

[65] Jessie M. Pangburn, *op. cit.*, p. 88.

CHAPTER 11

From Normal Schools
to Teachers Colleges

The development indicated by this chapter title is that of normal schools attaining recognition as institutions of college grade authorized to confer the baccalaureate degree on the basis of a four-year course of study. Chronologically this development overlaps that described in the preceding chapter and is in effect an extension of the endeavors of normal schools to achieve academic respectability. The immediate motive was the ambition to become recognized as approved institutions for the preparation of secondary teachers.

Insistence upon Preparation of Secondary Teachers As a Normal-School Function

At the meeting of the Normal School Department in 1900 it was recommended to the president that a place on the program of the next year be given to "The training of teachers for secondary schools." In 1901 James E. Russell presented a paper on this topic.[1] His position was that the preparation of teachers for secondary schools should be left to the colleges and universities, and he observed that if the normal school attempted to fulfill this function, it "must raise its standards and prepare

---

[1] James E. Russell, "The Training of Teachers for Secondary Schools," *Addresses and Proceedings* (National Educational Association, 1901), pp. 636-41.

291

to enter a new field." Russell did not elaborate, but it is apparent that he considered entering this "new field" as involving the development of respectable collegiate courses. In the subsequent discussion there was some difference of opinion in regard to the wisdom of the normal schools attempting to enter this "new field." In summing up, Russell expressed himself as much gratified that the consensus had been strongest on his side of the argument.

At the 1905 meeting of the Department of Normal Schools the president of the organization spoke on "A statement of the issues before the department." He referred to "the training of secondary teachers" as a "most serious problem" of concern to both normal schools and universities. He pointed out that college graduates generally were lacking in professional training and that those of the normal schools were "deficient in breadth and grasp of subject-matter." He seems to have been skeptical of the universities being able or willing to "present [professional] courses suited specifically and solely to the practical needs of the secondary teacher" and suggested that a solution of the problem might be attained by developing a plan of cooperation.[2] At the close of the session a resolution calling for the appointment of a committee to "formulate a statement of policy regarding the preparation and qualifications of teachers of elementary and high schools" was approved.[3] The committee was immediately appointed and presented a preliminary report the next day in which it was recommended that "it is the function of the normal schools to equip themselves for the preparation of secondary teachers."[4] The report was "filed" and the committee continued. The recommendation was repeated with only changes of phraseology in 1907 and 1908.

Having taken a "stand," the Department became concerned with the preparation of teachers for secondary schools. At the 1909 meeting the president read a paper on "The place of the normal school in a system of public education."[5] He observed that "for more than twenty years the Normal School Department of the National Education Association has been wrestling with the problems of the place and function of the normal school." His position was that of an emphatic endorsement of the training of secondary teachers as a normal-school function and he was able to refer to some institutions that had become "teachers colleges." A subsequent speaker began his paper as follows:

The work of training teachers for secondary schools is at present divided, in most of the states, between normal schools, colleges, and universities. There is,

[2] Charles C. Van Liew, "A Statement of the Issues Before the Department," *Addresses and Proceedings* (National Educational Association, 1905), pp. 519-24.

[3] *Addresses and Proceedings* (National Educational Association, 1905), p. 517.

[4] *Ibid.*, p. 518.

[5] H. G. Williams, "The Place of the Normal School in a System of Public Education," *Addresses and Proceedings* (National Education Association, 1909), pp. 548-56.

however, a well-defined movement in our higher institutions of learning, especially in universities, to limit the product of normal schools to the grades and to create a monopoly whereby only graduates of colleges and universities shall be eligible as teachers in secondary schools. On behalf of normal schools we unqualifiedly condemn such movement and protest against the creation of such monopoly. We propose to show: (1) That the normal schools are now doing a large part of this work and doing it so well that no sufficient reason exists for barring them from this field; (2) that universities and colleges are neither by equipment nor ideals properly fitted to train young people for the teaching process.[6]

Thus a significant controversy developed relative to the scope of the function of normal schools. It became prominent at the time when teacher educators tended to regard the purposes of teacher education (desired teacher qualifications) as being adequately defined (see Chapter 8), and in the "battle" of the following years there was limited attention to the development of more effective programs of teacher education. The normal schools tended to exhibit much of the attitude ascribed to them by De Garmo in 1892 relative to coordination with colleges and universities (see p. 288). The higher institutions, especially the state universities, exhibited considerable smugness stemming from their traditional prestige and their control of the accreditation of secondary schools. Both groups, however, included "liberals," some of whom exercised considerable leadership. To these leaders, particularly those functioning in the American Association of Teachers Colleges, much credit is due for the status of teachers colleges in 1930.

The Establishment of Teachers Colleges

There is uncertainty in regard to the date of the establishment of the first teachers college, i.e. a normal school authorized to confer the baccalaureate degree. Citing an unpublished study by E. R. Mosher, Pangburn [7] mentions the Michigan State Normal College (Ypsilanti) as the "first normal school to become a teachers college in the modern sense of the term." Legislative action occurred in 1903 and the first Bachelor of Arts degree was conferred in 1905. A tabulation of "date of legal establishment of teachers colleges" in the National Survey [8] gives 1897 as the date for the Michigan institution and lists the teachers college

[6] D. McGregor, "Professional Training for Teachers of Secondary Schools." *Addresses and Proceedings* (National Education Association, 1909), p. 581.

[7] Jessie M. Pangburn, *The Evolution of the American Teachers College* (Contributions to Education, No. 500 [New York: Bureau of Publications, Teachers College, Columbia University, 1932]), p. 42.

[8] Benjamin W. Frazier and Others, *Special Survey Studies*, National Survey of the Education of Teachers, Vol. V (U.S. Office of Education, Bulletin 1933, No. 10), pp. 52-53.

of New Mexico as being established in 1899.[9] A total of eighteen teachers colleges had been established by 1915, all but two being in the Middle West and West. Following this date the rate of legal establishment was much greater, the total by 1931 being 156 institutions.

Problems in the Development of Normal Schools into Teachers Colleges

In his address of 1901 James E. Russell observed that if the normal school attempted to prepare teachers for secondary schools it "must raise its standards and prepare to enter a new field" (see p. 291). This observation indicates two central problems in the development of normal schools into teachers colleges. Raising standards may be interpreted as meaning adopting the standards of contemporary colleges and universities. Entering a "new field" involved developing a four-year educational program of college grade. At the time of Russell's address a number of normal schools were offering curriculums extending two years beyond the level of high-school graduation, but these curriculums "consisted mainly of the common branches and purely professional subjects." [10] Some of the more ambitious institutions offered elective courses purporting to be of college grade, but the four-year educational program to be developed was largely new.

Such a development required additions to the staff of persons qualified to give collegiate instruction in the subject-matter fields. This required increased support. The limited appropriations obtained by tax-supported normal schools was a handicap in the development of their educational programs. In 1915 the salary schedules of state normal schools and teachers colleges were about two-thirds of those for comparable positions in tax-supported colleges and universities. In addition, the number of teaching hours per week in the normal schools was double the teaching load in the colleges and universities. The comparison for "pupils per teacher" was nearly of the same order.[11] Under these conditions the recruitment of an appropriate staff was a difficult problem.

Russell's position that the preparation of teachers for secondary schools

[9] Neither this tabulation nor Pangburn's statement refers to the use of the title "teachers college." According to a letter from H. H. Seerley, quoted by Hall-Quest, the first official change to this title was by the normal school at Cedar Falls, Iowa, in 1909. Alfred L. Hall-Quest, *Professional Secondary Education in Teachers Colleges* (New York: Teachers College, Columbia University, 1925), p. 19.

[10] Edward C. Class, *Prescription and Election in Elementary-school Teacher-training Curricula in State Teachers Colleges* (Contributions to Education, No. 480 [New York: Bureau of Publications, Teachers College, Columbia University, 1931]), pp. 28-29.

[11] Charles A. Harper, *Development of the Teachers College in the United States* (Bloomington, Illinois: McKnight and McKnight, Publishers, 1935), p. 279.

should be left to the colleges and universities was widely supported and until after 1920 there was considerable active opposition to the elevation of normal schools into teachers colleges.[12] This opposition increased the difficulty of obtaining adequate funds and the teachers-college development may appropriately be characterized as a "struggle."

Attitude of Normal Schools Toward Academic Standards

Within the movement to command recognition as institutions for preparing teachers for secondary schools and to obtain authority to confer the baccalaureate degree the normal schools gave little attention to "academic standards" beyond admission requirements and even here they tended to approve exceptions or to exercise "liberality" in accepting "equivalents" of a high-school education. Normal schools offered courses on the collegiate level, at least in the sense of granting "college" credit for them, which college and university authorities considered to be unworthy of such credit. Within this category were "review" courses and some pedagogical offerings. The collegiate courses were not "graded," i.e. senior-college students were enrolled in courses with freshmen and sophomores and even preparatory students.

College students in normal schools were rather typically permitted to carry programs of study considerably in excess of 15 semester hours which tended to be the standard in colleges and universities. The study of the normal schools of Missouri reported that in 1913-14 two-thirds or more of the programs of collegiate students in the regular session amounted to twenty or more class periods per week.[13] In four of the institutions 4 to 22 per cent of the collegiate students were permitted programs involving more than twenty-three class periods per week. The training of staff members assigned to collegiate courses was in many instances not up to "standard," particularly in the case of advanced courses, and the teaching load was above "standard." In the ambition to appear as colleges some normal schools expanded their offerings beyond their staff resources. On a survey visit to one of the Missouri normal schools in 1915 it was noted that the total number of collegiate students enrolled in one department was precisely equal to the number of courses listed in the catalog. When the instructor was asked for an explanation, his reply was, "The Board gauges a man by the class enrolments; hence instructors offer a large number of courses." [14]

Credit for "experience" was a rather common practice in at least one

---

[12] *Ibid.*, pp. 313f.

[13] William S. Learned, William C. Bagley, and Others, *The Professional Preparation of Teachers for American Public Schools* (New York: The Carnegie Foundation for the Advancement of Teaching, Bulletin No. 14, 1920), p. 434.

[14] *Ibid.*, p. 233.

of the Missouri normal schools. The "experience" thus recognized included not only teaching but also home experiences on a farm, labor on the local school farm, service as a desk attendant in the library, assistant in the laboratory, and the like. In some instances the credit granted was excessive. In one case "on account of her good record as a teacher in the state" seven and one-half hours in pedagogical subjects were allowed in addition to credit of one year of practice work. This student was also given an additional six and a quarter hours, apparently for merit as shown by "grades." [15] The school from which this practice was reported also granted a "conditional diploma" under which the recipient promised to return and make up the deficiency within a specified time or to surrender the diploma.

These findings from the Missouri study are perhaps not typical of the normal schools of the time, but it seems clear that these institutions were reluctant to adopt the "standards" of the academic world or, from a somewhat different point of view, to renounce their provincialism and freedom to adjust curricular offerings and other practices to the exigencies of their clientele and local situations. Although the "standards" of the colleges and universities of the time were not as specific as later and there was doubtless considerable liberality in their administration, such practices as those noted above were not considered to be compatible with the conditions of academic respectability.

Development of Standards for Normal Schools and Teachers Colleges

The slowness of normal schools in adopting high-school graduation or the equivalent as a condition of admission was noted in the preceding chapter. They were also slow in adopting other standards of the academic world. At the February meeting of the Department of Normal Schools in 1913 a "Preliminary report of committee on normal school standards" emphasized the "great lack of uniformity in the state normal schools of the country." [16] Although a "more definite report" was promised, it does not appear in the proceedings of subsequent meetings. A possible explanation is suggested by the resolution creating the committee which specified as its function: "to make a study of 'The Standards that Are Agreed Upon in the Proper Making of a Teacher.'" [17] Apparently there were no such standards.[18]

At the July meeting of 1915 a letter from Charles H. Judd was read in which he advocated the standardization of the normal schools. "On

---

[15] *Ibid.*, p. 333.

[16] W. T. Carrington, "Preliminary Report of Committee on Normal School Standards," *Addresses and Proceedings* (National Education Association, 1913), p. 542.

[17] *Addresses and Proceedings* (National Education Association, 1912), p. 851.

[18] The conditions described on page 277 had not changed materially.

account of the present chaotic conditions," it was stated, "universities refuse to recognize credits from normal schools at full value although they accept credits from colleges that are much inferior in equipment, training, and standard of scholarship." This communication stimulated the creation of a committee "to investigate the desirability and possibility of a standardization of the normal schools." [19] Subsequent proceedings of the department do not mention a report from this committee and it is apparent that this normal-school group was not friendly to standardization.

At the July, 1917, meeting two normal-school presidents discussed the question, "How far should the principle of standardization be followed by the normal school?" The first speaker expressed his position as follows: "The conditions in the different states of the Union are so varied that no standardization of courses of instruction in normal schools seems possible until the conditions in the different states become more nearly similar." [20] The second speaker said: "There is real need for some rational, helpful scheme of standardization that may be accepted by all these schools." This statement suggests a friendly attitude toward standardization, but it is apparent from the remainder of the paper that the speaker opposed the sort of standards being advocated by "outsiders." He referred to the action of his own institution in deciding against seeking admission to the North Central Association of Colleges and Secondary Schools and added: "Colorado State Teachers College [Greeley] maintains an ungraded school of adults without worrying much about entrance requirements and caring much more about the 'power unit' of the mature student's growth than about the 'time unit.'" [21] The secretary's minutes of the meeting mentioned a "spirited discussion" that "brought to light the extreme displeasure of the members over the treatment of the normal schools in the surveys conducted by the educational foundations [22] and by Commissioner Claxton." [23]

The first *Yearbook* (1922) of the American Association of Teachers Colleges, organized in 1917, included a summary of the proceedings of the earlier meetings. At the first meeting "the subject of chief interest

[19] *Addresses and Proceedings* (National Education Association, 1915), p. 785.

[20] C. G. Pearse, "How Far Should the Principle of Standardization be Followed by the Normal Schools?" *Addresses and Proceedings* (National Education Association, 1917), p. 384.

[21] J. G. Crabbe, "How Far Should the Principle of Standardization be Followed by the Normal Schools?" *Addresses and Proceedings* (National Education Association, 1917), pp. 387-88.

[22] William S. Learned, William C. Bagley, and Others, *The Professional Preparation of Teachers for American Public Schools* (New York: Carnegie Foundation for the Advancement of Teaching, Bulletin No. 14, 1920). 475 pp.

[23] Charles H. Judd and S. Chester Parker, *Problems Involved in Standardizing State Normal Schools* (U.S. Bureau of Education, Bulletin, 1916, No. 12). 141 pp.

was the establishment of an educational honor society." This matter and
the formulation of a constitution and by-laws are the only specific items
mentioned with reference to the second meeting. The establishment of a
"national honor society" received further consideration at the third meeting and two committees were appointed — one to "investigate the possible relation of the teachers colleges of the country with the Association
of Collegiate Alumnae" and the other to classify the teachers colleges.
The latter committee reported at the next meeting (1920) classifying
forty-two institutions as follows: Class A, "teachers colleges that have
conferred degrees" (35); Class B, "teachers colleges that have authority
to confer degrees, but have not availed themselves of the authority" (4);
Class C, "institutions that have four-year courses, but do not have
authority to grant degrees (3). The discussion at the 1921 meeting centered about the qualifications and classification of faculty members. Thus
according to the "official" summary of the proceedings the American
Association of Teachers Colleges was concerned during the first five
years of its existence with obtaining some of the labels of a collegiate
institution rather than with the nature and quality of the educational
program leading to the baccalaureate degree.

At the 1922 meeting of the American Association of Teachers Colleges
one of the approved items was the "slogan of the Association for the
year" — "The forward movement of the normal schools toward making
them technical, vocational Teachers Colleges with adequate standards." [24]
In his address Thomas W. Butcher stressed the desirability of meeting
"the standards of other colleges and of graduate schools." [25] A report by
the Committee on Teachers Colleges of the National Council of Education [26] provides information in regard to the observance of collegiate
standards in the member institutions of the American Association of
Teachers Colleges. In three-fourths of them the admission requirements
were the same as those in the respective state universities. Thirty-six institutions reported a minimum requirement of work for the baccalaureate degree in courses to which freshmen were not admitted. Since only fifty-one
of the teachers colleges were reported as granting degrees, the relative
observance of this standard was probably somewhat greater than the
absolute value of reported frequency indicates. The teaching load was
reported as exceeding 16 hours per week in twenty-four of fifty-five institutions providing this information. Eleven schools permitted students to
carry 20 or more hours of work requiring preparation but the modal
practice was 16 hours.

---

[24] *Yearbook* (American Association of Teachers Colleges, 1922), p. 22.

[25] *Ibid.*, pp. 27-28.

[26] The following statements are based on the report as published in the *Yearbook*
of the American Association of Teachers Colleges for 1922.

In 1923 the American Association of Teachers Colleges adopted "standards for accrediting teachers' colleges and normal schools," the "first set of normal school standards" adopted by an authoritative body.[27] Admission on the basis of "satisfactory completion of four years of work in a secondary school approved by a recognized accrediting agency, or equivalent of such course" and "average teaching program of a teacher" not to exceed "16 hours of 50 to 60 minutes each" were listed as "minimum standards" but apparently were not intended to be mandatory. There was no reference to other academic standards except class size.

There was interest in the development of more adequate standards for teachers colleges. In 1924 Guy E. Maxwell [28] reviewed the record of the Department of Normal Schools and commented on the standards adopted by the American Association of Teachers Colleges in 1923. The 1924 and 1925 *Yearbooks* of the Association include reports on various practices. In 1926 mandatory standards relative to admission, preparation of faculty, teaching load, and gradation of courses were adopted.[29] This action may be taken as marking the turn of the tide toward a willingness on the part of teachers colleges (four-year institutions granting a baccalaureate degree) and normal schools to conform to standards along the lines of those prevailing among reputable colleges and universities. Twenty years earlier a committee of the Department of Normal Schools had proposed that colleges and universities *should* give full credit for normal-school work provided the admission standard had been met. Now the American Association of Teachers Colleges acted to apply to its membership not only the admission standard (more rigorously defined) but also standards relative to faculty preparation, teaching load, and gradation of courses. Provisions in the 1926 action for gradual enforcement of the standards and for classification of member institutions on the basis of the extent to which the several standards were met suggest that some of the normal schools and teachers colleges of the time were not conforming to the standards. It is significant that institutions failing to meet certain standards, including those relative to faculty preparation, teaching load, and gradation of courses, were to be designated as Class C colleges.

[27] Guy E. Maxwell, "Working Conditions Essential to Highest Efficiency and Economy," *Addresses and Proceedings* (National Education Association, 1924), pp. 614-24. These standards are not mentioned in the 1923 *Yearbook* but are given in the Report of Committee on American Teachers Colleges of the National Council of Education, *Addresses and Proceedings* (National Education Association, 1923), pp. 483-84.

[28] *Ibid.*

[29] "Standards for Accrediting Teachers Colleges," *Yearbook* (American Association of Teachers Colleges, 1926), pp. 9-12.

Observance of Standards

A study of the catalogs of approximately 180 normal schools and teachers colleges [30] reported in 1927 revealed that the stated admission requirements specified or implied completion of secondary-school work. However, Earle U. Rugg, who reported the study, appeared to entertain some skepticism in regard to the complete enforcement of this requirement, and it is not unlikely that in at least some of the institutions some exceptions were made or the credentials presented were liberally interpreted.

The Committee on Accrediting and Classification reported in 1928 [31] that as a group the member institutions were weakest with respect to the "academic and professional preparation of the faculty," but that the standards relative to "entrance requirements, requirements for graduation, teacher's load, and student load" were rarely violated. A subsequent statement in the report suggests doubt relative to conformity with the standard specifying gradation of courses. An inquiry reported in the National Survey indicated general, but not complete, observance of the restriction that "senior college courses must not be open to freshmen who have not taken the prerequisites for these courses." The restriction that "programs consisting mainly of freshmen and sophomore courses, carrying full credit, shall not be available for students in the junior and senior years" was not observed in one-third of the institutions from which information was obtained. Other pertinent findings were also reported. Two-fifths of the 1,719 courses studied were not assigned a position in a sequence and 29 per cent of 2,309 courses were listed as for all undergraduates. About two-thirds of 1,798 courses had specified prerequisites.[32] These findings apply to all courses, subject-matter and professional, and in view of the inherent sequential nature of mathematics, foreign languages, and some other subject-matter fields, it is not unlikely that findings for professional courses alone would indicate a somewhat less degree of conformity with the standard.

Reports of the Committee on Accrediting and Classification during the following years afforded evidence that as a class, normal schools and teachers colleges continued to develop in the direction of academic respectability. In 1938 when the standards became completely mandatory,

[30] Earle U. Rugg, "The Trend Toward Standardization in Teachers Colleges," *Yearbook* (American Association of Teachers Colleges, 1927), pp. 84-99.

[31] Charles McKenny, "Report of Committee on Accrediting and Classification," *Yearbook* (American Association of Teachers Colleges, 1928), pp. 25-28.

[32] Earle U. Rugg and Others, *Teacher Education Curricula*, National Survey of the Education of Teachers, Vol. III (U.S. Office of Education, Bulletin 1933, No. 10), pp. 514-15.

there were no reported violations among the 157 classified member institutions of the American Association of Teachers Colleges.[33]

The Educational Program

As normal schools became teachers colleges, i.e. institutions requiring high-school graduation or the equivalent for admission and authorized to confer the baccalaureate degree, they expanded their educational programs, especially in subject-matter areas. The extent of this expansion is indicated by findings reported for the normal schools of Missouri which had announced programs for the A.B. degree in 1904.

In 1917-18 the total collegiate offerings ranged from 698.8 semester hours at Kirksville to 506.3 semester hours at Springfield. The degree of the expansion of offerings is emphasized by noting the number of semester hours offered in certain "departments": — "history and political and social science" (Kirksville) 100, ancient languages (Cape Girardeau) 91.3, agriculture (Kirksville) 45, and English (Warrensburg) 80.[34] The staffs of the several departments were not commensurate with the number of offerings. For example, there was only one instructor for the 91.3 semester hours in ancient languages offered at Cape Girardeau. Furthermore the departmental enrollments were very limited in many instances. During the regular session of 1915-16 more than one-third of the collegiate classes in the five institutions had fewer than ten students. In Latin the proportion was 88 per cent.

Two motives are indicated for such extensive arrays of departmental offerings — "keeping up with the Joneses" (the University of Missouri and the other normal schools of the state)[35] and departmental and instructor prestige under the elective system. In order not to be at a disadvantage in attracting students the administration of a normal school encouraged the offering of a large number of courses, both academic and pedagogical. Although not explicitly expressed it seems to have been the policy of each institution to extend its list of course offerings so that it could claim that it provided all the opportunities for teacher education which were provided by the competing schools. At least one of the normal schools of Missouri seems to have been aggressive in developing teacher-education opportunities beyond those afforded by its competitors.

Such practices are perhaps not typical of the normal schools and

---

[33] "Report of the Secretary," American Association of Teachers Colleges, *Addresses and Proceedings* (National Education Association, 1938), p. 324.

[34] William S. Learned, William C. Bagley, and Others, *The Professional Preparation of Teachers for American Public Schools* (New York: Carnegie Foundation for the Advancement of Teaching, Bulletin No. 14, 1920), p. 411.

[35] *Ibid.*, pp. 228, 232, and 235.

teachers colleges of the time which were attempting to establish themselves as collegiate institutions, but they do indicate the tendency to expand course offerings beyond a level commensurate with class enrollments and staff resources. In a study of the catalogs of fifty-nine teachers colleges for 1923-24 Hall-Quest [36] reported an average of 271 courses for all departments. The mean number of courses per subject-matter department ranged from 28.1 in English, 25.5 in science, and 23.3 in history, civics, and social sciences to 10.1 in classics, 9.3 in agriculture, and 1.0 in philosophy, ethics, and logic.[37] The number of semester hours is not given, but it is stated that the average number of "lecture hours" was 42.4 per course. This indicates an average credit value of 2.5 semester hours or possibly slightly more.

The teachers colleges studied by Hall-Quest varied with respect to the number of courses announced for 1923-24, the range being from 61 to 713. Ten of the fifty-nine institutions offered more than four hundred courses. Four of the five teachers colleges of Missouri offered 325, 383, 418, and 474 courses, respectively. These data are not comparable to those given above for 1917-18, but it seems probable that these institutions had increased their course offerings. A study reported in the National Survey gives an average of "about 15 courses per department or the equivalent of about 42 semester hours" per department for 1930-31.[38] Institutional totals are not given, but since seventeen subject fields were recognized in the tabulation, it is apparent that the average total number of course offerings was of the same order as reported by Hall-Quest for 1923-24. There were marked variations among the teachers colleges and normal schools studied. The range for the course offerings in English was from 2 to 99. The averages of the reported ranges are 3 to 58.

Within the expansion of the offerings in subject-matter fields little attention was given to the professional quality of the courses. Active argument for the teaching-knowledge qualification disappeared about the time of the beginning of the teachers-college development (see p. 196). Furthermore, the argument had been made relative to the preparation of teachers for elementary schools. In colleges and universities of the time it was generally assumed that the specialization represented by an academic major provided an adequate teaching knowledge for secondary instruction in that field. As teachers colleges developed, their subject-matter offerings tended to be similar to those of the colleges and universities.

In the National Survey it was concluded that there was very little

[36] Alfred L. Hall-Quest, *Professional Secondary Education in Teachers Colleges* (New York: Teachers College, Columbia University, 1925), p. 68.
[37] *Ibid.*, p. 71.
[38] Earle U. Rugg and Others, *op cit.*, p. 59.

professional treatment of subject-matter courses. A considerable proportion of subject-matter instructors claimed some professionalization of their courses, but visitation of selected teachers colleges "did not result in the impression that there was wide acceptance of the theory of professional treatment of subject matter," and an attempt to identify the "concrete ways" of professionalizing the courses was not successful.[39]

Curricular Requirements and Practices

As normal schools evolved into teachers colleges the institutions generally retained their two- and three-year curriculums which were mainly for the preparation of elementary teachers. Various four-year curriculums for secondary teachers were introduced. In his catalog study of fifty-nine teachers colleges for 1923-24 Hall-Quest reported 390 professional secondary curriculums, "no two of which are exactly alike." [40] These curriculums are tabulated under fifty-eight titles. All but three of these titles indicate a type of teaching position, some of them being subject combinations. Hall-Quest does not give an analysis of the requirements within these curriculums.

The National Survey gives an analysis of the catalog requirements for all four-year curriculums (636) of thirty-one teachers colleges. The following median semester-hour requirements are reported: total for graduation, 129; major (including special methods), 26; first minor, 17; second minor, 12; education and psychology (including student teaching and observation), 16; restricted electives, 31; free electives, 39; required contacts outside of major field (total medians in 14 fields), 73.[41] Since the medians of the restricted and free electives total 70 semester hours, the median prescribed work amounts to 59 semester hours. The distribution of the prescribed courses is not indicated, but it is significant that nearly 55 per cent of the total requirement for graduation is classified under restricted and free electives.

The analysis included 636 curriculums distributed among thirty-one teachers colleges, or an average of slightly more than 20 curriculums per institution. It may be inferred that a curriculum was generally for a particular type of teaching position and that it was the policy at this time to permit the students preparing for a given type of teaching position to exercise considerable choice in determining their programs of study. The sample data [42] in regard to the choices made indicate that some students extended their major beyond the minimum requirement; others

[39] *Ibid.*, p. 93.

[40] Alfred L. Hall-Quest, *op. cit.*, p. 40.

[41] Earle U. Rugg and Others, *op. cit.*, p. 62.

[42] *Ibid.*, pp. 65-66.

extended their technical-professional study. Adding to one or both minors appears to have been a typical practice.

The median technical-professional requirement, including special methods and professional courses in the major, is 20 semester hours. The totals for "education and psychology" and "special methods" in the sample data exceed this amount in 18 out of 24 cases. Most of the extreme cases are in art, industrial arts, and music majors, but the amounts for the sample mathematics' majors are 23, 31, 43, and 26, respectively. Thus it appears that the elective privilege was typically used to extend technical-professional study beyond the minimum requirement (median, 20 semester hours), in a few cases to a relatively high level.

In another place [43] it is stated that practice "indicates that students use their electives in fields in which they have already taken work." This suggests that students were influenced by departmental instructors who were doubtless motivated by the desire to increase their course registrations. Other evidence supports the conclusion that during the years preceding 1930 teachers colleges had not developed effective guidance programs.

In connection with the median requirements of 636 curriculums in thirty-one teachers colleges the National Survey also gives the ranges — semester hours for graduation, 120-163; major, 2-89; first minor, 6-36; restricted electives, 2-101; free electives, 1-79; education and psychology, 4-29; special methods and professional courses in major, 1-40; student teaching and observation, 2-32. Similar ranges are given for some of the "required contacts outside major field" — English, 3-33; foreign language, 3-24; science, 1-47; social science, 2-35. These extremes are doubtless contributed to by special-subject curriculums and those designed for kindergarten and elementary teachers. The departmental placement of courses may have been a factor. Bearing in mind these and other possible explanatory conditions, it seems clear that the teachers colleges of 1930 differed significantly in their curriculum requirements. It may be inferred that they had not adequately defined the desirable preparation for a given type of teaching position.

Some Comparisons with Colleges and Universities

As normal schools developed into teachers colleges, there was limited observance of the practices and standards of the colleges and universities of the time, and teachers colleges were generally regarded as inferior collegiate institutions. These newly organized institutions, however, gradually adopted the practices and standards of the academic world. By 1930 the teachers colleges tended to be similar to liberal arts col-

---

[43] *Ibid.*, p. 111.

leges and the liberal-arts unit of universities relative to the education of secondary teachers. Some data supporting this statement have been noted in the preceding pages. Additional data are provided by the National Survey and other studies.

Findings for 1923-24 reported by Hall-Quest were cited above as indicative of the expansion of the educational program of teachers colleges. He also reported data for thirty colleges and universities.[44] The tabulation of the courses in the departments corresponding to all departments of a teachers college revealed an average of 474.2 courses per institution. This is materially greater than the average of 271 courses for the fifty-nine teachers colleges studied, but the universities and some of the colleges offered graduate programs and apparently Hall-Quest included graduate courses in his counts. One can only speculate in regard to the average for colleges and universities if only undergraduate courses had been counted, but it is clear that in expanding their educational programs the teachers colleges were following a practice that is obvious in the colleges and universities of the time.

The findings reported in the National Survey in regard to the number of courses offered in the two classes of institutions [45] permit only limited comparisons, but it appears that normal schools and teachers colleges tended to offer fewer courses than were offered in corresponding departments of colleges and that their educational programs were much less elaborate than those of universities. The variations among normal schools and teachers colleges were somewhat more extreme than among the colleges and universities. These findings support the statement that by 1930 the educational program of teachers colleges was of about the same order with respect to number of courses offered as that of colleges and of the undergraduate liberal-arts unit of universities.

The National Survey provides data for other pertinent comparisons. Class size was much the same.[46] The average prescription for a major was about 5 semester hours greater in colleges and universities.[47] More than half of the members of the faculties of colleges and universities had had three or more years of graduate work. The corresponding preparation for state normal schools and teachers colleges was 25.2 per cent.[48] This difference is doubtless due largely to the greater amount of graduate work offered in colleges and universities, and in view of other find-

[44] Alfred L. Hall-Quest, *op. cit.*, pp. 70f.

[45] Earle U. Rugg and Others, *op. cit.*, pp. 58, 179.

[46] *Ibid.*, p. 181.

[47] *Ibid.*, p. 235.

[48] E. S. Evenden and Others, *Teacher Personnel in the United States*, National Survey of the Education of Teachers, Vol. II (U.S. Office of Education, Bulletin 1933, No. 10), p. 162.

ings it seems likely that there was little difference in the training of the
instructors in the undergraduate programs of the two classes of institutions. "Inbreeding" of staff was somewhat less in normal schools and teachers colleges. Years of service in the institution were about the same.[49] The
median years of secondary-school experience of the teaching staffs of
state normal schools and teachers colleges was 4.7; that for the teaching
staffs of state universities and land-grant colleges was 3.5.[50] The median
teaching load (clock hours) in state universities and land-grant colleges
was 15.0; in state normal schools and teachers colleges, 16.7. The corresponding findings for total time devoted to institutional responsibilities
were 44.7 and 41.8.[51] The teaching staffs of state normal schools and
teachers colleges produced relatively fewer books and articles than the
staffs of state universities and land-grant colleges.[52]

Concluding Statement

In retrospect one may criticize the normal schools and teachers colleges
for a number of practices during the period of development considered
in this chapter, but fairness requires that the educational and social setting of the time be recognized. Many normal-school presidents, perhaps
most of them, believed that high-school graduation, or the equivalent,
should be required for admission and their reluctance to adopt this standard was due largely to the demand for teachers and their belief that it
was important to increase enrollments. A few argued that the immediate
adoption of high-school graduation as a condition of admission would
deprive some young people, especially from rural areas, of the opportunity to prepare for teaching. Institutional competition and other influences stimulated an expansion of the educational program beyond staff
capacity and in some instances beyond the needs of secondary-school
teaching. The lack of adequate funds was a severe handicap. In view
of these and other factors of the setting it is significant that by 1930 the
teachers colleges were similar to liberal arts colleges in many respects.

[49] *Ibid.*, pp. 168, 169.   [51] *Ibid.*, pp. 182, 188.
[50] *Ibid.*, p. 172.   [52] *Ibid.*, p. 194.

CHAPTER 12

Teacher Education in Colleges
and Universities

The development of teacher education in colleges and universities following 1890 differs in significant respects from that in normal schools and teachers colleges. By this date the "normal-school idea" was generally accepted but in colleges and universities provisions for the professional training of teachers were at the level of "small beginnings."

In 1890 "teachers' courses" were offered in 114 colleges and universities out of a total of 415 such institutions.[1] In commenting on the nature of these offerings it was stated: "With few exceptions these departments, or courses, are nothing more than normal schools, which are usually classed among institutions of secondary grade." At this time most institutions classified as "colleges and universities" maintained a "preparatory department" and this characterization presumably meant that "with few exceptions" the pedagogical work for teachers was offered in this department and was designed for the preparation of elementary teachers.[2]

The "few exceptions," which were not enumerated, represent the status of the professional education of secondary teachers in colleges and uni-

---

[1] United States Commissioner of Education, *Report for 1889-90*, Vol. 2, p. 1020.

[2] G. W. A. Luckey, *The Professional Training of Secondary Teachers in the United States* (New York: The Macmillan Company, 1903), pp. 62f., 101.

versities. A "chair of didactics" had been established at the State University of Iowa in 1873 and a "chair of science and art of teaching" at the University of Michigan in 1879.[3] In 1887-88 William H. Payne, the incumbent of the chair at Michigan, offered seven courses: history of education (2), comparative education, school supervision, practical (art of teaching and governing), theoretical and critical, and seminary. In addition, teachers' courses were offered by several subject-matter departments.[4] All of these courses were designed as electives for juniors or seniors or for postbaccalaureate students. One course offered by the Professor of the Science and the Art of Teaching and one departmental teacher's course were requirements for the Teacher's Diploma.[5] Similar "teachers' courses" were offered in some other institutions but the number of instances was not large, and where offered the number of courses was less. Thus in 1890 the professional education of teachers for secondary schools in colleges and universities was at the level of "small beginnings."

Another difference is reflected in the motivation of the development in the two classes of institutions. The establishment of state normal schools was an expression of the desire of the people for better elementary schools,[6] and the new institutions were dedicated to the education of teachers for these schools. Any other function was considered incidental or even extraneous. In contrast, the development of professional education for secondary teachers in colleges and universities "seems to have originated with scholars and professional men" who had become impressed by the "great waste and inefficiency of college graduates" that obtained employment as teachers, mainly in secondary schools.[7] Luckey does not define this group of "scholars and professional men," but it included some college and university presidents, especially in the North Central and Western states, and some public school men.[8] A few faculty members were interested, but they tended not to be aggressive beyond developing departmental teachers' courses. As professorships of education were created the persons appointed were among the aggressive promoters.

[3] For a detailed account of this development, see Allen S. Whitney, "The First Chair of Education in an American University," *School and Society,* 53 (1941), 257-61.

[4] Allen S. Whitney, *History of the Professional Training of Teachers at the University of Michigan for the First-half-century, 1879 to 1929* (Ann Arbor: George Wahr, Publisher, 1931), pp. 46-47.

[5] *Ibid.,* p. 48.

[6] G. W. A. Luckey, *op. cit.,* pp. 53f.

[7] *Ibid.,* p. 104.

[8] Allen S. Whitney, *op. cit.* Chapters II and III reveal the leaders at the University of Michigan.

A more significant difference is that the colleges and universities were established institutions[9] devoted to certain recognized functions and committed to academic ideals and practices which had developed over a long period. Their attitude toward new lines of work was highly conservative. This attitude was accentuated in the case of the proposed professional training for teachers. The offering of pedagogical work in preparatory departments and the reputation of the normal schools of the time contributed to the opinion that professional courses for teachers would not be of college grade. Furthermore, teaching was thought of as an art and hence pedagogical instruction was not needed for secondary teachers, except possibly a departmental teachers' course. As a means providing a basis for understanding the development of teacher-education programs and of the organizational provisions for this function, attention is given to some aspects of colleges and universities and to the concept of qualifications desired for secondary teachers.

Functions Recognized by Colleges and Universities

The major functions of colleges and universities had been to provide the means of a liberal education and mental discipline.[10] The traditional means for these purposes was a prescribed curriculum, but by 1890 a number of institutions had adopted the elective system. This development continued and by 1910 some form of the elective system was to be found in practically all liberal arts colleges.[11] Associated with this adoption of the elective system there were other significant changes.

By the time of the "present" (median year 1918) studied by Koos and Crawford, the relative emphasis upon a "liberal education" remained unchanged, but there had been a marked decrease in the relative emphasis on "mental discipline" and a corresponding increase in emphasis on education for "civic and social responsibility." There had been also an increase in the recognition of "occupational training," which presumably included any specific mention of teacher education, but this recognition appeared in only about one-third of the "present" statements analyzed. The appearances of "development of scholarly interest and ambition" increased from 2 to 11. This change is probably a reflection of the development of graduate work as an extension of the undergraduate liberal-

[9] Certain exceptions may be cited: for example, Stanford University where a department of education was included in the initial organization, and Wayne University where teacher education had been an activity for years before the institution was organized.

[10] Leonard V. Koos and C. C. Crawford, "College Aims Past and Present," *School and Society*, 14 (1921), 499-509.

[11] R. Freeman Butts, *The College Charts Its Course* (New York: McGraw-Hill Book Company, Inc., 1939), p. 239.

arts program. As graduate work developed, departments tended to plan
their undergraduate courses, especially the more advanced ones, as
preparation for graduate study. Administrative emphasis upon scholarly
production and reputation accentuated the academic ideal.

The adoption of the elective system was also accompanied by an expansion of the course offerings. In this development there was much controversial discussion of the relative merits of the traditional subjects and
the newer subjects as means toward the purposes of a liberal education
and mental discipline.[12] Gradually the conservatives gave ground, but
the proponents of the newer subjects recognized that their offerings
should conform to academic standards. And both conservatives and the
progressives of the time tended to oppose the introduction of practical
(vocational) subjects.

As noted above, "mental discipline" had been one of the announced
purposes of colleges and universities, and this function was a major one
in the thinking of college faculties until after the turn of the century.
As advocates of new subjects urged their recognition, a major point of
the argument was that the content and its organization were such that
these subjects would contribute to the mental-discipline function.[13] The
essential qualities of content relative to this function do not appear to
have been clearly defined, but a general criterion was that the content
should be the product of scholarly study. Any apparent or claimed practical (vocational) value was a liability rather than an asset.

By 1915 the findings of scientific studies of transfer of training and
the appearance of Thorndikean psychology of learning had caused many
educators to renounce the mental-discipline function, but the effect was
less in liberal arts colleges. Influential men, administrators and professors, continued to insist that the disciplinary function was important and
to judge proposals of new subjects on the basis of their apparent contribution to this function.[14] The influence of these conservatives varied.
In some institutions it was minor, but, in general, it was sufficient to
cause proponents of practical (vocational) subjects to give attention to
their academic qualities.

This continuing conservative attitude toward practical (vocational)
subjects was supplemented by the development of the major and minor
adaptation of the elective system and by the development of the graduate school as an extension of the liberal arts college. A department endeavoring to develop and maintain a graduate program had to have

[12] *Ibid.*, pp. 204-30.

[13] Stuart G. Noble, *A History of American Education* (New York: Farrar & Rinehart, Inc., 1938), pp. 309-29. In these pages Noble shows the influence of the mental-
discipline function in the development of the secondary curriculum from 1860 to
1900. This function was probably more dominant in the thinking at the college level.

[14] R. Freeman Butts, *op. cit.*, pp. 309f.

students prepared for and interested in graduate work. Undergraduate majors and also undergraduate minors, if the program of study was somewhat extended, were sources of supply. Departments tended to develop advanced undergraduate courses that would stimulate interest in and prepare for graduate study.

Internal Organization of Colleges and Universities
Relative to Function

In the internal organization of a college or university a department represents a grouping of staff for providing instruction and promoting scholarly endeavor within a recognized field of knowledge. Within a university a college is an organization of departments and reflects a broader function represented by one or more curriculums leading to a baccalaureate degree. Under the administrative and legislative procedures of the institution a college, i.e. its faculty, determines the conditions of admission, its curriculum, and its requirements for graduation, and recommends candidates for degrees. Its administrative head (usually designated as dean) or persons under his authority or that of the faculty advise students.

Colleges within universities vary with respect to providing instruction for their enrollees. A college of law offers within its organization all or practically all of the work specified in its curriculum. Curriculums of other colleges frequently include courses in one or more fields represented by departments in another college of the institution. For example, engineering curriculums include courses in mathematics which is the field of a department of the college of liberal arts. In such cases the college usually does not attempt to provide the desired instruction but solicits the cooperation of the department in the other college to develop and offer the desired courses. The effectiveness of this arrangement depends upon the department's understanding of the purpose of the college represented by the curriculum and upon the freedom and support of the staff members involved in the particular courses.

A school within a university is usually a less autonomous unit than a college, but in some institutions the "school of education" has been in effect a college of education; in other cases, the "school of education" has been little more than a glorified department. This variation in meaning is confusing in considering the organizational development for teacher education. The situation is further complicated by the fact that a few college-of-education units have been explicitly or in effect schools of education in the restricted sense.

Concept of Qualifications Desired for Secondary Teachers

The record of the thinking in colleges and universities about desired qualifications for secondary teachers is fragmentary, but the general outline of the development seems clear. In 1890 the essential qualification was considered to be a good liberal education resulting from four years of college study. Beyond this qualification a teacher's success depended upon his "divine skills." However, the contention that teaching is an art was being vigorously attacked (see pp. 57f.) and some qualification proposals were advanced. For example, the *Register* of the University of California for 1892-93 included requirements for teachers' certificates: (a) Special knowledge, 20 semester hours "in the subject or group of closely allied subjects that the candidate expects to teach"; (b) Professional knowledge, 12 semester hours in pedagogy (which may include the Philosophy of Education); (c) General knowledge, courses representing four of six named fields of knowledge. Such a statement of the qualifications desired for secondary teachers was in advance of the general thinking of the time and perhaps it is not a valid representation of the beliefs of the faculty of the University of California.[15] The statement is indicative of the developing recognition of pedagogical training as essential in the preparation for secondary teaching. The spread of this recognition is indicated by the *Report of the United States Commissioner of Education for 1896-97* which listed 220 colleges and universities as providing instruction in "pedagogy," an increase of 106 institutions since 1889-90.

In Part Two the report of the Committee of Seventeen in 1907 was taken as the event marking the general acceptance of pedagogical training as being essential in the preparation of secondary teachers (see p. 203). During the following years the requirement of a substantial amount of work in education became the practice. By the time of the National Survey (1930) the average requirement in colleges and universities was 18.4 semester hours.

This development of practice, however, should not be interpreted as indicating universal acceptance of pedagogical training as desirable for secondary teachers. Although members of subject-matter departments were not very vocal about the matter, it seems clear that a considerable number of the members of college and university faculties did not consider pedagogical training to be a desirable qualification and that some were hostile to the idea. A Report of Committee Q of the American Asso-

---

[15] One student of the development in California refers to the University as being reluctant to establish work in pedagogy and stresses the operation of influences outside of the institution. Evelyn Atkinson Clement, *The Evolution of Teacher Training in California as a Phase of Social Change* (Unpublished Ph.D. dissertation, Berkeley: University of California, 1936), pp. 145f.

ciation of University Professors in 1933 expresses a position which doubtless was maintained in 1907 and during the following years by a considerable number of members of subject-matter departments. This report, based on a rather extended study, asserted:

> The amount of professional training should be as restricted as possible, for it
> does not increase the teacher's knowledge of the subjects he actually teaches
> . . . it is a grave question whether a beginner can profit much from any pro-
> fessional courses prior to having considerable classroom experience – save for
> work in methods which is actually associated with such experience.[16]

The special-knowledge qualification of the California statement indicates another significant development. The teacher's function was regarded as being to teach subjects and it was logical that he should be
competent in the field or fields of his subjects. This position fitted in
with the developing major and minor modifications of the elective system
and provided an argument for a department that wished to encourage
students to elect additional courses from its offerings. The idea of a
strong subject-matter major being a desirable, or a necessary, qualification became firmly incorporated in the thinking about the qualifications
of secondary teachers. In fact, this qualification tended to become the
dominant one in the thinking of many persons.

In this development little or no attention was given to the constitution
of the major. Practically any accumulation of course credits within a
department was acceptable, provided the total was sufficiently large. The
advisement of a major department relative to courses to be taken was
likely to be biased in the direction of preparation for further study in the
department.

Development of Departments of Education

In some institutions professional work, beyond departmental teachers'
courses, appeared as one or more courses offered by a member of the department of philosophy or some other established department, but a
"department of education" became the fashion. This organizational provision reflects institutional recognition of professional education for secondary teachers as a function on a par with that of providing instruction in English, mathematics, and the like. This recognition, however,
must be interpreted in terms of the nature of the courses offered by these
new departments of education.

The Report of the Commissioner of Education for 1896-97 listed 220
colleges and universities as providing instruction in "pedagogy." In com-

---

[16] Committee Q, "Required Courses in Education," *American Association of University Professors Bulletin,* 19 (1933), 189.

menting on this tabulation B. A. Hinsdale [17] suggested that a person who was acquainted with the situation could identify three general types of work: (a) "some lectures or a course of textbook instruction or possibly a combination of the two, in the elements of the theory and practice of teaching to such students as see fit to elect the work"; (b) the "normal-school" type of program; (c) education as "a university or college subject, equal in rank to other subjects." Hinsdale stated that probably no one had sufficient information to classify the 220 institutions under these categories, but he indicated that very few would qualify under the third.

The professors of education wished their courses to be recognized as "academically respectable," i.e. as being "equal in rank to other subjects." The meaning of this qualification does not appear to have been very explicit, but some implications may be noted. Apparently a course was regarded as being "academically respectable" if the instructor was a person of adequate academic standing within his institution and the course was clearly different from the "pedagogy" taught in normal schools. Where a department of education had been established, the emphasis was on history of education, educational psychology, and the like. "Practical courses" — reviews, practice teaching, observation, classroom management, and the like — appear to have been considered unworthy of credit toward the baccalaureate degree.

Luckey's tabulation [18] of courses in twenty "representative universities" indicates limited attention to the field of "methodology." For 1899-90 a total of 13 courses was classified under "method of instruction" and 4 under "art of teaching." In contrast a total of 35 courses was classified as "historical." Similar conditions were reported by Bolton [19] in 1907. History of education was the most largely attended course with educational psychology and principles of education next in order. "General method as a separate subject does not seem to be very much stressed" (p. 147) and "special methods" attendance was reported by a smaller number of institutions.

The effort to offer "respectable" courses in the place of "normal-school methods" is suggested by the following from the catalog of the University of Illinois for 1895-96:

2. *The Aim or Motive in Teaching.* (a) The true, or universal, aim as determined by the nature of life. (b) The various aims as consciously or unconsciously held at present by different countries and classes of people. Such

[17] B. A. Hinsdale, "The Study of Education in American Colleges and Universities," *Educational Review*, 19 (1900), 105-20.

[18] G. W. A. Luckey, *op. cit.*, p. 157.

[19] Frederick E. Bolton, "The Relation of the Department of Education to Other Departments in Colleges and Universities," *Journal of Pedagogy*, 19 (1906-7), 137-76.

diversity accounted for and unified. (c) The aim as shown in variation through historical development — the study of historical ideals. Winter term.

3. *The Universal Form of Method in Education,* as determined by the nature of life. (a) In its subjective aspects. (b) In its objective aspect. (c) The three forms of the relation of (a) and (b), giving rise to the logic, ethics and esthetics of educational categories. Spring term.

4. *The Universal Law and Problem of Thinking.* Special movements of the mind in learning discriminated. (a) How to think objects into organic unity. (b) How to think objects into class unity. Fall term.

5. *The Logical and the Psychological Factors in Educational Method,* that is, the foregoing process modified by the psychological factor. (a) The sketching of the lessons in recognition of the two factors. (b) The course of study as determined by the two factors; the chronological and logical arrangement of studies. Winter term.

The College-of-Education Development

In 1905 A. Ross Hill addressed the Department of Higher Education of the National Education Association on the question: "Should chairs of pedagogy attached to college departments of universities be developed into professional colleges for the training of teachers, co-ordinate with those of law, medicine, and engineering, or should they be abolished?" [20] This title and other evidence indicate that by 1905 a number of persons did not consider a department of education to be an adequate provision for the professional education of prospective secondary teachers.

In his argument for a "professional college for the training of teachers" Hill, then dean of the recently established Teachers College of the University of Missouri, pointed out that "courses in the philosophy of education, the history of education, and in genetic and educational psychology ... have the same right to place in a scheme of liberal education that have general philosophy, ethics, sociology, and the like." He placed "courses in the theory and practice of teaching, in school management and the like" on the same level as "technical courses in law, engineering, or medicine," and asserted that "time spent in observation [in a model school] cannot be expected to count toward the A.B. degree." In the following paragraph he argued for "practice teaching" which would belong in the same category as "observation." Thus one point in Hill's argument for a "professional college for the training of teachers" was that such a unit would provide a means for recognizing credit in "observation," "practice teaching," "methods," "manual training," and other technical-professional subjects which were not sufficiently academically respectable to be counted toward the A.B. degree.

[20] A. Ross Hill, "Should Chairs of Pedagogy Attached to College Departments of Universities be Developed into Professional Colleges for the Training of Teachers, Co-ordinate with Those of Law, Medicine, and Engineering, or Should They be Abolished?" *Addresses and Proceedings* (National Educational Association, 1905), pp. 512-15.

Hill also argued that the establishment of a college of education would serve to focus the attention of the various departments contributing to the liberal education of teachers upon the teacher-training function of the institution and that students enrolled in such a unit, being subject to its graduation requirements and the advisement of the dean of education, would obtain a more appropriate liberal education. Furthermore, enrollment in a college of education would serve to stimulate student interest in preparation for teaching.

At the time of Hill's address a professional college for the education of teachers had been established in a few universities.[21] A study reported in 1904 listed a "teacher college" at Columbia University, University of Chicago, University of Missouri, and University of Texas,[22] and the trend was in the direction of this type of institutional organization. In 1906 Sutton [23] reported a "teachers college" at nine other universities. He also reported education organized as a department coordinate with that of English, mathematics, history, and the like in eighteen institutions. The provision for education courses varied in the other eleven colleges and universities from which responses were received, assignment to the department of philosophy being most frequent. A total of thirty-four state universities were listed as having established a college of education by 1923.[24]

The National Survey reported 105 colleges or schools of education "largely in universities but also in some colleges." [25] The date of establishment ranged to the period 1931-34. The highest frequencies were for the periods 1916-20 (20), 1921-25 (22), and 1926-30 (18). The 105 units are described as "independent schools or colleges of education" which suggests that they were much alike except for the designation, but they differed in certain significant respects.

---

[21] For an account of the development in certain institutions, se Leigh G. Hubbell, *The Development of University Departments of Education in Six States of the Middle West* (Ph.D. dissertation, The Catholic University of America Press, 1924). 126 pp.

[22] Manfred J. Holmes, "The Present Provision for the Education of Secondary Teachers in the United States," *Fourth Yearbook,* Part I (National Society for the Study of Education, 1904), pp. 63-82. (See p. 69.) The inclusion of the University of Texas was due to a misinterpretation. Until 1920 the University of Texas used "school" in the sense of "department." In 1904 the education unit at Texas was a department. From a statement to the writer by B. F. Pittinger, November 29, 1949.

[23] W. S. Sutton, "The Organization of the Department of Education in Relation to the Other Departments in Colleges and Universities," *Journal of Pedagogy,* 19 (1906-7), 81-107.

[24] J. B. Edmonson and A. H. Webster, *Policies and Curricula of Schools of Education in State Universities* (U.S. Office of Education, Higher Education Circular No. 30, August, 1925). 32 pp.

[25] Earle U. Rugg and Others, *Teacher Education Curricula,* National Survey of the Education of Teachers, Vol. III (U.S. Office of Education, Bulletin 1933, No. 10), p. 164.

Variations in Organization and Function

At Harvard University the emphasis was on professional study at the postbaccalaureate level and the Graduate School of Education was established in 1920.[26] Teachers College, Columbia University, developed from the "New York College for the Training of Teachers" which was incorporated as a part of Columbia University in 1889. The charter provided for both baccalaureate and graduate degrees.[27] However, Teachers College did not become an "independent" unit for some years. A School of Education was formed within Teachers College in 1911-12. By 1918 this unit had become essentially a graduate school of education.[28]

Due to an accumulating surplus of secondary-school teachers in California, the idea of a graduate school of education appeared at the University of California by 1900. It was supported by the action of the State Board of Education in 1905 requiring a full year of postbaccalaureate study for the general secondary credential.[29] In 1913 the Academic Senate defined the "School of Education" as a designation for professional courses in Education.[30] This action marks the beginning of the School of Education of the University of California at Berkeley. Although juniors and seniors were admitted [31] the emphasis was on postbaccalaureate work. The "general secondary credential" required one year of such study and in 1916 the professional degree of "Graduate in Education" requiring two years of graduate study was established.[32] Four years later this degree was replaced by the Doctor of Education [33] requiring three years of graduate study.

Thus at Harvard, Columbia, and California the "department" of education evolved into a "professional" school for teachers and other educational workers. The emphasis was on graduate work and except at California the unit became essentially a graduate school of education. The implied concept of teacher education was a "liberal education" *plus* professional study at the postbaccalaureate level.

A contrasting view of the organization for teacher education is reflected in the developments at Ohio State University and the University of Minnesota. At Ohio State University a college of education was established in 1907. This unit included the department of psychology and "the professors and instructors in other colleges of the university offering

---

[26] Timothy F. O'Leary, *An Inquiry into the General Purposes, Functions and Organization of Selected University Schools of Education* (Ph.D. dissertation; The Catholic University of America Press, 1941), p. 50.

[27] *Ibid.*, p. 97.   [31] *Ibid.*, p. 397.

[28] *Ibid.*, pp. 117, 120.   [32] *Ibid.*, p. 386.

[29] *Ibid.*, pp. 369-70.   [33] *Ibid.*, p. 389.

[30] *Ibid.*, p. 374.

academic and vocational subjects of interest to prospective high-school teachers were listed as members of the staff." [34] Later the departments of Fine Arts, Music, and Physical Education were added and the designation of persons from other colleges was referred to as "selected persons." [35] The college of education enrolled prospective teachers in all subjects as freshmen. Although there was cooperation with other units of the institution and on occasion members from other colleges were asked to serve on a college-of-education committee, the "central and controlling responsibility" for matters of teacher education was in the College of Education.[36] Thus the College of Education of Ohio State University appears to have been an *independent* four-year undergraduate college. A strong program of graduate work has been developed but at the graduate level education is a department of the Graduate School.[37]

The College of Education of the University of Minnesota was established in 1905. "On June 7, 1916, the Board of Regents of the University of Minnesota passed a resolution to the effect that the responsibility for teacher-training be placed upon the College of Education; that all courses of a professional character should be given in the College of Education; and that all candidates for teaching should be certificated by the College of Education." [38] This action became fully effective by 1921. Students preparing for teaching in art, physical education, and music might register in the College of Education as freshmen. In other cases registration was restricted to juniors and seniors. In the case of students preparing to teach agriculture and home economics there was "joint registration" in the College of Agriculture, Forestry, and Home Economics. In 1930 the faculty numbered 111 including 35 representatives from departments in other colleges or schools. The executive faculty of the College of Education consisted of the heads or chairmen of the departments within the college and two representatives from the faculty of the College of Science, Literature, and the Arts.[39] As at Ohio State University, education was a department in the Graduate School of the University of Minnesota.

The undergraduate organizational provision at Ohio and at Minnesota

---

[34] Leigh G. Hubbell, *op. cit.*, pp. 28-29.

[35] A. J. Klein, ed., *Adventures in the Reconstruction of Education* (Columbus: Ohio State University, 1941), p. 18. See also p. 245.

[36] *Ibid.*, p. 16.

[37] *Ibid.*, p. 153.

[38] Victor H. Noll, "The Growth of the College of Education," in *The Changing Educational World, 1905-1930,* ed. Alvin C. Eurich (Minneapolis: University of Minnesota Press, 1931), p. 277.

[39] Melvin E. Haggerty, "The University College of Education as Related to Other Divisions of the University," in *The Changing Educational World, 1905-1930,* ed. Alvin C. Eurich (Minneapolis: University of Minnesota Press, 1931), pp. 99-100.

reflects the concept of teacher education as consisting of liberal (academic) study *combined with* professional study under the direction of a college devoted to the teacher-education function. The faculty of the college of education was commensurate with the scope of the total education of teachers.

At the State University of Iowa a School of Education was established in 1907. This School of Education was *in* the College of Liberal Arts and not an independent college unit. Although glorified by the designation "School of Education," the organization was in effect only a department in the College of Liberal Arts and in the Graduate School. Students graduating from the College of Liberal Arts obtained the endorsement of the School (Department) of Education by satisfying the requirements of the School of Education Certificate.[40] In 1913 a College of Education was created, but this action seems to have been essentially a change in the designation except that in budgetary matters, education having college status, the dean dealt directly with the central administration of the institution.[41] The College of Education has not "exercised the right of granting degrees," students preparing to teach being enrolled in other college units.[42] The functioning of the College of Education at Iowa seems to have been very limited with respect to the administration of preservice teacher education. Although the designation has been maintained and it has its own budget, the College of Education has been in effect a service department for other units of the institution which have retained administrative jurisdiction over the education of prospective teachers. Indirectly, the dean of the College of Education has exercised considerable influence over the advisement of students by reason of the fact that recommendations for a license to teach are made over his signature.

A fourth type of organization is illustrated by the development at the University of Michigan. Education continued as a department in the College of Literature, Science, and the Arts until 1921 when the School of Education was established with junior standing as an admission requirement,[43] except for the four-year curriculums in physical education, school health, athletics, and public health nursing. An attempt was made to restrict the granting of the life certificate to students obtaining the baccalaureate degree in the School of Education but the proposal was opposed by the Faculty of the College of Literature, Science, and the Arts and did not become effective.[44] Thus, at the University of Michigan the School of Education was only one unit for administering the education of teachers. Students in the College of Literature, Science, and the

---

[40] Timothy F. O'Leary, *op. cit.*, pp. 261-63.

[41] *Ibid.*, p. 278.   [43] Allen S. Whitney, *op. cit.*, pp. 136f.

[42] *Ibid.*, p. 278.   [44] *Ibid.*, pp. 141f.

Arts could satisfy the requirements for a life certificate by electing the necessary education courses.

The differences in the teacher-education units in universities indicated in these brief descriptions were due to several influences. A major influence was the local liberal-arts unit which, under institutional procedure, "controlled" such actions as the establishment of a new major unit and the definition of its function and jurisdiction. The college of liberal arts was the traditional teacher-education unit [45] and the establishment of a college of education in which all prospective teachers were required to enroll would mean the relinquishment of the control of this function to the new unit. This would result in a material decrease in the liberal-arts enrollment and this effect was doubtless a factor in the attitude toward the establishment of a college of education.

A more important consideration appears to have been the concept of essential teacher qualifications held in liberal-arts circles. Although educationists generally agreed that a teacher should have a "good liberal education," which would require that prospective teachers take a large portion of the total requirement for the baccalaureate degree of the college of education in subject-matter departments, the liberal-arts group feared that with different graduation requirements and student advisement under the college of education, the "liberal education" of prospective teachers would not be "good."

Members of subject-matter departments emphasized major specialization as an essential qualification for secondary teaching in their respective fields. Although educationists agreed that a prospective teacher should have a major in his first teaching subject, they believed that the teacher's preparation should include one or two minors to qualify him for instruction in other areas. Furthermore, a college of education would require a sixth to a fifth of the total undergraduate program to be in education courses. The preparation for a second teaching subject and the required work in education would limit the time available for major specialization. This restriction and the possible control of elections in the major field would handicap subject-matter departments in getting registrants for their advanced undergraduate courses which they were developing as "feeders" for graduate study.

Involved in the attitude of the college of liberal arts was a concept of teacher education which differed from that implied by the establishment of a college of education. Many, especially in academic circles, insisted that the education of a teacher should be thought of as a "liberal education" (graduation from a college of liberal arts or the equivalent) *plus* professional (pedagogical) study taken as extras or at the post-

---

[45] Bailey B. Burritt, *Professional Distribution of College and University Graduates* (U.S. Bureau of Education, Bulletin, 1912, No. 19). 147 pp.

baccalaureate level. According to this view, the college of education would tend to be a graduate school of education. In contrast, there were some who maintained that the jurisdiction of the college of education should begin at the level of college admission or at least not later than the junior year and that all prospective teachers should enroll in the unit. This position implied a concept of teacher education in which liberal (academic) study was *combined with* professional (pedagogical) study under the advice of the dean of the college of education. Within this view there was the implication, seldom expressed until later, that the "liberal (general) education" of a teacher and his subject-matter specialization should be professionalized, i.e. adapted to the needs of the profession of teaching.

The attitude and strength of the liberal-arts group varied. At the University of California (Berkeley) it was sufficiently powerful to add a fifth year to the preservice education of secondary teachers thus protecting its undergraduate program. The continuation of education as a department at the University of Michigan until 1921 and the retention of its teacher-education prerogative by the College of Literature, Science, and the Arts are indicative of the influence of this group. The development of the college of education at the University of Minnesota and at Ohio State University indicates a more liberal attitude.

Although it is not possible to document the statement adequately, two other influences seem apparent — the president's interest in and his understanding of teacher education and the personal and scholarly qualities of the head of the education unit. The positive influence of Marion L. Burton, president of the University of Michigan 1920-25, is apparent in the development at that institution.[46] The positive influence of the head of the education unit is illustrated by the development at Stanford University. Education was one of the twenty-five departments when the institution opened in 1891 and conditions in the state as well as within the institution were favorable. However, when E. P. Cubberley was appointed head in 1898, President Jordan told him "that the department was in thorough disrepute, and that if it were left to a vote of the faculty they would be almost unanimous for its discontinuance." [47] In the development from this status Cubberley's influence was a major factor. Evidence of the operation of negative influences from these sources is mainly inferential or not available in public records, but as the present writer inquired into institutional developments, it seemed clear that what was done or was not done in certain institutions could be explained largely

[46] Allen S. Whitney, *op. cit.*, pp. 126-49.

[47] Elwood P. Cubberley, "A Response to Many Toasts," in *School Administration in the Twentieth Century*, ed. Jesse B. Sears (Stanford, California: Stanford University Press, 1934), pp. 74-75.

in terms of the president's lack of interest in teacher education and/or the personal and scholarly qualities of the head of the education unit.

The National Survey gives the following information in regard to the organizational status of teacher education in the 105 colleges and universities in which a college or school of education had been established. In 8 per cent the teacher-education curriculums were at the graduate level, in 28 per cent the curriculums began with the junior year, and in more than half of the institutions with the freshman year. In 11 per cent the level at which prospective teachers enrolled in the education unit depended upon the field of teacher preparation. In 76 per cent of the institutions preparation for teaching was not restricted to the college or school of education, i.e. students enrolled in other colleges could qualify for teaching by taking education courses and meeting other requirements for certification. Only 73 per cent of the teacher-education units reported "practically independent status." [48]

In his address of 1905, Hill [49] proposed a college-of-education faculty consisting of staff members giving instruction in education courses, free-hand drawing, manual training, and vocal music, which were to be included in the college of education, plus "professors representing the various liberal subjects of school instruction who are qualified to give courses on the teaching of the subjects which they respectively represent." In an institution such as the University of Missouri at that time this faculty would include about twenty-five persons. Incidentally, it may be noted that "professors of education" would not constitute a majority within the faculty proposed by Hill. The "professors" offering courses on the teaching of subjects (special methods) were to hold "joint appointments," i.e. were to be considered as within the college of education.

This type of faculty was formed at the University of Missouri but after about twenty years the plan was discontinued. In 1930 the faculty of the college of education of the University of Minnesota included thirty-five representatives from departments in other colleges or schools. Such a faculty, however, did become popular and it is likely that in most teacher-education units the faculty was limited to the "professors of education" and the members of the other "departments" included in the organization or at least that the representation from subject-matter departments was very limited. Thus a college of education became thought of as an organization of educationists or at least as a unit dominated by this group.

The preceding account of the development of certain colleges of edu-

---

[48] Earle U. Rugg and Others, *op. cit.*, pp. 164-65.

[49] A. Ross Hill, "Should Chairs of Pedagogy Attached to College Departments of Universities be Developed into Professional Colleges for the Training of Teachers, Co-ordinate with Those of Law, Medicine, and Engineering, or Should They be Abolished?" *Addresses and Proceedings* (National Educational Association, 1905), pp. 512-15.

cation makes it clear that this teacher-education unit varied in significant respects. The condition should be kept in mind in the further consideration of teacher education in colleges and universities.

The Educational Program

The elective system, which had been adopted in some form by practically all colleges and universities by 1910, and the development of graduate schools as extensions of the liberal-arts college encouraged the expansion of course offerings in the several academic departments. In addition, new lines of work were gradually introduced — art, music, physical education, vocational fields (agriculture, home economics, and industrial education), and the like. In describing the educational program of teachers colleges comparative data were given for colleges and universities (see p. 305). These show that in most corresponding departments the offerings were more extensive in the latter institutions. Along with the expansion of course offerings there was some subdividing of departments which stimulated the development of additional courses. There was variation among institutions with respect to the number of courses within departments. Although the variation in number of departmental courses was not as great as in the case of teachers colleges,[50] there tended to be no typical educational program.

With the exception of teachers' courses (special methods) the offerings of academic subject-matter departments beyond the elementary level were designed mainly as preparation for more advanced study. Many of these courses provided for intensive study within a narrow area. In very few courses was any attempt made to adapt the work to the needs of secondary teachers. There was more professionalization in special subject fields.[51]

The establishment of a college (school) was usually followed by an expansion of the technical-professional offerings, but again there was wide variation among institutions, due largely to the number of types of school positions for which preparation was offered and the development of graduate work. The technical-education program in independent liberal arts colleges was modest.[52]

Undergraduate Curriculum Requirements and Practices

The most prevalent modifications of the elective system was in terms of a major and one or more minors. Under this plan there were usually, at least in later years, some prescribed courses in addition to the minimum requirements for the major and one or two minors. At the time of

[50] Earle U. Rugg and Others, *op. cit.*, pp. 59, 179.
[51] *Ibid.*, p. 277.   [52] *Ibid.*, p. 179.

the National Survey the median requirement for an academic major was 25 semester hours. In slightly more than half of the institutions there was also a median requirement of a first minor of 15 semester hours. A second minor (median, 12 semester hours) was required in only 18 per cent of the institutions. The median requirement in special vocational subjects was 37.5 semester hours. In connection with such majors a first minor was required in only 30 per cent of the cases. A smaller proportion required a second minor.

Requirements relative to the general-education qualification for academic majors are described as follows: "All institutions required a median of 4 semester-hours of physical education during the four years. Not quite all specified 8 semester-hours of English. Nine-tenths of them included 12 hours of foreign language. In four-fifths of the institutions a median of 9 hours of science was specified. Only three-fourths of the prescriptions required 7 semester-hours of social studies, usually specified in history." For special-subject majors the requirements were much the same except that there were fewer prescriptions of foreign language and the median prescription of science was nearly twice as large.

The median requirement of education (all courses) was 18 semester hours for both academic majors and special subject majors. However, a number of the institutions offered an education major in which the median requirement of courses in education was 25.5 semester hours. There is no information in regard to the number of the institutions, from which this finding was determined, having a college (school) of education, but it is likely that some of these majors were offered outside of such a unit.

The median of the free electives was 24 semester hours for academic majors and 23 semester hours for special-subject majors. In addition, there was a median of slightly more than 15 semester hours of restricted electives outside of the major and other general requirements.[53]

With reference to the preparation of secondary teachers for academic subjects, the fact that 49 per cent of the prescriptions did not include a first minor and only 18 per cent a second minor suggests that these institutions as a group gave little attention to the nature of the probable teaching assignments of beginning teachers. The variations from the medians given above also suggest, at least in the case of some of the extremes, a lack of understanding of the needs of teachers. For example, the range of academic major prescriptions was 15 to 80 semester hours and that for "all education" 6 to 35 semester hours. Although major

---

[53] *Ibid.*, pp. 193-95. The findings cited in these paragraphs are based on analytical study of the catalogs of twenty-nine universities and twenty-eight colleges selected as representative of such institutions. Since a separate study had indicated that the curriculum patterns in the two types of institutions did not differ significantly, the analysis was made for only the total group.

specialization somewhat in excess of 25 semester hours may be appropriate in some academic fields, several of the upper limits given [54] indicate specialization beyond the needs of secondary teachers. Furthermore,
excessive specialization at the undergraduate level restricts a student's
preparation for teaching outside of his major and/or his general education. A requirement of only 6 semester hours in education is not regarded
as consistent with the need of teachers for technical-professional training.
A requirement much in excess of 25 semester hours at the undergraduate
level may be questioned.

No information is given in regard to the organizational provisions for
teacher education in the twenty-nine universities and twenty-eight colleges from which the above findings were derived, but it is likely that
some of these institutions did not have a college (school) of education
and that a number of the institutions having such a unit also had teacher-
education curriculums outside of it. Hence the findings cited should not
be interpreted as applying to the colleges of education. It is likely that the
requirements in this unit were somewhat different. In another place, the
median education prescription for academic majors in colleges of education is given as 21 semester hours, including general psychology only if
classified by the institution as education. The range of the middle 50
per cent was from 19 to 26 hours. About four-fifths of the colleges
(schools) of education designated the fields for teaching majors and
minors and the courses, elective and prescribed, that might be included.[55]

The National Survey also gives an analysis of sample transcripts of
prospective teachers graduating from twenty-four colleges and universities.[56] It is stated that the findings probably represent the better practices in the education of teachers. The median of the work taken in the
major field exceeded the median prescription given above except in physical education for men, commercial education, and physics. Most of the
median excesses were not large, but the ranges indicate that a considerable number of prospective teachers materially exceeded the prescribed
amount of work. The significance of the extensive specialization is limited
to some extent by the fact that in all major areas some of the prospective
teachers extended their study beyond the minimum number of total
hours required for graduation. However, it is clear that these prospective teachers typically extended their major study beyond the prescription, in some cases by substantial amounts. With the exceptions of the
majors in elementary education and general education the median credits
in education ranged from 17 to 23 semester hours, but again the ranges
for the several majors show that some of these prospective teachers took

---

[54] *Ibid.*, p. 530.   [56] *Ibid.*, pp. 197-99, 534-36.
[55] *Ibid.*, pp. 164-67.

large amounts of education courses. The upper limits range from 29 to 94 semester hours.

An analysis of the majors of these prospective teachers [57] revealed much variation in the courses taken within a given field. For example, of 100 mathematics majors, 97 had taken calculus, 82 analytic geometry, 66 college algebra, 60 trigonometry, and 40 theory of equations. The remaining credits in the 100 transcripts were distributed among 26 other courses, no one of which had been taken by as many as 40 per cent of these mathematics majors.

In the study of the general education of prospective teachers, i.e. work taken outside the major field, the analysis included high-school transcripts as well as those for the four years of college. The tabulation of the "non-specialized contacts with the principal fields of knowledge" shows much variation in the general-education preparation of the sample of one thousand prospective teachers from twenty-four colleges and universities. All had taken, either in high school or in the higher institution, English, mathematics, and history, but in some other fields the proportion having taken work was relatively small.[58] The authors of the report do not commit themselves to an appraisal of the findings, but by calling attention to certain "basic challenges" imply probable weaknesses in the areas of "music and fine art" and "sociology, political science, and economics." [59] In another place [60] the findings are interpreted as showing that prospective teachers are "generally deficient in the contacts made in high school and college with the larger fields of organized knowledge" and "in their contacts with the special fields, such as art and music." This condition was attributed to the lack of effective guidance for prospective teachers.

Teacher Education on the Postbaccalaureate Level

Technical-professional courses in education are taken on the postbaccalaureate level by three classes of students: (1) those having a baccalaureate degree who wish to qualify for teaching by taking the necessary education courses; (2) students who have completed an undergraduate teacher-education curriculum and wish to extend their preparation, frequently as a means of qualifying for a different type of school position; and (3) students who wish to qualify as instructors in education in a normal school, teachers college, college, or university. Our concern in the following pages will be mainly with the second of these groups. The work for the first tends to be similar to that of undergraduate professional programs and will be given only incidental mention.

---

[57] *Ibid.*, pp. 241-43.   [58] *Ibid.*, p. 208.   [59] *Ibid.*, pp. 210-12.

[60] E. S. Evenden, *Summary and Interpretation,* National Survey of the Education of Teachers, Vol. VI (U.S. Office of Education, Bulletin 1933, No. 10), p. 92.

Up to 1890 education courses were offered for postbaccalaureate students in only a few institutions. Courses in education on the graduate level were announced by Johns Hopkins University in 1884-85 but the "Department of Psychology and Pedagogics" was discontinued in 1888 when G. Stanley Hall left the institution to organize Clark University. The work at Johns Hopkins did not "lead to a degree," but since pedagogy was considered "a field of applied psychology," [61] the courses in education could be counted toward a degree in psychology. Following the appointment of W. H. Payne as "Professor of the Science and Art of Teaching" at the University of Michigan in 1879 education courses were offered as a means for "one receiving a Bachelor's or Master's degree" to obtain a "teacher's diploma." Although the principal purpose was doubtless to provide courses which might be elected by college seniors, it is significant that professional study on the postbaccalaureate level was explicitly recognized. Luckey's description [62] of the development of professional work in other "leading universities" does not indicate explicit recognition of the postbaccalaureate level, but it is not unlikely that some of the students enrolled in the courses offered had received the bachelor's degree.

During the period since 1890 professional (education) study at the postbaccalaureate level has become a prominent field of major graduate study leading not only to the usual graduate degrees (master's and doctor's), but also to the professional degrees of a Master of Education and Doctor of Education. In addition, departments of education in colleges and universities and during recent years in teachers colleges have served increasing numbers of postbaccalaureate students, especially in summer sessions, who did not become candidates for a graduate degree. An understanding of this development, which may be regarded as phenomenal, requires that attention be given to the development of graduate work in American universities, especially the standards relating to degrees and to the clientele of departments of education.

Prior to the establishment of Johns Hopkins University in 1876, the opportunities for graduate study in the United States were largely extensions of liberal arts colleges. The courses offered tended to be extensions of the advanced courses designed for undergraduates. Under such conditions a large proportion of the students interested in graduate study, especially at the advanced level, went abroad, particularly to German universities. In these institutions the development of "initiative, self-direction, and self-reliance" was emphasized. The "graduate school" was a body of professors and students working together, typically in small groups. This graduate school was an "independent" unit rather than an extension of a liberal arts college.

---

[61] G. W. A. Luckey, *op. cit.*, p. 116.   [62] *Ibid.*, pp. 117f.

Johns Hopkins University was established as a "graduate" institution, and during the period from 1876 to 1900 several other American universities attempted to develop opportunities for graduate study along the lines of German universities, but the liberal-arts influence was potent. Most of the graduate instruction was provided by staff members from the liberal arts college who typically devoted a major portion of their time to undergraduate teaching. Other conditions tended to retard development along the lines envisaged by the founders of Johns Hopkins and other leaders of the time.[63]

Meanwhile the number of graduate students was increasing. The total graduate enrollment in colleges and universities was 460 in 1880-81. By 1890 graduate enrollments totaled 2,382; by 1910 the total was 9,370. The number of advanced degrees conferred increased from 1,135 in 1890 to 2,541 in 1910.[64] The significance of the development indicated by these quantitative increases depends upon the definition of "graduate student" and the nature of the requirements for the "advanced degrees" conferred. It is likely that in the above enrollment figures a "graduate student" was one possessing a baccalaureate degree and not counted as enrolled in a professional school or unit of the institution. This definition of a graduate student does not include any specification of the character of the courses being pursued nor the quality of scholarship being exhibited. However, the requirements for advanced degrees and discussions of the period relating to graduate work indicate a distinction between being classified as a graduate student and being recognized as a candidate for an advanced degree, especially the doctor of philosophy. The conditions for this recognition were basically qualitative — the scholarly qualities of the student and the nature of the program of work which he pursued.

Beginning in 1893 there was a concerted attack on the problem of defining graduate-school standards, first by the Federation of Graduate Clubs and a few years later by the Association of American Universities.[65] The motivation stemmed from the desire to establish "standards" and thus to create a high degree of prestige for advanced degrees, especially the doctor of philosophy. The National Association of State Universities, the Association of Land-Grant Colleges and Universities, the American Association of University Professors, certain philanthropic foundations, and regional accrediting associations also contributed to the standardization movement.[66] By 1910 the formal requirements (admission, residence,

[63] Ernest V. Hollis, *Toward Improving Ph.D. Programs,* Commission on Teacher Education (American Council on Education, 1945), pp. 12-21.
[64] Walton C. John, *Graduate Study in Universities and Colleges in the United States* (U.S. Office of Education, Bulletin, 1934, No. 20), pp. 12-13.
[65] *Ibid.,* pp. 23f.
[66] Ernest V. Hollis, *op. cit.,* p. 23.

examination, etc.) for the doctor of philosophy were fairly well standardized. Before a student was admitted to candidacy for this degree his record, both secondary and college, was "carefully scrutinized" and he was required to satisfy by examination or otherwise the specific requirements of the institution in which he was seeking admission to candidacy. He was also required to demonstrate ability to read French and German and other languages needed in his field of research. Before the degree was conferred the candidate was required to "pass" an examination designed to reveal the extent of his mastery of his major and minor fields of study and to present an acceptable dissertation "involving research and some new contribution to knowledge or an original treatment of the subject." Although the formal requirements for the degree of doctor of philosophy were fairly well standardized by 1910, the actual administration varied. For example, at some institutions the examination was of the order of "a brief and informal 'quiz' in the professor's office by a committee of three"; at others the examination was a formal and elaborate affair.[67]

The requirements for the master's degree (M.A. or M.S.) were not well standardized. A thesis and an examination were generally required,[68] but the criteria by which they were evaluated varied. In some institutions the master's degree was regarded as a "little Ph.D.," and although the thesis was not expected to represent independent research, it was judged by relatively high standards and the examination was relatively searching in the student's field of study. At the other extreme there were institutions in which the master's degree represented primarily a year of study at the graduate level, the thesis requirement being satisfied by an "essay" and the examination tending to be perfunctory. In a few institutions a thesis was not required or was optional, and in a few instances there was no examination.

The formal requirements for these advanced degrees imply that candidates for them should be students possessing superior qualities of scholarship, and that the program of work pursued should be characterized by intensive study in a given field superimposed upon undergraduate specialization and by progressively independent study and research. These implications refer to qualitative matters and attempts to deal with them were effective only to a limited degree. However, by 1910 there was general agreement that in graduate study toward the degree of doctor of philosophy the emphasis should be upon research and preparation for research and that the thesis should represent "some new contribution to knowledge or an original treatment of the subject." There

---

[67] Edwin E. Slossen, "Universities," in *A Cyclopedia of Education,* ed. Paul Monroe (New York: The Macmillan Company, 1913), V, 667f.

[68] Walton C. John, *Graduate Studies in Universities and Colleges in the United States* (U.S. Office of Education, Bulletin, 1934, No. 20), p. 148.

was less agreement in regard to what the master's degree should stand for. In fact, there was some discussion of the question of continuing the degree.[69] However, at least among the members of the Association of American Universities, there seems to have been a disposition to have the degree represent a year of *"bona fide* graduate study." The courses taken for the master's degree should be ones that were acceptable as work toward the doctor's degree.

Such was the general institutional setting within which education developed as a field of major graduate study. At the turn of the century education was a field of major graduate study at New York University in its School of Pedagogy. The aim was to "furnish thorough and complete professional training for teachers." Although the degrees conferred (Master of Pedagogy and Doctor of Pedagogy) had graduate designations, the School of Pedagogy was considered a professional unit corresponding to a school of medicine or a school of law rather than a graduate school in the conventional sense. Furthermore, it appears to have been administratively independent of the graduate school of the institution.[70] At Clark University education (pedagogy) was a subdepartment of psychology and the work was recognized as a minor for the degree of doctor of philosophy.[71] In a number of other universities students holding a baccalaureate degree enrolled in education courses as a means of obtaining a teacher's diploma. Courses specifically designated for such students were introduced in Teachers College, Columbia University in 1898-99.[72] In some institutions education was recognized as a major for a graduate degree. On the basis of data furnished by officials of the twelve institutions studied, the National Survey [73] reported masters' degrees in education granted in 1900 at University of California (1) State University of Iowa (4), Harvard University (3), and Teachers College, Columbia University (23). A doctor of philosophy in education was granted during this year at University of Chicago, State University of Iowa, and Teachers College, Columbia University.[74] Thus in effect, if not in name, education was a department of major study in the graduate school at five universities [75] in 1900. Since the study from which the above information

---

[69] *Ibid.,* p. 43.

[70] G. W. A. Luckey, *op. cit.,* pp. 139-41.

[71] *Ibid.,* p. 127.

[72] James Earl Russell, *Founding Teachers College* (The Grace H. Dodge Lectures [New York: Bureau of Publications, Teachers College, Columbia University, 1937]), p. 38.

[73] Earle U. Rugg and Others, *op. cit.,* p. 450.

[74] *Ibid.*

[75] Teachers College, Columbia University, did not attain control over its graduate degrees until 1915. See Russell, *op. cit.,* p. 48.

was taken included data from only eleven universities for 1900, it is possible that a similar status prevailed at a few other institutions.

Following 1900 education developed rather rapidly as a field of major study at the graduate level. In 1907 Bolton [76] obtained enrollment data from 37 colleges and universities. Two hundred sixty graduate students in education were reported for Columbia (Teachers College) and 259 for New York University. In the other 35 institutions the number of such students ranged from 0 at 5 universities to 49 at the University of California. The relative status of education as a field of graduate study is indicated by the fact that in the colleges and universities, other than Columbia (Teachers College) and New York Universities, the graduate students in education amounted to approximately 12 per cent of the total graduate enrollment. The National Survey [77] showed 134 masters' degrees and 15 doctors' degrees in education granted in 1910 at the eleven institutions from which data were obtained.

In general, the announced purpose of education courses designed for postbaccalaureate students was to provide advanced professional training, but since many of the students desired to obtain a graduate degree as evidence of completing a period of study beyond the baccalaureate degree it was necessary to make the content and method of conducting the courses such that they received the approval of the graduate school of the institution. The difficulty of making a course sufficiently professional (practical) so that it appealed to students as a worthwhile opportunity for advanced training and at the same time attaining the approval of the graduate school was rather frequently accentuated by a large enrollment. However, it appears that for some years following 1900 professors of education in universities tended to accept the proposition that the emphasis in graduate study should be on research, broadly conceived, and there is little evidence of opposition to the requirements and administration of graduate schools. The areas of history of education, philosophy of education, and educational psychology, being specializations of established fields of graduate study, afforded opportunity for research and as statistical methods and related techniques were developed, other areas of research were opened up. But education was a field of professional training as well as research and increasingly there were students in education at the graduate level who were interested primarily in additional training for their respective jobs or in training leading to better positions. If they evinced an interest in research, it was mainly as a means to professional prestige. Thus there developed opposition to the conventional standards of graduate work and to the administration of graduate study in education by the graduate school.

---

[76] Frederick E. Bolton, *op. cit.*

[77] Earle U. Rugg and Others, *op. cit.*, p. 450.

During the period following 1910 the graduate-student enrollment continued to increase — 1910, 9,370; 1920, 15,612; and 1930, 47,255. The increase in number of advanced degrees conferred was proportionately greater — 1910, 2,541; 1920, 4,853; and 1930, 14,495. The growth of graduate work was contributed to by the development of graduate departments in institutions previously offering opportunity for only undergraduate study, but a large portion of the increases was due to increased enrollments in institutions offering graduate work in 1910. The total number of masters' degrees in education conferred in twenty-six such institutions increased from 1,401 in 1910 to 9,401 in 1930.[78]

Within the quantitative development of graduate study there were significant qualitative changes. The student group became more heterogeneous relative to interests. Social developments, especially following World War I, accentuated the need for professional training at the postbaccalaureate level in various areas — personnel services in business and industry, social work, library science, public administration, business education, physical education and recreation, and the like, as well as education. As enrollments increased, graduate schools tended to develop more restrictive standards — admission, residence, examination, etc. — and more formal administrative organizations and procedures, but these developments were within the general framework of the liberal-arts tradition and the emphasis upon research. Thus a fundamental problem developed. If graduate schools persisted in maintaining their standards and policies, social pressures would force development of other postbaccalaureate units to meet the demands for advanced professional training.

Criteria for differentiating between undergraduate courses and those worthy of approval as graduate work had not been developed beyond the general level. In graduate schools a "scholarly literature" and a record of "research" in the area of a proposed course were generally held to be important, if not essential, conditions for approval. However, in "new" areas these conditions could not be satisfied beyond a relatively low level. In the more liberal graduate schools "standards" relative to courses were relaxed, especially in the case of ones designed for first-year students. In the more conservative graduate schools the "standards" were more rigidly maintained.

Within this general situation there were persistent pressures for an expansion of the graduate program in education and for modifications of standards relative to graduate degrees. Various areas of professional service in our schools were being expanded and systematized — curriculum, guidance, supervision, business management, psychological service, measurement, and so on. Specialized preparation for these areas

---

[78] Walton C. John, *op. cit.*, pp. 13-15.

of service called for new courses, and since these areas were "new," there was neither an adequate "scholarly literature" nor a "research tradition." However, courses to meet such needs were introduced in many institutions, particularly the larger universities. The variation in number of courses listed in institutional announcements (see Chapter 14) suggest a variation in graduate-school policies relative to approving new course proposals. In some institutions the department of education seems to have been given a high degree of autonomy; in others it was materially restricted by graduate school standards and policies.

In spite of the efforts of the Association of American Universities and other organizations directed toward the development of standards for the master's degree compatible with the concept of graduate work implied by the emphasis upon research, it appears that most institutions either declined to adopt the proposed standards for this degree or allowed exceptions as a common practice. The committee on graduate degrees reporting to the North Central Association in 1928 noted "the apparent decline in the standard of requirements for the master's degree by some of the recognized universities." [79] In an address before the Association of American Universities Dean Slichter of the University of Wisconsin stated that only eleven members of the association did not "advertise short-cuts to the master's degree." [80]

Attention was given also to the Ph.D degree, but there was little change in the quantitative standards for this degree beyond a more critical evaluation of the baccalaureate degree upon which admission to the graduate school was sought. The general position relative to qualitative aspects of the degree is indicated by a committee of the American Association of University Professors reporting in 1918. The report stressed the desirability of differentiating between admission to the graduate school and admission to candidacy for the doctor's degree. The committee was "unanimous in holding that the doctor's degree should be conferred only upon persons of unusual intellectual endowment with unequivocal capacities for research." [81]

Under the restraining influences in the situation outlined [82] in the preceding pages, it is to be expected that departments of education would seek to become "independent" graduate units. In 1920 a Graduate School of Education was established at Harvard University. This action, which appears to have been the first of its kind among American

<hr/>

[79] *North Central Association Quarterly,* 3 (1928), 171.

[80] Charles S. Slichter, " 'Debunking' the Master's Degree," *North Central Association Quarterly,* 3 (March, 1929), 463-67. Reprinted from the *Proceedings* of the 29th Conference of the Association of American Universities.

[81] See Walton C. John, *op. cit.,* pp. 48-52.

[82] For a more extended account see Hollis, *op. cit.,* pp. 28f.

universities,[83] is indicative of the developing dissatisfaction among departments of education relative to the standards of graduate schools and the administration of graduate degrees. Several causes contributed to this development. The enrollments of graduate students in education were heavily weighted with practitioners — school superintendents, high-school principals, teachers, and others — who were interested in professional training rather than research. The objections of these graduate students centered about the language requirements and the thesis for the degree of doctor of philosophy. Relatively few had attained a reading knowledge of both French and German; some were deficient in both languages. Hence the language requirements represented a deterrent for a considerable number of students who seemed otherwise qualified to pursue work leading to the doctorate. In the matter of the thesis practitioners frequently wished to work on a practical problem or at least to select a problem that appealed to them as worthwhile. At the master's degree level, the objection to a thesis was less strenuous, but students attempting to complete the work for this degree during summer sessions frequently found the thesis a formidable task.

Admission requirements of graduate schools created a second contributing cause. As graduate-school administration was systematized a baccalaureate degree from an "approved" institution tended to become a minimum requirement. Many graduate schools specified requirements in certain fields of instruction such as foreign language. The development of normal schools into teachers colleges conferring baccalaureate degrees created a growing source of supply, but in numerous instances a teachers college was not an "approved" institution and if "approved," the graduate may not have satisfied undergraduate requirements specified by the graduate school. If the applicant was admitted, it was with a deficiency. There were also graduates of "nonapproved" liberal arts colleges. The pressure from agencies accrediting secondary schools for a baccalaureate degree as a teacher qualification resulted in normal-school graduates and others taking correspondence courses, seeking credit for teaching experience, and in other ways endeavoring to obtain this degree. In many, perhaps a majority, of such cases the person had attained recognition as a competent teacher or school administrator, and from the point of view of ability to pursue graduate study in education, there was a strong argument for admission to full graduate standing, but his transcript included credits that were not "respectable."

Among institutions there were marked variations in regard to admission to the graduate school. For example, Linton found on the basis of questionnaire data obtained in 1926 that although slightly more than

<hr>

[83] Henry W. Holmes, "The New Requirements at Harvard for Degrees in Education," *School and Society,* 25 (1927), 707-11.

half of the institutions reporting did not make any prescription in regard to the nature of the undergraduate curriculum, among the remaining institutions the undergraduate prescriptions ranged from 3 to 100 semester hours.[84] Linton reported a growing tendency to admit graduates of four-year teachers colleges to full graduate standing, but eighteen of the sixty-seven institutions did not do so and in eleven others the decision was on individual transcripts.

Another problem in the administration of graduate study in education was due to the variation in previous professional training of those applying for admission. At one extreme there were applicants who had taken no education courses; at the other there were those who had credits well beyond the typical requirements for an undergraduate major in education. Among the sixty-seven institutions studied by Linton, twenty-five had no prescription of undergraduate study in education for admission to major graduate study in education, eleven did not reply, and the range of requirements in the other thirty-one institutions was from 5 to 9 semester hours to 35 to 39 semester hours.[85] Although a lack of undergraduate study in education may be compensated for by requiring certain education courses in addition to the usual total requirements for the master's degree, Linton interpreted his data as indicating that this was not the practice. Thus it appears that for some students a master's degree in education represented formal study in education during only one year while for others it represented a graduate major in addition to undergraduate study in education amounting to 30 semester hours or more.[86] Granting a master's degree on the basis of only a year of total study in the designated field was not compatible with graduate-school standards and presumably such practice occurred at the insistence of the department of education, which in turn had been influenced by the pressure from college graduates for a degree which would command recognition as a certification of satisfactory completion of a year of study beyond the baccalaureate degree.

A fourth contributing cause was the desire of graduate students in education to complete a portion, or even all, of the work for a graduate degree by attendance during summer sessions. The trend of the times is indicated by the increase in the total summer-session enrollment in twenty-three colleges and universities from 27,640 in 1913 to 83,971 in

[84] Clarence Linton, *A Study of Some Problems Arising in the Admission of Students as Candidates for Professional Degrees in Education* (Contributions to Education, No. 285 [New York: Bureau of Publications, Teachers College, Columbia University, 1927]), p. 85.

[85] *Ibid.*, p. 87.

[86] Leonard V. Koos, *Standards in Graduate Work in Education* (U.S. Office of Education, Bulletin, 1921), No. 38. 18 pp.

1931.[87] It is likely that the relative increase in graduate enrollment in education was larger. In 1931 the median graduate enrollment in sixty-three universities was 265. That a large proportion of the graduate enrollment was in education is indicated by the ratio of five graduate courses in education to one in the total of five other departments in twelve institutions.[88] In most institutions the number of graduate students in education was materially larger in the summer session than during the regular year. Furthermore, graduate students in education in summer sessions were less interested in research than those of the regular session.

Education departments tended to be sympathetic to student protests against graduate-school standards and administrative practices. Although staff members tended to emphasize research as a means of developing a science of education and did not disregard education as a field of scholarly study for those who aspired to positions in colleges and universities, they recognized that the need of practitioners was for further professional training. Furthermore, graduate departments of education desired to increase enrollments. In part this was a manifestation of the desire to develop departmental prestige within their respective institutions and among institutions of their class. Education was a relatively new graduate department and with respect to obtaining adequate budgetary allocations from institutional funds the situation was similar to that faced by normal schools during the years following 1890.

Institutional policies relative to financing summer sessions contributed to the aggressiveness of departments of education in attracting students. In 1931 only two of 65 universities and one of 137 colleges reported that provision for a summer session was included in the "regular year budget" of the institution. In more than half of both groups of institutions the summer session was reported as self-supporting.[89] In such a situation summer-session advertising to attract students was a general practice.[90] As the largest department within summer sessions, education needed a major allocation of funds, and hence the department was under pressure to meet the desires of prospective students. Thus in institutions where the standards and practices of the graduate school were a handicap in attracting students, the policy of financing the summer session operated as an incentive to the department of education to become independent of the graduate school or to obtain concessions in administering graduate work in education.

The establishment of the Harvard Graduate School of Education in

---

[87] Ivan A. Booker, "Educational Research and Statistics," *School and Society*, 37 (1933), 230-32.

[88] Earle U. Rugg and Others, *op. cit.*, pp. 412, 428.

[89] *Ibid.*, p. 415.

[90] *Ibid.*, p. 416.

1920 included setting up two professional degrees — master of education (Ed.M.) and doctor of education (Ed.D.). Since this date these
degrees have been established at other institutions. By 1929-30 six institutions had announced requirements for the doctor of education — Boston
University, California, Harvard, Johns Hopkins, Southern California,
and Stanford.[91] At the time of the National Survey (1931) the degree
was offered at twenty-two institutions.

The distinction between the doctor of education and the doctor of
philosophy in education is suggested by the terms "professional training" and "research." Professional competence rather than research ability
is the goal in the case of the doctor of education. The principal modification of the requirements for this degree were: (1) foreign language
requirements contingent upon the need for one or more languages in
the area of the student's specialized interest or no language required;
(2) a liberalization of the concept of the thesis to permit studies of
current school problems, organizations and applications of existing
knowledge, and the like; and (3) a minimum of successful professional
experience.[92]

Thus the development of study in education on the postbaccalaureate
level shifted from a tendency to conform to graduate school standards
to emphasis upon courses and degree requirements considered by "professors of education" and by the students to be more compatible with
the purposes of professional training at the graduate level. The institutional organization attending this development varied. At Harvard University a Graduate School of Education was established. At several universities education was a department within the graduate school with
few if any special concessions. In between these extremes there are many
compromise organizations. The result is that programs in education on the
postbaccalaureate level became mixtures of courses designed to meet
immediate practical needs of practitioners and courses designed in conformity with graduate-school standards.

Professional Status of the Provisions for the Education of Secondary Teachers in 1930

A criterion of the professional status of the provisions for an educational function is the adaptation of the provisions, organizational as well
as the courses of instruction, to the desired outcomes. In the case of
the education of secondary teachers the outcomes desired depended
upon the interpretation of our secondary schools relative to the qualifications of the teachers needed for the realization of the recognized purposes

---

[91] Walter S. Monroe, "A Survey of the Requirements for the Doctor of Philosophy
in Education," *School and Society*, 31 (1930), 655-61.

[92] Earle U. Rugg and Others, *op. cit.*, pp. 456-57.

of these schools. Thus the professional status of the provisions for the education of secondary teachers is to be appraised as high from this point of view if the organization and the courses of instruction for this function are considered to be effectively adapted to engendering the teacher qualifications judged to be needed for realizing the recognized purposes of our secondary schools. If adaptation of the provisions to the teacher-education function is considered not to be effective, the professional status will be judged to be low.

By the time of the National Survey a college (or school) of education had been established in most universities and in some colleges (see p. 316). However, the nature of this organization and the degree of its autonomy varied and this situation must be kept in mind in attempting any summary appraisal. Another complicating condition is the fact that in many institutions the college of liberal arts and even some other colleges functioned as teacher-education organizations in the sense that students enrolled in them could qualify for a license to teach by electing the necessary pedagogical (education) courses and meeting other requirements. In the National Survey [93] it is stated that in 76 per cent of the institutions having a college of education prospective teachers might enroll in other colleges, taking education courses as a means of meeting licensing and accrediting requirements. In other words after twenty-five years of the college-of-education development, three-fourths of these institutions maintained two administrative organizations for teacher education.

The presence of two administrative organizations for the education of teachers raises the question of the professional status of the provisions for this function, especially of those outside of the college of education. Of course, the administrative organization is only a means and the significant criterion is the adaptation of the provisions to engendering the teacher qualifications needed for effective service in our secondary schools. But here we find a difference of opinion in regard to the qualifications needed for effective service. In understanding this difference of opinion it is helpful to note certain aspects of the development of secondary education.

By 1890 the public high school had become the major type of secondary institution. Although a variety of "practical" subjects were offered in particular high schools, the traditional subjects dominated the curriculum. The Committee of Ten (1894) asserted that the "main function" of the secondary schools was to prepare their pupils for the "duties of life" rather than for college admission. This statement is not very meaningful because the Committee thought of mental training as the significant outcome of instruction and also asserted that the curriculum

---

[93] *Ibid.,* p. 164.

should be the same "no matter what the probable destination of the pupil may be."

The recommendations of the subject Conferences of the Committee of Ten outlined subjects which, for the most part, were elementary phases of college fields of instruction. These recommendations, the development of accreditation, and the Report of the Committee on College-entrance Requirements (1899) practically fixed the secondary curriculum except for such additional subjects of a "practical" nature as the schools might choose to offer as "extras," i.e. as subjects not counted toward college admission. The instructional task was conceived of as being to *teach the subjects* of the curriculum (See Chapter 3). Thus during the years following the turn of the century, when professional training for secondary teachers was being developed, the instructional task of the teachers of accredited subjects was thought of as being similar to that of college instructors in the corresponding elementary courses. Hence members of college departments tended to regard the preparation which experience had convinced them was adequate for success in teaching at the lower college levels as also adequate for success in secondary schools. The essential qualifications were the culture and mental training resulting from four years of college study and academic competence in the teaching field. A teacher's course by an experienced member of the department was considered by some academic people to be a desirable supplement to subject-matter preparation.

During the second decade of the century significant developments began to appear in the secondary schools. In 1890 the total enrollment was less than 300,000; by 1910 it exceeded 1,000,000; and by 1920 it exceeded 2,000,000. The pupil population had become more varied with respect to interests, purposes, and capacity to learn. The trend of the thinking of secondary-school leaders relative to purposes is indicated by the "seven cardinal principles" formulated by the Commission on the Reorganization of Secondary Education (1918). The report of this commission may be regarded as a "declaration of independence," a revolt against the domination of secondary schools by colleges and universities through entrance requirements and accreditation. Curriculum practice lagged behind curriculum theory, but new courses and new selections and organizations of old content began to appear, and by the end of the third decade the secondary curriculum had become very different from that of 1900.

Also by this time a significant change in teaching-learning theory had emerged. The teacher's task as an instructor was being conceived of as *directing learning* rather than *teaching subjects*. This change in the concept of the teacher's task made the understanding of the teaching-learning process an important qualification.

Curriculum change in secondary schools did not exhibit an even front. In some, the traditional subjects were retained with little change and new subjects were few. At the other extreme there were "progressive" secondary schools in which the curriculum bore little resemblance to the program of 1900. Insofar as liberal-arts faculties were informed in regard to curriculum practices in secondary schools, they tended to interpret the situation as one of uncertainty and confusion. Many members were not in sympathy with "progressive" practices and looked upon the more conservative schools as representing what should be. Some, perhaps many, were not informed. Furthermore, they were not aware of the change in teaching-learning theory. Due to these conditions, members of academic departments tended to think of the task of the secondary teacher, at least as it should be, as being much the same as it was during the first decade of the century and to consider the qualifications deemed adequate at that time to be still sufficient.

From the point of view of this concept of desired teacher qualifications, there were grounds for a favorable appraisal of the professional status of the organizational provisions for teacher education outside of the college of education. The more conservative subject-matter instructors would have considered the provisions more desirable if the required work in education were restricted to 12 semester hours or even less.

In considering the status of the provisions for educating secondary teachers in colleges of education, it should be recognized that these units were not professional schools in the sense of colleges of agriculture, engineering, law, or medicine. The college of education, except in some special subject fields, typically offered through its own staff only a sixth to a fifth of the total undergraduate program pursued by its enrollees. Outside of some special subject fields, most of the undergraduate program for prospective teachers was offered by subject-matter departments, typically in the college of liberal arts. Thus under the college-of-education organization the college of liberal arts continued to be the major contributor to the total undergraduate education of prospective teachers for secondary schools, i.e. it provided the means for a liberal (general) education and the teaching-knowledge qualification. Teacher education was a joint enterprise, and in such undertakings the degree of success attained depends upon the cooperation of the partners. In the National Survey the study of the situation led to the following general appraisal: "This cooperation between educationists and other departments is apparently getting closer and more cordial, as it should, but there is much to be desired along these lines in some institutions.[94]

The effect of this "closer and more cordial" cooperation upon the general education and subject-matter specialization of prospective secondary

[94] *Ibid.*, p. 166.

teachers is not made clear. The professionalization of the liberal (general) education phase of teacher education was not systematically dealt with in the National Survey but Chapter IV, Volume III, provides a basis for some observations. Analysis of high school and college transcripts of one thousand prospective teachers in terms of "nonspecialized contacts with the principal fields of knowledge" revealed a pattern of general education heavily weighted with mathematics and languages. Slight attention was given to political science, sociology, economics, arts, music, or philosophy. In contrast, opinion strongly favored a pattern of general education more appropriate for teachers. In fact, the opinion was almost unanimous except in the cases of "academic instructors" and "special-subject instructors." This finding probably should not be interpreted as implying acceptance of the thesis that the general education for teachers should be professionalized.

In many cases the provisions for subject-matter specialization were considered not to be adapted effectively to the needs of teachers in secondary schools. Analytical studies of college records of teachers revealed "gaps" in subject-matter preparation,[95] and there appears to have been a fundamental difference in the concept of the nature of adequate subject-matter preparation for secondary teaching.[96] Although this difference was probably not very clearly defined in the minds of either the "professors of education" or their academic colleagues, it appears that the former tended to emphasize breadth of study in the major field and substantial study in related (minor) fields and that many of the latter stressed specialized intensive study in the major field or even in a phase of it and considered an introductory course adequate preparation for teaching in related fields.

Although educationists, especially in teachers colleges, were urging the professionalization of subject-matter specialization, the proposal had not become a matter of much concern in academic circles. In the National Survey it was observed that the proposal had received little publicity.[97] In fact, it does not appear that professionalization of subject-matter courses had been adequately defined, and in practice very little was being attempted.[98] Expressed opinion among university and college faculties was strongly in favor of "some professionalization."[99] The explanation of this apparent contradiction seems to be in the concept of professionalization. The dominant view in academic circles seems to have been that adequate professionalization of a subject-matter major could be accomplished by means of a "special methods course" supplementary to the conventional subject-matter specialization. The concept of professionalization held by "education instructors" is not clear, and

[95] *Ibid.*, pp. 238-45.   [97] *Ibid.*, p. 273.   [99] *Ibid.*, p. 276.

[96] *Ibid.*, pp. 222-23.   [98] *Ibid.*, p. 277.

it may be inferred that this group had not yet clarified its thinking relative to what was desirable.

On the basis of responses of deans it appears that almost universally an "independent" college (school) of education exercised general control over "most matters entering into the education of teachers" and guided "students in preparing to be teachers in their entire program while enrolled in the school or college of education." The effect of this general control and student advisement is not specified, but it is likely that in most institutions it did not extend beyond curriculum specifications in terms of existing courses and the regulation of course elections. In situations where the cooperation was "closer and more cordial," the college of education probably was able to stimulate the development of some courses designed for teachers.

In any appraisal of the provisions for preparing secondary teachers under the college-of-education organization it is important to recognize institutional variations. In a few universities the provisions for teacher education under the college-of-education organization appear to have been rather effectively adapted to the needs of secondary teachers, but developments since 1930 (see Chapter 14, pp. 352f.) suggest that some educationists entertained doubts in regard to the efficacy of the contemporary college-of-education organization as a means of educating teachers for secondary schools.

Concluding Statement

The quantitative development of professional education for secondary teachers in colleges and universities from the "small beginnings" of 1890 to the status of 1930 is impressive. In 1890, 114 colleges and universities announced "teachers' courses," but very few of these institutions offered pedagogical courses of college grade for prospective secondary teachers. By the time of the National Survey approximately one thousand colleges and universities offered at least the education courses necessary for obtaining a license to teach.[100] In 105 of these institutions a college or school of education had been organized as a means of more effective teacher education. Three-fifths of these units had been established between 1915 and 1930.[101] Graduate work leading to at least a master's degree in education was offered in 128 colleges and universities.

The qualitative aspects of this development cannot be described in definite terms, but some suggestive statements can be made. In the group of colleges and universities studied in the National Survey the median prescription of courses in education, excluding general psychology, amounted to 18.4 semester hours.[102] The median prescription of such

---

[100] E. S. Evenden, op. cit., p. 76.
[101] Earle U. Rugg and Others, op. cit., p. 164.
[102] Ibid., p. 258.

courses, general psychology included only if so classified, in colleges of education was 21 semester hours.[103] Although some questioned the efficacy of courses in education on the preservice level (see p. 313), the general approval of such study suggests that the preservice education of secondary teachers was significantly higher in quality in 1930 than in 1890, when pedagogical training for secondary teachers was offered by very few colleges and universities.

Changes in the nature of the general education and the special-knowledge preparation of secondary teachers probably had been in the direction of better qualifications. The statement that the cooperation between educationists and subject-matter departments was becoming "closer and more cordial" supports this inference. On the other hand, the analysis of sample transcripts of graduates suggests that in a considerable proportion the content of the major was not very well adapted to the needs of secondary teaching. Also the general-education preparation seemed to be inadequate in certain respects.

The organizational development for teacher education is probably significant. The establishment of a college of education in a university expresses recognition of teacher preparation as a major function, and it is reasonable that this type of organization resulted in improving the preservice education of secondary teachers. Although the National Survey reported only 105 colleges or schools of education from the approximately one thousand higher institutions preparing teachers, it is stated that "a median of 71 percent of all undergraduate students who receive degrees with complete qualification for certification were reported as enrolled in the schools of education." [104] If a college of education is a superior provision for the preservice education of teachers, practice in colleges and universities had been favorably affected.

In connection with the statements just made it should be noted that in "only 24 percent of the institutions was preparation for teaching restricted to the school or college of education." [105] On the basis of visitation and conferences this plan was judged to be best in institutions large enough to support such an organization.[106] The fact that, after twenty-five years of development, this "best plan" was found in only twenty-five institutions is probably a significant indication of the status of the education of teachers for secondary schools.

The development of professional study on the postbaccalaureate level is significant. Five-year programs and the extension of professional study on the graduate level doubtless result in better teachers. It also should be noted that the development on the postbaccalaureate level provided professional training for a variety of school positions other than classroom teaching.

[103] *Ibid.*, p. 167.
[104] *Ibid.*, pp. 165-66.
[105] *Ibid.*, p. 165.
[106] *Ibid.*, p. 166.

CHAPTER 13

Organizational Developments
Since the National Survey

The National Survey of the Education of Teachers was an expression of a serious concern about the preparation of teachers for our schools that had been developing for several years, particularly within the membership of the American Association of Teachers Colleges. The Survey report furnished extensive information in regard to the status of teacher education in normal schools and teachers colleges and in colleges and universities for around 1930, and this date has been taken as the end of the period dealt with in Chapters 11 and 12. The Survey revealed that by this time most of the normal schools had become collegiate institutions, typically with the designation teachers college, and that these institutions were similar to liberal arts colleges and to liberal-arts units within universities in many respects. In considering the development of teacher education since 1930 it is not necessary to deal separately with the two groups of institutions.

Following the National Survey, the concern about teacher education became more widespread and intense and the period has been one of unprecedented activity directed toward the improvement of the preparation of teachers for our schools. Before sketching the major developments, the general setting of the period will be noted briefly.

General Setting of the Period

The depression beginning in the autumn of 1929 added to the over-supply of teachers which had been accumulating for several years (see p. 262). In 1932 only 40 per cent of those completing teacher-education programs obtained employment as teachers. Following this year, the proportion of graduates securing teaching positions increased and by 1941 a shortage of teachers was developing. During the period of World War II the teacher shortage became critical.[1] Although the lack of qualified teachers continued beyond the end of hostilities, by 1949 the production of secondary teachers exceeded the demand in most states. At the elementary level, however, the supply was about one-third of the demand.[2]

The depression and other social forces of the period stimulated many changes in our schools. These changes together with the developing teaching-learning theory (see pp. 156f.) made the work of the teacher different. In classroom instruction the teacher's function developed in the direction of guiding pupil experiencing and/or directing learning activities. In addition, teachers were called upon to assume more responsibilities in the area of pupil personnel work and to participate in curriculum development, formulation of school policies, and the like.

The period has also been one of much ferment in higher education. The multiplication of course offerings during the preceding years, the effects of the elective system, the increased variability of the student population, and other conditions stimulated deliberation and action relative to the undergraduate programs of colleges and universities. With respect to the present purpose, probably the most significant development is that commonly designated as "general education."[3]

The period from 1907 to 1933 was characterized by studies of teachers as they are. The National Survey, which may be regarded as the culmination of this approach in attempting to improve the preparation of teachers, presented a mass of status information relative to teachers and teacher education. Following the publication of the National Survey, the emphasis shifted to constructive action. This development is indicated by creation of commissions, councils, and committees.

The Commission on Teacher Education. This group was created by

---

[1] Earl W. Anderson, "Teacher Personnel—V. Supply and Demand," in *Encyclopedia of Educational Research,* ed. Walter S. Monroe (Rev. ed.; New York: The Macmillan Company, 1950), pp. 1424-27.

[2] Ray C. Maul, *Teacher Supply and Demand in the United States* (Washington: National Education Association, 1950). 36 pp.

[3] For an account of this development, see T. R. McConnell and Others, "General Education," in *Encyclopedia of Educational Research,* ed. Walter S. Monroe (Rev. ed.; New York: The Macmillan Company, 1950), pp. 489-500.

the American Council on Education following the publication of *Major Issues in Teacher Education* in 1938. The Commission interpreted its "mandate" as being "cooperative demonstration in living situations," i.e. "implementation as over against research or controlled experiment." [4] Cooperative demonstrations were organized in twenty selected institutions — six universities (Columbia, Ohio State, Stanford, Nebraska, North Carolina, and Texas); five colleges of liberal arts (Claremont College, the College of St. Catherine, the College of William and Mary, Middlebury College, and Oberlin College); seven state teachers colleges (Alabama State Teachers College at Troy, Colorado State College of Education at Greeley, Eastern Kentucky State Teachers College at Richmond, New Jersey State Teachers College at Newark, Southern Illinois State Normal University at Carbondale, Western Michigan College of Education at Kalamazoo, and Wisconsin State Teachers College at Milwaukee); and two Negro colleges (Prairie View State College and Tuskegee Institute).

The cooperative demonstrations in these institutions, initiated in August, 1939, and terminated in June, 1942, may be thought of as a group of uncontrolled (single-group) experiments. Each institution planned its "experimental program" under the general stimulation and "leadership" of the Commission. The planning included a cooperative formulation of purposes (objectives), the development of a program in the light of these purposes, and the development of methods of evaluation relative to the objectives.

The reports of the Commission do not provide systematic accounts of the changes in teacher-education practice represented in the several cooperative demonstrations. However, certain areas of development are apparent: student personnel work, preservice selection and recruitment, general education, advanced subject-matter preparation, child growth and development, social understanding, direct experience (observation and student teaching), and larger instructional units. In several of the institutions subject-matter people and educationists cooperated in certain activities.

Although evaluation was emphasized as a process in developing teacher-education programs, only a general appraisal of the cooperative demonstrations is reported.[5] Most of the colleges and universities were "well satisfied" with their accomplishments and the Commission concurred in this appraisal. The Commission noted that in addition to "progress" in the education of teachers for our schools, there were

[4] W. Earl Armstrong and Others, *The College and Teacher Education* (Washington, D. C.: American Council on Education, 1944), p. 3.

[5] Commission on Teacher Education, *The Improvement of Teacher Education* (Washington, D. C.: American Council on Education, 1946), pp. 67f.

"changes in the persons who bore institutional responsibilities, changes in their ideas and in their ways of working together." [6] The Commission regarded these latter changes as "the more fundamental and fruitful."

At the time of this writing one can only speculate in regard to the effect of these cooperative demonstrations upon the general development of teacher-education practice. Their occurrence is probably indicative of an increased concern about the education of teachers and a trend toward greater cooperation in teacher education. Perhaps the work of the Commission will come to be recognized as a significant stimulus in the development of teacher-education practice.

Other commissions, councils, and committees. The National Commission on Teacher Education and Professional Standards, created by the Buffalo Delegate Assembly of the National Education Association in July, 1946, grew out of the conviction "that teaching must be made into a real profession, and that the organized teachers themselves must take the lead in accomplishing that result." This Commission is becoming an influence of considerable importance in the preservice education of teachers. In its Annual Report for 1948-49 the progress of the year is reviewed under eighteen "major aims and goals." It publishes a newsletter, *The Journal of Teacher Education,* and various reports. Perhaps more important are the regional and national conferences held under its sponsorship.

The Council on Cooperation in Teacher Education grew out of cooperative activities of the American Council on Education beginning during the mid-thirties. At present (1949) it is a council of seventeen national organizations recognizing the improvement of teacher education as a major purpose. The Council sponsors cooperative meetings, especially of the clinic or work-conference type. It published a newsletter and bulletin materials.

Two general types of state organizations deserve mention. In 1949 there were twenty-seven state teachers associations with commissions or committees paralleling the National Commission on Teacher Education and Professional Standards of the National Education Association and four additional associations were in process of establishing such commissions. A State Council on Teacher Education has a "membership representing at least (*a*) the state department of education, (*b*) the state education association, and (*c*) individual colleges and universities." [7] In 1948 there were nineteen such councils. Although these two agencies have the same general purpose, i.e. to improve education within the state, they play somewhat different roles to this end. A state commission pro-

---

[6] *Ibid.*

[7] L. D. Haskew, editorial chairman, "State Councils on Teacher Education," *American Council on Education,* 1949), p. 68.

vides a means for the members of the teaching profession to participate in the formulation of goals and standards. The council is a means for converting these goals and standards into action programs.[8]

Developments in Teachers Colleges [9]

A significant development has been that of the expansion of a number of teachers colleges into general colleges, i.e. institutions explicitly recognizing one or more functions other than teacher education. Although some institutions may have aggressively promoted the expansion of function as a means of increasing their prestige, it appears that this development was largely the result of other influences. High-school graduates residing in the local community and in the surrounding area sought admission even though they had little or no interest in preparing for teaching. State normal schools and teachers colleges could not afford to deny admission to these applicants and increasingly during the thirties enrollments included nonprofessional students. By 1935 in California, where the teachers colleges were devoted to the preparation of elementary teachers, the number of such students was approximately equal to the number preparing for teaching, even though these institutions required a minimum of twelve upper division units in education of all candidates for graduation. In this year the state legislature, "in response to petitions" from students not interested in preparing for teaching, took action specifying that "no student who was not a candidate for a teaching credential should be required to take professional courses in education as a prerequisite to graduation." [10] The names of the institutions were also changed to state colleges.

Although the development in California is probably not entirely typical, it does illustrate the trend. Following the cessation of the hostilities of World War II, the pressure of the demand of veterans for educational opportunities forced teachers colleges to admit large numbers of students who were not interested in preparing for teaching. The result has been the expansion of a considerable proportion of teachers colleges into state colleges.[11]

---

[8] *Ibid.*, p. 56.

[9] Chapter 8, which deals with the development of desired qualifications, should be read in connection with this and the following sections.

[10] Frank W. Thomas, "Twenty Years of Bilateral Education," *Twenty-sixth Yearbook* (American Association of Teachers Colleges, 1947), pp. 21-28.

[11] In 1947 the administrators of 57 per cent of 127 teachers colleges reported their respective institutions as "multiplepurpose" regional colleges. Warren C. Lovinger, *General Education in Teachers Colleges* (Oneonta, New York: American Association of Colleges for Teacher Education, 1948). 119 pp. The present number of such institutions is not known, but a letter from Charles W. Hunt, secretary-treasurer of the American Association of Colleges for Teacher Education dated May 6, 1950, gives an estimate of 75.

There has been some discussion of this development,[12] but there appears to have been little opposition. Where the expansion of function has been established, it appears to be generally approved.[13] The possible unfortunate effect of multiple-purpose institutions is generally discounted. On the positive side, it is claimed that a state college attracts a more representative group of students and that thus it affords an opportunity for guiding a number of promising young people into teaching.

Certain general developments in teachers colleges are reflected by the annual lists of institutions accredited by the American Association of Teachers Colleges. A total of 196 institutions were accredited for the period March 1, 1947 to March 1, 1948, including fourteen colleges of education within universities.[14] In only one instance was the longest approved curriculum less than four years. Graduate work was approved in 22 institutions other than the education units of universities. The Committee on Accrediting and Classification reported 53 violations of standards for 1947, but due to the conditions of the time it recommended no disciplinary action.[15] These facts may be compared with corresponding ones for 1931-32. The membership list of that year included 175 institutions for which the longest curriculum is specified. There were 24 cases in which the longest curriculum was less than four years. Graduate work was offered in 13 teachers colleges.

Certain curricular changes in teachers colleges are revealed in a study by Sprague.[16] From 1928 to 1938 increased attention was given to the general-education qualification, the principal change being increases in "broad orientation or survey courses and so-called functional courses" and decreases in "short unit courses and traditional courses." The number of majors in comprehensive fields increased and the total semester-hour requirements increased for nearly all majors. These changes indicate increased attention to the teaching-knowledge requirement. Sprague indicates some qualitative change in the direction of more functional courses and professionalized courses.

In the technical-professional area there was a change from "courses which emphasize teaching skills and routine in management" toward "courses or types of subject matter which emphasize 'points of view' or 'interpretative background.'" Added attention to student teaching was

[12] For example, see *Nineteenth Yearbook* (American Association of Teachers Colleges, 1940), pp. 23-35.

[13] For a fairly typical appraisal, see Frank W. Thomas, *op. cit.*

[14] *Twenty-sixth Yearbook* (American Association of Teachers Colleges, 1947), pp. 152-56.

[15] *Ibid.*, p. 137.

[16] H. A. Sprague, *A Decade of Progress in the Preparation of Secondary School Teachers* (Contributions to Education, No. 794 [New York: Bureau of Publications, Teachers College, Columbia University, 1940]). 170 pp.

also noted. A decrease of 10.5 per cent in the total semester-hour requirements in education was interpreted as indicating a reduction of duplication and better integration of closely related material.

Developments in Liberal Arts Colleges

This designation refers to independent liberal-arts collegiate institutions and liberal-arts units within universities. In 1948 the membership
of the Association of American Colleges included 627 such institutions
and units in the continental United States.[17] Of this number 112 institution either offered no education courses or less work than was required
for certification.[18] Findings from a subparticipating group of 157 institutions are probably indicative of certain trends. Meyer [19] reported that
from 1900-1904 to 1925-1929 the proportion of college graduates entering
teaching increased from 18 to 45 per cent. Morris reported 39 per cent
of the senior class of 1937-38 becoming secondary teachers. The corresponding finding for 1947-48 is 27 per cent. However, the absolute number of teachers produced is approximately the same.

Although a comparison of the two studies should be made with
caution, the findings suggest that during the period since the National
Survey a decreasing proportion of liberal-arts students have become
secondary teachers. It is also perhaps significant that Meyer reported 98
per cent of the institutions he studied as maintaining a teacher-education
program. This finding may be compared with the 82 per cent reported by
Morris. However, the responses obtained by Morris relative to future
plans reveal that 61 per cent of the institutions plan to expand their
teacher-education programs,[20] and it appears likely that the liberal arts
college will continue to be a major source of teacher supply, the proportion of seniors preparing to teach possibly increasing.[21] Hence the points
of view of these institutions relative to teacher education and their current efforts to improve the preparation of teachers are matters of importance.

A general indication of the concern about teacher education on the
part of liberal arts colleges is the creation of a Commission on Teacher

---

[17] Van Cleve Morris, *The Education of Secondary School Teachers in the Liberal
Arts College* (Ed.D. thesis; New York: Teachers College, Columbia University, 1949),
p. 33.

[18] *Ibid.*, p. 38. This number is estimated from data supplied by the 368 institutions
participating in the study. The author expresses the opinion that the return from
institutions not maintaining teacher-education facilities was probably relatively high.

[19] Jacob G. Meyer, *Small Colleges and Teacher Training* (Bloomington, Illinois:
Public School Publishing Company, 1928), p. 133. This study is based on returns
from 156 members of the Association of American Colleges.

[20] Van Cleve Morris, *op. cit.*, p. 59.

[21] *Ibid.*, p. 61.

Education by the Association of American Colleges in 1937. This Commission cooperated with the Commission on Teacher Education of the American Council on Education and in 1947 it planned a "course of action" for the future. The study by Van Cleve Morris noted above represents an initial step in a campaign of the Association to improve the preparation of teachers in liberal arts colleges.

The liberal arts college is giving attention to recruitment and preservice selection.[22] The time allotted to general education has increased during the past ten years in two-fifths of the institutions and 47 per cent of the presidents or deans expressed the desire for a further increase. The corresponding findings relative to advanced subject-matter preparation and technical-professional training indicate a relatively stable condition.[23] In commenting on the findings Morris observed that they "do not support, indeed they contradict, the widely held notion that the educationists have steadily upped professional offerings and requirements and are impatient to do still more." [24] The presidents and deans believe that teacher education should be recognized as a responsibility of the whole faculty [25] and, in general, the members of noneducation staffs were reported as being somewhat more than "moderately friendly" toward teacher education.[26]

Morris found only slight support for the proposition that "the liberal arts college should undertake to prepare elementary-school teachers," the opinion being most favorable in the North Central area.[27] However, the continuing shortage of teachers for elementary schools and the accumulating surplus of secondary teachers [28] are resulting in an increasing number of liberal-arts students seeking preparation for elementary-school teaching, and it may be that an increasing number of independent liberal arts colleges will provide such teacher education.

Organizational Developments in Universities

By the time of the National Survey a college or school of education had been established in most universities. Although the National Survey expressed approval of such a unit as an organizational provision for preservice teacher education,[29] this plan became a point of attack. In fact,

---

[22] *Ibid.*, pp. 60f.   [24] *Ibid.*, p. 80.   [26] *Ibid.*, p. 129.

[23] *Ibid.*, p. 78.   [25] *Ibid.*, p. 132.   [27] *Ibid.*, p. 110.

[28] The current situation is emphasized by recently reported facts. The number of college and university graduates in 1950 who qualified as elementary teachers was less than a fourth of the number of new teachers needed this year. In contrast, the number of graduates meeting the requirements for secondary teaching was more than twice the demand for new teachers at this level. "Building a profession," *The Journal of Teacher Education*, 1 (1950), 176.

[29] Earle U. Rugg and Others, *Teacher Education Curricula*, National Survey of the Education of Teachers, Vol. III (U.S. Office of Education, Bulletin, 1933, No. 10), pp. 348-49.

before the National Survey was published the organization for teacher education had been radically changed at the University of Chicago and study leading to a reorganization was under was at Syracuse University. At the University of Chicago a School of Education was organized in 1901 and by 1909 it consisted of four units. For some years the School of Education functioned as an "independent" unit, but students in the College of Arts, Literature and Science also qualified for teaching by taking education courses. In 1931 the School of Education was discontinued, being replaced by a department of education within the division of social sciences. As such this "department of education" assumed no responsibility for the undergraduate education of teachers beyond providing education courses. The advisement of students was assigned to the departments of subject-matter specialization. The administration of teacher education was by an "all-university committee" with the assistance of subcommittees.[30]

Shortly after 1930 the organization for teacher education was studied systematically at Syracuse University. As a result of the deliberations of twenty-seven committees, an All-University School of Education was established in 1934. The resolution establishing this unit specified that its faculty "shall consist of from thirty-five to fifty members, including approximately fifteen from Liberal Arts, approximately ten from the present Teachers College, and the balance from other colleges and schools in which prospective teachers are enrolled." Students in other colleges and schools preparing to teach were required to enroll in the All-University School of Education at the junior level on the basis of "dual registration." Transfer students registered only in the All-University School of Education.[31] Instruction in subject-matter courses was in other colleges and schools, the All-University School of Education exercising no direct control. Indirectly it appears to have influenced the nature of these courses by pointing out the needs of teachers. The report of the operation of this organization indicates that it functioned as an effective means of desirable cooperation in teacher education.[32]

In these two developments there is explicit recognition of the principle that the organization for the education of teachers within a university should include, at least on a representative basis, all departments of the institution which contribute materially to the preparation of teachers. This principle was not new in 1930. It is apparent in Hill's proposal of

[30] Frank N. Freeman, "History of the Department and College of Education of the University of Chicago," *Zeta News,* 18 (May, 1933), 5-12.

[31] Curriculum Committee of the School of Education, Syracuse University, *A Functional Program of Teacher Education* (Washington, D. C.: American Council on Education, 1941), p. 201.

[32] *Ibid.,* pp. 23f. *et passim.*

1905 (see p. 315) and in the college-of-education organization that developed in a few institutions. But in 1930 the typical college-of-education faculty included few if any members from subject-matter departments.

The developments at Chicago and Syracuse reflected a second principle, namely, that within a university there should be only one organization for the administration of the teacher-education function. At the University of Chicago this organization was an "all-university committee" plus a group of subcommittees; at Syracuse University it was the All-University School of Education. Although these two plans have a common purpose, namely, the facilitation of whole-hearted cooperation of all departments that contribute to the collegiate education of a teacher, it appears that the two forms of organization imply different concepts of teacher education.

In the description of the Syracuse "experiment" it is stated [33] that a substantial majority of the faculty accepted the "basic assumption" that "all objectives of education, including teacher education, should derive from the needs of society." Thus the approach at Syracuse was to examine the "needs" of the schools, elementary and secondary, as a basis for formulating the concept of education for teachers. Although the report of the Syracuse plan is not explicit, it seems clear that teacher education was conceived of as consisting of general education and subject-matter specialization, both professionalized to a considerable degree, *combined with* pedagogical training. The present writer has not been able to locate an explicit statement of the concept of teacher education at the University of Chicago, but in the article by Freeman referred to above and in other sources certain statements [34] seem to imply the concept of general education and subject-matter specialization, with little or no professionalization, plus pedagogical training, especially emphasized at the graduate level.

Another implication should also be noted. In universities it is the custom to express recognition of a major function by the establishment of a college or school organization and hence the All-University School of Education at Syracuse may be interpreted as evidence of the recognition of teacher education as a major function. A committee is the typical provision for a minor or subordinate function and the all-university committee at the University of Chicago suggests recognition of teacher education at this level.

There seems to have been little immediate support of the Chicago

---

[33] *Ibid.*, pp. 7-8.

[34] For example, see Frank N. Freeman, *op. cit.*, p. 7, and University of Chicago Announcements, *The Preparation of Teachers*, Sessions of 1943-44, 43 (October 1, 1943), 5f.

plan.[35] In commenting on a similar organizational change in Western
Reserve University in 1945, W. C. Bagley stated that so far as he was
informed colleges (schools) of education in state universities "still retain
their professional designations." [36] A survey of educationist opinion reported in 1937 revealed a practically united stand for a college (school)
of education in a university.[37] Although this study included the opinions
of only a limited number of "professors of education," the general finding is doubtless fairly representative. Stiles [38] reported that 71 per cent
of his jury favored a "separate school of education." However, within the
"united stand" for a college (school) of education there is little published evidence of systematic study of the problem of organization for
teacher education within a university.

At several institutions having a college of education, an all-university
council or committee has been created [39] as a means of facilitating cooperation. The constitution of such a council or committee varies, but
typically it is intended to be representative of the entire university faculty.
The functioning is generally at the advisory level. In a letter of July 25,
1945, Stiles stated that he found no institution that "indicated that it had
developed this type of organization to the extent that it assumes a large
amount of jurisdiction over the teacher-education program of the university."

The discontinuance of the School of Education at the University of
Chicago did not create much of a disturbance in teacher-education
circles, but a similar organizational change at Western Reserve University
in 1945 stimulated a number of controversial writings.[40] Some authors
argued for placing the administration of preservice teacher education in

[35] For one supporter, see Thomas E. Benner, "Teacher-Training and the Liberal
College," *School and Society*, 35 (1932), 577-82.

[36] William C. Bagley, "Another Professional School for Teachers Loses Its Professional Identity," *School and Society*, 61 (1945), 372.

[37] Harry N. Irwin, "The Organization of Teacher-preparation in a University,"
Educational Administration and Supervision, 23 (1937), 454-60.

[38] Lindley J. Stiles, *Preservice Education of High-school Teachers in Universities*
(Unpublished Ph.D. thesis, University of Colorado, 1945).

[39] Stiles reported this form of organization in 30 per cent of the universities he
studied, but a number of relatively small institutions were included and presumably
the proportion would be larger for a group of large state universities. Lindley J.
Stiles, *op. cit.*

[40] For example, see William C. Bagley, *loc. cit.* Frederick E. Bolton, "What To Do
with University Schools of Education," *School and Society*, 62 (1945), 432-33.
Harry A. Brown, "Teachers Colleges and Schools of Education as Units in University,"
Educational Administration and Supervision, 31 (1945), 463-74. Charles H. Judd,
"Should University Schools of Education Cease to Exist?" *School and Society*, 62
(1945), 141-42. W. C. Ruediger, "The Sins of 1839," *School and Society*, 62 (1945),
294-95. Benjamin R. Simpson, "The Professional Training of Teachers and the Liberal
Arts College," *School and Society*, 63 (1946), 89-92. A. M. Withers, "For Educa-
tional Accord," *Journal of Higher Education*, 17 (May, 1946), 249-52.

the college of liberal arts contending that prospective teachers should not be "isolated" by enrollment in a teacher-education unit, that they needed to "rub elbows" with students interested in other vocational purposes. The proponents of this position stressed the importance of a liberal education, including subject-matter specialization, and contended that such preparation was best obtained under the administration of the liberal arts college. It was also noted that the undergraduate education of teachers extended beyond the college of education as generally organized, that most prospective teachers took four-fifths or more of their work in other units of the institution, and it was contended that under such conditions a college of education was not an appropriate administrative unit.

The proponents of a college-of-education organization contended that the education of teachers is a major function and hence should have the organizational recognition of college status and that teacher education would be better in a unit devoted to this function than in the liberal-arts unit which recognizes a number of aims.[41] The advocates of this position tended to admit that very few colleges of education were adequately organized and equipped,[42] but they contended that the thing to do was to create units commensurate with the function to be fulfilled.

The problem of the organization for teacher education in an independent liberal arts college or in a university is dealt with in a report from the Commission on Teacher Education.[43] After describing several of the cooperative demonstrations, the authors say: "We have no blueprint to offer on how institutions of higher learning should prepare teachers for their professional duties because we believe, in all sincerity, that there is more than one 'best' way" (p. 292). However, these authors did have convictions in regard to certain essential conditions whatever the formal organization may be. "Everybody in any way concerned with teacher education must learn to think and speak and act from the same basis of experience and with the same guiding values in mind" (p. 309). Such organic unity requires that subject-matter instructors and educationists work together in all study of teacher-education problems, in all planning, and in all curriculum development.

There is little evidence bearing on progress toward these conditions. The above report mentions "dual or liaison professors," which are to be found in a number of colleges and universities, as contributing materially to organic unity. In his inquiry the present writer found varying attitudes among educationists relative to dual professors or representatives from

[41] Earle U. Rugg and Others, *op. cit.*, p. 156.

[42] For example, Frederick E. Bolton, "A Lost Opportunity in Training High-School Teachers," *School Review*, 54 (1946), 342-50.

[43] W. Earl Armstrong and Others, *The College and Teacher Education* (Washington, D.C.: American Council on Education, 1944). 311 pp.

subject-matter departments. In a recent letter (April 6, 1950) Dean Harry S. Ganders, of Syracuse University, refers to joint appointments as "a delicate mechanism in university organization" and emphasizes that the success of a "dual professorship" depends upon the person appointed. However, after fifteen years of experience with the plan, he indicated no disposition to abandon it. At the University of Minnesota, where the college-of-education faculty has included representatives from subject-matter departments, the plan appears to be generally approved by the educationists.[44]

In contrast, conversations with persons at other institutions revealed little interest in joint appointments and some opposition to including subject-matter representatives in the college-of-education faculty. Recent criticisms of educationists and colleges of education [45] suggest the continuation among some subject-matter groups of the attitude expressed by Committee Q of the American Association of University Professors in 1933 (see p. 313). Among educationists the present writer found some evidence of the attitude: Let the liberal arts college give its general education and subject-matter specialization and then we will endeavor to make teachers out of the product.

The Bowling Green Conference, sponsored by the National Commission on Teacher Education and Professional Standards, included a group on the "organization and administration of the teacher-education institution." In the official report of this group [46] considerable space is given to "institutions of complex organization." The group declared that the organizational provision for teacher education should be comparable to that for law, medicine, engineering, or commerce and that all students preparing for teaching positions or for other forms of educational service should be registered in the teacher-education unit. No recommendation was made relative to the constitution of the faculty, but it was asserted: "Under all circumstances the teacher education division has a continuous obligation to utilize, through close cooperative relationships with other divisions, the total resources of the institution insofar as they are needed in teacher education."

Thus it appears that the present situation is one of considerable confusion and some disagreement in regard to the organizational and ad-

[44] This statement is based on a letter from Assistant Dean Marcia Edwards, May 11, 1950.

[45] For example, Harold L. Clapp, "The Stranglehold on Education," *American Association of University Professors Bulletin,* 35 (1949), 335-48; Albert Lynd, "Quacking in Public Schools," *The Atlantic,* March, 1950, pp. 33-38.

[46] John R. McLure, "Organization and Administration of the Teacher Education Institution," *The Education of Teachers—as Viewed by the Profession* (Washington, D.C.: National Commission on Teacher Education and Professional Standards, 1948), pp. 31-38.

ministrative provision for teacher education in multiple-purpose institutions. However, it seems clear that there is an emerging belief that the organization for teacher education should include, at least on a representative basis, all departments of the institution that contribute materially to the preparation of teachers for our schools. Although this position is not new, its present emphasis is a significant development.

Accreditation of Institutions for Teacher Education

An institution may be regarded as accredited for the education of teachers when a state department of education recognizes it as one from which recommendations are accepted as the basis for issuing licenses to teach. In such cases the accreditation has legal significance due to the fact that the accrediting agency, the state department of education, has authority to grant certificates to teach. An institution is also regarded as accredited when it is included in a list of institutions issued by a voluntary association of institutions or a professional group or association which has set up standards or requirements relative to such a list. The significance of such accreditation depends upon the standards and influence of the accrediting agency.

The adoption of "standards for accrediting teachers colleges" by the American Association of Teachers Colleges in 1926 marks the beginning of systematic accreditation as a means of improving the education of teachers. The record of the revision of these standards reflects a shift from quantitative items to emphasis upon qualitative standards. This development is illustrated by a comparison of the original standard on the "training school and student teaching" with the 1950 standard on "professional laboratory experiences." The former consists mainly of quantitative items — number of hours of supervised teaching to be required, the supervisory load of training-school teachers, and the like. The 1950 standard is an elaborate statement covering numerous qualitative items.

The present writer did not discover any formal list of accrediting standards issued by a state department of education, but a systematic accrediting procedure has been developed in some states. In California, for example, the accrediting is by curriculums leading to specific teaching credentials. An institution applying for accreditation files a somewhat elaborate report with the Committee on Accreditation. Then the institution is "inspected" by a committee.

There are about twelve hundred teacher-training institutions in the United States accredited by one or more agencies, but the criteria of accreditation vary and hence the designation "accredited" or "approved" has no standard meaning. Currently there is considerable discussion of the feasibility of a nation-wide program of accrediting institutions for the preparation of teachers and other school personnel.[47] The development of such a program involves numerous problems, but the fact that it is being advocated is evidence of the widespread interest in the improvement of teacher education.

Preservice Selection and Recruitment

The oversupply of legally qualified teachers during the thirties stimulated interest in preservice selection. There has been a large amount of research directed toward defining criteria of teaching success and identifying factors related to such criteria.[48] Although the prediction formulas developed are subject to significant limitations, a considerable number of teacher-training institutions have adopted some form of selective admission and/or selective retention. In some states quotas were assigned to the several state normal schools and teachers colleges.[49] The plans of selective admission vary with respect to the factors included, but usually the plan was highly objective. In a recent study [50] only 42 of 237 institutions reported a plan involving character evaluation. Selective retention is commonly based on scholastic record and examination scores.

During recent years considerable interest has developed in recruitment, i.e. encouraging young people of high ability and appropriate personality qualities to enter teacher-education programs. This interest was doubtless stimulated, at least in part, by reported findings indicating that the prospective teacher group was inferior to most other corresponding college groups.[51] There were also the facts of the economic and social status of teaching.

There is little information relative to practice. A study of seventy-seven universities in 1945 revealed little effective use of available methods and techniques.[52] It is not unlikely that this finding is typical of the general

---

[47] W. E. Peik, "The Accreditation of Colleges and Universities for the Preparation of Teachers and the Building of a Profession," *Journal of Teacher Education,* 1 (1950), 14-23.

[48] For a brief summary, see Charles W. Sanford and J. Lloyd Trump, "Teacher Education—IV. Preservice Selection," in *Encyclopedia of Educational Research,* ed. Walter S. Monroe (Rev. ed.; New York: The Macmillan Company, 1950), pp. 1390-96.

[49] *Ibid.,* pp. 1393-94.

[50] Douglas E. Lawson, "A Study of Selective Admission Based upon Character Evaluation as Practiced in Teacher-training Institutions Throughout the United States," *Educational Administration and Supervision,* 35 (1949), 421-26.

[51] For example, see William S. Learned and Ben D. Wood, *The Student and His Knowledge* (Carnegie Foundation for the Advancement of Teaching, Bulletin No. 29, 1938), pp. 38f. See also Arthur E. Traxler, "Are Students in Teachers Colleges Greatly Inferior in Ability?" *School and Society,* 63 (1946), 105-7.

[52] Lindley J. Stiles, "Recruitment and Selection of Prospective High-school Teachers by Universities," *Educational Administration and Supervision,* 32 (1946), 117-21.

situation. Another recent writer [53] noted a tendency among teacher-training institutions to push the problem of recruitment back into high schools. In a few states special appropriations are made for scholarships as inducements to enter teaching.[54]

Five-Year Programs for Secondary Teachers

The introduction of required study of education in the four-year program leading to a baccalaureate degree decreased the time available for general education and subject-matter specialization. Liberal-arts groups were not friendly to this curtailment of the time for academic study. In California when the State Board of Education in 1902 adopted a rule requiring that a recommendation for a high-school certificate show that the applicant had twelve semester hours of credit in education, the University of California (Berkeley) took action to require a half year of postbaccalaureate study for the teacher's recommendation. Later this additional requirement was increased to a full year. Although the action at the University of California was not typical, it does reflect an attitude that has become rather general. The establishment of the Harvard Graduate School of Education in 1920 was an expression of the belief that adequate preparation for secondary teaching required more than four years.

In the National Survey it was reported that in 8 per cent of the colleges and schools of education the enrollment of students was at the postbaccalaureate (graduate) level.[55] In other institutions many teachers were extending their preparation to the level of a master's degree.[56] In 1930-31 29 per cent of the senior-high-school teachers studied reported one or more years of graduate work.[57] In his study of the liberal arts college in 1949 Morris [58] reported 56 per cent of the independent colleges in "five-year states" offering "a master's degree or fifth year program." The proportion for "four-year states" was 9 per cent. The corresponding findings for university liberal-arts units were 92 and 58 per cent respectively.

The extension of a teacher's education to include a year beyond the baccalaureate degree raises the question of the nature of the additional work and also that of its relation to the undergraduate program. At the

---

[53] Dorothea Blyler, "The Pretraining Selection of Teachers," *Educational Administration and Supervision*, 34 (1948), 275-84.

[54] Clifford P. Archer, "State Scholarships in Teacher Education," *School and Society*, 71 (1950), 245-48.

[55] Earle U. Rugg and Others, *op. cit.*, p. 164.

[56] *Ibid.*, p. 173.

[57] E. S. Evenden, *Summary and Interpretation*, National Survey of the Education of Teachers, Vol. VI (U.S. Office of Education, Bulletin 1933, No. 10), p. 42.

[58] Van Cleve Morris, *op. cit.*, pp. 112f.

time of the National Survey there was much difference of opinion on the first of these questions.[59] No findings are given relative to the second, but it is implied that the idea of a five-year integrated program was "gaining momentum" (p. 314). The present writer was not successful in locating information on which to base a general statement of current status of this development. Findings reported by Morris reveal considerable difference of opinion among heads of departments of education in regard to the content pattern of the fifth year.[60] A 1940 report of practice in New York State indicated varying degrees of integration.[61] Obviously efforts to develop an integrated five-year program for a teaching position are seriously handicapped when the certification requirements for the position do not specify a fifth year of preservice preparation. It is likely that an integrated five-year program is an ideal rather than a practice except where a fifth year is required for a teaching credential.[62]

Technical-Professional Study at the Advanced Graduate Level

The development of graduate work in education was traced in Chapter 12 and the offering of the professional degree of Doctor of Education (Ed.D.) was noted (see p. 337). From 1930-31 through 1939-40 the number of persons receiving the Doctor of Education degree annually increased from 39 to 162. In 1940 there were living a total of 804 persons who received the degree during the decade 1930 to 1940. Of this number 715 were employed in educational positions in 1940. The reported analysis of this employment indicates that in the majority of cases the work engaged in called for professional competence rather than training in research. Only 16 per cent were employed at the university level; 44 per cent held administrative positions, apparently mainly in public schools; and only 5 per cent were reported as engaged in educational research. These facts reveal the popularity of the Doctor of Education (Ed.D.) degree and indicate the demand for technical-professional training at the advanced graduate level. However, it may be noted that during the decade 1930 to 1940 the Doctor of Philosophy (Ph.D.) in

[59] Earle U. Rugg and Others, *op. cit.*, p. 312.

[60] Van Cleve Morris, *op. cit.*, p. 114.

[61] Harold E. B. Speight, *Report on Plans for Five-year Programs of Teacher Education* (Committee on Teacher Education of Association of Colleges and Universities of the State of New York, 1940), 21 pp. (Mimeographed.)

[62] No state requires a fifth year for an elementary-school certificate. Three states, California, New York, and Washington, require a fifth year for a high-school credential. A five-year requirement is to become effective in Arizona, September 1, 1950. T. M. Stinnett and Others, "Interstate Reciprocity in Teacher Education-certification," *The Journal of Teacher Education*, 1 (1950), 56-80.

education was conferred on some 2,700 persons.[63] A recent study [64] reported the Ed.D. degree being conferred at 31 institutions in 1945.

The master of education was adopted less rapidly. A questionnaire study of twenty-nine universities in 1938-39 revealed the degree as being offered at only seven of these institutions.[65] In a study of the catalogs of forty "representative large universities" reported in 1949, it is stated that twelve had established the degree of Master of Education, thirty-two provided for the Doctor of Philosophy in Education, and fourteen conferred the Doctor of Education.[66] Two causes contributed to this condition. In 1927 the Graduate School of Education at Harvard increased the period of graduate study for the Master of Education degree to two years and this gave it a new meaning.[67] Thus the establishment of the Master of Education tended to become a matter of creating a degree standing for two years of graduate work rather than merely providing an alternative degree at the first-year level. A more potent cause was the greater liberality of graduate-school standards and practices relative to the established master's degrees. Of the sixty-four institutions studied by Powers five had no thesis requirement for the master's degree and eight others permitted the substitution of other work for the thesis.[68] A foreign language requirement had not been a common practice.[69] Relatively few institutions did not permit students to obtain the master's degree by summer residence.[70]

[63] Ernest V. Hollis, "Two Doctoral Degrees," *Journal of Higher Education*, 13 (May, 1942), 256-62.

[64] Clifford Woody, *Requirements for the Degrees of 'Doctor of Philosophy in Education and Doctor of Education*, Monograph No. I (National Society of College Teachers of Education, 1947). 54 pp.

[65] J. G. Gwynn and W. T. Gruhn, "Research and Statistics," *School and Society*, 53 (1941), 93-96.

[66] George C. Kyte, "Educational Requirements for Various Degrees in Education Granted by Representative Universities," *Educational Administration and Supervision*, 35 (1949), 401-18.

[67] Henry W. Holmes, "The New Requirements at Harvard for Degrees in Education," *School and Society*, 25 (1927), 707-11.

[68] J. Orin Powers, "The Administration and Requirements of the Master's Degree in Education," *Nineteenth Yearbook* (National Society of College Teachers of Education, 1931), pp. 5-20.

[69] Leonard V. Koos, *Standards in Graduate Work in Education* (U.S. Office of Education, Bulletin, 1921, No. 38).

[70] The contrast with the practice relative to the degree of Doctor of Philosophy was marked. In the study by Koos just referred to, only five of fifty-one institutions did not permit the master's degree to be obtained by summer residence while of the twenty-five institutions granting the doctor's degree, nineteen did not permit it to be obtained by summer residence only.

Concluding Statement

Although only fragmentary data are available relative to the current (1950) status of teacher-education practice, it is clear that during the period since the National Survey there have been significant changes in the preparation of teachers for our schools. Possibly more significant than these changes is the widespread interest in the improvement of teacher education. The various commissions, councils, and committees currently studying teacher education and promoting developments in practice should result in significant changes in the coming years.

CHAPTER 14

The Technical-Professional
Program

In the preceding chapters there have been references to the courses designed to engender the desired pedagogical knowledges and skills, but a systematic treatment will give a more adequate picture of the development of the pedagogical (technical-professional) program in normal schools and teachers colleges and in colleges and universities. After noting general aspects of the development, attention will be given to certain details. The development of teaching-learning theory was traced in Part One and this account, especially Chapters 3 and 4, should be considered a part of the total story.

General Developments

According to a study of "representative" normal schools [1] in 1889, the typical program of professional courses consisted of "history of education," "science of education" [principles of teaching], "methods in elementary branches" [special methods], "mental science" [educational psychology], "school economy" [classroom management], and "practice teaching." In 1895 the recommendations of the Sub-committee (of the

---

[1] "Report of the 'Chicago Committee' on Methods of Instruction, and Courses of Study in Normal Schools," *Addresses and Proceedings* (National Educational Association, 1889), pp. 570-87.

Committee of Fifteen) relative to "professional work" for elementary teachers were in essential agreement with this reported typical practice.[2] Deyoe [3] reported five courses as being required in 1902-3 in the curriculums for elementary teachers in more than half of the institutions he studied — general methods and principles of teaching, 82 per cent; history of education, 89 per cent; observation, participation, and teaching, 91 per cent; psychology — general and/or educational, 95 per cent; and school and class management, 61 per cent. On the basis of his inquiry Krusé stated: "By 1910 the standard professional course in normal schools and teachers colleges consisted of the following courses: (1) educational psychology; (2) history of education; (3) classroom management; (4) principles of teaching; (5) practice teaching; and (6) a group of special methods." [4]

Luckey [5] reported a frequency tabulation of the "principal courses offered by the departments of education" in "twenty representative universities" during the academic years 1890-91 to 1899-1900. Only seven institutions are represented in the data for 1890-91. The sum of the frequencies was nineteen or slightly less than an average of three courses per institution. By 1899-1900, all twenty institutions being represented, the grand total was 115 courses or an average of slightly less than six courses per institution. Since Luckey tabulated only "principal courses offered by the departments of education," these findings do not adequately reveal the extent of the average program of technical-professional courses in these institutions and his descriptive reference to other courses designed for teachers (p. 158) suggests that the total number offered in some institutions was materially greater, especially for the second date.

Luckey's data suggest the following program of course offerings as the typical practice in "representative universities" around the turn of the century.

1. *History of education* — one course, more frequently two courses, and sometimes three or four courses. (Under this head are included courses bearing such titles as Education Classics and History of Educational Thought.)

[2] *Addresses and Proceedings* (National Educational Association, 1895), pp. 240-48.

[3] George P. Deyoe, *Certain Trends in Curriculum Practices and Policies in State Normal Schools and Teachers Colleges* (Contributions to Education, No. 606 [New York: Bureau of Publications, Teachers College, Columbia University, 1934]), pp. 75-76. The sources of Deyoe's study were catalogs and other official publications of a total of forty-five selected normal schools and teachers colleges distributed among thirty-three states. Evidence of the representativeness is not given, but he indicated considerable confidence in the reliability of the sampling (pp. 2-5).

[4] Samuel A. Krusé, *A Critical Analysis of Principles of Teaching as a Basic Course in Teacher-training Curricula* (Contributions to Education, No. 63 [Nashville, Tennessee: George Peabody College for Teachers, 1929]), p. 62.

[5] G. W. A. Luckey, *The Professional Training of Secondary Teachers in the United States* (New York: The Macmillan Company, 1903), p. 157.

2. *Educational psychology* — one course, occasionally two or more courses. (The titles vary, Child Psychology and Applied Psychology frequently being used; in some cases the course included considerable content in the field of general method.)

3. *Principles (philosophy) of education* — one course.

4. *Methods (general) of teaching* — one course.

5. *School management* (school economy) — one course.

6. *Special methods and observation and practice teaching* — Offering special methods was the more common practice. (Luckey listed only five courses under the head of observation and practice teaching in the twenty institutions in 1899-1900; during this year Teachers College, Columbia University, offered fourteen special methods courses for secondary subjects.)

Comparison of this outline with the program of typical course offerings in normal schools of the time reveals a general similarity, but there are certain differences. The work in the universities studied by Luckey was on the collegiate level while that offered by the normal schools was not recognized as academically respectable, i.e. of college grade. This qualitative difference is reflected by the greater emphasis on history of education in the universities, by the offering of "principles (philosophy) of education" which had no counterpart in the typical program of the normal schools, and by the limited offerings under "observation and practice teaching" in the universities.

Luckey's study included a report of the opinions of fifty professors of education in colleges and universities in regard to the essential professional subjects.[6] Although the data were questionnaire responses, it is likely that the relative emphasis in practice is indicated by the sequential order in the following enumeration of subjects thought to be of most importance:

History of education, with a probable course in Educational systems, foreign and domestic; Educational psychology, including Child study; Theory of education, including the science and philosophy of education; Methodology, including both general and special methods; School administration, including organization, supervision, and management; and Observation of actual school work and practice-teaching.

Bolton's questionnaire study [7] reveals the number of courses actually conducted in "all of the leading colleges and universities" during the first semester of 1906-7. The tabulation is in terms of student registration under twenty-four course categories (including the designation "other"). For the total group of thirty-one institutions the average number of course categories under which registrations were reported is slightly under seven. The list of institutions included all but two (University of North Carolina and Clark University) of the "twenty representative uni-

---

[6] *Ibid.*, pp. 160-79.

[7] Frederick E. Bolton, "Relation of the Department of Education to Other Departments in Colleges and Universities," *Journal of Pedagogy*, 19 (1906-7), 137-76.

versities" studied by Luckey. For the eighteen institutions represented in both studies the average number of course categories for the first semester of 1906-7 is eight. Although the two studies are in terms of different data, the findings from Bolton's investigation indicate an increase in the average number of technical-professional course offerings at these institutions, perhaps three or four, within a period of seven years.

In a similar study of courses being given in 1913-14 in twenty-eight institutions Bolton [8] employed sixty course categories in his tabulation. The larger number of categories is due in part to a more analytical classification, but an increase in the number of courses being given is apparent. A tabulation by Wilson made from the catalogs of thirty-two colleges and universities for the same year (1913-14) revealed an average of eighteen courses and 43.5 semester hours per institution.[9] A study [10] of the course offerings of fifty representative teacher-training institutions in the seven fields of educational psychology, school administration, curriculum, supervision, history of education, philosophy of education, and educational sociology revealed that the grand total of courses offered in these fields increased from 959 in 1921-22 to 2,095 in 1931-32. In this compilation a course that was repeated during the year was counted only once and the figures do not include courses offered only during the summer session, correspondence courses, extension courses, introductory courses in general psychology, thesis courses, courses listed under the departments of physical education, vocational training, business, or social psychology, and courses listed as not given during 1921-22 or 1931-32. Hence the average of nineteen courses in 1921-22 and that of forty-two courses in 1931-32 do not fully represent the size of the institutional programs of professional courses at these respective dates.

In the studies thus far noted no distinction was made between courses designated for undergraduates and those which might be taken for graduate credit. The National Survey [11] reported a careful tabulation from the catalogs of 12 institutions, "which may be considered typical to a certain extent," of the courses listed for "graduates and undergraduates" and for "graduates only" from 1900-1901 to 1930-31. Excluding seminar and research courses the average number of such courses per institution increased from slightly less than 10 in 1900-1901 to slightly more than 107

[8] Frederick E. Bolton, "Curricula in University Departments of Education," School and Society, 2 (1915), 829-41.

[9] G. M. Wilson, "Titles of College Courses in Education, Educational Monographs, No. VIII (Society of College Teachers of Education, 1919), pp. 12-30.

[10] Felix H. Ullrich, "The Status of Professional Training in Educational Psychology," Journal of Educational Research, 27 (1933), 200-206.

[11] Earle U. Rugg and Others, Teacher Education Curricula, National Survey of the Education of Teachers, Vol. III (U.S. Office of Education, Bulletin 1933, No. 10). 547 pp.

in 1930-31.[12] The average number of courses under the two categories was approximately the same at the beginning of the period, but the increase of the number of courses open to both "graduates and undergraduates" was much greater until after 1925-26.

Crabb's tabulation of the course titles given in the catalogs of six state normal schools in 1900 shows an average of slightly less than nine professional courses per institution.[13] The corresponding average for 1910 (including four additional institutions) is eleven and for 1920 (the same ten institutions) it is nineteen. Walk's study [14] was directed toward revealing variations in normal-school practice (to be noted presently) and does not afford findings comparable with those derived from Crabb's report, but in his conclusions Walk referred to the "multiplication of courses in general" during the period from 1904 to 1914. From a study of the catalogs of fifty-nine teachers colleges for 1922-23 Hall-Quest [15] reported an average of 30.5 professional courses (psychology and education) for secondary teachers. Crabb also presented data for twenty-three normal schools and sixty teachers colleges for about 1925. The average number of courses in "psychology and education" was thirteen for the first group of institutions and twenty-five for the second.[16] Data collected in the National Survey from sixty-one normal schools and teachers colleges revealed a median of 14.4 courses in education. These findings, derived from questionnaire returns for the year 1930-31 refer only to courses offered in the department of education. Psychology appears to have been a separate department in some institutions. Furthermore, some technical-professional courses were doubtless listed under other departments. Hence the average for all such courses would have been somewhat larger.

Although the findings cited from such studies should not be interpreted too literally and chronological comparisons should be made with caution, because there were doubtless variations in the recognition of technical-professional courses, the general picture of the expansion of the institutional program of pedagogical courses is clear. In 1890 the typical (average) program in universities purporting to provide technical-professional training for teachers consisted of about three "principal"

---

[12] *Ibid.*, p. 449.

[13] Alfred L. Crabb, *A Study in the Nomenclature and Mechanics Employed in Catalogue Presentations of Courses in Education* (Contributions to Education, No. 21 [Nashville, Tennessee: George Peabody College for Teachers, 1926]), p. 12.

[14] George E. Walk, "A Decade of Tendencies in Curricula of State Normal Schools," *Education*, 37 (1916), 209-29.

[15] Alfred L. Hall-Quest, *Professional Secondary Education in Teachers Colleges* (Contributions to Education, No. 169 [New York: Teachers College, Columbia University, 1925]). 125 pp.

[16] Alfred L. Crabb, *op. cit.*, p. 59.

courses in psychology and education (pedagogy) plus one or more other courses such as school law, school hygiene, and special methods (typically offered in subject-matter departments). The size of the typical program in normal schools appears to have been slightly greater, possibly including one additional course. By 1910 the typical program in the "leading colleges and universities" consisted of more than ten courses, perhaps as many as twelve. The size of the program was about the same in normal schools. Thus within a period of twenty years the average number of professional courses in both classes of institutions had increased by about 100 per cent. By 1920 the average technical-professional program in normal schools and teachers colleges consisted of about twenty courses. Due to the development of graduate study in universities the average number of education courses offered in these institutions was greater. In the twelve institutions studied in the National Survey the average number of advanced undergraduate and graduate courses, exclusive of research and seminar courses, was approximately fifty in 1920. One can only speculate in regard to the size of the essentially undergraduate program in such institutions, but it is likely that it included a slightly larger number of courses than indicated for normal schools and teachers colleges.

Following 1920 there appears to have been some increase in the average number of technical-professional courses offered by normal schools and teachers colleges, but the data afforded by the National Survey [17] indicate that by 1930-31 the average program in these institutions was about the same as in 1920. The story of the undergraduate program in colleges and universities is probably about the same. At the graduate level the increase in number of technical-professional courses was phenomenal. In the twelve institutions studied in the National Survey [18] the average number of nonresearch courses in which graduate credit was given increased from 50 in 1920-21 to 107 in 1930-31. For courses "open to graduates only" the corresponding increase was from 13.5 to 50.4.

The data presented in the preceding pages reflect an expansion of the area of professional training and the production of research workers and other students of educational problems. In 1890 school administration was practically nonexistent as an area of professional training; today it is an area of major graduate study. Other new areas of the technical-professional program include the curriculum, educational measurements, pupil personnel work, and supervision. Evidence of the production of research workers is furnished by the 1950 edition of the *Encyclopedia of Educational Research*, a compactly written volume of 1,500,000 words.

[17] Earle U. Rugg and Others, *op. cit.*, p. 59.
[18] *Ibid.*, p. 449.

Institutional Variations

Within the average picture of the development of the program of technical-professional courses there has been wide variation among institutions in the number of courses offered, especially since about 1910. As of 1913-14 Wilson [19] reported a range from three courses in Toledo (Ohio) University and five in the College of Emporia, Missouri Valley College, and Yankton College to forty-one courses at the University of Missouri and sixty-four at the University of Kansas. Ullrich's study [20] of fifty representative teacher-training institutions revealed an institutional range in the field of educational psychology from two to eighteen courses in 1921-22 and from three to forty-nine courses in 1931-32. A portion of these variations in institutional practice is due to some universities offering a program of graduate study and providing training for a wider range of positions. However, it seems clear that there was considerable variation among colleges and universities in the number of undergraduate courses offered when only preparation for similar types of positions is considered.

There have also been variations among institutions with respect to the titles employed as designations of the technical-professional courses offered. This condition has been noted by practically every one who has studied institutional programs, but it will be sufficient to note the findings reported by Crabb [21] who made an extended inquiry. The analysis of the catalogs of six state normal schools for 1900 showed only one common course title, practice teaching, and nineteen titles with a frequency of one. The analysis for ten institutions for 1910 showed two course titles, practice teaching and history of education, with a frequency of ten and thirty-six course titles with a frequency of one. The results of the more elaborate analysis for about 1925 are given in Table 2.

Crabb pointed out that some variations in titles are inconsequential and such findings should be discounted, but his study and other evidence do reveal that within the phenomenal growth of technical-professional content there has been striking variation among institutions with reference to the organization of courses as well as the number of courses offered. In such a situation it is difficult to identify the content pattern of the typical technical-professional program. However, certain general characteristics may be noted.

---

[19] G. M. Wilson, *op. cit.*, pp. 12-30.

[20] Felix H. Ullrich, *op. cit.*, pp. 200-206.

[21] Alfred L. Crabb, *op. cit.*, p. 12.

TABLE 2. Frequencies of the appearance of courses titles in catalogs of
three groups of normal schools and teachers colleges.[a]

Frequency	Group 1 (23 institutions)	Group 2 (60 institutions)	Group 3 (4 institutions)
1	97	699	499
2	27	70	19
3	17	34	3
4	8	13	0
5	5	9	
6	1	10	
7	1	3	
8		1	
9		6	
10	3	2	
11		6	
12		4	
13		1	
14		1	
15		2	
16		2	
17		2	
18		2	
24		1	
34		1	
35		1	

[a] Crabb, *op. cit.* The date is not given but presumably it was 1924-25. The institutions of group 1 were normal schools offering two- and three-year curriculums. Those of group 2 were teachers colleges and those of group 3 were "outstanding teacher training institutions."

The Developing Technical-Professional Program

The typical normal-school programs of 1889 and 1910 (see pp. 363-64) suggest historical and theoretical content amounting to about half of the pedagogical work. There is little information in regard to the content pattern of the evolving pedagogical program in normal schools and teachers colleges, but it has been frequently referred to, especially in university circles, as being heavily weighted with methods courses. In reporting a study in 1925 Rainey [22] referred to this characterization and presented evidence from an analysis of the offerings of seventy-one teachers colleges. He classified 31 per cent of the technical-professional courses as "methods." This finding suggests a somewhat limited emphasis upon such work, and it does not appear that the evolving technical-professional program in normal schools and teachers colleges should be characterized as being heavily weighted with methods courses. It should be noted that Rainey classified an additional 17 per cent of the courses as "management" or "tests and measurements." Hence when student teaching is also recognized, it appears that in 1925 more than half of the program is to be regarded as "practical." Thus the development had been in the direction of less attention to historical and theoretical content.

[22] Homer P. Rainey, "A Study of the Curricula of State Teachers Colleges," *Educational Administration and Supervision*, 11 (1925), 465-72.

In his tabulation of the "principal courses" in "twenty representative universities," Luckey [23] employed fourteen course designations: (1) history of education, (2) school systems, (3) educational classics, (4) theory of education, (5) science of education, (6) philosophy of education, (7) institutes of education, (8) supervision and management, (9) method of instruction, (10) art of teaching, (11) observation and practice teaching, (12) applied psychology [educational psychology], (13) genetic psychology, and (14) child study. Luckey stated that he was not able to classify all courses under these categories and indicated that among the courses grouped together in the tabulation there was considerable variation in content. No course category was represented in all of the twenty institutions during a given year, except history of education in 1898-99. In 1899-1900 the highest frequencies were: history of education, 18; school systems, 14; supervision and management, 14; method of instruction, 13; child study, 12; and applied psychology, 11. Thus on the basis of Luckey's tabulation only six of the course categories were represented in a majority of the institutions during the year 1899-1900.

Luckey grouped his course designations under four more general heads: (a) historical (history of education, school systems, and educational classics); (b) theoretical (theory of education, science of education, philosophy of education, and institutes of education); (c) practical (supervision and management, method of instruction, art of teaching, and observation and practice teaching); (d) psychological (applied psychology, genetic psychology, and child study). In percentages the distribution of the courses tabulated for 1899-1900 is: historical, 30; theoretical, 16; practical, 31; and psychological, 23. This distribution is probably valid as an indication of the general content pattern of the professional program in universities at the turn of the century.

Bolton's study [24] of 1907 is in somewhat different terms but the following distribution has been computed: historical, 22; theoretical, 23; practical, 38; and psychological, 17. In the computation "principles of education" was included under theoretical, but it is likely that the content of this course was rather heavily weighted with psychological material. It is probable that there had not been much change in the relative attention to "theoretical" and "psychological" content. It appears that there had been some decrease in the relative emphasis upon historical material and an increase in "practical" courses. Bolton reported a similar study [25] in 1915. With reference to the content pattern of the program of courses, he noted history of education as continuing to be "one of the leading sub-

[23] G. W. A. Luckey, op. cit., p. 157.

[24] Frederick E. Bolton, "Relation of the Department of Education to Other Departments in Colleges and Universities," Journal of Pedagogy, 19 (1906-7), 137-76.

[25] Frederick E. Bolton, "Curricula in University Departments of Education," School and Society, 2 (1915), 829-41.

jects," the increasing prominence of special methods, a "very definite tendency toward making all of the work in education concrete and scientific and less abstractly theoretical," the emergence of attention to social aspects of education, and an increased emphasis upon practice teaching. In reporting his study of college and university catalogs for 1913-14 Wilson [26] noted that comparison with Luckey's findings of 1907 shows "a considerable decrease in the number of historical courses and a very rapid increase in the number of practical and special methods courses."

Referring to the undergraduate course offerings in colleges and universities toward the close of the second decade Douglass [27] listed the same courses as Krusé (see p. 364), except for the omission of "classroom management" as the "core" or "Big Five" of the institutional program. Although it should be recognized, as Douglass noted, that numerous other courses were offered and that there were variations in title and content of these "standard" courses, the studies by Bolton and by Wilson tend to support the assertion by Douglass. A course in history of education was very generally offered. The tabulation reported by Bolton in 1907 shows enrollments for "educational psychology" in just half of the institutions studied, but the data were obtained by questionnaire and presumably were as of the semester of responding. Hence the findings are not strongly contrary evidence. Bolton's study of 1915 indicates "educational psychology" was a very common professional subject and Wilson's study of approximately the same date furnishes supporting evidence. The supporting evidence is similar for the other three courses.

Thus within the expansion of technical-professional offerings in colleges and universities a "core" program persisted. On the basis of data of 1923-24, Edmonson and Webster reported the following as the most frequently required courses: (1) Psychology of education, (2) General methods, (3) Observation and practice teaching, (4) History of education, (5) Principles of secondary education.[28] These authors noted variations relative to the specific courses listed as required but stated that "the central tendency of schools of education, taken as a whole, is to require the same specific courses but different numbers of semester hours."

There have been few more recent studies of the content pattern of institutional programs but findings reported by Ullrich [29] probably indicate the trend. The average number of courses per institution in school

---

[26] G. M. Wilson, *op. cit.*, pp. 12-30.

[27] Harl R. Douglass, "Integration of Courses in Education," *Journal of Educational Research*, 34 (1941), 665-68.

[28] J. B. Edmonson and A. H. Webster, *Policies and Curricula of Schools of Education in State Universities* (U.S. Office of Education, Higher Education Circular No. 30, August, 1925), p. 24.

[29] Felix H. Ullrich, *op. cit.*, 200-206.

administration, curriculum, and supervision, which may be regarded as "practical" in terms of Luckey's categories, increased from 8 in 1921-22 to 20.5 in 1931-32. The corresponding averages for the general field of educational psychology are 6.5 and 14. In contrast, the averages for history of education are 3 and 4 and for philosophy of education and educational sociology combined 1.5 and 3. Thus relative to the total program as tabulated — history of education declined, philosophy of education and educational sociology combined remained at about the same relative status, while the "practical" courses (school administration, curriculum, and supervision) and educational psychology increased. The relative increase of courses in these areas becomes more impressive when it is noted that of the total courses tabulated for 1921-22 about 40 per cent were "practical" and 30 per cent were psychological.

The figures cited in the preceding paragraphs should not be interpreted too literally. Practically all of the investigators noted the difficulty of classifying titles and it has been shown that a title is a dubious indication of course content. However, some aspects of the development are apparent. Although a "core" program of required courses tended to persist, history of education declined as a specific requirement. At the time of the National Survey it was a prescribed course in only about one-fourth of the colleges and universities and had been taken by only slightly more than half of the prospective teachers whose records were analyzed.[30] At the turn of the century educational theory (philosophy of education and other courses centering about educational purposes) was a minor course area and despite the influence of John Dewey and other educators interested in the area of educational theory, it continued at about the same status up to about 1930.[31] In the report of the National Survey philosophy of education does not appear among the ten most frequently required courses and such a course had been taken by only about 10 per cent of the prospective teachers whose records were analyzed.[32] In contrast, "practical" courses, which constituted about a third of the program at the turn of the century, had increased both absolutely and relatively. The study by Ullrich suggests that by 1930 half or more of the course offerings belonged under this category. Likewise psychological courses increased both absolutely and relatively.

The period since around 1930 has not been studied sufficiently to provide much quantitative evidence of the trend of the development of the content pattern of institutional programs of technical-professional courses.

[30] Earle U. Rugg and Others, *op. cit.*, p. 260.

[31] Obed J. Williamson, *Provisions for General Theory Courses in the Professional Education of Teachers* (Contributions to Education, No. 684 [New York: Bureau of Publications, Teachers College, Columbia University, 1936]), p. 63.

[32] Earle U. Rugg and Others, *loc. cit.*

Considered with reference to Luckey's general categories — historical, theoretical, practical, and psychological — the content pattern does not appear to have changed materially since 1930. In 1936 Williamson [33] presented evidence indicating an increasing interest in educational theory since about 1930, but he noted also that there seemed to be "a pronounced lag between the importance ascribed to the teaching of general educational theory by certain leaders in education and the curricular practices of teacher-training institutions." [34] This statement and other comments indicate that Williamson did not find evidence indicating increased attention to educational theory as a professional subject up to the date of his study. Although no specific evidence can be cited, it is likely that the situation has not changed materially since that date. On the other hand, there has been considerable infiltration of educational theory into a number of courses not designated as such. For example, Jensen [35] found that considerable emphasis was being given to "aims pertaining to philosophy of education" in the "first course in education."

Since about 1920 there have been numerous developments of new course organizations directed toward making the program more coordinated and functionally effective. At the University of Kansas two sequential courses (Fundamentals of Education I and II) were developed and in 1925 the School of Education solicited teacher-graduate evaluations as a means of obtaining data on which to base a revision of these courses. [36] Numerous studies have been made at the University of Minnesota. [37] Among normal schools and teachers colleges the Colorado State Teachers College (Greeley) pioneered in organized curriculum reconstruction. [38] A state-wide, organized endeavor to reconstruct the curriculum for elementary teachers has been described by Dearborn. [39] The development of a more effective program of student teaching has been a matter of systematic study in many institutions. [40]

[33] Obed J. Williamson, *op. cit.*, pp. 98-123.

[34] *Ibid.*, p. 163.

[35] Harry T. Jensen, "Selecting Aims and Purposes of the First Course in Education," *Educational Administration and Supervision*, 28 (1942), 401-13.

[36] F. P. O'Brien, "Employing Student Criticism in Revising Courses in Education," *Educational Administration and Supervision*, 11 (1925), 394-98.

[37] For a summary account of studies up to 1926, see M. E. Haggerty, "Specialized Curricula in Teacher-Training," *Fifteenth Yearbook* (National Society of College Teachers of Education, 1926), pp. 3-25.

[38] E. A. Cross, "A New Curriculum for a Teachers College," *Educational Administration and Supervision*, 15 (1929), 549-58.

[39] Ned H. Dearborn, "Curriculum Revision in the New York State Normal Schools," *Elementary School Journal*, 30 (1930), 519-24.

[40] For an illustration, see Faculty of the Maryland State Normal School at Towson, "A Plan for the Closer Coordination of Professionalized Subject-Matter and Student-Teaching in a Normal School," *Educational Administration and Supervision*, 16 (1930), 257-86.

In this curriculum reconstruction the "standard" (traditional) courses — history of education, philosophy of education or principles of education, general method or principles of teaching, and educational psychology — tended to be replaced by new selections and organizations of professional subject matter. As yet there is considerable variation in such courses among institutions, but the general purpose is to develop a group of integrated core courses which will be functionally effective. The nature of the movement may be illustrated by noting the "three core courses" developed at the University of Wisconsin [41] — (1) The child: his nature and his needs; (2) The school and society; and (3) The nature and direction of learning. The first of these courses is psychological, but it represents a new selection and organization of content. The second course is a more radical innovation. It consists of four units: (a) bird's-eye view of the American school system, (b) the organization and administration of American education, (c) the teaching profession in the United States today, and (d) social conditions and problems as they influence and are influenced by education. As the title suggests, the third course includes content from psychology, especially psychology of learning, and methods (principles) of teaching. There is also a unit on "evaluating learning experiences." In commenting on this program of core courses Willing indicated that it might be designated as "general and theoretical," but he hastened to emphasize that the courses were intended to be "practical," i.e. "the department wants its work to count on the job."

The general character of the "three core courses" developed at the University of Wisconsin and the comment just noted appear to be indicative of a growing trend in the general content pattern of institutional programs.[42] The categories (historical, theoretical, practical, and psychological) which Luckey employed and which appear to have entered into much of the thinking of his time and for several years afterwards are disappearing. The "new" courses are intended to be "practical" in the sense that, as Willing expressed it, they will "count on the job," but in terms of content these courses include historical, theoretical, and psychological material as seems appropriate. It is not yet apparent what categories, if any, will emerge from the current reconstruction of technical-professional courses.

The problem of selecting and organizing technical-professional content for engendering the desired teacher qualifications is complex. A

---

[41] Mathew H. Willing, "The Program at the University of Wisconsin," *Journal of Educational Research*, 34 (1941), 641-49.

[42] Additional evidence is afforded by accounts of the development of courses at other institutions which will be noted in considering efforts directed toward improving professional education of teachers.

recent analysis lists fifteen subordinate questions.[43] Such complexity precludes any simple comprehensive statement beyond saying that the record of the period since 1930 reveals much experimentation and hence much variation among institutions. With reference to the general organization of the program Horrocks states that the "trend of the past 15 years" has been toward some form of integration, but he recognizes that at the date of his writing a considerable number of institutions still offered programs of separate courses. Michaelis did not deal specifically with the question of integrated programs, but his tabulations of required courses suggest little organizational integration in the universities studied.[44] Possibly integrated programs are more frequent in colleges and teachers colleges. Some content seems to be rather typically included in certain general courses. Horrocks mentions principles of education, guidance, curriculum, statistics and measurement, and educational sociology. In other areas trends are not apparent due to continuing variation in practice and controversial discussion. This seems to be true of educational psychology, introduction to education, and secondary education.

In institutions where an integrated program has not been developed, student teaching and educational psychology (some variation in title) are required. Beyond these courses there is much variation in specific requirements. In the forty-nine universities [45] studied by Michaelis ten courses were required for secondary teachers by five or more institutions and twenty-two courses by one to four institutions.

The development of the thinking about desired teacher qualifications (See Chapter 8) reveals an increased emphasis upon understandings, especially of the child, the school, the community, and the American way of life. The effect of this emphasis in the thinking about the purposes of teacher education upon the technical-professional program has not been systematically studied, but it appears that there has been some shift from the emphasis upon immediately practical courses (specifics) to an increasing recognition of the importance of "theory" courses. In this emerging development some educationists are aggressively advocating courses under the designation "foundations of education," [46] but the companion categories are not yet evident.

---

[43] John E. Horrocks, "Current Issues and Trends in the Secondary Teacher Education Curriculum. I. Content and Organization," *Educational Administration and Supervision*, 34 (1948), 193-207.

[44] John U. Michaelis, *An Overview of Teacher Education in State Universities* (Berkeley: University of California, May, 1948), pp. 31-32. (Mimeographed.)

[45] The number for this item was 49.

[46] For example, William Stanley, "A Charter for the Foundations of Education," *Educational Administration and Supervision*, 35 (1949), 321-33; Committee on Social Foundations, *The Emerging Task of the Foundations of Education*, ed. Harold Rugg (National Society of College Teachers of Education, 1950).

The Content of Certain Courses

The nature of the content of courses bearing the same or essentially equivalent titles may be considered as another aspect of the development. There have been several analytical studies of the content of the course commonly designated as educational psychology. In 1909 a committee of the American Psychological Association presented a report on the "teaching of psychology" in normal schools, colleges, and universities. The section on normal schools, prepared by G. M. Whipple,[47] summarized "questionary" returns from one hundred institutions (eighty-four public, sixteen private). In the portion of the report dealing with details it appears that the course content varied with respect to the topics included and especially with respect to the distribution of time among the various topics. For example, the time devoted to "learning, habit, educative process" ranged from two lessons to six weeks. This condition suggests a divergence of opinion concerning the specific purposes of the course. This inference is supported by several other statements in the report. Crabb [48] included an analysis of the catalog descriptions of "educational psychology." The tabulation showed fifty-three topics out of a total of eighty-five appearing in only one description. Some of the topic designations may be regarded as substantial equivalents and so this finding should be discounted, but the evidence does indicate considerable variation among institutions in regard to the content of this most highly "standardized course."

Further evidence on this point is provided by analyses of texts designed for the course. In 1927 Worcester [49] concluded, from an analysis of five educational psychology texts that had been reported as most commonly used, that "one would be somewhat put to it to discover five texts on supposedly the same subject which vary more than these do." Worcester also reported briefly an analysis of the outlines for the first course in educational psychology from ten colleges and universities. It appears that the course as taught exhibited marked variation in both content and emphases.

A systematic analysis of ten psychology textbooks "most frequently used in 1927" in normal schools and teachers colleges revealed marked variations in the space devoted to topics in a composite list compiled

---

[47] G. M. Whipple, "The Teaching of Psychology in the Normal Schools," Report of the Committee of the American Psychological Association on the Teaching of Psychology, *Psychological Review*, Monograph Supplement, 12 (April, 1910), 2-40.

[48] Alfred L. Crabb, *A Study in the Nomenclature and Mechanics Employed in Catalogue Presentations of Courses in Education* (Contributions to Education, No. 21 [Nashville, Tennessee: George Peabody College for Teachers, 1926]). 98 pp.

[49] Dean A. Worcester, "The Wide Diversities of Practice in First Courses in Educational Psychology," *Journal of Educational Psychology*, 18 (1927), 11-17.

from the indexes of the volumes.[50] Of the twenty-seven topics, five — attention, intelligence (and its measurement), learning (including habits), perception, and traits (nature) — were treated in all of the ten texts, but the emphasis varied. For example, in the case of "learning" the proportion of space ranged from 19.0 to 4.4 per cent. Among the topics not dealt with in one or more of these texts the proportion of space in other texts was frequently large. For example, "individual differences" was omitted from two texts, but in two others it occupied slightly more than 10 per cent of the space. "Central nervous system" was omitted in two texts but in one, 17.2 per cent of the space was devoted to it. On the basis of questionnaire responses from instructors, Robinson also reported that in the normal schools and teachers colleges the staff members were "expected to determine either without restrictions or within generous limits the content of the courses given" and that "there is too great a disparity of aims in the teaching of [educational] psychology" (pp. 81, 83). An analysis of thirteen texts published during the period 1940-46 revealed marked variation in the relative emphasis given to 26 topics.[51] A few topics were omitted in certain texts. A study of five texts published in 1948 yielded similar results.[52]

In a study [53] reported in 1935 it is stated that a tabulation of the chapter headings in eighteen texts in educational psychology published during the preceding five years resulted in a list of 250 different items and that replies to a questionnaire inquiry justified the conclusion that "only about twenty per cent of the chapter headings most frequently used in recent educational psychology textbooks" are preferred by instructors giving the introductory course in this field. Another writer [54] after noting certain recent texts asserted: "Evidently there is still need for some guiding principle or frame of reference in the selection of topics for educational psychology texts." A review of "Three books on educational psychology" [55] published in 1940 and 1941 suggests a similar conclusion. In addition to being dissatisfied with the content of current texts instructors and others have criticized them as being too abstract and too diffi-

[50] Clara L. Robinson, *Psychology and the Preparation of the Teacher for the Elementary School* (Contributions to Education, No. 418 [New York: Bureau of Publications, Teachers College, Columbia University, 1930]), p. 65.

[51] An unpublished study by Leonard D. Nelson reported by G. M. Blair, *Educational Psychology, its development and present status* (Bureau of Research and Service, College of Education, University of Illinois, 1948), pp. 20-24.

[52] See Glenn M. Blair, "The Content of Educational Psychology," *Journal of Educational Psychology*, 40 (1949), 269-72.

[53] Noel B. Cuff, "What Should Be Included in Educational Psychology?" *Journal of Educational Psychology*, 26 (1935), 689-94.

[54] James Lynch, "Functional Textbooks in Educational Psychology," *Journal of Educational Research*, 33 (1939), 1755-82.

[55] Homer B. Reed, *School and Society*, 54 (1941), 619-22.

cult in the matter of terminology.[56] The sarcastic description of educational psychology as "putting what everybody knows in language which nobody can understand" has been repeated many times.

Other areas of professional study exhibit the same general picture in regard to content of texts and courses. Osburn [57] reported that out of a total of 2,711 items of content, three texts designed for a course in principles of teaching had only 26 items in common. Garber [58] found that the nine books designed as texts in secondary education which he studied differed "rather widely both with regard to the topics discussed and with regard to the amount of discussion given to each topic." In commenting on the results of an analysis of eighteen introductory texts published before 1934, Burton and Ibanez made the following comment: [59] "It is evident that, from book to book, the greatest differences exist in regard to method of approach, scheme of organization, inclusion and exclusion of content, fidelity to announced scheme, and in scope and distribution of content."

The studies of the content of educational psychology have been accompanied by continued efforts to improve the selection and organization of psychological content for teachers in the program of teacher education in practically all institutions purporting to give systematic attention to this function.[60] Presumably every text designed as a basis for the first course in this area represents a considered judgment in regard to the topics to be included and the relative attention to be given them. In addition, several persons, some authors of texts, have set forth their ideas concerning the content of the course [61] or have reported consensus studies.[62] The Yearbook of the National Society of College Teach-

[56] Blair reported a vocabulary analysis of eight texts in educational psychology. He found wide variation in the psychological terminology. Of the fifteen "most used psychological words" in each of the texts, only one, "psychology," appeared in all lists. Some words with a relatively high frequency in one or more texts did not appear in one or more others. Glenn M. Blair, "The Vocabulary of Educational Psychology," *Journal of Educational Psychology*, 32 (1941), 365-71.

[57] W. J. Osburn, "Constitution of Our Courses in Principles of Teaching," *Educational Administration and Supervision*, 17 (1931), 544-51.

[58] Lee O. Garber, "The Content of Textbooks in Courses in Secondary Education," *School Review*, 44 (1936), 759-63.

[59] W. H. Burton and D. M. Ibanez, "Introductory Courses in Education," *Journal of Educational Research*, 29 (1935), 186.

[60] Clara L. Robinson, pp. 7f.

[61] J. Mace Andress, "The Aims, Values and Methods of Teaching Psychology in a Normal School," *Journal of Educational Psychology*, 2 (1911), 541-54.

[62] Alfred L. Crabb, *op. cit.*
Oscar E. Hertzberg, "The Opinion of a Teacher-training Institution Concerning the Relative Value of Subject-matter in Educational Psychology to the Elementary School Teacher," *Journal of Educational Psychology*, 19 (1928), 329-42.
Goodwin B. Watson, "What Shall Be Taught in Educational Psychology?" *Journal of Educational Psychology*, 17 (1926), 577-99.

ers of Education in 1932 bears the title, *The Direct Contribution of Educational Psychology to Teacher Training*. Although no course outlines were presented in this committee report, several of the contributors dealt with questions bearing on the matter. A more recent committee report is published in the *Journal of Educational Psychology*.[63]

In view of the persistent criticism and the equally persistent effort to develop a better selection and organization of psychological content for teachers, it is pertinent to ask why has not greater progress been made toward the desired end. One contributing factor has been the differences among psychologists in regard to basic theory. In addition to several "schools of psychology" there have been differences within the "schools" (see pp. 36f.). A more potent influence, however, has been the absence of recognized criteria for the identification of the content of educational psychology. In a summary statement on criteria Gates listed the following as being identifiable:

1. Practical value: Value as applicable to the regular classroom work of the typical teacher.
2. Theoretical value: Value as basis of stimulating thinking concerning the objectives, methods, and means of education in modern society.
3. Cultural value: Value as basis for assisting teachers to become liberal, balanced, and intelligent members of modern society.
4. Propaedeutic value: Value as a necessary preparation for, rather than intrinsic in, a fact or principle justified by one or more of the preceding values.[64]

In his comments Gates stated that published criticisms of educational psychology indicated a general agreement that, although several of the writers stressed the first criterion, the last two tended to dominate the selection of content in practice. This summary statement was qualified by the observation that there was a "feeling that these criteria are rather loosely applied."

The situation appears to have been one of "too many cooks spoiling the broth." Among those who have written texts or planned courses there have been at one extreme psychologists with limited understanding of the teacher's work and with little genuine interest in developing a functional educational psychology. At the other extreme there have been educationists with limited training in psychology but with a faith in psychological research as providing important instructional content. In between there have been psychologists with an understanding of the

[63] *Journal of Educational Psychology*, 40 (1949), 257-94.

[64] Arthur I. Gates, "The Place of Educational Psychology in the Curriculum for the Education of Teachers," *Twentieth Yearbook* (National Society of College Teachers of Education, 1932), p. 25.

teacher's work and an interest in teacher education and educationists with extended training in psychology, but up to 1930 relatively few of these persons exhibited much concern about reaching an agreement in regard to the criteria which should be recognized in selecting the content of educational psychology. The analyses of recent texts noted above do not indicate much progress toward agreement relative to the first course in educational psychology, but perhaps the continuing interest will bear fruit in the near future.

Practice Teaching

In his list of the qualifications of the "roundly-equipped teacher" Parr included "such an acquaintance with the art of teaching as a reasonable experience will give" (see p. 184). In his discussion [65] he observed, "it seems plain that ultimately normal schools must afford facilities for imparting familiarity with the art, equal to that attempted in the science of education." At the same meeting of the Department of Normal Schools Charles H. Allen presented a paper under the title "The training school as an adjunct of the normal school." [66] Although he referred to the training school as an "adjunct" of the normal school, he insisted that it was a "necessary adjunct" and "should be the most prominent feature of the normal school." Apparently Allen's concept of the training school was "ideal" rather than descriptive of conditions in the normal schools of the time. "I am aware that in some normal schools the practice is chiefly or entirely provided for by forming classes from adult pupils, 'playing' they are children" (p. 499).

In a study [67] of normal schools in 1887, fifty-five institutions out of seventy-four reporting provided for practice teaching in a "school of children." Several of the institutions, including a few of those maintaining a "school of children," provided for practice upon classes formed of classmates, but this plan was generally regarded as a makeshift. Gray also noted that "observation" was reported by about half of the normal schools. In most cases it appeared to be a rather incidental element in teacher education, but in a few schools it was a systemized activity regarded as an effective means of training. In a discussion at the meeting of the "Congress of Professional Training of Teachers" in 1893, a normal school president referred to "the recent revival of the plea that

[65] S. S. Parr, "The Normal-School Problem," *Addresses and Proceedings* (National Educational Association, 1888), pp. 467-76.

[66] *Addresses and Proceedings* (National Educational Association, 1888), pp. 496-503.

[67] Thomas J. Gray, "Methods of Instruction in the Normal Schools of the United States," *Addresses and Proceedings* (National Educational Association, 1887), pp. 472-80.

practice-teaching is unnecessary in the preparation of normal school pupils for teaching, and that observation of class-work furnishes sufficient basis, on the practical side, for the graduation of pupils from [normal] schools." [68]

In 1895 the Committee on Normal Education of the National Council of Education reported a summary of information received from sixty-three normal schools (fifty-seven state, one county, and five city). Only four of the schools reported no provision for practice teaching. In 40 per cent of these institutions practice teaching was provided for in public schools. Although diversity was noted, the most common plan was to assign the pupil-teacher to a class of five to fifteen children for "one, two and sometimes three periods each day." The average duration of this type of assignment was about 30 weeks. Diversity was also reported with respect to the connection between the practice work and the other phases of the student's study and to the supervision of the practice teaching. The report is not very critical and the committee seems to have been reluctant to take a positive stand in regard to what should be.[69] However, the appearance of the report and the attention given to practice teaching that year by the Department of Normal Schools indicate a growing concern about this phase of teacher education. At the 1896 meeting the entire program of the Department was devoted to the "practice school." The papers presented and the ensuing discussion indicate general agreement in regard to the desirability of including practice teaching and/or observation in the professional training of teachers.

Normal-school leaders, however, were not in agreement in regard to the facilities that should be provided. Some favored a "model school" to be used only for observation. At the other extreme, there were those who advocated the utilization of the "town schools" as a means of practice teaching.[70] Some, perhaps the majority, favored a combination of observation and practice teaching. Snyder advocated a year of observation (five days per week) in conjunction with a "seminar" under the "superintendent" followed by a year in the "practice department." The Report of the Committee on Normal Schools in 1899 included a section on "Training Schools" in which twenty-nine theses [71] were formally stated. The central theses were that "in comparison with other lines of work in a normal school, actual teaching is capable of ranking as the most valuable course for the student, since it furnishes, at the same time, both theory and practice" and "the training school should be the correlating

[68] *Addresses and Proceedings* (National Educational Association, 1893), p. 408.

[69] John W. Cook, "Report of the Committee on Normal Education—The Kind and Amount of Practice-Work and Its Place in the Normal School Course," *Addresses and Proceedings* (National Educational Association, 1895), pp. 501-9.

[70] Z. X. Snyder, "The 'Training School' in the United States," *Addresses and Proceedings* (National Educational Association, 1898), pp. 751-55.

[71] *Addresses and Proceedings* (National Educational Association, 1899), pp. 845-54.

center of the normal school." [72] The secretary's minutes of the meeting do not record a vote on the report, but the discussion (pp. 896-903) does not reveal any opposition to the several theses.

Although the "recommendations" of 1899 presumably represent the advanced thinking of the time rather than typical practice, it is significant that the envisaged training school was stressed as the "correlating center" of the normal school. Heads of departments in the normal school were to be "supervisors in fact" of their respective subjects in the training school and the "method of teaching in the normal school should be essentially the same as that pursued in the training school." At the 1902 meeting David Felmley advocated an intimate working relationship between "heads of departments" and the training school. The "supervisor of practice" should also be an "instructor in general method." The normal instructors should visit practice teachers, and occasionally teach classes in the training department.[73] The discussion indicated general agreement with this position, provided the training school was protected from domination by the "heads of departments." Although the discussion furnishes no direct evidence of contemporary conditions, there is some suggestion that the "ideal" advocated by Felmley was far from being attained in practice.

In the study of Missouri normal schools the authors [74] referred to the "training department" as the "weakest part of the structure" of these institutions and indicated that this was "probably true in many, if not most, of the state normal schools in this country." Later the "lack of cooperation" between the training department and the rest of the school was emphasized.[75]

There was little practice teaching in colleges and universities until after 1900. In the twenty colleges and universities studied by Luckey [76] "observation and practice teaching" was not offered until 1895-96 [77] and

[72] "Report of the Committee on Normal Schools," *Addresses and Proceedings* (National Educational Association, 1899), pp. 846, 852.

[73] David Felmley, "The Relations of the Heads of Departments to the Training School," *Addresses and Proceedings* (National Educational Association, 1902), pp. 530-34.

[74] William S. Learned, William C. Bagley, and Others, *The Professional Preparation of Teachers for American Public Schools* (Carnegie Foundation for the Advancement of Teaching, Bulletin No. 14, 1920), p. 192.

[75] *Ibid.*, pp. 193f.

[76] G. W. A. Luckey, *op. cit.*, p. 157. See also pp. 206-13.

[77] Practice teaching was introduced on a very limited scale at the University of Illinois in 1893-94, but it was discontinued after one year and not revived until 1906-7. The innovation of 1893-94, which was at the primary-school level, has been characterized as "probably the first practice-teaching in any American University." The second effort, which was discontinued after two years, was at the secondary level, the work being carried on in the Academy of the University of Illinois. Frances Morehouse, *Practice Teaching in the School of Education, University of Illinois, 1893-1911* (University of Illinois, School of Education Bulletin, No. 7, 1912). 15 pp.

it was reported for only five of the institutions in 1899-1900. At Harvard University and Brown University a form of internship or cadet practice teaching was developed.[78]

The slow development of practice teaching as a phase of professional training in colleges and universities was contributed to by several influences. There was limited recognition of technical-professional training as an essential part of the education of secondary teachers. Furthermore, a considerable proportion of college graduates had had some teaching experience prior to entering college or during the period of collegiate study. Luckey expressed agreement with the prevailing opinion that prospective secondary teachers needed "less drill in practice-teaching than do elementary teachers" and noted a minority opinion which questioned "the advisability or necessity of any practice-teaching on the part of secondary teachers." However, practice teaching gradually became an established phase of professional training in colleges and universities. In 1905 practice teaching or observation was reported by twenty-one of fifty universities and sixteen of forty-two colleges.[79] The increase in the number of colleges and universities offering such work was phenomenal during the next ten years.[80]

In the National Survey it was reported that twenty-five states required some credit in student teaching for one or more types of certificates and the proportion of beginning teachers without such experience was relatively small.[81] Practically all normal schools required student teaching in their curriculums and all of the colleges and universities studied offered it in academic fields, but 15 per cent did not require it of students majoring in these fields. In some of the special-subject fields the proportion requiring student teaching was substantially greater.[82] In both groups of institutions the range of time spent in this work was astonishingly great, 18 to 270 clock hours in college and universities and 30 to 500 clock hours in normal schools and teachers colleges.[83]

Practice-teaching instruction depended upon the development of facilities. A campus training school, especially of the "model" type, involved considerable expense and, as normal-school enrollments increased,

[78] James E. Russell, "The Training of Teachers for Secondary Schools," *Addresses and Proceedings* (National Educational Association, 1899), pp. 285-96.

[79] Manfred J. Holmes, "The Present Provision for the Education and Training of Secondary Teachers in the United States," *Fourth Yearbook* (National Society for the Study of Education, 1905), pp. 63-82.

[80] A. R. Mead, "Report of a Study of Institutions with Teacher-training Departments," *Practice Teaching for Teachers in Secondary Schools* (U.S. Bureau of Education, Bulletin, 1917, No. 29), pp. 7-25. For the school year of 1914-15, 117 colleges and universities reported "supervised student-teaching."

[81] Earle U. Rugg and Others, *op. cit.*, p. 380.

[82] *Ibid.*, p. 381.

[83] *Ibid.*, p. 398.

a campus training school of sufficient size to provide adequately for practice teaching became a material factor in the educational program of the local community. Some normal schools developed arrangements for utilizing local public schools for practice teaching.[84] A few institutions extended this utilization to neighboring towns. However, a campus training school was the dominant practice. A survey in 1909 revealed that in 95 out of 117 normal schools all of the practice teaching was provided for in the campus training school,[85] but the trend was in the direction of greater utilization of public schools. A study reported in 1925 revealed that "approximately three out of every five state teacher-training schools" depended wholly or partly on public schools for practice-teaching facilities.[86] About the same situation prevailed among colleges and universities.[87]

The National Survey revealed the use of affiliated schools (presumably mainly of the local community) to be the dominant practice. Only 11 of 129 colleges and universities and 19 of 65 normal schools and teachers colleges reported exclusive use of a campus school. Larger proportions of these groups of institutions made use of both a campus and an affiliated school. This was the most frequent practice in normal schools and teachers colleges, but an affiliated school was the dominant type of facility in colleges and universities.[88] A study of 131 normal schools and teachers colleges reported in 1942 showed the exclusive use of this type of facility in slightly less than 10 per cent of these institutions. In contrast, a combination of a campus and an affiliated school was reported by 68 per cent of the 131 institutions.[89]

A variety of activities was included in or associated with the course in practice teaching. In a study reported in 1921 William S. Gray recognized eleven categories in addition to a miscellaneous group.[90] A more

[84] Charles H. Judd and S. Chester Parker, *Problems Involved in Standardizing State Normal Schools* (U.S. Bureau of Education, Department of the Interior, Bulletin 1916, No. 12), pp. 48-52.

[85] E. E. Lewis, "Practice Teaching in Model Schools," *Elementary School Journal*, 13 (1913), 434-44.

[86] J. O. Engleman, "A Study of Student Teaching in State Normal Schools and Teachers' Colleges," *Elementary School Journal*, 26 (1925), 256-63.

[87] Joseph L. Henderson, "A Statistical Study of the Use of City School Systems by Student-teachers in Colleges and Universities in the United States," *Educational Administration and Supervision*, 12 (1926), 326-39.

[88] Earle U. Rugg and Others, *op. cit.*, pp. 387-88.

[89] E. I. F. Williams, *The Actual and Potential Use of Laboratory Schools* (Contributions to Education, No. 846 [New York: Bureau of Publications, Teachers College, Columbia University, 1942]), p. 109.

[90] William S. Gray, "The Use of a Time-record Blank in the Standardization and Supervision of Student-teaching Courses," *Educational Administration and Supervision*, 7 (1921), 121-32.

elaborate analysis was employed by Armentrout.[91] In another study Williams recognized three general categories of practice-teaching activities — observation, participation, and student-teaching.[92] "Observation" typically included a number of related activities — written reports, conferences with instructor, reading, etc. Usually there were some preparatory activities.[93] In many institutions an outline form was developed for use in reporting the observations. "Participation" included such activities as marking papers, sitting as a member of the class, making lesson plans, instructing individual pupils, and sharing the instruction of the class as a whole. "Student-teaching" ("complete conduct of the class under the direction of a supervising teacher" and related activities) was analyzed by Nelson. Her "Master Activity Check List" included eleven major divisions.[94]

In addition to the possible variations within the general categories of observation, participation, and student-teaching there are many possible patterns of combinations of these types, other professional courses, and subject-matter courses. Williams found a total of twenty-seven patterns in a group of 128 state normal schools and teachers colleges.[95] Observation, participation, and student-teaching combined into a single course was the most frequent pattern, being reported by forty of the institutions. The total frequency of other combinations of these "laboratory courses" was also forty, making a grand total frequency of eighty. The corresponding total for combinations of "laboratory courses" and other professional courses was seventy-two, the most frequent combination being observation with one or more other professional courses. In addition to the variations in the pattern of practice-teaching (laboratory) activities there have been differences among institutions in the amounts of the several activities.[96] In the National Survey it was reported that with few exceptions normal schools and teachers colleges provided experience in a greater number of the sampled activities than did colleges and universities, but

[91] W. D. Armentrout, *The Conduct of Student Teaching in State Teachers Colleges* (Educational Series, No. 2 [Greeley, Colorado: Colorado State Teachers College, 1927]). 198 pp.

[92] E. I. F. Williams, *op. cit.*

[93] Elisha L. Henderson, *The Organization and Administration of Student Teaching in State Teachers Colleges* (Contributions to Education, No. 692 [New York: Bureau of Publications, Teachers College, Columbia University, 1937]), p. 55.
Esther Marion Nelson, *An Analysis of Content of Student-Teaching Courses for Education of Elementary Teachers in State Teachers Colleges* (Contributions to Education, No. 723 [New York: Bureau of Publications, Teachers College, Columbia University, 1939]), pp. 37f.

[94] Esther Marion Nelson, *op. cit.*, pp. 43-61.

[95] E. I. F. Williams, *op. cit.*, pp. 58f.

[96] A. R. Mead, *Supervised Student-teaching* (New York: Johnson Publishing Company, 1930), Chap. XV.

both groups of institutions tended to emphasize the more routine activities.[97]

Fragmentary studies of practice reveal significant changes in student teaching and associated activities in some institutions. Participation with adolescent groups was developed at Syracuse University.[98] Developments at several institutions are described briefly in a report of the Commission on Teacher Education.[99] A study of forty-seven state universities [100] reveals a number of required activities not directly connected with classroom teaching — attend school assemblies, assist with extracurricular activities, arrange bulletin boards, attend teachers' meetings, assist in guidance program, supervise study hall, work with student government, assist in library, attend community meetings, meet with curriculum committee, sponsor social clubs, do a community study. The proportion of these universities mentioning such activities ranged from 63 to 5 per cent. Certain developments are suggested in the "cooperative demonstrations" of the Commission on Teacher Education.[101]

Such evidence makes it clear that in a number of institutions, perhaps in most, student teachers engage in a number of activities in addition to those involved in classroom instruction. Comparison with findings reported in the National Survey [102] indicate that the content of the student-teaching course is becoming more commensurate with the scope of the activities in which teachers are being asked to engage. This interpretation is supported by the "preliminary and tentative" recommendations for the revision of Standard VI, Professional Laboratory Experiences, including Student Teaching, of the American Association of Teachers Colleges submitted in 1948.[103]

The requirement of observation as a prerequisite for student teaching and the specification of courses to be taken concurrently constitute another development. In the study by Michaelis 68 per cent of the institutions reported that they required a period of observation (median 16 clock hours) before student teaching. The interpretation of this finding is not clear. Luckey's designation, "observation and practice teaching"

---

[97] Earle U. Rugg and Others, *op. cit.*, p. 400.

[98] Curriculum Committee of the School of Education, Syracuse University, *A Functional Program of Teacher Education* (Washington, D.C.: American Council on Education, 1941), pp. 93f.

[99] W. Earl Armstrong and Others, *The College and Teacher Education* (Washington, D.C.: American Council on Education, 1944), pp. 180f.

[100] John U. Michaelis, *op. cit.*

[101] Lindley J. Stiles, "Contributions of the Commission on Teacher Education to Student Teaching," *Educational Administration and Supervision*, 33 (1947), 141-48.

[102] Earle U. Rugg and Others, *op. cit.*, p. 396.

[103] *First Yearbook* (American Association of Colleges for Teacher Education, 1948), pp. 90-98. This standard was adopted in 1950.

(see p. 371), indicates that observation was an activity in some universities before the turn of the century and some observation in the student-teaching course became a general practice. In some institutions students enrolled in the practice-teaching course devoted some time to observation before taking charge of a class. In such cases observation might be regarded as prerequisite to actual student teaching, but it seems likely that Michaelis refers to a course in observation taken before enrolling in student teaching. On the basis of this interpretation the reported requirement of "observation before student teaching" probably indicates a developing trend.

It is a fairly common practice to specify one or more education courses to be taken concurrently with student teaching, special methods in the major teaching subject being most frequently required.[104] Concurrent requirements promote integration of learnings, but in the present writer's visitation another purpose became apparent. In some institutions the special methods course or a curriculum course, taken either concurrently or as a prerequisite, was considered a means of compensating for the lack of professionalization in major and minor study.

Although practice in student teaching and associated activities has doubtless developed in the direction of greater effectiveness, it seems generally agreed that further improvement is possible and desirable.[105] The development of facilities is a prerequisite problem. Typical facilities consist of a campus laboratory school supplemented by public schools located near the institution. A laboratory school adds materially to the annual budget of a teacher-education unit. In the study by Michaelis [106] the median amount was $79,124.00. The utilization of public schools involves considerable expense, if the teacher-education institution contributes materially to the salaries of the cooperating teachers and provides an adequate supervisory staff.

No recent survey of student-teaching costs was located, but a recent analytical study at the University of Illinois revealed a per student cost of about $150.00 for a five-hour course. This finding is typical of corresponding data released by other institutions. In view of the general opinion that few teacher-training institutions have yet developed optimum facilities, it is likely that the per student cost of an optimum program would be materially greater than $150.00. In any case student teaching is the most expensive course of the technical-professional program, and this condition should be recognized in interpreting the development of practice.

---

[104] John U. Michaelis, op. cit., p. 49.

[105] For example, see Lindley J. Stiles, "Preservice Education of High-school Teachers in Universities," School Review, 54 (1946), 162-65.

[106] John U. Michaelis, op. cit., p. 12.

Efforts Toward Greater Uniformity of Courses and Programs

The lack of standardization relative to course titles and the variation of content under the same title or essentially equivalent titles were the subject of explicit criticism by practically all who have studied the matter. Although there have been variations in emphasis and some reservations, it appears to have been generally agreed that these conditions were indicative of immaturity and inefficiency in teacher education and that progress would include change in the direction of greater uniformity. On the other hand, the "professors of education" as a group have tended to resist efforts in the direction of standardization of courses.

The typical contemporary appraisal of the developing program and the general position relative to the desirability of standardization are reflected by the proceedings and addresses of the Department of Normal Schools, the American Association of Teachers Colleges, and the National Society of College Teachers of Education. The first of these organizations was formed in 1870 as the successor of the American Normal School Association which dated back to an informal meeting in 1855. In 1925 the Department of Normal Schools was combined with the American Association of Teachers Colleges which had been initiated in 1917 [107] and strengthened in 1923 by the merging of it and the National Council of Teachers Colleges.[108] The Department of Normal Schools was not an accrediting agency and hence its actions must be considered as only expressions of opinion by the persons voting, which seem to have been largely normal-school presidents. Committee members and participants in the programs were also largely presidents. Hence the record of this organization should be regarded as primarily one of the opinion of this group. The American Association of Teachers Colleges became an accrediting agency and hence its standards functioned as extra-legal controls. In view of this fact the actions of this organization have probably lagged behind the typical opinion among teachers college presidents in regard to what should be.

The proceedings and addresses of the Department of Normal Schools during the years prior to 1890 reveal several individuals urging that steps be taken in the direction of developing a "standard" program of professional work,[109] but there was no decisive action by the organization. In 1897 the Department instructed its committee which had been study-

---

[107] *Addresses and Proceedings* (National Education Association, 1925), pp. 863, 1054-55.

[108] *Yearbook*, American Association of Teachers Colleges, 1923, p. 27. For an account tracing the development from 1858, see Guy E. Maxwell, "Working Conditions Essential to Highest Efficiency and Economy," *Addresses and Proceedings* (National Education Association, 1924), pp. 614-24.

[109] For a brief summary account, see Samuel A. Krusé, *op. cit.*, pp. 57-61.

ing the "work of normal schools" to "submit a course of study with minimum professional requirements for the state normal schools of the United States." The 1899 report was presented under the title, "Function of the normal school." The proposals relative to "minimum professional requirements" were in terms of "psychology," "pedagogy," "observation," and "teaching." In the "ideal" outline the committee specified philosophy of education, science and art of teaching, history of education, and school economics. Such general description of the "professional work" was in keeping with the committee's explicit stand against any standardization. "The course of study is beginning to be as variable as individuals. This is as it should be, and it should be expected in this *nascent* period of pedagogics." [110] Thus a committee, which had made an extended study of current conditions and had presumably given serious consideration to the question of what the course of study of normal schools should be, in effect, proposed "free experimentation" in regard to the nature of technical-professional courses. The explanation seems to be that although the technical-professional program was generally regarded as unsatisfactory and many individuals deplored the variation among normal schools and the generally chaotic situation, normal-school people, especially the presidents, were unwilling to submit to any control, or even to "go on record" as favoring a specified program of studies. In any case the 1899 report seems to have set the "fashion."

A committee, appointed in 1904 to formulate "a statement of policy regarding the preparation and qualification of teachers of elementary and secondary schools," reported in 1908 but did not mention technical-professional courses. The report of the Committee on Resolutions in 1909 provided for the appointment of a committee "to investigate conditions and to prepare a report for this department on standards and courses to represent a standard American normal school." [111] Although this resolution was "unanimously adopted," there is no record of the appointment of the proposed committee. Presumably the failure to appoint the committee was due to opposition to standardization. The 1914 report of the Committee on Resolutions included the following: "We commend the present efforts of normal-school presidents and faculties to revise and adapt directly to teaching work and classroom needs the present courses in psychology, pedagogy, and other so-called professional subjects; and we commend the effort of normal schools to resist undue standardization. . . ." [112]

In 1926 E. S. Evenden, a member of the Committee on Standards and

[110] *Addresses and Proceedings* (National Educational Association, 1899), pp. 838-45.
[111] *Addresses and Proceedings* (National Education Association, 1909), p. 548.
[112] *Addresses and Proceedings* (National Education Association, 1914), p. 540.

Surveys of the American Association of Teachers Colleges, reported a
study of the courses in "education and psychology" required in the four-
year curriculums for intermediate teachers in a selected list of twenty-
five teachers colleges and then proposed a "standard" program of such
courses. The general situation revealed is indicated by the fact that
twenty-three classifications were employed in tabulating the "required"
courses in education and psychology. The only courses generally required
were practice teaching and educational psychology (frequencies of
twenty-three and twenty-two respectively). At the other extreme there
were ten courses listed as being required in only one institution each.[113]
A revealing statement is: "The two most discouraging elements in any
attempt to study the curricula of teachers colleges are the variations in
titles for the same courses and the even greater variations in the content
of courses with the same title." [114] Evenden's proposed courses to be required in the four-year curriculum for intermediate teachers consisted
of (1) introduction to teaching, (2) elementary educational statistics and
measurements, (3) educational psychology, (4) classroom procedures,
(5) practice teaching, (6) history and principles of education, and (7)
observation and specialized practice teaching. For each of these courses
Evenden outlined the "general purposes" and stated "reasons for a place
in the curriculum." Although the study and the proposals appear to have
been made by Evenden as an individual, it is perhaps significant that
the following year he was re-elected to the Committee on Standards and
Surveys and designated as chairman. However, the association did not
act on the proposals and up to 1930 there was no official action indicating concern about the nature of technical-professional courses.

The constitution of the National Society of College Teachers of Education (1925 revision) specifies that "membership shall be confined to
teachers and administrators in recognized colleges and universities who
are engaged in teaching and research in education." As a matter of fact
the membership for some years had included a considerable number of
teachers and administrators from normal schools and teachers colleges.
However, the Yearbooks of this organization may be regarded as reflecting the thinking of the group designated by the membership specification.
The content of technical-professional courses and curriculums has been
a major center of interest of the Society since its formation in 1902. At its
second meeting in 1903 a "Committee on College Courses in Education"

---

[113] Some of the titles are indicative of the specialized nature of these "required"
courses—psychology of speech, educational biology, heredity and education.

[114] E. S. Evenden, "What Courses in Education Are Desirable in a Four-year Curriculum in a State Teachers College? What Should Be Their Scope?" *Yearbook*
(American Association of Teachers Colleges, 1926), pp. 57-71.

was appointed,[115] and at least six additional committees concerned with the general problem have been created since that date.[116] There have also been numerous individual papers presented at annual meetings which have dealt with aspects of the problem.

The committee reports and other writings in the publications of the Society have reflected a persistent conviction that greater uniformity in the content and scope of technical-professional courses was desirable, at least in the case of the more fundamental ones. But usually, especially in committee reports, support of the principle of uniformity has been qualified by an endorsement of continued experimentation in the development of courses. A statement by William C. Ruediger, chairman of the committee reporting in 1919, expressed the attitude and the hopes that are reflected in many other writings:

> While we all feel keenly the need of greater uniformity in the fundamental courses, the chairman of your committee, and doubtless the other members as well, feel just as keenly that progress toward greater uniformity should not be forced. It should not come by a majority vote. It can come only by reaching a rock-bottom foundation on self-evident principles. . . . The uniformity we are seeking must be rational, not authoritative. Granted forbearance, experimentation, and open-minded discussion, this type of uniformity will in the end settle itself.[117]

In 1924 the National Society of College Teachers of Education appointed a committee with the following functions:

(1) To summarize the general principles which should govern the determination of the curriculum for teacher training. (2) To initiate and supervise

[115] William C. Ruediger, "Introductory Statement Outlining a Tentative List of Basic Courses," *Educational Monographs*, No. VIII (Society of College Teachers of Education, 1919), pp. 5-11. Efforts to locate the report of this first committee were not successful, but a number of individual studies appeared within the next few years which may be taken as a record of the first efforts of this Society to improve professional courses in education. Studies by Sutton and Bolton, which as reprints are listed later by the Society as its publications, were reported in the *Journal of Pedagogy* for December, 1906, and March, 1907. There was also a bulletin dealing with the work in *The History of Education* by Burnham and Suzzallo in 1908, and a report on the *Aims, Scope, and Methods of a University Course in Public School Administration* by Spaulding, Burris, and Elliott in 1910.

[116] The *Sixth Yearbook* (1915) of the Society (published as a School Review Monograph) includes a committee report on the "Work in education in colleges and universities." The *Eighth Yearbook* (1919) includes the report of a Committee on College Courses in Education. This yearbook also includes the membership of two additional committees, (1) Professional Curricula for Different Types of Teachers and (2) Standardizing Colleges, Schools, and Departments of Education. A "Curriculum Committee," appointed in 1924, made a very brief report in 1926. The *Twenty-third Yearbook* (1935) is devoted to the education of teachers, one chapter bearing the title "Curriculum Content and Pattern."

[117] William C. Ruediger, "Introductory Statement Outlining a Tentative List of Basic Courses," *Educational Monographs*, No. VIII (Society of College Teachers of Education, 1919), pp. 5-6.

one or more specialized studies in job analysis within some restricted field of teacher training.[118]

In 1926 the chairman of this committee reported that the variations in terminology and point of view of the members of the committee relating to principles of curriculum construction were so diverse that any reconciliation appeared to be an impossible task at that time. Apparently this committee made no further effort in this direction, but it did initiate the Commonwealth Teacher-training Study [119] which was published in 1929. Although this study was motivated by the recognition of the chaotic and variable character of institutional programs of courses, it was directed toward deriving information relative to the traits and duties of teachers which would serve as a basis for a reorganization of professional courses. Thus the functions designated by the Society's action in creating its committee in 1924 and the ensuing study suggest a shift in focus of attention from direct means of standardization to the formulation of fundamental principles of curriculum construction which were expected to lead to reorganization of technical-professional courses. This interpretation is supported by the subsequent record of the Society.

The 1929 Yearbook, *Current Educational Readjustments in Higher Education*, included a chapter on "Current efforts to improve instruction in schools, colleges, and departments of education, and in teachers colleges and normal schools." In the summary for the section on "curriculum construction," after noting that "much is being done in all types of teacher-training institutions to modify and improve the purpose and content of entire curricula and of specific courses," the committee stated: "Unfortunately, only a limited number of studies are in progress which deal specially with the basic principles underlying curriculum construction and which promise to supply data on which valid changes may be based in the future" (p. 40). The committee does not appear to have been much concerned about the matter of standardization.

The committee report on "Principles of curriculum construction for the education of teachers" in the 1935 Yearbook began with a reference to the desirability of "greater uniformity," but none of the sixteen principles presented refer explicitly to standardization. The general position of the committee was that if "practical agreement" is reached in regard to valid basic principles of curriculum construction, "the details of form can be safely determined by local factors and problems" (p. 73). Since 1935 the matter of the program of course offerings in education has

[118] W. W. Charters (Chairman), "Report of the Curriculum Committee of the National Society of College Teachers of Education," *Fifteenth Yearbook* (National Society of College Teachers of Education, 1926), pp. 1-2.

[119] W. W. Charters and Douglas Waples, *The Commonwealth Teacher-training Study* (Chicago: University of Chicago Press, 1929). 666 pp.

not received explicit attention in either the programs or yearbooks of this Society.

Thus the record provided by the Department of Normal Schools and the subsequent American Association of Teachers Colleges and by the National Society of College Teachers of Education reflects continued concern about the diversity among institutions relative to the program of technical-professional course offerings and also persistent reluctance to take action directed toward standardizing professional courses. Since about 1925 the focus of attention has been in the direction of developing principles of curriculum construction which would afford valid guidance in a reconstruction of the program of technical-professional education. This reconstruction has been envisaged as being "radical," but there has been no official action toward defining the principles which should govern the reconstruction of the program of professional work.

Concluding Statement

The account given in the preceding pages justifies certain summary statements relative to the development of the technical-professional program since 1890. (1) There has been a phenomenal increase in the number of education courses in the average program of offerings in both normal schools and teachers colleges and in colleges and universities. The development of courses for graduate study is especially impressive. (2) The course pattern of this expanding program has varied widely among the institutions of both categories. Within this varied expanding program there have been both new organizations of technical-professional content and courses consisting largely or wholly of new content. (3) Up to about 1910 there was considerable emphasis in colleges and universities on developing education courses that would be accepted as "academically respectable." Following this time there was an expansion of "practical" courses. More recently there have been attempts to develop functional foundation courses, i.e. courses with fundamental content which would "count on the job." (4) When courses and texts bearing the same or similar titles have been analyzed, wide variations have been apparent. There have also been variations in the program of offerings and in course requirements. These findings reflect the immaturity of education as a field of organized knowledge and as an area of professional training. Throughout the period there has been a persistent belief that a "standard" program should be developed. Practice, especially since about 1920, has been characterized by experimentation relative to developing an optimum technical-professional program. Significant improvements have doubtless been effected in some institutions, but the problem persists.

CHAPTER 15

Appraisal and Interpretation

In the development of teacher-education practice during the past sixty years certain general changes are apparent. In 1890 normal schools were generally of secondary grade, applicants being admitted with little or no attention to schooling status and few students extending their period of attendance beyond one or two years. During the period since this date these schools have become collegiate institutions requiring secondary graduation as a condition of admission and conferring the baccalaureate degree on the basis of a four-year curriculum. A considerable number of teachers colleges have become general colleges; a few have developed graduate programs.

In the colleges and universities of 1890 teacher education in a professional sense was a the level of "small beginnings"; today some 1,200 institutions provide for the professional preparation of teachers. The organizational provision for teacher education varies, a department of education being most common. Most universities and a few colleges have a college or school of education. A number of institutions offer a graduate program leading to a doctor's degree.

These developments represent gains in the preparation of teachers for our schools. The elevation of the education of teachers for elementary schools to the collegiate level, the acceptance of technical-professional training as an essential phase of the preparation of secondary teachers, and the expansion of teacher-education facilities are especially significant. The development of technical-professional content should also be noted.

These gains are mainly quantitative, and as the qualitative aspects of teacher-education practice are considered, it is appropriate to ask: Is the record of the period one of commendable progress or has it been characterized by sins of omission and commission? What does the record, especially that of recent years, promise relative to the future? The answers to these questions depend upon the concept of the qualifications needed by teachers in our schools, and certain developments in this area will be considered first.

The Evolving Concept of Desired Teacher Qualifications

In Part Two, three chronological periods were recognized: 1890 to 1907, 1907 to 1933, and since 1933. During the first period, especially up to the turn of the century, there was considerable penetrating thinking in normal-school circles from the functional approach expressed by Parr in 1888: "What the teacher must be is determined by the nature and needs of the training process" (see p. 183). Personal fitness was generally regarded as an important qualification with emphasis upon "good moral character" and such personality traits as sympathy, tactfulness, and "magnetism of kindness and justice." There was general acceptance of the "law" that an elementary teacher should have a secondary-school education and that a teacher in a secondary school should have completed a college course. Thus a teacher's general education was emphasized in a quantitative sense. The teaching-knowledge qualification was stressed by some leaders as transcending a good "academic knowledge" of the subjects to be taught. However, few arguments for explicit recognition of this qualification area are to be found in the literature after 1903.

Considering the status of practice relative to professional training of teachers, the frontier thinking of this period about pedagogical qualifications is to be commended in the case of the education of elementary teachers. As technical-professional training was recognized as a desirable phase of the education of teachers for secondary schools, the purposes tended to be defined in terms of the total amount of such preparation and one or more required courses. In retrospect this seems to have been a weakness. Instead of approaching the matter from the functional point of view the "professors of education" concerned with the education of teachers for secondary schools tended to be interested in developing professional courses that would meet with the approval of their academic colleagues — history of education, educational psychology, principles of education, and the like.

During the period from 1890 to 1907 it was the fashion to regard technical-professional training as a phase of the education of teachers to be *added to* their liberal (academic) education. This fashion was most prominent in academic circles, but it is reflected in the development of a number of the normal schools of the period. From the point of view of our present thinking it is unfortunate that as pedagogical study became recognized as desirable in the education of teachers for secondary schools it was regarded as something to be *added to* academic study.

During the years from 1907 to 1933 there was little systematic discussion of purposes and the record reflects a shift in the approach from the "nature and needs of the training process" as the basis of defining purposes to the scientific study of teachers as they are as a means of identifying the desired qualifications. The "professors of education," especially those exercising administrative functions, tended to regard the definition of purposes as accomplished, at least in general outline. This attitude and the trust in research as a means of identifying and evaluating the details of teacher qualifications seem now to have been unfortunate in that there was little recognition of the changing purposes of our schools in the thinking about teacher education.

The amount of research directed toward identifying and evaluating personality traits of teachers suggests emphasis upon this aspect of personal fitness, but until the development of programs of selective admission, toward the close of the third decade of the century, relatively little attention was given to it in the thinking about the purposes of teacher education. Insofar as attention was given to teacher personality the trend in defining the desired traits was the direction of emphasis upon those making for leadership, good judgment, self-control, and the like. There was also increased emphasis upon physical and health aspects of fitness.

There was a tendency to increase the quantity of general education for elementary teachers, especially during the later years of the period, and probably more significant to define the general education of teachers with respect to the needs of the profession. The definition of teaching knowledge was largely in terms of minimum quantitative specifications for majors and minors. The thinking about pedagogical qualifications reflects little attention to qualitative aspects.

Insofar as the evolving concept of personal fitness functioned in the thinking about teacher education the development is to be regarded as commendable. The same appraisal applies also to the tendency to define the general education of teachers with respect to the needs of the profession. The prominence of quantitative considerations in the thinking about teaching knowledge and technical-professional training and the consequent minimization of concern about qualitative aspects must be regarded as a weakness.

Differentiation of teacher education with respect to type of position became rather prominent in the thinking about purposes during the later years of the period and this development is to be regarded with approval, with perhaps the qualification that in their enthusiasm teacher-educators tended, at least to a degree, to carry specialization to an extreme and to lose sight of the importance of general education and the general aspects of technical-professional training.

Following 1933 there was increased concern about the definition of purposes of teacher education and a shift in the approach to the functional point of view which was noted as a characteristic of the first period. There was, however, a difference in the interpretation of the "nature and needs of the training process" due to the changed concept of the purposes of our schools and the contemporary teaching-learning theory. Although it is difficult to appraise the developments of so recent a period, it is likely that there has been progress toward a definition of purposes of teacher education which will be recognized in the future as a commendable achievement. Possibly the most significant development is the emerging tendency to think of desired teacher qualifications in terms of competencies rather than accumulations of credits.

There is some evidence of a tendency to think of personal fitness in terms of desired qualities of teacher-pupil relations rather than personality traits of the teacher. The thinking of educationists, and to some extent that of instructors in subject-matter areas, is in the direction of a concept of teaching knowledge compatible with the evolving curriculum in our schools. Although there are still differences of opinion and much confusion in regard to the nature of pedagogical training, there seems to be a tendency to think of the technical-professional phase of a teacher's education as being *combined* (integrated) *with* his general education and teaching knowledge. Some writers urge that we think of the total program beyond the second year of college as professional, i.e. as explicitly planned relative to the work of the teacher in our schools.

Thus it appears that the teacher-education group, after making a commendable beginning during the nineties in the direction of defining purposes, turned their attention to other matters and maintained a policy of waiting until scientific studies of "teachers as they are" revealed the objectives of teacher education. The lapse of interest and the shift in the approach to the definition of purposes are explainable, but they mark a deviation in the development that cannot be regarded as commendable. The return to the functional approach during the thirties and the growing interest in teacher education are to be commended.

The development of the concept of desired teacher qualifications may be considered as the record of the answers given to the question of the significant differences between the educational qualifications needed by a teacher and those possessed by any well-educated person. In 1890 there was general agreement that an elementary teacher should have some pedagogical training, but relative to the preparation of secondary teachers the dominant opinion in 1890 and for some years afterwards, especially in academic circles, was that a well-educated person was adequately qualified. Teachers' courses offered by subject-matter departments were provided in a number of colleges and universities, but such courses were generally regarded as extras and were considered to contribute little to the preparation of secondary teachers. By 1907 there was widespread support of pedagogical training for secondary teachers and during the following years discussions of this phase of the question shifted to the nature and amount of such training.

An adequately qualified teacher may also differ from a well-educated person with respect to general education and subject-matter specialization. The differences may be of two types — the selection of courses and the nature of some or all of the courses. In 1890 the general education provided by secondary schools and higher institutions was accepted as adequate preparation for teachers in this qualification area, but within a few years it was being argued that certain subjects should be required for teachers. At the time of the National Survey practice in teachers colleges revealed a selection of courses which made the general education of teachers somewhat different from that of typical well-educated persons. Practice in colleges and universities reflected little difference.

In 1890 a number of normal-school leaders, perhaps a majority, argued that subject-matter courses should be professionalized, i.e. they should be adapted to the needs of teachers. However, the argument soon subsided and the subject specialization provided for in a good liberal education tended to be considered adequate for teachers. At the time of the National Survey practice in teachers colleges and in colleges of education in universities revealed some selection of courses from the point of view of the needs of teachers. The offering of professionalized courses was not the typical practice in teachers colleges.[1] In colleges and universities there was very little professionalized treatment of subject matter.[2] Thus the general position in practice seems to have been that there should be no significant difference in the content of particular courses. The subject-matter courses, with relatively few exceptions, were designed to be taken by other students as well as by prospective teachers.

During recent years technical-professional training has been almost universally accepted as an essential phase of teacher education, but there

---

[1] Earle U. Rugg and Others, Teacher Education Curricula, National Survey of the Education of Teachers, Vol. III (U.S. Office of Education, Bulletin, 1933, No. 10), p. 93.

[2] Ibid., p. 273.

still. are differences of opinion relative to the nature and amount of such training and to its placement in the total program. Relative to the differences between an adequately prepared teacher and a well-educated person in the areas of general education and subject specialization, the current situation appears to be one of considerable confusion and little penetrating thinking, especially in the development of practice. Since the National Survey there has been an increasing tendency to distinguish between academic majors and minors and teaching majors and minors on the basis of course selection. The development of general-education programs has probably resulted in better teacher preparation in this area, but there has been relatively little planning of programs for teachers. In his inquiry into the current situation the present writer learned of relatively few courses in academic fields that were designed for teachers. Thus current practice appears to support the position that satisfactory general education and subject-matter preparation can be accomplished by wise selection from the courses offered and by subject-matter study included in student teaching and other technical-professional courses.

The position just expressed may not be the final answer to this basic question. Currently subject-matter groups are exhibiting a developing interest in the preparation of teachers and as they attain an understanding of the purposes of our schools, their programs, and the nature of the service asked of teachers, it is not unlikely that these groups will modify their course offerings, perhaps developing some courses especially designed for teachers.

Appraising the Development of Teacher-Education Practice

The teacher-education practice of a given time may be regarded as commendable if it appears to have been effective in engendering the qualifications needed by teachers in the schools of the time. In thus appraising the development of teacher-education practice one is dealing with a complex educational activity as well as with an evolving service resulting from our developing schools. The following appraisal is limited in two respects. Attention is focused on two aspects of practice, the organizational and administrative provisions for teacher education and the educational program, and developments along these lines will be judged relative to certain general criteria.

Criteria of organizational and administrative provisions. The organizational and administrative provisions for teacher education are means for facilitating the development and functioning of the educational program. Criteria for appraising these provisions have been given little systematic attention outside of the deliberations of the American Association of Teachers Colleges and its successor the American Association of Colleges for Teacher Education in developing accreditation standards. These standards are suggestive, but they do not seem suitable for the present purpose. Hence certain criteria are suggested from general considerations.

The preparation of teachers for service in our schools is an important social function, and an institution purporting to educate teachers should give this function distinctive recognition. Such recognition is evidenced in several ways — the formulation and adoption of teacher-education objectives, the organization and announcement of curriculums, and so on, as well as the organizational provisions.

A second criterion derives from the fact that the education of teachers is a cooperative undertaking involving the participation of a considerable number of persons. These persons, or at least appropriate representatives from the several instructional units, should be organized as a faculty group for teacher education. Such an organization is necessary for appropriate participation in planning and legislating.

Finally, the effective functioning of a faculty group requires leadership. In the case of teacher education this leadership should be vested in persons having an understanding of and continuing contacts with our schools and a major interest in preparing teachers for service in our schools.

Criteria of the educational program. The basic criteria for appraising the educational program are the teacher qualifications to be engendered as preparation for effective service in our schools. These qualifications, which constitute the objectives of teacher education, are to be derived from the purposes of our schools, the scope and general nature of the service required of teachers, and the nature of the teaching-learning process. Through the period since 1890 there have been changes in each of these areas and consequently in the concept of desired teacher qualifications.

The evolving concept of desired teacher qualifications has been traced in a preceding section, but it should be emphasized that a valid appraisal of the educational program of a given time requires that the desired qualifications employed as criteria be consistent with the purposes of our schools at that time, the contemporary service asked of teachers, and the contemporary teaching-learning theory. Hence no one statement of desired qualifications can be used as a basis of appraising the educational programs of different times. However, certain general statements may be made.

The educational program should reflect four categories of teacher qualifications: (*a*) personal fitness, (*b*) general education, (*c*) teaching knowledge (subject specialization), and (*d*) professional (pedagogical) training.

The education of workers for our schools should be appropriately differentiated relative to the areas of service, but narrowness of specialization should be avoided, especially at the undergraduate level, so that the teacher may have the capacity for adaptation to the evolving educational program of our schools and to some extent to different areas of service. With respect to a given area of service the curriculum and other requirements should be compatible with the demands of that service.

The courses of instruction and the curriculum organization should provide for integration of learnings, especially those of the pedagogical area and of subject-matter specialization.

Course specifications and other requirements should be supplemented by an effective guidance program.

Appraisal of Normal Schools and Teachers Colleges

The normal school was established as an institution to provide the "special preparation" which it was contended teachers needed to be most effective in instructing children. Following 1890 some normal schools gave attention to nonteaching purposes, but, in general, these institutions were devoted to the education of teachers; at least it was explicitly recognized as the dominant function. As normal schools became teachers colleges this devotion to the preparation of teachers for our schools continued. Normal schools and teachers colleges may appropriately be referred to as single-purpose institutions.

Charles H. Judd referred to the establishment of normal schools as a "major catastrophe," thus emphasizing his opinion that separate institutions for the preparation of teachers were undesirable.[3] The issue raised by this position now tends to be academic because many of the normal schools have become general colleges (multiple-purpose institutions), but it may be noted that beginning in 1834 New York subsidized academies as a means of providing for teacher education. It is significant that this plan was not considered effective and the normal school at Albany was established in 1844. In Judd's criticism of normal schools there is the implication that they had not been effective institutions for the education of teachers. Although the record reveals practices that seem to have been unwise, at least in retrospect, it appears that the normal schools contributed significantly to the improvement of teaching in our schools, especially at the elementary level.[4]

---

[3] Charles H. Judd, "Should University Schools of Education Cease to Exist?" *School and Society,* 62 (1945), 141-42.

[4] Argument for this statement has been forcefully presented by Charles A. Harper, *A Century of Public Teacher Education* (National Education Association, 1939). 175 pp.

The normal schools of 1890 were characterized by much diversity of opinion and practice. Some normal-school leaders maintained that completion of the secondary school should be required for admission and that the "special preparation" should be restricted to pedagogical training. Others maintained that the normal school should offer instruction in subject-matter areas and thus provide for combining pedagogical study with subject-matter instruction. In practice most normal schools offered subject-matter courses and during the years following 1890 a number of normal schools aggressively sought students who desired additional schooling of the conventional sort (see pp. 279, 286). The emphasis upon academic work and the correlative minimization of the "special preparation" was accentuated by the ambition of normal schools to attain recognition as institutions for the preparation of secondary teachers.

The differences in practice, and especially the tendency of some normal schools to emphasize a program of liberal education in addition to one of teacher education, seem to have been unfortunate. In view of the relatively small size of the institutions and their limited resources, devotion to teacher education would seem to have been a wiser course of action. However, in defense of the state normal schools of the time it should be noted that appropriations for their operation were niggardly, and consequently they were under pressure to attract students as a means of increasing their incomes as well as supporting their requests for increased appropriations (see pp. 273, 282). Hence the responsibility for what seems to have been a weakness of normal schools from 1890 to 1907 and even later must be shared by the public which in practice tended to neglect normal schools after they had been established.

The ambition of normal schools to attain recognition as "approved" institutions for the education of teachers for secondary schools is understandable. In the culture of the time, the higher schooling levels had an increased prestige. Teaching at the secondary level tended to be thought of as *higher* than teaching in elementary schools. Hence an institution "approved" for the preparation of secondary teachers tended to be thought of as "superior" to one that devoted itself to the education of elementary teachers. However, one may raise the question whether teacher education would not have been advanced if the normal schools had restricted their function to the education of elementary teachers. Certainly the situation in many states in which the teachers colleges competed with the state university and other collegiate institutions in the education of secondary teachers does not seem to have been socially efficient, especially when it is noted that the number of teachers being prepared for elementary schools has been generally grossly inadequate.

In 1890 and for some years afterwards the president of a normal school exercised almost unlimited administrative prerogatives. There was little staff organization, and faculty participation in the formulation of policies and program was very restricted. As the normal schools increased in size, and especially as they became teachers colleges, their organization tended to be patterned after that of "standard" colleges. In this development the subject-matter departments tended to be isolated from the department of education, and pedagogical training was something to be added to academic study rather than integrated with the other phases of the teacher's preparation. This development was unfortunate, but it should be noted that the isolation has decreased during recent years.

Due to policies and practices not in conformity with academic standards of the time and other conditions, normal schools up to about 1920 were generally regarded as not being academically respectable institutions. In particular cases this appraisal was doubtless too severe and it appears that the aggressiveness in attracting students, which was a cause of some of the criticized practices, was due, at least in part, to the niggardly support given to normal schools. As normal schools became teachers colleges, especially since about 1925, these institutions have exhibited commendable concern about conformity with academic standards. The American Association of Teachers Colleges has been an instrument of considerable influence in this development, especially among its member institutions.

Although the development of teachers colleges into general colleges has been due largely to social pressures, it seems to be generally regarded with approval among teacher educators. The effectiveness of teacher education in multiple-purpose institutions depends upon the organizational and administrative provisions for this function. As will be noted presently, relatively few colleges and universities appear to have developed optimum provisions for teacher education, but it may be that the normal-school and teachers-college background of these "new" institutions will minimize the difficulties.

Organization for Teacher Education in Colleges and Universities

Although "teachers' courses" were offered in slightly more than a fourth of the colleges and universities of 1890, in most cases the work was of normal-school grade and not a part of the collegiate program. Thus with few exceptions teacher education was not recognized as a function except in the sense that a good liberal education was considered adequate preparation for teaching in the secondary schools of the time. The State University of Iowa and the University of Michigan had created a professorship in education, but in most universities the teachers' courses of college grade were offered in subject-matter departments and in the department of philosophy or psychology. Following 1890 colleges and universities gradually recognized the teacher-education function by establishing a department of education. Beginning about 1905 a college or school of education was established in a number of these institutions. At the time of the National Survey there were 105 colleges (schools) of education, mostly in universities and 485 departments of education, mostly in independent liberal arts colleges.[5] These organizational developments indicate institutional recognition of the teacher-education function, but in appraising them the nature of this recognition must be considered.

A department of education is an organization for offering technical-professional courses; it is not a unit for the development and administration of a program of teacher education. Whatever is done along these lines is by the central administration of the institution or by some subordinate agent. An independent liberal arts college emphasizes a general (liberal) education. Within this function it typically provides for major and minor specialization and some free electives. A student interested in teaching may utilize these electives as a means of satisfying the education requirement for certification, and it is likely that in many of these institutions teacher education was on this level. Some liberal arts colleges outlined teacher-education curriculums and assigned the advisement of students to the head or some other member of the education department. Such provisions may be regarded as an informal teacher-education unit and probably many independent liberal arts colleges were relatively effective in preparing teachers for our schools, but the lack of a formal organization for teacher-education creates the possibility that this function may be subordinated to the major purpose of the institution.

In large institutions the educational and administrative organization is more important. If it is the policy of the institution to express the recognition of major functions by establishing autonomous college organizations, failure to do this for the preparation of teachers implies that teacher education is considered a subordinate function. At the time of the National Survey 73 per cent of the colleges and schools of education reported "practically independent status," but in 76 per cent of the institutions prospective teachers were also enrolled in other college units.[6] These findings make misleading the statement that there were 105 colleges and schools of education. The number of institutions in which the recognition of the teacher-education function was on a par with that of agriculture, engineering, and the like was not more than twenty-five.

The problem of the educational and administrative organization for teacher education in multiple-purpose institutions is not a simple one and perhaps there is no single best plan. The essential condition is that there

[5] Earle U. Rugg and Others, op. cit., p. 160.
[6] Ibid., pp. 164-65.

be adequate provision for and encouragement of wholehearted cooperation of the several staff units involved in the preparation of teachers under
the leadership of persons having an understanding of and continuing
contacts with our schools and a major interest in educating teachers for
our schools. Evidence for a general appraisal of colleges and universities
on the basis of this criterion is fragmentary, but from the present writer's
study of the literature and from his visitation it appears that a large proportion of these institutions has not yet developed organizational and
administrative provisions which conform to this criterion.

Although a college or school of education is the typical provision for
teacher education in universities, there is some evidence that it is not
considered a satisfactory one. Of the 105 institutions reported in the
National Survey as having a college or school of education, 27 per cent
gave the unit only partial independence and 76 per cent did not give the
unit exclusive jurisdiction over teacher education. These restrictions suggest reservations in regard to desirability of a college or school of education. The disestablishment of the School of Education at the University
of Chicago and the arguments of Charles H. Judd are more explicit evidence. The creation of an all-university council or committee in a number
of institutions indicates recognition of the need for something more than
the typical college-of-education organization.

The central thesis of the criticism of the typical college-of-education
organization is that "the preparation of teachers should be a clearly
recognized function of the University as a whole, with appropriate administrative provisions for it." [7] The first part of this assertion is merely
a way of saying that the general education and subject-matter specialization of a prospective teacher should be recognized as essential phases of
his preparation. This view is not new; it has been generally accepted
throughout the years since 1890. The acceptance of this view, however,
merely specifies the scope of the teacher qualifications to be considered; it
does not define the nature of the teacher's general education and his
subject-matter specialization or the relation of these phases of his preparation to his technical-professional study.

Practice in colleges and universities reflects varying answers to the
question implied in the above statement. At one extreme a teacher is
considered to be adequately prepared if he has a good liberal education
including academic specialization, and has included the necessary amount
of technical-professional study in his undergraduate program or has
added such study at the postbaccalaureate level. The general education
and subject-matter specialization of a well-educated person plus the
necessary amount of technical-professional work constitute adequate

[7] *The Preparation of Teachers,* University of Chicago Announcements, 43, No. 14
(October, 1943), 5.

preparation for teaching. This concept of desired teacher qualifications appears to be more prevalent than is generally recognized. It is apparent in some institutions having a college of education, especially when the unit is at the graduate level.

In contrast, practice in some institutions reflects the view that a prospective teacher's general education and his subject-matter specialization should be adapted to the work he is to do and that his technical-professional study should be integrated with the other phases of his preparation. This concept of desired teacher qualifications is found mainly in institutions having an undergraduate college of education in which all prospective teachers are required to enroll.

The issue represented by these contrasting concepts of desired teacher qualifications is not new. It was being debated in normal-school circles in 1890. Some normal-school leaders contended that all academic training should be left to the common schools and the function of the normal school should be to add pedagogical training. Others maintained that the study of subject matter was an essential phase of professional preparation and should be adapted to the needs of teachers, and hence should be included in the normal-school program. Following the turn of the century, there was little discussion of the issue, especially with reference to the education of teachers for secondary schools. The lack of attention to this fundamental issue in connection with the development of organizational and administrative provisions for teacher education in multiple-purpose institutions is to be regarded as a "sin of omission."

Since about 1930 colleges and universities have become more concerned about the education of teachers, and as shown in Chapter 5, there has been significant progress in the definition of desired teacher qualifications. However, the thinking about desired teacher qualifications does not appear to have functioned widely in discussions and actions relative to the organizational and administrative provisions for teacher education in multiple-purpose institutions, and the controversy noted above persists. Many persons, including a considerable number of educationists, appear to believe that a "roundly equipped" teacher can be produced by adding a program of technical-professional study to a good liberal education. Others hold that both the general education and subject-matter specialization of prospective teachers should be adapted to the work they are to do. In spite of the opposing beliefs, the issue is not receiving the explicit attention its importance justifies.

The persistence of the divergent beliefs and especially the lack of penetrating thinking about the interrelationship of desired teacher qualifications, and the organizational and administrative provisions for teacher education make it difficult to predict the future. The record of the All-University School of Education at Syracuse University suggests this type of provision as a possible development, but it should be noted that the Syracuse plan is similar to the proposal of A. Ross Hill in 1905 (see p. 315). As colleges of education were established, relatively few were patterned after Hill's proposal. The faculty of the college of education tended to be limited to "professors of education" or at least there was not adequate representation of the departments involved in the total education of teachers.

In the absence of records of the deliberations leading to the establishment of the several colleges of education, one can only speculate why there was not greater conformity with Hill's plan. It seems plausible to assess blame to both educationists and their academic colleagues. Among educationists there were many who thought of technical-professional study as something to be *added to* a teacher's general education and subject specialization, and so they were not concerned with the need for the cooperation of their academic colleagues. In some cases educationists tended to regard their academic colleagues as persons who were not interested in the education of teachers, except in terms of conventional subject specialization, and if interested, they were lacking in competence because they were not in touch with secondary schools. Furthermore, since it was the function of educationists to provide the training that would make teachers out of liberally educated persons, and they had frequent occasion to study our schools, they were sufficient for planning the program of teacher education and for administering it.

On the other hand, subject-matter departments had vested interests and the liberal arts college, in which most of them were included, had been the teacher-education unit of the institution. Under such circumstances there was reluctance to relinquish curriculum-making and student advisement to a new college unit. In some cases there was actual hostility toward education as an area of professional training. There was a tendency to minimize the independence of the college of education and there was little disposition toward cooperation in the education of teachers.

Today conditions are more favorable for developing an effective organization for teacher education, but there are practical difficulties in developing programs of general education and subject specialization adapted to the needs of teachers, and in integrating this work with technical-professional study. Appropriate adaptation requires courses, especially in subject fields, designed relative to the needs of teachers. If the staff of a subject-matter department is aware of the evolving teaching-knowledge demands in the corresponding area in secondary schools, interested members face difficulties. First, there is no agreement on what the content outline of courses for engendering appropriate teaching knowledge should be, and instructional materials are scarce. Second, if an instructor develops an effective professionalized course, he adds little to his standing in the department. In some institutions systematic attention to the development of "courses for teachers" tends to be a liability. Finally, if effective teaching-knowledge courses are developed, there is the problem of identifying and segregating prospective teachers. These difficulties, however, are not insurmountable, and an interested department should be able to develop effective means for engendering teaching knowledge commensurate with the demands of the modern secondary school.

Another means of providing teaching-knowledge instruction is to develop subject-matter departments within the college of education. There are obvious objections to such an organization for teacher education in universities. However, it may be the solution, at least to the extent of providing a limited number of professionalized subject-matter courses in the several areas. Some practice in this direction is to be found in certain institutions, but it does not seem likely that colleges of education will generally develop comprehensive subject-matter departments.

In a few institutions the teacher-education unit is at the postbaccalaureate level. Under this plan a prospective teacher completes the requirements for the baccalaureate degree in the college of his choice, possibly taking one or more education courses, but his enrollment in the teacher-education unit does not begin until the fifth year. Since five years of preparation are involved, such organizational provision for teacher education is not likely to become popular until such a period of schooling is required for certification. In considering it as a possible future development, its implications relative to teacher qualifications should be noted. Deferring explicit teacher education, at least beyond one or two introductory courses, until the fifth year implies acceptance of the general education and the subject specialization of the liberal arts college as adequate preparation in these qualification areas. Furthermore, the technical-professional training is to be *added to* the other phases of the teacher's education. Placement of the teacher-education unit at the postbaccalaureate level does not appear to be the answer to the organizational problem unless one accepts these implications, or unless the program of preservice education is extended beyond the fifth year and includes provisions for supplementing the undergraduate general education and subject specialization.

It may be presumptuous to predict the eventual organization for teacher education in universities where the preservice education of teachers is on a four-year basis, but there are "signs" pointing in the direction of an organization along the lines of the College of Education of the University of Minnesota and the All-University School of Education at Syracuse University, with perhaps a more formal provision for communication between the "department" of education and the several subject-matter departments.[8] The essential conditions are that the organization provide: (1) for adequate participation of the several staff units contributing to the education of teachers in policy making, planning, and legislation; (2) for the encouragement of wholehearted cooperation; and (3) leadership under persons having an understanding of, and continuing contacts with, our schools, and a major interest in educating teachers for them.

General Aspects of the Educational Program

A very significant development is the increase in the amount of preparation for elementary teachers. Although there was general support in 1890 of the "law" that an elementary teacher should have a secondary education, teachers' certificates were issued on the basis of examinations with little or no attention to the amount of schooling of the applicants. Even when a license to teach was obtained by completing a normal-school curriculum, the total schooling frequently did not amount to more than nine or ten years. By 1950 four years of college study were required in seventeen states for the lowest regular certificate for teaching in elementary schools and only two states specified no college study.[9] Of the college and university students completing preparation for elementary teaching in 1950, 63 per cent were enrolled in four-year curriculums. Of the elementary teachers employed in thirty-five states nearly 47 per cent had completed 120 or more semester hours of college study.[10]

Although there was general agreement in 1890 that secondary teachers should be college graduates, the schooling status of such teachers was typically below this level, many having completed only a year or two of college study, some probably not having extended their schooling beyond the twelfth year. By 1950 the minimum requirement in four states was five years of college study and in thirty-seven states, four years.[11]

Within these quantitative increases in the preparation of teachers there have been qualitative changes in the educational program. In 1890 the curriculums of normal schools were largely prescribed, and these institutions tended to confine their offerings to the required courses. The situation was much the same in colleges and universities, but as the elec-

---

[8] For reports of recent progress at three institutions, see W. Earl Armstrong and Others, *The College and Teacher Education* (Washington, D.C.: American Council on Education, 1944), pp. 96-126.

[9] T. M. Stinnett, Harold J. Bowers, and E. B. Robert, "Interstate Reciprocity in Teacher Education Certification," *Journal of Teacher Education*, 1 (1950), 56-80.

[10] Ray C. Maul, *Teacher Supply and Demand in the United States* (Washington: National Education Association, 1950), pp. 6, 32-33.

[11] Stinnett and Others, *op. cit.*, p. 64.

tive system was adopted, the program of offerings was expanded and college graduation was defined in terms of an accumulation of credits, including limited prescriptions. Normal schools and teachers colleges also adopted the elective system and expanded their programs of offerings, in some cases beyond staff resources.

Under the elective system the curriculum actually pursued by a prospective teacher consisted of the rather limited prescriptions and courses selected on the basis of more or less casual advisement, student interest, and convenience. The educational program of prospective teachers varied within institutions as well as among institutions, and further consideration of qualitative aspects of the developing program is limited to certain general characteristics.

Critics of normal schools have insisted that these institutions gave too much time to pedagogical study and consequently neglected general education and subject-matter preparation. This wholesale appraisal of normal schools during the years following 1890 should be interpreted in the light of contemporary conditions. Normal-school leaders of the time generally believed that an elementary teacher should have academic preparation, represented by the completion of a secondary school and an adequate knowledge of the subjects to be taught. It did not seem appropriate to require secondary-school graduation as a condition of admission and the student body was typically heterogeneous relative to schooling level (see p. 278). Many students attended only one or two terms before leaving to teach, mainly because the economic status of teaching did not justify extended preservice preparation. There was a difference of opinion in regard to the nature of an adequate teaching knowledge and especially in regard to the nature of the subject-matter instruction the normal school should provide. A number of normal-school leaders maintained that the program of these institutions should be confined to professional work, general education and subject-matter preparation to be left to the common schools.

The heterogeneity of the student body and the short periods of attendance contributed to the offering of review courses and other short subject-matter courses, and to registering students on the basis of expediency. Under such conditions it is doubtless true that the actual curriculums of many normal-school students were heavily weighted with pedagogical courses, or, at least, they included little subject-matter work considered to be academically respectable. But when the regular courses of study of the better institutions are examined, it appears that the relative emphasis on pedagogical study was not as extreme as many of the critics asserted it was. In any case the trend was in the direction of greater emphasis on subject-matter study, and by the time of the National Survey the average pedagogical requirement in four-year curriculums of teachers colleges was about the same as in corresponding curriculums of colleges and universities.

When the compatibility of the program with the nature of the service asked of teachers is considered, the record reveals considerable effort toward increasing it, especially since 1920. However, in general, programs of teacher education have not been adequately adapted to the needs of the teaching profession. During the years following 1900, a major motivation of normal schools was to attain recognition as academically respectable institutions. Some form of the elective system had been adopted by normal schools and teachers colleges, as well as by colleges and universities, and the design of subject-matter courses and student advisement tended to be on the basis of preparation for further subject-matter study rather than the needs of teachers in our schools. In colleges and universities especially, there was a considerable lag in understanding the purposes of our schools and the nature of the work teachers were being called upon to do.

In the National Survey it was concluded that the general education of teachers was deficient in several respects. It was stated that this was due more to the "failure to provide professional and vocational guidance for prospective teachers" than to the lack of courses of instruction and other facilities.[12] Data presented in the National Survey suggest the inadequacy of the subject-matter preparation of many teachers.[13] Following the National Survey normal schools and teachers colleges gave systematic attention to the formulation of objectives from the point of view of the work teachers were asked to do, and there has been a consequent improvement in the educational program. Developments along these lines were slower in colleges and universities.

As one examines the record since 1890, and even as one inquires into present programs, it is easy to point to practices that seem to represent serious weaknesses in the preparation of teachers for our schools. Numerous influences have contributed to these weaknesses and they should not all be charged to the educationists of the times. The responsibility for them must be shared by subject-matter departments, by institutional administrations — especially in colleges and universities — and by the public which has failed to provide adequate support for teacher education. The public has also been a factor in the slow development of more adequate certification requirements and in the continuing low economic

---

[12] E. S. Evenden, *Summary and Interpretation*, National Survey of the Education of Teachers, Vol. VI (U.S. Office of Education, Bulletin 1933, No. 10), pp. 92-93.

[13] Earle U. Rugg and Others, *Teacher Education Curricula*, National Survey of the Education of Teachers, Vol. III (U.S. Office of Education, Bulletin 1933, No. 10), pp. 80-81, 238-45.

status of teaching. In view of the nature and complexity of the reasons for the "sins" of omission and commission of the past, the improvements of the educational program during recent years should be regarded as a commendable achievement. The current interest in the improvement of teacher education suggests that the programs will continue to develop in the direction of better adaptation to the needs of the service.

The Technical-Professional Program

In 1888 Parr [14] outlined the professional work of "the normal school in its final and completed form": (1) not general psychology but educational psychology, "based on the application of the laws of the mind to an interpretation of the process of growth under stimulation"; (2) method, general and special, "purged of the flood of devices which properly belong to the art"; (3) history of education, a "philosophic exposition" rather than a "register for births, deaths, and anecdotes"; (4) an unnamed course, not "called by the contradictory and impossible name of philosophy," devoted to "the science of the nature of mind, of development and stimulation, and of aims, tests, and the relation of the powers of mind to kinds of education"; and (5) "training in the art" (practice teaching). This description of the "ideal" technical-professional program implies that Parr considered contemporary practice unsatisfactory. From time to time other educationists expressed adverse appraisals, and through the years there appears to have been rather widespread agreement among "professors of education" that the pedagogical courses offered were not highly effective in engendering the professional knowledges and skills desired for teachers in our schools.

The multiplication of education courses in institutional programs (see pp. 366f.) has been regarded as indicative of undesirable overlapping among related courses, thinness of content, and inclusion of content of doubtful value. Bolton was especially emphatic in reporting his second study.[15] He directed attention to certain course titles which seemed to him to designate a topic that might be included within a course but not an area of study sufficient to be worthy of recognition as a course. But Bolton's major emphasis was upon the multiplication of offerings as symptomatic of overlapping among courses. "A study of the titles and descriptions of courses gives the impression that there are many courses in some institutions which mean essentially the same thing." In the summary of his study of the catalogs of sixty normal schools for 1903-4 and 1913-14

[14] S. S. Parr, "The Normal School Problem," *Addresses and Proceedings* (National Educational Association, 1888), pp. 467-76.

[15] Frederick E. Bolton, "Curricula in University Departments of Education," *School and Society*, 2 (1915), 829-41.

Walk [16] referred to the "multiplication of courses in general, and incident to this, enormous variations in the scope of the work done" as "indicating the absence of definite underlying conceptions of the appropriate sphere of professional training."

In his study of the courses offered in the general field of educational psychology in fifty colleges and universities, Ullrich observed that the "study tends to show that there is no direct relationship between the adequacy of professional training and the number and variety of courses offered." [17] From this statement it may be inferred that he questioned the efficacy of the program in educational psychology in at least some of those institutions which offered the larger numbers of courses in this field. In 1932 Gates [18] summarized a number of criticisms: "Courses in [educational] psychology are not organized sequentially in the program to avoid outright repetition and to provide effective extension, review, and integration. New courses, it is urged, are merely added without adequate reorganization of the whole program to produce the most fruitful total pattern."

The belief that the multiplication of pedagogical courses and the variation in content of courses bearing the same or an essentially equivalent title are indications of weaknesses in the program is implied in suggestions in regard to the maximum number of courses needed for effective pedagogical training of teachers. In the study referred to above, Bolton expressed the judgment that the program of offerings including initial graduate work should not exceed about twenty courses. In 1926 Monroe[19] suggested that "ten courses with an average credit of 3 semester hours plus practice teaching and a group of special methods courses would constitute a very comprehensive array of offerings for undergraduate students preparing to teach in high schools." He also suggested by implication that the number of courses beyond the undergraduate level should be restricted. In the National Survey, after presenting data bearing on existing conditions in colleges and universities, the topic, "suggested content in education," is approached with the following introduction:

Any subject matter in a new field like education is changing. It is always dangerous to crystallize curricular subject matter, but it would seem from the general trend of evaluation studies and from courses most frequently required

[16] George E. Walk, "A Decade of Tendencies in Curricula of State Normal Schools," *Education,* 37 (1916), 209-29.

[17] Felix H. Ullrich, "The Status of Professional Training in Educational Psychology," *Journal of Educational Research,* 27 (1933), 200-206. (See especially p. 205.)

[18] Arthur I. Gates, "The Place of Educational Psychology in the Curriculum for the Education of Teachers," *Twentieth Yearbook* (National Society of College Teachers of Education, 1932), pp. 21-35.

[19] Walter S. Monroe, "The Undergraduate Curriculum in Education," *Fifteenth Yearbook* (National Society of College Teachers of Education, 1926), pp. 26-34.

that it is possible to select the 5 or 6 courses in education which for a short period of years might serve as a logical core offering to prospective teachers in liberal arts colleges and universities.[20]

Evidence of the functional quality of the technical-professional program has been sought by soliciting the opinions of "recently trained and successful teachers and school administrators." In a recent study of the opinions of about 1,700 secondary teachers and principals in California "professional education courses" were rated as highly valuable by only one-third of the respondents. "Student-teaching," which appeared as a separate item, received this rating from slightly more than half of the respondents.[21] The low appraisal of "professional education courses" is emphasized by the fact that only five out of the total of twenty-three items received a lower rating. Of the six factors of "college experience" only "social life in college" was rated lower.

The extent to which this group of teachers and the institutions in which they had received their professional training may be regarded as typical is not known. Furthermore the opinions of teachers and school administrators may not be a valid basis of appraisal. However, the findings do raise the question of the efficacy of the present technical-professional program, especially of courses other than student teaching. In this connection it is perhaps significant that the lapse of time since the "professional education courses" were taken made little difference in the value assigned to them.[22]

The constructive efforts in some teacher-education units have doubtless resulted in more effective technical-professional training, but the persistent contemporary criticisms and other evidence strongly indicate that through the years the program has been generally lacking in effectiveness. This interpretation leads to the question of why the "professors of education" did not develop a more effective instructional program. In considering this question it should be noted that in 1890 pedagogical subject matter was very limited. The *Bibliography of Education,* by G. Stanley Hall and John M. Mansfield published in 1886, recorded some 2,500 titles classified under 60 captions. However, in the Preface the "strictly pedagogic literature" was referred to as "relatively limited" and under the head, "works in systematic pedagogy" there are only three titles in English, one of them being a translation. In the following section, devoted to works of a "less systematic character," there are 21 titles in Eng-

---

[20] Earle U. Rugg and Others, *op. cit.,* pp. 262-63.

[21] Jesse A. Bond, "Contributions of General Factors to Effective Teaching in Secondary Schools," *Educational Administration and Supervision,* 34 (1948), 479-87.

[22] Jesse A. Bond, "The Effectiveness of Professional Education in the Preparation of High-school Teachers," *Educational Administration and Supervision,* 35 (1949), 334-45.

lish, 8 of them being foreign publications. Although these figures should not be taken as literal measures of available texts and reference sources for use in the technical-professional training of teachers at the time, they are suggestive of the very limited pedagogical subject matter at the beginning of the period considered here.

Following 1890, the production of pedagogical works by American authors increased. A "bibliography of education for 1899"[23] included 618 entries, approximately 60 of them designating "books" of American publication.[24] Wyer and Lord compiled annual bibliographies through 1906, the number of entries varying from 319 in 1901 to 665 in 1905. Since 1926 an annual list of "educational books," compiled for several years by Joseph L. Wheeler and associates, has been published in *School and Society*. The 1926 list included only 225 titles, but in 1932 the number was 831 and in 1939 "approximately 900." The increase from "approximately 60 books" in 1899 to "approximately 900 volumes" in 1939, although not a precise measure, shows that the development of the technical-professional program involved incorporating a continuing stream of new content. This condition encouraged the organization of new courses.

The development of new courses was also contributed to by the trend toward differentiation of curriculums relative to type of position during the second and third decades and by the contemporary emphasis on "specifics." New courses, or at least new titles, became a "must" if an institution was to be regarded as "progressive."

Such conditions contribute to an explanation of what happened in the development of technical-professional courses for teachers, but recognition of them does not provide a satisfying answer to the question of why, in the light of contemporary criticisms and the constructive proposals, there was not greater progress toward a functionally effective program. In commenting on the "lack of uniformity" among university departments of education, Luckey expressed his conviction "that much of the variation is due to the inefficiency and lack of proper training of the professors themselves."[25] In the study of the Missouri normal schools it was found that the training of teachers of professional subjects was inferior to that of teachers of academic subjects.[26] The number of teachers of education who appeared "to have been drawn directly from superintendencies with-

---

[23] J. I. Wyer and Isabel E. Lord, "Bibliography of Education for 1899," *Educational Review*, 19 (1900), 384-93.

[24] It is interesting to note the presence of the following: Dewey's *School and Society*, James's *Talks to Teachers*, Hanus' *Educational Aims and Educational Values*, and Russell's *German Higher Schools*.

[25] G. W. A. Luckey, *The Professional Training of Secondary Teachers in the United States* (New York: The Macmillan Company, 1903), p. 154.

[26] William S. Learned, William C. Bagley, and Others, *The Professional Preparation of Teachers for American Public Schools* (New York: Carnegie Foundation for the Advancement of Teaching, Bulletin No. 14, 1920), p. 283.

out special training in education" was also commented on.[27] Since the dates of these appraisals, education staffs have been improved with respect to training. From a study of faculty personnel in a selected group of teachers colleges reported in the National Survey [28] it was concluded that the instructors were "fairly well prepared quantitatively at least." *The Survey of Land-Grant Colleges and Universities* (1930) revealed that with respect to training teachers of education, exclusive of supervising teachers in the training schools, compared very favorably with the total staffs of these institutions.[29]

Amount of training is not a satisfactory measure of competence for developing courses and programs of courses and one can only speculate in regard to whether an appraisal of the order of Luckey's would be applicable to the period since the turn of the century. On the basis of his acquaintance with teachers of education, the present writer is not inclined to point to the "inefficiency and lack of proper training of the professors themselves" as a significant cause of what occurred in the development of technical-professional courses during this period.

Probably the major contributing cause has been the general "atmosphere" within which those responsible for the development of technical-professional courses and programs have worked. A prevailing attitude is suggested by the characterization of the normal schools of around the turn of the century as "wonderful provincial institutions," and by the comment that a given school tended to reflect the theories and ambitions of its head. It was maintained that each institution should be free to minister to its constituency as it saw fit. Since enrollment data were objective measures of "institutional success" which were influential in obtaining appropriations and even in attracting more students, this freedom was not infrequently interpreted as an authorization to offer "new" courses and to modify the content of old courses as might appear to be advantageous. Within an institution the "success" of a department and of individual instructors tended to be measured in terms of the number of course registrations.[30]

---

[27] *Ibid.*, p. 284.

[28] Earle U. Rugg and Others, *op. cit.*, p. 125.

[29] Arthur J. Klein (director), *Survey of Land-Grant Colleges and Universities* (U.S. Office of Education, Bulletin, 1930, No. 9), II, 160.

[30] Evidence supporting these statements is provided by numerous sources of which the Learned and Bagley study of the Missouri normal schools may be noted. Typical of numerous statements relative to the Missouri institutions in 1915 are the following: "Under present conditions the measure of success [of the president and of the institution] is chiefly the size and prominence of the institution" (p. 275). ". . . the instructor faces a class composed of individuals who have selected him out of several possible choices that would advance them equally toward their diploma. He knows . . . that unless his course can be given a savor of modernity surpassing those of his competitors . . . his numbers will ebb away. . . . Not only one's salary but one's assistants, equipment, class accommodations, and indirectly one's prestige depend on the same factor [success in attracting students]" (pp. 277-78).

In his study of "twenty representative universities" Luckey made the comment that "a few institutions seem to be a law unto themselves." [31] In general, however, institutional individualism was somewhat restrained among colleges and universities due to the pressure to be academically respectable, but the academic-freedom tradition was capitalized to justify a large degree of freedom to the individual instructor to modify his courses as he desired. In commenting on the "multiplication of courses" in 1915, Bolton mentioned the desire to attract students as the "only reason" for the existing condition.[32] Following this time the pressure for production (books, reports of research, and other writings) as a means of advancement and prestige contributed to the spirit of "rugged individualism" in college and university circles.

In addition to the attitudes of "rugged individualism" and academic freedom, the "atmosphere" has been clouded by persisting controversial issues. For example, in 1888 Parr employed the caption "educational psychology not general psychology" in presenting his ideas of what the content should be in this area of professional training.[33] In the *Twentieth Yearbook* of the National Society of College Teachers of Education (1932) a chapter is devoted to the "Relation of general psychology to educational psychology." After reviewing reported studies the author concluded that "much of what is taught in educational psychology is nothing more than general psychology with a different label." [34] In the following chapter of the Yearbook, Fowler D. Brooks discussed "Educational psychology as cultural or functional." In the light of Webb's conclusion this discussion suggests a statement of the issue as of 1932 somewhat as follows: Should the course in educational psychology consist of a systematic organization of content selected from general psychology with perhaps incidental indications of applications in teaching, or should the course be organized about specific teaching problems, psychological facts and principles being introduced as they are applicable. The purpose of the first type of course would be "cultural"; that of the second "functional." Thus the issue implied by Parr in 1888 had persisted through the years, the change being essentially one of terminology.

Other controversial issues might be cited, but more pertinent to the present argument is an attitude reflected in discussions of them. Until comparatively recently there was much either-or thinking, and it tended to be fashionable to establish a position as one's own. Although there were

[31] Luckey, *op. cit.*, p. 159.

[32] Frederick E. Bolton, *op. cit.*

[33] S. S. Parr, "The Normal School Problem," *Addresses and Proceedings* (National Educational Association, 1888), p. 470.

[34] L. W. Webb, "Relation of General Psychology to Educational Psychology," *Twentieth Yearbook* (National Society of College Teachers of Education, 1932), p. 38.

many middle-of-the-roaders, they were not very vocal and there was little effort toward rapprochement. This aspect of the "atmosphere" contributed to partisanship and individualism among educationists.

Assuming that the "atmosphere" indicated is a valid interpretation, one may raise the question as to its source. To some extent it doubtless stemmed from the general spirit of the times, but it seems appropriate to say that considerable responsibility should be charged to ambitious presidents of normal schools and teachers colleges, administrative heads of departments of education, and popularity-seeking professors of education. At least it seems that persons in administrative positions could have contributed to a more favorable "atmosphere" if they had directed their talents toward cooperative, systematic study of the problems of teacher education within and among their institutions, reconciliation of opposing positions, and minimization of student registrations as the measure of institutional prestige and instructor success.

Concluding Statement

In the preceding pages certain aspects of the development of teacher education have been considered relative to the two general questions raised on page 396. It seems clear that teacher-education practice since 1890 reflects a number of *sins* of omission and commission, but it is equally clear that there have been significant improvements in the preparation of teachers for our schools. Perhaps more significant than the improvements effected are the developing interest in teacher education and the present organized efforts to improve it. The record since about 1930 justifies optimism relative to the future.

In contemplating the future, it should be recognized that a number of the issues and difficulties of the past are found in the present situation. There are still the questions of the qualitative nature of general education and subject-matter preparation for teaching. Is conventional academic study in these areas adequate, or should the program include professionalized courses, i.e. courses designed with reference to the needs of teachers in our schools? Most colleges and universities face the problem of developing an effective organizational and administrative provision for teacher education. Educationists have the problem of developing an optimum technical-professional program for the preservice preparation of teachers.

The point of attack in dealing with these and other issues and problems is the formulation and adoption of a definitive statement of the desired teacher qualifications derived from the purposes of our schools, the services requested of teachers, and the nature of the teaching-learning process. This step has been taken by most of the member institutions of the American Association of Colleges for Teacher Education (formerly the

American Association of Teachers Colleges). In the absence of evidence of action in other higher institutions one suspects that the matter has not received much penetrating and systematic attention.

The formulation and adoption of a statement of desired teacher qualifications is not something to be done by educationists; all instructional groups that contribute to the preservice education of teachers on the college level should be involved. In view of the developing character of our schools and of the nature of the teacher's work, continued attention must be given to possible revisions. The initial formulation should not be mere opinion; it should be derived from adequate information about our schools and the work of teachers. If the institutional group is not well informed about these matters, appropriate studies should be undertaken. The record of the teachers-college group suggests that the problem of formulating an adequate statement of teacher qualifications does not involve serious difficulty, provided it is attacked with the proper attitude.

In developing the means of engendering the desired qualifications there are likely to be some major differences of opinion and some practical difficulties. If the problem is approached with open-mindedness and with an appreciation of its importance, it should be possible for an institution to develop effective means — both organizational and administrative provisions and an instructional program. The social importance of teacher education justifies intensive and persistent effort in this direction.

Developing a more effective technical-professional program is the responsibility of educationists. Some recent efforts in this direction are probably to be commended, but, in general, it appears that much remains to be done. In addition to developing more functionally effective courses and programs of courses, more attention should be given to engendering greater respect for technical-professional study. The continued criticism of education courses and colleges of education suggests that educationists have not been sufficiently concerned about "selling" their work to their academic colleagues. Salesmanship in this connection will not be easy, but educationists should recognize it as a challenge.

INDEX

Ability grouping, 106, 108

Academic emphasis in normal schools, 274, 286-88

Academic environment, 269, 309-11, 328f.

Accreditation of institutions for teacher education, 357-58

Activity movement, 91-98

Adapting instruction to individual differences, 101-10; to stage of child's development, 115, 124f., 157

Admission to normal schools, 271-72, 278-79, 281; to teachers colleges, 298-99, 300

American Association of Teachers Colleges, 297, 301, 389, *et passim*

Apperception, 17, 33, 127

Appraisal of the development of teacher-education practice, in normal schools and teachers colleges, 402-4; in colleges and universities, 404-10; general aspects of educational program, 410-13; technical-professional program, 413-19

Assignments, 133-36, 142; differentiated, 106-7

Attitude toward technical-professional training in colleges and universities, 191, 308-9, 312-13, 320

Background developments in psychology, general, 9-14; the child and child development, 14-30; psychology of learning, 30-46; individual differences and educability of children, 46-51

Behaviorism, 28, 39

Certification of teachers, 262-67, 359

Charters on motivation, 78-79

Child development, concepts of, 14-30, 114-15, 157, 162-64

Child-centered school, 95, 109, 145

Class teaching defended, 102

Classroom management, 88-89, 93-94

College of education, defined, 311; development, 315-23, 351-57

Colleges and universities, compared with teachers colleges, 304-6; coordinated with normal schools, 288-90; education courses offered; *see also* Technical-professional program

Colleges and universities, provisions for teacher education in 1890, 307-9; recognized functions, 309-11; internal organization, 311; concept of teacher qualification, 312-13; development of departments of education, 313-15; college of education development, 315-16; variations in organization and function, 317-23; educational program, 323; curricular requirements and practices, 323-26; teacher education on the postbaccalaureate level, 326-37; professional status of teacher education in 1930, 337-42; modification of organization following 1930, 350-57; an appraisal, 404-10

Commission on Teacher Education, 242, 250, 345-47

Committee of Seventeen (1907), 203-4, 215, 222, 230

Committee of Ten, 200, 243, 338

Committee Q of American Association of University Professors on technical-professional training for teachers, 313

421

Incidental (instrumental) learning, 81, 82, 100, 159, 170
Individualized instruction *versus* class teaching, 101-10
Individual differences and the educability of children, 46-51, 101-10, 115
Initial discovery of adequate response, 43
Instructional procedures and aid for "assisting" pupils, 136f.
Integration in teacher education, 251
Intelligence, nature, 47f.
Interest, as motivation, 126, 128, 158; definitions of, 73-74, 77
Interest *versus* effort, 71f.
Issues in teacher education, nature and extent of technical-professional program, 370-76, 389-94; organizational provisions for teacher education in multiple-purpose institutions, 307-8, 313-23, 351-57; professionalization of general education and subject-matter specialization, 302-3, 323, 341, 406f.; standardization of normal schools and teachers colleges, 296-99; training secondary teachers in normal schools, 291-93; *see also* Liberal education, Teaching knowledge
Issues in teaching-learning theory, shifts of "majority" opinion—teaching as an art *versus* method of teaching, 57-70; conditions for effective learning, 70-87; teacher control, mechanization, conformity *versus* pupil freedom, self-expression; independent thinking, 87-101; individualized instruction *versus* class teaching, 101-10; current disagreements, 159-78

James's laws of association, 31

Kilpatrick's concept of project, 80-81

Law of effect, 35, 36, 39, 40, 44, 84
Law of exercise emphasized, 36, 39; modified by Thorndike, 40
Laws of learning, behavioristic, 39; Thorndike's, 35, 38

Learning, general problem, 34; conditions for effectiveness, 70-86; types (Freeman), 36-37
Learning activities, S. C. Parker's types, 131-32
Learning as a psychological topic, 31f.
Learning as problem solving, 34-35, 42f., 68
Learning, optimum conditions for, 77-86; outcomes of, 165-66; psychology of, 113-14, 127, 132; types of, 132-33; *see also* Effective learning
Learning psychology; *see* Psychology of learning
Lesson planning, 60, 120-21, 123-24, 129
Lesson types, 59-60, 68, 132, 156
Liberal arts college, teacher education following 1930, 350-51; *see also* Colleges and universities, provisions for teacher education
Liberal (general) education, 186, 203, 206, 221-24, 253, 326, 406f.

"Majority" opinion, shifts on certain continuing issues, teaching as an art *versus* method of teaching, 57-70; conditions for effective learning, 70-87; teacher control, mechanization, conformity *versus* pupil freedom, self-expression, independent thinking, 87-101; individualized instruction *versus* class teaching, 101-10
Measurements (objective test scores) as revealing effectiveness of teaching, 61f.
Method of teaching *versus* teaching as an art, 57-70
Methods of teaching, 57-70, 175-77; *see also* Teaching-learning theories
Mode of educational progress, 155
Motivation procedures, 71f., 86
Motivating condition in learning, 35, 42f., 70f.
Multiple-purpose institutions, teacher education in, 348-49, 404f.; *see also* Organization for teacher education in colleges and universities

National Commission on Teacher Education and Professional Standards, 347

National Education Association, Committee of Seventeen (1907), 203-4, 215, 222, 230

National Herbart Society, 4, 58, 124, 130

National Survey of the Education of Teachers, 213-14, 223-24, 241-42, *et passim*

Nature and nurture, 14-30, 50

"Nature is Right" doctrine, 18, 22, 27

Normal-school attitude toward academic standards, 295-96, 299

Normal-school curriculum in 1890, 273-74; during following years, 282-86

Normal-school function, 271, 277, 286-87, 291-93

Normal-school leaders of 1890, thinking of, 190-91

Normal-school students, 272-73

Normal schools, education courses; *see* Technical-professional program

Normal schools, of 1890, 271-77; major problems following 1890, 277; admission requirements, 278-79; practices in attracting and holding students, 279-81; support of normal schools, 282; curriculum developments, 282-86; as institutions for nonprofessional purposes, 286-87; increasing academic emphasis, 287-88; coordination with colleges and universities, 288-90; an appraisal, 402-4

Organization of subject matter, 124

Organization for teacher education in colleges and universities, 307-8, 313-23, 338, 351-57

Organizational developments since the National Survey (1930), general setting of the period, 345-48; developments in teachers colleges, 348-50; in liberal arts colleges, 350-51; in universities, 351-57; accreditation of institutions for teacher education, 357-58; preservice selection and recruitment, 358-59; five-

year programs, 359-60; technical-professional study at the advanced graduate level, 360-61

Outcomes (products) of learning, 33f., 165-66

Parr's approach to the definition of teacher qualifications, 183-84

Pattern methods of teaching, 175-77

Pedagogical knowledges and skills, 182, 188-89, 190, 197-204, 230-38, 254-55

Pedagogical program; *see* Technical-professional program

Periods of development, teaching-learning theory, 111-12; concept of desired teacher qualifications, 192

Personal fitness, 184-85, 202-3, 206, 216-21, 252-53

Philosophical atmosphere of 1890, 9, 10-11

Philosophy and research, 66f.

Postbaccalaureate teacher education, 326-37

Practice teaching, 381-88

Preservice selection and recruitment, 351, 358-59

Principles of teaching, 57f.

Problem attitude in motivation, 85

Professional institutions for teachers, 276

Professional status of education of secondary teachers in colleges and universities in 1930, 337-42

Professionalization of subject-matter courses; *see* Teaching knowledge

Progressive Education Association, 55-56, 64, 152

Progressive theories of learning and teaching; *see* Project method; Teacher control, mechanization, conformity *versus* pupil freedom, self-expression, independent thinking; Teaching-learning theory of 1950

"Progressives," general characteristics, 53f.

Project method, 64-65, 78, 80f., 145f.

Psychology, general development, 10-13

Psychological background, 9-51